Rethinking Uncle Tom

The Political Philosophy of Harriet Beecher Stowe

William B. Allen

LEXINGTON BOOKS

A division of
ROWMAN & LITTLEFIELD PUBLISHERS, INC.
Lanham • Boulder • New York • Toronto • Plymouth, UK

LEXINGTON BOOKS

A division of Rowman & Littlefield Publishers, Inc.
A wholly owned subsidiary of The Rowman & Littlefield Publishing Group, Inc.
4501 Forbes Boulevard, Suite 200
Lanham, MD 20706

Estover Road
Plymouth PL6 7PY
United Kingdom

British Library Cataloguing in Publication Information Available

Library of Congress Cataloging-in-Publication Data

Allen, W. B. (William Barclay), 1944–
Rethinking Uncle Tom : the political philosophy of Harriet Beecher Stowe / William B. Allen.
p. cm.
Includes bibliographical references.
ISBN-13: 978-0-7391-2798-8 (cloth : alk. paper)
ISBN-10: 0-7391-2798-5 (cloth : alk. paper)
ISBN-13: 978-0-7391-2799-5 (pbk. : alk. paper)
ISBN-10: 0-7391-2799-3 (pbk. : alk. paper)
eISBN-13: 978-0-7391-3354-5
eISBN-10: 0-7391-3354-3
1. Stowe, Harriet Beecher, 1811–1896—Political and social views. 2. Stowe, Harriet Beecher, 1811–1896. Uncle Tom's cabin. 3. Uncle Tom (Fictitious character) 4. Equality in literature. 5. Liberty in literature. 6. Slavery in literature. I. Title.
PS2958.P6A66 2009
813'.4—dc22 2008039313

Printed in the United States of America

∞™ The paper used in this publication meets the minimum requirements of American National Standard for Information Sciences—Permanence of Paper for Printed Library Materials, ANSI/NISO Z39.48-1992.

Written for and with special regard to
Susan, Danielle, Lauren, Emma, and Sarah

Contents

Acknowledgments

This work owes more than can be expressed to numberless individuals. Certainly the late Joseph S. van Why and Diana Royce stand first in that list, however. As President and Librarian respectively at the Stowe-Day Center in Hartford, Connecticut, they welcomed me as a researcher and greatly facilitated the reflections that have matured here. Mr. van Why, in particular, was a helpful critic. The successor staff at the Stowe-Day Center have also been most encouraging. Similarly, I found a congenial respite at the Huntington Library in San Marino, California. Among readers Professors Colleen Sheehan and Jack Doody have been immensely helpful, and Professors Lucas Morel, Alfred Brophy, John Callahan, Charles Johnson, and William Dennis have been encouraging.

My family has supported this work through decades of labor, and I am particularly grateful to them. I owe greatest thanks to my wife, Carol M. Allen, who provided invaluable assistance as an editor and annotator and, most importantly, as a reader who could push me toward clarity. It is fair to say that the work would not have ended so well, and perhaps not at all, without her assistance.

Many libraries, such as that at Northwestern University, have been most accommodating in providing access to rare resources, enabling discoveries of long-hidden links in the chain of reasonings developed here.

The Schlesinger Library, Radcliffe Institute, Harvard University, has provided permission to reproduce the photograph appearing on the cover (or as frontispiece). And the extensive citation from the letter from Francis Lieber to George Ticknor of March 14, 1853 was made available courtesy of the Huntington Library (LI 4381).

I owe thanks to the Earhart Foundation in Ann Arbor, Michigan, for support of sabbatical leave at the James Madison Program in American Ideals and Institutions at Princeton University. The time they afforded me for research enabled me to complete the preparation of this work. My colleagues at the Madison Program were both encouraging and inspiring.

Preface

I. THE MYTH OF UNCLE TOM

Each day we awaken like children. By the time our feet find our slippers, we have restored our place in yesterday's promises. Until that instant, wakening, we are blithely free of the sedimented constructions that define our place in the flux of being. Child-like we behold the truth of infinite story; grown-up we imagine the vision of only one way out. In the most recent times critics and interpreters of Uncle Tom have constructed a one-way view of Uncle Tom, albeit offering a few kind words for Uncle Tom along the way. Nevertheless, they have stolen my promised hero, and I write to reclaim him.

Recovering Uncle Tom requires retelling his story. Accordingly, a comprehensive review of scholarly analysis is deferred to the section following part I of book I. Those who are innocent will find this approach rewarding, while sophisticates may choose to move straightway to the critique. They will find there the specific that restores lost innocence. Uncle Tom truly is Uncle Tom only for the child-like. For the grown-up he is a pasteboard construction of social, cultural, and philosophical perplexities. This closing discussion clears away the pasteboard, so that adults may become open to the real Uncle Tom—it is a form of vision correction that distorts reality for those who already have 20/20 vision, but enables the myopic to see clearly for the first time.

Uncle Tom's Cabin[1] generated enormous circumstantial criticism. By circumstantial criticism I mean that form of analysis that concentrates on the political and social milieu in which the novel was written and the audience to whom it was addressed.[2] Until recently, it was never imagined that the text might well bear analysis in its own right. In particular, it was never imagined that *UTC* might present *sustained* arguments about human nature and human knowledge. This book explores those large issues, beginning from the center of the novel and the role of its two principal myths: the myth of "little Eva" and the myth of Uncle Tom.

II. THE DRAMA OF UNCLE TOM

The reader familiar with the plot of *UTC* will not need the reminder that a sharp break distinguishes the first and second portions of the novel. Initially, Uncle Tom is seen in the midst of slavery as the patriarchal institution. A trusted slave and even manager on his master's plantation, ensconced in a relatively comfortable and certainly charming cabin amid the love and charms of wife and children, and himself a moral patriarch among his peers, his life conforms to a portrait of slavery adorned with every conceivable mitigating grace. But necessitous circumstances led to his sale, and he began a journey southward from his old Kentucky home.

Though the slavery Tom next encounters is mild and even pleasurable, his circumstances peculiarly reflect the advanced stages of modern individualism. The anomic interlude at the St. Clare mansion was eventually followed by the utter, atomistic degeneracy of the Legree plantation, but meanwhile, in the context of advanced individualism, Stowe introduces the myths of Eva and Tom. By means of these myths, Harriet Stowe succeeds in characterizing the moral and intellectual limits of modernity.[3]

In Stowe's view modern morality rested on an ideal morality that admitted exceptions in the interest of self-preservation. In an early chapter of *Uncle Tom's Cabin* (chapter xii) she labored to tie every consequence of slavery to the law and morality that permitted it. She derived a debauched "public sentiment" from the force of slave law and its practices. The entire edifice fell with the refutation of the slavetrader's, Haley's, humanity. She made him a representative of the law, of the city. And her purpose was to question the whole of the city's teaching.

Stowe concluded that chapter with an example of the "exception" at work. America strove to rid the seas of the foreign slave trade, while the interstate slave trade flourished. The point may not be made clearer: the guiding principle of humanism (her name for modern liberalism) is the universalism of an ideal morality, subjected to particular exceptions. The ordinary abolitionist's approach was to oppose ideal morality (the higher law) to the exception. Stowe's myth of Uncle Tom presents an alternative to that provisional connection between self-preservation and morality, one that does not require abstraction from an earthly way of life.

The reader must be careful not to afford Uncle Tom too much credit. So far as we can judge of things as they are, Tom is but a slave. Indeed, he is rather an inoffensive and pathetic slave, however sympathetic his character. Safe it is to imagine that no compelling alternative can be built on that foundation alone. Stowe realized the difficulty, but she ascribed it rather to the reader than to her hero. We see only with what she regarded as "the light of the present," which rather obscures by blinding than illuminates things as they are. Her claim was that Tom is far more than we perceive. To prove this, it seems, she introduced a new set of characters in the novel's second part. The foremost of these characters is "little Eva." Eva is explicitly presented as a myth through which the reader may comprehend the "ideal" character of Uncle Tom. But such indirection is insufficient, insofar as we require to witness the myth in action.

Tom knows the truth—it is not bleak—and that alone keeps him alive, or at least a slave, for the moment. The truth that Tom knew explains not only the fate that awaits him, but some residuum of hope in this world. The Bible in its earthly bearings is the chief theme, or at least the chief element of his understanding as it relates to the apology for his course of action. Tom apparently came to terms with his condition and his faith, but the reader does not see how without the myth of little Eva. Eva is Tom's very own myth, the myth within the myth of Uncle Tom. The present work unfolds the larger myth, and all of the lesser myths out of which it is constructed.

III. THE MEANING OF UNCLE TOM

The story of Uncle Tom is perhaps as well known as any other single story. Indeed, extraordinary numbers of people who have never read the novel still believe to understand its purpose and "message." This is partly to be explained as the legacy of the phenomenally diverse and worldwide distribution of the novel. It is also partly to be explained by the persistence of the judgment that the novel is simplistic and uncomplicated.[4] On that view, the act of reading the novel is rather an act of indulgence—if moral—than an act of reflection.

The author of the novel did not share this judgment. Stowe believed the work to be "subtle" and marked by "finer shades" of meaning. This sentiment was expressed in a letter, written from Paris in 1856, to her husband. And there is other evidence external to the novel that she considered it complex. Indeed, at least two full works (*The Key to Uncle Tom's Cabin* and *Sunny Memories of Foreign Lands*) were subsequently published to defend and explain the novel (a fact not widely known).[5] But the most defensible claim for treating the novel and its author seriously emerges from the novel itself.

And a careful reading of the novel—and its various editions—reveals the care with which it was written.

This fact has not been generally recognized by persons believing to know the story of Uncle Tom. Nor have many persons been aware that, in addition to *Uncle Tom's Cabin*, Harriet Stowe published over fifteen major titles as well as hundreds of shorter works, articles, and poems. Stowe is a major American author, with a considerable corpus in which serious and well-developed social, moral, religious, and political reflections are coherently set forth.[6]

The present work attempts to set forth that claim to reflective consideration. Only with considerable timorousness can a contemporary scholar, descended from America's slaves, undertake so sensitive a task. Even when the task itself is not arduous it is so laden with social and political portent in our day that one scarcely knows how to speak the truth. Stowe was once attacked for contributing to the subjection of women, on the one hand. And while the charge has not stood up under investigation—indeed, much of the current scholarship on Stowe praises Stowe for what is perceived as her belief in the salvific grace of women in general and mothers in particular—it has reflected the kind of tendentiousness that has often infected Stowe scholarship. On the other hand, the truth leads me to reveal that Mrs. Stowe's work was considerably influenced by Mr. Stowe. And that seems equally well calculated to affront the legions that, having disavowed her on other grounds before, would now draw her into a protective circle of warm indignation. Further, Stowe has been accused of disseminating racist stereotypes and bigotry.[7] And who can welcome the opportunity to correct that misunderstanding at the cost of being wrongly taken to question the judgment of her accusers? But correcting that misunderstanding results necessarily from the demonstration that black political thought has its roots in the milieu of Uncle Tom,[8] the debate between Stowe and Frederick Douglass ("What Country Have I?"). It is most significant that, in Douglass's own eyes in the end, she won the debate.[9]

This study has produced some important findings. They may aid in our understanding of the quality, character, and tensions of American life and thought in the nineteenth and twentieth centuries.[10] In spite of the pain invariably associated with changing established but faulty conceptions, Harriet Beecher Stowe deserves reconsideration and Uncle Tom deserves rethinking. Fortunately, recent work on Stowe has tended in the same direction, making a clear case for a major restatement. When this work was undertaken in 1974 there was little encouragement available. The state of Stowe scholarship seemed to have been irrevocably set in the passionate outbursts of Baldwin's essay on "Everybody's Protest Novel" and Furnas's *Good-bye to Uncle Tom*. Furnas welcomed the era of civil rights, an era of awakened consciousness, by celebrating the rejection of Stowe as creator of that backwardness in blacks that came to be called "Uncle Tom-ism."[11] And there matters stood until the last decades.

The late Ellen Moers, among many others cited in this work, revealed how strongly creative that tension is which emerges from responding to Stowe—to *Uncle Tom's Cabin*—at the same time one attempts to respond to received judgment about the cultural, literary, and historical merits of Stowe's work. Moers's stout defense of Stowe's merit, of her *place* in the American literary tradition, constitutes the kind of summons to which this writer and others responded.[12] Moers' reasoning was precise: apart from the literary question, strictly speaking, Stowe was the *only* great American writer to address *frontally* the most sensitive, the most pressing, and the most difficult question of antebellum America.[13] Her work "just growed" out of the moral and theoretical necessities of the peculiar life being constructed in the New World.

The present work begins with the consciousness that no other nineteenth-century work of stature—apart from direct political speech—places readers in subsequent centuries in as direct contact with nineteenth-century America as the work of H. B. Stowe. Fittingly, therefore, I begin with the great novel, *Uncle Tom's Cabin.* Fully the half of this work was the *first* actual explication of that text. Because Stowe's political philosophy is almost entirely present in her first novel, such concentration is appropriate. The novel we all know becomes a guiding light by means of which we can illumine the slants and themes of Stowe's other works.

The next substantial portion of this text focuses on Stowe's only directly didactic work. It is a work of political reflection, not fiction, and a conscious defense of the didactic use of the novel. The work is *Sunny Memories of Foreign Lands*, an ostensible travel diary that is, in fact, a conscious though inexplicit adaptation of the Tocquevillean perspective. Stowe used a trip through England as occasion to reflect on America. She wrote the travelogue so as to reveal this. In opening the account of her journey she claimed to have sailed in the ship "Niagara," in spite of accurate published accounts that she sailed in the "Canada." Indeed, her personal diary, from which "Sunny Memories" was compiled, correctly names the ship "Canada." But "Niagara" served Stowe's purpose, as became clear at the end of her tour when the Niagara, which is shared between New York and Canada, served as the theme for profound philosophical reflection. Stowe wanted to use that name to emphasize her concentration on America, starting with the metaphor of a troubled ship of state and ending with a vision of a renewed way of life.

The conclusion of this work presents the end, the goal Stowe envisioned. It is drawn from her other major works, but above all from her most important non-slavery novel, *Oldtown Folks*. Starting with the title, that work is an account of three historical or moral stages: Oldtown, Needmore, and

Cloudland, and the names of the three villages in which the drama occurs. The story is an account of the impossible tensions that emerge from unreflective abandonment of the *ancien régime*. The Cloudland utopia is revealed as incapable of generation and hence no true city. Then we are prepared for Stowe's anutopia, the ultimate life of decency and order that is proof against false dreams of rationalized life (Needmore). The neologism, anutopia, is an appropriate characterization of Stowe's vision. It is a double negative. Since utopia originally meant nowhere, the refutation of utopia comes to stand for a definite somewhere. Stowe's political philosophy was not a conservative defense of the status quo (as the attack on slavery alone would reveal). It was rather a defense, a demonstration of the permanent necessity of moral and prudential judgment in human affairs and of those political conditions that could best guarantee these conditions of decency.[14]

The conclusion of book I is the introduction proper. It establishes the questions to be raised by Stowe and describes the historical milieu from which they emerged. The central portion of that task is the demonstration that Calvin Stowe—theologian, social critic, educationist, political philosopher—articulated those questions. His wife proved a more than able interlocutor and respondent. Through her his scholarly musings were transformed, metamorphosed into world historical significance.

The leading question is the "identity of disinterestedness and benevolence," on which foundation the evil of slavery was originally argued. But by the end that question, in Stowe's hands, had turned into the suggestion that man is suspended between God and nature by the strings of poetry and philosophy. It is by these, her two disciplines, that I have sought to re-discover the care—the art—and thought of H. B. Stowe.

Finally, this is a long work, plain in some ways and intricate in others. General readers will find it engaging through a presentation that directly addresses topical issues, while scholars will find here opportunity to focus researches anew. For thoughtful readers it will require patience to find what lies beyond the topical and the scholarly.

NOTES

1. The text cited throughout is the Oxford edition, edited by John A. Woods, 1965. Hereafter, *UTC*, with page references noted parenthetically.

2. Indeed, in his introduction to a series of essays on the novel, Sundquist reflected that "*Uncle Tom's Cabin*" can now barely be read with an open mind." Eric Sundquist, ed., *New Essays on Uncle Tom's Cabin* (Cambridge: Cambridge University Press, 1986), p. 5 (hereafter cited as New Essays).

3. White suggests that ". . . Stowe argues against the logic of individualism in *Uncle Tom's Cabin.*" Isabelle White, "The Uses of Death in *Uncle Tom's Cabin,*" *American Studies* 26 (1984): 14.

4. Although not alone, Hovet is among the small number of readers who understand that Stowe uses "slavery not only as a frightening example of social sin but also as a symbol of the profound theological and philosophical issues facing American society . . ." He errs, however, in the meaning he ascribes to the symbol. Theodore R. Hovet, "Modernization and the American Fall into Slavery in *Uncle Tom's Cabin*," *New England Quarterly* 54, no. 4 (1981): 500.

5. Gail Smith speculates, "The title of the *Key* links it with numerous 'keys' to the scriptures published before and after [*Uncle Tom's Cabin.*] It suggests that [the novel] is not immediately self-evident as a text—that it is a hieroglyphic Bible . . . " Gail K. Smith, "The Sentimental Novel: The Example of Harriet Beecher Stowe," in *The Cambridge Companion to Nineteenth-Century American Women's Writings*, ed. Dale M. Bauer and Philip Gould (Cambridge: Cambridge University Press, 2001), p. 227 (hereafter cited as "The Sentimental Novel").

6. Notwithstanding comments such as this one by Romero, in fact Stowe addressed in depth a wide range of such issues: "Stowe's novel [i.e., *Uncle Tom's Cabin*] reduces the complex array of antebellum social relations into a single, apocalyptic contest between a patriarchal power which destroys selfhood and a womanist resistance which reinstates it." Lora Romero, *Home Fronts: Domesticity and Its Critics in the Antebellum United States* (Durham, NC: Duke University Press, 1997), p. 70. Happily, there are a few critics who acknowledge the true scope of Stowe's endeavors. Rexroth, as an example, is emphatic: "*Uncle Tom's Cabin* is not only an attack on slavery, the greatest and most effective ever written, it is a book of considerable philosophical or religious and social importance." Kenneth Rexroth, *The Elastic Retort: Essays in Literature and Ideas* (New York: The Seabury Press, 1973), p. 105 (hereafter cited as Elastic Retort).

7. The list of accusers is far too long to cite in its entirety and this category of Stowe scholarship is sufficiently well known to require minimal rehearsing here. Thus, brief excerpts from a few such works are cited here only as representative: In describing the antebellum black response to *Uncle Tom's Cabin*, Banks concludes that "what initially appeared as a blessing to convert the hearts of the nation to abolition became for black readers . . . a curse that encouraged continuation of the doctrine of white supremacy in America." Marva Banks, "*Uncle Tom's Cabin* and the Antebellum Black Response," in *Readers in History: Nineteenth-Century American Literature and the Contexts of Response*, ed. James L. Machor (Baltimore: Johns Hopkins University Press, 1993), p. 225 (hereafter cited as "*Uncle Tom's Cabin* and the Antebellum Black Response). Sundquist cautions that "the novel's characterization of black Americans, whether slave or free, has often rendered it objectionable to modern sensibilities." Sundquist, *New Essays*, p. 1. Nearly every contributor to a recent guidebook to teaching *Uncle Tom's Cabin* shares the perspective expressed by Ammons, the volume's editor: "Stowe wanted slavery to end and racial inequality to remain. There is no other conclusion." Elizabeth Ammons, "*Uncle Tom's Cabin*, Empire, and Africa," in *Approaches to Teaching "Uncle Tom's Cabin,"* ed. Elizabeth Ammons and Susan Belasco (New York: Modern Language Association, 2000), p. 75 (hereafter cited as "*UTC*, Empire, and Africa"). Loebel likewise praises Stowe's desire for a just ending of slavery but bemoans her unjust representation of black characters in her fiction: "Can justice be advocated for and received in the name of others when justice is not even rendered to them in representation?" Thomas Leon Loebel,

"Legal Fictions: Representing Justice in Nineteenth-Century American Literature" (Ph.D. diss., State University of New York at Buffalo, 1996), p. 162 (hereafter cited as "Legal Fictions"). Stowe's most recent biographer, Hedrick, is unable to exculpate her entirely: "Stowe's political achievement was to make a national audience see the subjectivity of black people, but what she herself saw was filtered through a white woman's consciousness." Joan D. Hedrick, *Harriet Beecher Stowe: A Life* (New York: Oxford University Press, 1994), p. 210 (hereafter cited as Harriet Beecher Stowe). Even the editor of the 150th anniversary edition of *Uncle Tom's Cabin*, Charles Johnson, sees in the work "a portrait of black people that, from a twenty-first-century perspective, is ineluctably racist. . . . [Stowe's characterization] simply replaces one racist stereotype with another that is equally condescending and unacceptable." Charles Johnson, introduction to *Uncle Tom's Cabin*, by Harriet Beecher Stowe (Oxford: Oxford University Press, 2002), p. ix. These critics would do well to heed Stowe's own admonition to readers in general: "One would think it a matter of common sense, that in order to criticize justly you must put yourself for the time being as nearly as possible at the author's point of sight . . . [and] form a sympathetic estimate of what he is striving to do, and then you can tell how nearly he obtains his purpose." Harriet Beecher Stowe, *My Wife and I: Or, Harry Henderson's History* (Boston: Houghton, Mifflin & Company, 1899), p. 184.

8. Cf. Levine: ". . . some of the key debates of the early to mid-1850s on race and nation were spawned by the African-American response to *Uncle Tom's Cabin*. Stowe's novel worked with and contributed to what Floyd Miller characterizes as 'the basic instability of black ideologies at this time.'" Robert S. Levine, *Martin Delany, Frederick Douglass, and the Politics of Representative Identity* (Chapel Hill: University of North Carolina Press, 1997), p. 60 (hereafter cited as Martin, Delany, Frederick Douglas, and the Politices of Representative Identity). Much of Levine's unorthodox work focuses on the complex ways in which Stowe, Frederick Douglass, and Martin Delaney influenced and were influenced by each other.

9. Although Levine might argue that Douglass won the debate ("If Stowe in her 1851 letter set out to 'correct' Douglass, the rhetoric of her novel suggests that Douglass, through the columns in his newspaper, 'corrected' Stowe instead." p. 149), he nevertheless acknowledges Douglass's respect and praise for Stowe's work. Robert S. Levine, *Martin Delany, Frederick Douglass, and the Politics of Representative Identity* (Chapel Hill: University of North Carolina Press, 1997). Steptoe makes the questionable assertion that both Douglass and Stowe were winners in this debate; however, his analysis is seriously flawed in a number of respects. Robert B. Steptoe, "Sharing the Thunder: The Literary Exchanges of Harriet Beecher Stowe, Henry Bibb, and Frederick Douglass," in *New Essays on Uncle Tom's Cabin*, ed. Eric J. Sundquist (Cambridge: Cambridge University Press, 1986), p. 152.

10. Cf. Strout: " . . . the images, rhetoric and ideas [of *Uncle Tom's Cabin*] are deeply connected with the ideological tensions of the most critical period in our history. . . . *Uncle Tom's Cabin* is surely one of the most American books in our literature." Cushing Strout, "*Uncle Tom's Cabin* and the Portent of the Millennium," *The Yale Review* n.s. 57 (1968)," 385 (hereafter cited as "*UTC* and the Portent of the Millennium"). Also, Kaye writing of *Uncle Tom's Cabin* and of *Ceclia Valdes* comments: "The achievement of both of these great novels lies in the accuracy with which they

reproduce the conditions of the societies which produced them and predict the nature of those crises whose inevitability is so carefully documented in their pages." Jacqueline Kaye, "Literary Images of Slavery and Resistance: The Case of *Uncle Tom's Cabin*," *Slavery & Abolition* (1984): 117.

11. J. C. Furnas, *Goodbye to Uncle Tom* (New York: W. Sloane Associates, 1956). So pervasive is this misreading of the novel, that in his recent work, *Not So! Popular Myths about America from Columbus to Clinton*, Boller includes the myth of Uncle Tom as one of those he exposes, stating, "Stowe's Uncle Tom was 'no Uncle Tom.'" Paul F. Boller, "Uncle Tom as a Black Hero," in *Not So! Popular Myths about America from Columbus to Clinton* (New York: Oxford University Press, 1995), p. 66. Yet even during the period when the term "Uncle Tom" was most intensely reviled, there were critics such as Hudson, who could perceive the truth of the novel: "The term, 'Uncle Tom,' does not deserve the connotation which it has today. The memory of this humble slave should be a source of inspiration and pride, not of shame." Benjamin F. Hudson, "Another View of 'Uncle Tom,'" *Phylon* (1963): 87.

12. Ellen Moers, *Harriet Beecher Stowe and American Literature* (Hartford, CT: The Stowe-Day Foundation, 1978; hereafter cited as *HBS and American Literature*).

13. Cf. Rexroth: "Hawthorne, Cooper, Washington Irving ignore the reality of slavery. Yet slavery was the great fact of American life. Harriet Beecher Stowe alone of the major novelists faced the fact and worked out its consequences in the humanity of those involved in it." Kenneth Rexroth, "*Uncle Tom's Cabin*," *Saturday Review of Literature* (1969): 71. Kazin lists the negligent authors, citing Thoreau and Stowe as exceptions and adding: "What is missing in [Thoreau's] opposition to slavery . . . is the presence of an actual, living, breathing slave. Harriet Beecher Stowe was to supply one in *Uncle Tom's Cabin*, and this, she claimed, not without the assistance of God." Afred Kazin, *God and the American Writer* (New York: Alfred A. Knopf, 1997), p. 74. From a British perspective, Newman notes, "None of the male novelists of the American Renaissance tackled the topic of slavery, with the honourable exception of [Herman Melville's 'Benito Cereno']." Judie Newman, "Introduction," in *Dred: A Tale of the Great Dismal Swamp* (Halifax, England: Ryburn Publishers, 1992), p. 10.

14. While numerous critics understand Stowe to be pointing toward a utopia in her works (Cf. Rodgers-Webb, Ryan, Brown, and Tompkins among others), Karafilis recognizes that this is not Stowe's intent, and utilizes Foucault's concept of heterotopia to explore Stowe's aim as rather the use of real, material places (such as the Great Dismal Swamp in *Dred)*, from which to critique other spaces, including utopias. Angelic Tina Rodgers-Webb, "Looking Forward and Backward: The Utopian Impulse in American Women's Fiction from Stowe to Gilman" (Ph.D. diss., University of Southern Mississippi, 2001). Susan M. Ryan, "Charity Begins at Home: Stowe's Antislavery Novels and the Forms of Benevolent Citizenship," *American Literature* 72, no. 4 (2000) (hereafter cited as "Charity Begins at Home"). Gillian Brown, *Domestic Individualism: Imagining Self in Nineteenth-Century America* (Berkeley: University of California Press, 1990; hereafter cited as *Domestic Individualism*). Jane P. Tompkins, *Sensational Designs: The Cultural Work of American Fiction, 1790–1860* (New York: Oxford University Press, 1985; hereafter cited as *Sensational Designs*). Maria Karafilis, "Spaces of Democracy in Harriet Beecher Stowe's *Dred*," *Arizona Quarterly* 55, no. 3 (1999).

Another rare critic who discerns that Stowe's vision is not utopian is Donovan: "Had Stowe made Tom a George Washington instead of a Christ, we would have a very different novel—a utopian novel that elides the problem of evil . . . [but] this is not the novel [Stowe] intended to write." Josephine Donovan, *Uncle Tom's Cabin: Evil, Affliction, and Redemptive Love* (Boston: Twayne Publishers, 1991), p. 56 (hereafter cited as *UTC: Evil, Affliction and Redemptive Love*).

Book I

THE GHOSTLY CRY: *UNCLE TOM'S CABIN*

I

1

The Question of Equality

Uncle Tom's Cabin deals with the question of equality.[1] It depicts the meaning of equality through the vehicle of the greatly superior man: the human model of surpassing excellence.

Dred, on the other hand, deals with liberty. There the question of equality is not openly raised. And the really free man is in the state of nature—a state in which moral equality is necessarily present but not of great consequence.

Hence, it is Dred's physical prowess that Stowe emphasizes, though he is great-souled; and it is Uncle Tom's spiritual strength that she emphasizes, though he possesses great physical prowess.

Stowe believed that an emphasis upon liberty constituted a danger so far as the purposes of civil society were concerned. Where men self-consciously enjoy liberty understood as an essential freedom of will they become conscious of their differing capacities. Liberty gives birth to desires that may otherwise be repressed. But not all who experience the desire possess adequate means of satisfaction. Only they who can both desire a thing and obtain it, therefore, seem to be fully free. And all who fall short seem justly restricted.

Yet, they who are deficient in one respect may not be so in another. And even if they are deficient in all respects, they yet retain the capacity to adapt some means to some ends. In their case liberty is also possible. But it will seem a mean thing in comparison to the liberty of all who command superior means. And the superior will find it difficult to show any respect for the inferior. Without mutual respect for their respective capacities, superior and inferior human beings cannot associate in a single polity devoted to liberty. For the one will enslave the other, from contempt, or be himself enslaved in the default of decisive action, from envy. There is no ground of respect for difference in liberty.[2] Liberty can constitute a principle of civil association only if it emerges itself from a ground of respect for difference. This necessary condition was the object of consideration in Stowe's first major slavery writing, "The Two Altars."

Equality is the ground of respect for difference. Stowe believed that all appeals to civil purposes had to address the polity as if it emerged from a care for moral equality. The emphasis on moral equality establishes a willingness to obscure distinctions based on capacity as the condition of forming society. Thus, every member of society stands in relation to every other as morally competent to judge no further than his own good. By insisting on a general incompetence or deficiency, however, men undermine all claims to mastery. Thus, they save each for everyone the liberty to command such means as he may to the fulfillment of appropriate desires.

In the "Preface" to the European edition of *Uncle Tom's Cabin*, in 1852,[3] Stowe maintained that compromise on slavery was no longer possible. She invited Europeans to emigrate to America, prepared to vote against slavery. The liberty she wished to defend required vigilance still. But beyond vigilance was the preeminence of moral equality.[4] Liberty for all, by necessity, means that moral equality is more important than liberty. For moral equality guarantees but cannot be guaranteed by liberty.

Where liberty is worshipped and nature rules, the superior will subdue the inferior, whether by force or persuasion. Because of nature's indifference to the hopes of human morality, mere law cannot command the hierarchy nature prescribes. Where liberty is worshipped and nature rules, law will be undermined. *Dred* is a story of the violent undermining of law. The underlying assumption of *Dred* is that the test of strength underlying the institution of slavery must sooner or later reverse its consequences. The existence of slavery affirms the absence of moral equality as the bond of the master class.

Slavery in the modern world is based on the absolutization of liberty as the right of the strongest. And *Dred* argues that sooner or later the force of this principle must give the lie to the pretense of social convention. Sooner or later must a strong man emerge who is conventionally a slave or inferior. And in applying this regnant principle of justice he will trod the in fact weaker under his foot. *Dred* portends a world of ugly and violent recrimination, logically consistent with the regnant morality. Stowe employs this portent to warn of the necessity to abandon a principle of justice that distinguishes men radically.[5]

This prospect is subdued in *Uncle Tom's Cabin*, where a defense of moral equality reveals that law or social convention may indeed succeed in masking the hierarchy of nature. In fact, Stowe believed that the purposes of civil society require masking the hierarchy of nature. Nonetheless, the underlying assumption of *Uncle Tom's Cabin* agrees with the assumption of *Dred*:

that institutions or social conventions can impose *only* a social hierarchy. The crucial question is whether the social hierarchy will be amenable to the incidence of natural superiority in goodness. The answer is, not where superiority must resist the impulses of law. Moral equality successfully masks the natural hierarchy only because it does not demand the submission of the superior, especially those superior in goodness.

Yet, superiority in goodness, if it is possible, seems to deny the basis of moral equality. It seems to raise a claim to command which both respects differences in men and distinguishes men radically. As if to emphasize this paradox, moral equality also cannot distinguish one people from another, as liberty may. A people dedicated to liberty is distinguished from a servile people. But a people affirming moral equality, as the basis of their claim, is not thereby distinguished from another people ignorant of that principle. That is, they claim no superiority vis-à-vis another people, because the principle they affirm asserts a universal deficiency. Only as their attachment to moral equality leads to their enjoyment of liberty can they be said to live a relatively better life. The attachment to moral equality not only disallows radical distinctions among fellow citizens; it disallows radical distinctions among humankind.

Moral equality respects the differences in men only if it is false to say that superiority in goodness confers a title to rule. Distributive justice is giving to every man his due, what is fitting to him. It requires respect for the differences in men. Superiority in goodness is a superiority of judgment with respect to what is fitting. But every member of society stands in relation to every other as morally competent to judge no further than his own good. That men are possessed of differing capacities of judgment does not dispossess them of the claim to judge. Those superior in goodness must possess a superior wisdom about the things good for men; they must be human models of surpassing excellence. If they do not enjoy a title to rule men, it must be that ruling others is not among the good things individual men require as such.

Ruling oneself is a greater good than ruling others. And although they who rule others may, nay, must still rule themselves, they who are ruled are prevented from ruling themselves. Thus, they are denied the greatest human good. It would be singularly unaccountable that they who are superior in goodness would gain, by their goodness, the right to impair the goodness of others. The arbitrary power of judging for others is not good for the judge. The absolute power of judging for oneself is morally necessary. That power is exercised best by those superior in goodness. But they preserve that power for themselves only as all men possess it. When that power is exercised arbitrarily by those inferior in goodness, the good of all is imperiled. Those of inferior capacity require to be guided if moral equality is to be preserved.

How can men be guided by the wise if the wise possess no power to rule them? The model of Christianity provides the answer for Stowe. Those superior in goodness are mainly so because they serve the good of others.[6] They do not usurp the right of judgment, but they supply the appropriate ends or desires and the means suited to the capacities of their fellow. They acquire a mastery over others, largely through opinion.[7] And they do so without respect to their own conventional status. The truest form of mastery not only does not depend upon the law, but also may not do so. Moral equality is the principle that could assure that men are not deprived of the beneficence of superior wisdom at the same time they are protected against despotism.

The strongest defense of moral equality is the demonstration of superior goodness at work under the worst conditions: despotism. *Uncle Tom's Cabin* presents an ideal case: the man so far superior by nature that he will rule the opinions of others, including those called his masters, though himself enslaved. But the ideal does not teach the indifference of goodness to conventions so much as it demonstrates the character of the goodness that was possible were impediment removed.[8] We grasp Stowe's intent best when we become mindful of the alternatives she confronted. She wished to attack slavery and to reveal the erroneous principle of justice that was its support. She could do so by inveighing against the abridgment of the liberty of men often the equal or superior in capacity to their masters. (This alternative was reflected in the sub-plot of George Harris's escape from slavery.) But in that she had to attack the regime itself and thus to undermine the notion of an American common good as America then stood. Or, she could appeal to the common good of the American polity. And in that she was required to show what were the true American principles and wherein the practice of slavery departed from them. Thus, she could reveal the prospects for good—even for the lawful masters themselves—threatened by the existence of slavery.

As if to show how her choice was made, Stowe incorporates both alternatives in the almost parallel plots of the novel. We have the story of George Harris's escape and education as well as the story of Uncle Tom. Indeed, to explain the novel it will be, finally, sufficient to answer the question: Why was Uncle Tom rather than George Harris named as the "hero of our story"? George Harris certainly fits the more traditional—Patrick Henry—model of the American hero. Thus we wonder why the unusual, uncommon man should be chosen as the hero in order to ensure our sympathy for the many, the lowly. Why does the democratic American polity require a human model of surpassing excellence in order to attain democratic happiness?

The first critic properly noting the tension between George Harris and Uncle Tom nevertheless failed to perceive the significance of that tension, although he acknowledged the complexity of the novel. Fiedler's *Love and Death in the American Novel* relates the tension in the following terms:

> Poor George—his existence is fictional only, not mythic. Unlettered Negroes to this day will speak of a pious compromiser of their own race, who urges Christian forbearance rather than militancy, as a "Tom" or "Uncle Tom;" it has become a standard term of contempt. But no one speaks of the advocate of force who challenges him as a "George," though Mrs. Stowe's protagonist of that name was a very model for the righteous use of force against force.[9]

This may doubtless be explained by the fact that Americans—including "unlettered Negroes"—already have the example of Patrick Henry and other exponents of the righteous use of force against force from the American founding. (See the artfully colored portrait of George Washington that hangs from Uncle Tom's cabin wall.)[10] But the criticism was meant to go deeper than that. Fiedler understood Uncle Tom merely as the exponent of a "primitive piety." For that reason he did not consider George Harris's "challenge" as a genuine alternative. It is the *only* way. And Uncle Tom's sentimental character is but the mythic creation of a guilt-ridden conscience, hungering for real expiation and not the mere contempt a George offers. The righteous use of force against force was unproblematic for Fiedler and not an affirmation of the right of the stronger. Stowe's view was more sublime and less optimistic. Thus, George was for her an admirable but too limited character, with whom she identified the American founding in some respects.[11]

NOTES

1. The novel's evident focus on equality is, however, missed by too many scholars, such as Saunders who goes so far astray as to assert that it "failed to advance the cause of equality." Catherine Elizabeth Saunders, "Houses Divided: Sentimentality in the Function of Biracial Characters in American Abolitionist Fiction" (Ph.D. diss., Princeton University, 2002), p. 17 (hereafter cited as "Houses Divided").

2. Boyd's analysis of the models of power in *Dred* acknowledges the enslaving potential of such unbounded liberty, although he errs in his belief that Stowe saw matriarchy as its alternative. Richard Boyd, "Models of Power in Harriet Beecher Stowe's *Dred,*" *Studies in American Fiction* 19, no. 1 (1991).

3. Published by Berhnard Tauchnitz at Leipzig, and reprinted in the 1965 Oxford edition of *Uncle Tom's Cabin.* Page references refer to the reprint edition.

4. *UTC,* p. ixiv: "For they who enslave others cannot long themselves remain free."

5. It is common enough for those who have analyzed *Dred* to emphasize that the novel voices warning; Hartshorne, for example, describes it as a "novel about that day of vengeance," and Berghorn as "a jeremiad warning" and a "prediction of impending apocalypse." Sarah Dickson Hartshorne, "'Woe Unto You That Desire the Day of the Lord:' Harriet Beecher Stowe and the Corruption of Christianity in *Dred, a Tale of the Great Dismal Swamp,*" *Anglican and Episcopal History* 64 (1995): 287.

Donna E. Berghorn, "'The Mother's Struggle': Harriet Beecher Stowe and the American Anti-Slavery Debate" (Ph.D. diss., University of Pennsylvania, 1988), pp. 178, 246 (hereafter cited as "The Mother's Struggle"). Several critics share Hamilton's sense that, in the end of *Dred*, "Stowe pulls back in horror from a vision of black retributive justice and insurgency." Cynthia Hamilton, "*Dred*: Intemperate Slavery," *Journal of American Studies* 34, no. 2 (2000): 277. None of these critics, however, have uncovered the deeper, philosophic underpinnings of this warning, although Cotugno moves in this direction with her understanding that in *Dred*, "Stowe attempts to move the nation back to its founding principles . . . " Clare Degree Cotugno, "Form and Reform: Transatlantic Dialogues, 1824–1876" (Ph.D. diss., Temple University, 2001), p. 188 (hereafter cited as "Form and Reform").

6. Steele emphasizes the good done by Tom, seeing in his character an intentional echo of "the Suffering Servant of the synoptic tradition." Thomas J. Steele, S.J., "Tom and Eva: Mrs. Stowe's Two Dying Christs," *Negro American Literature Forum* 6, no. 3 (1972): 85 (hereafter cited as "Tom and Eva"). Smylie discusses the ways in which "Tom demonstrates the 'sympathies of Christ'" and "shows his willingness to become a vicarious sacrifice, to give up his own life protecting others." James H. Smylie, "*Uncle Tom's Cabin* Revisited: The Bible, the Romantic Imagination, and the Sympathies of Christ," *Interpretation* 27 (1973): 82. Lewis likens Tom to "the head servant, a 'patriarch in religious matters,' Christian teacher, friend to women, the downtrodden, and oppressed in the model of Christ." Gladys Sherman Lewis, "Message, Messenger, and Response: Puritan Forms and Cultural Reformation in Harriet Beecher Stowe's *Uncle Tom's Cabin*" (Ph.D. diss., Oklahoma State University, 1992), p. 205 (hereafter cited as "Message, Messenger, and Response").

7. Note Stowe's youthful appreciation of the role of sound opinion in guiding conduct in chapter 17, note 25.

8. A point Shipp cogently described in his dissertation. See note 95 **[AU2: please correct note number and provide corresponding chapter]**of this work. Robert Hosford Shipp, "*Uncle Tom's Cabin* and the Ethos of Melodrama" (Ph.D. diss., Columbia University, 1986; hereafter cited as "*UTC* and the Ethos of Melodrama")

9. Leslie Fiedler, *Love and Death in the American Novel* (New York: Stein and Day, 1960; reprint, 1966), p. 264 (hereafter cited as *Love and Death*). One must, however, note that "to this day" hardly dates back further than 1940. Until then Uncle Tom was highly regarded by blacks as well as others and not generally considered a "pious compromiser." See chapter 8, note 4. A latter day statement which seems closer to the mark is Irving Kristol's plea for fairness to Uncle Tom: "If none reproached him for not demanding his freedom, it was because he evidently already possessed it—that inner transcendent freedom which all noble souls possess, and which the human race will never cease to venerate. So long as it venerates anything beyond its material self." Irving Kristol, "A Few Kind Words for Uncle Tom," *Harper's Magazine* 230 (1965): 98.

10. While numerous Stowe scholars have noted the presence of this portrait in Tom's cabin, none seem to have understood the device. Consider these examples: Riss states that "rather than seeing this 'negrification' of Washington as Stowe's effort to expose the hypocrisy of distributing liberal rights according to race, I will argue that this moment exemplifies Stowe's belief that racial homogeneity can provide

the only secure foundation for either a familial or political community." Arthur Riss, "Racial Essentialism and Family Values in *Uncle Tom's Cabin*," *American Quarterly* 46, no. 4 (1994): 514 (hereafter cited as "Racial Essentialism"). To Brown "the portrait of George Washington (in blackface) . . . poignantly underscores . . . the marketability of slaves." Gillian Brown, *Domestic Individualism: Imagining Self in Nineteenth-Century America* (Berkeley: University of California Press, 1990), p. 48.

11. Note the character of his "Declaration of Independence," which affirmed his liberty but neglected its basis in moral equality as such. *UTC*, Ch. 12, "The Freeman's Defence."

2

The Real Alternatives

Stowe reveals the status of George's righteousness at the end of the novel, where she engages him in an argument in which she gets the last word. But we are running ahead of our narrative. To slow down and begin at the beginning, we can perceive what is at stake between the political and moral alternatives she offered in the first section of the novel,[1] where the differences are initially formulated. In the final chapter of the first section and the first chapter of the second section, Stowe introduced a character who serves as the vehicle to express this difference. The character, "an honest drover," is a slaveholder but a slaveholder who is uncharacteristically uncertain about the basis of his authority. The circumstances are, on the one hand, a Kentucky tavern that is the first stop on George Harris's route of escape from slavery and, on the other hand, a riverboat upon which Uncle Tom is carried deeper into slavery.

The isolated appearance of John the Drover in these selected and separate incidents provides a bridge between the plots that otherwise goes unnoted. Besides emphasizing again how little time is required for George Harris to acquire his liberty, following his direct, step-by-step approach, the bridge serves to make clear what may have been in doubt: Uncle Tom and George are reacting to the same slavery. The distinction between the kindness and brutality of their masters in no way mitigates our understanding of their circumstances. The reader should not, therefore, depend upon meeting Simon Legree before Uncle Tom's motivation becomes questionable.

It is the dark cloud that overhangs the administration of slavery in every case that produces ambivalence in the Kentucky drover about the basis of the institution. His doubts lead him to eliminate all appearance of coercion in his relationship with his own slaves. This requires that he be ready to give up his slaves to freedom. But he does not in fact give up his slaves. His honesty, therefore, is nothing other than his openness to a demonstration of the true demands of justice, which he is predisposed to follow. And he recognizes that such a demonstration must turn on the account of the slave as fully a man. Thus it must reveal the nature of the duties men owe to men and the differences in men. His situation, in other words, is the ideal situation of Stowe's audience. He occupies within the novel the role of the ideal reader of the novel. And he confronts the two alternative accounts of justice.

In the first of these two chapters, chapter XI, Stowe presents the drover's account of his own opinion. She depicts his character suitably to his role as a surrogate reader: complete republican simplicity. He is a loose-jointed, heavy-boned, tobacco-chewing Kentuckian, who wears indoors the liberty his forefathers donned out of doors as they pushed back the frontier. Seated in a tavern at which George will soon appear, he greets his fellow lodgers with a hearty "bonhomie." With them, he meets George Harris before George's arrival at the tavern. The encounter is via an advertisement for a runaway slave. Among other things, the handbill related that the "boy, George," was very intelligent, speaks handsomely, can read and write, will probably try to pass for a white man, and was branded with an "H" in his right hand. The handbill was read aloud by Mr. Wilson, also a traveler and George Harris's former, kindly employer in a hemp factory. After the reading, John, the Drover, raised himself from his post by the fire, walked up to the handbill, and let fly a charge of tobacco juice. Letting it be known that that expressed his opinion on the subject, he returned to his seat.

John was challenged to further explanation by the tavern host, and he indicated a preference that his target had been the "writer of that ar paper."

> Any man that owns a boy like that, and can't find any better way o' treating on him, *deserves* to lose him. Such papers as these is a shame to Kentucky; that's my mind right out, if anybody wants to know! (122, original emphasis)

He next related how he handled his own gang: he offers them their liberty. "That's the way I keep mine" (122). When they are free to run, they no longer wish to do so. This method, according to John, produced better results than anyone in the region can boast. And the method is based on treating the "boys" "like men."

> Treat 'em like dogs, and you'll have dogs' work and dogs' actions. Treat 'em like men, and you'll have men's works. (122)

John employs an interesting adaptation of Aristotle's advice as to the method of dealing with slaves. Having previously argued the injustice of slavery,[2] Aristotle nonetheless recognizes the possibility that a decent (indeed, "ideal") republic cannot be constructed without slavery. In that pre-modern era the labor of slaves was a necessary source of the leisure required for gentlemanliness. To prove the injustice of slavery, Aristotle demonstrated that slaves should differ from free men as fully as such men differ from beasts. Then some men could by nature rule others despotically, just as any man may by nature rule dogs despotically.

Harry Jaffa has developed this argument in its comprehensive form, whereby we see that the relationships among natural beings must be derived from their respective relationships to the whole of nature. A comprehensive view of the relationships of natural beings (those with some capacity of self-movement) begins with God and descends to beasts. Because of the difference between God and man, God rules man despotically. That is the same relationship that man has to beasts. To justify the despotic rule of man over man, differences among men of the same nature as those between God and man and man and beasts must be found.[3] Aristotle's proof denies the existence of such vast differences among men. His provisional acceptance of slavery, therefore, relies on a conventional understanding of slavery and seeks to accommodate it to natural principles. Aristotle achieves this by insisting that the *treatment* of the slave must be based on his capacity for freedom. That is, although he will be a slave, the slave's treatment must essentially deny that his slavery is the proper form of expression of his humanity.[4] This is also the essential form of John the Drover's distinctions between "dogs' works" and "men's works." The difference is that Aristotle suggested holding eventual freedom before the slave in order to motivate the slave to acquit himself well in slavery *as a means of escaping* slavery. John offers his slaves present freedom as a means of motivating them to acquit themselves well in slavery, simply.

The Drover found it necessary, in other words, to forgo the appeal to law in dealing with his slaves. He assumed full personal responsibility for the subsistence of the relationship between himself and his slaves because, as he saw it, men cannot otherwise be held in slavery—at least, not as men. But John fully recognizes that the relationship is still slavery. Its justification is provisional in his case, resting on the likelihood that none of his men will wish to pursue "men's actions." The significant omission of men's actions as what one might get when slaves are treated like men reaffirms the presumption that they who will be enslaved will not be subject to the full range of human ambitions. John can be satisfied with slavery if his slaves deserve to be ruled by him. But he cannot be sure of this unless he provides them opportunity to escape his rule. They are ruled by their own wills. He gets "men's works" and not men's actions, because men's works alone are suited to their capacities. This, at least, he is entitled to assume under the precautions he has taken.

In addition, John added the more significant fact that he considers law incapable of making these distinctions. Hence, "more 'n all" he provided for the freedom of his slaves in the event of his death. The force of law could not extend his *de facto* superiority to someone else, perhaps an inferior, by way of the fiction that law judges according to nature. To the drover, slavery is based on the right of the stronger, or best, and it relies, therefore, on a natural hierarchy that requires individual and not general determination. Hence, law can only obscure the distinctions men are required to make and, as a consequence, necessarily produces injustice. It is perfectly consistent for him to shield his slaves from the law and to refuse to give them up.

But the drover's argument is subject to a weakness and does not go without challenge. There are other slaveholders who cannot justify their title by their capacity to rule other men. They face rather bleak prospects in accepting that argument. Mr. Wilson, George's former employer, fully agrees with the drover but rather because he knows and likes George Harris than because he recognizes any insufficiency in the law. As his conversation with George Harris shows later, the gentleman is utterly incapable of any abstraction in this matter. He supports John's analysis by relating his acquaintance with George and the fact that George had invented a hemp-cleaning machine on which George's owner, Mr. Harris, held the patent. That was, of course, among the reasons that Harris took George away from the factory and attempted to "break him." To the drover this is a clear example of the owner failing to perceive his own good. He pushes the paradox of Harris's enjoying the profits from the patent he held, while destroying the source of those profits. John, in other words, accepts the identity of self-interest and benevolence.

It is at this point that another traveler intervenes in the discussion and challenges the drover by defending Harris's position. To the new interlocutor "bright niggers" are the special problem, which disproves John's argument. Under his system of openness, owners would be left with no control over them—at least those owners inferior to their gifted chattel. Given the chance to leave, such slaves would betray their own interest to stay. And sooner or later it would become evident that the principle of slavery is not race, *per se*, but an individually determined natural hierarchy. At that point Mr. Harris and his defender would be threatened with enslavement, and the pretense of equality in the master class would be completely shattered. If, therefore, slavery is good for no man, the drover is wrong. Harris does not misperceive his own good. It is in the interest of the institution of slavery, once established, to replace the appeal to strength with the appeal to law. The institution as such cannot be defended where the defense reposes entirely in the relationship between the capacities of the individual masters and the individual slaves.

The drover does not fully respond to the address of the new interlocutor, who is identified no further than as "a coarse-looking fellow from the other side of the room." In fact, he only intimates that the objection does not so much prove the justice of slavery as to suggest a fundamental injustice. The drover ascribed what the "coarse fellow" considered "aggravatin' and sarcy" behavior to the fact that the slaves were men, not easily gotten "down into beasts." The exchange continued:

> "Bright niggers isn't no kind of 'vantage to their masters. . . . What's the use o' talents and them things, if you can't get the use on 'em yourself? Why, all the use they make on 't is to get round you. I've had one or two of those fellers, and I jest sold 'em down the river. I knew I'd got to lose 'em first or last, if I didn't."
>
> "Better send orders up to the Lord, to make you a set, and leave out their souls entirely," said the drover. (123)

Now both of these responses must be considered seriously. The poor, coarse old slaveholder has a genuine problem and has struck upon a practical solution in his own case. "Talents and them things" cannot be naturally commanded by men who do not enjoy them themselves. In their case, the connection between self-interest and benevolence does not hold because they would naturally be the objects of benevolence rather than dispensers of benefactions. At the same time, the purpose of slavery where the talented may be enslaved is to serve the advantage of the master. And unless a master without talents wants to place himself under the tutelage of a slave, he must be content to obtain limited advantages from creatures in still worse condition than himself. His power must be extensive enough to permit this. But it can only be that extensive if supplemented by law, since he has not such powers by nature. With the aid of law, the master without talents creates an artificial hierarchy that does not threaten his own freedom but still resembles the drover's natural hierarchy.

The drover's response, on the other hand, raises a doubt as to the legitimacy of an artificial hierarchy. If the hierarchy does not emerge by nature, the suggestion is that it emerges from violence to nature—the creation of soulless anthropoids. If, however, violence to nature was the source of slavery, it is questionable whether any genuine or just advantage is served by it.[5] What was thought to be merely the acknowledged right of the stronger looms as something perverse. In fact, if the original title were based on the appeal to strength, it would seem unlikely that law—moral obligation—would constitute a force sufficient to repress continued appeal to strength. Thus, the appeal to strength—the right of the stronger—would not be the origin of this institution or of any institution. The moral principle itself would be at the origin. And the principle originating slavery would be an impeachment of nature—a doing violence to the natural hierarchy—to which men fall prey because of their very openness to moral principle. The perversion would consist in taking advantage of men's moral sensibility to undermine the very end of that sensibility, the realization of a natural hierarchy. The honest, open, good-natured drover, however liberal, is faced with the prospect that even his benign administration of slavery must be illegitimate. In shielding his slaves from the law, he shields them from the only principle that defends their slavery!

The conversation ends abruptly because of an interruption. John seemed prepared for the doctrine of moral equality, to which he had already given full theoretical if not practical assent. But a practical difficulty remains. Although moral equality may be granted as a consequence of human origins, it is still the case that men differ in their capacities. Further, if moral principle is at the origin of human institutions, it is necessary that men share some form of relationship. And, whatever the form, the relationship cannot avoid reflecting the differences in capacities. The doctrine of moral equality cannot be accepted until the full implications of the principle can be spelled out in practical terms.

We discovered why the strong among the slaves were not continually enslaving the weak among the masters by revealing that the right of the stronger was not, in fact, the basis of slavery. The principle of moral equality faces a similar challenge from "bright niggers." If it means, in general, that no man rules another by nature, then it must certainly mean, in particular, that no man ever rules the very best men in fact. But it is not manifest that "bright niggers," however "aggravatin' and sarcy," are not in fact ruled by their masters.

The principle of moral equality is defensible only if the very best men cannot in fact be ruled, and the injustice is rather in the attempt than the event. They may remove themselves from proximity to their masters and avoid being ruled by inaccessibility. But that is not a sufficient test. The liberty gained already presupposes what is not proved: the utmost capacity to govern oneself. The very best men can accept that their superiority gives them no title to rule if they can at the least ensure that they are not thereby ruled by men worse than themselves. Moral equality is compatible with moral excellence only if moral excellence is unimpeachable even in a defenseless condition. It follows that the best demonstration of the illegitimacy of slavery and the practical safety of moral equality are one and the same: that is, to show the limitation of slavery morality by showing the impossibility of enslaving, of actually ruling, the best souls. That is the same thing as to say that John the Drover need not be concerned to defend the natural hierarchy from the moment he is shown that it cannot in fact be violated. The George Harris model cannot serve this end. The fact is, if all the slaves were to follow that model, nothing would have been decided about the nature of either man or slavery. It must be shown that human law or morality, though it may do violence to nature or mask nature, cannot in fact overthrow nature. From the moment that is shown, John may give up his slaves without yielding his appreciation of the differences in men or abandoning his own interests.

But this moral insight he cannot find in his country—for good reasons. He understands liberty in relationship to the right of the stronger. Thus, he can provide a defense for George Harris even against the law. But the limitations inherent in that view require that he return to law or morality to seek a more comprehensive answer as to how differences in capacity can be reflected in human relationships, if mastery and submission are not the model. And when he turns to morality he finds only contradictions *he* is unable to resolve. So we are introduced to him a second and final time in chapter 12, as he accompanies Uncle Tom down river.

There the question is no longer how to exempt—liberate—the brightest men from slavery, but the justice of slavery itself. Again, the drover has to consult fellow travelers. In fact, as before he casually enters an established conversation. On this occasion, however, he has no opinion to offer; he is unsure. Consequently, he phrases in terms of action the alternate possibilities, using the occasion to jostle the conscience of slave-trader, Haley.

In chapter 12 we are provided further acquaintance with Uncle Tom before John the Drover makes his appearance, in contrast to the order of chapter 11. We learn, above all, that the author also considers her hero an unusual character. Indeed, he seems so stolidly unmoved by a desire for vengeance or even an energetic demand for liberty that he almost seems a just victim of injustice. Nevertheless, the drover's discussion of the justice of slavery will not touch particularly on Uncle Tom. Tom is rather only an unnamed member of the slave coffle brought aboard the riverboat, *La Belle Rivière*, by Haley the trader.

The discussion is in fact initiated when one of the little angels aboard ship reports the appearance of the slave gang to his mother. Her gentlewomanly oaths and cries of shame are the occasion, once again, for a fellow traveler to defend the institution. Unlike the "coarse fellow" from the tavern, who defended slavery by the interest of the master, however, the defense drawn from this "genteel woman" rests on the benefit of slavery to the "negroes," in particular. In this discussion a subtle change occurs. The attack on slavery still comes from a southerner. But the initial defense of slavery is placed in the mouth of a northern woman. Stowe does not explicitly avow this, but she has the genteel northerner say, "I've been South, and I must say I think the negroes are better off than they would be to be free" (141). This unacknowledged first occurrence of what will become a major theme of the novel, culminating in a Vermonter's slaying Uncle Tom, underscores the importance of the opinion here expressed. Rather than proceeding from a view to the good of the master, it is predicated on a radical distinction between blacks and whites. Stowe believed that liberating the country from the evils of slavery as distinct from slavery itself depended more on refuting this positive good opinion than upon demonstrating the injustice of the right of the stronger.

The discussion aboard *La Belle Rivière* turned upon the question whether slaves were as fully human as the master class. The southern lady who attacked slavery attacked most bitterly its "outrages on the feelings and affections" of the slaves. She cited specifically the separation of families. The northern lady accepted the general truth of this statement as it relates to human affairs, but eventually maintained that "we can't reason from our feelings to those of this class of persons" (141). After a warm response from the anti-slavery gladiator, the genteel woman rested herself in a repetition of her initial reflection. She had begun with a preface that there was much to be said on either side of the question. But her entire case amounted to the twofold assertion that negroes were sub-humans who were improved by the moral guidance of their masters. In this she implicitly accepts the argument that among the fully human, each must be supposed competent to judge of his own good. And Stowe implicitly argues that this is the state of northern opinion on the matter.

As a consequence, there falls upon northern opinion and the entire positive good school the necessity to demonstrate the generic deficiencies of negroes. The northern lady shrinks from this task, but just as she shrinks into silence an unidentified parson speaks up.

> It's undoubtedly the intention of Providence that the African race should be servants,—kept in low condition. . . . "Cursed be Canaan; a servant of servants shall he be," the scripture says. (141)

Earlier in the novel Stowe attributes this position to some of the southern clergy, in particular. Thus we may assume this parson is a southern parson, and his appearance—out of nowhere—demonstrates the support and origin of that northern opinion which impedes the struggle against slavery.

But there is a slight difference in application. For the genteel woman, the slaves were sub-humans who were being improved. But in the parson's use of holy text, they are fully human beings who are being punished. We must emphasize the passage, "kept in a low condition," which interdicts attempts at improvement. In this we find a moral or biblical basis for the artificial hierarchy—the necessity of breaking "bright niggers." Thus, what the northern lady sees as the work of nature is in fact the work of men—if under divine guidance. The origin of the northern prejudice—the view of negroes as sub-human—is the rigorous application of an artificial hierarchy designed to keep the slaves in a low condition.

> It is at this point, on his own ground, that we re-encounter John the Drover. "I say, stranger, is that ar what that text means?" said a tall man standing by. (141)

John confesses that he has not heretofore viewed the matter in that light. We saw why in chapter 11. But we remember that John was open to moral guidance on the subject. So the parson responds, again, "undoubtedly." For reasons "inscrutable" the divinity decreed the doom of bondage for the African, the son of Canaan, "and we must not set up our opinion against that" (141).

Now this seems comprehensive enough, although its reliance on "inscrutable reasons" ought to leave some room for doubt in John's mind. Nonetheless, he tries out the practical implications, perhaps sarcastically, perhaps not.

> "Well, then, we'll all go ahead and buy up niggers, . . . if that's the way of Providence,—won't we, Squire?" said he, turning to Haley, who had been standing . . . intently listening to the conversation. "Yes . . . we must all be resigned to the decrees of Providence. Niggers must be sold, and trucked round, and kept under; it's what they's made for. 'Pears like this yer view's quite refreshing, an't it stranger?" said he to Haley. (141–42)

Because John ends his statements in questions, needling the slavetrader, Haley, we are entitled to assume that he finds this view singular rather than refreshing. But Haley, at least, responds seriously. He never really thought about the matter, but would not have gone so far himself. He was just a man in business, who, if it turned out to be wrong, "calculated to 'pent on 't in time" (142). Now John enjoys himself, congratulating Haley on having been saved the trouble of reflection and repentance. All of which blessing comes from knowing the scripture, like the good parson.

> "Ye could jist have said, 'Cussed be'—what's his name?—'and 't would all have come right.'" And . . . the honest drover . . . sat down and began smoking, with a curious smile on his long, dry face. (142)

Only at this point does Stowe explain that the troublesome stranger is John the Drover, connecting this conversation with the previous discussion. John still doubts. This new view is insufficient to alter his relationship with the human beings he holds as slaves. Still, he had not found and cannot offer the moral guidance to assure himself that even his minimalist approach is just.

Again, from nowhere a parson speaks. He utters but one statement. Opposing the New Testament to the first parson, he quotes, "'All things whatsoever ye would that men should do unto you, do ye even so unto them.' I suppose . . . *that* is scripture, as much as 'Cursed be Cana'" (142, original emphasis). Matters are at a standstill, which fact John promptly notices. The boat's coming into a landing temporarily interrupts the discussion. But on the way to the guards John ascertains what we were not yet told, when a fellow passenger nods to his question, "Both them ar chaps parsons?" (142). The contradiction between the two serves to indicate why John cannot find comprehensive moral guidance. Something needs to be added to take him beyond the minimalist position he occupies—something in the way of doing unto others what one would want done to himself that yet takes account of differing capacities. Until that is provided, the drover's opinion comes closest to recognizing the necessity of moral equality. Christianity simply understood is a provisional account of man's duty to man.

During the break in the discussion a practical example of the effect of slavery is given. A distraught slave-wife rushes on board to cry farewell to her slave-husband, one of those chained in the coffle. The author describes the event in her own words, and reduces it, in general application, to what *she* considers the essence of slavery, "the weak broken and torn for the profit and convenience of the strong" (143). That is, they are not improved—ruled for their own good—nor kept in a low condition by divine injunction. But the "strong," who profit from it, are nonetheless made strong by the protections afforded them through the opinions of such as these. In that sense the weak are not necessarily the naturally weak but rather those kept weak by reason of exclusion from social and political intercourse.

Francis Lieber mildly criticizes *Uncle Tom's Cabin* because "*the minister* does not appear once." His review was generally favorable and certainly kindly but noted an absence of practical guidance on the question of slavery. This last criticism is sufficiently answered by the concluding sentence of the review: "Could I mount the scaffold for the abolition of slavery, I would do it tomorrow."[6] But beyond that, and more importantly, is the connection between the two criticisms.

Lieber apparently meant the minister in his accustomed role—actually ministering to consciences and preaching sermons. But it is safe to say he overlooked the passages we have just cited, for they explain, in their contradictions, the "absence of the minister." The appeal to the church, simply, is an appeal to the very source of many of the opinions subtending slavery and, in any event, to the contradictions, which resulted in the paralysis of opinion that left the drover in doubt of how far he need go.[7] The practical guidance in *Uncle Tom's Cabin* results from its demonstration both of the opinions required to end slavery and the means necessary to establish those opinions. The minister does appear—but in order that we discover the need to go beyond the church. The minister here serves an earthly purpose greater than himself.

The discussion resumes with the anti-slavery parson vehemently attacking Haley as the cause of all the bitterness seen in that tearful separation of husband and wife. He assured the trader that he would be called to divine judgment on account of this sin. Haley turned from him in silence, but could not escape the omnipresent drover.

> "I say now," said the drover, touching his elbow, "there's differences in parsons, an't there? 'Cussed be Canaan' don't seem to go down with this 'un, does it? . . . And that ar an't the worst on 't . . . *mabbee* it won't go down with the Lord, neither, when ye come to settle with Him, one o' these days, as *all on us must,* I reckon." (143, emphasis added)

We add, by way of voiding suspense, that Haley managed to escape to a neutral corner and there reflected on the increasing "danger" of his enterprise, resolving to end it apparently soon.

But we are here concerned only with John, who finally stopped asking questions and turned a bit serious himself. The differences in ministers, he reasoned, provide no measure of safety with respect to God, nor, we might say, with respect to justice. Thus, his concluding statement is as much a reflection upon his own circumstances, as he duly notes, as upon Haley's. And the problem is that he is left to himself to reconcile the demands of justice, since the authoritative interpreters of the just—those officially designated as such—fail to recommend a course either consistent or sufficiently comprehensive when all are considered together.

The reader of the novel occupies the same position, save that he has the further advantage of being able to read beyond these isolated passages. John the Drover appears nowhere else in the novel. And, considering his good intentions, we may freely imagine that he has now joined us in reading the rest of the novel and continuing these reflections. And what we seek, above all else, is to discern what it is that John owes his slaves beyond liberty, the attainment of which nonetheless requires their freedom. We wish to discern how John can provide for their good without ruling them, since in his case the slaves are inferior in capacity to himself. We wish to discern, therefore, why the indefeasible liberty of all relies more surely upon the right of the weaker than upon the right of the stronger—why, that is, George Harris is an inappropriate hero for the defense of moral equality and the demonstration of man's duty to man.

What we require is a single account of the three dilemmas presented through John the Drover's appearance in the drama. *The first,* we recall, was to know that human morality could not overthrow nature, though it might mask it. This would permit John to accept a principle that would defend the freeing of his slaves without risking either his own enslavement or, more importantly, the occasion to pursue what is good. *The second* was to know if the slave class was as fully human as the master class. John is predisposed to this view, but is uncertain as to either its practical consequences or the results if, acting upon this view entirely, it is subsequently shown to be in error. Thus, *the third* and most significant dilemma must be resolved as a condition of resolving the first two. If it is true that the artificial hierarchy masks a true natural hierarchy but cannot override it, the strong kept artificially weak must, even in their weakness, be capable of demonstrating their human superiority to the naturally weak. They must be more than "bright niggers." Clearly shorn of all conventional supports and wholly without occasion to rule other men by established authority, they must nonetheless manifest their "talents" and one talent above all others, the capacity to judge what is good for men.

> But to live,—to wear on, day after day, of mean, bitter, low, harassing servitude, every nerve dampened and depressed, every power of feeling gradually smothered,—this long and wasting heart-martyrdom, this slow, daily bleeding away of the inward life, drop by drop, hour after hour,—this is *the true searching test* of what there may be in a man or woman.[8]

John demands what it is very difficult to provide: the human model of surpassing excellence drawn from among the misery of the slaves. This is a thing difficult to provide, but the author will make the attempt. And, as if to create the suspense she had already removed in the avowal that Uncle Tom was her hero, she continues the parallel plots with the teasing question, who will be our model?

NOTES

1. In these terms, chapters 1–11 constitute the first section of the novel, and chapters 12–21 constitute the second section. By page number rather than chapters a different center is found and yet new questions introduced.
2. Aristotle, *Politics*, 1245a15–1255a1.
3. Harry V. Jaffa, *Crisis of the House Divided* (Seattle: University of Washington Press, 1973; hereafter cited as *Crisis of the House Divided*). Also, Harry V. Jaffa, *Bicentennial Celebration* (Durham, NC: Carolina Academic Press, 1978).
4. *Politics*, 1325a24; 1327b; 1328b24–1329a25; and 1330a20.
5. Aristotle, *Physics*, Book V, Chapter 6.
6. Francis Lieber, "Uncle Tom: A Review of Mrs. Stowe's Book," 1853, ms# LI469, Huntington Library, San Marino, California (hereafter cited as "Uncle Tom").
7. Cf., book I, part II, "The Genealogy of Uncle Tom," chapter 15.
8. *UTC*, Ch. 38, p. 443 (emphasis added). Stowe proceeds as though the entire novel were, in effect, a refutation of Hegel's view of the African, in *The Philosophy of History*. But in order to rescue the African, it proves equally necessary to demonstrate the subordinate importance of consciousness as such—subjective knowledge of the

present state of moral development—in the consideration of human moral possibilities. Thus, Stowe appeals to that substratum—once called nature—which both determines and is available as a guide to action. The reason or logic of history, in this view, will extend no farther than particular appeals to reason may carry it—there is no general, abstract development of the *logos.* Thence is derived the significance of Stowe's concluding citation of missionary reports from Africa: "It has often been found among them, that a stray seed of truth, borne on some breeze of accident into hearts the most ignorant, has sprung up into fruit, whose abundance has shamed that of higher and more skillful culture" (p. 451).

3

Standards of Humanity

To know George Harris and Uncle Tom we must return to the beginning of the novel. We may take the foregoing discussion as a guide to the reading of the novel. We now attempt an explication of the text. One of the most difficult problems faced in explicating *Uncle Tom's Cabin* is the incongruity between some chapter headings and the texts of those chapters. The fact is, four of the chapters do not offer much of what their titles promise. And to understand the novel it is necessary to understand why this should be so. The chapters which present special difficulties are chapter 1, "In Which the Reader Is Introduced to a Man of Humanity"; chapter 2, "The Mother"; chapter 18, "Miss Ophelia's Experiences and Opinions"; and chapter 33, "Cassy." Much of the power of the novel depends upon the effect of these odd chapters. Indeed, it is because of them that the "hasty" and improbable conclusion—tying far too many diverse strands together in a happy and beautiful whole—may in the end be seen to be not hasty however improbable.

To begin at the beginning, these four chapters serve to highlight the mechanism through which we will view the action of the hero and its contrast with his alter ego. That mechanism is indirection.[1] It is a fact that, throughout the novel, every significant development of Uncle Tom's character is revealed indirectly, in the process of discussing some other primary character or event. Meanwhile, save for his first appearance, the very reverse is true of George Harris. Uncle Tom's character is rooted in relatedness to others in an extreme degree, to a degree equivalent to the individualism if not isolation of George Harris. (And in the end the consequences of Tom's relatedness overcome the consequences of George's individualism.)

The problem to which the reader's eye is directed in the first chapter is the characterization of the man of humanity, the man whose character is rooted in relatedness to the human things. More precisely, that chapter's title promises the reader that he shall meet such a man. The author in that chapter directly introduces only two men. The one is a Kentucky gentleman and slaveowner, Mr. Shelby. The other is the slavetrader, Haley. Two other men are introduced, but only through the mouths of Shelby (Uncle Tom) and Haley (a fellow slave-trader, Tom Loker). As will subsequently emerge, neither Shelby, Haley, nor Loker can be called a man of humanity in the fulsome sense the novel intends to establish. The reader, therefore, must either take the account of Uncle Tom by the non-humane slaveowner as nonetheless revealing some measure of Uncle Tom's humanity, or he must consider the chapter intentionally ironic.[2] In either case, it would emerge that this indirect and perhaps ironic introduction of our hero (he was the subject of a commercial transaction) would properly phrase the problem of the novel. The character of property as such is primarily comprehended from the opinions of those who employ it. What exists of the human in such property (character derived independent of the opinion of the user) amounts to refutation of the argument that it is rightly treated as property.

The difficulty in chapter 2 is more readily discerned: the chapter promises the reader a "mother." In fact, two mothers are introduced, and it is very unclear which was intended to bear the title. The suggestion is strong that Mrs. Shelby is certainly as much the mother to her servant, Eliza, as Eliza is to her little boy. But these questions occupy hardly a third of the chapter. The remaining two-thirds introduces George Harris, husband to Eliza. The author offers the introduction in her own words, but it too is indirect. George does not speak, not even when the dialogue, in his presence, turns to the question of his fate. His master had come to retrieve him from a factory to which his services had been let. And against the protests of the factory owner, the property was reclaimed.

Manifest in this chapter is what is only tacit in the opening chapter. The character of soul in the slave has been derived independent of the opinion of the owner. George's owner is at least intelligent enough to realize that the situation is untenable, and Stowe even emphasizes the owner's "consciousness of inferiority" to his intelligent chattel. But the owner fails to realize that once the distinction has been admitted, he cannot rationally re-assert the priority of his property right in the slave. Mr. Harris's sense of inferiority is the tacit emancipation of George Harris.

There is no irony in this second chapter, though indirection is again employed to reveal the slave's status. And, unlike the first chapter, the status of the slave in this chapter is limited, particular. George Harris is comprehended rather more through his relationship with Eliza, a mother and wife, than through his master. After this chapter, the reader never meets George indirectly. And in the following chapter, "The Husband and Father," George is already a free man—he announces to his wife his intention to escape. The reader never meets George's master, after the second chapter, except through George's mouth.

Indirection, then, is the method through which the character of the slave who is yet a slave is revealed, when that character is not slavish. Stowe respects the formal requirement that the slave as slave has no will. The slave will speak up as a man when he ceases to be a slave.[3]

Most of the story of George Harris is the story of a free man. Uncle Tom remains a slave for long after George Harris is free. Chapters 18 and 33, therefore, continue to insinuate Uncle Tom into the drama, rather than to make him the central character. That is, though by this point he does speak, strictly speaking his speeches continue to be subordinated to the purpose of developing other characters. This is at least the appearance. For it is manifest, by the end, that Uncle Tom bears a primary responsibility for the events that have unfolded. In chapters 18 and 33, therefore, the distance between the chapter titles and the centrality of Uncle Tom in those chapters is heightened.

Chapter 18 reveals Uncle Tom's coming to rule in the St. Clare household on the analogy of Joseph's coming to rule in Egypt. Uncle Tom begins to occupy—and *pursue*—the position of spiritual guide to the least of the slaves as well as to the master. Then, in chapter 33—the last occasion of a mere insinuation of Tom—we have the fullest description of our hero that the novel contains. Though that chapter apparently fulfills the promise of its title, "Cassy" (we do meet Cassy, by name that is, for the first time), it is uncontested that its dramatic pitch—and that of the novel—is Uncle Tom's declaration of independence, "but this yer thing I can't feel it right to do;—and, Mas'r I *never* shall do it,—*never*!" (407, original emphasis). (The woman Tom refuses to whip at Legree's command is not Cassy, incidentally.) Thereafter, Tom speaks to us directly and freely. And it must not be neglected that Tom's emancipation comes in his first couple of weeks on Simon Legree's plantation, and he will remain there two or three years longer. Thus, the point of chapter 33 is Tom's resistance to Simon Legree.

Chapter 1 introduces a problem: the necessity for a redefinition of humanity. Chapter 2 offers the open and obvious example of one form of the expression of humanity, the example of George Harris. In chapter 18 we see a counterexample, a form of humanity represented by Uncle Tom and which remains essentially hidden.[4] And in chapter 33 we encounter the question of whether humanity or humaneness endures in the form it assumes in Uncle Tom in a way that it cannot endure in the form it assumes in George Harris. The novel's account of this perplexity is its account of the standard by which Uncle Tom is the chosen hero over and above George Harris. To understand that choice we must look still more closely at the drama of the novel. More precisely, to understand why the method of Uncle Tom's emancipation is morally more persuasive to John the Drover than the method of George Harris's emancipation, we must return to the drama of the novel.

NOTES

1. Camfield quotes an 1868 reader of *Uncle Tom's Cabin* (E. P. Parker) who was alert to Stowe's use of indirection: "'She does not *tell,* but *shows* us what it is. She does not analyze, or demonstrate, or describe, but, by a skillful manner of indirection, takes us [there] . . . and allows us to see [the system of slavery] as it really is.'" Gregg Camfield, "The Moral Aesthetics of Sentimentality: A Missing Key to *Uncle Tom's Cabin,*" *Nineteenth-Century Literature* (December 1988): 322 (hereafter cited as "Moral Aesthetics:), quoting S. M. Betts, "Harriet Beecher Stowe," in *Eminent Women of the Age* (Hartford, CT: S. M. Betts, 1868), p. 318. Likewise, Shipp emphasizes that "Mrs. Stowe's characters *are* what they *do.*" Shipp, "*UTC* and the Ethos of Melodrama," p. 64. Original emphasis.

2. Donovan, for example, concludes that the chapter title "sets the ironic tone for the opening episodes of the novel" and reads it as "an ironic epithet for Mr. Haley . . . " Donovan, *UTC: Evil, Affliction, and Redemptive Love,* p. 48.

3. The conclusion here may be doubted, if one takes "Persistent Sam," Aunt Chloe, and Cassy to "speak up" independently in their expressions either of angst or ambition. I would insist, however, that each of these examples, as we shall see, represents the fundamental submission to slavery on the part of the slaves. That is particularly true of Cassy, whom Uncle Tom must reclaim from this character deforming submission. Mullen discusses the resistant orality that was part of the slave oral tradition, noting that "nineteenth-century black women writers struggled in their texts to reconcile an oral tradition of resistance with a literary tradition of submission." Harryette Mullen, "Runaway Tongue: Resistant Orality in *Uncle Tom's Cabin, Our Nig, Incidents in the Life of a Slave Girl,* and *Beloved,*" in *The Culture of Sentiment: Race, Gender and Sentimentality in Nineteenth-Century America,* ed. Shirley Samuels (New York: Oxford University Press, 1992), p. 245. She presents the "resistant orality," however, as a means to defend oneself rather than to free oneself.

4. So hidden, in fact, that Baldwin does not see it before him, in his condemnation of *Uncle Tom's Cabin* above all else for what he calls "its rejection of life, the human being, the denial of his beauty, dread, power, in its insistence that it is his categorization alone which is real and which cannot be transcended." James Baldwin, "Everybody's Protest Novel," *Partisan Review* 16 (1949): 85.

4

Stowe's Own "Introductions"

To begin once again at the beginning, Stowe's own explanations are helpful in fathoming how the novel should be read. She wrote many and varying prefaces and introductions to *Uncle Tom's Cabin* as it appeared in its several editions in many lands.[1] We may take the "Introduction" to the 1878 American edition as the last though not necessarily most authoritative statement on the work. There, for the first time, Stowe revealed that the story of Uncle Tom had been thought through *before* a word was written. It was carefully planned.[2] The importance of this fact resides in the fact that it is a cornerstone of a secular version of the composition of *Uncle Tom's Cabin,* which seems intended to supplant the earlier "inspired" version.

Add to these reflections the fact that the 1878 "Introduction" was the final comprehensive statement Stowe made on *Uncle Tom's Cabin* in her own name,[3] and we see that it must serve as our beacon to the author's intention. In that light, one thing stands out more dramatically than all else: *Uncle Tom's Cabin* is viewed by its author as comprehensive, complete. It can stand entirely on its own. This fact is all the more remarkable because, as we have seen, the very challenges to that work called forth "defenses" and the novel, *Dred,* seems a necessary sequel. Nonetheless, by 1878 it seemed to be complete in itself. This "Introduction"—written at a point when all of Stowe's *major* works have appeared—fails to make direct mention of any other single work! Although the burden of the "Introduction" is to reveal the novel's role in the struggle against slavery, none of the assistance it received from subsequent works is mentioned. Neither is the initial essay, "The Two Altars," mentioned.

One might suspect that these facts are accounted for merely by the fact that the author intended only to provide a bare summary of the process that led to writing that particular novel and expounding the teaching it contained. But the 1878 "Introduction" carries the "process" from the author's initial personal encounters with slavery (*UTC*, xxv). through her husband's struggles over the question in the church to the ultimate and complete emancipation of the slaves (*UTC*, lii–liv). She describes the Cincinnati and Alton, Illinois riots without mentioning her "Franklin" essay. She describes in lengthy and personal detail the circumstances of the "Fugitive Slave Law" without mentioning "The Two Altars." She describes her "surprise" at abolitionist and southern reaction to *Uncle Tom's Cabin* without mentioning her defensive efforts in the *Key*. She describes her 1853 journey to England without mentioning "Sunny Memories." She does not describe the political events subsequent to 1852–1853—save for the progress of Emancipation—but she does include among a numerous correspondence (almost entirely with Europeans) an edited 1856 letter from Macaulay in which a mention of *Dred* is retained (*UTC*, p. xxxiv). In the face of this almost studied silence about all her other work, we can only conclude that *Uncle Tom's Cabin* may stand alone. *Dred* is indeed a sequel, but perhaps only incidentally so.

This conclusion is further bolstered by the stated reason for reissuing the novel in 1878:

> Now the war is over; slavery is a thing of the past; slavepens (*sic*), bloodhounds, slave-whips, and slave-coffles are only bad dreams of the night; and now the humane reader can afford to read *Uncle Tom's Cabin* without an expenditure of torture and tears. (*UTC*, liv)

Perhaps it is not *until* 1878 that *Uncle Tom's Cabin* can stand alone. It presumably still has a task to perform, quite independent of its role in the immediate political struggles of 1850–1860. It has a teaching for free men, quite independent of the solace it brought to slaves. Although Stowe was perhaps optimistic about the humane reader's political objectivity,[4] her belief in a continuing role for the novel commits us to search for this teaching of *Uncle Tom's Cabin*. John the Drover, it seems, was more than a man of his times.

What did Stowe believe to be the essential teaching of the novel? The 1878 "Introduction" both clarifies and obscures that question. The clarification stems from the explicit depiction of the novel as serving a political purpose, bolstered by the secular version of its composition. This theme repeats what Stowe was willing to say to Englishmen (though not to Americans or Frenchmen) in 1852. The justification of the character of Uncle Tom was in artistic license.[5] And the artistic purpose was dominated by the political purpose.

> In shaping her materials the author had but one purpose, to show the evils of slavery were but the inherent evils of a bad system. . . . (*UTC*, xxxi)

This, as we shall see, enters *Uncle Tom's Cabin* in the lists supporting Calvin Stowe's refusal to judge the slaveholder as opposed to the system of slavery. The problem was not the sinfulness of the slaveholder but the evil of the system.

This purpose led Stowe to expect opposition primarily from abolitionists, such as Amos Alonzo Phelps, as indeed her husband had encountered. Hence, her surprise that the abolitionists accepted and the slaveholders raged against the novel is genuine. Experience suggested the reverse. Through poetry, Calvin Stowe's argument seemed to have overcome the high-minded abolitionists. But this was perhaps illusory, and that is the point that was clarified in the "Introduction." The abolitionists' acceptance was only momentary—long enough to carry through the *Key, Dred,* and the end of slavery (that is, long enough!), but momentary. Already in 1878 the tide was reversing. And by the late twentieth century it was reversed.

It is clear then. The character of Uncle Tom was never meant to support the simple-minded attack on slavery. That the name has become an epithet is but testimony to the resurgence of the fundamental misconception of political life that characterized abolitionists. We explained that misconception above as the notion that political rights are derived from extra-political sources. It is the idea that men can claim rights and privileges from their fellow citizens on the basis of something other than their consociation. Uncle Tom argues that even if men possessed his every excellence—especially the knowledge of "natures"—without a political appreciation of those excellences they would stand radically dissociated one from another. But since men do not generally possess his excellences, the appeal to extra-political sources leaves them no hope but to encounter or be distantly affected by an Uncle Tom. Uncle Tom is not just. He is benevolent, even magnanimous.

But to the same extent that this somber truth is clear, it is not clear what "good" Christianity offers men in this world. And this Stowe obscures, pointing the return to the novel. As if to underscore this obscurity, Stowe specifically addresses the Christianity of the novel in the 1878 "Introduction." Its religious influence, she holds, has not been its "least remarkable" feature. But that feature of the book is presented, equally remarkably, as entirely unpolitical—as universal.

> The Christianity represented in the book was so far essential and unsectarian, that alike in the Protestant, Catholic, and Greek church, it has found sympathetic readers. (*UTC*, lviii)

The three great divisions of the Christian church all find themselves reflected in *Uncle Tom's Cabin*! And not only these, but non-Christian sects are drawn to it! This poses a problem of interpretation. Were this merely a statement of the author's intention, we might attempt an account of the adaptation of Christianity—always a political problem heretofore—to genuine universal politics. But the author's account is rather an account of the "history" of the book. Indeed, this *was* the character of its reception, whatever her intent.

An additional element of difficulty enters. The 1878 "Introduction" accomplishes much of its task through the medium of correspondence. Stowe reprints letters from and to her concerning the novel. Partially, she reveals that she undertook a campaign to spread the book abroad as part of the struggle against slavery—part of the struggle for world opinion and even more tangible signs of opposition to slavery. On the very *day* the book was published,[6] she was found writing to notable Englishmen, enclosing a copy of the book and requesting their assistance in the crusade. But, on the other hand, virtually all the correspondence is with Europeans, some of it unsolicited. Thus, practically the only testimonial reaction to the novel—outside of her intimate circle—is from Europeans. There was American reaction, as her biography testifies and the *Key* before that.[7] But in 1878 Stowe chooses to publish the European reaction almost exclusively. Why?

I believe the answer to this question is connected with the problem of the role of Christianity in the novel. But to answer it, we must consider, first, other statements of her objective in Europe—in particular, the prefaces to the French editions. By way of anticipation, however, let us respond to a likely objection to this mode of proceeding. The objection runs thus: Stowe was as surprised as everybody else at the European reaction to *Uncle Tom's Cabin*. She never anticipated any particular effect there and, therefore, could not have written the novel with such things in mind.

The response is two-fold. I believe it is the way in which Stowe herself would respond. First, it is certainly true that the European reaction was a surprise, as indeed was the American reaction. But the surprise was almost entirely as to the *magnitude* of the reaction. That so many people would occupy themselves with the novel in either Europe or America could not have been predicted. This was true even though prior serialization of the work had given some evidence of great popularity in America. By the same token, it was still possible to anticipate some impact on certain segments of American and European communities. In particular, French and English abolitionists and liberals were specific objects of her hopes, as her letter writing campaign revealed. Secondly, the fact that she undertook her foreign campaign on the very day of the book's release—before even the American results were in—reveals as fully as anything can—aside from the work itself—that she thought she had written to them as well.

What were Stowe's European objectives? They were not merely to enlist European aid in the struggle against slavery. This is what the refusal to couple

European with American correspondence in the 1878 "Introduction" suggests. This is also suggested by the differences between, on the one hand, the French prefaces and, on the other hand, the British and American prefaces. At bottom, Stowe's appeal is for a conscious application of Western moral principles on a universal basis. The prevailing notion of "humanity" or "humanism" at that time accounted for non-Westerners as peoples in their nonage. On this basis, such peoples were excepted from the moral demands emanating from the conjunction of Christianity and natural rights. They were subject to proselytizing—to conversion and improvement—but they were not regarded as in possession of the distinctively human faculties in any other form than as something promised in the future.

Stowe regarded this conception of an exception to otherwise commanding principles of universal morality as alone subtending the continued existence of modern liberal societies as particular or exclusive regimes. To that extent, this conception undermined the very principles of modern liberal societies. That is, the actions necessary to the defense of a particular regime could extend so far as to constitute an attack on Western morality itself, as Stowe conceived it. The maintenance of slavery on the basis of the exception was but an extreme example of the problem. The contemporary notion of the equality of peoples as prior to the equality of men is a more limited expression of the same principle. A humanism based on such a foundation was regarded as radically flawed because insufficiently cosmopolitan (insufficiently founded in human nature itself). Only a fully cosmopolitan humanism could generate a notion of reciprocal duties between any human beings on the basis of natural rights.

Nonetheless, politics and therefore Christianity remain a problem in this view. Stated most succinctly, the problem was to derive a source of particularity in societies without depending on exclusivity. In the "Preface" to the European edition, Stowe implicitly claims to have resolved this difficulty.

> In authorising the circulation of this work on the continent of Europe the author has only the apology that the love of *man* is higher than the love of country. (*UTC*, lxi)

The author makes clear that what she meant by "man" is human beings regarded apart from their particular distinctions—mere human beings. She emphasizes this by holding that American slaves are "now to a very wide extent a mixed race." The dominant element in the mix is, apart from African blood, the "best of Anglo-Saxon blood."[8]

For this reason, Stowe claims to be justified in disregarding the argument, which excepted Africans from the demands of freedom or the morality of natural rights. Nature, she implicitly argues, has disregarded human particularities and, thereby, points the way to the resolution of this vexing question.

But for Stowe context is almost everything. So we cannot neglect the fact that this argument seems to be contradicted in the American and British prefaces and is entirely unstated in the specifically French prefaces.

In the "Preface" to Bosworth's English edition[9] she speaks of "an injured and helpless race." She does not distinguish the "mixed" American from the African and, hence, does not remind English readers of the Anglo-Saxon component of the mix. And the "Preface" to the first American edition[10] is still more directly contradictory.

> The scenes of this story, as its title indicates, lie among a race hitherto ignored by the associations of polite and refined society; an exotic race, whose ancestors, born beneath a tropic sun, brought with them, and perpetuated to their descendants, a character so *essentially* unlike the hard and dominant Anglo-Saxon race, as for many years to have won from it only misunderstanding and contempt. (*UTC*, 1)

The American "Preface" is as close as Stowe ever comes to accepting the exception of the African from the demands of Western morality. Whether this preface or rather that of the European edition is her true view, we may judge only by attempting to penetrate the relation of each statement in its context to her ultimate purpose.[11]

The problem is to come to a decision about the meaning of "race." The European edition explicitly maintains that race is not predicated on any essential human differences. But in that preface Stowe is addressing a people whose own political life is not yet bedeviled by the question in the way that British and American political life was seen to be.[12] It could be said that she predicates the argument, in each case, on an appeal to the prevailing prejudice of each people. But that would be inaccurate. In the first place, she manifestly wished to alter these prejudices in some degree. And in the second place, Europeans cannot be said to have held the kinds of opinions she suggests. What is more likely, therefore, is that Stowe appeals for a change in views to the precise extent that prevailing sentiments will permit. And we must not overlook the fact that, however various the prefaces, they respectively bring the readers to a single and identical text wherein Stowe speaks with the same voice to all. Whatever errors are tolerated in the preface may be corrected in the text.

A very particular demonstration of the flexibility of the prefaces is to be found in Bosworth's English edition. As noted above, she there obscures her argument from the mixed bloodlines of the slaves. The reason for this is apparent: Stowe judged that English pride (itself rooted in the "exception" view) could not support such a direct connection. This is shown by the fact that substantial portions of that preface are literally reproduced from a letter she wrote to Sir Arthur Helps.[13] In that letter her purpose was to encourage his efforts to disseminate the novel more widely but still more importantly to calm fears that she had impugned the English character.

As we shall see, a critical section of *Uncle Tom's Cabin* compares the lot of American slaves to English laborers—and favorably. This drew from many English liberals gentle but determined refutations (*UTC*, xliv). Helps was among those offended by the passages. For, he argued,

> there is . . . even in our poorest districts and in the worst of times, all the difference that exists between humanity and barbarism; between the dignified suffering of a man oppressed by untoward circumstances and the abject wretchedness of another driven about like a beast. . . .[14]

And to the author he recommended a deeper appreciation of the Anglo-Saxon heritage.

> If she were to study this country well, she would find that with the self-helpfulness belonging to the Anglo-Saxon race (for we too are Anglo-Saxons) individuals are making exertions in every way to benefit the poor people around them. . . .[15]

> Do you think that if our poor were like your slaves, they would love law and order as they do?[16]

Hence, to Helps the material comparison must be subordinate to the moral comparison. It was the case however that he thought the material comparison favored the English laborer as well. He maintained the "exception" view of Christian-natural right morality ("Was Christianity set in a world so complete in its social arrangements that you had only to perfect them in detail, and then that all would be right?"). But he could support the condemnation of American slavery as so manifestly unjust in the circumstances as not to qualify under the exception.[17]

Stowe's response did not meet the challenge head-on. Had she done so, she would have had to come perilously close to anticipating Nietzsche's "God is dead" in making explicit her understanding of the biblical notion, God "is no respecter of persons." Instead, she explained the nature of literary device. The offensive speeches were in the mouths of slaveholders, not her own. The historical source of this opinion she identifies as John C. Calhoun, who maintained that "slaves were infinitely above the condition of the English poor." According to Stowe, she would not have introduced such speech into her book, except that her purpose required her to "state the most plausible argument of slaveholders in the most plausible way."

> And the thing has been done—I desired to make a book that they would *read*—and in order to do it, it was necessary that I should do them every justice, and if needful throw in a little on the side of mercy—and the consequence is that

> *at last* the bars are down and an anti-slavery book is actually pouring full tide into the Southern States.[18]

It is considered a fundamental axiom that to affect the sentiments of men, it is necessary to appeal to their prejudices. And that required phrasing those prejudices as plausibly as is possible.

In writing to Helps, Stowe's avowed purpose is to marshal further the *"public sentiment of nations"* against the South. She claims more for the effect of her work alone than is strictly true. The 1878 "Introduction" assured us that the work in fact met violent resistance in the South. It was indeed read there. It was also very soon barred from many places in the South. In addition to this slight mistruth, she never revealed her own opinion about the plight of the English poor.[19] Instead, she manages to place the burden entirely on Helps's shoulders.[20] The manner in which she accomplishes this is directly related to Bosworth's "Preface."

Stowe ultimately appeals to that identical Anglo-Saxon "self-helpfulness" as a means of converting Helps's indignation into both assistance for American anti-slavery efforts and *support* of the argument about the material circumstances of the English poor.[21] The first substantive paragraph of the letter (rewritten for publication) is wholly incorporated into the "Preface."

> I am perplexed how to reconcile the impression received from your article as to the condition of the English poor, with those I have received from much current English literature. I will name for example Charlotte Elizabeth's "Helen Fleetwood," and the "Little Pin Headers"—many of Dickens' writings, and latterly "Alton Locke" and "Yeast."[22]

In the letter, this paragraph suggests that the argument Helps opposes is an English argument, not American. But Stowe does not develop this point. Instead, she turns to the Calhoun thesis and treats the argument as a southern argument. (The "Preface," we shall see, does not make this concession.) The consequence is that she never resolves her own "perplexity" in the letter. Rather, she challenges Helps to undertake this task—not only as to herself but also as to America generally.

> *If* the charges are not true, she says, then *he* should show this. Suppose you write something like a comparative estimate of the condition of your poor with those held in slavery in this country—or an account of their conditions, in which you constantly graduate your shadings and statements with a *mental* reference to such a comparison, without formally announcing it. . . . An article written in England in the tone of a dispassionate spectator, willing and disposed to show all justice to the South . . . would have great effect here . . .
>
> . . . ought we not to feel that our Anglo-Saxon brethren look on us with a brotherly interest? All who speak one language and cherish one literature, and

> who have in the main one great type of character ought to be one in sentiment, and the wise and good in each ought to feel for the cause of right in each.[23]

To consider these passages in detail, we discover that Stowe reserves but does not disclose a mental reservation as to what the results of the proposed material comparisons will show. She allows Helps to assume a positive result, thereby allowing him to connect his defense of England (and the Anglo-Saxon race) with the undermining of slavery. The emphasis is entirely on the undermining of slavery, without respect to the truth of the comparison. Hence, the purpose of including it in her book is justified without respect to its being merely a literary device.

Further, she appeals to Helps's identification with Anglo-Saxon culture to produce the conclusion that, if the comparison's findings are negative, then will reason have been provided for generalizing anti-slavery's concern to the English poor—the "cause of right" among *all* Anglo-Saxons. But this can be defended on this ground solely because Helps is convinced of Anglo-Saxon particularity. For it is the very aim of *Uncle Tom's Cabin* to show that Anglo-Saxons do not share "one great type of character." It is this that constitutes the ultimate attack on slavery. The appeal to a principle she does not hold, therefore, reveals Stowe's purpose in making the appeal.

The "Preface" to Bosworth's edition makes this clear, initially by reversing the order of the discussion of the views of the plight of the English poor. Stowe there repeats the argument from literary device. But Calhoun is dropped. The view is generally held in the South. But the derivation of the view, in that paragraph, is simply "statistics." In the following paragraph one source of such statistics is identified: "Helen Fleetwood," which contains parliamentary reports establishing the "worst details." To underscore the derivation of this view from the English sources indicated in her letter, Stowe speaks in this paragraph entirely in the first person plural, showing the view to be American and not just southern. "Our ideas with regard to the condition of the English poor are drawn from current English literature." Where she distinguished her own "perplexity" from what "Calhoun said" in the letter, no such reservation remains in the "Preface."

Neither is there any reference at all to the Anglo-Saxon race in the "Preface." But this is consistent with her respect for English prejudice. As indicated above, the slaves are known only as a "helpless and injured race" and thus far distinguished in the views of men like Helps from the "self-helpful" Anglo-Saxons. Her own view of the Anglo-Saxons differs, however. In the original preface, the American preface, she refers to the Anglo-Saxon race as "hard and dominant." This cannot be repeated in the English preface. Nor can she invoke the subsequent reference of the European "Preface," where the blood of slaves was seen to be thoroughly mixed with "the best of Anglo-Saxon blood." If there is but one striking element to this systematic appeal to various national conceptions of race, it is the manifest recognition of an American capacity to hear the worst and the best.

What, then, was her own view on the question of race?[24] I suggest that the European edition is controlling. It offers the freest expression. It bears a direct relation to her interpretation of Christianity (discussed below). And most importantly, it receives the most substantial and direct support in the novel itself. In the text, excluding the American "Preface," there are eighty-one plausibly categorical references to "race," if I do not miscount. And the single emphatic element of these references, taken as a whole, is the variability of the "human substance" which provides the ground for a judgment of racial affinity. By far the greater number of references are rooted in signs of character, with the attendant result that the hero, Uncle Tom, ends up belonging to some eight explicit races by the time the novel ends.

From the European "Preface" we read the following:

> It cannot be that so monstrous a solecism [meaning slavery, which was called a sacrilege in the opening paragraph—"the worst form of sacrilege"] can long exist in the bosom of a nation which *in all other respects* is the best exponent of the great principles of universal brotherhood. In America the Frenchman, the German, the Italian, the Hungarian, the Swede, the Celt all mingle on terms of equal right—all nations there display their characteristic excellencies and are admitted by her liberal laws to equal privileges; everything is tending to liberalise, humanise, and elevate and for this very reason it is, that the contest with slavery grows every year more terrible. (lxii–lxiii, emphasis added)

This is clearly an artful appeal to the racial distinctions that Europeans see among themselves. Brotherhood among Europeans can be envisioned even if attended by insurmountable difficulties. And because Europeans themselves will attach great importance to these in principle bridgeable differences, they can be brought to consider on the same basis differences between Africans and already amalgamated Europeans (in America). Once the insurmountable difficulties of amalgamation are viewed as political rather than essential they become surmountable.

In the novel itself Stowe presents this same view as a source of disagreement between George Harris and herself (the same point is represented symbolically in the fact that, at the beginning of the novel George is almost completely "white" but, by the time he makes this argument at the end of the novel is virtually as "black" as Uncle Tom). His list of "races" differs slightly, as he refers to America's Irishmen, Germans, and Swedes (494). But he does not wish the Africans to become one of them. He holds to a modified view of the exception of non-Western peoples from Western morality. That is, he argues that they are included in the teachings of Christianity and natural rights, but rather as separate peoples. The view is roughly akin to the contemporary notion of self-determination for peoples instead of individuals, or cultural relativism.[25]

But Stowe rejects that view, even after portraying it as sympathetically as possible in the character of George Harris. Ultimately, she calls for the indefinite "moral and intellectual" integration of the ex-slaves in America itself as a precondition of their returning to Africa (508). And in practical terms this can only mean adding them to the list of races which "mingle on terms of equal rights" in America. George denied the possibility of this. And, in fact, this makes his appearance in the novel an even greater paradox and much more important. For the original "plan" of the novel was to demonstrate the capacities of the slaves for the life of freedom in America.[26]

The purpose of the novel became instead the demonstration of the fundamental principles underlying *any* specific intention to prove the capacities of slaves for the life of freedom. This is the thrust of the statement in the "Preface" to the European edition. The first and second French prefaces are more directly revealing of the same purpose. They are more directly religious, especially Catholic. She consistently writes of "l'apôtre saint Paul" rather than the more Protestant, "l'apôtre Paul." And she concludes the first French "Preface" with "Amen, Amen." In these prefaces, especially the second, she also specifically describes the intent of the character of Uncle Tom. As has always been recognized, Uncle Tom is *the* vehicle of the book's religious sentiment. What has not been recognized is that his Christianity is not so strongly juxtaposed to the slaveholder's religion as it is juxtaposed to the view of human nature underlying the character of George Harris. This is so because George Harris's principles are but the principles of the slaveholders applied with greater rectitude. Christianity, therefore, is adapted to the articulation of a fundamental cosmopolitanism free of political embarrassments.

The underlying assumption of this view is that the chance of human excellence or virtue stems from individual capacities of soul rather than from political circumstances (George thought he might be able to become a Christian once he was free, but not before!). And Christianity—or Uncle Tom's Christianity—provides the formulation of the possible reaches of individual excellence. It is that body of tenets or opinions which describes man's essential capacities and which incidentally reveals the extent to which these capacities may or may not be suppressed. The appeal for "universal brotherhood" is an appeal for the recognition of this principle as prior to the particular distinctions among men, such as Anglo-Saxon brotherhood. Nonetheless, the appeal as such simultaneously recognizes the necessity for some form of political protection of "human nature." Thus is derived its cosmopolitanism.

Such cosmopolitanism once established, it follows that political arrangements which "*obstruct*" the development and expression of excellence are perverse, hence unjust, even though no specific political arrangement can be the *cause* of individual excellence. Against this background, we may discover a standard of judging political institutions in the extent to which it is possible (and states in fact do permit or facilitate) that human excellence may emerge. Humanity or humanism will then be understood as a solicitous and universal regard for the expression of human excellence or virtue.

This seems to be the content suggested in the particular account of the novel's Christianity in the several prefaces and the second French "Preface" in particular.

> In the author's country this book has had in view a special object; its mission has been particular and local. The intention of the author has nonetheless been to express in the tale she has written, something other than some truths applicable to temporary facts and to a given situation. The heart of the tale is for all times and for all places. The story of Uncle Tom is the story of the relations of the human soul, by itself poor, without strength, defenseless, with the Help of the Divine Redeemer, through whose aid the soul becomes strong, exalted and divine.[27]

Uncle Tom's Christianity makes available to him what heretofore was available only to the smallest number of human beings. The Divine Redeemer aids him. But with the "instruction of Jesus Christ" he aids himself.

> (He) acquired an energy, a patience, a calm, a courage in reverses, and, in the middle of the greatest afflictions, a peace that could make the greatest philosophers envious.[28]

Through this body of tenets the capacities of the human soul are shown rising from the worst possible human circumstances to the highest human eminence.

This worst-case demonstration would wholly undercut Stowe's argument, but for the fact that she regards it as necessary only for establishing the irreducible basis of the correct view of human nature. This is the lesson "for all times, and for all places." But she also has a "particular and local" objective. The general or universal case is intended as a guide for the particular case. That Uncle Tom triumphs in the worst case proves mankind's capacity. That others might triumph only to the extent they escape the worst case proves the necessity to avoid the worst. She sees this task as entirely political—though founded on right sentiment.[29]

This seems to be denied in the American "Preface," where "human liberty" is said to be in the hands of God and where Stowe says the "object of these sketches is to awaken sympathy and feeling for the African race, as they exist among us" (*UTC*, 1). But we are entitled to doubt this not only because we doubt that she accepts the distinction of the "African race"[30] in its full force. We doubt it also because, in the other prefaces, she proceeds unerringly to the crucial political problem: the territorial expansion of slavery. And it is her conclusion that the key to ending slavery is to keep it bottled up.[31] In addition, she appealed to the prospective emigrants from Europe to choose their political party before they came. They were to come prepared to "vote against the institution of slavery." And, finally, the appeal to public sentiment was itself the quintessentially political act.[32]

Stowe's European purpose was two-fold. She wished to begin the construction of that political Christianity which she saw as necessary to modern liberal society. In addition, she wished to bring European opinion directly to bear on the specific problem of slavery in America. She conceived that *Uncle Tom's Cabin* was so constructed as to be able to accomplish this task, largely because of the book's "catholic religious spirit." For no one of the prefaces, in itself, could have borne this burden very far. The teaching of *Uncle Tom's Cabin*, therefore, presents in comprehensive fashion the following principles.

1. The defect of the conception of Western liberalism or humanity in its exception of peoples in their nonage from the demand of Western morality.
2. The necessity to derive particular societies or cultures strictly from the requirement of protecting human nature, if they are to be considered just.
3. The view of human nature as revealed through individual excellences or virtues.
4. The possibility of a fundamental cosmopolitanism (political Christianity) free of political embarrassments.

NOTES

1. Harriet Beecher Stowe, introduction to *Uncle Tom's Cabin: or, Life among the Lowly, Writings of Harriet Beecher Stowe* (Boston: Houghton, Mifflin, 1878). This introduction is reprinted in 1965 Oxford edition of *Uncle Tom's Cabin*; page references to this introduction refer to the reprint edition.

2. *UTC*, pp. xxx–xxxi. The writing of the death of Uncle Tom, before any other part of the story, still involved connections with every other detail except the story of George Harris. And even this last would be included if by "the death" Stowe means the *two* chapters containing both the fatal blow and the eventual expiration.

3. Although that introduction is written entirely in the third person, there was no attempt to hide her authorship.

4. If, at least, a fairly large sample of French university students are to be an example. For the present author, assigning the novel to them in a class in 1971, found yet—over a hundred years later—abundance of tears. It seems Plato was nearer the truth

about the effect of literary genres than Stowe, who seemed to think that men would temper their reading with political sensibility. Cf. Plato, *Laws*, Books II and VII.

5. *UTC*, p. lxviii, "Preface" to Bosworth's English edition. Cf., 1878 "Introduction," and French and American prefaces.

6. March 20, 1852.

7. Charles E. Stowe, *The Life of Harriet Beecher Stowe* (Boston: Houghton, Mifflin, 1889; hereafter cited as *The Life of Harriet Beecher Stowe*).

8. Gossett incorrectly interprets this passage by confounding the syntax and grammar in such a way as to render the expression, "whatever may be said of the African race by itself," an independent clause rather than an element in composition with all the possible traces of genealogy. The natural meaning is that African blood is the dominant element, and next in order is Anglo-Saxon blood. Stowe's "whatever" is precisely a "whatever" and not an exclusion. Gossett's usage is obviously a violent handling of the language. No definitive reflection upon so-called pure-blood Africans is in any way conveyed by this passage, but Gossett concludes: "The phrase 'whatever may be said of the African race by itself' would seem to leave Tom and the other blacks in the novel without white intermixture as among those who are, at best, doubtful material for good citizenship. One can argue that this was a mere debating point and that Stowe did not mean to say that blacks without white intermixture are unfit for freedom. She herself was apparently unaware that she had cast doubt on the fitness for freedom of Tom or any other wholly black person. . . . Yet the . . . comment should warn the reader that there is an ambivalence in Stowe's conception of the inherent character of blacks and that he should expect inconsistencies." Thomas F. Gossett, *Uncle Tom's Cabin and American Culture* (Dallas: Southern Methodist University Press, 1985), pp. 109–10 (hereafter cited as *UTC and American Culture*).

9. The Bosworth edition referenced here is that published October 13, 1852, and reprinted in the 1965 Oxford edition of *Uncle Tom's Cabin*; page references refer to the reprint edition.

10. Harriet Beecher Stowe, preface to *Uncle Tom's Cabin, or, Life among the Lowly* (Boston: J. P. Jewett, 1852). This preface is reprinted in the 1965 Oxford edition; pagination here refers to the reprint.

11. Compare the refutation of George Harris's defense of African uniqueness, in the concluding chapter of the novel.

12. See the discussion of Carlyle's "Occasional Discourse on the Nigger Question," book I, part I, chapter 11, and also note 36.

13. H. B. Stowe to Sir Arthur Helps, August 22, 1852, Brunswick, in Sir Arthur Helps, *Correspondence of Sir Arthur Helps* (London: John Lane, 1917), pp. 133–37.

14. Letter to C. E. Norton, July 1, 1852, in Helps, *Correspondence*, pp. 114–15.

15. Ibid., p. 116.

16. Ibid., p. 117.

17. For a discussion of Helps's review and of the response to Helps's arguments made by Edward J. Pringle in his 1852 commentary on *Uncle Tom's Cabin*, see Stephen Keck, "Slaves or Labourers: Revisiting the 1852 Debate between Sir Arthur Helps and 'A Carolinian' (Edward J. Pringle)," *Proceedings of the South Carolina Historical Association* (1997).

18. Helps, *Correspondence*, p. 134.

19. At least, up until she writes "Sunny Memories," where it is clear that the slaveholder's view is not so far from her own. On that subject, see book II, part I, especially chapter 23.

20. Although unawares, Helps fully accedes to shouldering this burden. His judgment of her letter: "Her letter impressed me with the strongest belief of her earnestness and devotion to the cause—and by the cause I mean the cause of truth, not of any fanatical party whatsoever." *Correspondence,* Letter to C. E. Norton, Oct. 18, 1852, p. 145.

21. Hedrick briefly mentions the exchange with Helps, categorizing it as an example of "Stowe's visceral and largely unsystematic responses to injustice . . ." which she concludes "had the weaknesses as well as the strengths of anarchistic political thought." Hedrick, *Harriet Beecher Stowe,* p. 243.

22. Helps, *Correspondence,* p. 133.

23. Ibid., pp. 136, 137.

24. Commentary on Stowe's view on the question of race has, perhaps, received more ink than any other aspect of her work. While there is a long list of critics who seek to show that her work is racist (whether that racism is seen as malevolent or as the unavoidable consequence of "the times") or to demonstrate its racist effects, there are also those who understand her treatment of race more accurately. A few examples are cited here, but none make use of Stowe's technical writings in geography to address the issue comprehensively (as is done in the "Coda" to this work in chapter 27). Rexroth points out that Stowe "made the Negro, slave or free, visible as an essential member of American society, and she made the full humanity of the Negro visible to all, black or white, all over the world." Rexroth, *Elastic Retort,* p. 103. Graham reasons that Stowe "shared many of the misperceptions about race common in her lifetime . . . " but stresses "the remarkable degree to which she was able to rise above the sentiments then ascendant and to establish a humanitarian and sometimes uncommonly perceptive point of view . . . she hoped to make her readers see Negroes as fellow human beings . . . " and concludes that "the salient argument of her writings was for the full, equal brotherhood of all men." Thomas Graham, "Harriet Beecher Stowe and the Question of Race," *New England Quarterly* 46 (1973): 614, 615, 622 (hereafter cited as "HBS and the Question of Race"). Hada finds that Stowe "envisions a society where a black man is not considered animalistic but humane, with feelings for his wife, children, and indeed everyone he encounters." Kenneth Hada, "The Kentucky Model: Economics, Individualism, and Domesticity in *Uncle Tom's Cabin,*" *Papers on Language and Literature* 35, no. 2 (1999): 184. Anderson insists that "Stowe was fighting to convince her audience not only that black men and women should be granted freedom but were full human beings." Beatrice Anderson, "Uncle Tom: Hero at Last," *ATQ* 5: 106. Fluck believes that at the time that Stowe wrote "blackness may have held connotations of various possibilities, but not that of genuine morality" and that Stowe "for the first time in American history may have managed to make the black visible as a moral human being." Winifried Fluck, "The Power and Failure of Representation in Harriet Beecher Stowe's *Uncle Tom's Cabin,*" *New Literary History* 23: 325, 328. Ipema settles the question of Stowe's perspective on race thus: "Stowe recognizes differences between the races, but argues that those differences in no way affect what one critic

calls 'the equality and freedom promised by American political principles.' All races are entitled to equality and freedom." Tim M. Ipema, "The Voice of Protest in *Uncle Tom's Cabin* and *Native Son*" (master's thesis, Eastern Illinois University, 1990), p. i (hereafter cited as "The Voice of Protest"). Meyer provides a thoughtful analysis of not only Stowe's views but also the "willful overlooking of the other elements of black and white equality signaled by other events in the novel," which is perpetuated by numerous modern critics; he encourages readers to "continue to assert the value of discourse by nonminorities about minorities. . . . " Michael J. Meyer, "Toward a Rhetoric of Equality: Reflective and Refractive Images in Stowe's Language," in *The Stowe Debate: Rhetorical Strategies in Uncle Tom's Cabin,* ed. Mason I. Lowance, Ellen E. Westbrook, and R. C. De Prospo (Amherst: University of Massachusetts Press, 1994), p. 252.

Scholars trying to determine Stowe's views on race would do well to consult all of her writings and not focus solely on *Uncle Tom's Cabin.* Several Stowe scholars see a more positive (or revised) perspective on blacks in *Dred.* Levine, for example, writes: "Insofar as it explodes critical myths about her purported blindness to African American realities, *Dred* is critical to an understanding of Stowe's career." Levine, *Martin Delany, Frederick Douglass, and the Politics of Representative Identity,* p. 147. Moreover, what could be clearer than these words, which Stowe wrote in her preface to Nell's 1855 *The Colored Patriots of the American Revolution*?

> It is to be hoped that the reading of these sketches will give new self-respect and confidence to the race here represented. Let them emulate the noble deeds and sentiments of their ancestors, and feel that the dark skin can never be a badge of disgrace while it has been ennobled by such examples.
>
> And their white brothers in reading may remember, that generosity, disinterested courage and bravery, are of no particular race and complexion, and that the image of the Heavenly Father may be reflected alike by all.

Harriet Beecher Stowe, preface to *The Colored Patriots of the American Revolution,* by William C. Nell (Boston: R. F. Wallcut, 1855), p. 6 (hereafter cited as *The Colored Patroiots*).

25. Although much of her dissertation seriously misreads *Uncle Tom's Cabin,* Kosnik is alert to this aspect of George Harris, which she categorizes as his refusal to "pass" for an American. Kristin Costello Kosnik, "The Alien in Our Nation: Complicating Issues of 'Passing' and Miscegenation in the American Narrative" (Ph.D. diss., Columbia University, 2001; hereafter cited as "The Alien in Our Nation").

26. The debate among Stowe scholars about whether she was a "colonizationist" has been fierce and too extensive to do more here than mention some examples. Banks highlights the extent to which even those of Stowe's own generation were troubled by what they saw as her endorsement of the colonization project. Banks, "*Uncle Tom's Cabin* and the Antebellum Black Response." Strout offers a more nuanced perspective on this question but nonetheless concludes that "it is in her policy of exporting free Negroes . . . that she betrays a moral evasion of the deeper dilemmas inherent in the history of American race relations." Strout, "*UTC* and the Portent of the Millennium," p. 383. Powell expresses the point of view voiced by many Stowe critics, saying "the colonization ending of *Uncle Tom's Cabin* . . . calls into question the credibility of Stowe's project to overcome the racial prejudice of the North. . . . " Timothy Burgess Powell, "The Beautiful Absurdity of American

Identity: Confliction Constructions of the Nation in 19th Century American Literature" (Ph.D. diss., Brandeis University, 1995), p. 102.

A few scholars provide an alternate viewpoint. Henry, for example, suggests that "Stowe, through George, allows for the possibility that blacks will be like Biblical Hebrews not only in the Exodus myth, but in the establishment of a nation as well, and on this model, Liberia becomes the new Jerusalem." Nancy Elizabeth Henry, "Originating Fictions: Harriet Beecher Stowe and George Eliot" (Ph.D. diss., University of Chicago, 1994), p. 188 (hereafter cited as "Orginating Fictions"). Ammons expresses a similar viewpoint, but in a harsher voice: "Yet if Stowe's endorsement of emigration reflects her racism, and it does, it also and paradoxically signifies her respect for African Americans' full equality, as fellow Christians, world missionaries, and therefore potentially glorious imperialists." Ammons, "*UTC*, Empire, and Africa," p. 74.

Much of the discussion of this question—like the discussion of Stowe's overall views on race—suffers from its focus solely on *Uncle Tom's Cabin*, ignoring the rest of Stowe's *oeuvre* while trying to judge her stance on colonization. However, several writers point to *Dred* as evidence either of a change in Stowe's thinking on this subject or as evidence that she simply did not endorse colonization. Ryan, for example, proposes that "*Dred's* conclusion can be read as Stowe's attempt to envision a cooperative interracial United States, one in which African Americans occupy a variety of positions within household and within benevolent dyads." Ryan, "Charity Begins at Home," p. 772. Henry, Levine, Cotugno, and others also read *Dred* as a rejection of the colonization project. Nancy Elizabeth Henry, "Originating Fictions: Harriet Beecher Stowe and George Eliot" (Ph.D. diss., University of Chicago, 1994). Levine, *Martin Delaney, Frederick Douglass, and the Politics of Representation.* Cotugno, "Form and Reform." On the other hand, Gruner contends that even in *Dred*, "Stowe stuck to her guns on the colonization issue" by placing Henry Clayton's enclave of former slaves in Canada and that she was unable "to imagine a future America in which blacks have any legitimate place." Mark Randall Grüner, "Stowe's *Dred*: Literary Domesticity and the Law of Slavery," *Prospects* 20 (1995): 12, 11.

27. *UTC*, p. lxxiii (my translation of the French).

28. Ibid., p. lxiv (my translation).

29. Hence, in the prefaces to the American and European editions, Stowe invokes the testimony of the few—poets, orators, artists, the literati—to show that the "divine faculties" in man profit most from freedom. And they advance "the great master chord of Christianity" in regarding freedom as for the sake of human excellence.

30. "As they exist among us" is a significant qualification.

31. *UTC*, "Preface," European edition, and "Preface," Bosworth's English edition, pp. lxiii and lxv.

32. See the discussion of the purpose of influencing public sentiment, book II, part I, chapter 19.

5

A Little Wine and Brandy: The Narrative Begins

We need no longer wonder why chapter 1, "In Which the Reader is Introduced to a Man of Humanity," is ironic. It is the purpose of the novel to consider the meaning of "humanity." And it is Stowe's position that it is sufficient to show it in one man in order to establish it for mankind. But to show "humanity" in a man through a discussion of slavery encounters the difficulty of disentangling the human and the "property" elements in the man. The original subtitle for *Uncle Tom's Cabin* was "The Man Who Was a Thing." To demonstrate the error of slavery, Stowe must build a foundation which not even slavery can shake. The prevailing view of "humanity" was insufficient because it allowed exceptions. It accords full human status to men only in the best case. Stowe constructs a new view of "humanity," deriving the measure of humanness from a man in the worst case.[1] The method of indirection she employs, at least in the case of Uncle Tom, is but the historical analog of his ascent—of our ascent from an imperfect political vision to a perfect political vision. The novel begins with men as they understood themselves.

That the understanding men have of themselves is not without many ambiguities is the lesson of the first chapter. The novel opens with the slaveowner, Shelby, and the slavetrader, Haley, seated in Shelby's home and negotiating an exchange of notes, in Haley's possession, for slaves. The two are at once particularized, as the author refers to them as "two Gentlemen." That is certainly their self-understanding, and that understanding is rooted in the acquisition of what they regard as the graces of civil life. In the best case, the man of humanity would be identical with the perfect gentleman—the Christian gentleman, perhaps. But as men understand themselves, gentlemanliness is acquired through conformity to the regulative principles of a regime. In these terms a gentleman is not a gentleman simply, for he is some particular kind of gentleman—American or British or European, etc. Nor, in broader terms, does the gentleman by convention possess that independence of mind and character that is otherwise the mark of the gentleman.

The expression, "two gentlemen," was used just as a matter of convenience or convention: a means of introducing the underlying question of the relationship between gentlemanliness and humanity. "One of the parties, however, when critically examined, did not seem, strictly speaking, to come under the species" (3). The "critical" approach would clearly distinguish the characteristics of gentlemanliness as the consequence of a general case (species) which in itself may be recognized as whole, but which nonetheless is subordinated to some genus. It nonetheless partakes of this distinction only by virtue of what commonly (with reference to the species) identifies it as part of the genus (humanity?). In the same way, we may see that "man *qua* man" is distinguishable from the genus "living being" but is yet identifiable as "man" only on the basis of belonging to the genus. If reason is the essential human distinction, it is nonetheless the "reason of a living being" and, therefore, to be ultimately derived from life or the capacity of being ensouled. The capacity for gentlemanliness, therefore, is derived from the broader capacity of humanity.

The person excepted from the class of gentleman by appearance was the slavetrader. This does not mean that he cannot claim humanity, for that is broader and prior to gentlemanliness. The accompanying description of Haley—as yet unnamed and thus merely a man—portrays tastelessness. He is distinguished from the apparent gentleman by such expressions as "coarse, commonplace features" and a "low man." His character is such that "not even the desire to be graphic" can induce the author to transcribe his "various profane expressions." (To avert the obstinate and wrongheaded notion of Stowe's prudishness, it should be noted that, in *Dred*, no such squeamishness interfered with the transcription of Tom Gordon's profanities. The squeamishness here is propaedeutic as opposed to being a matter of principle.) She seems to take the high ground to emphasize the nature of the gentlemanliness for which we seek. But the wine-tasting drama (discussed below) will reveal how uncertain we might be in finding precisely where the high ground is, even if we limit ourselves to judging merely by accepted behavioral signs.[2] How profound, then, is the conflict between exterior and interior signs of highness!

Of Shelby, it is said that he "had the appearance of a gentleman." The accompanying description notes the "arrangements of the house" and "the general air of housekeeping" as signs of "opulent circumstances." Thus, two signs of gentlemanliness are framed: the sign of character; the sign of circumstances. The stage for opposing Uncle Tom's black visage to his angelic soul is well set. But before that is done Haley and Shelby must be reduced to recognizable terms, in order that we see the method at work. When we pursue the task of unraveling the real and the apparent in each and inquiring after the true picture of a gentleman, we see that neither Shelby nor Haley is a gentleman.

The author begins with a double irony: she calls "two gentlemen" men, neither of whom is in fact a gentleman. And although this does not, in itself, disprove their claims of humanity, it eliminates a certain and easy possibility for identifying one or both as human. (Where the species is found, the genus is necessary.) Of the two, he who least appears to be a gentleman joins the apparent gentleman in claiming to be the "humane man" to whom the reader is being introduced. But the questionable status of that claim is shown by virtue of the fact that Shelby, who appears to be a gentleman, gives occasion and some credence for both claims by appealing to the "conscience" of the "low man." Thus explicitly is the question raised not only as to who the true gentleman is, but indeed whether the gentleman alone is the "man of humanity."

The author subtly but beautifully and dramatically confirms this appraisal in the exchange between the two over a matter of taste (hence, habituation or good breeding): the judgment of the adequacy of wines. The very first sentence of the novel reads, "two gentlemen were sitting alone over their wines," after which Stowe speculated on the characteristics of gentlemanliness. Stowe opens the dialogue, with Shelby making an offer in trade, and Haley, rejecting the offer, "holding up a glass of wine between his eye and the light." Shelby counters by praising the virtues of his offer. And Haley inattentively brushes aside the praise, hardly finishing his response before "helping himself to a glass of brandy." Nowhere is mention made of Haley's drinking the initial glass of red wine! It seems quite clear that he did not; he rejected it as inadequate after examination. As the bargaining went on hot and heavy (Shelby appealed to Haley's conscience), "the trader sighed contemplatively and poured out some more brandy." Throughout this process, Shelby took no apparent notice of Haley's judgment of his cellar. The bargaining continued to the point that Shelby had clearly gained the ascendancy when the lovely slave, Eliza, appeared to reclaim her wandering son. Haley was taken. He sought to close the bargain by making an additional offer for her, promising Shelby a "fortune."

> "I don't want to make my fortune on her," said Mr. Shelby, dryly; and, seeking to turn the conversation, he uncorked a bottle of fresh wine, and asked his companion's opinion of it. "Capitol, sir,—first chop!" said the trader; then turning, and slapping his hand familiarly on Shelby's shoulder. . . . (7)

Shelby's attempt to distract Haley failed in its particular purpose. But it succeeds in revealing two facts to the reader.

First, Shelby had intended to keep his distance from Haley. He offered him an inferior wine, initially, thus reflecting his judgment of the slavetrader's status. Secondly, he was not unaware of Haley's harsh judgment of his cellar. Implicitly defending his gentlemanliness against the invasion of Haley's apparent uncouth, Shelby sought to maintain a hierarchical relationship between themselves. But that relationship was untenable.[3] It was assaulted first by the fact of the negotiations. It was assaulted by Haley's simultaneous disrespect for and condemnatory judgment of Shelby's status. And, finally, it was also assaulted by Shelby's own recourse to conscience. When the difficulty of Eliza arises, there remains to Shelby nothing but an appeal to the fundamental equality of their attainments (he seeks a judgment of the wine to vindicate himself, to win respect for his taste, and to accord respect to Haley). Thereafter they address each other as gentlemen, and their honor becomes the seal of their agreement. They become gentlemen by agreement.

Now, the agreement between Shelby and Haley succeeds in concealing from them just how violently their self-understanding has been overthrown. (When Eliza escapes before Haley takes the slaves away, Shelby exclaims, "It touches upon my honor!") But the reader cannot conceal from himself that the bottom of their understanding had been exploded. (Little wonder Stowe's "sympathetic portrait" was condemned in the South!) Out of the wreckage of Shelby's and Haley's views a new foundation must be laid, and upon this foundation the shattered fragments of conscience must be recast into a monument to human prudence.

The matter of conscience between Shelby and Haley, the slavetraders, is a question of distributive justice: what must Shelby, the slaveowner, pay to Haley in order to cancel some outstanding debts. Ordinarily, such a matter is easily settled by the principle of commutative justice. The debts are stated in terms of some currency, and what one owes is that precise amount of currency. Or, the debt is to be paid in goods, and there must be some value established for the goods. Normally, one consults market prices and settles on some prevailing rate.

In this case, however, the goods reflect a high degree of individual variability, such that the determination must be made anew in each case. Hence, in offering the slave, Tom, as alone of sufficient value to cancel his debts, Shelby explains that the valuation is not so high as it seems, because "Tom is an uncommon fellow; he is certainly worth that sum anywhere,—steady, honest, capable, manages my whole farm like a clock" (4). Haley resists. He sees the value of these qualities of soul—as we might call them—but either feels that Shelby overvalues them (Haley has not met Tom) or that, in calculating the value of the goods, such qualities cannot be taken entirely into account. If we assume the latter to be the case,[4] our problem is framed thusly: Why does the author have Shelby (an apparent gentleman) maintain that it is necessary to take such matters into account, "if you have any conscience"?

Where the slaveowner or slavetrader must consider his property not only as an available body but also as endowed with those characteristics least determined by the body, does not one undermine the very notion of slavery? That is, can one—with conscience—hold a slave under such circumstances? If the answer is yes, does it remain so if those characteristics (steadiness, honesty capacity, prudence) prove to be the very sources of gentlemanliness? With respect to what does Shelby implore Haley to be conscionable?

A partial answer is found in Haley's response. He considers Shelby's appeal as mere oath-swearing:

> "Well, I've got just as much conscience as any man in business can afford to keep,—just a little, you know, to swear by, as 't were, and, then, I'm ready to do anything to 'blige friends; but this yer, you see, is a leetle too hard on a fellow—a leetle too hard." (5)

The appeal, in Haley's view, is a form of argument—but it can be successfully employed only to the extent that it does not cut into profits. Since Shelby is also a businessman, Haley implies that Shelby uses the appeal as a way of striking a balance—adding friendship—in the scales. But, Haley retorts, weigh the scales with what conscience I have, and I am still not receiving what is equal or fitting. In this case, the friendship does not strike a balance.

Whether Haley fully accounts for Shelby's conscience is left unclear by the author. She has Shelby proceed to suggest that something akin to friendship also exists between himself and his slaves. "I don't like *parting* with any of my hands, that's a fact" (5, emphasis added). Though a fool is soon *parted* with his money, more frequently does one *lose* property. In common speech, parting is the sorrow of friendship. Shelby suggests, therefore, that this sale is occasioned by necessity. Where friendship would warrant rejection of such transactions, necessity commands it. Such friendship implies attachment to the slave in some way other than his status as property. It is in this manner that conscience might come to exist, and there remains only the question of whether it can do so short of the fulsomeness that a reciprocal bond requires, or whether the friendship of the huntsman for his well-reared assistant or companion might suffice. As only gentlemen can genuinely be friends only a gentleman genuinely experiences the conscientiousness of friendship.

Shelby's friendship for Tom encounters the same difficulty his claim of humanity encounters: it imposes upon him conditions he cannot meet.

Shelby offered Haley the finer wine as a means of turning the conversation away from Eliza. At the same time, he extended to Haley the status of a gentleman, offering intangible benefits in place of the tangible benefits he was unable to offer. But the consequence of his decision to pretend that Haley is a gentleman is that Shelby is forced to defend his own gentlemanliness. In this he fails. The occasion for Eliza to become a subject of discussion was created by Shelby's successful attempt to charm the trader with the antics of Eliza's boy. Thus, having been refused the sale of the mother, the trader naturally resumes bargaining about the son.

> "I would rather not sell him," said Mr. Shelby, thoughtfully; "the fact is, *sir*, I'm a humane man, and I hate to take the boy from his mother, *sir*." (7, emphasis added)

The claim of humanity does not carry the same force as "I say no, and I mean no," which was the response to the request for Eliza. And this first and emphatic use of the civil "sir" reflects an acceptance of the show of familiarity with which Haley opened the negotiations, "clapping his hand on Shelby's shoulder." It is therefore unsurprising to find in Haley's immediate response a recognition that Shelby had agreed to the sale. "I understand, perfectly," he said. What he understood, of course, was that he would get the boy on the condition of supporting a proper show of regret. This leads to the most humorous but also the most serious section of the first chapter, a lengthy disquisition by Haley on the subjects of human nature and humanity.

Haley's disquisition begins with the distinction between the slaves and "white folks." But the distinction derives from the variable influence of differing social conventions, as his conclusion reaffirms. At the bottom of his own practices is recognition of the transience of human sentiments that are not reinforced. Thus he has a regard for the feelings of the slaves. This regard allows him to succeed through modern principles of management, "and humanity, sir, . . . is the great pillar of *my* management" (9, original emphasis). From this climax of the disquisition, Haley proceeds through an account that distinguishes the transient human feelings as natural and the mature "spectations" as conventional. The end of humanity is the proper recognition of the differing expectations of different peoples.

At the conclusion of this involved theory, Shelby remains unsatisfied that it is his own "humanity" that he has heard described. But in fact it is. Shelby is forced to rely on the slavetrader to defend his position either because he lacks the courage to do so himself, or because he is himself aware that that position is controverted at least in the person of his wife. He reflects on the latter possibility when he admits to Haley, toward the end of the disquisition, that his slaves had not been raised in accordance with this view. Mrs.

Shelby had rather been the source of the *mature* expectations of Shelby's slaves. Having relied on the trader to state his notion of humanity, he is prepared to complete the deal only if he can go a step further and convince the trader to assume to himself the squeamishness of conscience which is Shelby's own: "If *you* want the matter carried on in the quiet way you speak of . . ." (11, added emphasis). Haley, of course, spoke so only in response to Shelby's need. Shelby has succeeded in defending his gentlemanliness and humanity *only* if Haley may truly be regarded as a gentleman.

Shelby cannot be humane if he is proved not to be a gentleman, because his only possible claim to humanity arises from his claim to gentlemanliness. In its absence, he is moved only by an egoism, which it is the purpose of gentlemanliness to avert. Because he is not a gentleman, he is wholly exposed to "those temptations to hardheartedness, which *always* overcome frail human nature *when* the prospect of sudden and rapid gain is weighed in the balance, *with no heavier counterpoise* than the interest of the helpless and the unprotected" (11, emphasis added). A heavier counterweight would be the conscience derived from true gentlemanliness and humanity. It must be the purpose of gentlemanliness, not to convince man to care for the "helpless," but to convince him that regard for the "interests of the helpless" is in fact regard for the gentleman's own advantage. There is irony in the portrait of the mildness of Kentucky slavery, which is not generally forced to meet this test of its apparent gentility. For Shelby's circumstance is precisely the circumstance in which such a test occurs, and he is found wanting in resources that would permit him to rise above the necessary "human frailties." It should be no surprise that Haley could not accept friendship as balancing the scale in their transaction.

That the expressed trust with which Shelby regards Tom may be reasonable cannot also establish that it is reasonable for Tom to trust Shelby. Just as the friendship Haley insinuates between himself and Shelby constitutes an unbalanced relationship (although Shelby capitulated), the relationship Shelby insinuates between himself and Tom also constitutes an unbalanced relationship.[5] That suggests already that what we have to seek in the matching of Shelby and Tom is a sense of distance equivalent to the distance between the non-gentleman, Haley, and the apparent or pretended gentleman, Shelby. In chapter 1 but four men are introduced, and the chapter title promised that in at least one of them (unless Mrs. Shelby was meant) the reader will find a man of humanity.

We saw that the two signs of gentlemanliness were circumstance and character. That must be corrected. What, in fact, we initially saw in Haley were "physical" signs of character—crude features, gaudy dress, and swaggering pretensions, in short, tastelessness. The implication is that a sophisticated Haley would be indistinguishable from a Shelby. Granting, as Aristotle says, a certain equipment as necessary to gentlemanliness, it may be wondered whether the gentlemanly character might exist independently of gentlemanly circumstance? That is, though one may not be a gentleman without appropriate position and property, might one in fact possess the same character of soul? In this we begin to recognize the Christian pauper. We also note that "virtue" does not necessarily bring the human goods. That is, we see what appears to be an explicit teaching: that one can acquire the pleasant things without (before) one acquires goodness of soul and, possibly, acquiring goodness of soul may mean never acquiring the pleasant things. And, most importantly, we begin to recognize in "humanity" that specific character of soul that is the property of the gentleman but which may be, in the nature of things, independent of the circumstances of gentlemanliness. That is, if one already endowed with riches and status then acquires the character called "humanity," he will then become a gentleman. But if he acquires that character, he will have done so independently of his riches and status.

The chief circumstance of gentlemanliness had always been thought to be a decent polity. In this light, the virtue of humanity comes to be seen as not only independent of ease of circumstances but possibly apolitical as well. If we yet maintain that ease of circumstances and a decent polity are *signs* of gentlemanliness, however, we point to the extraordinary difficulty of ever identifying true gentlemanliness or humanity. To be unquestionably identified, it must be sought where there is no possibility whatever of confusing an image or appearance of gentlemanliness for the real thing. The obvious analogy of this procedure to modern philosophy's state of nature theories is no accident.[6] And it is even more effective for it forbids simply taking civil man and imagining him without laws in order to conceive the true human condition. What identifies the slave more effectively than anything else is his disqualification for honor or gentlemanliness. Uncle Tom enjoys neither ease of circumstance nor a decent polity. The physical signs of his character suggest lowliness. To complicate matters further, we do not properly see his character or even trustworthy signs of his character in this chapter. The medium used, we remember, is indirection. What we do see is Shelby's appreciation of Tom's character. And that, under the circumstances, is a questionable appreciation.

Still, Tom is introduced in some fashion, and he and one other Tom—a brutal slavetrader—are the only other men introduced, the one by Shelby, the other by Haley. We have Shelby's Tom, the novel's hero, and Haley's Tom, who also ascends in the end. For reasons that will emerge, Haley's Tom need not be considered (any more than Haley) in responding to the chapter title. It is Shelby's Tom, Uncle Tom, who concerns us then. It is he who is least (in some eyes, not at all) in a position to be gentlemanly and who presents, therefore, the supreme test of that ignoble truth: the humane life is choiceworthy even if the choice lies between the humane life and the human goods. That Tom's character is not discussed in this chapter—nor even the character of the "man of humanity" as such—is not a problem. It may be that we get, quite literally, only an "introduction" to a *humane* man.

NOTES

1. Shipp is rare, if not unique, among Stowe scholars in his recognition of her intent in this regard. He develops a powerful argument that the chief lesson of *Uncle Tom's Cabin* is the importance to human beings of "an informed heart"—a phrase he adopts from Bruno Bettelheim's book of that title. "Although Dr. Bettelheim uses the principles of psychology in a non-fictional exploration of the problems created by such extreme circumstances [i.e., a Nazi concentration camp], and Mrs. Stowe used the principles of Christian humanism in a fictional exploration of the same problems, the question for both writers is the same: how does one maintain an integrated personality, beneficial to oneself and others, in circumstances so dehumanizing that the complete disintegration of personality would seem to be the only possible response to the environment? Each writer assumes that the personality capable of surviving in the extreme circumstances will inevitably flourish in a less extreme one. . . . Moreover, society improves and becomes more conducive to this type of personality as an increasing number of such people influence it." Shipp, "*UTC* and the Ethos of Melodrama," p. 23–24.

2. Levin is one of the few critics who has observed Stowe's deft use of manners to advance plot, theme, and characterization; labeling *Uncle Tom's Cabin* "a romance of manners," he suggests that "Mrs. Stowe's dramatic action highlights one major function of the grand folks' superior manners: to protect gentlemen from the direct recognition of the brutal reality that makes them as mean as traders." David Levin, "American Fiction as Historical Evidence: Reflections on *Uncle Tom's Cabin*," *Negro American Literature Forum* 5, no. 4 (Winter 1971): 133, 134 (hereafter cited as "American Fiction as Historical Evidence"). A contemporary of Stowe's likewise praises her as a student and recorder "of *men and manners* . . . of elemental human nature . . . [and] of this great life-drama." "Novels: Their Meaning and Mission," *Putnam's Monthly Magazine* 4 (1854): 394.

3. Cf. Marks: ". . . Haley is in control of the social situation." Pamela Ann Marks, "A Voice in Ramah: Rhetorical Structure and Cultural Context in *Uncle Tom's Cabin*" (Ph.D. diss., University of Rhode Island, 1991), p. 147 (hereafter cited as "A Voice in Ramah"). Also Brommell: " . . . try as he might, Shelby simply can't keep his distance—physical, social, or moral from Haley. They are implicated together in the evils of slavery. So, too, then, are the readers who have cast their lot with Shelby by identifying with him." Nicholas K. Brommell, *By the Sweat of the Brow: Literature and Labor in Antebellum American* (Chicago: University of Chicago Press, 1993), p. 166 (hereafter cited as *By the Sweat of the Brow*).

4. That this is correct is shown in the paradox of Haley's humanity. He views not just slaves but all men as primarily determined or formed through stimulus-response mechanisms. The characteristics stem from this process. But as yet the art

of producing the characteristics—and, of course, judging them—is entirely too limited. He has a just appreciation for the crude level of art.

5. Tom does not capitulate. He does not act on the basis of the supposed friendship. His knowledge of natures liberates him from dependence while allowing him fully to account for or even excuse Shelby's actions.

6. See the discussion of Calvin Stowe's account of state of nature theories in book I, part II, chapter 15. The change in the conception was motivated by the same concern manifest in this search for gentlemanliness. "It is rather the formulation of that way of living which can affirm that all men have an equal right to justice without leaving all at the mercy of the least understanding of justice."

6

Patriarchy, Matriarchy, and Other Myths of Slavery

Stowe's concern to identify a *man* of humanity in the opening chapter is connected with her rejection of a "patriarchal legend" of slavery. *Uncle Tom's Cabin* does not offer the frontal attack on that view that is to be found in *Dred*. But she does maintain that so long as the foundation of slavery is that "law" which regards men as transferable property, it cannot be a patriarchal institution (*UTC*, 12). On the other hand, the refutation of the "patriarchal legend" does not in itself refute the possibility of a matriarchal order. Indeed, it was only from fear of Mrs. Shelby that Mr. Shelby would not countenance the sale of Eliza. And it was rather she than he who was responsible for raising their slaves with false "expectations" (10 and 39). And the author further emphasizes the possibility of a matriarchy in the first chapter by describing Mrs. Shelby in terms that would befit the character of a gentleman.

> Mrs. Shelby was a woman of high class, both intellectually and morally. To that natural magnanimity and generosity of mind . . . she added high moral and religious sensibility and principle, carried out with great energy and ability into practical results. (13)

And, finally, confronted with Eliza's fear of a pending sale, she responded, "I would as soon see my own children sold." This is even more dramatic than it seems, since, from all appearance, Mrs. Shelby had but one child!

Stowe wished particularly to deal with the possibility of a matriarchal pattern for slavery that would make it an acceptable form of humane life. This is more than additional testimony to the important role of mothers in the novel.[1] In one sense, the many sensitive mothers and children serve but to remind the readers of the origin of mankind's concern with decent human life—just as Aristophanes' *Ecclesiazusae* accomplishes the same end from an opposite perspective. And, after all, a man remains central to the novel's development and its every expression of hope for humanity. Nonetheless the problem of a possible matriarchal pattern is important. It provides occasion to measure the countervailing tendencies of law and charitable sentiment, without obscuring the central task of the novel.

Appropriately, therefore, Stowe's second chapter is entitled, "The Mother." In this chapter we discover the ground and manner of the matriarchal pattern, but Stowe does not render her judgment of its capacity to mitigate the excesses of slavery until three chapters later. Indeed, all of the principal characters of the novel are introduced and Uncle Tom is even partially characterized before Stowe reveals, in chapter 5, that the matriarchal pattern cannot work. The principal characters are introduced under the shadow of a matriarchal presence which ordinarily is powerless over—and indeed even blind to—their fundamental condition.

Stowe's view of the character of maternity is that it is peculiarly responsible for the development of moral sentiments—at least in liberal democracy.[2] To that extent, it fulfills the primary task of preparing the young for citizenship.[3] It is not accidental, therefore, that Shelby's slaves have come to assume participation in a form of citizenship—let us call it partial citizenship—under Mrs. Shelby's guidance. The purpose of the consideration of matriarchy is to judge how far the slaves can come to really enjoy citizenship. And it is further to reveal the consequences to the slaves themselves of accepting partial citizenship.

We saw in chapter 1 that Shelby's highest praise for his slaves was based on the influence of Mrs. Shelby's moral guidance—so far as he knew. In the second chapter, we find the basis of that judgment. Mrs. Shelby raised her slaves as if they were her own children—at least Eliza. And this included the effort to bring them to "maturity" unharmed by the ordinary dangers and temptations of human life. In chapter 3 Eliza reveals that Mrs. Shelby's method in part relied on the inculcation of Christian precept. And in chapter 5 Mrs. Shelby reveals the full method and its end.[4]

> I thought, by k\ess, and care, and instruction, I could make the condition of mine [slaves] better than freedom. (40)

She does not restrict her claim to Eliza. She regards the selling of Tom as "tearing him from all *we* have taught him to love and value." These virtues include the "duties of the family, of parent and child, and husband and wife." The very attempt to induce moral sensibility creates reciprocally binding moral ties, she holds.

We need not judge here how far Mrs. Shelby's efforts are the cause of the attainments of *all* of her slaves. This is at least problematic in the case of Uncle Tom, who was already eight years old at the time Mr. Shelby was born and perhaps as old as twenty-eight by the time Emily became Mrs. Shelby.[5] It is important, however, to consider the characters and circumstances of the slaves independently of her account. And, as it happens, all of the principal slaves on the Shelby estate are introduced in some manner in these first five chapters.

In listing the moral characteristics she sought to induce, Emily notably omitted any reference to political duties (although she does call Uncle Tom a "noble-hearted soul"). This is perhaps consistent with the Christian perspective from which she speaks. It is also consistent with the conception of partial citizenship. And when we learn from the slaves themselves what is the tendency of their morality, it is clear that the "condition better than freedom" is one from which the onerous burdens of civic duties have been lifted. For Eliza, what Christianity means is that she must be obedient. In the discussion of Uncle Tom no clear indication is given as to how he understands the relationship between his Christianity and his slavery. But even in his case there is strong identification with the political system which is the formal expression of the morality to which he has ostensibly been committed—if the portrait of Washington which hangs from his cabin wall is an indication.

What ties these first five chapters together is the development of the slave's connection to the political regime through Mrs. Shelby. Her crowning achievement in this regard was arranging the marriage of George and Eliza Harris. When George emerges as the chief subject of chapter 2, it is clear that the reader will both come to know the truth about Eliza as a reflection of George and also to discern the character of Emily Shelby's influence, the extent of the matriarchal influence. Indeed, nothing so dramatically if only symbolically suggests the extent of the matriarchal influence as the description of Mrs. Shelby's caring for and arranging Eliza's wedding. Emily considered George and Eliza particularly well "suited" in their match. This judgment ostensibly rests on the fact that both were of mixed blood. But beyond that, which remained unstated as a particular reason, was the very strong emphasis on the strength and dignity of George's *position*. At the time of the marriage he was employed at the factory, and "he had free liberty to come and go at discretion." The initial introduction of George emphasized his intelligence and inventiveness. He spoke "fluently," bore an "erect" carriage, and "looked so handsome and manly." In almost every respect, at the time of the marriage, the reader sees in George Harris a man indistinguishable from the republic's free citizens, on the surface.

It is the manifest incongruity of this virtual free man being owned by "a vulgar, narrow-minded, tyrannical master" that establishes the dramatic context for development of the character of George Harris. With all his "superior qualifications," "this young man was in the eye of the law not a man, but a thing." The application to George Harris of the novel's original proposal for a subtitle alerts the reader to consider in his character the defect that is peculiar to slavery. That is, one must regard what there is in the man that is sacrificed to his thingness. This establishes the theoretical context for the development of his character. And because this is all accomplished in the chapter that frames the relationship of Eliza and Emily, we discover what there is in matriarchy that allows it to suppose a state "better than freedom."

In the eyes of some, George's condition might have been viewed as better than freedom, though he was only indirectly under Emily Shelby's influence. He enjoyed relative ease, leisure, and respect. It was this fact that induced his master to "reclaim" him. In a dramatic confrontation George welcomed this news with slave-befitting silence. It was the work of "a power that he knew was irresistible." The gravest defect of George's "happiness" was precisely this "knowledge" of an irresistible power. What it means to a great extent is that he indulged his "happiness" on the prospect of nothing more than that, by chance, he should have a kind or at least benign master. However so great were his "superior qualities," they were indeed not the source of his happiness. Whatever George may have thought previously, the fall from grace was the revelation of his untenable status.

> He had been able to repress every disrespectful word; but the flashing eye, the gloomy and troubled brow, were part of a natural language that could not be repressed,—indubitable signs, which showed too plainly that the man could not become a thing. (16)

What George had previously sacrificed in the acceptance of "a power that he knew was irresistible" was the power to determine his own happiness. He had accepted the theoretical possibility that the despotic control of one man over another might be better than freedom.

In chapter 3 George liberates himself from his earlier thralldom and, in the process, explains the basis of his previous error—hence, that of his wife. That chapter, "The Husband and Father," finds George cursing the birth of his son and cursing the fact that he had ever seen his wife. He loves them nonetheless. But he now realizes that they are not "his own"—and cannot be. The problem is not that they are "owned" by the Shelbys—which is problem enough. The problem is that George is "owned" and hence can have nothing of his "own." Possession unlike use is entirely a capacity of freedom. Because freedom is a particular state or condition of the exercise of the will, and because will, itself, is rooted in reason, possession like freedom is an attribute of rational beings. What George has discovered, however, is that rational capacity is *not* the foundation of freedom or possession.[6]

> Who made him my master? . . . What right has he to me? I'm a man as much as he is. I'm a better man than he is. I know more about business than he does; I'm a better manager than he is; I can read better than he can; I can write a better hand,—and I've learned it all myself, and no thanks to him,—I've learned it in spite of him. (19)

Such a massive demonstration would prove compelling indeed to John the Drover. But that is an accident. And as accidents go, George did not come into the "property" of John the Drover.

George has no answer—in theoretical terms—for his discovery. That, in the end, is the great distinction between himself and Uncle Tom. He thinks only that he is illegitimately denied his freedom—the use of his reason. He does not know what the basis of that freedom might be—apart from the reason itself. He does not know that his master's inferiority—weakness—is not in itself a moral defect and therefore a disqualification for ruling him. But he senses that the existing arrangement does violence to nature, as he is brought to curse child, wife, and life itself.

> What's the use of our trying to do anything, trying to know anything, trying to be anything? What's the use of living? I wish I was dead! (19)

Of all the many wishes that were beyond George's power, in his circumstances, this is the one wish of the power to realize which he could in no way be deprived. But he is not merely whining. He is sensing—though ignorant—that human capacities must point to some end and are not in themselves the end of human endeavor. Rational capacity is not the basis of human freedom and possession because, as capacity, it points to a human end which itself is a source of those principles that defend human freedom and possession. If the human end were possession simply, or life for life's sake, the connection with reason would become indefensible. Possession is not rational in itself any more than is freedom in itself rational. It is true that there are rational means to sustain life (one of which might well be to destroy slavery), but life in itself cannot be thought rational on that account. Because he assumes a rational form for life itself, George's despair is grounded in a fundamental optimism about the human condition.

It is perhaps this optimism that restrains George from the attempt to realize his wish for death. But he is in addition fortunate to have Eliza's restraining influence work upon his soul. At this point (chapter 3), they do not know that their own son has been sold. But they do know of the radical change in George's condition. Thus Eliza greets him with a "why don't you smile?" and a "look at Harry—how he grows" in this instance of by now infrequent visits. She sought to charm him with the very things that he had now come to curse. And his despair of living completes her shock: "Dear George, that is really wicked."

George, we will soon see, is not unmoved by his own things. Nor does he fail to bring Eliza around to a less sanguine view. But he must first give an adequate response to Eliza's counsel of patience and suffering obedience. It was her affirmation, "after all he is your master, you know," which brought forth George's detailed demonstration of Mr. Harris's inferiority. When he compounds this judgment with the announcement that he has taken about as much "insult and torment" as "flesh and blood" can bear, Eliza despairs for the course he is likely to take. Where he questions the legitimacy of his master's powers, she "always thought" it was her duty to "obey my master and mistress, or I couldn't be a Christian." George begins to win Eliza to his side—and, himself, to discover a single ground for restraint and opposition to tyranny—when he concedes the justice of her view.

> "There is some sense in it, in your case; they have brought you up like a child, fed you, clothed you, indulged you, and taught you, so that you have a good education; that is some reason why they should claim you. But I have been kicked and cuffed and sworn at, and at the best only let alone; and what do I owe? I've paid for my keeping a hundred times over. I *won't* bear it. No I *won't*!" he said, clenching his hand with a fierce frown. (20, original emphasis)

George's argument is a particular statement of that view of slavery which sees a people of advanced civilization bringing improvement to a people in its nonage. In recognizing the validity of this claim, George reveals his essential flaw: "happy" slavery is perhaps acceptable precisely because it brings to the slave the same objectives he would seek in freedom. That George accepts this, even in the face of Eliza's admission that her religion or civilization induces submission, is the fact that separates him from Uncle Tom.[7] Even Emily and Arthur Shelby could teach no more than submission for the sake of religion, and Uncle Tom's faith—as we shall see—is categorically opposed to this.

Nonetheless, in the present case this variant of contemporaneous humanism does serve to motivate a noble effort in the name of freedom. Even if the freedom consists only in being well fed, well clothed, and well educated, it can serve to avert the worst forms of despotism. That George Harris could find a ground for opposition to masters in Eliza's ground for submission serves to prepare her for the test she will encounter: must she, on her master's just claim, submit to the sale of her son? The perplexity George induces will make the answer to that question easier.

> She had never seen her husband in this mood before; and her gentle system of ethics seemed to bend like a reed in the surges of such passion. (21)

George completes Eliza's conversion with two facts, each of significance. The first is that he refused his master's orders to drown his own pet dog—the only comfort he had in those dark days. Instead, he submitted to a flogging after having watched the master and his master's son pelt the drowning dog with stones. George's refusal to kill the dog is a counterpoint to Uncle Tom's subsequent refusal to whip the slavewoman on Legree's plantation. But George's refusal is complexly tied up with his own connection with the dog—it was not a matter of principle or right, simply.

Again, Eliza counsels faith and righteousness—though now lauding George's disobedience: "O, George, you didn't do it!" She seeks to embrace a wider view of Christianity than mere submission, one which, promising right and good after much wrong and evil, can lend encouragement to human effort on behalf of right. But George denies that one can be a Christian under his circumstances. The promise of the good that follows evil is more readily believed by those "sitting on their sofas and riding in their carriages!" No, not even Eliza could strive for excellence, were she in George's place. But, of course, she *is* in his place if her initial appeal to hearth and home is genuine! By introducing the second and last fact in this paradoxical manner, George reveals that he cannot curse wife, child, and life. He might die for them; he cannot commit suicide before them. He relates the worst and most revealing fact last of all (they are still unaware of the sale of their son, despite Eliza's suspicion). Mr. Harris intends to prohibit George's visits altogether and unite him to someone on his own plantation.

> "Why—but you were married to *me*, by the minister, as much as if you'd been a white man!" said Eliza, simply. (22, original emphasis)

Eliza's incredulity is a direct consequence of her moral sensibility. The tenuousness of the connections of hearth and home reveal more profoundly the import of the defect of partial citizenship. George now sees it correctly, though he would have accepted partial citizenship and thought it alright for Eliza.

After this George announces that he will escape. He receives no resistance whatever from Eliza. To "be free" or die becomes the necessary form of expression for the preconditions of humanity. George provides the answer to his own question about the reason of life. The entire pathos in his character centers on the identification of life with freedom. This is not a comprehensive answer, although it serves sufficiently to inspire particular exertions. As if to underscore the partial perspective in this view, Eliza gives final counsel. She agrees that he must go—but not for freedom! Instead, where she noted his inclination to wicked things earlier, she now notes that to remain would mean giving in to orders to sin—to commit adultery. She urges him to go to avoid sinning. At the same time, she urges him to avoid sin in going. Her conversion is not to George's entire view of the conditions of human goodness: that is, the necessity to settle the question of life and the comforts of life before raising the question of goodness. She is rather converted to a broader Christianity. We might say she is forced to cast off the limits on her Christianity that her partial citizenship imposed. Hence, she is for the first time capable of *opposing* Christianity to "master's" wishes.

Throughout the development of these characters there is a tension between the recognition of signs of nature—say, being at ease or in comfort—and the recognition of signs of humanity—that is, straining toward the possibility of human improvement even where it appears impossible. The materialism-spiritualism dichotomy cannot be substituted for this formulation, because the tension is created precisely by the necessary but ambiguous relationship of those two factors. Their connection with matriarchy's hope for a condition "better than freedom" is seen in the transformation of Eliza's submissiveness into manly righteousness. In that process, it seems that freedom must be viewed as a minimum condition of human goodness because of the connection between goodness and one's own things. That is to say, the good that one is bound to by the reason of one's relationships necessarily implies liberty sufficient to pursue it. Eliza will at no time speak of seeking freedom herself. Yet, she will do so—almost automatically—for the sake of achieving the good for her son. When she flees with her son she tacitly recognizes that it was chance that connected her with Mrs. Shelby. To insist that matriarchy can produce a condition "better than freedom" is to maintain tacitly that chance is superior to art in framing human institutions. By refusing to entrust her son to such chance, Eliza tacitly rejects the foundation of her own education and with it, her partial citizenship.[8]

NOTES

1. Since feminist literary criticism first aimed its sights on Stowe in the mid-1980s, her thinking on "the woman question" has perhaps received attention nearly equal to her thinking on race. This scholarly trend generally portrays Stowe as advocating the replacement of traditional patriarchy with matriarchy. A few examples of this strain of Stowe scholarship are cited here. Tompkins dubs *Uncle Tom's Cabin* the "*summa theologica* of nineteenth-century America's religion of domesticity . . . the story of salvation through motherly love," adding that for Stowe, "the new society will not be controlled by men, but by women." Tompkins, *Sensational Designs*, p. 125, 145. Ammons reports that Stowe led the way in creating an American literary tradition, which postulates "an ideal community as something defined by family (rather than work), measured by relationships (rather than products), and ruled by women (rather than men)" and asserts that Stowe's "desire . . . to reconstitute the

world along female rather than male lines, for, in short, the coming of the female Christ—animates *Uncle Tom's Cabin*." Elizabeth Ammons, "Stowe's Dream of the Mother-Savior: *Uncle Tom's Cabin* and American Women Writers before the 1920s," in *New Essays on Uncle Tom's Cabin*, ed. Eric J. Sundquist (Cambridge: Cambridge University Press, 1986), pp. 157, 169 (hereafter cited as "Stowe's Dream"). Likewise, Lang perceives that Stowe "hopes to establish that women, because they do not themselves engage in the slave trade, are exempt from its corrupting influence—are, in fact, its natural opponents." Amy Schrager Lang, "Slavery and Sentimentalism: The Strange Career of Augustine St. Clare," *Women's Studies* 12 (1986): 36 (hereafter cited as "Slavery and Sentimentalism"). To Joswick, " . . . motherly love, not law, is the novel's highest authority . . . [it] is the very source of a moral awareness of good and evil and provides the earthly measure of salvation or damnation." Thomas P. Joswick, "'The Crown without the Conflict': Religious Values and Moral Reasoning in *Uncle Tom's Cabin*," *Nineteenth Century Fiction* 39, no. 3 (1984): 259. In Brown's Marxist reading of the novel, Stowe "sought . . . the replacement of the market economy by a matriarchal domestic economy." Brown, *Domestic Individualism*, p. 24. Kimball is far from alone in maintaining that "Stowe's advocacy of women as the central agents of salvation . . . [is] . . . the basic foundation of her work." Gayle Kimball, *The Religious Ideas of Harriet Beecher Stowe: Her Gospel of Womanhood* (New York: Mellen Press, 1982), p. 65. Generally speaking, these and similar discussions do not grasp the full complexity of Stowe's views on matriarchy.

2. See book II, part 1.

3. Stowe's belief in the vital role women played in educating the young is widely acknowledged in the literature. See for example Loebel ("the source of national and social repair is to be found in the nature of women. Women's ability to love, and their role as the educators of the family in the home, can convert male brutality and lift the fallen") and Sawaya ("In Stowe's and [Catharine] Beecher's eyes, women have extraordinary power to control the fate of the nation because of their ability to control the home environment of the child"). Loebel, "Legal Fictions," p. 367. Frances Josephine Sawaya, "The Home Front: Domestic Nationalism and Regional Women's Writing" (Ph.D. diss., Cornell University, 1992), p. 19 (hereafter cited as "The Home Front"). I also discuss this role for women in my article, "The Manners of Liberalism." ("The question [for Stowe] was not whether women would be the subordinate enforcers of traditional manners; it was rather whether the decisive form or content of the manners of liberalism would be the responsibility of women as, in other ages, it had been the care of aristocracy.") William B. Allen, "The Manners of Liberalism: A Question of Limits," *Improving College and University Teaching* 30, no. 4 (1982): 167 (hereafter cited as "The Manners of Liberalism"). Kimball echoes this comment: "Women replaced the influence of aristocracy . . ." Kimball, *The Religious Ideas of Harriet Beecher Stowe*, p. 77.

4. Brown accurately perceives the limits of a slavery grounded in matriarchy; however, she somehow overlooks Stowe's firm dismissal of this alternative. "Stowe replaces the master-slave relationship with the benign proprietorship of mother-child, transferring ownership of slaves to the mothers of America. . . . In Stowe's matriarchal society, slaves are synonymous with children because they lack title to themselves and need abolitionist guardianship. . . . Uncle Tom wants not emancipation but this protective ownership: 'the Lord's bought me and is going to take me

home. . . . Heaven is better than Kintuck.' By imitating God's parental economy, mothers approximate heaven in their home." Brown, *Domestic Individualism*, p. 32. Saunders likewise misses Stowe's dramatic commentary on the vision articulated by Mrs. Shelby: "Stowe places the argument that the slave[s] are unable to conduct their lives independently of their masters . . . in the mouth of a sympathetic southern character [Mrs. Shelby], then lets it pass without comment." Saunders, "Houses Divided," p. 418.

5. In a dissertation that, overall, distorts Stowe's message about patriarchal and matriarchal aspects of slavery, Saunders, nonetheless, accurately notes that "even in his spiritual life, [Tom] is surprisingly independent of Mrs. Shelby's ministrations." Saunders, "Houses Divided," p. 5.

6. Several Stowe critics focus on this question of ownership, albeit drawing some errant conclusions in this regard. Brown, for example, finds as a central theme of the novel "the liberal tradition of possessive individualism, in which individual rights are grounded in the principle of self-ownership." Brown, *Domestic Individualism*, p. 59. Riss states that Stowe approves certain instances of persons being "owned," basing this assertion on the fact that George speaks approvingly of owning his wife when they are reunited and Tom speaks approvingly of being "bought and paid for" by his Savior. He concludes that "Stowe does not object to the principle of persons being owned but to the way that slavery institutionalizes the wrong kind of ownership" and that "in response to this significant moral problem at the heart of the slave system, Stowe proposes that biology can serve as the only reliable test for proper ownership." Riss, "Racial Essentialism," p. 532.

7. Saunders recognizes that Stowe charts quite separate courses for the journeys of George and Uncle Tom; however, her characterization and assessment of their destinations is far from what Stowe intends. Saunders praises George's valuation and eventual ownership of his own family and faults Tom for "thinking of himself more as a part of the larger plantation family than as the head of his biological family or a member of a community made up of slaves alone" (424). The "larger family" Saunders refers to here is the plantation family and she says that "throughout the book, Tom seems to choose his masters and their welfare over his own interests and those of his biological family" (422). Because Saunders understands that Stowe has clearly made Tom the hero of the novel and because Stowe never reunites Tom with his biological family, she concludes that Stowe had "difficulty in truly valuing the slave families and potential for black self-sufficiency they represent over the paternalistic plantation family and the hierarchical version of black/white relations it represents" (394). Saunders, "Houses Divided."

8. Saunders misses Eliza's tacit rejection of Mrs. Shelby's teaching and her new found manly righteousness, stressing instead that Eliza's virtues all seem to have come from "her attachment to and emulation of a white mother-figure. As a result, the virtues Eliza exhibits continue to be associated with the white race despite the fact that a biracial woman possesses them." Ibid., p. 393.

7

The Birth of Uncle Tom

The connection between Uncle Tom and Mrs. Shelby is much more elusive. He virtually ignores her existence—in his own speeches. And although she claims to have taught him the duties of hearth and home, there is no evidence of this. Uncle Tom and Aunt Chloe, his wife, never once cite a teaching of Mrs. Shelby's—as Eliza does when she quotes that the soul of "one child is worth more than the whole world." And, as we noted above, it is certain that Uncle Tom could not have been raised by Emily—as Eliza was—since he was surely from eight to ten years her senior. Nevertheless, she claims to have taught him, and we are committed to a search for her teaching.

This is, perhaps, as good a place as we shall find to note that the novel is entitled not "Uncle Tom" but "Uncle Tom's *Cabin*." This is odd. For, on the surface, the cabin plays almost no role in the novel.[1] And we see Uncle Tom, himself, in the cabin only for the briefest of spaces. Unless I am mistaken and unless any place in which Uncle Tom resided is thought to be his "cabin," there are but five appearances of *the* cabin in the entire novel and two additional mentions, only one of which was explicit. It is true that this last, explicit mention of the cabin apostrophized it as a memorial to the freedom of those on the Shelby plantation, whose freedom was given as a consequence of the influence of Uncle Tom. Thus it may be said to have symbolic character quite apart from its character as domicile. Still, any number of possible symbols were available. The novel might have been called, for example, *Uncle Tom's Bible, or Life among the Lowly*. The oddity of this novel's actual title is perhaps its most perplexing feature.

The first introduction of Uncle Tom—in person—and his cabin occurs in chapter 4, "An Evening in Uncle Tom's Cabin." This chapter also provides the only explicit discussion of the cabin itself. Whatever we must at last conclude about the novel's title must be derived primarily from this chapter. Our present purpose, however, is to begin the development of Uncle Tom's character—to discover its dramatic and theoretical contexts. We begin with the assumption that Uncle Tom's character is somehow reflected in his cabin or at least in the fact that it is his cabin rather than himself which is celebrated in the novel's title. Nor can we neglect the designation of Uncle Tom's final abode on earth, the hovel at Legree's plantation, as his "cabin." This creates a strong presumption that his cabin is wherever he is. Nevertheless, Stowe does particularly describe his Kentucky cabin where his wife remains after Tom has left.

Of the many possible accounts of the cabin, none are offered by Stowe. Although no other slave appearing in the novel has his own "cabin," the reader is given no indication of how Tom comes to enjoy this privilege. Perhaps he built it himself. It was a "small log cabin" constructed of "rough logs." Perhaps Master Shelby had it built for him, in recognition of his prime ministerial functions on the plantation. Perhaps it was occupied by some prior prime minister and descended to Tom along with the responsibilities of the office. There are surely other possibilities as well. But all of these possibilities, save the first, share a common liability: they would reflect some qualification of Tom's ownership of the cabin. Only the first, Tom's building the cabin, would make it unquestionably his—the work of his own hands in spite of the legal infirmities to which he was subject. The author comes close to suggesting this view but once, in the close of chapter 21, where it is revealed that the cabin, after Tom's *and* Chloe's departure, is "shut up." Hence, the property seems not to have been regarded as descendible—except perhaps to their children who were yet in their nonage. The cabin is regarded as distinctly Tom's cabin.[2]

Kirkham's important work, *The Building of Uncle Tom's Cabin*, is appropriately named. He had in mind, of course, rather the author's work of building the novel than Uncle Tom's building the cabin. But we can now see that an important dimension in building the novel must have concerned the distinction to be accorded the subject celebrated in the title. Having established this much, it is then ironic that no account of the origin of the cabin is given. Nor, indeed, is there revealed any particular attachment Tom has to the cabin. It is rather Aunt Chloe—Mrs. Uncle Tom—who shows a particular attachment to the cabin and the solidity and standing it affords her. It is through Chloe that we come to understand the cabin as belonging to Uncle Tom. It belongs to him in precisely the manner that his wife and children belong to him. They are all "of him." They are his own things. The cabin, as distinct from Tom's "dependents," stands as the counterpoint to the hemp-cleaning machine that George Harris invented. In spite of the fact that Mr. Harris held the patent and enjoyed the fruits of the invention, George Harris owned the machine in a way that made it an inseparable part of himself. And Tom and Chloe enjoyed the fruits and flowers which "flourished under careful tending" about their cabin.

It is no more necessary to account for the cabin's origin than it is necessary to account for the origin of the hemp-cleaning machine. The reference, in each case, is to the "inventor." That is a big jump to make, by way of an assumption. Yet, the assumption in the case of Uncle Tom seems tenable. For his cabin is the source of his contact not only with the reader, but with his fellows in the novel as well. The story's subtitle amplifies the purpose intended in the celebration of the cabin: "or, Life among the Lowly." Tom's character is initially made manifest in his cabin, but especially in the service his cabin performs as the forum for his own moral and spiritual leadership among the slaves.

The ultimate question for the critic will be, "What is the relationship between Tom's pre-eminence among the slaves and his submission to his master?" But we are entitled to consider the much more immediate question, "What is the substance of Tom's moral leadership, and what is its relationship to the matriarchal principle?" At the surface we know from Eliza's case that Mrs. Shelby's influence is chiefly (though not exclusively) religious. And, if we expect Tom's cabin to symbolize or reflect the truth about his faith, we cannot escape wondering whether it, too, were constructed with his own hands.

The author offers little direct portraiture, though she promises much. Let us quote at length the initial account:

> Uncle Tom, Mr. Shelby's best hand, who as he is to be the hero of our story, we must daguerreotype for our readers. He was a large, broad-chested, powerfully-made man, of a full glossy black, and a face whose truly African features were characterized by an expression of grave and steady good sense, united with much kindliness and benevolence. There was something about his whole air self-respecting and dignified, yet united with a confiding and humble simplicity.
>
> He was busily intent at this moment on a slate lying before him, on which he was carefully and slowly endeavoring to accomplish a copy of some letters, in which operation he was overlooked by young Mas'r George, a smart, bright boy of thirteen, who appeared fully to realize the dignity of his position as instructor. (26)

Nothing strikes us so forcefully and immediately in our hero as the almost complete contrast with George Harris. Tom is *really* African. He has not the tortuous self-doubts and crises of self-confidence that afflict George. But, on the other hand, when his frank illiteracy and awkward attempts to learn to write are the medium through which we view his "*expression* of grave and steady good sense," the image of a massive stolidity is almost inescapable. And this is contrasted with George Harris's teaching himself to read and write and his fervid intellectual temper. George is "the man who was a thing," while Tom is "among the lowly." And, of course, Tom—too old to have been taught as a child by Emily Shelby—takes his lessons from her thirteen-year-old son. She, at least, has not taught anything in the line of rudimentary literary achievements. One thing counts heavily in Tom's favor: his determination to learn quite independently of Emily. And his determination is the equal or more of George Harris's own determination.

But is this strength of will—apparent only in the recognition of a manifest defect—a sufficient explanation of Tom's moral leadership? Stowe thought not. For she appealed rather to his "greater breadth and cultivation of mind" to explain his leadership. The image of stolidity is thus erased. But on what basis is so shocking a transition performed? Uncle Tom's moral leadership, having lasted already for an "indefinite length of time" (32), is said to depend in a particular way on "morale," that is, the character and disposition of soul in those led or governed. His rule was based on his influence. And his influence depended on the preservation of a positive and receptive will in those affected by him. There was in his teaching the complete absence of appeal to coercive authority.[3] Mrs. Shelby's influence, as we saw, was mixed with the necessity of submissiveness. Tom's teaching, therefore, if it is independent of Emily's, will necessarily be contrary to her teaching although not necessarily a contradiction.

The opposition would stem from the abandonment of obedience as a motivation or means to fulfillment of the teaching. And Tom's appeal to his fellow slaves would be based on a silent rejection of the form though not content of Mrs. Shelby's teaching. But, as we shall see, the rejection of the form of her teaching—"a life better than freedom," partial citizenship, founded in submissiveness—does alter or expand the content of the teaching.[4] To understand, first, the form, let us again quote at length:

> Uncle Tom was a sort of patriarch in religious matters, in the neighborhood. *Having naturally*, an organization in which the *morale* was strongly predominant, *together with* a greater breadth and cultivation of mind than obtained among his companions, he was looked up to with great respect, as a sort of minister among them; and the simple, hearty, sincere style of his exhortations might have edified even better educated persons. But it was in prayer that he especially excelled. *Nothing could exceed* the touching simplicity, the child-like earnestness of his prayers, *enriched* with the language of Scripture, which seemed so entirely to have wrought itself into his being, as to have become a part of himself, and to drop from his lips unconsciously; in the language of a pious old negro, he "prayed right up." And so much did his prayer always work on the devotional feelings of his audiences, that there seemed often a danger

> that it would be lost altogether in the abundance of responses which broke out everywhere around him. (36, emphasis added)

Now the several elements of this caricature are distinct. Tom had an "organization," whether used loosely or strictly, which accorded well with certain natural powers of his own. Those powers are revealed if not named in the combination of a certain kind of greatness of intellect with emphasized simplicity. And, finally, we see a respect of audience—the power to move an audience—in the form of an address to God. Hence, the powers exercised by Tom remain obscured by the very means and channels that he adopts for the exercise, whether by choice or necessity. And the exercise of these powers depends upon recognition of differing "natures" or capacities in human beings. His singular "prayer" works on plural and presumably differing "audiences." In summary, we may say that Tom exercises a wisdom that is largely if not wholly obscured by innocence or simplicity. Those who are moved by Tom will be moved before they know by what they are moved.

A distinct element of the caricature we have not touched upon is Tom's relationship to Scripture. To the extent it has become "a part of himself," he has been liberated from Emily's teaching. This is seen most clearly in a consideration of the particular teaching of the "meeting" on this evening in his cabin.

It may be thought that Mrs. Shelby is indirectly present, since her son, who gave Tom reading lessons earlier, is called upon to read for *Tom's audience*. But George Shelby does not choose the reading himself—the only substantive portion of the teaching that is suggested here. And we shall see that his mother would not or could not have chosen the readings from *Revelation*. The author offers no more than the following, in chapter 4:

> Mas'r George, by request, read from the last chapters of Revelation, often interrupted by such exclamations as "The *sakes* now!" "Only hear that!" "Jest think on 't!" "Is all that a comin' sure enough?" (35, original emphasis)

But, in chapter 7, Aunt Chloe refers back to this evening with vengeful anger, as she anticipates the slavetraders' groans in hell.

> "I tell ye all!" she said, stopping, *with a fork uplifted in her hands;* "it's like what Mas'r George reads in Ravelations,—souls a callin' under the altar! and a callin' on the Lord for vengeance on sich!—and by and by the Lord he'll hear 'em—so he will!" (63, emphasis added)

Though George is here credited with reading such tales, let us be reminded that he read them upon request! The evidence points to Uncle Tom as the "requester," and he hastens to correct Chloe's interpretation—a fact to which we will return. But, on the basis of this description, I would suggest that Tom's text for the evening was *Revelation* 14–22 (a text to which he returns in chapter 22 with little Eva).[5] As we undertake the interpretation of this text, let us bear in mind that Chloe's analysis followed revelation of the news of Tom's sale, but that Tom's decision to use the text came *before* this calamity.

That *Revelation* 14–22 is the text is suggested only by the barest of references. The only direct reference is to the "last chapters of Revelation." Therefore, the text must include some series of chapters, concluding with the twenty-second. A less direct reference is the text chosen by Tom and read by Eva. It seems, among others, one of Tom's favorite texts. The point at which Eva interrupts her reading, "a sea of glass mingled with fire," is the second verse of the fifteenth chapter of *Revelation*. We cannot know where her reading began. And still less direct are the mere allusions Chloe makes to the content of the text. But, in light of the above, these allusions may suffice. We have to search for a point at which "souls under the altar" are invoking the "vengeance" of the Lord. We have chosen chapter 14 (later passages make such allusions albeit less clearly) primarily because of the weight of Eva's reading combined with the necessity to see these imploring souls as distinctly human rather than angelic. And the fourteenth chapter unquestionably opens with reference to the human subjects of salvation.

> . . . no man could learn that song but the hundred and forty and four thousand, which were redeemed from the earth. (*Revelation* 14:3)

And, when Andy seeks assurance that "sich'll be burnt up forever, and no mistake," we have an almost direct echo of verse 11, "And the smoke of their torment ascendeth up forever." No matter how justly the query may be posed, by what assurance do Tom, Chloe, and their fellows assume themselves to be among so select a group, that question has no place here, for we desire only to understand the relevance of the text as applied to their earthly status. They may be in error, and we may still see how easily earthly "servants" come to imagine themselves as the favored heavenly "servants." And this is surely one of the necessary concomitants of Emily's teaching.

One clear interpretation of these chapters—which include the prospect of the direct rule of Christ on earth—is that a promise of justice is given to some human beings vis-à-vis others. And that justice is retributive. As is always the case with retributive justice, it is highly ambiguous whether justice resides most in the fact that they who are punished receive their due reward or whether those who suffered the crimes for which the criminals are punished are thereby receiving their due reward. *Revelation* is clear that the punishment of the sinful is not for the sake of the holy. It is instead the pure application of divine wrath. Nonetheless, the promise is implicit if not explicit in this text that God will not forbear in his wrath. Hence, though he may not be moved by human supplication, sufficient ground is surely given for the inspiration of human hope.

> For true and righteous *are* his judgments: for he hath judged the great whore, which did corrupt the earth with her fornication, and hath avenged the blood of his servants at her hand. (*Revelation* 19:2)

Aunt Chloe is surely just in glorifying in the sternness of God.

But Uncle Tom seems not to choose the text for such reasons. The last two chapters center on the prophesied refounding of Jerusalem—the arrival of the perfect earthly city. By inference, therefore, these passages reveal the imperfections of ordinary political life—not just for slaves but also for all men. "What *city* is like unto this great city!" (*Revelation*, 18:18) serves as an apostrophized reflection on earthly things *as they stand*. From the point of view of life here and now, *detachment* is emphasized—not submission.

> He that overcometh shall inherit all things, and I will be his God, and he shall be my son. (*Revelation* 21:7)

This promise of perfection—unlike the promise of wrath—is more than a testimony to divine power. It is a contract. And, as such, it is divine recognition of human power or capacity. Human beings of character and power sufficient may bind God to the performance of this contract.

> Blessed are they that do his commandments, that they may have *right* to the tree of life, and may enter in through the gates into the city. (*Revelation* 22:14)

Thus is established an impossible tension between the natural right that engenders political justice and a divine right that demands transcendence of ordinary politics for the sake of perfection. The test of this religious principle reposes in the character and power of men. Where they are found wanting their religion will fail. But the issue of the *attempt* to succeed is the utter destruction—or trivializing—of political right as such—political prudence is no match for religious perfection. Alternatively, we might argue that such a wager (pursuing divine perfection at the cost of certain impoverishment of earthly things and principles) is humanly justified only if, in the end, it is humanly possible—only if at least one human being may possess such character and power. And, in that event, the conditions of ennobling human political life—refounding—become possible.

But *Revelation* itself limits this possible implication of the text. Its most stringent prohibitions are directed not to the ordinary sinner but to the human being who would, precisely, test this religious principle.

> For I testify unto every man that heareth the words of the prophecy of this book, if *any* man shall add unto these things, God shall add unto him the

> plagues that are written in this book: and if *any* man shall take away from the words of the book of this prophecy, God shall take away his part out of the book of life, and out of the holy city, and from the things which are written in this book. (*Revelation* 22:18–19)

Thus, the prophecy of *Revelation* raises for the second time the paradox of the forbidden fruit. Since, in either case, the motive for testing the religious principle must arise from the desire to realize powers that liken and approach men to God, the divine prohibition of the end intended reveals the motive as corrupt, proceeding from disobedience.

In the face of the interdiction, to wish to add or subtract from the prophecy could proceed *only* from the desire to test the powers implied. The correct attitude toward the prophecy, therefore, would be that reflected in the meeting in Tom's cabin: "'The *sakes* now!' 'Only hear that!' 'Jest think on 't!' 'Is all that comin' sure enough?'" And Chloe's invocation of the text, against the slavetrader, seems an appropriate response to these wonderings. But Uncle Tom insists that Chloe and the others are in error. He corrects them and we must wonder whether he corrects *Revelation* also. That is the same thing as wondering whether someone adding to or subtracting from the prophecy, though possibly barring heaven to himself, might nonetheless succeed in transferring the grounds of politics to a supra-political plane.

Tom begins his correction by qualifying the promise of eternal perdition. He never suggests that that is *not* the promise of the prophecy. But he cautions Chloe and the "chill'en" that *they* must not implore eternal perdition for any "human crittur." "Forever is a *dre'ful* word," he reminded them, intending to replace the desire for vengeance with a desire for the conversion of sinners. They respond to their religious patriarch that they cannot help themselves and that no one could. Chloe, in particular, appeals to "natur herself." To her mind the systematic and brutal violations of nature require retribution in the extreme degree. "Lor, if the devil don't get them, what's he good for?" Her reasonable appeal—may not corrective justice bring at least a little justice to victims?—leaves her in tears as she confronts the alternative. Tom is soon to phrase it, opposing scripture to scripture: "Pray for them that 'spitefully use you, the good book says"(63).

So far, no violent wrenching of the prophecy occurs. Tom might vigorously debate God on the point whether one part or book of the prophecy is to overmaster others. Chloe's anticipatory and yielding tears suggest that God, if he dared take that side, is a loser in the debate. In spite of that, Chloe finds it too tough to pray for them—requiring more in character and power than she can summon. At this point it would seem appropriate for Tom to counsel that she pray for the strength—the character and power—to pray for her enemies. That she could have done—and even have let out a good bit of venom in the process—without, technically, violating the precept, "and in their mouth was found no guile" (*Revelation* 14:5). But Tom surprises the reader. He counsels Chloe instead to recognize her weakness in this regard as the power of nature! The very nature—or something like it—which Chloe considered violated is pointed to as the source of human imperfection—that is, as the source of the inability to achieve divine detachment.

The signs of nature to which Chloe pointed—maternity, matrimony, parentage—are for Tom the signs of human weakness. The identification of what is one's own—the imperfect worldly state to which *Revelation* referred—is but a reflection of a fundamental weakness, the lack of character and power sufficient to overcome.[6] It is *this* that the "Lord's grace" restrains, according to Tom, and thus paves the way to salvation. Conceding this virtually generic human weakness, it is not then idle for Tom to commend to Chloe thankfulness for not being *even* worse!

> . . . you oughter thank God that you an't *like* him [Haley], Chloe. I'm sure I'd rather be sold, ten thousand times over, than to have all that ar poor crittur's got to answer for. (64, orginal emphasis)

Tom's science of natures is the ultimate foundation for his counsel to Chloe. The identical science informed his advice to Eliza, that she escape, while reserving to himself the role of sacrifice. And we see that the hierarchy of human souls disclosed by this science reaches beyond the one-dimensional view of domestic attachments through the example of Tom himself, initially, and now by the addition of Haley. But we may say by way of hypothesis that the *character* of human attachments is understood by Tom to reveal the character and power of individual souls. Thus, the hierarchy extends, provisionally, from Haley[7]—who cares but for himself and of himself primarily for his body—to Eliza, Chloe, et al.—who care for their domestic and implicitly political attachments—to Tom himself—whose attachments have not been made precise but are clearly supra-political.

It is clear that Tom views this hierarchy as not simply accidental—the differences are natural. And it is this that he *adds* to *Revelation*. Nowhere does the text itself suggest that any human beings are sinners if not of necessity at least by inherent circumstances. It was implied in the text that the saved few would possess character and power out of the ordinary. But the drawing out of this implication was interdicted as an adding to the prophecy. Tom cannot escape the charge that he has done this. It is important to ascertain why. This we cannot do comprehensively until much later. But a provisional response will be found if we work our way back to the theme, matriarchy.

Chloe's cry that "natur herself" was being violated carried with it the implicit claim that the slaves would find it impossible to submit to such violations save on the hope of *both* retribution and salvation. This was precisely the motivating principle of George Harris's resistance. The recognition of natural rights and the founding of politics on such rights emerge precisely from awareness of a similar impossibility.[8]

When Chloe claims that the devil would be of no good otherwise, she means that the religion of which he is so central a part is intimately connected with her submission—and presumably Tom's. In this view, the slaves have a great stake in upholding the truth of the prophecy of *Revelation*—neither adding to it nor subtracting from it. Emily Shelby's teaching joins Chloe's view at precisely this point—ironic though it be,—and both oppose the result of Tom's teaching. He urges a contrast between natural human sentiment and "perfected" human sentiment—that is, man overcoming natural weakness to attain something higher. On that view, the slaves—without respect to their formal position—would have to eschew submission for the sake of salvation if for no other reason.

It should now be clear that Uncle Tom's faith is in fact as much the product of his own hands—vis-à-vis Emily's teaching—as we have assumed his cabin to be. It is a singular dramatic fact that Uncle Tom, in the entire novel, offers not a single word of address to Emily Shelby (though she several times addresses him directly) and but one reflection, his dying expostulation:

> Give my love to Mas'r and dear good Missis, and everybody in the place! (477)

It is safe to say that he understood her goodness in the light of her "nature." The partial citizenship she extended to her slaves—in the form of a condition "better than freedom" and hence without the onerous duties of citizenship—was surely enjoyed by Tom and Chloe, by virtue of their positions, as much as anyone save, perhaps, Eliza. But the question is not whether they enjoyed relative ease so much as whether Tom, in particular, understood his condition to be a reflection of his faith—as we know Eliza did.

And before making the necessary judgment, it might just as well be said now that Tom was, indeed, attached to the Shelbys—especially to Mr. Shelby. This seems incongruous because Shelby was so nearly a worthless character. But the fact remains. Tom loved him, whom he had served since Shelby's infancy, and Tom loved him *although* he recognized a weakness in Shelby's nature and although Tom had essentially operated the farm and could not expect Shelby to do so well as he, Tom, had done. But was he in fact submissive? Or, did he understand himself to have "freely" undertaken these connections and attachments to the extent to which he was conscious of them?

If Tom's faith is to provide the answer, at this level, the answer must be that he maintained the attachments in spite rather than because of Emily's teaching. The emphasis Tom placed upon the imperfections of human political efforts (which Emily comes to share only after these tragedies intrude upon her optimism) directly contradicts her matriarchal intentions. The protection she intended to provide her slaves depended ultimately on the Shelbys's own prudence *and* on the existence of decent laws defending that prudence. And, of course, Tom's appeal to differences in natures—instead of prayerful submission—was a silent rejection of the form of Emily's teaching.

Again, to the extent that Tom took seriously *Revelation*'s promise of divine paternity for those who would "overcome," matriarchy would find it impossible to compete with such a lineage save through immaculate conception. And the author's account of Tom's acquisition of the "language of Scripture" reveals that, between Tom and the prophecy, there remained no room for Emily to intervene. In the end, the detachment necessary to Tom ("What city is like unto this city!") is a formidable barrier to Emily's matriarchal project. She had staked all on limiting the slaves' horizon. But the means or form she adapted (teaching the "duties of family, of parent and child, of husband and wife") belong to a realm which is both less than Tom's concern and, at the same time, insufficient in the present case (What to do when the sale and its conditions have been announced?). The matriarchal plan turned on the possibility that some human beings could happily be the subjects of humanism (the moral graces of others), without striving to acquire the humanistic character themselves. The matriarchal plan failed to recognize the disqualification for honor or gentlemanliness (that is, full political standing) as a liability. Tom does not directly contradict this, as he aims higher still.[9]

NOTES

1. At the time that the project of this book was initiated, few Stowe scholars had analyzed the use of the cabin as a trope in any depth. One early critic to do so is Oliver who wrote in 1965 that "the 'cabin' figure is a central and dominating metaphor giving form and meaning to the entire novel." Like many subsequent critics, Oliver saw the cabin as a symbol of "domestic understanding and consideration," and pointed out that Stowe "has taken us to the cabin of a slave to show us the potential, even the temporary actual, that man can achieve." Egbert S. Oliver, "The Little Cabin of Uncle Tom," *College English* 26, no. 5 (1965): 356, 357. During the past two decades of Stowe scholarship, this trope has received greater attention. Useful discussions are found in Short ("The cabin functions as a trope . . . [it] becomes a combined metonymy, metaphor, and synecdoche for 'home.' . . . The novel becomes, both for George and others, a quest for 'home' understood best by Tom

and Eva—a home located within the heart and attained only in death, the cabin of the heavenly city, an inconceivable future that puns, in an act of temporarily dislocating syllepsis, a lost past.") and Sachs ("the cabin provides the keynote that organizes and harmonizes the novel's seeming structural peculiarity into an almost starkly straightforward design. With the cabin at the structural and geographical center of the novel, the two essentially discontinuous plot lines resolve quite simply: they are Northern and Southern radiations of successive depictions of virtuous and villainous households, out of a central household paradigm. Even the literal, physical layout of the book gains a dimension of coherent significance through a consideration of the cabin. For, like the cabin itself, which is delimited and defined by its physical boundaries, the book too is framed and defined at its boundaries by the presence of the cabin"), among other sources. Brian C. Short, "Stowe, Dickinson, and the Rhetoric of Modernism," *Arizona Quarterly* 47, no. 3 (1991): 11. Elizabeth Evans Sachs, "Describing a Sphere: A Definition of Space in American Women's Domestic Fiction in the Nineteenth Century" (Ph.D. diss., University of Wisconsin, 1992), p. 76 (hereafter cited as "Describing a Sphere"). Speaking about Rachel Halliday's home, Shipp comments on the overall use within the novel of "home" as trope: "Like other ideal homes in the novel, this home both mirrors and prepares its occupants for an ultimate spiritual home. The religious associations of a home are conveyed by Mrs. Stowe in a variety of ways. Tom's cabin is transformed into a church; the atmosphere in the Halliday's kitchen is profoundly if unconsciously evangelical . . . " Shipp, "*UTC* and the Ethos of Melodrama," p. 12. Earlier in his text Shipp notes that "ironically, Tom's cabin is a home in a way that his master's mansion is not. The exemplary life Tom and his wife Chloe have managed to create within their severely limited means is a powerful suggestion of the slave's capacity to improve both his private environment and that of the society around him, if only he is given the freedom and power to do so." Ibid., p. 7. Fisher, on the other hand, considers the cabin a symbol not of accomplishment, but rather of failure. He first discusses the cabin as a symbol of heaven (as have numerous other critics): "That the cabin is mentioned in the title is odd because the cabin plays very little part in the novel. In fact the key detail is that, from the first act of the novel on, Tom no longer lives in the cabin and never returns there. It is therefore the place where he isn't. . . . The title therefore asserts his homelessness, his possession of a home that he has not yet reached" (p. 119–20). Fisher then compares it to "ruins" which are used metaphorically in Romantic literature, saying that they are all "places that testify to the human inability to prevail . . . [the cabin] is an inverse monument: a witness to human failure rather than to human glory or accomplishment. It is in this sense that the title names the empty cabin and the book itself, in which the story of Tom is told from the point of view of his death, is Tom's monument" (p. 121). Philip Fisher, *Hard Facts: Setting and Form in the American Novel* (New York: Oxford University Press, 1985; hereafater cited as *Hard Facts*). Lewis also sees the cabin as a monument, but not a monument to failure: "Uncle Tom's Cabin, as Christ's empty tomb, serves as a memorial to the *exemplum.*" Like several other critics, she comments on Stowe's images of home as pointers toward man's heavenly home; however, she concludes that "Tom's cabin can't be the *exemplum* for home as heaven because of its basic flaw; he cannot own it. . . . Tom's cabin cannot endure except as a memorial to his martyrdom to save those whom it houses." Later, she adds: "Tom is true Christianity; his empty cabin signifies his empty house church, robbed of spiritual presence." Lewis, "Message, Messenger, and Response," p. 220–21, 271.

Sawaya draws attention to Stowe's symbolic use of buildings in some of her other writing, in particular in *Old Town Folks*: "The building [i.e., the church meeting house] both explains and enforces unity and enables democracy and equality to grow. . . . In fact, in this story, the house does not represent a separate, divided, private, solely familial space, but an open and public space. . . . Similar to the meeting house, the effect of [Grandmother Badger's] house on those who gather in it is to foster democracy." Sawaya, "The Home Front," p. 81, 82, 83.

2. Cf. Brown: ". . . the cabin that despite Stowe's title is not his . . ." Brown, *Domestic Individualism*, p. 48.

3. Shipp points out that Stowe's "larger philosophy . . . eschews control in favor of influence" and notes also that this message is one commonly developed in melodrama: "The plots of melodrama unfailingly involve a conflict between a force that aims to control and the human object of that aim. . . . Because it is a didactic genre, melodrama counsels against control as a mode of interaction, presenting even benevolent or well-meaning control as destructive, and frequently presents the attempt to influence others in a positive manner as the ideal way to interact." He also describes Tom as "himself the possessor of an informed heart and is, inevitably, a good manager. He . . . is able to translate the principles based on his feelings into practical results." Shipp, "*UTC* and the Ethos of Melodrama," p. 186, 188, 36.

4. Although they do not discuss this point as a rejection of the alternative of "partial citizenship" as offered by Mrs. Shelby's matriarchy, a handful of Stowe critics have understood that Stowe does not, after all, in *Uncle Tom's Cabin*, propose a transition from patriarchy to matriarchy as the means to end slavery or to otherwise reform society. See, for example, Levin ("[Tom] is in absolute command of his cabin. . . . This is a patriarchal, two-parent household, and the young children in it know that the father who loves them enough to weep at the prospect of leaving them is strong enough to enforce his domestic authority"); Sundquist (who asks whether the novel does "in fact subvert all patriarchal and paternalist governance, or does it . . . allow for a different, less harsh form of paternalistic governance?"); Yarborough and Allen ("Even though in this novel the people with proper feelings are often women, *Uncle Tom's Cabin* in no way promotes matriarchy or any other radical change in the social structure"); and Steele ("But to say that masculine and feminine roles have been reversed in *Uncle Tom's Cabin* is less accurate than to say that they have been merged . . . "). Levin, "American Fiction as Historical Evidence," p. 132. Sundquist, *New Essays*, p. 32. Richard Yarborough and Sylvan Allen, "Radical or Reactionary? Religion and Rhetorical Conflict in *Uncle Tom's Cabin*," in *Approaches to Teaching Uncle Tom's Cabin*, ed. Elizabeth Ammons and Susan Belasco (New York: Modern Language Association), p. 66. Steele, "Tom and Eva," p. 90.

5. Boots, on the other hand, speculates that George reads chapters 24 and 25 of Revelation and also sees in George the fulfillment of the prophecy: "'Blessed is he who keeps the words of the prophecy of this book. . . . Blessed are those who do his commandments, that they may have the right to the tree of life, and may enter the gates into the city [of eternal life].'" Cheryl Charline Boots, "Earthly Strains: The Cul-

tural Work of Protestant Sacred Music in Three Nineteenth-Century American Popular Novels" (Ph.D. diss., Boston University, 2000), p. 161, 169. That account, however, is inconsistent with the fire and brimstone version that Chloe recalls. Boots relies upon the expression "last chapters," which would mean more than one and therefore at least the last two, taken literally. However, every chapter after chapter 13 would qualify as the "last chapters," as in the second half of the book. And it is surely the case that the language of *Revelations* 14: 11 and 19, 1–3 is captured explicitly in Chloe's "quotation of 'souls a callin under the altar'" and Andy's "'Sich'll be burnt up forever.'" Finally, the book of *Revelations* ends at chapter 22!

6. It is this point, in particular, which eludes Saunders when she faults Tom's seeming lack of attachment to his biological family. Saunders, "Houses Divided."

7. He would sell his own mother, Shelby says, if he could get a good price.

8. Cf. Locke, *2nd Treatise on Civil Government*, Chs. 8–16, but especially paras. 168 and 176 and paras. 233–35 of Ch. 19.

9. An intention that is overlooked by those who believe that domestic matriarchy is the ideal that Stowe urged in this novel and her other works.

8

The Kinesis of Slavery and the Science of Natures

Having demonstrated that Tom's faith is not directly implicated in the matriarchal project, Stowe then renders her judgment of that project's capacity to mitigate the excesses of slavery. She does so in a direct contrast of Emily and Arthur Shelby. This is accomplished in chapter 5. That is, perhaps, the easiest of the forty-five chapters to explicate. It has a title of beautifully balanced ambiguity and precision: "Showing the Feelings of Living Property on Changing Owners."

The two senses of "changing" are equally involved in the chapter. In the ordinary sense—Tom's transference from Arthur's ownership to Haley's—we have ground to consider both the effect of the "living property" on Arthur's feelings and the "feelings" of the "living property." In Arthur's case, the feeling is of embarrassment and shame. It is summarized in his announcement that he cannot bear to witness the consummation of the transaction. When Tom is carried off he intends to be "off." This seems to be the form of winking hard at some of the necessary incidents of worldly practices that Arthur recommends to Emily. Indeed, he argues, the morality of such a regime cannot too far exceed its necessities.[1] Hence, his shame seems to result from some moral residuum which, strictly speaking, is out of place. Stowe uncharacteristically refrains from making any comment during the dialogue between Emily and Arthur, in which dialogue he confesses the sales. But against the background of chapter 1, it is clear that Arthur's candidacy for "Man of Humanity" had ended—even in terms of that defective humanism which, itself, does a lot of hard winking at moral necessities.

The second sense of "changing" applies to Emily. That is the sense in which the "owner" is seen to be transformed in outlook or expectation. The change in Emily results from recognition of the failure of the matriarchal project. Emily's moral guidance for her children and slaves was indissolubly tied to the condition of Arthur's worldly success.

> I can't help myself. I didn't mean to tell you this, Emily; but, in plain words, there is no choice between selling these two and selling everything. (40)

Arthur is a worldly failure who cannot afford the only morality that might defend the life he lives. It was this revelation which led Emily to curse slavery, declare her opposition to it and the laws which preserve it, and to confess her previous, erroneous hope to "make the condition of mine better than freedom." By the "laws like ours," it is clear that Emily means laws which rigidly separate temporal and spiritual or worldly and moral concerns. These can be contrasted only with the comprehensive community of the past, in which the command of the law and the command of morality were meant to be identical. In such a community, it would not be possible, by law, to sacrifice conscience to self-interest.

> Emily spurns Arthur's suggestion that she, too, refuse to witness the event. I'll be in no sense accomplice or help in this cruel business. I'll go and see poor old Tom, God help him in his distress! They shall see, at any rate, that their mistress can feel for and with them. (42)

Having recognized the failure of the matriarchal project, she too retains a moral residuum that seems out of place. But her moral residuum results from the conscious determination not to accept hard winking at moral imperfections. As such, Emily represents the first step in the articulation of a new humanism. In her it is politically impotent, but no less significant. If the reader could conceive Emily to be the "Man of Humanity," he would already have discovered the foundation for recasting humanism without the baggage of moral relativism.

Emily can "feel for and with" Tom and Chloe. The "Feelings of Living Property" have their effect on "changing owners." Tom and Chloe also have their own feelings—still more complex than Emily's and Arthur's. Chapter 5 is almost exactly divided between Emily's and Arthur's dialogue and Eliza's discovery of the sale, escape from the home with her son, and confrontation of Tom. Eliza's feelings are less complicated and less important. She, after all, overheard Emily's curses as she hid herself in a closet. Indeed, she leaves behind a note in which she apologizes for leaving, just as Tom must apologize for staying.

Eliza is enabled to tell the entire story—including the condition that the sale was the means of saving everything else—before Tom has a chance to react. But he has not opportunity to confront the significance of Eliza's decision, for Chloe immediately challenges him to pack and leave or explain why not. We must note, before considering Tom's reply, the oddity of Chloe's demand. She joins with George Harris in her sentiments: "I'd a heap rather die than go" where "they kill niggers with hard work and starving." But, all the time rallying Tom, she tacitly volunteers to stay behind! It may be sufficient to say, *à la* Banfield, that she is present-oriented and simply has not reflected on the consequences to herself.[2] But more is involved than the question of whether she, in turn, may be sold. As we noted above, when Chloe curses Haley she appeals to matrimony, maternity, and parentage. Can it be explained why her attachment to family, in itself, is overlooked in her advice to Tom? If George Harris is the model for Chloe, might it not be that the foundation of liberty is so thoroughly connected with individual preservation that, of itself, it allows no consideration of the social principle *per se*? On these grounds, it is comfortable preservation that makes the thought of family possible. But, by the twentieth century, did we not come to wonder whether placing comfort before family inverted the necessary order?

Chloe has no occasion to answer and clarify. Tom is emphatic. He will not escape. Eliza has given the reason. Either he is sold, or "all the people on the place" must be ruined. Tom is a martyr. But why should this be? What are his grounds? Consider. Of Eliza—and her boy—he approves the decision to escape. Indeed, he is an accomplice. Surely the sale of the boy also affects the others! Arthur had said, "either these *two*" or all. But Tom takes the burden entirely on himself—he even repeats his formulation:

> It's better for me alone to go, then to break up the place and sell all. (46)

Is it reasonable for him to think he is worth that much—and that the child was but a bauble for the trader? It is reasonable only if the foundation of his advice is still more true of himself:

> Let Eliza go—it's her *right*! (emphasis added) I wouldn't be the one to say no—'t an't in *natur* (original emphasis) for her to stay. . . . (45)

Nature in some way distinguishes Eliza and Tom. And the distinction affects the manner in which they exercise the right which derives from nature. While Eliza is free to pursue her "own things," Tom is, apparently irreparably, attached to specific social considerations—to the city.

Lest it be thought that the "nature" invoked here be nothing more than maternal instinct, the reader is reminded of Chloe's appeal to nature and Tom's use of that appeal to correct *Revelation*. Tom's knowledge of natures—now including his own—is apparently comprehensive. It is the apparent foundation of his martyrdom. And it is the certain foundation of his rule over his "masters." It may be well to indicate the range of that knowledge here, in order that we attach the greatest significance to Tom's decision.

If we examine only Tom's direct references to nature and natures we find six passages. In addition, we find one passage in which the author speaks, but so as to amplify our understanding of Tom's understanding. There are seven passages in all. They are spread evenly through the book. The first regards Eliza. We discussed it above. The second (the longest discussion of nature and natures) regards Chloe and Arthur Shelby. As regards Chloe, we have discussed it; as regards Shelby, Tom attributes to Shelby's nature his desire to run away before the trader returns. This compares with the third passage, in which Tom holds that "it's natur I should think a heap" of Shelby although Shelby, as a master, may naturally neglect the services Tom has done for him (109). It is clear that the "nature" in this case is acquired, both by masters and servants, whereas the first two examples seem less variable.

In the fourth passage, Stowe herself speaks. Respecting his residence in the St. Clare home, she explains how Tom came to rule. Among other things,

> Tom had every facility and temptation to dishonesty; and nothing but an impregnable simplicity of nature, strengthened by Christian faith, could have kept him from it. But, to *that nature*, the very unbounded trust reposed in him was bond and seal for the most scrupulous accuracy. (233, emphasis added)

It is unclear whether "that nature" is the combination of the former elements or the "nature" apart from its simplicity and Christian faith. But we see him throughout the novel engaged by nothing so readily as by the appeal to his honesty (151).

Like the third and fourth, the fifth passage addresses Tom's nature primarily. On this occasion he again speaks. Having been told of his impending freedom by St. Clare, Tom exults. St. Clare, somewhat hurt and asserting that Tom has not had it so bad, seeks an explanation.

> Mas'r, I'd rather have poor clothes, poor house, poor everything, and have 'em *mine*, than have the best and have 'em any man's else,—I had *so*, Mas'r; I think it's natur, Mas'r. (349, original emphasis)

For Tom, in other words, freedom is not connected with comfort and, in his case at least, this is the natural formulation. There are three dimensions to Tom's nature, each of which he understands. First, he is attached to those things for which he has had peculiar care and responsibility. He differs from the others in this only insofar as, in him, this characteristic is primarily other-regarding. Second, he is by nature moderate; by nature, he replaces the claims of self-interest with self-control. Third, he considers it natural to prefer self-rule to all other good things.

The sixth and seventh passages again refer to others. The sixth passage, Tom speaking, celebrates the natural capacity of Christ to endure suffering. Taking the Passion as a human model, Tom distinguishes men from Christ by the reflection that "it seemed to come so natural to him, and we have to fight so hard for 't!" (413). Self-rule, for men, is naturally superior to other goods. But men differ in their capacities to attain it. Hence, the seventh and final passage returns us to the first. As he did with Eliza, Tom advises a slave to flee. This time it is Cassy. But on this occasion Tom makes clear the natural foundation. Cassy must flee in order to avoid further degradation. Moderation and self-rule is simply not possible for her—given her capacities—in the circumstances of Simon Legree's plantation. Tom confides that even *he* would have fled Legree's terror, save that he felt it a duty to minister to "these yer poor souls" who would have been left behind. The circumstances are the opposite of those at Shelby's plantation, but Tom's apology for staying is the same. Similarly, Cassy is in Eliza's shoes and must follow Eliza's example. It is even Tom who originates the idea of Cassy's escape![3]

> It's different with you; it's a snare to you,—it's more'n you can stand,—and you'd better go, if you can. (454)

Cassy's deficient nature qualifies her for a different mission. But that mission—like George Harris's—is primarily that she acquire sufficient ease of circumstance at least to have the chance of ruling herself.

Tom's knowledge of natures seems to produce a hierarchy that ends in Christ.[4] But we must bear in mind the distinction between preferring self-rule by nature and being capable of achieving it by nature. Each of the three dimensions of Tom's own nature is independent of the inspiration of Christ. As such, they constitute a model of strictly human excellence. The connection with the model of Christ is that it serves rather to measure what is nonetheless a distinctively human achievement. The end suggested in the model of Christ would in fact be the logical end of the model of Tom. But that is restricted to suffering. Tom would have escaped in differing circumstances. The model must then serve other circumstances as well. Hence, it becomes as important to distinguish this new foundation for human attachments and moral endeavors from the self-preservation, natural rights foundation as it is to distinguish men from God. Tom retains respect for natural rights by advising Eliza and Cassy to flee. But he suggests that something will be required in addition, if they are not merely to become Shelbys in their own turn. That is, something more is required if the tone of society is not to be set by Shelbys merely—however lovable they be.

Tom's apology for not fleeing with Eliza boils down to the assertion that, for superior natures, there was at the time no greater opportunity for acting wisely outside of slavery than in slavery! His apparent commitment to existing social relationships may be deceptive. But the failure of Emily's matriarchy would seem of necessity to create a crisis. The partial citizenship that she had offered requires a reformulation of the question whether Tom has transcended the city or not. If there is sense in Tom's position, it can arise only from the reflection that there is no phoenix to spring from the ashes of Emily's matriarchy. The flaw seems to lie not in the law that she would correct, but in the very moral principles themselves.

The key, perhaps, is found in the enduring connection between comfort and goodness. The partial citizenship offered to the slaves seems not sufficiently distinguished from the full citizenship of a regime based on such principles. The slave seems to face the dilemma of confirming and deepening his slavery by accepting the amelioration partial citizenship offers (worldly comfort). But, of course, Emily's matriarchy failed this test. It could not deliver the partial citizenship or, what is the same thing, mitigating moral graces.

Of the novel's several caricatures used to suggest this argument, one is worthy of comment. That is "persistent Sam," who saw in Tom's demise his own ascent. Sam's story is the story of the slave who has accepted the promise of partial citizenship in the liberal democratic regime, and who struggles to master the conditions of that citizenship. It is in this story that we find the obvious, heavy-handed parody of the Declaration of Independence. The parody involved in George Harris's "declaration" is more subtle and becomes apparent only when the tension between George and Tom is recognized. "Persistent Sam" is introduced into the drama just as the slaves get wind of the impending sale and Eliza's escape. He is introduced for the purpose of leading the chase to capture Eliza, in which pursuit he intends not to be lax. In the end, however, he proves the earthly cause of her salvation. And this change of circumstance merits particular explanation. The explanation is the account of the citizenship Sam thinks to enjoy.[5]

> The author is blunt and direct in opening this phase of the drama. Black Sam . . . was revolving the matter in all of its phases and bearings, with a comprehensiveness of vision and a strict lookout of his own personal well-being, that would have done credit to any white patriot in Washington. (50)

The personal reflection to which Sam was led was none other than his own chance to replace Tom as "grand Cuffee." Sam's soliloquy was interrupted by a messenger from his master, who announced the need to ride after Eliza. This sign of providence inspires Sam to "cotch her." But events move too swiftly for any ordinary politician, as the servant, Andy, adds that Mrs. Shelby would prefer Eliza's successful escape. The perplexity is short-lived as Sam enters the task of satisfying the despot's whim. Before he even speaks to Emily directly, he commences delaying tactics by placing a beechnut burr beneath the saddle of Haley's mount. The resulting fall and melee delay the start from nine o'clock to near one. And on the road Sam skillfully diverts

Haley yet another two hours with a wild chase along a deserted path. Still, they arrive at the banks of the Ohio before Eliza's crossing (she had a fourteen hour advantage altogether, but she was afoot). It is for Sam, then, to alert her and give the start to her mad dash across the ice-floe clogged river. The thing done, Sam joyfully returns to report to his mistress and to regale his peers with the account of his heroism and of his principles.

Sam did not regard the events unfolding around him as human drama. He rather thought of it merely as a change of political administration. Now that Tom was down, thought he, "der's room for some nigger to be up—and why not dis nigger!" His perspective is not false, insofar as it was the case that engines of social adjustment were turning and might just respond to his touch. Neither was there moral insensitivity, insofar as such moral conceptions as would apply would wholly transcend the realm he knew. His perplexity is genuine when he wonders why Emily does not want Eliza caught, since he thought she "would a scoured the varsal world after Lizy." But the surest indication of his perspective is found in the non-servile manner in which he deals with Haley. The actions he undertook required recourse to every liberty he might have taken if his intention were to escape slavery himself or even to avenge its injustices. Shelby, who, after hearing Sam innocently relate the whole, cautions him not to make a habit of such practices, indirectly affirms the extent of Sam's liberties. Haley may well have been killed by his fall, though Sam clearly intended no such end. He would not have done so. He could not have done so. The opportunity is again spurned when he and Andy lead Haley into a dense and deserted wild. They may easily have slain him, left him there, and rode on toward Eliza with an extra mount to ensure freedom for all of them. Haley could not have been missed or found before they had safely secured their freedom. This they did not do. This decision to remain in slavery differs qualitatively from Tom's and requires a different kind of apology.

Stowe suggests the view that informed Sam's horizon at the opening of this section, when she notes that the chief news making the rounds of the slave quarters was the news of Tom's "fall." Eliza's escape—though "an unprecedented event"—was only "accessory" if great in "stimulating excitement." Sam's vested interest in the order on the plantation is in fact a reflection of the perspective of the slaves generally. They imagine themselves to participate in a comprehensive political order—as did George and Eliza before catastrophe struck. Sam's "comprehensiveness of vision" is comprehensive in precisely this sense. He understands the grounds for the arrangement of offices in this social order. And that ground is self-interest strictly speaking.[6] Nonetheless, the liberation of self-interest is said to require certain concessions to principles of community and, foremost, the commitment to defend this political principle.

It may be that Sam's connection of the defense of liberty with exercise of the liberty of indulgence is an inaccurate reflection of the master upon whom he patterned himself. It was his frequent attendance on his master at political gatherings that inspired his "burlesques and imitations" of his masters. But he seems rather serious as he settles into his new role as "prime minister," in the midst of an outflux of meats, pies, and other edible rewards for his day's working, regaling his fellows with the tale of heroism and a pledge to defend them to the end. Sam's apology made no mention of the self-interest which began the day's reflections for him. His speech was an embellishment of "all for one and one for all." And he produced a flourish in defense of statesmanship: "I'm the feller for yer all to come to, bredren,—I'll stand up for your rights,—I'll fend 'em to the last breath!" (87). But the younger Andy revealed the original intention to capture Eliza. Hence, Sam was called upon to reconcile his apparent moral contradiction.

Two things should be noted, in order to make Sam's apology intelligible. First, his speech reveals a full acquaintance with the language of rights and the heavy responsibilities such principles entail. Hence, ignorance is an insufficient account of Sam's acceptance of slavery. He is not ignorant of such things (in fact, he learned of them in the identical manner George Harris learned of them), even if he is ignorant that he has no such rights in slavery. Partial citizenship may be a more powerful illusion than we are willing to concede.[7] Second, Sam's claim that he sacrificed himself "fendin' fer yer all, yes, all on yer" by defending one from the slavetrader is nearly identical to Tom's "It's better for me alone" than for "all" to go. The irony is that Sam is aware that, for him, this claim is made possible only by the sale of Tom! The "all," for Sam, is exclusive of the one—and therefore anyone—who would embarrass his claim to preside and to profit from his administration. The "all," for Tom, is exclusive of himself. Tom does not for himself as he does for others. Sam does for others as he does for himself. With that distinction in mind, we can understand his appeal to principle in order to remove the suspicion of moral inconsistency.

Sam began by invoking "conscience." He confronted the moral challenge head-on, explicating a Christian concept of especial force.

> "Dat ar was *conscience*, Andy; when I thought of gwine arter Lizy, I railly spected Mas'r was sot dat way. When I found Missis was sot the contrar, dat ar was conscience *more yet*,—cause fellers allers gets more by stickin' to Missis' side,—So yer see I 's persistent either way, and sticks up to conscience, and holds on to principles. Yes, *principles*," said Sam, giving an enthusiastic toss to a chicken's neck,—"what's principles good for, if we isn't persistent, I wanter know?" (87–88, original emphasis)

Sam is explicit. Conscience is the source of moral guidance. But it is variable specifically because it must take as its standard a principle that is peculiarly responsive to changing circumstance. The principle is self-interest. Sam's public teaching is identical to his private teaching. This causes no embarrassments, for the variability in the demands of conscience is amply compensated by consistent attachment to principle. Sam feels to possess a sure guide for conscience. He explains, therefore, that the ordinary judgment that a man is inconsistent because he prefers one thing one day and another the next is in error. For the variable preferences are but so many different means for reaching the unvarying end. Conscience is the means for pursuing the specifically human end, and as a means it must be informed by the end itself. The principle that reveals the end is the guide for all even if but a few recognize it. Sam ends in a flourish.

> —jest anything that I thinks is principle, I goes in to 't;—I wouldn't mind if they burnt me 'live,—I'd walk right up to de stake, I would, and say, here I comes to shed my last blood fur my principles, fur my country, fur der gen'l interests of s'ciety. (88)

That a principle of self-interest could inform such public-spiritedness seems and is ironic. But look beneath the irony and discover Sam's apology. He is a true revolutionary. If ever the day should come that men begin to kill men for being willing to die—to feed men for desiring to eat—to torture men for not fearing pain—then indeed will he have something to fight for! His conscience would dictate it.

To those who conceive the project of modern liberalism to be based entirely on the fear of pain, Sam's citizenship will seem full rather than partial. But it must not be neglected that Sam is utterly incapable of breaking his habit of taking the Lord's name in vain.[8] That is, his rather stark presentation of these principles is stark just because it is unadorned by any mitigating moral graces. There is, in Sam's version, no room for the humanistic distinction between civilized and uncivilized. Insofar as modern liberalism bears within itself the promise of human improvement (which it characteristically does), it at least promises more than Sam promises.[9] Where the damage is done in Sam's suggested version is that the mitigating moral graces—the demand for moral consistency—prove to be nothing more than the facility with which one can demonstrate the rectitude of following one's own passion.

As such, this is but a minimum condition of social life. Where one cannot assert the rectitude of following one's own passion, that passion is suspect and, perhaps, prohibited. But the only thing about which there can be moral certainty is the propriety of following such passions for which a principled defense can be made. It is true that this undermines any conceivable defense of slavery, insofar as slaves no less than freemen are subject to the passions. But it is also true that, in principle, no difference between slave and freeman should in fact remain. In these terms, the conditions are identical as the men are identical. "Persistent Sam" has indeed deepened his slavery in the endeavor to realize the promise of partial citizenship. But he has done so only in terms of the risks he takes in surrendering and forgoing the exercise of all coercive or punitive authority. He believes that the condition of self-indulgence may be advanced in slavery even more than in freedom. That is at best an error in judgment and not a moral problem.

NOTES

1. And, indeed, it *cannot*. See the account of "persistent Sam" later in this chapter.
2. Edward C. Banfield, *The Heavenly City* (Boston: Little, Brown, 1968; reprint, 1970), Ch. 3 or, to take the original example, De Tocqueville's *Democracy in America*.
3. Notwithstanding the claim made by Lant, that "Cassy herself devises" the plan for her escape. Donovan reminds us that "one cannot . . . ignore the role of Tom in their escape." Kathleen Margaret Lant, "The Unsung Hero of *Uncle Tom's Cabin*," *American Studies* 28 (1987): 58. Donovan, *UTC: Evil, Affliction, and Redemptive Love*, p. 111.
4. Cf. Shipp (writing about the dramatizations of *Uncle Tom's Cabin*): "Acknowledging the sacred quality of all human life need not blind the audience to distinctions between those lives which are better lived than others." Shipp, "*UTC* and the Ethos of Melodrama," p. 149.
5. Bush overlooks this aspect of the significance of the character of Persistent Sam, dismissing his importance to plot and theme with the statement that " . . . Sam's function is to highlight and mock the hypocrisies of much public rhetoric." Harold K. Bush, "The Declaration of Independence and *Uncle Tom's Cabin*: A Rhetorical Approach," in *Approaches to Teaching Uncle Tom's Cabin*, ed. Elizabeth Ammons and Susan Belasco (New York: Modern Language Association, 2000), p. 180 (hereafter cited as "The Declaration of Independence and UTC". Bense comes closer in his analysis: "As the case of Sam will also show, Stowe worked subversively within the rhetoric and culturally invented myths that held sway over slavery propaganda to convert the most egregious kind of slave stereotyping among her contemporaries into a shape-shifting, encompassing figure who would, through his words and enactments, deflate major tenets of American ideology that had made his 'creation' possible. . . . Through his performance as a speaker, Sam's roles as providential agent, self-taught orator, community protector, bragging humorist, and homespun philosopher result in significant humor at the expense of white male authority." Also: "Through Sam's emblematizing of self-reliance, success, and salvation, Stowe projects a comically conceived, inward view of the North's popular mind, its self-congratulatory compounding of the influences of Emerson and Franklin with the religious tradition of exemplary 'perseverance.'" James Bense, "Myths and Rhetoric of the Slavery Debate and Stowe's Comic Vision of Slavery," in *The Stowe Debate: Rhetorical Strategies in Uncle Tom's Cabin*, ed., Mason I. Lowance, Ellen E. Westbrook, and R. C. De Prospo (Amherst: University of Massachusetts Press, 1994), p. 189, 195, 200.
6. Gossett notes Burgess's comment in this regard and adds a rejoinder: "In 1966, Anthony Burgess would comment on this passage. 'The speech is the speech of a

whole tradition of fictional negroes . . . but the argument is that of the modern African politician.' It is also the argument of shrewd and self-interested people of any race anywhere." Gossett, *UTC and American Culture*, p. 112.

7. Tocqueville, at least, argues so in *Democracy in America*; but we must note that Stowe was not entirely in agreement that the slave "appears insensible to his extreme wretchedness." Sam is still trying to "make something of himself." Alexis de Tocqueville, *Democracy in America*, tr. Henry Reeve (New York: Schocken Books, 1961), vol. I, p. 395 (hereafter cited as *Democracy in America*).

8. Cf. the account of George Washington's *single* resort to swearing, in Harriet Beecher Stowe, *Poganuc People: Their Loves and Lives* (New York: Fords, Howard & Hulbert, 1878; reprint, Hartford, CT: Stowe-Day Foundation, 1987), Ch. 13 (hereafter cited as *Poganuc People*). Citation pagination refers to Stowe-Day edition.

9. Cf. Thomas Jefferson, *Notes on the State of Virginia*.

9

"What Country Have I?"

The motif and motive of George Harris's escape reveals both the wisdom and limitation of "Persistent Sam's" view. The wisdom is revealed through the circumstance that George's run to liberty is, in fact, a run to law. Sam is right to strive for a ground upon which to stand in the context of a political order. It was the law called "English liberty" which could, with one touch, "dissolve every incantation of slavery, no matter in what language pronounced, or by what national power confirmed"(*UTC*, 442). When George declares of Canada, "that shall be my country," (129) he exercises in the anticipation the liberty he expects to result. That George runs to law confirms the ambiguous status of liberty. That he eventually abandons "English liberty" for the hope of Liberian liberty confirms how little he understood the ambiguous status of liberty. What he in fact understood was only sufficient to reveal the limitations inherent in Sam's view: the ground upon which Sam sought to stand was as the Slough of Dispond. It was in the nature of the law of American slavery that the promises of partial citizenship could not be delivered; it was a pit of quicksand. By discovering that partial citizenship was much more uncertain than Sam realized (i.e., the risks involved in surrendering all coercive or punitive authority uniformly end badly [133]), George realizes that the slave has no choice but to reject partial citizenship and to reclaim the right of being a man.

The problem of the character of George Harris, then, is wholly revealed in consideration of his understanding of what it means to be a man. The thematic presentation of this problem involves testing how far his understanding satisfactorily responds to the urgencies of John, the Drover. Analysis of his understanding begins with his motive for escaping. We have seen above that he formulates the intention as a specific response to the hardships to which he has been reduced. George begins with the fear of pain. He is not so narrow a character as to focus wholly on pain, however. The complete statement of his motivation is given in the second half of chapter 11, the chapter in which John, the Drover, is introduced. There George initiated his escape and was called upon to justify his course by Mr. Wilson, his former employer.

Some attention must be given to circumstances before we consider George's own words. George, like Eliza, escaped in the guise of a white. Stowe makes much of this fact in both cases. George, indeed, is so white that in order to disguise himself, he *darkens* his features![1] It has commonly and erroneously been thought that Stowe's treatment of mulattoes and quadroons and octoroons, etc., is a sign of her own racism: she preferred lighter-skinned to darker-skinned Africans.[2] So far is this from being true that George's case proves the opposite: she understood the foundations of race prejudice in her own day—especially at the North—and capitalized on it with the intention of embarrassing it in a contradiction. We noted above the apparent contradiction between the European "Preface" and the American and English prefaces. We noted, too, that in the case of the latter the text could serve to correct faulty impressions. George Harris serves precisely this purpose. And his understanding of liberty is closely related to the achievement of that end.

In the first place, let it be noted that Stowe's repeated emphasis on slaves of mixed race is an implicit criticism.[3] It suggests that there were many full Africans, highly prized, in order that there be so many mulattoes. But that is a passing criticism in the text. The deeper criticism is found in the fact that George and Eliza *change color*! While slaves and in the South, both are practically white. George, for example, received virtually no physiognomic characteristics from his mother and, opposed to the legal definition, Stowe considered him white or European (125). This has the effect of eliminating the racial defense of slavery; whites, too, are enslaved; indeed, the heirs of slaveowners are enslaved. It is easier for some to see the horror of slavery when there is no appreciable difference between the slave and the master.[4] As a consequence, it is easier for the northerner to identify with the slave—practically a near relation!—and to condemn the institution. This accounts for the miracle of the Harris's changing color. Every step they take closer to freedom brings them richer African physiognomic characteristics. George, for example, as he stood on northern soil, at a rocky pass in the dead of night, successfully defending himself against would-be slave catchers, was a "youth of African descent," with "swarthy cheek"(226). As he prepared to board a boat for the final leg of his journey, he bore the "tint of African blood in his cheek"(438), and their son—disguised as a little girl—possessed a "dark beauty"(441) although Eliza had still less African "blood" than George. And, at the end of the novel, we find George desiring a specifically African way of life as distinguished from white ways to realize through ordinary generation the apparent promise of his magical transformation.[5] To that consideration we later return. Here, however, we see that this sympathetic hero wins the sympathy of his audience as a white but seeks to retain it as a black man. Thus does the northerner whose heart is moved to pray for the liberty of the white man—more intelligent than his master!—find himself praying for the liberty of a black man—whose capacities as such he had learned to suspect. Far from revealing, under shrewd psychoanalytic consideration, Stowe's unconscious prejudices, this device reveals a subtle attack on race prejudice as incident to the attack on slavery. Hence, at the end of the novel Stowe consummates her efforts with assimilationist proposals and even the passing detail of an interracial marriage.[6]

There is a connection between the attack on prejudice and George Harris's struggle for liberty. The liberty he seeks—a form of law, as we noted—is likened to the liberty defended by America's citizens. Hence, Stowe argues at once that that liberty as such is only defensible on universal ground and, insofar as there is any defect in George's conception, is an inadequate foundation of political life. Where Sam's conventional view was defective because wholly conventional, George's universal—hence, natural—view, must be defective on the basis of other considerations. To discover these considerations one must consider the way in which George's view is natural.

Stowe makes the task easier by immediately confronting George's action with the contrary force of law. Although the dialogue sufficiently reveals the nature of the opposition, the device of a reference to Bunyan's *Pilgrim's Progress* assists the reader (125). In the specific reference Mr. Wilson, who presents the demands of the law, is said to be "much tumbled up and down in his mind." His confusion apparently stems from the fact that his own inclinations are opposed by a fear aroused by the clamorous command of the law. Thus, he is likened to Christiana and her company, who would be admitted into the way to Heaven, but are frightened by the loud barking of a dog within the gate. In that section of *Pilgrim's Progress* the dog is actually kept by the devil for the purpose of frightening pilgrims away. The dog is not really in the way, because he is on the devil's nearby estate. Since, however, he can come right up to the wall, he appears to be directly in the path of right. In *Uncle Tom's Cabin* the connection is not to be made on the basis of interpretation of that passage. Instead, it seems intended for fairly literal construction. Earlier Stowe had borrowed yet another portion of the same story. She attributed to one of the slave catchers a "doggish nature,"[7] when expanding upon his account of his trade which she considered the work of the law. The law, then, stands in the way as a source of bedevilment for human inclinations to decency. And the law-dogs are the means of fighting off such inclinations.[8]

Mr. Wilson managed to conquer his fear of the frightful consequences—for George—and to assist George in his escape. But George first must out shout the law-dogs. He is assisted in this by the fact that Wilson is rather more concerned with George's obedience to the law than with his own! George may not have been able, on his own principles, to rebut the argument that Wilson should uphold the law. But the argument that he, George, should uphold the law is withered with scorn. George denies Wilson's belief that George is indeed a citizen—if partially.

> Mr. Wilson, *you* have a country; but what country have *I*,[9] or anyone like me, born of slave mothers? What laws are there for us? We don't make them,—we don't consent to them,—we have nothing to do with them; all they do for us is to crush us, and keep us down. Haven't I heard your Fourth-of-July speeches? Don't you tell us all, once a year, that governments derive their power from the consent of the governed? Can't a fellow *think*, that hears such things? Can't he put this and that together, and see what it comes to? (127, original emphasis)

Now, at a minimum, southern Fourth of July speeches were not intended for slaves. That they should prove a source of inspiration to slaves is testimony to a power they possessed beyond the intention of their creators. Sam, too, understood this. The difference is that George can see the impossibility of realizing their aim in slavery. But there is a paradox in his wishing to realize such aims. Fourth of July speeches incontestably belong to the United States. That George wishes to realize their promise, while acknowledging that he has no country, is tantamount to wishing to be what he believes he cannot be: an American. The only solution is to maintain that these principles are realizable apart from their source of origin. Their natural foundation must be sought.

Wilson repeatedly held before George the demand of obedience to the laws of his country. George rejects it specifically because those laws admit of a difference between Wilson and himself. Wilson insists that disobedience is wicked and unchristian. George resists the conclusion, maintaining that the Bible does not apply to his circumstances: "My wife is a Christian, and I mean to be, if I ever get to where I can . . ." This reservation is the key to understanding George's demands. He regards moral considerations, in some degree, as a luxury. Under necessitous circumstances they cannot be indulged. Similarly, under necessitous circumstances, human intentions can never be more than provisional. The stages of George's escape are indicative of this. He does not know what the end of his efforts will be, both in the sense of what he may encounter and in the sense of what he shall choose. Hence, he wishes first to die free, then to be a Canadian, then to be educated, and moves through successive stages until he wishes to return to Liberia in order to perfect a Christian life in an African land. The provisional character of George's intentions is clearly related to self-preservation.

And we are able to note that, to the extent self-preservation becomes less problematic, George's horizon is widened. And to the extent his horizon is widened, he more easily indulges other-regarding moral considerations. This seems to be the universal or natural foundation of George's understanding of liberty. The securing of immediate self-interest will widen one's horizons.

This formulation carries within it the implicit humanist formulation: to the extent men are chiefly concerned with preservation, by necessity, they are equally liberated from the moral considerations. The reason for this is simple. The moral considerations—Christianity in this case—are regarded as the only sources of genuine political distinctions or particularities.

> "*Is* there a God to trust in," said George. . . . "O, I've seen things all my life that have made me feel there can't be a God. You Christians don't know how these things look to us. There's a God for you, but is there any for us?" (133, original emphasis)

Hence, the proper formulation of the humanistic exception is to emphasize that a faith or culture is for not only those who may believe or practice it, but also those who may derive comfort or profit from it. In those terms, every people in its nonage is a people under necessitous circumstances. Mr. Wilson—goodly though he be—is a parody of civilization. Almost his every utterance to George is in the form of a direct biblical quotation. And his opposed moral inclinations are entirely inexplicable. The same thing was essentially true of the Ohio senator—freshly home from drafting a fugitive slave law—who assisted in Eliza's escape. What is insufficient in the natural account of liberty is precisely its inability to include these virtually instinctive moral or humane sentiments. The genuinely humane exception is apparently less concerned with circumstances than is formal humanism.

Stowe uniformly maintains that what modernity requires is a principle to check the career of formal humanism, which consistently falls victim to worldliness. That principle is a form of matriarchy—indeed, Emily Shelby's matriarchy—with the proviso of moral hardheadedness as its necessary condition. Emily's failure lay in the fact that she did not recognize the insufficiency of the original formulation of modern liberty to her own project. Her project would work only insofar as her "slaves" could truly say that they had a country. But in that, they could not be slaves. This, too, is brought into the story of George Harris's escape.

It is in the reunion of George and Eliza at a Quaker settlement that Stowe finds occasion to commence an inquiry into a non-provisional connection between self-preservation and morality. It is here that she—as distinguished from George—pronounces them free. Their reunion is only part of the condition of freedom. The most significant condition lay in the fact that both began there to formulate a new conception of happiness. Their previous capacity to accept certain conditions of slavery as happy was a fatal flaw in their moral possibilities.[10] And it is against the extreme of apparent Quaker indifference to earthly comforts that they begin to discern wider possibilities.

George considered himself free and equal when he paused at the tavern where he met Mr. Wilson. He boasted of traveling through the land, stopping at the best establishments, and dealing on equal terms (131, 133). But he was disguised throughout this process. And in Stowe's terms he was still enslaved. Her judgment is opposed to his own when she declares that he "sat down on equal terms at (a) white man's table" for the "first time" in the Quaker household of Rachel Halliday (161). It is correct to speak of Rachel's "household," for Stowe is ironic in her reference to a "white man's table." She describes Rachel as seated at the head of the table and gently presiding but nonetheless presiding over the household. Rachel's rule is founded on a mature chastity which Stowe considers the peculiar vehicle of moral instruction and command in "our modern days."[11] This mature chastity replaces the ancient *eros* identified with the Cestus of Venus[12] with the gentler ties of Christian *philia*. Under its influence, heads are not "turned" so easily and things "go on harmoniously." It offers a non-utopian moral horizon.[13] The moment at which Eliza's dream of presiding over her own household in this manner is declared to be reality is the moment of George and Eliza's freedom (160). Stowe does not call this regime a matriarchy. But she does emphasize the "anti-patriarchal" rite of shaving, in which Simeon Halliday is engaged. Thereby, she completes the suggestion of a feminine check to masculine intemperance.

There is yet irony in this account. The Quakers are an extreme, not the true example of modern morality. Where mere humanism sacrifices morality, Quakerism sacrifices self-preservation. Their nominal rejection of all violence, including self-defense, is not accepted by Stowe.[14] And they, too, must come to terms with law—the principle that must mediate between self-preservation and morality while tyrannizing neither. Their profound submission is tacitly likened to the slave's acceptance of Christianity as a doctrine of obedience. But in the provisional account (chapter 13) the emphasis is placed entirely on their subordination of worldly concerns to moral duty (162). They do not answer the question as to the non-provisional connection between morality and self-interest. They rather serve the provisional purpose of giving ground (security) for the sprouting of belief in George's soul.

> This indeed, was a home,—*home,*—a word that George had never yet known a meaning for; and a belief in God, a trust in his providence, began to encircle his heart, as, with a golden cloud of protection and confidence, dark, misan-

> thropic, pining, atheistic doubts, and fierce despair, melted away before the light of a living Gospel, breathed in living faces, preached by a thousand *unconscious acts* (emphasis added) of love and good will which . . . shall never lose their reward. (162)

This genuine Quaker humanity, itself a reflection of the influence of Rachel's mature chastity, serves to remove doubt but without formulating any conscious principles of guidance for the opposition to tyranny. When, therefore, Simeon assures George that Quakers take these risks to preserve their way, Stowe tacitly reveals their entire principle is the elimination of doubt, simply. Simeon transforms the biblical "wherefore are we sent into the world?" into

> . . . for therefore are we sent into the world. (162)

To the Quakers, all the questions are seen to disappear in the appeal to a higher law—a higher law that is incapable of political distinction (they render unto Caesar!). In short, George is confronted—through the Quakers—with an apolitical Christianity. Hence, he is allowed to abandon the appeal to skepticism as the justification of his action. This achievement is only provisional, because George's run to liberty, as we have seen, is a run to law. And the Quakers expressly acknowledge an inability to distinguish the various versions of law.

Effectively, George's and Eliza's story ends here. We must seek yet higher ground to distinguish the various versions of law. They flee toward a city the character of which they do not in fact know. This is a direct result of their reliance upon men who either know no cities or cannot transcend their connection to their own cities. The results are briefly summarized. Insofar as liberty for the slave and the necessity to disobey unjust laws are concerned, the incentive of material well-being seems to be the first motive. But the means of achieving this—the motif—seems to require the emergence of a care for spiritual well-being. This, in turn, should supplant the original end.[15] Indeed, it is Simeon's willingness to suffer for his own spiritual well-being that facilitates for George the very material well-being which may give occasion for a concern with spiritual health. Hence, George's relationship to law—his attempt to escape from bad to good law—is fully developed if we regard his motives in the light of the motives of those who assist him. George is not attached to the law he flees, but he is assisted by men who submit to it (Mr. Wilson as well as the Quakers), all of whom stand at a higher spiritual level than he. Yet, George's appreciation of law is superior to their appreciation even as it subordinates spiritual health to physical health. What is required is a means of preserving George's appreciation of law while achieving the reversal of his motivating principles. This is accomplished for George even as he is unaware that it happens. It is the generation of belief that is properly the first step toward attachment to law, the Quakers to the contrary notwithstanding. Yet, insofar as that belief cannot be generated apart from such example, we inherit a touchy problem. It would seem that all who must depend on such examples cannot free themselves, apart from the provisional appeal to skepticism. That is, they remain unable to see a connection between law, morality, and self-preservation, because every moral example is forced to appeal beyond the law.

George's story ends here precisely because he is never able to see this dilemma. To discover a solution we have to consider Uncle Tom, in whose story the problem is made explicit. Yet, George ends with much more than he began. Through him, therefore, Stowe continues to place the American Founding in perspective. George attains a kind of spiritual attachment—a vision of a *home* divinely ordained—which is the grist of martyrdom. This runs counter to the traditional model of spiritual detachment, but Stowe does not explain the discrepancy here. Instead, the story of George's heroism, as the news of his later progress, is inserted only parenthetically in the tale that follows this confirmation of his freedom. Tom's story is primary in the subsequent chapters and consideration of this question. We may, however, be forgiven for jumping ahead and completing what was said of George.

George appears in a new light in chapter 17, "The Freeman's Defence." The story of his slavery is ended. What remains of his saga helps to reflect the primary story. We need suggest but two considerations from that chapter. First, Quaker absolutism is qualified by the principle of self-defense. In the reconstructed view, it is acknowledged that the "more excellent way" is not always available to men who might, on occasion, have to "resist evil." Apart from that, George grows under the Quaker influence—acceding to Eliza's moral influence (mature chastity), pledging to send back the price of Eliza and her son, and declaring against primarily worldly concerns. But because his family still stands for him where the Quaker God nominally stands for them, he is determined to "fight to the last breath" to defend it.

The strong contrast of George's indignation with Quaker docility demands the qualification of Quaker principle. His fiery sentiment was addressed to a people who could—or at least believe they could—if necessary "stand by and see them take my wife and sell her" to avoid spilling the blood of others. This declaration heightens the apparent contrast between George and Uncle Tom. But what distinguishes them still more is the Quaker willingness—*even* Quaker willingness—to concede the possibility of a duty of resistance or an inkling of unjust laws (217). Simeon conceded much in that statement. The author presumably considered this reasonable, for she entrusted the escort of George's party to a converted Quaker—woodsman and hunter capable and willing to defend himself—whose conversion followed his "having wooed a pretty Quakeress (and) been moved by the power of her charms . . ." In short, Quaker certainty obscures the founding principle of the Quaker way.[16] It is, therefore, still less capable of suggesting the founding principle of an American way.

The second element of this chapter borrows of the first to make its point. George's party is pursued by the slave catchers to a rocky defile, from which the pursuers are precipitously "tumbled." This situation is the conscious parallel to verse 18 of Psalm 73, from which Simeon read to breathe a calming and strengthening influence into George.

> Surely thou didst set them in slippery places, thou castedst them down to destruction. (220)

But it was George's gun and Phineas's (the converted Quaker) arm that did the Lord's casting. Hence, what Simeon's reading neglected was the necessity of men to be the instruments of the Lord's work, including his works of wrath.[17]

The work of the Lord that George must perform in this case is the consummation of his "Declaration of Independence." To the importunate demands of the slave catchers, in the name of the law, George responds:

> We don't own your laws; we don't own your country; we stand here as free, under God's sky, as you are; and, by the great God that made us, we'll fight for our liberty till we die. (226)

It was at this point that Stowe describes George as reaching the pitch of his African physiognomy. And the reason was clear. George was running from one law to another law precisely because Americans' own Declaration of Independence had neglected to defend, in her view, the liberty of men. It rather established the liberty of a nation. She attacks the reader with the vulgar impossibility that George's manly stand was not "sublime heroism" simply because he was African rather than Hungarian.[18] The American habit of supporting resistance to established laws in other countries, she suggests, is valid only insofar as it informs the American way itself. Only thus could it rest upon the rights of man rather than the rights of nations.[19] George's run to law—to another city—has been described throughout as the attempt to escape rule by the right of the stronger. Beyond the irony intended in the thought that Mr. Harris was stronger than George, this is ironic precisely because the determination of rights or liberties on the basis of nationhood must, in the end, depend on strength. The Quaker view has been qualified only to reveal the genuine dilemma that induces that view. In the process we discover with how little conviction we are able to defend the life of freedom on the basis of sects, cultures, or nations. Though there must be cities, as such, it now emerges that the defense of the life of freedom must transcend the city as such. The greatness of man must exceed the greatness of cities if John, the Drover, is to be reassured. George asked, "What country have I?" But his question is the wrong question!

NOTES

1. There may be some validity in Kosnik's comment that "the success of George's performance relies on the failure of his 'body' to serve as a legitimate signifier of race"; but there is more to George's changing complexion than this alone. Kosnik, "The Alien in Our Nation," p. 23.

2. Here are two examples of this widespread charge: Crane ("But George Harris's eloquent embodiment of higher law jurisprudence . . . is plainly dependent in Stowe's formulation upon his racial resemblance: he looks like 'us.'") and Young ("Stowe . . . replicates racial stereotypes, privileging light-skinned over dark-skinned black characters.") Gregg David Crane, *Race, Citizenship and Law in American Literature* (New York: Cambridge University Press, 2002), p. 68. Elizabeth Young, *Disarming the Nation: Women's Writing and the American Civil War* (Chicago: University of Chicago Press, 1999), p. 31.

3. This criticism is surfaced by several Stowe critics such as Sarson ("The various shades of color in the story are not designed to illustrate how clever whites are in relation to browns, nor browns in relation to blacks. What the abundance of mulattoes does highlight, however, is the fact of miscegenation, and, therefore, the reality of the sexual abuse of black women by white men.") and Strout (" . . . the relative whiteness of her blacks [in *Uncle Tom's Cabin*] . . . was a vivid symbol of evil because the white man who exploited a black woman violated the integrity of two families, his own and hers."). Steven Sarson, "Harriet Beecher Stowe and American Slavery," *New Comparison* 7 (Summer 1989): 34 (hereafter cited as "HBS and American Slavery"). Strout, "*UTC* and the Portent of the Millennium," p. 376.

4. Cf. Nelson: " . . . Abolitionists tried, by making many of their characters almost white, to work on racial feeling as well. This was a curious piece of inconsistency on their part, and indirect admission that a white man in chains was more pitiful to behold than the African similarly placed." John Herbert Nelson, *The Negro Character in American Literature* (Lawrence: University of Kansas, Department of Journalism Press, 1926), p. 83–84.

5. Brown is quite wrong in her assessment that "Stowe dismisses [the] potential of black to become white by reminding us of the blackness of blacks. At the moment in the novel when slaves become free and ready to pursue their entitlements, they appear simultaneously most self-possessed and most black." Brown, *Domestic Individualism*, p. 58.

6. This is at page 492. The marriage, however, may be a French one. Emmeline, the former slave, married the first-mate of an unidentified ship. But the marriage takes place in France, and we know not where the couple took up residence.

7. *UTC*, p. 76. Gayle Wilson notes, further, that one could envision Tom Loker's name as "low cur" and recites other devices that Stowe uses to convey his "doggish nature." Gayle Edward Wilson, "'As John Bunyan Says': Bunyan's Influence on *Uncle Tom's Cabin*, " *ATQ* n.s. 1 (1987): 158–59.

8. This was the common abolitionist perspective, as is manifested in the attack on the "Fugitive Slave Law." Cf. chapter 9, "A Senator Is But a Man," and chapter 12, "Select Incidents of a Lawful Trade."

9. This may be a conscious repetition of Frederick Douglass's query, addressed to the American Anti-Slavery Society in 1847. If that be so, it may also be that Douglass has the strongest claim to be the model for George Harris. In that event, her quarrel with George would be nothing more than her quarrel with Douglass's initial rejection of America and assimilation. [Cf. Philip Foner, ed., *The Life and Writings of Frederick Douglass* (New York: International Publishers, 1950), vol. I, p. 236.] Note, for example, Moer's hypothesis: "Surely [Stowe] drew the character of George Harris after Frederick Douglass. . . . George Harris is Frederick Douglass to the life and in many of his opinions." Moers, *HBS and American Literature*, p. 15. And Levine demonstrates throughout his monograph the many ways in which Stowe and Douglass conducted a literary conversation. Levine, *Martin Delany, Frederick Douglass, and the Politics of Representative Identity.*

10. Cf. *UTC*, pp. 153, 129, 42, 18–19, and 17 and contrast with Uncle Tom, pp. 349, 345, and 135.

11. Fielder refers to Rachel Halliday as "an aging and chaste Venus." Leslie Fiedler, *The Inadvertent Epic: From Uncle Tom's Cabin to Roots* (New York: Simon and Schuster, 1982), p. 19. Shipp sees both Rachel and Simeon Halliday as "in full possession of informed hearts." Shipp, "*UTC* and the Ethos of Melodrama," p. 26.

12. A cestus is a woman's belt or girdle, and especially the symbolic one worn by a bride, and hence, a virgin. Mature chastity is the grandmotherly gentleness identified in book II, part II.

13. "All have sinned and come short of the glory of God." *Romans* 3:23.

14. See book II, part I, chapter 22 and chapter 23. Among the critics who point out that no characters in the novel accept the Hallidays' invitation to stay at their home is Riss (" . . . although the Quakers may welcome all, no one seems to want to join their family"). Riss, "Racial Essentialism," p. 533.

15. Cf., especially, Simeon's counsel at p. 220.

16. Consider Simeon's reading of *Psalm* 73, which omits several passages that justify *doubt* by faith in God's goodness. The passages he read suggest a certainty of salvation and of his own way. All of which is made clear by the "oversight" of retaining "Nevertheless" at the start of verse 23, in spite of the fact that the antithesis of doubt to which it refers in verses 21–22 is omitted.

17. Cf. *Psalms* 73, verse 27 and the final clause of verse 28.

18. A reference to the Hungarian freedom fighters of the 1840s and 50s for whom there was much popular sympathy in America.

19. Hedrick's assessment of Stowe's political astuteness is far too limited: "Had Stowe been politically attuned, it is unlikely she would have whole-heartedly embraced Kossuth, who drew the wrath of the abolitionists for his refusal to speak out on behalf of slavery during his American tour." Hedrick, *Harriet Beecher Stowe*, p. 235.

10

We Have No City

The story of George Harris ends where the story of Uncle Tom—that is, the account of his principles—literally begins. Chapter 12, a "Select Incident of Lawful Trade," we discussed previously insofar as it laid the conditions for the account of moral equality.[1] We will discuss it below insofar as the idea is broached, for the first time, that humanism is founded on false principles and may be recast.[2] There remains to discuss, therefore, the central figure of the chapter, Uncle Tom.

This chapter begins the second section of the novel. Its importance is highlighted in many ways. It is the first chapter headed by a thematic biblical epigram: Jeremiah's prophecy of the birth of the Messiah.[3] In this chapter, for the first time, the discussion of justice as the right of the stronger appears to be at the exact center, with the definitive response following exactly at the center of the novel itself. And it is the chapter in which thematic development of Tom's character begins. The method of indirection becomes attenuated, though it is not entirely abandoned.[4]

Before considering the bold declaration of Tom's independence of the city, and the elaboration of the character befitting that condition, we must pause to reflect upon the setting of our drama. For it is in this chapter that the origin of Stowe's twin themes of ascent from and descent into slavery, centering around the Ohio River, clearly emerges.[5] The idea is derived from the contrasts in the conditions of American freedom and equality on the opposite banks of the river. That contrast was thematically developed in *La Démocratie en Amérique*.[6] We suggest in part II, chapter 15, the relevance of Tocqueville to Calvin Stowe's project. That project eventuates in the need to confront the challenge of slavery. And we find in Harriet Stowe's last major writing[7] the reflection of this concern with Tocqueville's analysis. We can, however, suggest independent evidence for the view that Tocqueville inspired the confrontation of George Harris with Uncle Tom. For the opening theme of this chapter—Tom's independence of the city—is directly reflected in the discussion that precedes Tocqueville's account of the relationship between freedom and equality along *la belle rivière*.

The opening of Tocqueville's chapter 18 strongly resembles, though perhaps *only* resembles, our interpretation of the break between chapters 11 and 12 of *Uncle Tom's Cabin*.

> The principal part of the task which I had imposed upon myself is now performed: I have shown, as far as I was able, the laws and manners of the American democracy. Here I might stop. (Tocqueville, p. 393)

Just as we have found trans-political reflection necessary to answer the most serious questions raised with regard to slavery in America, Tocqueville found it necessary to regard the political account, as such, of the American people insufficient. Where for Stowe, however, the problem is to suggest some insufficiency in the law, Tocqueville seems to suggest a sufficiency in the law apart from transcendent considerations. In this category does he in some measure place the consideration of America's slave and Indian populations. His account of "these two races" follows the full account of "laws and manners in the American democracy."

This unquestionably means that the moral judgment that Tocqueville ultimately renders is not to be understood—in its own terms at least—as compromising the political judgment he had already made. He carved out an exception! Nonetheless, he still provided the standard, which the Stowes followed. Although he does not regard the problem of slavery as a "democratic" problem, he does regard it as an "American" problem. That is, for Americans the political question is indissolubly connected with slavery.[8] This reflection, indeed, is a foundation for Calvin Stowe's effort (discussed below) to make the question-problem of slavery prior in the consideration of America's principles.

What accounts for Tocqueville's judgment is the entirely legitimate argument that the slaves are not in fact Americans. Unlike Justice Taney's *Dred Scott* opinion,[9] however, this judgment has nothing to do with whether America's principles will tolerate citizenship for blacks. The answer to that question is unquestionably affirmative for Tocqueville. In his mind, what stands in the way is not American theory but American opinion and practice. The unfortunate consequence is that the blacks, no longer able to be removed from America, are nonetheless countryless—barred from participation in any of the saving graces of civilization. This perspective is the same as that which informed George Harris's rebellion. But for Tocqueville such examples in no way mitigate the harsh truth that, for most, such routes of escape are forever closed. Hence, no principles applicable to political life may be derived from that source. The sad fact is that the "negro's" only "country" is his "home," the shelter "afforded by his master."[10]

This sad state is principally explained by Tocqueville with reference to the differences between ancient and modern slavery. And those differences turn especially on the crucial fact of prejudice in the modern world having assumed an ineradicable status. Among the ancients, the slave was usually of the same race as the master, and often "the superior in education and instruction."[11] Manumission, therefore, was a ready and frequently used resort. To be clear: the condition for the recognition of the ancient slave's humanity—even his superiority—was the absence of a racial distinction. The implication is that that is the universal condition: positive differences in human capacities are recognizable only on the basis of previously established terms of common identity. A man radically unlike oneself in social, cultural, racial constitution will never be judged one's superior in non-trivial matters. Hence, "we scarcely acknowledge the common features of mankind in this child of debasement. . . . " In order "to induce whites to abandon" their prejudices, "the negroes must change" in character *and* physiognomy. The miraculous changes in George Harris's physiognomy reflect precisely this demand. Tocqueville, however, believed such miracles to be impossible: "But as long as this opinion subsists, change is impossible." The condition for the change in character and physiognomy (through intermarriage) is a change in that very opinion which thwarts every attempt to change the condition![12] It is this judgment that assimilation was impossible—capable of producing only crude caricatures of the Europeans/Englishmen—which creates the need for a demonstration of some ground for the change of opinion apart from the politically desirable goal of assimilation.

The story of George Harris reflects Stowe's acceptance of Tocqueville's argument, so far as it goes. But he continued the argument to suggest the form of modern prejudice. Moderns, he held, have "three prejudices to conquer." These are "prejudice of the master," "prejudice of the race," and "prejudice of colour."[13] The Stowes, however, argue that only the "prejudice of the master" is crucial—that, in fact, the two latter are included in this one. Hence, the necessity of moral equality. Moral equality is precisely the vehicle that permits moderns to recognize—as the ancients did—those positive differences in capacity among men. Unlike the ancient *ethnos*, however, it is understood to be defensible on its own terms and not as an accident of birth. Thus, the story of Uncle Tom reflects the Stowes' refusal to accept Tocqueville's argument that modern opinion cannot be changed.

The story of Uncle Tom specifically refutes the exception carved out by Tocqueville. Nonetheless, Tom's story begins under the guidance of

Tocqueville's transcendent principles, for the Stowes do not disagree with him there, and they carefully distinguish him from full-fledged defenders of modern humanism. The dramatic form of the novel itself is inspired by his account of the differences between the two banks of the Ohio. In that account, Tocqueville provided a parallel account of the life in the free and slave states, for the specific purpose of revealing how far slavery is inferior to freedom—for the masters. The following discussion of Stowe's *Geography* (see chapter 27, Coda, 437) is crucial here. Tocqueville could not have informed what she wrote in 1833; what she wrote in 1855 plainly was so influenced.

> Were I inclined to continue this parallel, I could easily prove that almost all the differences which may be remarked between the characters of the Americans in the Southern and Northern States, have originated in slavery . . . (Tocqueville, p. 434)

Harriet Stowe may have wished but did not require that the parallel be extended, for the argument that preceded this conclusion is fully reflected in *Uncle Tom's Cabin.*

Tocqueville begins by noting that still more stringent social barriers to contact between blacks and whites have accompanied the increasing appearance of legal equality in the North; while, in the South, the unfettered rules of despotism admit of a much more casual relationship between masters and servants. This argument serves to repeat and affirm the disqualification of blacks for any kind of citizenship. But it also reveals the foundations of partial citizenship—the limited amenities granted to slaves in the South almost constitute an advance, compared to the infirmities they would suffer in the North. Tocqueville, however, presents this argument not in order to minimize the slave's plight, but to heighten the contrasts between the lives of slaveowners and free men. And nothing stands out so sharply as the fierce and prideful industriousness of the northerners. Thus, as slave states decline in produce and population, free states are fruitful and multiply.

> But this truth was most satisfactorily demonstrated when civilization reached the banks of the Ohio. The stream Indians had distinguished by the name of Ohio, or Beautiful River, waters one of the most magnificent valleys which has ever been the abode of man. Undulating lands extend upon both shores of the Ohio, whose soil affords inexhaustible treasures to the laborer; on either bank the air is wholesome and the climate mild; and each of them forms the extreme frontier of a vast State: that . . . upon the left is called Kentucky; that upon the right bears the name of the river. These . . . only differ in a single respect; . . . slavery . . . Thus the traveler who floats down the current of the Ohio, to the spot where that river falls into the Mississippi, may be said to sail between liberty and servitude . . . (Tocqueville, pp. 430–31)

The parallel comparison concludes with a preference for liberty, as decidedly less costly *and* more productive than servitude.[14] But three elements affect this conclusion and are important to our story. First,

> The white inhabitant of Ohio, who is obliged to subsist by his own exertions, regards *temporal prosperity as the principal aim of his existence.* (Tocqueville, p. 433, emphasis added)

Secondly, Tocqueville does not fail to notice here, as he did earlier, the effect of the Louisiana Purchase on American principles. He argues that the *entre-pot* of New Orleans, as part of a slave state, contributes so to raise the price of slaves as to make any economies impossible in the more northerly slave states. They must live with the market.[15] And, finally, nearly every energetic and enterprising slaveowner is a northern émigré.[16]

It is clear that, to Tocqueville, the call of self-interest and the improvident political act of expanding slavery into a highly demanding market have joined to perpetuate the institution. Equally clear in his analysis is the expectation that the lure of profit would have led—and might yet lead—to the abolition of slavery if, first, no new market impetus is provided and, second, some way could be found to be rid of the slaves. He had earlier claimed that the "opposite consequences" of slavery and freedom "suffice to explain" the differences between ancients and moderns.[17] The ancients, it turned out, did not understand the call of self-interest,[18] that it could advance freedom. There results the formula of modern humanism: slavery "may be attacked in the name of the master; and, upon this point, interest is reconciled with morality."[19]

How does this affect the building of *Uncle Tom's Cabin*? In the first place, Stowe uses each of the three elements of Tocqueville's conclusion in constructing her drama, in addition to the dramatic form of the contrast between Ohio and Kentucky. We know that she gets it from Tocqueville because the name of her fictitious steamer, La Belle Rivière, has no particular reason to be French, apart from the fact that that is the tongue in which the story of the Ohio's Indian name was related in the version of *Democracy of America* probably read by Calvin Stowe.[20] It is certain, at least, that the translation used in his 1839 essay differs markedly from the English translation then available and is a much more literal rendering.[21] One expression shows this more than any other. The French, *sentiment*, is usually rendered as "opinion" in English. So it is in the Reeve translation.[22] But, throughout his essay, Calvin Stowe repeatedly uses the expression "public sentiment" where one would expect the more common "public opinion." The inference is fair: his head was full of *le sentiment publique*. Many will concede this and *still* maintain that Calvin Stowe's essay is not shown to have any relation to *Uncle Tom's Cabin*. Note, then, that we will discuss below the use of

Thomas Carlyle in this chapter 12 we are now discussing. Calvin's essay cited but two philosophers: Tocqueville and Carlyle!

Now, if Stowe named her steamer La Belle Rivière specifically to call Tocqueville to mind rather than as an incidental reflection of her first exposure to these themes, we should expect what we indeed find, and that is the recurrence of the themes of his discussion of slavery. The slave's countryless status is foremost. We have seen it in George, and will shortly consider it yet more profoundly in Tom. In addition we have been introduced to the role of self-interest in modern liberalism. We soon begin to construct a new version. The argument from self-interest to humanity is thematically raised in this chapter. And every schoolboy knows the extent to which Stowe relies on the northerner-cum-southern slaveowner as a dramatic device. Simon Legree was thought her most successful characterization. We can now have regard for the Tocquevillean implications of that device—Stowe's demonstration that self-interest and morality are not identical; or, what is the same thing, demonstration of the mistaken appeal of rational humanism.

The position we seek offers a response to each of the dilemmas posed through George Harris. We seek the specific form of "moral hardheadedness."[23] That seems to be a necessary condition for the discovery of a "nonprovisional connection between self-preservation and morality." We look to a middle ground, having learned that, where humanism sacrifices morality, Quakers sacrifice self-preservation. Tocqueville is the starting point of the middle ground. Through consideration of his argument we learn that morality is the victim of humanism precisely because of humanism's utopianism when logically extended. The requirement of an "exception" reveals the defect of the principle. Hence, it argues the necessity of a non-utopian moral horizon. Such a horizon will comprehend or suggest the realm of law. For Stowe believes that the generation of belief is the first step toward attachment to law.

How incongruous then! Chapter 12 opens with the declaration that Uncle Tom has no city. In the light of our discussion of Tocqueville, that may mean only that his slavery is complete. We must be careful. We require to know the way in which Tom may be said to have no city, even more than we require to know the kind of city George will eventually have. We begin by proving that Tom is not a naïf.

In chapter 10, Tom was being carried off by Haley, who had stopped at a blacksmith's to have the fetters enlarged to suit Tom's build. During the interval, young George Shelby caught up with them. He had been speeding on horseback, since Tom was off before George had ever heard of the sale. George was furious. He rated Haley for his monstrous inhumanity—buying and selling men and women. The trader was out of earshot as the young boy promised Tom, "I'll knock that old fellow down—I will!"

> No you won't, Mas'r George; and you must not talk so loud. It won't help me any, to anger him. (115)

We may almost add to Tom's prayer, "needlessly," as Tom demonstrates for the first time acute awareness of his general situation—of the political reality. This much is clear. He is not stupid. And he is not acculturated—at least not in ordinary terms. George was calmed but momentarily. As he heated up again, Tom became emphatic: "it won't do *me* any good" (116, original emphasis). A moral outburst on his behalf, which ends in harm to himself, seems unreasonable.

From thence Tom turned to finishing touches of his contribution to the education of young George. He begins with the counsel of respect to his father, apparently for George's own good, and to "keep close" to his mother. George is perfectly acquiescent. But Tom knows the temptations to which he will be subject and so continues. George is to realize that, by nature, he will be inclined to some degree of evil thought or deed. But he must resist nature by cultivating gentlemanliness. All the time Tom is cautious to acquire George's permission for speaking so. But he reminds the lad of his great seniority and complete concern for George's own good. He ends by advising George to be a "good Mas'r like yer father; and be a Christian, like yer mother." George is calmed. He promises to be a "first-rater." Tom's double-awareness of his perilous circumstances and solicitousness for George's welfare raises a delicate but unavoidable difficulty.

Though not blinded to slavery's defects, Tom seems to wish to make the best of it. He assumes that slavery will continue to exist and asks only that it be ameliorated by being transformed wholly into Emily's matriarchy. Young George is to become the man-woman who guides this refounding. If Tom, himself, were not governed by Emily's conception, as we argued, is this perspective consistent?

Perhaps the notion of the man-woman points a way out. Emily wished to effect mitigating moral graces through her own—noiseless feminine—influence. She would improve the lot of slaves without ending slavery. However, to keep slavery means to rely upon Mr. Shelby, masculine ineptitude and self-interest. That seems to preserve still too great a distinction between masculine worldliness and what, fully developed, mature chastity must be.[24] Masculine worldliness, tempered as Tom suggests, would seem incapable of preserving slavery as such. Arthur Shelby is a worldly failure, and Tom knows it as well as the reader. We get glimmers—if not light—when we suspect that the use of Arthur as a model for George envisions not the perpetuation of slavery but rather subjection to influences friendlier to freedom than to further slavery. Emily employs noiseless influence and not rule in behalf of right, while Arthur Shelby attempts rule unsuccessfully in behalf of interest. Shelby's moral defect is that he lacks Emily's purpose and is unfit to rule, while Emily's practical defect is that she lacks the capacity to rule. Meanwhile, Tom acquires mastery of souls while neither ruling nor attempting to rule. Using Shelby as model raises the prospect that only someone who does not, and moreover may not, rule can be a "soul" master. Tocqueville's ancient slavery raises its head. Only if this view is correct are we able to understand in a non-Tocquevillean way Tom's independence of the city and, on this occasion, his only apparently contradictory awareness of his political situation and the future of slavery.

Chapter 12 opens with the Bible:

> We have here no continuing city, but we seek one to come; wherefore God himself is not ashamed to be called our God; for he hath prepared for us a city. (134)

We recognize in these passages from the "letter to the *Hebrews*" the thrust of the passages in the last chapter of *Revelation*.[25] Stowe said that these words "kept running through his head" as Tom set off on his journey with Haley. Since he was working from memory—though she assuredly was not—we may be allowed to quote the two separate passages she has brought together as one. The first, here, is actually subsequent in *Hebrews*.

> That we have here is not a continuing city, but we will seek one that is coming. *Heb*. 13:14.

> But now they desire a better *country*, that is, an heavenly: on account of which God is not ashamed of them, to be called their God, for he hath prepared for them a city. *Heb*. 11:16 (emphasis added)

In the "letter to the *Hebrews*" the contexts of the two passages is the development of contrasts between Sinai and Zion. And in the earliest passage, the reference to "country" involves discussion of the "promised land" as well as reference to the land the Jews would leave. The context of the old law is the concern with an earthly city. By eliminating the first clause of *Hebrews* 11:16, Stowe succeeds in collapsing Sinai and Zion into a single conception. But, by taking the result clause of *Hebrews* 11:16 (wherefore . . .) and transforming it into a result clause for *Hebrews* 13:14, she makes the task of seeking a future city the specific cause or origin of divine grace. Just as the earthly Sinai is eliminated, so is the transition to Zion, or the heavenly city. And the human effort of seeking a future city is paralleled with God's preparation of a city. The conclusion: where God has prepared for men a city, it can only bear divine sanction that men should seek a city. The correction of *Revelation* is exculpated!

The contrast between "country" and "city" is also meant to be instructive. A country is a place where men live, presumably in a city. Its status is not only earthly, but also exclusive. One country is always distinguished with reference to another. A "better country" is a country that is better *than* some other country as well as better *for* men. A city, on the other hand, is a way of life, whether in this world or the next. In the Gospel, it seems clear that the earthly way of life itself does not endure, but an enduring way of life approaches. In Stowe's version, ambiguity surrounds the word "continuing" as it surrounds the Sinai/Zion conception. It may mean that the earthly city, as it is, is not continuing and thus follows the suggestion in *Revelation*. Or, it may mean, with the Gospel, that the earthly city as such is not continuing. In the latter view, the defects of the earthly way of life are irredeemable in this world. In the former view, there is hope of earthly salvation.

Through Tom we may be able to conceive which of the two views is intended. That he should be independent of the city—that he should have transcended—will have differing consequences depending on the view we adopt. If the earthly way of life as such is defective, his independence will bear disregard for earthly things in general as opposed to disregard for mere specific practices. If the earthly way is correctible, his independence will bear the mark of a superior conception of human life on earth. And the principles of the Gospel, thus interpreted, will give rise to a course of action.

> These words . . . kept up, somehow, a strange sort of power over the minds of poor, simple fellows, like Tom. They stir up the soul from its depths, and rouse, as with trumpet call, courage, energy, and enthusiasm, where before was only the blackness of despair. (135)

The trumpet does not only herald the opening of the gates of heaven. It also gives the peal of approaching battle. And the characters of soul aroused—"courage, energy, enthusiasm"—seem more generally to be appropriate to the struggle for the life and death of morality than to the enjoyment of beatific felicity. Though none may doubt of Tom's evident heavenly aspirations throughout the novel, it is not clear that he may have had other—earthly—aspirations as well.

Tom is an unusual character. His detachment from earthly concerns has not blinded him to the regard for such things. The exchange with young George Shelby shows the negative foundation of this concern. In those terms, his own good was the standard of earthly measure. But Stowe seems to envision the concern with self-preservation as an exception to the chief concerns of an earthly way of life. Hence, the positive conception presents an alternative—and, for Tom, a more common point of reference. We begin to see the emergence of moral hardheadedness in chapter 12, when Tom is informed, at once, that Haley will be pausing in their journey to purchase more slaves and, accordingly, will "clap you in jail" for the sake of security. Tom's reaction proceeded, first, through the attempt to imagine the circumstances of these new victims. Did they have families? Would they feel as Tom did about separating from them? Then did he reflect upon the indignity of being thrown into jail.

> (He) had always prided himself on a strictly honest and upright course of life. Yes, Tom, we must confess it, was rather proud of his honesty, poor fellow—not having very much else to be proud of . . . (135)

Tom's reaction yielded first space to others, even others unknown to him. And even his concern with himself centered not on any possible discomfort, but upon the indignity. What is omitted, too, is important. Stowe's understated and reluctant confession reveals that she, too, regards her hero as unusual (even if pride in one's honesty were sufficient!); he almost seems a just victim of injustice, wholly unmoved by vengeance—the indignant defense of his own things—or even an energetic demand for liberty.[26] The very honesty upon which he placed so great emphasis seems an entirely private affair. If it has a social bearing, it is indirect. This is reflected in his quiet concern for others.

Tom's situation differs not at all from that of all of the other slaves. What explains his different reaction? Must not he too deal with Aunt Hagar's question, sobbed out when she was counseled to "trust in the Lord" upon Haley's acquisition of her son, "What good will it do?" (139). His answer lies, perhaps, in the very private nature of his moral hardheadedness. His belief is as much for his own sake as for the Lord's sake and more for his own sake than for others in spite of his regard for the welfare of others and contempt for his own. The contrast between Tom's self-controlled, dignified parting and that of every other slave—including Eliza—is striking. His seemed far the less passionate though so much more filled with pathos (even Aunt Chloe rose to the occasion, refusing to "cry 'fore dat ar old limb," Haley). It fully reflects a lack of attachment to this life and city. Tom has transcended his time and city. And every apparent attachment results rather from a voluntary will (informed by private moral standards). He is free to attach himself to such earthly things as he will, precisely because he is not attached by his own prejudices. Tom seeks no country, for there is no country for the only city he is prepared to recognize.

What remains of chapter 12 serves to affirm that Tom is the model of the "man of humanity" to whom the reader was to be introduced in chapter 1 (hence, his ability to instruct George in gentlemanliness). The author commences the story, in effect, by putting an end to the irony she had originally created. Haley is explicitly rejected as the humane man—the irony has served its purpose (148). So, too, are rejected the "enlightened, cultivated, and intelligent" men who support him by maintaining the system. Stowe attributes the character of their principles to their capacity to generalize and to that view of habituation that Haley presented in chapter 1. It was there that he described his system of dealing with the natural human emotions that embarrass the trading business. He resorted to management principles based on "humanity." And the foundation of Haley's humanity was the recognition that habituation could so direct people's "'spectations" that they would get used to all sorts of things. Their affections, in his view, are largely social conventions, and there is an appropriate set of conventions for slaves, which are neither worse nor better than any one else's (9–10).

The specific occasion for Stowe's rejection of Haley is an example of his management at work. At a stop above Louisville, he acquired a woman and her ten-month-old son. The previous owner, however, neglected to tell her she was being sold. Entering into Haley's "quiet way" of managing the business, he told the woman she was off to Louisville to hire out as a cook and join her husband. Once she was aboard *La Belle Rivière* and nothing was to be done for it—following his method—Haley broke the news. She protested, but was soon quieted. Subsequently, Haley negotiated the sale of the baby to a fellow passenger who was happily disembarking at Louisville. This sale, too, was not announced beforehand. As the steamer reached Louisville and the slave woman departed to the guards in prayer of a glimpse of her husband, the new "father" walked away with the child who had been left sleeping. Again, the ship departed, and the woman returned to confront Haley's management. The child was gone, the ship afloat, and nothing to be done for it. There was less to be said on this occasion. The woman's great grief inspired doleful but silent remorse. Haley surrendered to her plea to be let alone, convinced that she would come around. She left the ship in the dead of night (*UTC*, 144–50).

Haley's attempt to cultivate a form of detachment to facilitate the business of trading seems almost a parody of Tom's stoic if not cowardly detachment. But Stowe employs the parody to demonstrate the self-cultivation to which Haley and the nation were subject. The habit of generalizing so about habit, she suggests, induces blindness as to the character of soul that could enter into such practices. Because the practice of habituating others habituates oneself, it makes a difference for oneself what habits one seeks to induce in others. Tom, who suffers through this transaction, is the direct contrast, for "he had not learned to generalize, and to take enlarged views" (149). *His* detachment comes not at the cost of denying a common humanity. The example is completed when Haley, in search of the woman, questions Tom. Tom saw no need to provide this information; he judged his actions by consideration of the necessities of the system of slavery. In short, he did not regard Lucy's suicide as any of Haley's business. But Haley persisted, for he was sure that Tom, from proximity, must have known. And fortunately for himself, he resorted not to threats, but an appeal to Tom's honesty: "Tom, be fair about this yer." Tom's private morality brings the response and reveals the source of every objection to Tom's character. Tom's morality is incapable of making, in its turn, the kind of exception that Haley's morality would permit had Haley found it of profit to break his promise to place Tom in a good family.

The title of chapter 12 is "Select Incidents of Lawful Trade." In the chapter, Stowe labored to tie *every* consequence of slavery to the law, which permitted it. She derived the debauched "public sentiment" from the force of the law and practice. All fall with the rejection of Haley's humanity. She has made him a representative of the law, of the city. The purpose is to question the value of the city's teaching. She concludes with an example of the "exception" at work. America strives to rid the seas of the foreign slave trade; the interstate slave trade flourishes. The point may not be made clearer: the guiding principle of humanism (her name for modern liberalism) is the universalism of ideal morality, subjected to particular exceptions. The ordinary abolitionist approach is to oppose the ideal morality (higher law) to the exception. Stowe's Uncle Tom presents an alternative to the provisional connection between self-preservation and morality, which does not require abstraction from an earthly way of life.

NOTES

1. See book I, part I, chapter 2.
2. See book I, part I, chapter 11.
3. Cf., *Matthew* 2:17–18 and 2:1 for the fulfillment of the prophecy.
4. In her insightful explication of the novel and particularly of Stowe's skilled use of rhetorical devices in it, Marks emphasizes the importance of this chapter, also pointing out that it is the first to be headed by a biblical epigram. She states that in this chapter, "Stowe's narrative voice . . . climbs into a pulpit and delivers a sermon where it may combine most or all of the rhetorical elements of intensification at once . . . " Marks, "A Voice in Ramah," p. 209.
5. Among the critics who have mapped the contours of Stowe's moral geography in *Uncle Tom's Cabin* are: Lang ("the moral geography of the novel" is one in which "the Ohio River divides heaven from hell . . . "); Bellin (who notes the paired plots of "Tom's journey South, deeper into enslavement, and the Harrises' journey North, closer to freedom . . . "); Steele (who equates North with good and South with evil and finds in the Harrises' journey "a comic counterpoint to the tragic-melodramatic southward and deathward movement of Uncle Tom"); and Moers (in describing the "astonishingly rich river motif" of the novel, she points out "its elaborate journeyings of black man and white, crisscrossing down the river to hell and up the river to peace and freedom . . . "). Lang, "Slavery and Sentimentalism," p. 32. Joshua D. Bellin, "Up to Heaven's Gate, Down in Earth's Dust: The Politics of Judgment in *Uncle Tom's Cabin*," *American Literature* 65, no. 2 (June 1993) 275 (hereafter cited as "Up to Heaven's Gate"). Steele, "Tom and Eva,"p. 89. Moers, *HBS and American Literature*, p. 10.

6. Tocqueville, *Democracy in America*, vol. I, Ch. 18, especially pp. 430–31.

7. Catharine Esther Beecher and Harriet Beecher Stowe, *The American Woman's Home, or, Principles of Domestic Science* (New York: J. B. Ford & Co., 1869; reprint, Hartford, CT: Stowe-Day Foundation, 1975; hereafter cited as *The American Woman's Home*).

8. Tocqueville, op. cit., p. 394.

9. *Dred Scott v. Sandford*, 1856.

10. Tocqueville, op. cit., p. 395. May this reflection have inspired the title, *Uncle Tom's Cabin*? Consider Tom's hovel on Legree's plantation, which was called his "cabin"—"a fact critics seem to have overlooked," as Donovan points out. Donovan, *UTC: Evil, Affliction, and Redemptive Love*, p. 101.

11. Tocqueville, op. cit., p. 424.

12. Ibid., p. 426.

13. Ibid.

14. Ibid., p. 432.

15. Ibid., and cf. *UTC*, p. 163, and the discussion in book II, part I, chapter 19.

16. Ibid., p. 434, and cf. *UTC*, Ch.15, p. 174, the description of the St. Clare family, and the account of Simon Legree.

17. Ibid., p. 431.

18. Ibid., p. 434.

19. Ibid., p. 435.

20. Hedrick mistakenly attributes the naming of the steamboat, *La Belle Rivière*, to Stowe's having "worked the details of Charles Beecher's New Orleans experience into her story" (p. 222). She claims that Beecher traveled on a steamboat of this name on his journey down the Mississippi and cites *Chariot of Fire: Religion and the Beecher Family* by Marie Caskey as the source of this information. She is mistaken. Here is what Caskey actually wrote: "Charles left for New Orleans in late December of 1838, taking passage on a boat headed down 'La Belle Rivière' to the Mississippi" (p. 151). Caskey, of course, means that Beecher traveled down the Ohio River (often called "La Belle Rivière" because "Ohio" means "beautiful" in the Indian tongue in which it was christened) to reach the Mississippi. Harriet Beecher's first book, the reader must always recall, was a "geography"! She needed no help to understand the contours of the Mississippi, no literary metaphor to move north, east, south, west (or to change the order for moral purposes, as noted in book II, part II, Coda). Hedrick, *Harriet Beecher Stowe*. Marie Caskey, *Chariots of Fire: Religion and the Beecher Family* (New Haven: Yale University Press, 1978; hereafter cited as *Chariots of Fire*).

21. Calvin indicates his knowledge of French in the account of his study of Bible manuscripts in his *Origin and History of the Books of the Bible*. Among the many libraries he visited in 1836 was the Imperial Library in Paris, where he apparently got on swimmingly with the director. See page 76. Paige Savery, "Life of Calvin Ellis Stowe: A Chronology," unpublished pamphlet (Hartford, CT: Stowe-Day Foundation). This pamphlet cites a letter of 1847, wherein Stowe writes his mother that "after 25 years of study he now reads 'Latin & Greek, Hebrew, Syrian, Chaldee, Arabic, German, French, Spanish, & a little Persian.'"

22. Tocqueville, *Democracy in America*.

23. In applying Bettelheim's concept of the "informed heart" to *Uncle Tom's Cabin*, Shipp describes a condition similar to my concept of moral hardheadedness.

He writes of the character George Harris: "Mrs. Stowe never presents George's passionate feelings as unjustified; in fact, she supplies him with more than ample justification. Nevertheless, she invariable suggests that any emotion uninfluenced by intelligence is as potentially life-threatening as intelligence uninfluenced by emotion." The type cast in George Harris is contrasted with the type cast in Miss Ophelia, whose spiritual journey in the novel entails opening her heart. But, as Shipp reminds us, "Feeling alone does not give one an *informed* heart" (original emphasis). Shipp finds an admirable model of the "informed heart" in the character of Mrs. Shelby in whom he perceives that "'sensibility' precedes 'principles,' and together they combine to produce 'practical' results. Here, then, is the most fundamental formulation of Mrs. Stowe's prescription for humankind." Shipp, "*UTC* and the Ethos of Melodrama," pp. 42, 34, 35.

24. Remember that Rachael Halliday presided in her matriarchy "noiselessly."

25. As often but not always occurs, Stowe does not identify the source of these passages. In this case, the reason seems to be that she wants them to be regarded as a single passage, rather than separate and distinct.

26. It is this aspect of Tom's characterization, perhaps, that has led to misperception of his overall character by many; see, for example, Saunders: "The very qualities that made [Tom] an effective argument for abolition also helped to sustain a belief in racial inequality. . . . Tom is an ineffective vehicle for an argument for racial equality because he is insufficiently masculine." Saunders, "Houses Divided," p. 411.

11

The Light of the Present

Our story is at a standstill. So far as we can judge of things as they are, Tom is but a slave. Indeed, he is rather an inoffensive and pathetic slave, however sympathetic his character. Safe it is to imagine that no compelling alternative can be built on that foundation. Stowe realizes the difficulty, but she ascribes it rather to the reader than to her character. We see only with what she regards as "the light of the present," which rather obscures by blinding than illuminates things as they are. She claims that Tom is far more than we suspect. To prove this, a new set of characters is introduced. The foremost of these is the famous "little Eva." Eva is explicitly presented as a myth through which the reader may comprehend the "ideal" character (which is to say, the myth) of Uncle Tom.[1] But we require to witness the myth in action and not merely as an analogy. Hence, another contrast to Tom is introduced. That is Augustine St. Clare, Eva's father and Tom's new, kindly master. St. Clare possesses *almost* the identical ideal character, save that the claims of morality are compromised in his soul. The contrast between Tom and himself is precisely the contrast between moral softness and moral hardheadedness.[2] And it emerges most strongly in St. Clare's climactic and penultimate challenge to humanism in the exact center of the novel. The characters about Eva and St. Clare serve in a minor way to reveal Tom's nature by virtue of their distance from Eva and St. Clare. Through the central portion of the novel, a comprehensive view of human knowledge and morality is offered. Before we present clearly the structure of the "myth of Eva" and the character of Tom, however, we must briefly survey the range of these many characters. But it is fit to begin with the demonstration of the existence of the myth.

Chapter 14 accomplishes this end. The chapter seems to have two purposes. One is to record the nature of Tom's understanding of the Bible and its relation to life. The second is to record his power over the opinions of others. The first discloses the need for a myth. The second provides the specific means for the introduction of Eva.

Tom, it is said, studies over his Bible rather than simply reads it. He seems bent on discovering something that he supposes to be found there. But his concern with learning is shadowed by the recognition of a fixed and eternal alteration in his earthly circumstances. The reflection waters the pages of Tom's Bible with teardrops, as he directs his attention to a future home in heaven.[3] But Tom's study was fatally flawed, for he had nothing to desire to know. The promises recorded there were simply true.

> . . . so evidently true and divine that the possibility of a question never entered his simple head. It must be true; for, if not true, how could he live? (166)

This is not exactly the philosophic posture—the willingness to face even the bleakest of possibilities in order to gain certain knowledge of the truth. But how does one study without questioning—when, that is, one already knows? But one alternative suggests itself. One then studies to fill in the details. One reflects upon the appropriate means to the end. The study is secondary. Tom knows the truth—it is not bleak—and that alone keeps him alive, or at least a slave for the moment. This may seem incongruous, since death may speed the pleasant consummation of the truthful promise he beholds. Surely the details of the afterlife are not his affair. That question can apply only to earthly existence. Stowe hastens to qualify the formula.

> . . . his Bible seemed to him all of this life that remained, as well as the promise of a future one. (166)

Hence, the truth Tom knows explains not only the fate that awaits him, but some residuum of hope in this world. The Bible in its earthly bearings is the chief theme, or at least the chief element of his understanding so far as it relates to the apology for his course of action. Tom has apparently come to terms with his condition and faith. But the reader does not see it. And that requires a myth, the myth of little Eva.

Eva enters Tom's life as the third and most significant of the victories recorded in this chapter. Haley was first, as Tom wins his confidence and gains release from the fetters that had bound him. Free to move about the boat, he then "won the good opinion of all the hands" (164). The author boisterously casts these developments in the language of victories for Tom, as a prelude to the elaborate discussion of his consciously formulated designs upon little Eva. "He resolved to play his part right skillfully." The character of Eva is responsible for the wooing. She roamed freely about the boat, winning the hearts of all. The little "fairy" had presence, a presence noted and appreciated by Tom. We must quote at length to convey fully the significance of Tom's reaction to Eva.

> Her form was the perfection of childish beauty, without its usual chubbiness and squareness of outline. There was about it an undulating and aerial grace, *such as one might dream of for some mythic and allegorical being*. Her face was remarkable less for its perfect beauty of feature than for a singular and dreamy earnestness of expression, *which made the ideal start* when they looked at her, and by which the dullest and most literal were impressed, *without exactly knowing why*. (166–67, emphasis added)

Stowe imagined Eva as an allegory. And the purpose is to reveal what it is that the "ideal" Tom exactly knows which the "dullest and most literal" do not know. This is the correct interpretation, at all events, if Tom's reaction to his first sight of Eva is given its fullest weight. The "impressible" (168), though hardly "susceptible,"[4] Tom regarded her as "almost divine." Coming upon her suddenly, "he half believed that he saw one of the angels stepped out of his New Testament." To this author, the sight of an angel is cause for a "start." And using himself as an example, this author can only surmise that the sight of Eva made Tom start. Thus, he is indeed "ideal." That he sets to work to cultivate her friendship, "to tame her," reveals however that he was not awed. Eva is Tom's very own myth.

Tom is not *merely* ideal. For, in the passage in which he is, in effect, declared to be ideal, the possibility of the myth is raised. But the myth is connected to Uncle Tom, the one man in the novel fully aware of Eva's nature. He, in other words, knows the foundation of his ideal status. He sees beyond the myth. The reader does not understand even the myth. But it would seem crucial to do so, in order to understand the novel. We can begin at the surface, presuming to respond to John, the Drover. Some obvious possibilities for the interpretation of the myth suggest themselves.

Perhaps, for example, the myth of universal union or brotherhood among men is intended. Eva unites opposites. She unites Tom and her father, the impish slave girl, Topsy, and the stern Yankee, Ophelia, and others. But she fails with the analogous team of her mother and Mammy. If this were a myth of brotherhood the myth would have a defect—like Plato's myth of the cave. Also, like the cave, there is a tenuous relationship between Eva and worldly things, between Eva and the city. She is demanded—even ordered—to remain on earth but leaves anyway, unlike the philosopher of the cave in the ideal situation. But in that case it is the philosopher alone who suffers the impositions of his fellow citizens. Eva is not alone—she has Tom who alone does not demand that she remain and even understands why she must leave. He alone "sends" her where she must go—and, interestingly, is left behind. Just as Eva is ordered to stay and goes, Tom is constantly beseeched to go, but stays. The myth of Eva, then, is meant to explain the character of Tom and, consequently, that of his knowledge.

The myth is only partly approached by considering the relationship between Tom and Eva. There is really a triad. And we must consider the relationship between Tom and St. Clare and St. Clare and Eva also, in order to complete the analysis. Partly, our understanding of Tom's relationship with St. Clare is built only through our perception of St. Clare's relationship with Eva. Stowe suggests the relationship between Eva and her father, and thus the reason he, too, must die.

> All the interests and hopes of St. Clare's life had unconsciously wound themselves around this child. It was for Eva that he had managed his property; it was for Eva that he had planned the disposal of his time; and, to do this and that for Eva,—to buy, improve, alter, and arrange, or dispose something for her,—had been so long his habit, that now she was gone, there seemed nothing to be thought of, nothing to be done. (347)

Thus was the worldly St. Clare so completely in the service of an otherworldly being. Because he misperceived her nature, he misperceived the nature of those activities in which he had to engage in order properly to say that he did them "for her."

Perhaps, then, the myth of Eva has to do with the end of human life. Whatever makes the human end inaccessible to the individual as such (such as universal brotherhood) leaves man without hope or character when the end is taken away. The unworldly Eva ennobled St. Clare's worldly activities, but made them no less worldly. Hence, those activities were yet a part of what Stowe calls the "otherwise unmeaning ciphers of time"—for he could not subordinate them to a transcendent possibility. The worldly life must be counted meaningless unless there is a higher life—the slave who escapes, escapes to nowhere if there is not more than the immediate: He escapes to a world in which the best men, the St. Clares, die without undertaking the only kind of activities that can ennoble their characters in this life.

We have gone as far as we can in the way of interpreting the content of the myth of Eva without introducing further dramatic detail and discussing the other characters of the central portions of this novel. The insufficiency of our understanding of the myth of Eva seems to be connected with an insufficiency in our understanding of the earthly circumstances as opposed to the heavenly circumstances to which the myth relates. Chapter 14 then, accomplishes no more than to reveal the dimensions of the inquiry into the character of Uncle Tom. But we are not yet released from the method of indirection. Even the fact that Tom was ideal could only be revealed indirectly. Let us consider how far the other characters—their characters—can enlarge our frame of reference.

That our approach is correct, we may be assured by an incidental consideration: the character of the primary chapter titles beginning with chapter 14 and continuing to chapter 22, "The Grass Withereth—The Flower Fadeth," wherein, under the shadow of the prophecy of Isaiah, the meaning of the myth is revealed. Those chapter titles? "Evangeline." "Of Tom's New Master . . ." "Tom's Mistress and her Opinions." "Miss Ophelia's Experiences and Opinions." "Topsy." In chapter 22 we return to the relationship between Tom and Eva. The intervening chapters thus are formally devoted to delineations of character. And we argue that the delineations are designed to broaden our understanding of Tom's character.

The stereotypes of these characters are in fact established in chapter 15, "Of Tom's New Master, and Various Other Matters," save for Eva and Topsy at the beginning and end. The subsequent chapters, therefore, serve the purpose of inquiring how such souls phrase and pursue the moral demands and what they conceive to be the foundation of slavery. The stereotypes are designed to accord with the moral perspectives.[5] The compound is designed to challenge Tom's understanding. Chapter 15 opens by affirming that we have begun explicit discussion of things high and low, since the "humble hero" now is placed among "higher ones."

The first of the "higher ones" is St. Clare himself. He is the scion of a Canadian family now descended into a Vermont branch and a Louisiana branch. In himself he bears the novel's moral theme—in attenuated form. He is the man-woman.[6] As before, he is characterized as worldly, but it becomes clear that he is worldly only in a general philosophic or deistic sense. He has no *taste* for mundane activities and no conception of transcendent activities. The highest human activities are thus esthetic—cultured. The cultured obscures but does not regard the "real."

> The *real* remained,—the real, like the flat, bare, oozy, tide-mud, when the blue sparkling wave, with all its company of gliding boats and white-winged ships, its music of oars and chiming waters, has gone down, and there it lies, flat, slimy, bare, exceeding real. (176)[7]

Marie St. Clare, wife of Augustine, is the character who gives the lie to the naiveté that Stowe could only characterize very, very good women. She is pervasively masculine—in Stowe's terms—entrenched in an impregnable self-concern. Contrasted throughout with her openhearted, benevolent servant, Mammy, the two seem to be introduced for the sole purpose of demonstrating the impossibility of reconciling self-interest and benevolence. Marie is the first of only two characters in the novel who are said in most unchristian manner to be beyond salvation.[8] She is *perfectly* self-centered; i.e., she recognizes none of the claims of humanity to an extent, which is the opposite equivalent of her husband's secular humanism. He recognizes only the claim of humanity. The reader is not surprised that Marie is unfit for the maternal role.[9] St. Clare imports a "mother" from the North.[10] Genuine mothers *among the slave-owners* are rare indeed in this novel. Emily Shelby is the only one![11]

Ophelia St. Clare, Augustine's Yankee cousin, is the particular model of the Yankee mother—a spinster mother! But the Yankee mother is almost an independent character in the novel, a model toward which Ophelia might aspire. She is characterized by two traits: efficiency and moral sternness. The full weight is not given to those principles in *Uncle Tom's Cabin*, for the original of the Yankee mother antedates the regime of modern liberalism. The efficiency is comparable.

> . . . the lady in the snowy cap, with the spectacles, . . . sits sewing every afternoon among her daughters, as if nothing ever had been done, or were to be done,—she and her girls, in some long forgotten fore part of the day, *'did up the work,'* and for the rest of the time, it is *'done up.'* (179)

But the moral sternness has changed appreciably, in direction if not in intensity. Comparable but not identical devices are used in *Uncle Tom's Cabin* and the subsequent *Oldtown Folks* to review the nature of this moral sternness.

> In the former, the New England mother has a . . . respectable old book-case, with its glass doors, where Rollin's History, Milton's Paradise Lost, Bunyan's Pilgrim's Progress, and Scott's Family Bible, stand side by side in decorous order. (179)

But this is a "complete change of base" from the old time religion, a change induced by the age of revolution in America. The change worked "a constantly ameliorating power"[12] upon the foundation of Oldtown morality.

> On the round table that stood in her bedroom, next to the kitchen, there was an ample supply of books. Rollin's Ancient History, Hume's History of England, and President Edward's Sermons, were among these.[13]

These were well used, but still secondary to "Grandmother's Blue Book," "Bellamy's True Religion delineated, and distinguished from all Counterfeits." The old New England mother enjoyed comprehensive moral guidance and lived in the comprehensive community, able to distinguish itself from others at the same time as it distinguished the true religion and history of the universe. A religion directed rather more to the common condition of humanity comes to replace the old just as ties of particular history are surrendered to the demands of universal history. The new religion addresses the unadorned, unchained individual. The new New England mother has lost the comprehensive moral guidance of Oldtown, because she lives in a new city. Her books, in ascending order, declare a simple piety-faith to replace the lost paradise.

Ophelia St. Clare—aspiring to the model of the new New England mother[14]—is *the* prototype of the good citizen in a decent modern regime: she requires only to be shown the "right" or "ought" in order to ensure that she would pursue it.[15] As such, then, she is the civil analog to Uncle Tom, who only does what he *knows* to be right.[16]

Chapter 16 opens the discussion of the status of religion and morality for such characters and for Tom. The consideration turns rather less on the question of salvation, however, than on the question of rule. Though she employs—perhaps we should say, in addition to employing—the imagery of Christianity, Stowe directly raises the question whether slavery is, first, a legitimate form of rule and, second, whether it is capable of ruling even against the legitimate claims of superior strength or wisdom. The question is introduced by yet another generalization about the race to which Tom belongs. And she follows with a panegyric to mighty Africa and the "highest form of the peculiarly Christian life," which it is to develop, and Africa's coming rule—at the instance of God—in the last kingdom on earth, wherein the first shall be the last and the last first.[17]

But it is difficult to take Stowe seriously because she places these words in Marie's mouth *as well as* her own: "Was this what Marie St. Clare was thinking of. . . . Most likely it was." And true enough, Marie does hold an opinion similar to this, at least in its general if not in its particular terms.

> "Dr. G—— preached a splendid sermon. . . . Well, I mean all my views about society, and such things," said Marie. "The text was, 'He hath made everything beautiful for its season,' and he showed how all the orders and distinctions in society came from God; and that it was so appropriate, you know, and beautiful, that some should be high and some low, and that some were born to rule and some to serve, and all that, you know; and he applied it so well to all this ridiculous fuss that is made about slavery . . . !" (209)

St. Clare demurs from all this, and surprises Ophelia, who questions whether he does not believe these things. His response is a gruff defense of self-interest as the only defense of slavery. Hence, Ophelia asks whether that excludes any question of the right and wrong of slavery—are utilitarian considerations the only moral ground? But St. Clare refuses an answer—though he proceeds to elaborate general notions on religion and society, which conclude that any absolute right that does seem to exist seems not to be a concern of men. Religion is essentially a myth, and myth possesses no morality beyond the utilitarian or pragmatic (212). This is not satisfactory to Ophelia.

In chapter 18 St. Clare gets a reprieve—another opportunity to face up to the moral dilemma (245). But before it occurs, the reader is shown George's heroic defense of his freedom, and Tom's gaining of ascendancy in the St. Clare home. We see that Tom comes to rule (i.e., "escapes" slavery) as Joseph came to rule in Egypt, and that this process commenced before the death of Eva. We find that Tom's Christianity is not constitutional but is added on to an "impregnable simplicity of nature" which is, itself, the guarantee of his righteousness. Tom is always engaged by appeals to his honesty—not the general legal rules, but the personal commitment held him. "An odd mixture of Fealty, reverence, and fatherly solicitude" becomes the basis of his relationship with St. Clare. And immediately we discover which of those three is the most important. Tom could speak his mind, not as a fearless babbler, but as a moral teacher. Hence, he commences St. Clare's education in goodness by revealing the evil of one's unknowingly harming oneself.

Tom's growing power is in some measure the consequence of St. Clare's disposition to being moved by ideals: his unworldly worldliness; but it is in part a consequence of that by virtue of which Tom claims the right to rule. Dinah, too, displayed a power of ruling, as she defended her kingdom in the kitchen through a perfect diplomatic art which "unites . . . subservience of manner with . . . inflexibility as to measure." But she manifests this character in no other respect; what characterizes Tom in matters of the highest importance, characterizes her in ordinary—indeed, trivial—affairs. Hence, the trait is not itself heroic, nor any victory won by it. Dinah "rules" her mistress, but remains a slave; only rule with respect to the highest things makes slavery problematic.

Now, St. Clare's despairing of any men ever acting on the basis of an absolute right amounts to a denial that any men ever rule on the basis of absolute right—that is, no human rule is founded on the mastery of the highest things, and slavery is just another form of human rule. It should, therefore, be normally the case that the high and the low (with respect to capacity) would indiscriminately and promiscuously be found to be masters and slaves. All human rule or morality is founded upon the necessity for a complete confusion of the various types of soul, and hence of the various hierarchical possibilities. Surpassing excellence has no political home. But, under such circumstances, morality must be understood as in direct conflict with any presumed natural hierarchy. Ophelia cannot, of course, accept such a consequence. And it is with such notions in the background that she gives St. Clare a new occasion to defend the high or right as consistent with the best political hopes.

St. Clare rejects Ophelia's concern about the moral character of the slaves as out of place. He finds that they cannot possibly be moral under such circumstances—including those who might most naturally incline toward virtuousness. Only two slaves might escape this fate. The naturally continent, who are by nature "simple, truthful, and faithful," are one kind. And the *moral miracle*, Tom, is another kind. Tom is distinguished from the first *only* insofar as we imagine his conversion to be related to his developed character; for then, he could not have been fully distinguished by nature (244).

And what of the slaves' souls—more than a few of which may have been worth saving? St. Clare does not find that that affects the requirements of life in this world. It is, then, Ophelia's cry of "Shame!" that constitutes the second challenge. Her righteous indignation presumes a moral superiority to which St. Clare is called to respond. But to him the response is the same: No men live otherwise. All political arrangements are reducible to a struggle between upper and lower classes. Thus, moral indignation cannot be leveled at southern institutions. Ophelia objects that a different, need we say new, order of society exists in Vermont. To which statement he not only assents, but also agrees to widen the attribution to include all New England (and, by implication, virtually all the United States save the slave states).

The occasion for a review of his initial formulation about the absolute right would seem to have arisen. He would seem called upon to justify his lack of concern with the morality of his action, from the very moment he consciously recognizes the actual existence of a superior alternative. But we are again cut off. He does not run off. He is rather interrupted by the dinner bell. But it is noteworthy that it is he, St. Clare, who reports the ringing of the dinner bell, and neither Ophelia nor the author. We are entitled to believe that he still hesitates to address the question, but he no longer does so with such ease to his own conscience.

The stage is now set for the final assault on St. Clare's moral sensibility. But before we can consider that we must consider two factors as prefatory. The first arises from a discrepancy between the *National Era* serialization of *Uncle Tom's Cabin* and the published volume. And the second is Thomas Carlyle's "Discourse on the Nigger Question," which is prefigured in that discrepancy. As to the first fact: At the beginning of chapter 12, we recall, Stowe reveals what is the nature of Tom's participation in the earthly regime. It was there made clear that Tom never accepted citizenship, partial or otherwise. What is more, but for his apparent citizenship in the "heavenly city" or "city of god," he would have been sunk in despair. He was never at all happy, not really happy at that moment. Tom expressed his posture in Pauline severity, quoting from *Heb.* 13:14, "We have here no continuing city, but we seek one to come"; and adding, "wherefore God himself is not ashamed to be called our God; for he hath prepared for us a city." Stowe describes the peculiar power of these words over the "minds" of "poor, simple fellows like Tom," and considers them the source of that "courage, energy, and enthusiasm" which replaces the "blackness of despair." At this point, the published text is happily consistent with the tone of the epigram at the head of this chapter, the first such epigram in the book and presumably underscoring the intention to render a biblical critique of slavery. The form of that critique, again, depends on the identification of Sinai with Zion. The epigram is taken from *Matthew* 2:18. But Stowe omits the last clause: "because they are not." "Rachel is weeping for her children, and would not be comforted, *because they are not.*" Stowe allows us to imagine that the children still are or may be. That is the gloss on her interpretation of the fulfillment of the prophecy of *Jeremiah* 31:15,[18] which is found in *Matthew* 2:1. She leads the reader to anticipate relief from the "blackness of despair."

But, the published version has deleted the conclusion of the same paragraph as it appeared in the serialization. That read as follows:

> I mention this, of course, *philosophic friend, as a psychological phenomenon.* Very likely it would not do such a thing for you, because *you are an enlightened man, and have outgrown the old myths* of past centuries. But then you have Emerson's Essays and Carlyle's Miscellanies, and other productions of the latter day, suited to your advanced development . . . [19] (emphasis added)

Textually, two facts stand out in this passage. First, after the deletion, there remains in the text no other direct address to the reader as a philosopher. Secondly, the author eliminated a direct characterization of religious faith as a "psychological phenomenon" and of religion as "myth"—thus, leaving the introduction of Eva as the *first* discussion of myth (a veiled discussion). It cannot be said that the author did not wish to publish such sentiments, for they had already been published and disseminated across the nation. Further, it is clear that the principle thrust of the book is the critique of the particular humanistic perspective that is directly broached in this passage. But the critique is muted by the elimination of this passage, and there must be a reason for it.

As it happens, the serialization contained no preface. Nor did it include the last two chapters. And the two chapters, 18 and 19, are in reality a single chapter, as we note. The order of the chapters, then, is changed by the arrangements undertaken for book publication. Chapter 12, the chapter under question, occupied no special seat of honor, by position, in the newspaper version. Hence, the importance of its statements was not underscored. In book form, chapter 12 becomes the central chapter of the first half of the book. That position, then, underscores the importance of the first use of biblical epigram in the novel, and the characterization of Uncle Tom's detachment. At the same moment, elimination of the critique of humanism prevents a premature emphasis on that central argument, and permits a more patient development of Uncle Tom's character—that is, it permits a stronger basis to be laid for depicting the alternative to contemporary humanism. Thus, we come to the direct encounter with Tom's role as a teacher of the good and the paradox of the opposition between goodness and morality before we genuinely undertake the critique. As is said in the sports world, Stowe guarded her enterprise against peaking too soon.

Uncle Tom's Cabin does, then, prove that the humanistic perspective is not the authoritative defense of modern republicanism—that is, decent republican life. In the space between this initial opportunity and the actual attack, the character of Uncle Tom and of humanism (through St. Clare) are developed side by side. Then, that humanism can be directly confronted—represented by thinkers such as Emerson and Carlyle, as the deleted passage reveals.[20] In particular, it is represented in Carlyle's *Miscellanies*, among which is the much disputed "Occasional Discourse on the Nigger Question." We find there a version of modern liberalism, albeit in satirical form, that provides the grist for Stowe's mill. Accordingly, we shall review it in detail, to get a sense of how "humanism" came to be seen as problematic in her eyes.

Carlyle's essay takes the form of unauthorized publication of a curious manuscript by one Dr. Phelim McQuirk (who reminds us of Vermont's Dr. Botherem, though quite the opposite). It is not clear, therefore, how far it represents the opinions of Carlyle and how far it is a satire or parody of other opinions. But let us put aside that question, and attempt an understanding of the surface of the argument as it is presented. The essay begins at page 303 of the Everyman edition. It announces the purpose of its attack as counteracting the influence of contemporary "rose-pink" sentimentalism. Abolitionism or Christian sentimentalism endangers the universal work of serious men.[21] Further, this sentimentalism is associated with the Dismal Science, founded on economic rationalism. But mere economic rationalism is insufficient, for it interests men in none other than themselves.[22] The logic of economic rationality is the impoverishment and suppression of the masses.

The alternative is a moral guidance in accord with the teaching of Fact and Nature—the universal command. All human beings have a single purpose: to labor to the full reach of their ability.[23] This labor must be in useful work, for only thus does it achieve its end. This is the condition of the happiness of all as it is of one—and as such, a model of utopia.[24]

Quashy, then, must be forced to work. But he is likable. Alone among savages, he is capable of humane relationships. Neither indiscriminate slavery nor moral indifference is acceptable in regard to him.[25] He is a fellow man. And no moral justification of oppression is possible. But, "hardships, oppressions, and injustices" are not limited to slavery. They are the condition of human life in this world. Slavery, in fact, is the general human condition.[26] Men do not, universally, abide in an absolute morality.

The greatest examples of slavery occur in the noblest countries—and, as such, are the accompaniment of civilization to this point. *Wisdom is enslaved by folly, the strong by the weak.* Majority rule, democratic equality, and the pursuit of material pleasure are the forms of this rule—utility the standard. The claim of equality in wisdom among men destroys any chance for the good. It does so by denying the basis of humanity.

> What are the true relations between Negro and White, their mutual duties under the sight of the Maker of them both; what human laws will assist both to comply more and more with these? The solution, only to be gained by earnest endeavour, and sincere reading of experience, such as have never yet been bestowed on it, is not yet here; the solution is perhaps still distant. But some approximation to it, various real approximations, could be made, and must be made:—this of declaring that Negro and White are unrelated, loose from one another, on a footing of perfect equality, and subject to no law but that of supply-and-demand according to the Dismal Science; this, which contradicts the palpablest facts, is clearly no solution, but a cutting of the knot asunder; and every hour we persist in this is leading us towards *dis*solution instead of solution! (Carlyle, pp. 330–31)

Thus slavery is none other than tyranny—or, it is *but* an instance of the tyrannical form of rule.[27]

Only a clear conception of true mastership and servantship can successfully oppose tyranny or slavery. The relationship must be established on the basis of permanency (taking it to be based on the rule of folly by wisdom).[28] Let the Black man voluntarily bind himself, and you clear away all the abuses of slavery. The "thing itself" becomes something precious. The motivating idea or force behind it is to bring the Negro to the level of civilization—to "save the baby."[29] Unless this is done, resistance will and *should* increase. But as it happens, injustice will be protested by unjust men. Hence, the occasion for protest ought to be removed and perfect abolition granted. Perfect abolition is a minimum requirement of "human" souls.

All questions of right reduce to the limited attachment to as much as possible in this world.[30] Each society approaches its "mights" in some specific fashion; but none approaches perfection. All seek to supply the things needful for human life, and hopefully do so in a way that leads to civilization: commerce, arts, politics, and social development. *The noblest things are earthly, but beyond the "groslly terrene."*[31] The first or highest right or claim to the earth belongs to him who is best able to "educe" from it the noblest things.

We may return to St. Clare's dilemma. But it is first necessary to remind ourselves that the notion of humanism as the enemy Stowe attacks is not without its paradoxes. These stem from the fact that there seem to be two distinct and opposing conceptions of that moral virtue called humanity. We recall that the author introduced us to "a man of humanity" in the very first chapter. There, we imagined, it was an intentional paradox, since one man who claimed to have humanity, Haley, seemed obviously inhumane. The author, it seemed, wished to teach by way of contradiction or contrast—by way of melodrama. As it turns out, however, Mr. Haley is not without some claim to be a man of humanity after all. And if this is true, the opening chapter is not just paradoxical, but ironic—as the wine-tasting episode revealed. For it would now appear that it is humanity itself that is doubtful, rather than Haley's humanity as such. The contrast would have concealed the profound wisdom in the author's conception of the nature of humanism; and the ordinarily careful reader would be brought to doubt that conception through the innocent and guileless simplicity of Uncle Tom, without suspecting the operation of superior wisdom.

It is that humanistic requirement that the "undeveloped" or "underdeveloped" be developed by their superiors (satirized by Carlyle but importantly defended by John Stuart Mill) which is most roundly undermined through the character of Uncle Tom. Under that requirement moral excellence as such is no longer the standard of human excellence. And, instead, the standard of human excellence becomes the degree of attachment to some specific conception of human life and, especially, human progress.[32] The appeal to surpassing excellence undermines all attempts at ideological standards of excellence.

At the conclusion of chapter 12, Haley is said to have overcome every humane weakness. But soon thereafter we discover that Haley is but the reflection of a more general and highly developed tendency. He was indeed "made" by forces greater than himself. The educated, the high, the refined, and the talented make possible the shamelessness of the ignorant, the low, the coarse, and the simple in these matters. And how is this accomplished? Through the teaching that the demands of morality are general or universal, but not susceptible to any precise *and* particular articulation. Tom, we recall, could sympathize with Lucy, whose suckling child was sold away, because he had not learned to *generalize* and see such evils as only what are "inseparable from any other relations in social and domestic life." Tom, in other words, did not judge the moral circumstances of individuals by their cities' rates of progress toward some supposed universal human end. If the guiding principle of humanism is the universalism of ideal morality, subject to particular exceptions, the particular exceptions are the cities in which men live and the stages of "progress" within those cities, by necessity. The description of Haley seems to portray him as the opposite of the humane type, until American legislators are called humane for struggling against the foreign slave trade (while leaving the domestic trade unchallenged). Stowe questions the value of the city's teachings only insofar as it is a city grounded in humanism.

In that extra chapter of *Uncle Tom's Cabin*, chapter 19, without which there would be no center by chapters and which contains, itself, the first center of the novel, by pages, St. Clare is brought to climax the attack on humanism—to abandon humanism—when he is portrayed as Haley's guardian, the defender of the system. He shows, before the charge is made, that he fully grasps the grounds of the arguments (252). Explaining why he closes his eyes to the outrages that occur, he begins with a characterization of the ways of the world—hence, the ways of necessity. In effect, his argument runs as follows: In the world there is mankind or humanity, which organizes itself into particular communities each of which forms its city or regime. Since the evils that occur are likely the result of the constitution of the city or regime (as opposed to the nature of man in general), the individual is in no position to resist them. Thus, one must not examine from too near the ways of men in cities—anywhere in the world; "'Tis like looking too close into the details of Dinah's kitchen."[33] This reference to a previous encounter with Ophelia, over the moral character of the slaves, constitutes a repetition of his refusal to discuss the right and wrong of slavery. And, as a repetition, it is intended as a final refusal.

But St. Clare must not have expected Ophelia to hold him directly responsible, and as a man rather than as a citizen. For her, every citizen is such by virtue of what makes him a man and not vice-versa. That is, it is the nature of man to be a citizen. She cannot accept the distinction of political life as artificial and flawed in comparison with what man could be without law. St. Clare, therefore, is put to the defense of the possibility of men doing, knowingly, what they consider to be wrong and, as such, harmful to themselves.[34] Though Ophelia accepts that men may do wrong knowingly, as a result of natural depravity, she cannot conceive it being the result of doctrine—particularly, doctrines of tolerance. Thus, she and St. Clare speak to different universes in this short exchange—a fact of which he is aware. Nonetheless, he charges her, like every human being, of doing things that she does not consider right—and even repeating the offense.

Because she considers his argument a charge of moral error, she takes it more seriously than he intended—that is, personally. But he abhors personal guilt—Christian sentimentalism. So he hastily retreats into frivolity and thereby convinces her that he was not serious at all.

Ophelia nonetheless persists. He must become serious. He hesitates, and—excusing himself by noting the languid effects of the climate—he suddenly conceives that all these moral questions might be reducible to environmental determinism. This accidental (i.e., non-climatic) moral discovery launches him upon an effort to explicate the problem. Thus, he commences:

> When in the course of human events, it becomes necessary for a fellow to hold two or three dozen of his fellow-worms captive, a decent regard to the opinion of society requires . . . (254)[35]

Again, Ophelia does not find him serious. He changes course—but is it a real change? It seems unconnected with the argument from climate or environmental determinism. But has he not revealed the origin of his ultimate account? The parody of the *principles* of the Declaration of Independence (the most consistent theme of the entire novel!) is intended as a true account of the *consequences* of the Declaration—that is, not just blacks but all men are enslaved by the establishment of government. And what is worse, they who enslave are the equals—the fellow-worms—of those who are enslaved. Hence, there is no moral or natural justification of the city as such. And there follows no moral or natural justification of citizenship. This seems, somehow, to deny the legitimacy of the consent of the governed. But among moral equals such consent can only be considered illegitimate if it is understood to proceed from folly rather than wisdom. As Carlyle suggests, what greater folly is there than the subjection of the wise to the foolish, a necessary consequence of the establishment of government on the basis of the principles of the Declaration?

But Ophelia, who *needs* to be told the ought, cannot conceive this as serious. St. Clare meets her at her level. He calls slavery the work of the devil—"abstractly considered." Ophelia is astonished, we need not say pleased. This is language she understands. But does she in fact understand? Why does St. Clare use the qualifier, "abstractly considered"? The answer is best seen by returning to Carlyle, whose essay is paralleled in the development of this argument. In declaiming against the African slave trade, Carlyle conceded the justice of arguments against it. But, he wondered, why is so much money and effort wasted in the attempt to chase and capture pirates on the seas and in Africa? Without the *entrepots* of sale, in Brazil for example, no business could exist. Hence, it makes far better sense to send a war party to Brazil and to counsel those errant men that they must either end their appetite for slaves or be destroyed. When they are destroyed, if need be, there can no longer be the noxious trade. And, he asks, why do we not do that, "if Heaven do send us?" Thus, Carlyle reveals both the nature of the action that follows moral certainty and the paradox of a humanism or cultural relativism which deprives itself of the power of indignation and the right of punishment. That absolute right of which St. Clare despairs would make prudential if not expediential hesitations unnecessary. From a wisdom certain flows facile judgment of human crimes and goodness.

Only because men cannot be certain that they are heaven sent, do they—nay, must they—defer to the possibility that someone else—however much man is one—possesses a genuine morality. St. Clare's invocation of the Devil is intellectually identical to Carlyle's argument (archetype of the argument against totalitarianism). Reasoning from the diversity of human practices, any conception of the necessity of a single human way as the only just way, produces the opinion that men live for the most part if not entirely in error. Hence, Ignorance or the Prince of Darkness is the cause of the human forms and not Wisdom or the Son of Light. To say the devil is responsible is the same as to say that human ignorance or irrationality is responsible.

Though St. Clare seems to shift his argument away from the Declaration, in fact, he shifts only his language. There results a final consequence of greater import. By interesting Ophelia in the discourse through the appeal to her moral sensibilities or prejudices, St. Clare commits himself to finishing. Hence, it is from this point that St. Clare comes to terms with his own moral sensibilities. The characterization of the humanistic perspective is complete. There remains but to judge whether he can live in accord with it.

St. Clare finally capitulates and makes his apology (255). He apologizes not for possessing slaves but for not freeing them. He begins by correcting Carlyle's account of the master's relationship to Quashy[36]—denying that the relation is maintained for Quashy's good and that the ultimate civilization of the savage is the objective. It is rather for the good of the master, and thus bottomed on the right of the stronger. In this he is in perfect agreement with Alfred, his twin brother (263). But St. Clare thinks it is in its nature an abuse—not a moral order or hierarchy. "Talk of the *abuses* of slavery! Humbug! The *thing itself* is the essence of all abuse!" The reason for this is that men are not animalistic, beastly, though they live perforce by "savage laws." The important question, then, is why are not savage laws replaced by human laws? St. Clare's apology consists precisely in his account of the impossibility of that consummation.

To Stowe, Augustine St. Clare had now "started up," and everything Greek in him rushed to the surface. So striking is the transformation that Ophelia had never before witnessed him in this particular mood. But he begins with the odd parenthesis that talking and feeling about "this subject" is of no use. Hence, the righteous indignation he displays is understood to be rather heuristic than practical. Thus does he declare that he would agree to perish with his fellows if the "whole country would sink, and hide all this injustice and misery from the light." What disgusts him particularly is the fact that this despotic power is placed into the hands of so many base creatures—creatures in whose hands cruelty must be the necessary result. But does not this imply that the abuses of slavery make the evil? Would it not be the case that the thing itself has no particular character, since every man is on his own with respect to ruling and being ruled (that is, with respect to his character)? Is St. Clare, then, ready, first, to curse his country and, secondly, the human race rather on account of the weakness of character in individuals than because of slavery itself? This is almost a necessary conclusion in light of the prior argument that the slavery itself is an abuse, without respect to how it is used. It must be the case that the thing itself is an abuse only because Carlyle's utopian expectations are impossible. It is the abuse of an abuse, the very civilization or morality to which humanism aspires is *itself* the denial of the possibility of human life in accord with natural hierarchy. The confused intermingling of the various types of human souls must be an absolute necessity, under whatever forms of ruling might be tried by man.

It is here that we begin to discover the necessity of not founding a defense of the slave's humanity on the character of the probable exercise of his rights in freedom. Here, Tom's importance reaches its climactic greatness, for he is the vehicle through which we prove the existence of the confused intermingling of souls—whatever their circumstances. St. Clare continues to demonstrate the particular application of these principles. It may suffice for us to continue our summary method of discussing chapter 19. Then we can return to our myth of Eva.

Ophelia was quite certain that Augustine had more than satisfied her desire for a moral accounting, for she had never heard such wrath "even at the North" (256). This provides the occasion for a descent, "a sudden change of expression," and resumption "of his habitual careless tone." A fair margin of safety and decent respect for civilization restored, she required him to explain how he, Augustine, came to be and continues to be a slaveowner. That St. Clare possesses slaves is but the work of "ordinary generation." He inherited his way of life. But why does he not free them? The short answer is that he "wishes" to care for his slaves[37] and has no conception at all of how they might live apart from him. But much in the way of moral struggle precedes that understanding.

It is in the account of the differences between his twin brother[38] ("active and observing," "truthful from pride and courage") and himself ("dreamy and inactive," truthful from "a sort of abstract ideality"), the one "Roman," the other "Greek," that Augustine confronts the consequences of his moral perspective.[39] As joint heritors of a plantation and a town home, they sought to manage their properties as a team. It was soon necessary to part company. Alfred retained the plantation; Augustine retained the town home and investments. The one ruled slaves for a profit; the other ruled slaves for pleasure. To Augustine, the difference lies in paternal versus maternal characteristics. His brother was the proud aristocrat their father had been, while he was the child of a saintly mother, imbued with a "passion for humanity," for equality (259). St. Clare sees in himself the rejection of aristocracy, and even of natural aristocracy. He thought his father a "born aristocrat," although "originally of poor and not in any way of noble family." Natural aristocracy seems a useful model of inspiration for the elimination of artificial barriers to individuals. But St. Clare holds that natural *aristoi* must draw an artificial line of "humanity" around themselves. They draw the line differently in differing climes and times. Hence, they readily except others from the claims of humanity.

"What would be hardship and distress and injustice in his own house, is a cool matter of course in another." In this we find the source of St. Clare's parody of the Declaration.

> My father's dividing line was that of color. *Among his equals*, never was a man more just and generous; but he considered the negro, through all possible gradations of color, as an intermediate link between man and animals, and graded all his ideas of justice or generosity on this hypothesis. (258)

As the parody revealed, St. Clare conceives this hypothesis as only the right of the stronger. This is the real moral problem for him—an insoluble problem in the end.

Natural aristocracy is taken to mean the inherent superiority of some men over others and, in its nature, cannot stop with racial differences. A moral order that escapes this self-immolation must be based on a conception of "natural democracy" which regards all men as equally distinguished from beasts. Presumably, it would be informed by St. Clare's love "for all kinds of human things." The difficulty St. Clare faces is that he has no answer for his father's homely wisdom. Unless his and his mother's "idea of the dignity and worth of the meanest human soul" (260) can eliminate a need for politics, it still must arrive that some men must be subjected to government. As such this idea shares in the character of cities and constitutions. "All government includes some necessary hardness. General rules will bear hard on particular cases." Beyond this St. Clare cannot go, although he doesn't know but that he "might have been a saint, reformer, martyr!" had he not lost his mother at his own so tender age.

Stowe rather believes that this view can proceed no further than he has pursued it. A fitting silence intervenes between his expostulation and a dramatic return to the theme of climatic determination.

> What poor mean trash this whole business of human virtue is! A mere matter, for the most part, of latitude and longitude, and geographic position, *acting with natural temperament*. The greater part is nothing but an accident! (261, emphasis added)

Thus are we returned to the "accidental" discovery of the initial theory of climatic determinism. The accident is now part of the theory, showing that nothing is determined in the larger sense, if everything is in the narrow sense. Virtue results when climate acts in accord "with natural temperament." St. Clare were, by natural temperament, not a slave owner. His apology is that he was not born where he might live as nature inclined him. What kind of accident would he have required? That which befell his uncle—as aristocratic as St. Clare's father—when he settled in New England "where all are, in fact, free and equal."

There is certainly one sense in which it is true that any individual is born into a given regime only by accident. But ordinarily one attaches the accident to the birth, not the regime. Some other cause of the regime's existence must be sought—namely, a concern with the human way of life. But Augustine seems to have another objective in mind. He persists in contrasting the elder St. Clares, by temperament alike.

> One fell into a condition where everything (democracy) acted against the natural tendency, and the other where everything (slavery) acted for it . . . (261)

According to this formulation natural tendencies may be successfully resisted or supported depending on whether the tendency is bad or good! The aristocratic tendency may be checked; the democratic tendency (Augustine himself) may rather be thwarted.

This is the most curious thesis in *Uncle Tom's Cabin*. It introduces us to St. Clare's final argument: slavery is the right of the stronger. But on its own terms it seems suspiciously like a positive, even utopian argument. Consider. If good democracy can counter inhuman, exclusive aristocratic tendencies, must there not follow every hope for successful refounding and earthly salvation? In addition, if evil aristocracy cannot corrupt however much it weakens good democrats, is there not in every despotism a permanent residuum of sound material as foundation for a successful revolution? That is, the principle differences in souls remain distinct and viable on these terms. The difficulty is readily noted if we inquire, Who may be enslaved? Insofar as enslavement means substitution of the will of the master for the slave's own will—even his "irresponsible" will[40]—the slave cannot be a "born democrat."[41] If the "born aristocrat" is the only human type left, we have accidentally refuted the argument from the natural tendencies. Aristocratic tendencies may be counteracted by democratic and aristocratic means.

The argument in fact depended on tendencies from men in communities—not natural tendencies. Political tendencies may counteract political tendencies. The argument does not apply to slaves, as formulated, because they are beyond the reach of the force of these political principles, whatever may be their natural tendencies. The future of slavery—as of man—depends not on natural tendencies but on forceful political endeavor. Natural tendency and accident cannot resolve the problem of slavery. If the types of soul he identifies are as he maintains and coincide with political tendencies, slavery as such is right or natural. If slavery is not right, he must be wrong. St. Clare must either accept slavery as in accord with nature; or he must insist that it contravenes nature. Because he insists upon the latter,[42] he *must* abandon the implications of his particular attachment to democracy. He can find no practical application of his moral principle, without bowing to Carlyle's "rule of folly over wisdom."

St. Clare retreats to the right of the strongest. He generalizes the argument from slavery to an argument of the relationship between higher and lower classes. He accepts his brother's abandonment of the distinction of race. Augustine is still opposed to Alfred's moral conclusion, but agrees that what is done in slavery is identical or similar to what obtains between English aristocrats and American capitalists, on the one hand, and working classes on the other hand. The low are compelled to work, not for their own good, but for the good of the high. Slavery is to some extent recommended by its more frank revelation of the necessary conditions of civilization.[43] St. Clare's apparent return to his original position contains a significant change. Earlier, he held that the debasement of the slaves did not concern him.[44] That argument, too, was based on the lower class being "used up, body, soul, and spirit, for the good of the upper." In the final formulation this remains the justification, but it has a great cost: degraded slaves degrade their masters. Yet, to improve them—to act upon the thesis that their slavery was for *their* good—would erode the basis of civilization.[45] St. Clare is unable to solve this dilemma for himself. His wish to care for his slaves is fundamentally an act of self-indulgence. As he confesses, he is "up to heaven's gate in theory—down to earth's dust in practice." His is the dilemma of secular humanism. St. Clare will not find his own way out. His salvation comes through discovery of a slave for whom he cannot care, and who, instead cares for St. Clare. St. Clare's system of rule—making his slaves dependent on his kindness—is reversed in his relationship with Uncle Tom.

NOTES

1. A number of critics see Eva as a myth or as a symbol; examples include: Ammons ("The child is pure symbol . . . [she] embodies the essence both of motherhood and Christianity"); Steele ("Eva evokes the Christ of the Last Discourse in St. John's gospel . . . she sums up in herself the essential message of the gospel of love"); Bush ("lily-white Eva epitomizes the Christian commission to become a 'doer of the word'"); Gossett ("a symbol of perfect innocence . . . "); Marks ("a child figure who is able to perceive evil and is willing to grapple with it"); Lewis ("Tom and Eva serve as *exemplum* of the Son and the Spirit . . . "; also, "Eva as the Lamb of God . . . "); and Short ("Without Eva the novel would not strike so deep . . . Eva, as synecdoche for soul, can 'fold into her bosom' a 'hieroglyphic' expressive potential which, unlike those of society, brooks no interpretation"). Ammons, "Stowe's Dream," p. 164. Steele, "Tom and Eva," pp. 84, 85. Bush, "The Declaration of Independence and *UTC*," pp. 180–181. Gossett, *UTC and American Culture*, p. 193. Marks, "A Voice in Ramah," p. 193. Lewis, "Message, Messenger, and Response," pp. 203, 236. Bryan C. Short, "Stowe, Dickinson, and the Rhetoric of Modernism," *Arizona Quarterly* 47, no. 3 (1991): 12.

Donovan is adamant: "Stowe was, I believe, trying to show what a purely good, uncorrupt person would be. Like the characters in Dante's *Paradiso* she is the embodiment of a beatific vision, and one simply has to accept her on this level and not apply realistic criteria." Donovan, *UTC: Evil, Affliction, and Redemptive Love,* p. 77. Numerous critics have commented upon the prevalence of a pure child and especially the death of a pure child in sentimental literature. Brooks points out that in melodrama, particularly when the protagonist is "beyond adolescence, a child may be introduced as the bearer of innocence." Peter Brooks, *The Melodramatic Imagination: Balzac, Henry James, Melodrama, and the Mode of Excess* (New Haven: Yale University Press, 1976), pp. 33–34 (hereafter cited as *The Melodramatic Imagination*). Szczesiul's non-standard analysis emphasizes the ways in which Stowe's portrayal of both Eva and Tom incorporates aspects of the Roman Catholic hagiographic tradition ("Eva is . . . a spiritual martyr in the tradition of the confessor saints" and "the locks of [her] hair take on the significance of religious relics of a departed saint"). Anthony E. Szczesiul, "The Canonization of Tom and Eva: Catholic Hagiography and *Uncle Tom's Cabin*," *ATQ* n.s. 10 (1996): 65, 67.

2. The character of Augustine St. Clare has attracted substantial critical attention, with much of it focused on either his inaction or his internal conflict. A few examples are cited here. Bellin sees St. Clare as "the key to *Uncle Tom's Cabin*"—as the fulcrum of Stowe's opposition of judgment and action. "St. Clare occupies the center of the novel because it is in him that the two alternatives he represents may be set in opposition to one another, examined, and then one cast into the fire and the other embraced." Bellin, "Up to Heaven's Gate," p. 285. Lang's view of St. Clare as the man-woman echoes Bellin somewhat: "He represents Stowe's effort to combine the knowledge and power of men with the goodness of women and thus to bridge the gap between private feelings and public action . . . St. Clare alone has the potential to translate virtue and understanding into right action: instead, he dies." Lang, "Slavery and Sentimentalism," p. 34. To Sundquist, St. Clare embodies "the South's spiritual devastation." Sundquist, *New Essays*, p. 27.

3. *UTC*, pp. 164–65.

4. *UTC*, pp. 329, 331, 336, and 342.

5. A few words, here, on the critical assessment of Stowe's use of characters may be in order. A significant portion of the scholarship faults Stowe for what is seen as the use of stereotypes in place of fully developed characters; this strain of scholarship especially condemns the depiction of black characters as mere stereotypes. For example, Banks reports that antebellum black readers found "Stowe's use of racial stereotyping" to be "troubling" and accuses her of "dramatizing the prevailing notion of black subjugation through her depiction of blacks as naturally obedient, Christian, childlike and forgiving." Banks, "*Uncle Tom's Cabin* and the Antebellum Black Response," p. 222. Ammons and Belasco insist that "the farther away a black character moves from those stereotypes in Stowe's novel, the whiter he or she is in ancestry." Elizabeth Ammons and Susan Belasco, eds., *Approaches to Teaching Uncle Tom's Cabin* (New York: Modern Language Association, 2000), introduction, p. 2. Countless examples of this perspective could be cited. There are, however, a handful of scholars who see it differently. Davis stresses the variety among Stowe's characters ("Both whites and blacks are remarkably varied . . . ") Richard Beale Davis, "Mrs. Stowe's Characters-in-Situation and a Southern Literary Tradition," in *Essays in*

Honor of Jay B. Hubbell, ed. Clarence Gohdes (Durham, NC: Duke University Press, 1967), p. 109. Rexroth rhapsodizes "How real, how convincing, this huge cast. . . . True, the Negroes are seen from the point of view of a white person, but any attempt to 'think black' would have been a falsification. Mrs. Stowe simply tries to think human. And human they all are . . . " Rexroth, *Elastic Retort*, pp. 104–5. Sarson notes that the novel "cover[s] the slave world as a whole . . . the book contains among its [black] characters Christians and heathens, rebels, brutes, buffoons, brilliance and everything in between." Sarson, "HBS and American Slavery," p. 37. Moers perceives a similar diversity: "In manner, speech, skin color, capacity, and moral life, Mrs. Stowe distinguishes her black characters as sharply one from another as her whites, one consequence of her dedication to the American Real that has been widely misunderstood." Moers, *HBS and American Literature*, p. 15. Occasionally, a critic concludes that the characters are stereotyped, but purposefully so. Tompkins explains that "figures like Stowe's little Eva . . . operate as a cultural shorthand." Tompkins, *Sensational Designs*, p. xvi. Camfield, for example, sees the stereotypes as "vehicles to carry [Stowe's] theological and philosophical beliefs." Camfield, "Moral Aesthetics," p. 327. Citing John Herbert Nelson's analysis of *The Negro Character in American Literature*, Saunders distinguishes between "stock characters" and stereotyped characters: " . . . Nelson sees typicality as one aspect of humanity, and hence of realism; people and realistic characters, in his estimation, derive their identity not only from their individuality, but also from the expression of group traits in a particular environment." Saunders, "Houses Divided," p. 66.

6. See chapter 18, note 2.

7. Bellins misreads this passage as implying that Stowe finds earthly existence filled with a darkness and violence that can never be fully vanquished and states that she does not wish "to explore the darkness fully; instead she prefers . . . to skip over this world and to welcome the world to come." Bellins, "Up to Heaven's Gate," p. 287. Moers, who recognizes and extols the realism of Stowe's writing, instead describes this passage as "not the least interesting permutation of the river symbolism which makes a literary whole of *Uncle Tom's Cabin*." Moers, *HBS and American Literature*, p. 11.

8. The other is Simon Legree, p. 386. The first case is implicit, the second, explicit.

9. Romero stresses that Stowe depicts Marie St. Clare not as a "whole woman," but "rather, as Stowe twice repeats, she is 'a fine figure, a pair of bright dark eyes, and a hundred thousand dollars.'" Lora Romero, "Bio-Political Resistance and Domestic Ideology and *Uncle Tom's Cabin*," *American Literary History* 1 (1989): 722 (hereafter cited as "Bio-Political Resistance"). Ammons surmises: "Progenitor and antithesis of this heavenly Eva is the worst mother in the novel, ironically named Marie (the most perfect of Christian mothers), a woman who is despised precisely because she so utterly fails to live up to the Victorian ideal of the loving mother . . . she represents in female flesh the double of the satanic Legree." Ammons, "Stowe's Dream," pp. 164–65. Shipp finds that "Mrs. Stowe demonstrates, in her portrait of Marie, how destructive emotions uninfluenced by intelligence can be." Shipp, "*UTC* and the Ethos of Melodrama," p. 45.

10. *UTC*, pp. 176–78.

11. An account of Augustine's mother is given, of course, but she is not "present."

12. Harriet Beecher Stowe, *Oldtown Folks* (Boston: Fields, Osgood, 1869), p. 376 (hereafter cited as *Oldtown Folks*).

13. Ibid., 369.

14. Grant reads Ophelia St. Clare as a symbol for the North itself and points out that initially "Ophelia wants to remake Topsy without remaking herself." Instead, Ophelia—like the northern states—must first transform herself. "No longer self-righteously equating slavery with Southern degradation, Ophelia reinvigorates the sources of her own Yankee virtue when she accepts her own measure of responsibility for Topsy's fate and commits herself to decisive action." David Grant, "*Uncle Tom's Cabin* and the Triumph of Republican Rhetoric," *New England Quarterly* 71, no. 3 (1998): 440, 443 (hereafter cited as *UTC* and the Triumph of Republican Rhetoric").

15. *UTC*, pp. 181–82.

16. Even Haley attests this! Cf. p. 173.

17. *UTC*, p. 206; *Mark* 10:31.

18. Kirkham is wrong to suggest that Stowe is misquoting from *Jeremiah*, because depending on her "memory" (a charge made as well by other Stowe analysts who deem her a careless writer). She is exact both in what she quotes and what she omits to quote. E. Bruce Kirkham, *The Building of Uncle Tom's Cabin* (Knoxville: University of Tennessee Press, 1977), p. 167 (hereafter cited as *Building*). Although Madison overlooks Kirkham's lapse in this regard, her own careful study results in this judgment: "There is no question that Stowe was revising and no question that she was a careful writer, much more careful than later critics or biographers, other than Kirkham, give her credit for." Ellen Louise Madison, "A Parallel Text Edition of *Uncle Tom's Cabin*: Materials for a Critical Text" (Ph.D. diss., University of Rhode Island, 1986), p. 47.

19. For a citation of the *National Era* text, collated with the first edition, see Kirkham's dissertation. E. Bruce Kirkham, "Harriet Beecher Stowe and the Genesis, Composition, and Revision of *Uncle Tom's Cabin*" (Ph.D. diss., University of North Carolina, 1968). The published version, his *Building of Uncle Tom's Cabin*, deletes the excellent treatment of this passage, apparently judging it of minor significance. Another useful source is Madison's dissertation, cited above. Madison, "A Parallel Text Edition."

20. Perhaps Carlyle himself recognized the attack. Gossett notes that "Carlyle wrote to Emerson in 1853 that true enlightenment would come to the world only when 'the strenuous effort and most solemn heart-purpose of every good citizen in every country of the world' would work to that end. In the meantime, mankind was suffering 'this malodorous melancholy "Uncle Tommery."' To his sister Jean, Carlyle wrote about the same time, '[T]o me for one, it [i.e., *Uncle Tom's Cabin*] seemed a pretty perfect sample of Yankee-Governess Romance, & I fairly could not and would not read beyond the first 100 pages of it.'" Gossett, *UTC and American Culture*, p. 247.

21. Thomas Carlyle, "Occasional Discourse on the Nigger Question," in *English and Other Critical Essays* (London: J. M. Dent & Sons, 1915; reprint, 1925), p. 306. For an attempt at "Carlyle's interpretation" which is most suggestive of an approach to this essay and useful in itself, see G. B. Tennyson, *Carlyle and the Modern World*. Lecture delivered to the Carlyle Society, March 6, 1971 (Edinburgh: Carlyle Society, 1971).

22. Ibid., p. 307.
23. Ibid., p. 309.
24. Ibid., p. 311.
25. Ibid., pp. 311–12.
26. Ibid., p. 313.
27. Ibid., p. 315.
28. Ibid., p. 320.
29. Ibid., p. 321.
30. Ibid., p. 324.
31. Ibid., p. 325.
32. While many Stowe critics explicitly or implicitly describer her as a zealous reformer, Bromell is rare in detecting her skepticism about "reformist optimism": "Stowe's target [i.e., in her description of Haley's arrival at "'Christian perfection and political perfection'] here is a reformist optimism in progress and a reformist faith in rationality. She hints that when it is detached from its roots in human instincts and affections—that is from the heart—the work of self-cultivating and self-perfection . . . may turn out to be the devil's work in a new disguise." Brommell, *By the Sweat of the Brow*, p. 168.
33. Grant sees in Dinah's kitchen "a microcosmic slave system. . . . Only the good will and passion of individuals is capable of salvaging some good from the system—and then only temporarily." Grant, "*UTC* and the Triumph of Republican Rhetoric," p. 437. Brown finds that "the variable state of Dinah's kitchen exhibits the antithesis of domestic economy: the fluctuating marketplace . . . [with its] reign of desires without 'logic and reason' other an personal interest . . . " Brown, *Domestic Individualism*, p. 15.
34. Remember, Tom has only shown him the danger of *un*knowingly harming oneself. Does Tom assume the impossibility of the alternative suggested by Ophelia?
35. Arner uses St. Clare's mocking of the Declaration of Independence, as well as other aspects of the novel, to argue that Stowe intends him as a portrayal of the failure of Jeffersonian idealism. Robert D. Arner, "Jeffersonian Idealism and the Southern Frontier: A Reading of *Uncle Tom's Cabin*," in *New Historical Perspectives: Essays on the Black Experience in Antebellum America*, ed. Gene D. Lewis (Cincinnati: Friends of Harriet Beecher Stowe House and Citizens' Committee on Youth, 1984).
36. Stowe's usage of this term may have been independent of Carlyle's essay, but that is not likely. The word came into wide currency only about the time her novel was written. And Carlyle's essay, written only two to three years earlier, seems only the second literary usage of the term. In fact, the *Oxford English Dictionary* which seems to be the successor to Craigie's *Etymological Dictionary* lists an earlier Western usage as a letter of *Mrs. Carlyle's*, written subsequently to Carlyle's own essay! Obviously, too little attention had been paid to that essay! Further indication of the likelihood that Stowe read Carlyle's essay is found in Legree's echo ("And isn't he MINE? Can't I do what I like with him?" *UTC*, p. 467) of McQuirk's question about " . . . the 'right of property' so-called, and of doing what you like with your own [?]" Carlyle, pp. 324–25. Both authors in all likelihood make an ironic reference to the New Testament landowner's question: "Is it not lawful for me to do what I will with mine own?" (*Matthew* 20:15).

37. *UTC*, pp. 265–66.

38. Arner posits that "in making Augustine and Alfred amiable twins except where issues of equality are concerned, Mrs. Stowe surely meant to symbolize, among other things, the tragedy of a South divided against itself, or of the South and the North divided against each other over issues of equality and slavery." He also wonders whether the light and dark contrast of the twins "may be intended to suggest the theme of brotherhood of dark and light, as in the South the slave cannot be defined without the master, the black man understood without the white and *vice versa*." Arner, "Jeffersonian Idealism," pp. 73–74. Marks says that "the twins, one bathed now in the dawn of moral enlightenment and the other in the darkness of ethical and religious failure, are another paradoxical contrary . . . " Marks, "A Voice in Ramah," p. 206. To Bush, "These twins act as two sides of the same coin that we have already detected in George's character . . . " Bush, "The Declaration of Independence and *UTC*," p. 181.

39. *UTC*, pp. 256–65.

40. *UTC*, p. 262.

41. *UTC*, p. 263.

42. *UTC*, pp. 262–63.

43. *UTC*, pp. 263–64; that is, the violation of rights.

44. *UTC*, p. 244.

45. *UTC*, p. 266.

12

Myth Making and the End

The peculiarity of chapters 18 and 19 was that they revealed the soul of St. Clare although they bore the title, "Miss Ophelia's Experiences and Opinions." Her opinions are rather revealed in chapter 20, in which she undertakes the task of mothering the impish, unhabituated Topsy. What is crucial in her opinions—as in the superior education in the North—is not Ophelia's lingering prejudice but her willingness to learn.[1] That it takes the miraculous or mythical power of Eva to achieve *this* lesson shows not so much its impossibility as the difficulty to be encountered.

The reader might forgive the absence of a detailed examination of that chapter, as it further prepares the field for the work of the myth. But it is important to note Stowe's closing statement, in its bearing on the myth. Topsy "is fairly introduced into our *corps de ballet.*" This is one of the few elements of explicit direction in the novel. The other notable such element is the designation of Tom as our hero. In a ballet one seeks to convey a truth by situation and music—harmonies—rather than words. We read the author in those terms. Although Tom is the key to the novel, the major chord in the harmony is obviously Eva. Through her or from her we derive the standard by which we are enabled to judge the other elements.

We find a difficulty in the harmony, one that bespeaks a difficulty in the myth we are forced to articulate if we are to understand Eva. Shortly before her death, in the chapter of that title, Eva addresses the assembled slaves. She delivers a powerful homiletic in which she reveals their prospects and their duties. Her language is, "you must," "you can," "Jesus will." But the homiletic—and thus the harmony—falters when she says, "you must read—"

> The child checked herself, looked piteously at them, and said, sorrowfully, "O dear! you *can't* read, poor souls!" and she hid her face in the pillow and sobbed. . . . (330, original emphasis)

After she reconciles herself to the unfortunate circumstance of the slaves, she continues—but her speech has become largely conditional, protreptic. And she concludes uncertainly, "I *think* I shall see you all in heaven" (Emphasis added).

If we take the content of this speech as the substantive or didactic element of the myth, we can see that at its heart is the necessity for real, worldly, political change as a necessary component of the effectiveness of the myth.[2] And we know the possible gravity of the problem from Stowe's account of the forces that interrupt a harmony.[3] We should, therefore, be able to articulate the myth in the general or theoretical terms that will account for the origin of discord in the harmony. We will at least point toward an answer as to whether it is soluble—that is, whether the harmony is wholly marred by the defect in the myth.

This task is achieved in the chapters that comprise the ascents-descents of Eva and her father. As it also happens, it is in these chapters that Tom's soul is most fully revealed. He radiates in the light of the myth, and we are entitled to imagine that that is not an accident.

Chapter 21, "Kentuck," opens by returning us to Tom's original cabin. This is next to the last time we encounter it, for by the end of the chapter the cabin, it will be revealed, is "shut up."[4] Uncle Tom no longer has a hearth. The next time we meet it is in the end, when George Shelby, freeing the slaves, points to it as a symbol.

This chapter was occasioned by the receipt of a letter from Tom at the Shelby plantation, which letter disclosed his whereabouts and conditions and renewed his hope for a return. Mr. Shelby—sufficiently removed from a possibility of an ugly scene—fails just as we anticipated and now proves less accommodating to the idea of a repurchase. Mrs. Shelby gives up on him. And the author is liberated—free to admit that Mrs. Shelby is "in every way superior" to her husband in character. Both Haley and Shelby have been eliminated as humane, in anything other than an invidious fashion.[5] Shelby became a willing defender of the slave regime, and, without any reservations as to the souls of the slaves, he forthrightly maintains that the slaves should not be given "a morality above their conditions"—that is, no more than the situation requires of partial citizenship. In other words, he abandons a "positive good" defense for slavery, and freely stands on pure expediency—already refuted by this point. We, too, are free, then, free to turn to a counter-humanistic myth.

Let us directly confront the meaning of the myth, and let us do so from the point of view of its meaning for Tom—although it has a general meaning also. The question is directly raised, what does Eva mean for Tom? The author provides no direct response, but says that he "loves her as something frail and earthly"—mundane—and "worships her as something heavenly and divine." As for the meaning of Tom to Eva, nothing definitive is said. But we do learn something of their interaction in chapter 22. From a consideration of that we can come to know the meaning of the statement about Tom.

The first account follows the characteristic pattern. Eva reads the *Bible* to Tom. But she in some way excels all other readers. In the attempt to please her friend, she discovers a source of pleasure for herself. Though Tom brings her to the *Bible*, she possesses a ready sympathy.

The two attempt an exposition—particularly of the acts of "Revelation" and "Prophecies." They find no particular answer or assurance, but they delight in this unknown, mystic thing. The author here distinguishes the physical or natural sciences and the moral sciences. Natural science requires concrete understanding to be "profitable"; moral science does not. This results from the nature of the soul, which sees only dimly an eternal past and an eternal future but finds the present brightly illuminated. Matters of moral science seem to be rooted in dimensions inaccessible to the soul. Nonetheless, it is said the soul "must yearn" for these inaccessible realms, since it is in its nature to respond to their promptings.[6]

But those answers in the soul that correspond to the unknown eternity are expressed in a mystic imagery—a mythicism. The soul does not really read such ideas in the present, so much as it *saves* them through myth to be read when the soul enters the realm of darkness.

Before attempting to account for this highly abstract relation of the nature and purpose of human understanding, it is required to comprehend more fully the relationship of men—or at least the principal characters of the novel—to the illumination and understanding of the present. Beginning from the argument that the present is the realm of natural science, one expects it to be dominated by a vigorous naturalism perhaps contending with and overmastering this mythic tendency. This expectation seems to be given some support when we learn that genuine experience of the mystical relies on a stilling of the senses.[7] Eva "sees" the spirits bright in her sleep. But awake she finds them reflected in natural objects. It is, presumably, when one is awake that the living soul, always dominated by the present, is truly alive to this present.

Following this train of thought, we should expect the more worldly characters to find a vast field for action in the present and the other-worldly characters to contemn the present in anxious anticipation of eternity. Yet, St. Clare "cordially hated the present tense of action," while Ophelia can never imagine any time but "now" (353). "Now is the only time I have anything to do with," says Ophelia, after hearing St. Clare read of the "Last

Judgment" and informing him of the necessity to repent, presumably for the sake of an afterlife. We find a paradox: Ophelia, who lives by the ought, lives only in the present; St. Clare, who lives by the universal maybe, lives outside of himself and hence outside of time. His objectivity seems to alienate him from the realm of human action. Since Ophelia's actions are clearly grounded in moral science, though perhaps dependent upon natural science, she does not perceive that truth that shines only on the present. She needs to be told the ought. St. Clare is the closest thing to a natural scientist (excepting "Persistent Sam") we find in the novel, as his enlightened humanism reveals. But the truth he knows paralyzes him; it makes him incapable of action. He is like the great poets of the day who somehow know but do not pursue the truths of moral science *because* they fear the truths of natural science.[8]

The paradox deepens. The truth that shines in a light around the present seems not to be a truth about human action. But the eternal past and eternal future are dim, dark, and inaccessible to the soul living in the present. There seems to be no ground—no foundation—for human life in the present by definition. Eva's faltering in relating her myth seems necessary, if there is no comprehensive account of human existence. Tom's sophisticated agreement with St. Clare that "the whole world is as empty as an egg shell"—his emphatic "I know it" (344)—seems to condemn him as a hopeless visionary who rejects the world he knows only to long for a world he does not know. As Tom confesses, however, this vague yearning does produce a concrete result (345). He never surrenders to the despair this empty world would produce only because he *felt* that "the good Lord" stood by him. In Tom, the *effect* of the dim presences of past and future are always manifestly present—so strongly so that at neither the peak of his earthly happiness (361) nor at the peak of his earthly misfortune (365) do we find him focused primarily on worldly concerns. In the first case, after Tom was told of his impending freedom (349), he watched his master walk away from the manor for the last time, then seated himself in quiet, peaceful reflection. His mind turned first toward the future. One might be tempted to say the immediate future in order to distinguish it from the afterlife. But the immediate future will not be as Tom expects, since chance or heaven intervenes with the death of St. Clare prior to completion of the manumission. The dimness of the immediate future is indistinguishable from the dimness of the eternal future. They are in fact one.

Tom's thought of the future was a reflection upon the action in which he would engage; it centered on his will and the strength of his body. He would be able to return to his home "at will." He does not reflect upon the question, when he might will to return, for he is mindful of his voluntary pledge to save his master, taking as long as required. Tom will wish to return home only after he has completed the task he has already willed for himself. "Then he thought of his noble young master, and, ever second to that, came the habitual prayer that he had always offered for him" (361). Finally, he turns to Eva and, as such, to the past. Though he considers her in eternity, "among the angels," his reflections make her appear as she *was*. Only such reflection is capable of revealing past and future as an unbroken moment—the undifferentiated eternity in which the present is but the illusion of consciousness. Thus "musing, he fell asleep and dreamed he saw her coming bounding towards him, just as she used to come . . ."[9] (361).

Tom's reflections constitute an ascent, in terms of content. He starts from the most earthly of reflections—"the muscles of his brawny arms"—and ends in the mystic imagery that relies on the stilling of the senses by inducing sleep. In terms of true understanding it is still an ascent. But that is difficult to notice, because it is a descent in the human expression of understanding. By moving from the future to the past, he seems to proceed from what is least known to what is most known. And the events seem to bear this out. He will not be freed, his master is finally saved, and Eva was in heaven. But this does not correspond to Tom's own understanding. For he thought that he knew that he would be freed, he did not know that his master could be saved, and Eva only seemed to be in heaven. Hence, in terms of Tom's or human understanding this is a descent. That it is proved an ascent by the events shows only that the meaning of events transcend human understanding. Tom is justified rather by the events than by his reasoning about them—and also by his inclinations. He devoted the least time to the present, least active hope to the future (he will return "at will"), and least doubt to the past. Tom's prejudices and attachments are yet genuine, though somehow unreal, since they do not attach. There is no more love reserved for them than for others. In fact, we ascend toward Eva—our myth of the good—and therefore place the good, and a good work—St. Clare—before Tom's own family and future. We know that his reflections ascend, finally, because it is Eva that induces sleep and brings pleasant dreams. It seems, then, that *what* one thinks about, and the order, is of greater importance than what one actually thinks!

For Uncle Tom the present is not so much contemned as overshadowed. In the second peak—the disaster portended in St. Clare's death—we discover the basis of Tom's inclination toward the good. He does not reflect on what will become of him, nor even of his family. To him the present is not the dagger that hangs above his head, though clearly it does so. It is rather the salvation of St. Clare. His "whole soul was filled with thoughts of eternity"—the least knowable things. The light of the present was not on his soul. Tom's eternity is a present—the only present he genuinely knows. However dim its outlines, he formulates all actions and hopes on the basis of a standard derived from his "thoughts of eternity."

This prototype—ascendance from naturalism to mythicism—provides a parallel, or analogy, which may be employed to comprehend the myth of little Eva. We must remind ourselves, then, that the question is, what does Eva mean to Tom? We know that he loves her as something mundane or natural, hence limited, and he worships her as something heavenly or mystical. Tom does not convert Eva, as he does so many others. She believes by virtue of her nature. What, perhaps, distinguishes Eva's faith from Tom's is her almost deistic capacity to discover good in virtually everything natural. Eva knows that men, in particular, do bad things; *she cannot account for it.* But, we recall, moral science is profitable in a way natural science with only an imperfect understanding of the whole cannot be. Eva's weakness or femininity, then, does not mar her goodness or perfection, as Ophelia's weakness, were she to persist in it, would mar her goodness. *The* human weakness is the inability to grasp the whole. But that weakness becomes a source of disorder only when it is conjoined with the merely human strength or masculinity, doubt or skepticism (that is, the attempt to turn the human weakness, ignorance, into a virtue).[10] Now, that disorder becomes a source of terror when it is conjoined with the "light of the present," a light which we know from Uncle Tom to be false or misleading.

NOTES

1. See Grant on Miss Ophelia's transformation, chapter 11, note 14.

2. A surprising number of critics claim that Stowe does *not* advocate real, worldly, political change in *Uncle Tom's Cabin.* Examples include Romero ("Rebellion in *Uncle Tom's Cabin* is not a political act but rather the radical separation of the individual from all political activity"); Bardes ("the book offers no solution to the slavery problem . . . "); and Mason ("Stowe's novel throws the responsibility for reform onto the individual . . . [her] recommendations subvert her own analysis of slavery as a system by reducing its reform to a personal level. . . . Stowe's sensibility demands emancipation, but she sees it more as a matter of individual conscience and moral suasion than as a problem demanding social and political action"). Romero, "Bio-Political Resistance," p. 727. Barbara Bardes and Suzanne Gossett, *Declarations of Independence: Women and Political Power in Nineteenth-Century American Fiction* (New Brunswick: Rutgers University Press, 1990), p. 59. Jeffrey D. Mason, *Melodrama and the Myth of America* (Bloomington: Indiana University Press, 1993), pp. 103–4 (hereafter cited as *Melodrama and the Myth of America*).

Other critics, however, do recognize that Stowe's message includes political change. See, for example, Grant ("the novel would make its most significant contribution to political antislavery rhetoric by modeling a way to channel the various internal forces born from a love of liberty into a course for effective action . . . ") and Sundquist (*Uncle Tom's Cabin* is "deeply *political* in nature. . . . Both Stowe and Herman Melville . . . wrote epic novels that drove to the heart of American democracy by infusing everyday materials with highly charged political purpose" [original emphasis]).

Grant, "*UTC* and the Triumph of Republican Rhetoric," p. 433. Sundquist, *New Essays,* pp. 1, 2. Siebald recognizes both the political and apolitical aspects of the novel, stressing that *Uncle Tom's Cabin* "is a book with two very different purposes and achievements. It is a propaganda novel aiming at social and political solutions in this world and, at the same time, the story of a spiritual pilgrimage to heaven. Whoever wants to do justice to the book as a whole must read it both ways and find out how Mrs. Stowe reconciled these seeming opposites." Manfred Siebald, "Harriet Beecher Stowe: *Uncle Tom's Cabin* (1852)—Walking through Fire and Singing of Heaven": Harriett Beecher Stowe's Vision of Heaven," in *Journey to the Celestial City: Glimpses of Heaven from Great Literary Classics,* ed. Wayne Martindale (Chicago: Moody, 1995), p. 104.

3. Cf. p. 295: "So well is the harp of human feeling strung, that nothing but a crash that breaks every string can wholly mar its harmony."

4. *UTC,* pp. 295–96. Actually, this is revealed in the beginning of chapter 22, but the letter read there is written at the end of chapter 21.

5. Cf. pp. 42, 92, 148, and 152.

6. Cf. Plato, *Phaedrus,* 249b8ff. Stowe was familiar with this teaching (for example, she refers to it in *The Minister's Wooing*) and cited it as authoritative. Kerr discusses, in some depth, Stowe's interest in the spirit world. Howard Kerr, "'The Blessed Dead:' The Transformation of Occult Experience in Harriet Beecher Stowe's *Oldtown Folks,*" in *Literature and the Occult: Essays in Comparative Literature,* ed. Luanne Frank (Arlington: University of Texas at Arlington, 1977).

7. *UTC,* p. 299. Cf. *Oldtown Folks,* Ch. 17, for example.

8. *UTC,* p. 348; Cf. Calvin E. Stowe, *Origin and History of the Books of the Bible* (Hartford, CT: Hartford Publishing Co., 1867), Ch. 8, p. 258 (hereafter cited as *Origin and History*).

9. See book I, part II, chapter 18.

10. Cf. May: " . . . [Stowe] was forced increasingly to give up the search for complete understanding of God's ways. According to her own repeated statements, she was able to conclude, in the worst crisis of her life, that the mystery of God's dealing with men was swallowed up in the greater mystery of the love of Christ" (May refers here to an undated letter from Stowe to her sister Catharine). Henry F. May, introduction to *Oldtown Folks,* by Harriet Beecher Stowe (Cambridge, MA: Belknap Press of Harvard University Press, 1966), p. 20 (hereafter cited as "Introduction"). Caskey demonstrates that Calvin Stowe led the way in that search when he "told his congregations" and his wife "that men could never settle such [theological] questions and ought humbly to admit it." Caskey, *Chariots of Fire,* p. 182.

13

An Unaccountable Prejudice

What Eva—or the myth of Eva—means to Uncle Tom is revealed rather through his conduct than his speech. In himself lies the earthly harmony that is idealized through Eva. Because Tom, however, is not mythical in the drama of the novel (however much we might assert a myth of Tom), the harmony that is demonstrated through him must have overcome the defect in the myth of Eva. The necessity of real, worldly political change must be evident in Tom himself. His own blending of naturalism and mythicism must be superior to Eva's, in precisely the same way that his metaphysics must bear a correlative ethics—i.e., it must be able to account for the fact that men do bad things and, hence, the manner in which they do good things.

Before we complete the account of Tom's metaphysics and ethics, a digression may be permitted. It is easy to demonstrate that Tom has substantial effect in this world. We do not refer here to his "victory" over Simon Legree—a disputed achievement. We rather refer to the novel's conclusion, begun in the chapter entitled "Results." Even if the reader still reserves his judgment on the question as to which hero is the superior model, George or Tom, an incontestable fact remains. Stowe's celebrated conclusion, improbably tying together every strand of the story in a single harmony, above all else traces every delightful outcome and success of the novel to Tom's initial influence. Where, therefore, Tom has nothing to do with George's escape, per se, he bears considerable responsibility for aiding the escape of George's wife. In addition, he is largely responsible for the escape of Eliza's mother,[1] thus setting afoot the train of events which bring George together with his sister—now become wealthy. George Harris's subsequent study in

Paris, worldly success, and venture to Liberia (from where the reader will "yet hear from him") remain tied to the sacrifices of Uncle Tom. In addition, Tom's moral education of young George Shelby bears the fruit of emancipation for Tom's many fellows on the Shelby plantation. The only result not tied to Tom, Ophelia's success with Topsy in Vermont, is, however, a direct result of Eva's influence.[2] Hence, Tom's refusal to accept slavery for anyone other than himself—if he accepted it for himself!—bore fruit for liberty.[3] George Shelby speaks for Stowe as well as himself when, freeing the slaves, he reminds them to "think that you owe it to that good soul."[4]

Critics may be right to suggest that all of the "everything ended happily" is too much for one novel—not to mention the shoulders of one man. It is dramatically unsound,[5] save in the situation where the requirements of the drama—themselves the result of aesthetic humanism[6]—are strictly subordinated to the grandeur of the principles defended. In that case, it were petty, nay, a crime, to do less!

The grandeur of Tom's metaphysics is expressed in earthly terms through his optimistic view that this is not the best of all possible worlds. This view contrasts strongly with St. Clare's cultivated pessimism: any other possible worlds could only be worse. This is the very pessimism which John, the Drover, most feared. It is refutable only insofar as the earthly superiority of Tom's view is demonstrable in deed. But what means might Tom possess that Eva did not to free his view from the defect of the myth? Why does he not falter when he regards the condition of the slaves, as did Eva? Perhaps conditions were too mild in the St. Clare home, and the more mature Tom less impressed by what seemed difficult. That would only require the Legree plantation—the ultimate test. Under conditions in which the slaves were literally reduced to the level of beasts, would he still not falter? Tom did not. Hence we know that he is better prepared.

What Tom possessed, that Eva did not, was the knowledge of natures; he knew of what things men were individually capable.[7] We have discussed this knowledge of natures above. We saw how it informed Tom's judgment of the moral demands to be made of others. But how might it relate to his metaphysics? The ultimate test would surely be to apply it to a soul such as his own! If Tom were to judge the nature of someone capable of his own surpassing excellence (or nearly so) and, in addition, to provide moral guidance for him, Tom must surely reveal to him the bridge between naturalism and mythicism. Such an *élève* was Augustine St. Clare. And the supreme test of Tom's knowledge of natures is his knowledge and command of St. Clare. The ultimate test of Tom's knowledge of nature precedes the ultimate test of the capacity of the mythicism—of his moral hardheadedness.

The same problem is accounted for on the novel's surface in the recognition that St. Clare's wish to care for his slaves is thwarted by the fact of Tom's superior caring for St. Clare. That Tom cares for St. Clare is problematic under the circumstances, but becomes doubly so when we recognize that Tom has an "unaccountable prejudice in favor of liberty" (369).[8] Ordinarily, a slave who recognizes the value of liberty eventually recognizes his relationship to his master as antithetical to liberty. Tom's love of liberty seems unaccountable—literally, not just sarcastically—because of his care for St. Clare.[9] If he truly loves liberty, his care for his master is not a badge of slavery. The apparent contradiction seems reconcilable only insofar as we doubt Tom's servitude. On the surface of the novel, consideration of Tom's knowledge of St. Clare's nature and of his command of St. Clare seem to require a denial of Tom's servitude to accompany the account of his metaphysics.

Let me state the content of the teaching frankly. Afterwards we may review Tom's attempt to govern St. Clare. Liberty is not an intellectual conception. At least, Tom's conception of liberty focuses almost entirely on the disposition of the body—the power to use the body to some purpose. There can evidently be degrees of liberty. Tom's love of liberty is a love of the power to dispose his own body—his own things. One's soul alone is capable of disposing one's body, apart from the intervention of a second party.[10] Thus far we do not disagree with St. Clare's definition of liberty, save that he conceived the liberty rather to reside in the *irresponsibility* of the willing soul—not to have to answer to another for one's choices. Tom's sense of liberty plays its part in overcoming the defect of the myth of Eva. The blending of naturalism and mythicism depends upon acknowledgment of an inherent power to dispose natural things. The counterpart to the intellectual ascent from naturalism to mythicism is an acute awareness of a connection between the natural body and the soul: the awareness that every opportunity for the soul is grounded in some specific possible disposition of the body. It profits little to commune with the soul's urgings, if one does not communicate with one's natural body or things without the intervention of a second body.

Tom's love of liberty is accounted for; it is the love of ruling his own body with his own soul. This does not, however, explain the manner in which he actually deals with the physical nature and circumstances he confronts. The original of all dispositions of natural bodies must surely be self-preservation. That seems to require placing the preservation of one's own body—self-interest—before all other good things. Tom subordinates self-interest to benevolence on the foundation of the lessons of moral science. Tom denies that he must choose to preserve his own body or things *before* he chooses any other good thing. Liberty presupposes the body's existence and, hence, its preservation in the instance of its existence. It does not make preservation an end. Self-preservation is a disposition of natural bodies, which is prior to liberty temporally if not logically. As such it is a subject not of moral science but of natural science.

Tom does not disregard the body; his regard begins where the moral significance of the body begins. Because the truths of moral science are directed toward the present, so far as action is concerned, they remain connected with natural science. That is, the counterpart of natural science's imperfect understanding of the whole is that less than perfect concern with the body that is required to give room to the works of the soul. Tom's attachment to earthly things, his love of liberty, is for the sake of his morality.

The body is a vehicle for the soul's endeavors. The exact concern with the body that is recommended is that which stops short of imagining that the body is the whole of being; or which remains unimpaired by skepticism as to the existence of a transcendent reality. The claims of the body must never be recognized as of sufficient breadth to describe the universe. It follows that one's attachment to one's own things is informed by rather than informs a transcendent reality.

An account of the ways of men, insofar as it distinguishes them on the basis of their attachments, disregards the true foundations of human life. Such an account regards the exception as the rule. Only the pretense that natural science is sufficient to the account of the ways of men has permitted thus obscuring the foundations of life. Comprehensive natural science is blind rather than illuminating, shining rather more upon the observer's understanding than upon the object of observation.

Moral science deals with the dim outlines of the past and future. It is never complete. Its force as the organizing principle for natural science, therefore, is rather derived from its independent status in nature than from demonstration of truths. It is the science of man. It suffices to generate beliefs. Beliefs suffice to rule natural science or, what is the same, dispositions of the body. Every concrete deed as such is conditional, though the principle which informs the deed be precise. Because St. Clare reversed this relationship, he treated the principles of choice and action as conditional, while regarding the deeds themselves as firm or absolute. Thus, his moral paralysis: the paradox of sustaining deeds—irresponsible will—that are not nor can be justified in principle. The blending of naturalism and mythicism is designed to free men from their dependence on natural science for a comprehensive account of human ways and, hence, to wean them from utopian expectations of a natural hierarchy.

Uncle Tom does not contradict himself. He may care for St. Clare without abandoning his love of liberty. In addition, though formally a slave he need not yield to servitude where circumstances permit him to rule. Tom's influence with St. Clare in the ordinary sense commenced shortly after his arrival in the household. He came to be the manager and the one trusted to come and go with money, as he had been on the Shelby plantation. But Tom soon attempted what he never did with Shelby, as far as we know. Having cared for St. Clare's debauched remains after an evening of wild conviviality, Tom was disturbed by the indulgence he witnessed. Next morning, in all docility and humility, he lay siege to St. Clare's conscience. On his knees and with tears in his eyes, he held fast until he won St. Clare's pledge of honor that he would be "good to himself." In the dramatic history the event was minor. But it was pregnant with significance for the major challenges to come. Tom broached his lecture on doing harm to oneself while still uncertain as to his influence. Thus, as he delivered the charge he turned to the door and grabbed the doorknob.

It was St. Clare who revealed that Tom could try more and practically invited the tearful scene that followed. For his response to Tom, "O, that's all, is it?" went farther than Tom expected. "O that's all!" would have dismissed Tom. "Is it?" recalled him. This event occurred before Eva's death and establishes Tom's authority independently of Eva's influence. When the loss of Eva greatly increased St. Clare's dependence on Tom, Tom's moral authority and his daring likewise soared.

Though St. Clare had two moral difficulties to confront, how to regard slavery and how to regard his own salvation, Tom focused only on the latter. The two, however, were not independent, and St. Clare's maturing conception of his moral responsibilities to his slaves paralleled his maturing conception of religious duties.

Augustine reveals the first concrete change in his view of the morality of slavery in the final thematic discussion of the "right of the stronger."[11] Augustine comes to realize that his wish to care for his slaves does not mitigate the injustice of slavery—he can no more make the lives of his slaves "better than freedom" than could Emily Shelby (349). The key to this change is the switch from a philosophic mode of expression to a largely biblical mode of expression. He indulges a reference to "All men are born free and equal," but this is rather to suggest its apparent inadequacy as catechism (306). Augustine's view of the relationship between deed and principle is changing. All life, he holds, is a matter of habituation—education.

> "Our system is educating them (the slaves) in barbarism and brutality. We are breaking all humanizing ties, and making them brute beasts; and, if they get the upper hand, such shall we find them." (307)

"All men are born free and equal" is not wrong; it is simply insufficient to inform deeds.

It is Alfred, Augustine's twin brother, who introduces the Gospel, but mockingly. "*Dies declarabit*" scorns Augustine's own "*dies irae.*" There can be no other purpose for the sole Latin rendering of the *New Testament* in the novel. The passage from *1 Corinthians* affirms that all deeds will ultimately be seen in the light of their principles.[12] And ultimately that is good enough for Alfred. In some sense, the same is true of Augustine. For, though he thinks human life on beastly principles wrong, he does not conceive of any alternatives. The "rising masses" merely represent a coming reversal in the sources of right. Alfred's dependence on "Anglo-Saxon blood" to keep the masses down is turned by Augustine into a syllogism. "There is a pretty fair infusion of Anglo-Saxon blood among our slaves now." And if it be true that the Anglo Saxon is superior, which judgment only by appearances may suggest (308),[13] then a system that infuses inferiors with Anglo Saxon blood creates equality in spite of itself. The irresistible principle of might makes right will override convention. The rising must come, whether by the light of natural rights and the equality of man or by the light of the right of the stronger.

Upon this ground does St. Clare turn to biblical principles, suggesting fundamental error in the principles as more compelling than the fear of consequences. When Alfred reaffirms the will to command, St. Clare applies the "proverb" that rule of others demands rule of oneself. And when Alfred concedes this flaw in the system—suggesting a northern education for his son, or drawing upon freedom for the preservation of despotism—St. Clare triumphs with the suspicion that something is amiss, "since training children is the staple work of the human race."[14] Since Alfred feels no embarrassment about drawing advantages from considerations of relative morality, however, St. Clare must reveal his full principle: it is not "Christian-like!"

St. Clare gains the rhetorical victory. Alfred therefore challenges him to act upon the basis of his wisdom. He might begin by educating his "own servants"—the necessity of which he now grants. But St. Clare has not matured thus far.

> "One man can do nothing, against the whole action of a community. Education, to do anything, must be a state education; or there must be enough agreed in it to make a current." (309)

Although Augustine no longer makes the humanistic exception based on cultural relativism, his humanity still suffers a weakness. *He has not learned that it is not necessary to await a noble regime before attempting a noble deed.* On the other hand, neither does he add anything to the prophecies of *Revelation*. He is eligible for salvation. Tom rightly concentrates on this, in spite of Alfred's shrewd retort to the last remark—he is the master of irony in the novel—"you take the first throw," which took the brothers into a game of backgammon!

St. Clare's views on slavery matured further, as he responded to challenges from Eva, Ophelia, and his own wonderings.[15] He finally resolved to free Tom, fulfilling his promise to the dying Eva, and the other slaves. The process of manumission, for Tom at least, was begun. But the deed was not done. St. Clare still wondered what might be the consequence of acting on his principles (359–60). His uncompromising moral judgment stopped just short of hardheadedness. Before he could arrive at the summit he was dead (360–63). Lightheartedly we find good fortune in that. For, had St. Clare really turned to good and survived to prosecute it, much of the luster of Tom's heroism need have been lost. There are advantages in the possession of conventional status!

St. Clare's salvation came on his deathbed, under the inspiring regard of Uncle Tom.[16] Tom struggled manfully to ensure that salvation. After Eva's death, Tom sought out St. Clare. In the passage in which Tom affirms the annihilation of St. Clare's worldly understanding—"this whole world is as empty as an egg shell"—we find Tom struggling with St. Clare concerning the extent of their respective knowledges. The word "struggle" is perhaps a bit melodramatic. A struggle emerges only after St. Clare is brought to the point of crisis. At this point he but resignedly affirms a prevailing skepticism in the face of Tom's reaffirmation of a superior understanding. Tom meets St. Clare on St. Clare's ground—the realm of the present and natural—but ironically. He agrees that the world is "as empty as an egg shell," but not necessarily so empty as an empty eggshell. St. Clare does not yet see clearly that the possible life contained in an unbroken eggshell is at once empty and full. It is the emptiness in worldly terms of an unbroken eggshell that Tom affirms (344–45).

In order to move St. Clare Tom employs two approaches, which reflect his own position. He likens St. Clare's circumstances to his own—he makes a confession. And he employs his conventional method of conversion, getting St. Clare to read to him from "all that remained of this world" (345–47). In the first case Tom stretches the truth, for he claims signs of weakness that are not in fact present in the novel.

> "[W]hen I was sold away from my old woman and the children, I was jest a'most broke up. I felt as if there warn't nothin' left; and then the good Lord, he stood by me, and he says, 'Fear not, Tom;' and he brings light and joy into a poor feller's soul,—makes all peace; and I's so happy, and loves everybody, and feels willin' jest to be the Lord's, and have the Lord's will done, and be put jest where the Lord wants to put me. I know it couldn't come from me, cause I's a poor, complainin' cretur; it comes from the Lord; and I know He's willin to do for Mas'r." (345)

Tom's intimate intercourse with the Lord is no more incredible than his self-deprecation, for we never once see him complaining in the novel. And it has its effect in Augustine's immediate response, "Tom, you love me," which is both wondering recognition and question. Tom does not reply, "yes," to this question—declining further to adapt the truth to the circumstances. He responds instead that he is "willin' to lay down my life, this blessed day, to see Mas'r a Christian" (345).

Tom's system of seduction was by then readied for use. In his helplessness and docility he called upon "Mas'r" to please read "this" for him, as "Miss Eva used to do" so beautifully. Upon reading the miracle of the resurrection of Lazarus, St. Clare challenged Tom, in effect, "How can you believe this?" Tom replied that he could even "see" it. He does not reveal that he sees with other than worldly optics.

> "But, Tom, you know that I have a great deal more knowledge than you; what if I should tell you that I don't believe this Bible?" [which Augustine has already done before]. "O Mas'r!" said Tom, holding up his hands with a deprecating gesture. "Wouldn't it shake your faith some, Tom?" "Not a grain," said Tom. "Why, Tom, you must know that I know the most." "O, Mas'r, haven't you jest read how he hides from the wise and prudent and reveals unto babes.[17] But Mas'r wasn't in earnest, for sartin, now?" said Tom, anxiously. (346)

The editor of the Oxford edition of *Uncle Tom's Cabin* points out the inconsistency between Tom's reference to a passage suggesting the incapacity of the "wise and watchful" for divine understanding, and the explicit claim of the text that St. Clare had read from *John* 11—the "account of the raising of Lazarus."[18] But we may justifiably remind ourselves that the context is the struggle between Tom and Augustine over respective knowledges. It would not be amiss to recognize the necessity for Tom to claim no more for himself than suffices to St. Clare's conversion.

In that light we note with interest that the present passages began with Tom's quoting the same passage from *Matthew*, but without specific attribution. When he subsequently claims that St. Clare had just read the passage, it is at least true that St. Clare had just "heard" it. And in that context—Tom refusing to relent before Augustine's superior "knowledge" and asserting his own mastery—it seems that Tom completely melds into one his application of biblical text and the text itself. That allows him to state his claim to understanding in the extreme degree, without confronting Augustine with the gulf that divides them.

This may be an entirely fanciful account, but it derives peculiar support from an odd turn in the text that the Oxford editor did not note. But ten pages later, in the same chapter, the account of St. Clare's death, St. Clare engaged Ophelia in a melancholy discussion centering on the precise question of "last judgment," as that is related in *Matthew* 11 and 25.[19] It was he that introduced the text. And his questioning soul comes to appreciate the nature—if not the extent—of Tom's wisdom.

> "What a sublime conception is that of a last judgment!" said he,—"a righting of all the wrongs of past ages!—a solving of all moral problems, by an *unanswerable* wisdom! It is, indeed, a wonderful image." (357, emphasis added)

The questioning soul, however, does not long to end its questions—to obtain "unanswerable wisdom." That is rather the character of soul of the good or wise, who, because of superior ability or insight, question reluctantly and wish to avoid questions. Such questions produce a paralysis in the soul—erode the foundation of action.[20] The questions return to St. Clare, although he is measurably beyond his initial moral perspective. In effect, he begins to understand though not entirely to heed his *"Dies Irae."*

Those lyrics, which plague his mind with Latin sonority, in the end turn out to be the foundation of Tom's confession. The author provided the standard translation, which she acknowledged to be "inadequate." The invitation to the reader to provide a better translation provides a measure of the distance between St. Clare and Tom:

> *Recordare Jesu pie*
> *Quod sum causa tuae viae*
> *Ne me perdas, illa die*
> *Querens me sedisti lassus*
> *Redemisti crucem passus*
> *Tantus labor non sit cassus.*
>
> Think, O Jesus, for what reason
> Thou endured'st earth's spite and treason,
> Nor me lose, in that dread season;
> Seeking me, thy worn feet hasted,
> On the cross thy soul death tasted,
> Let not all these toils be wasted.
>
> Think, O Jesus that I am the reason of your ways.
> Nor do you lose me, that day.
> Complaining and fatigued you have soothed me.
> You have redeemed the cross. A step
> So great should not be hollow labor. (356–57 and note)

The new body of humanism is fastened to the skeleton of Christianity, without forswearing the objectives of grace and personal salvation. The death and salvation of St. Clare—apart from "works"—reaffirm the traditional Christian view of the centrality of repentance, at the same time that the instrumentality of Tom in that salvation affirms an application of otherworldly principle in this world.

It is in this same chapter—between accounts of doctrine, as it were—that Augustine informs Tom of Tom's impending emancipation. After the exchange in which Tom decidedly declares for liberty and distinguishes the natural condition from concern with death and material well-being, St. Clare tacitly reveals his increasing dependence on Tom. He rather mournfully reflected on Tom's departure. But Tom reassured him that he, Tom, could not leave "while Mas'r is in trouble." Willing to stay for as long as St. Clare might wish or require, Tom freely committed himself to the good of another—to see "St. Clare a Christian." Tom engaged himself, perhaps for the rest of his life, without stopping to consider that, perhaps he was freely choosing never to see his wife and children again.[21] Not even Christian's singular abandonment of a reluctant family, in his search for the "city on a Mighty Hill," is comparable in its degree of transcendence of one's own things! The ethics of the myth of Tom seem rooted in a cosmopolitanism so obtuse to distinctions founded on relationship as to call into question every conceivable form of community as such.[22] In their defense, however, it may be that such ethics are called into being in opposition to a cosmopolitanism that regards but cannot defend distinctions founded on relationship. If the system of self-preservation and self-interest, which only permit an arbitrary or irrational attachment to one's own, is to be replaced by a system of benevolence, a necessary casualty seems to be the preference of one's own welfare—the welfare of one's own—to the welfare of others.[23]

The conversion of St. Clare reveals the force and foundation of Tom's benevolence to the fullest. Tom's benevolence, in turn, reveals the unaccountable nature of Tom's love of liberty. Only in the final chapters do we encounter the dramatic or historical form of that transcendence which is yet compatible with liberty. Tom's attachment to, or rather, preference of his family over a good deed would have depended on the certainty of his returning home as much as any other present hope-future prospect. We saw above how ill founded was that hope. We have not seen how Tom's particular character of soul enabled him to deal with the consequences to himself. That is, we have not considered how suitable Tom's ethics are to the human necessity to abide with chance. St. Clare's chance and premature death constitutes the moment of truth for Tom.

It is the addition of the influence of chance, alone, which sharpens Tom's benevolent cosmopolitanism, his moral science, into an ethical system not founded on relationship.[24] And by "chance," of course, nothing more is meant than the realm of natural bodies and the forces to which they are subject.

> Tom turned away; his heart was full. The hope of liberty, the thought of distant wife and children, rose up before his patient soul, as to the mariner shipwrecked almost in port rises the vision of the church-spire and loving roofs of

> his native village, seen over the top of some black wave only for one last farewell. He drew his arms tightly over his bosom and choked back the bitter tears, and tried to pray. The poor old soul had such a singular, unaccountable prejudice in favor of liberty, that it was a hard wrench for him; and the more he said, "Thy will be done." the worse he felt. (369)

Through the analogy employed in this passage, we can see the strength of Tom's attachments. But I submit that his tears are rather for his liberty—now threatened—than his family. His unaccountable prejudice is his *one* unconquered prejudice. It is controlled, by circumstance, but not conquered. Indeed, as matters worsened Tom ruminated the possibility of escape. His unconquered prejudice must be a necessity: commitment and transcendence require free will. In that case, however, Tom had never been really enslaved; he had always exercised free will, benevolence as his standard. Tom may be the hero of the novel because he is designed to demonstrate to John, the Drover, that no man need be a slave. Tom is higher than those who have their souls submit to the body's chains, even as his body is enchained. He is the hero because he's never been a slave! That this is the correct interpretation is revealed when Tom arrives at the Legree plantation and reverses the force of the above analogy. The circumstances are the same, but he imagines others as *lost to him* rather than himself lost to them.

> The foreshadowing of a whole life of future misery, the wreck of all past hopes, mournfully tossing in the soul's sight, like dead corpses of wife, and child, and friend, rising from the dark wave, and surging in the face of the half-drowned mariner! (399)

Our mariner Tom placed everyone else back amid the fatal wreckage of the ship earth, and regards himself as only "half-drowned" in the very case that is ordinarily considered annihilation. Of these two perspectives, the latter is the perspective of the free man.

NOTES

1. See chapter 9, note 8.
2. But remember, unlike so many others, Ophelia required only to be shown the "ought," not the "how."
3. MacFarlane entirely misses the point: "Tom's journey south leads paradoxically to physical enslavement and spiritual freedom. . . . Tom's failure to achieve political freedom seems in the novel to be almost a result of being African and feminized." Lisa Watt Macfarlane, "If Ever I Get to Where I Can: The Competing Rhetorics of Social Reform in *Uncle Tom's Cabin*," *ATQ* n.s. 4 (1990): 139.
4. *UTC*, p. 501. For the other examples, see pp. 488–501.

5. But not melodramatically unsound. See the defense of melodrama in book II, part I.

6. But, think, who would dare question the propriety of Vicenzio's resolution of the entanglements of *Measure for Measure*?

7. Cf. Brooks: "Saying one's one and one another's moral nature is an important part of melodrama's action and substance." Brooks, *The Melodramatic Imagination*, p. 37.

8. Rhodes, a historian and not a literary critic, is rare in his notice of this prejudice of Tom's and points out that this prejudice was widespread among slaves: "Even had the material condition of the slaves been as good as the apologists of slavery were in the habit of asserting, the eagerness of nearly every negro for liberty was a grave indictment of the system. One of the finest touches in *Uncle Tom's Cabin* is the joyful expression of Uncle Tom when told by his good and indulgent master that he should be set free. . . . In attributing the common desire of humanity to the negro, the author was as faithful as she was effective." James Ford Rhodes, *History of the United States from the Compromise of 1850 to the McKinley-Bryan Campaign of 1896*, 8 vols. (Port Washington, NY: Kennikat Press, Inc., reissue, 1967), vol. 1, p. 377.

9. *UTC*, pp. 349, 357, 365, & 369.

10. Cf. Boreham: "All through the book, Uncle Tom talks of himself as a soul—a divine, immortal and redeemed soul; a soul . . . can never be the property of any earthly owner. . . . You can no more buy a soul than you can buy a seraph." F. W. Boreham, *The Gospel of Uncle Tom* (London: The Epworth Press, 1956), p. 16.

11. This discussion comes in chapter 23, the central chapter. The final *dramatic* discussion is Tom's confrontation with Legree—Tom emerges as stronger, driving Legree into the *impotence* of insanity. The stronger do or may rule, but not systematically. That is the upshot of the myth of Tom.

12. "The deed of each will be brought to light; the day will make it clear."

13. Provided we conceive the deed rather than the principle to be absolute.

14. Cf. book II, part II.

15. *UTC*, pp. 317, 348, & 352–54.

16. See discussion in book I, part II, chapter 18, of Lieber's account of these events.

17. *Matthew* 11:25 and *Luke* 10:2.

18. *UTC*, p. 346, n. 1.

19. The "righting of all the wrongs of the ages" seems to come from *Matthew* 11, while condemnation "for not doing positive good" comes from *Matthew* 25, especially verse 35ff.

20. *UTC*, pp. 348 & 359.

21. Saunders falls short of comprehending the scope of Tom's ethics when she says, "Stowe portrays Tom as thinking of himself more as a part of the larger plantation family than as the head of his biological family or a member of a community made up of slaves alone." She does not see that is it the human family, in its entirety, to which he sees himself belonging. Saunders, "Houses Divided," p. 424.

22. But, we must not forget, the myth of Eva as articulated through Tom shows attachment to one's own to be rooted in knowledge of the present—a concern of the moment.

23. This general understanding of the thrust of modern liberalism is conveyed eloquently in Luc Ferry, *Man Made God* (Chicago: University of Chicago Press, 2002), translated from the original, *L'Homme-Dieu, ou Le Sens de la vie* (Paris: Grasset, 1996).

24. It follows, of course, that where familial distinctions become subordinate, less immediate distinctions such as race or *ethnos* become still more subordinate.

14

Triumph

We have considered Tom's "declaration of independence" above. As in the case of George Harris, it is the expression penultimate to the final refusal to surrender to slavery.[1] And, as George's "declaration" is preceded by an antepenultimate anticipation,[2] there is a parallel in the story of Tom. The point of chapter 33 is Tom's resistance to Legree. We may have more correctly declared resistance to Legree to be the point of chapters 30 through 40. For it is in the initial chapter of this series that it is said of Tom, "He had a master!" in spite of his *own* judgment, upon surveying the crowd of bidders attending the auctioning of St. Clare's estate, that there was not present a single man "whom he would wish to call master." And it is in the final chapter of this series that Tom's "victory" over Legree is consummated in the form of heightened consciousness—consciousness-cum-conscience. Tom's *conscience-raising* demonstrates its power in reclaiming the previously imbruted Sambo and Quimbo and in lighting the fire of Legree's fatal insanity.

> Yes, Legree; but who shall shut up that voice in thy soul? that soul, past repentance, past prayer, past hope, in whom the fire that never shall be quenched is already burning! (472)

Stowe's unchristian-like conclusion of the utter loss of Legree's soul directly contradicts Tom's plea for Legree's repentance. This points to a distinction between the hero and the author, which completely accounts for Tom's resistance and the character of his *conscience-raising*.

Legree is not a man to the author. He is always regarded as beyond redemption precisely because he is but a form of consciousness the foundation of which is refuted in the person of Tom.[3] Stowe does not deny the

Lord's forgiveness, she disagrees with the notion of an elect,[4] and it is she who has Tom implore Legree to repent. What she sees, therefore, is still more comprehensive than what Tom may see. The drama requires this massive intrusion of her own perspective. To her Legree is rather the "work of the law" than a man, and such law can only be overcome—it cannot be saved. The fire that is burning is the coming revolution, the overthrow of law. Thus, Stowe does not really undercut Tom. Where Tom speaks to the man—the human potentiality—Stowe speaks only to the institution[5]—the form of consciousness.

Legree becomes Tom's master by convention only. We have in this story the very model of the failure of the right of the stronger—in the form of law—to create the basis of human conscience. Tom judged that none of his prospective buyers was in fact a master to him. And we are entitled to inquire whether his finding a master did not depend, *à la mode de* Hegel, on his own consciousness of being mastered. If so, the Hegelian principle has been adapted to the refutation of Hegel by virtue of the dichotomy between legal or conventional slavery and actual slavery, and the resulting denial of a historical basis for the master-slave development of consciousness. That is, consciousness is independent of circumstances insofar as the objective consciousness is a product of the subjective consciousness. Only if subjective consciousness were wholly produced by objective consciousness—environmental determinism—could it then be said that consciousness emerges from circumstances. In addition, that consciousness would always be present or momentary—even in the absolute moment—and there could be no unfolding history, i.e., historical or trans-temporal consciousness, strictly speaking.

Masters and slaves as such, then, would be ephemera without significance. For transcending or overcoming depends on the possibility of a historical or non-momentary consciousness, one not only formed by circumstance but also preserved with reference to circumstance. Even the slave who becomes a master must become a master with reference to having been a slave. This rigidity, nay, ritual of role and type is refuted in the model of Tom, wherein it becomes clear that the transaction of consciousness between master and slave is not two-fold but four-fold. It is insufficient for each to recognize—impute—the special characteristic of the other, since the doing so presupposes what is not self-evident, the recognition of the special characteristic of oneself quite apart from the imputation of another and hence with regard to every possible other. That is, each is always master and slave in potential, and only accidentally either in fact. Consciousness as such derives from the recognition of the accidental as accidental and hence the resulting discovery of the relationship between the subjective consciousness and the objective consciousness.

I wish to make clear that I do not consider *Uncle Tom's Cabin,* nor even the work of Calvin Stowe, an attempt to articulate the philosophy of Hegel.

This is not a dialogue with Hegel insofar as no pretense whatever is made to answer his every point or every significant point. But it is equally clear that this *one* problem—recognized as deriving from Hegel—is seen as needing a solution. Its relationship to *Uncle Tom's Cabin* is also clear. We prove below that Calvin Stowe made a substantial contribution to the novel. Calvin's concern with Hegel is manifest and provable in his own work. These two facts could be admitted and yet be thought to be independent. But that is not the case. In the precise chapters we consider we find a textual connection with Calvin's attack on "the Hegelian philosophy."[6] In his attack Calvin Stowe characterized "the Hegelian philosophy" analytically as the complete identification of the perceiving subject and the perceived object.

> Admitting this as a fundamental principle, what is God? Is God the creator of man, or is man the creator of God?[7] The latter of course. The human mind is the only development of God,—only by the workings of the human soul does God arrive at self-consciousness; and if there were no men there would be no God, as there can be no color without an eye, and no sound without an ear. There seems to be recognized a sort of *natura naturans*, a sort of blind, unconscious, fermenting leaven, constantly working; but this never attains to personality or consciousness except in the human soul. ("The Four Gospels . . . ," 509 and also *Origin & History*, 260)

I have quoted Calvin Stowe's critique of Hegel at length in spite of the fact that the skepticism it describes is by now a cliché in the ears of modern philosophy. I quote it at length that we may say what the poetic (as opposed to analytic) characterization of "the Hegelian philosophy" is intended to convey.

> I have been admonished more than once to treat this philosophy with respect, to admire it at least as an "exquisite work of art if not a system of absolute truth." I shall do my best in this particular. I have acknowledged before, and here repeat the acknowledgement, that I have no very definite knowledge of it. It stands before me, in its bulk, and its unintelligibleness, as a huge, shapeless, threatening spectre, most fitly described in the words of Virgil" *Monstrum horrendum, informe, ingens, cui lumen adeptum.*" (A monster, horrid, hideous, huge and blind.) ("The Four Gospels . . . ." 508 and *Origin & History*, 258–259)

The precise Virgilian passage adapted by Calvin to the Hegelian *corpus* is adapted by Stowe in the opening of chapter 30 of *Uncle Tom's Cabin*, the account of the slave warehouse. What might the reader of the novel imagine a slave warehouse to resemble?

> They fancy some foul, obscure den, some horrible *Tartarus 'informis, ingens, cui lumen ademptum.'*[8] (372)

As the reader of these two passages immediately perceives, the application of Virgil is markedly different in each case. Stowe continues to reveal that the reader must not expect evil to come dressed in the role. While Calvin continues to reveal the imposing danger of Hegelian blindness, eventuating in the charge, "Atheistic liberty is the worst kind of tyranny" ("Four Gospels . . . ," 510 and *Origin & History*, 258–59). Nonetheless, it is surely a remarkable coincidence—all the more so since their purposes seem to differ—if Stowe and Calvin both found the applicability of the identical passage in Virgil quite independently. That they have not done so is revealed by the significance in each case of Virgil's description of Polyphemus. Nor may it be said that Calvin copies Stowe, for he cites Virgil *exactly*. Stowe, on the other hand, is forced to change the text. Virgil's *informe*, a neuter adjective, has to be changed to the masculine *informis* for the sake of agreement with the *Tartarus*, which replaces *monstrum*. Calvin's citation must have come no less directly from Virgil than Stowe's. And we are left to conjecture who inspired this happy coincidence. Where linguists write the one-tongued, like the one-eyed, can but lamely follow.

Polyphemus is the cyclops of Odyssean legend who, after having his single eye expunged, is described by Virgil as a horrid monster. The darkness in which he wandered is as necessary to his monstrousness as his shapeless gigantism. The connection between this account of "the Hegelian philosophy" and *Uncle Tom's Cabin* is found in the source and character of this darkness. In "the Hegelian philosophy" this is *produced* by the notion of subjective determination of objective fact—or, the discovery that human lights are the *only* lights of understanding and reality. Hence, the darkness is a moral darkness—an incapacity to relate the human things in any terms broader than immediate circumstance and conditioning. We have already seen the blinding force of human lights—the "light of the present"—in *Uncle Tom's Cabin*. There is, in addition, the characterization of Tom's transition to Legree's plantation as a transition to inhabiting "dark places."[9] Tom, you see, leaves the light of *St. Clare*. But the darkness of Legree's farm is imparted less by the dense tropical foliage that surrounds it than by the identical moral darkness Calvin Stowe finds in "the Hegelian philosophy." It is most significant that *all* of Tom's moral instruction on the plantation takes place at night, sometimes without even the light of a candle. Stowe agrees with Calvin: the dark place is but a space in the mind—consciousness willfully narrowed to a single principle, "the determinate force of will" (457). Whether Calvin is correct to have reduced "the Hegelian philosophy" to the one-eyed blindness of the "fact-value" distinction is a question that can occupy profound thinkers at a later time. Our task here is to make clear the myth of Tom. And it is undeniable that he serves to carve out of darkness a greater sphere for the moral work of active intellect.

At this point in our narrative it should be clear that but one thing is necessary to the consummation of this task. Tom need be conscious—demonstrably so—of the misfortune which has befallen him. Thus, he must reveal how he shall preserve his liberty in the obvious case where the whole point is to deprive him of it. The author wastes no time in furnishing the materials of this drama. In chapter 31, "The Middle Passage," Legree unwittingly (so little is he master) hurls down the gauntlet when he discovers Tom's Methodist hymn book.

> "I have none o' yer bawling, praying, singing niggers on my place. . . . *I'm* your church now! You understand,—you've got to be as *I* say." (386, original emphasis)

In chapter 32, with the slaves trudging along behind his wagon in a dusty trail, Simon ordered his tribe to produce mirth: "Strike up a song, boys." He was wholly surprised and not a little angered to be met from Tom's lips with

> Jerusalem, my happy home.
> Name ever dear to me!
> — — — (392)

Legree silenced Tom and demanded something "rowdy." "One of the other men" satisfied the master's craving to dispose of the bodies and souls of others. Here began Tom's resistance to Legree. In light of Legree's previously announced distaste for "Methodism" Tom's defiance was a declaration of hostility. The sequence of events following is a steady escalation of tension, culminating in Tom's declaration of independence in chapter 33. This declaration has been described previously. But I wish to reiterate that it comes in the first few weeks of Tom's presence at the Legree farm. There follow two years or more of struggle, culminating in Tom's triumph. We require now but to describe what that triumph consists of.

At the close of these chapters, Stowe provides a thumbnail summary of Tom's life.

> An eternal, inexorable lapse of moments is ever hurrying the day of the evil to an eternal night, and the night of the just to an eternal day. We have walked with our humble friend thus far in the valley of slavery; first through flowery fields of ease and indulgence, then through heart-breaking separation from all that man holds dear. Again, we have waited with him in a sunny island, where generous hands concealed his chains with flowers; and, lastly, we have followed him when the last ray of earthly hope went out in the night, and seen how, in the blackness of earthly darkness, the firmament of the unseen has blazed with stars of new and significant lustre. (466)

This summary would suggest that Tom was not at all conscious of the full nature of this struggle—"his chains" were "concealed" from him. That, however, would render both his judgment of Legree and his "unaccountable prejudice in favor of liberty" wholly inexplicable. This result is avoidable by only one device. The author's rare use of "we" in the expression "we have walked with our humble friend" suggests that the summary offers a perspective other than Tom's and not peculiarly the author's, namely, our own. The likelihood of this is greatly increased by the appearance of bright new stars, which expand or transcend the earthly horizon. The new stars or *lustre* come into our view as the completion of that common sense perspective which characterizes the summary. Hence, we see in and through Tom consequences of his triumph that, in the nature of things, could only be secondary or even unconscious in him. The summary is an objective account of Tom's life including the illusions.

Tom's triumph takes on a slightly different form for us when we attempt to understand it as he understood it. But let us note the author's coloring—a third level if we will—before attempting to recover Tom's sense. Throughout these eleven chapters the most common metaphor is the biblical "morning-star" frequently applied to Tom. The most common trope is darkness or some variant of that, including biblical characterizations. And the most common reference—if the indirect references through biblical allusions are permitted—is the reference to wisdom. The connection among the three is suggested in the epigram to chapter 35.

> And slight, withal, may be the things that bring
> Back on the heart the weight which it would fling
> Aside forever; it may be a sound,
> A flower, the wind, the ocean, which shall wound,—
> Striking the electric chain wherewith we're darkly bound.
> *Childe Harold's Pilgrimmage,* Canto 4 (421)

Stowe's abridgement of stanza 23, in the fourth canto of Byron's poem, replaces the repressed grief he described with a notion of the willful narrowing of the human horizon. Hence the darkness is self-induced. Or, moral incapacity is seen to result from the conscious effort to reduce the "weight" of cosmic relations in individual reflection. This application of Byron's poem is enhanced in chapter 34, when Stowe makes use of the excised second line to confirm her point. There, Tom challenged Legree with the latter's insignificance in the face of eternity. Where, in Tom, the same conception produced "light and power," its effect on "the sinner's" self-induced darkness was "like the bite of a scorpion" (434).

The light, the brightness, the morning-star which is Tom, is none other than the human horizon in itself.[10] Legree's darkness is the extreme recursion from that horizon. Wisdom is that saving instrument which serves rather more to alleviate than to forestall darkness.

> Few—none—find what they love or could have loved.
> Though accident, blind contact, and the strong
> Necessity of loving, have removed
> Antipathies—but to recur, ere long,
> Envenom'd with irrevocable wrong;
> And Circumstance, that unspiritual god
> And miscreator, makes and helps along
> Our coming evils with a crutch-like rod,
> Whose touch turns hope to dust—the dust we all have trod. (Byron, cxxv)

> Yet let us ponder boldly—'tis a base
> Abandonment of reason to resign
> Our right of thought—our last and only place
> Of refuge; this, at least, shall still be *mine;*
> Though from our birth the faculty divine
> Is chain'd and tortured—cabin'd cribb'd,
> confined,
> And bred in darkness, lest the truth should shine
> Too brightly on the unprepared mind,
> The beam pours in, for time and skill will couch the blind. (Byron, cxxvii)

Byron, of course, is not authority for Stowe's views beyond the version of the stanza she cited. But we have discovered already that the willful narrowing of the human horizon is related to the notion of circumstance as the human tutor. Stowe suggests a wisdom that transcends the circumstance yet answers to its every necessity. The initial epigram in this series of chapters invoked the complaint of divine indifference to evil prevailing over good (384). That complaint, of course, was the song of Legree's slaves. The final epigram in the series closes with Tom's song: "Deem not the just by Heaven forgot!"[11] which was "invented" by Stowe as a more apt expression of her purpose than the poet's "Nor let the good man's trust depart."[12]

Simon Legree's world of darkness is a world in which subjective consciousness of power is confused as objective evidence of power. When Legree reflected on Tom's persistent and belittling resistance, he was seized with paroxysms of anger and frustration.

> "I *hate* him!" said Legree, that night, as he sat up in his bed; "I *hate* him! And isn't he MINE? Can't I do what I like with him? Who's to hinder, I wonder?" And Legree clenched his fist, and shook it, as if he had something in his hands that he could rend in pieces. (467, original emphasis)

The characteristics of Tom that create Legree's frustration and doubt are such as lead irreversibly to Tom's triumph.[13] But Tom triumphs rather over Legree's world of darkness and only incidentally over Legree. Tom had answered Legree's incredulous "Isn't he MINE" some years earlier. In this moment of Legree's mortal attack, therefore, the question is but the faintest glimmer of a dawning consciousness of impotence in Legree. And it anticipates a vulnerability to conscience, which never takes redemptive shape in Legree but succeeds in torturing him.[14]

Tom's triumph consists of the mastery of conscience—a heightening of conscience to the point that it provides *the* defense against the false images of consciousness. Tom characterizes his triumph in that moment—following his declaration of independence—when Cassy counsels him to "give up!" The advice brings a shudder to Tom, partly because he recognized in it the voice of his own weakness. Cassy boldly asserts the incompatibility of right and strength—the former is subordinated to the latter. She boldly asserts God's indifference to the fate of at least some men. And she conceives of the circumstances on Legree's plantation as raising implacable barriers both to doing good and receiving good (410–11). As the author herself had done before (394–97), Cassy concludes the brutalization of the slaves to be complete. Paradoxically, Cassy counsels a prudent regard for oneself—attachment to worldly things—the precise foundation of the brutalization.

It is the specter of brutalization that governs Tom's triumph. He is motivated rather or primarily by the desire to preserve a certain character of soul. Tom commonly speaks in the singular of *his* struggle and *his* victory, while Cassy and the others characteristically speak in the plural of *their* submission and *their* degradation. Tom is a naïf.

> "Poor critturs!" said Tom,—"what made 'em cruel? and, if I give out, I shall get used to 't, and grow, little by little, just like 'em! No, no, Missis! I've lost everything,—wife, and children, and home, and a kind Mas'r,—and he would have set me free, if he'd only lived a week longer; I've lost everything in *this* world, and its clean gone, forever,—and now I *can't* lose Heaven, too; no, I can't get to be wicked, besides all." (411, original emphasis)

Tom's perspective of his life's history differs radically from our own. First, where we find an earthly illumination Tom sees the prospect of heaven. And secondly, what we regarded as an illusion ("his chains concealed with flowers") Tom clearly sees as mere misfortune. In consequence, the eternal and comprehensive loss of everything is nothing other than the matured insensitivity to worldly things—the discovery that such things are suspended by the rarest cords of unlikelihood and vitiated, shot wholly through with accident. In our perspective, Tom was deprived of hope. In his perspective, hope is radically founded on and limited to the power to form one's own soul. For this reason he considers Legree's slaves "poor critturs." Even as he describes the process of habituation—conditioning—he is incredulous as to its power.

It is proper that Tom struggles to avoid brutalization. Stowe had declared that "the whole object of training" of "the Negro" was "directed towards making him callous, unthinking, and brutal" (375). In resisting the intention of the training to which he is subject, Tom proves not only that he is wrongly enslaved but also, paradoxically, that he is no slave at all. Tom's triumph is a triumph over slavery—or, a triumph over the foundation of that form of consciousness suggested in the expression "callous, unthinking, and brutal." Cassy mistakenly believes Tom's appeal to Heaven to be the expression of a fear of Hell. She reminds him, again paradoxically, that the slave will not be held responsible for the wickedness he is forced to practice. Tom considers that the true defeat: to be deprived of responsibility for one's character. It may be that the wicked slave will not go to hell, Tom admits. But he will yet be wicked.

> ". . . it won't make much odds to me how I come so; it's the *bein' so,*—that ar's what I'm dreadin'!" (412, original emphasis)

Tom's triumph consists in the defense of the priority of self-control to all other forms of human endeavor. John, the Drover, has his answer. No other point in the novel produces a like intellectual experience. Cassy is awed, stupefied—"a new thought" had struck her.

> "O God a' mercy! you speak the truth! O—O—O!"—and with groans, she fell on the floor, like one crushed and writhing under the extremity of mental anguish. (412)

The light that floods Cassy's mind is the bright, new star we found in Tom. Our perspective differs from his, because we are yet in need of discovering what he already knows. Tom would have shocked us if he had originally declared that his victory did not consist in either winning his liberty or assuring his salvation. We could have thought those two to exhaust all possibilities. We now can see that it is of no consequence that Tom did not win his liberty in the conventional sense—a fact that he even recognized. And his salvation is not the end by which his victory is characterized, even if it is a fit reward.

Stowe entitles chapter 38, "The Victory." The chapter is headed by a biblical epigram, which suggests the two-fold victory over the fear of death and the pains of an afterlife.[15] But Tom does not die in this chapter nor is death threatened save as the constant companion of mortal combat. Here Tom met the test that exceeded the heroic and dramatic confrontation. He witnessed and endured day by day, week after week, and month after month the conditioning that corroded the slaves' humanity. No longer naive, "Tom no longer wondered at the habitual surliness of his associates" (444).

> The gloomiest problem of this mysterious life was constantly before his eyes,—souls crushed and ruined, evil triumphant, and God silent . . . Tom wrestled, in his own soul, in darkness and sorrow. (444)

Nor could holy word illumine this darkness.

> He . . . drew his worn Bible from his pocket. There were all the marked passages, which had thrilled his soul so often,—words of patriarchs and seers, poets and sages, who from early time had spoken courage to man,—voices of the great cloud of witnesses who ever surround us in the race of life. (445)

And Legree was attentive to the decline in his spirits—ready to assail naive faith and to couple the assault with an appeal to self-interest. Legree contrasts the "lying trumpery" of religion with his own concrete nature. However limited the concrete individual "can do something" and as such is a sure guide to the future. Tom did not descend so low. He resisted the ultimate despair, that there is absolutely no connection in the world between goodness of soul and justice of reward,[16] and he began the reascent with a vision of "one crowned with thorns." Tom discovered that it was insufficient to transcend the pleasant and desirable things, that indeed one must transcend the needful things, in order to ensure self-mastery even to the last degree.

> He that hour loosed and parted from every hope in the life that is now, and offered his own will with an unquestioning sacrifice to the Infinite. (446)

Thus did Tom pass through his wilderness.[17] He did not change, he simply had to face the ultimate test. Tom's victory is over himself. His victory over Legree is a secondary but natural result of his self-mastery.

This important chapter concludes with a demonstration of the kind of activity that accompanies heightened conscientiousness. Tom's ensuing cheerfulness and helpfulness become the standard (and threat) of the entire plantation. He began to master his "associates" even as he had begun to master Legree's opinion *before* the ultimate test.[18] He began to reestablish the moral authority he exercised in the Shelby plantation. In few words, Tom demonstrates the existence of the human residuum by reclaiming these imbruted souls to the ranks of humanity. He demonstrates the triumph of the human model of surpassing excellence in the worst of circumstances.

Finally, Uncle Tom-cum-Father Tom (he is never called "Uncle Tom" by any adult in the novel, save Eliza, who acquired the habit as a child!) recognizes and accepts his responsibility for having raised the hopes of a people who but the day before were resigned to life without hope. Challenged by an awakened Cassy to murder their common oppressor, Tom recoiled in horror. He stuck to his original argument, "good never comes of wickedness!" But this answer is insufficient in a way that the previous fear of being wicked was not at all. We might point out, by retort, that being good could be even more compelling than "not being wicked." And it is Tom who has awakened in Cassy and all the slaves a desire to be good. To Tom, as we have seen, the punishment of the unjust is the work of God. But may it not also be incidental to securing the good? Cassy thinks it is.

> "Any life is better than this. . . ." "What has he made me suffer? What has he made hundreds of poor creatures suffer? Isn't he wringing the life-blood out of you? *I'm called on; they call me*!" (452, emphasis added)

For most human beings the desire to defend the good is irresistible—as Stowe reminded the Quakers.[19] And they who arouse in others a love of the good must bear the responsibility for the consequences. Tom accepts his responsibility by offering the dual alternative of a blood-free escape for Cassy and his continued dedication to exercising moral leadership among the remaining slaves (for whom, eventually, must not the first alternative also become necessary?). The force of Tom's proposal results from its being inessential to deflecting Cassy from the murder she had meditated. Tom suggests the escape only *after* he has stilled the blood-lust, and in frank recognition that it "t'an't natur'" for Cassy to resist the passion to defend the good.

A brief postscript to the myth of Uncle Tom is in order. Tom dies in the arms of young George Shelby. As he did on the day he departed the Shelby farm, he finds it necessary to admonish George not to revile his (Tom's) "owner." But this last occasion is no mere political savvy, looking to his own interest. Tom has just instructed George in the manner in which the "myth of Tom" should be related back in Kentucky. ". . . it's nothing but love!" Tom wishes that his death scene will not be related truly. And he asks George not to pray for hell for Legree.

> "O, don't!—oh, ye musn't!" said Tom, grasping his hand; "he's a poor mis'able critter! it's awful to think on 't! O, if he only could repent, the Lord would forgive him now; but I'm 'feared he never will!" "I hope he won't!" said George; "I never want to see *him* (original emphasis) in heaven!" "Hush, Mas'r George!—it worries me! Don't feel so! He *an't done me no real harm* (emphasis added)—only opened the gate of the kingdom for me; that's all!" (477–78)

Tom lends support to Calvin Stowe: the institution is to be reviled as beyond salvation, not the men. Still, Phelps may be accorded this much: It may be that the men cannot be saved *within* the institution.[20] Legree's salvation may depend on abolition, as Phelps would have it, while Christians are restrained from damning him, as Calvin would have it. But even this generosity of sentiment must be judged rather by the absence of "real harm" than by the specific character of the sinner.

In her "Concluding Remarks" Stowe cites the examples of "nobility, generosity, and humanity" among many "individuals at the South" as saving "us from utter despair of our kind." But such superior souls are rare everywhere (504). She thereby makes it clear that the nature of man is more seriously in question than the nature of Christianity. It is necessary to affirm a natural tendency to justice in order to avoid despair. What Christianity may add or subtract from this tendency is a legitimate subject of inquiry, but it may not be the starting point. For this reason, the opening chapter of *Uncle Tom's Cabin* introduces "a man of humanity," while the center of the work seeks to unveil the differing kinds of humanism. And the conclusion, Tom's myth—accepting the argument from equality that man is never "a creature to be trusted with wholly irresponsible power"—finds it necessary to obscure the truth that "the honorable, the just, the high-minded and compassionate," never "the majority anywhere in this world," are accordingly subjected to the abuses of the low. Just as it is ultimately true that "nothing" can protect the slave "but the *character* of the master,"[21] it is equally true that nothing secures the good in this life beyond the character of the bad.

NOTES

1. What is a matter of weeks in George Harris's case, however, is a matter of years for Uncle Tom!
2. The conversation with Mr. Wilson.
3. Stowe's deliberate use of the conventions of melodrama and her defense of the genre is discussed in book II, part I of this work. Here, however, it is worth noting comments by Brooks that in melodrama "the villain is simply the conveyer of evil, he is inhabited by evil" and "the world according to melodrama is built on an irreducible manichaeism, the conflict of good and evil as opposites and not subject to compromise." Brooks, *The Melodramatic Imagination*, p. 33, 36.
4. Strout finds that *Uncle Tom's Cabin* "was in large part a protest against the Calvinist doctrine of human inability to merit salvation." Strout, "*UTC* and the Portent of the Millennium," pp. 379–80. To Donovan Stowe "seems to be moving away from the arbitrariness of orthodox Calvinism and toward a religion in which people can choose the path of salvation . . . by electing a change of heart within themselves . . . " Donovan, *UTC: Evil, Affliction, and Redemptive Love*, p. 46.
5. See book I, part II, chapter 17.
6. As we also saw in the climactic account of humanism, previously, and the discussion in book I, part II, chapter 15. Calvin Stowe launched an early attack upon

Hegelian philosophy in his article, "The Four Gospels as We Now Have Them in the New Testament and the Hegelian Assaults on Them," published in *Bibliotheca sacra* in 1851. He later incorporated much of that argument into his *Origin and History of the Books of the Bible.*

7. Cf. book II, part I, chapter 22, and chapter 25.

8. *Aeneid*, iii, 658.

9. Chapter 32. On the applicability of "the Hegelian philosophy" in this context, the following suggestive passage is relevant:

> Spirit in this case, therefore, constructs not merely one world, but a twofold world, divided and self-opposed. The world of the ethical spirit is its own proper present; and hence every power it possesses is found in this unity of the present, and, so far as each separates itself from the other, each is still in equilibrium with the whole. Nothing has the significance of a negative of self-consciousness; even the spirit of the departed is in the blood of his relative, is present in the self of the family, and the universal power of government is the will, the self of the nation . . . what is present means merely objective actuality, which has its consciousness in the beyond; each single moment, as an essential entity, receives this, and thereby actuality, from another, and so far as it is actual, its essential being is something other than its own actuality. Nothing has a spirit self-established and indwelling within it; rather, each is outside itself in what is alien to it. G. W. F. Hegel, *The Phenomenology of Mind*, trans. J. B. Baillie, 2nd ed. (New York: The MacMillan Co., 1931), p. 510–11.

10. In Lewis's analysis, "Star is the biblical morning star, Christ, and is used interchangeably for Eva, America, and in allusions to Tom. Eva is mythic, allegorical, noble, and if America can rid itself of slavery, it can be like the morning star in God's kingdom, as she is, restored to its innocence, and as Tom is when morning star (Christ) looks down on man of sin, purified by his sacrifice." Lewis, "Message, Messenger, and Response," p. 247.

11. *UTC*, p. 466, and note.

12. She substituted her line for the original first line in William Cullen Bryant's "Deem not that they are blest alone," fifth stanza.

13. Cf., pp. 113ff.

14. Compare p. 457, *UTC*.

15. *I Corinthians* 15:57. Cf. verses 55, 56, & 58.

16. Cf. Brooks on melodrama: "The *reward* of virtue . . . is only a secondary manifestation of the *recognition* of virtue." Brooks, *The Melodramatic Imagination*, p. 27.

17. That Tom should travel through such wilderness is intrinsic to the melodramatic structure, which typically includes " . . . a threat to virtue, a situation—and most often a person—to cast its very survival into question . . . " Ibid., p. 29.

18. *UTC*, pp. 400–401.

19. Cf. book I, chapter 9.

20. See the discussion in book I, part II, chapter 17.

21. Phelps is not right, in the last analysis, although despotic slaveowners must occur in some number. This result is in fact the work of human nature, as much as or more than the work of conditioning. While the institution is unjust or sinful, the men may or may not be.

II

15

The Genealogy of Uncle Tom

Calvin Stowe wrote *Uncle Tom's Cabin*. This shocking statement, though not true, is nearer the truth than a century and a half of interpretation of H. B. Stowe's novel.[1] In this work I assume the burden to explain the principles espoused in *UTC*, but this task cannot be completed without an account of Calvin Stowe's relationship to his wife's dramatic project. In a novel in which the genealogy and descent of the orthodox hero, George Harris, bears major importance, the genealogy and descent of Uncle Tom, the principal character, remains a mystery.[2] In fact Uncle Tom required no earthly forebearers. The defense and propriety of his character derive from moral, philosophical, and religious considerations. He was fathered in the minds of H. B. and Calvin Stowe. And the first appearance of those ideas that culminated in the conception of Uncle Tom is found in the early work of Calvin Stowe.

H. B. Stowe was a philosopher. This still more shocking and yet more nearly true statement has been as much neglected in over a century of interpretations as the mystery of the conception of Uncle Tom.[3] Stowe referred to herself as a philosopher on more than one occasion. We have occasion to discuss those claims in this work. But it is not obvious that such claims deserve to be discussed. We believe today that anyone who holds to a distinct idea is as such a philosopher. We believe that anyone may be a philosopher—or, *have* a philosophy. Under those lights a discussion of the political philosophy of H. B. Stowe is but a discussion of the political prejudices of H. B. Stowe. The philosophic tradition, however, requires that a distinction be made between those whose political prejudices or opinions are mere opinions and those whose political opinions are informed by theoretical insight.

What most practically distinguishes the lights of the philosophic tradition from our own lights is the necessity, under the former, for an appeal to reason in order to take any opinion whatever seriously. Under our own lights we can no more question our claims about philosophy than we can question the claims of philosophic tradition. Under our lights we cannot question H. B. Stowe's claim. Under the lights of philosophic tradition we may question her claim only if we take it seriously initially.[4] That is to do no less than Friedrich Nietzsche did and no more than Francis Lieber did.[5]

There is a connection between Stowe's claim to be a philosopher and my claim that Calvin Stowe wrote *Uncle Tom's Cabin*. The *prima facie* case for Stowe's claim would be her writing—but only if my claim is in error. That is, the novel may or may not be philosophic in character. If it is not, but Calvin Stowe wrote it, Stowe may yet be a philosopher. Each of the variants of this argument may also be true. But if we consider the likelihood that Calvin Stowe did not write the novel, that the novel is philosophic, and that Stowe is *not* a philosopher—a combination not altogether unlikely—the mystery of the conception of Uncle Tom will settle into seeking the source of the philosophic argument in the novel.

This is one way to answer the question—putting first things first—what is the source of *Uncle Tom's Cabin*? Let us inquire *why* and *how* Calvin's ideas are manifest in the novel. *That* they are so we strongly hinted previously, and now we will demonstrate the reasons that justify that conclusion. One of the chronologically earliest signs of the influence of Calvin's ideas on Uncle Tom is found in an unpublished "Dissertation on the Use of Wit in Matters of Religion." Calvin wrote this work while he was but twenty-two years old, before he entered on his studies at Bowdoin College. A circumstantial treatise on rhetoric—which means persuasion—it primarily concentrates on propriety in speech. Nonetheless, it also reflected on the dress appropriate to truth.

> More especially does this appear necessary at the present day, when a taste for light and superficial thought is so universally diffused, that it is impossible to induce many to attend to solid sentiments plainly expressed, when most readers are so fascinated by the foppish and gaudy outside of folly and falsehood, that truth, if she appears in her native simplicity, must . . . expose herself to the hazard of being hooted out of what is called good company as a very unwelcome and old-fashioned guest. . . . [S]he should deck herself with all the ornaments, that are proper to her; for still she will be likely to meet with but a cool reception from some, as she would no more assume all the petty embellishments of a popular style than a virtuous and modest woman . . . would appear in public with . . . the lascivious dress and languishing airs of the courtesan.[6]

The young child, Harriet Elizabeth Beecher, was composing poems in Latin at the time this was written—1823. She evidently profited from the training for, still adhering to this idea, Calvin Stowe asked her in 1857 to learn Greek, that she might still more assist him in dressing up his ideas.[7]

The first sign of Calvin's influence on *Uncle Tom's Cabin* emerges in his own two-fold recognition of the need to teach certain general, public truths and the necessity to do so in a non-scholarly fashion. The form of the novel was appropriate to this task. I began this study with the intention to explicate *Uncle Tom's Cabin*. The study has long since been forced out of that narrow channel. Nonetheless, it is precisely the explication of the novel—under the awareness of Calvin's intentions—which induces us to search for the elements of its teaching as revealed through its fancy garb. According to Francis Lieber, this teaching was of world-changing significance.

> This book is an historic event—I mean certain important public acts and actions and certain trains of thought—either new or old ones invigorated—will date from this book.[8]

The possibility of the existence of unexplored yet commanding resources enlivens the attempt to explicate the novel as "historical event" even if the analysis itself takes on some of the characteristics of a romance. In the nature of pure romance, according to H. B. Stowe, it is idle to search "for trap-doors."[9] *Uncle Tom's Cabin* is not a *pure* romance—if it is a romance at all. The search for Calvin's influence therefore, does not depend on the mysterious change in the novel's title. Forrest Wilson suspected "the hand of Calvin" in eliminating every reference to slavery in the title and thereby enhancing "the story's universality."[10] But he little suspected that the change more accurately expressed the purpose and teaching of the novel.[11]

An account of the novel as organic unity would find *its* chief evidence, of course, in an exegetical analysis of the novel itself. Such analysis does reveal that the novel's teaching is centered rather less on the evil of slavery than on the articulation of the conditions of democratic political life and the appropriate nature of modern humanism.[12] The two questions are posed through the parallel plots of George Harris's material ascent from slavery and Uncle Tom's material descent into slavery.[13] The answers, however, are both given through the vehicle of the main plot. They involve questioning the identification of moral goodness with disinterestedness (the precise articulation of the character assigned to Uncle Tom) and focus on the role of an aristocracy in a democratic polity. Because we are here chiefly concerned with pointing out the probable source of these concerns, we recur to the novel no further than to reveal how the dramatic structure and the narrative succeed in posing the questions. And this is accomplished in the novel in the critical eleventh and twelfth chapters, in which George Harris and Uncle Tom effectively begin their respective journeys (*UTC*, 118–53). These two chapters contain the novel's only extensive *debate* on the morality of slavery. The dramatic center of these chapters is the effort of an earthly, kindly slaveowner (John, the Drover) to discover a clear-cut moral foundation for keeping *or* freeing his slaves.

His deliberations posed three dilemmas that Stowe resolved only in the conclusion of the novel. First, he wished to be assured that *human morality cannot overthrow nature,* though it may mask nature. This would remove the risk of John's own enslavement in the action of freeing his slaves. Second, John wished assurance that *the slave class is fully as human as the master class.* That is his predisposition. But he remains uncertain of its foundations and of its practical consequences. And, finally, John wanted assurance that, even if an artificial (social) hierarchy can mask a possible natural hierarchy, *the strong kept artificially weak must yet be capable of demonstrating their own intrinsic capacity.* Clearly shorn of all conventional supports and wholly without recourse to established authority, they must nonetheless manifest their "talents" and one talent above all others, the capacity to judge what is good for human beings.

This abbreviation of the principles urged in *Uncle Tom's Cabin* suffers the defect of retrenchment. The argument was fully presented above, and here we address only the likely source of these now recognizable terms. That source is Stowe's husband, Calvin Ellis Stowe. In particular, these ideas are traceable to his 1839 essay, "The Advantages and Defects of the Social Condition in the United States of America."[14] A close analysis of this essay reveals its connection with H. B. Stowe's teaching, but further background is yet necessary.

Traditionally, Calvin Stowe is considered the weak, whining, and relatively inept shadow of a vastly more powerful wife. This caricature was given greatest currency by Forrest Wilson.[15] But an understated version of the same theme may be found in Kirkham still (see reference supra) and elsewhere.[16] Edward Wagenknecht came close to breaking that tradition entirely in a major work on Stowe.[17] In his biographical sketch of her life and work Wagenknecht includes a chapter entitled, "The Wife." And, though much space is still devoted to Calvin Stowe's hypochondria and domestic and business helplessness, Wagenknecht approaches the conclusion that Calvin Stowe gave his wife more than encyclopedic reference in her writing. Wagenknecht doubtless would have found what he nearly avowed had he studied their respective works *as well as* their correspondence. Gossett largely echoes Wagenknecht, insisting on Calvin Stowe's weaknesses ("hypochondria, feelings of hopelessness under stress, gluttony . . . and a lack of resolution and skill in handling practical problems") and commenting that "one of [Stowe's] difficulties was Calvin himself," yet nevertheless acknowledging that "if the Stowes did not always bear their burdens patiently, they could at least confide in and help one another."[18] Stowe's most recent major biographer, Hedrick, likewise rehearses her husband's weaknesses (for example, "He predicted gloom and doom so regularly that it is perhaps not surprising that occasionally he was right") but still more often joins Caskey in noting the strengths of their "intellectual comradeship," pointing out that[19]

> "[Harriet] turned to [Calvin] for information, relying on his scholarly command to direct her to sources she used in her writing. He relied on her narrative skill and attention to detail to enliven his journalistic pieces and biblical lectures. Harriet once likened her scholar-husband to a cormorant, putting more and more learning into his bottomless bill; but while he was content to store knowledge, Harriet fashioned information into useful articles, editorials, stories that would touch a nerve in the reading public. . . . With his support and encouragement, Harriet became 'a literary woman'" (referring to a letter from HBS to Henry Ward Beecher, February 1, [1872 or later] in the Beecher Family Papers at Sterling Memorial Library, Yale University) (Hedrick, 94, 100, 132) while Caskey pointed out what remained largely true until now, that . . . while acknowledging that [Calvin] Stowe was a noted biblical scholar, no historian has ever examined his scholarship or the effects of that scholarship on the changing religious ideas of his more famous wife. Not only his biblical studies but also his pulpit views were, as Harriet herself indicated time and again, the single most important influence on her theological development, particularly since they reinforced the liberal preachments of her brother Henry, who himself owed a considerable debt to Stowe. (Caskey, 180)

She proceeds then to analyze his contributions to his wife's "theological education" (181), particularly with regard to *The Minister's Wooing*—the work of H. B. Stowe to which Caskey gives the greatest exegesis. She further writes:

> Harriet herself aided Calvin materially in his major work, the *Origins and History of the Books of the Bible*, while her own nonfiction books, the *Key to Uncle Tom's Cabin* (1853), *Woman in Sacred History* (1873), and *Footsteps of the Master* (1877), resulted from collaboration with Stowe and, to a lesser extent, with Edward Beecher. Calvin read and criticized her drafts, suggested lines of investigation, and brought many sources, including apocryphal and traditional ones, to her attention. (Caskey, 181)

Because the focus of Caskey's monograph is entirely upon the religious thinking of the prominent Beecher family, she does not discuss Calvin Stowe's equally profound influence on the political philosophy that underpins Stowe's fiction.

That Calvin Stowe was materially concerned with H. B. Stowe's project is all too certain an implication of their relationship. Their correspondence reveals their mutual concern with both the form and content of her publications.

Long after publication of *Uncle Tom's Cabin,* Stowe wistfully invoked the pains they jointly suffered in writing it.

> The people have not got over *Uncle Tom's Cabin* in France—It goes everywhere. It has revived the gospel among the poor. . . . Is not this blessed, my dear husband? Is it not worth all the suffering of writing it?[20]

And if it is true that their mutual ideas entered into construction of the novel, and it is in addition true that the first evidence of these ideas appears earliest in Calvin Stowe's work, it is an inevitable conclusion that he strongly influenced his wife. In those terms, the gestation of *Uncle Tom's Cabin* commences at least in 1836, though the signs are not obvious until 1839. In 1836, Calvin Stowe wrote to Stowe from London, with direct reference to abolitionism and slavery. In 1839 appeared his essay, "Advantages and Defects . . ."

In the letter of October, 1836, Calvin Stowe refers his wife to his previously and fully expressed opinion on slavery. What occasioned the letter was his giving an address to a meeting of Methodists in London, in which meeting he again expressed his views on slavery.[21] He did so after having complained, earlier that summer, of fanatical abolitionists at a rally in Exeter Hall in London. They—along with their American counterparts—came in for harsh criticism.[22] Calvin does not spell out the just position, which he holds, but refers her to it. At a minimum this must refer to the "free speech scandal" at Lane Seminary, from which Stowe seems to date the concern with slavery.[23]

If we consult a later letter, written from Cincinnati on May 18, 1842, we get the idea that the 1836 reference to his views was richer than many have cared to think.[24] In this letter Calvin reveals that he listens to his wife as well as talks to her—and in the most significant matters. She is absent on this occasion, and his letter is a pining for her conversation. But he is not simply lonely, for he wants to discuss scholarly and religious questions.[25] And almost no one else satisfies him in these things so much as she. Her father, Lyman Beecher, comes close, but he falters on a significant point. He refuses to identify morality with disinterestedness. He cannot comprehend how anyone "believes *goodness* and *an enlightened regard to one's own happiness* are *not* one and the same thing . . ." (my emphasis). We are entitled to believe that Stowe does understand this principle and that they have discussed it—and its *likely source,* de Tocqueville—at length. But there is even further evidence from a letter written almost a month earlier. I quote at length:

> I have been thinking this week how much real communion of soul and mind we have had together, notwithstanding all the little territories of married life, of which we have had our share. In matters of religion and taste and opinions

> and feelings, things quite independent I intend by the use of the word, [we] are very much alike; and I believe there are very few husbands and wives in the world, who have so many real good talks together, in more matters, as we have.[26]

Calvin Stowe evidently considered his relationship with his wife to be founded on broader terms than are commonly associated with marriage. The fact that they think "very much alike," and think together, seems to him strong reason for associating his wife in his own efforts.

These letters I have cited from 1842 were all written during the period of a single absence, while Stowe was away. With one other in the series, that of May 19, 1843, one theme recurs with the greatest frequency: Calvin wishes her to write more for publication.[27] Indeed, to that point she had hardly written much at all and little that could be called serious. The letter of April 30 is cited in virtually every account of her life and work. It was in that letter that Calvin declared, "You must be a literary woman" and advised her to sign her name "Harriet Beecher Stowe," which was more euphonic than the cumbersome Harriet Elizabeth Beecher Stowe. But the entire series of letters is dedicated to the same end. The last of these even goes so far as to associate her in the task that he had undertaken four years earlier.

> Why don't you write some more? We look in every issue for a piece from you. The little magazine goes abroad finely. . . . You have it in your power, by means of that little magazine, *to form the mind of the West* for the coming generation.[28] (My emphasis)

We could not justly imagine this strong support for her writing career was wholly independent of that identity of mind Calvin had cited. But his interest goes deeper than that. She could be associated with his teaching project because, to him, theirs was a life of teaching and studying together. Just as he wished to associate her in his life-work in 1857, it seems he wished to associate her in his project of forming "the mind of the West for the coming generation" in 1842.

There was a time when I considered entitling this study "Superman was an Uncle Tom." That would surely have highlighted the central theme of Stowe's novel—the harmlessness and innocence and yet irresistible strength of goodness and wisdom. The Superman/Clark Kent dichotomy more nearly approaches Stowe's theory than it approaches Nietzsche's idea of the "Overman." Stowe's melodramatic appeal, couching great strength under the disguise of insipidity, was however but a means to a broader end.[29] In order to preserve this wider perspective I rejected the narrower title. Nonetheless the rejected title suggests a standard of judgment for the novel as well as direct access to the "project" and Stowe's own commitment to it. In the first sense, there is no more important question to ask than whether

Uncle Tom is or need be believable. The fictional Henry Morton, we know, cannot command obedience however much believed.[30] The suggestion that the demand for believability is misplaced invokes a different standard for the superman, the aristocrat, what—in *Uncle Tom's Cabin*—is the human model of surpassing excellence. The habitual self-deprecation that accompanies commerce between the few and the many under the aegis of modernity rather reveals the pain with which the few form such liaisons than wins belief or trust. The model of Uncle Tom prescribes a stature that so far exceeds the many that self-deprecation cannot be asked, but that so agreeably reflects the many that self-deprecation is unnecessary. Who, today, will trust a presidential candidate who "cannot laugh at himself"? Derision of the modern Uncle Tom conceals an express fear of the will of the many. Commanding, again, demands independence, even diffidence. Stowe has tried to picture the substance that the master formally suggested. Is this teaching compatible with democracy, natural rights? Edward Beecher—Stowe's brother—regarded the struggle over slavery (Elijah Lovejoy's struggle) as "solely the advocacy of freedom and equal rights."[31] It is safe to say that *almost* any defender of America would have given that answer.

Calvin Stowe reconsidered the question of natural right and political right. The most primitive political requirement, the right to live, he regarded as superseded by the formation of a political covenant. The traditional "state of nature"—so familiar to the theory of liberal democracy—is but the "savage state." In this state all men possess the right to live, but few do so securely. Making that right secure is essentially a privation, the wanted privation of pain. Men commence their political existence in this negative posture and, but for the emergence of some principle of addition, they would never go beyond this goal as the sum of human endeavor. Utilitarians are confused to think they find the basis of human life in the concept of good or enjoyment interpreted as realizing mere subjective preferences. To enjoy is to possess. Neither enjoyment nor possession can be associated with a privation.

Only a positive orientation toward the achievement of some decisively human way of life constitutes the true foundation of *human* politics. Self-interest is indeed the foundation of the first recognizably human political impulse: the affirmation that all *men* have an equal claim to live implies the necessity of subjecting all men equally to justice. But this self-interest, residing solely in the wish or desire for privation of pain, does not have as logical product the desire for comfortable preservation. The attainment of the latter is conditioned upon a factor of change, whereby the former, initial political impulse has come to be seen as the necessary but subordinate cause of concern with a specifically human way. All men have a right to live. Have all a right to live like men? That is, the agreement that eventuates in the privation of pain creates a problem that can be solved only by abandoning *that* agreement itself for one in which the right to live is supplanted by the right to live in a certain manner.

This conclusion is not merely the sum of those negative conditions that guarantee the lives of all; for the negative conditions only forced recognition of the problem. It is rather the formulation of that way of living that can affirm that all men have an equal right to justice without leaving all at the mercy of the least understanding of justice. The force of nature is such that, in the savage state, one's self-interest is so strongly present that one's interest in a civil self can only be established with great difficulty. And the only means of sustaining this "civil" self-interest is by rendering self-interest proper a thing subject to be forgotten. Enjoyment or acquisition is a means of keeping the desire for privation of pain ever obscure,[32] but only so long as it is guided by a specific conception of the human way of life. In transforming the right to live into a claim for justice, this agreement creates the basis for the human concern with commodious living.

The self-interest involved in comfortable preservation is the interest each has to stand in the most favorable position *vis-à-vis* efforts required by the concern with justice. Avarice no less than magnanimity is concerned with action. Human acquisitiveness can never be *the* basis though it may well be *the* instrument of *any* politics in this view. It can be instrumental in fulfilling the purpose of a regime in which avarice is specifically directed to the ends of the regime. Through these reflections Calvin is enabled to deny that the United States is or could be founded on narrow self-interest and the view of natural rights that is its corollary. The political covenant is *not* the necessary *and* sufficient condition of the political happiness of a particular polity. This means that the political covenant, like the divine covenant, gains its efficacy from the efforts to which it gives rise rather than the principle of its formulation. That divine covenants were a necessary *and* sufficient condition for the salvation of man *qua* man, advanced American Puritanism would continue to believe. But the force of covenants in the case of particular men was always the great hurdle. The choice of rejecting either particular providence or the efficacy of human will was unenvied. The sophisticated atheism of some Puritanism, to which this choice gave occasion, Calvin would counter only by the argument that the divine covenant, as to the salvation of particular men, was a necessary but not a sufficient condition. The evidence is analogical.[33] The opposite case (general providence) identifies general and particular causes, since God could not fail to provide salvation for all to whom he intended it. If salvation is intended for men in general, yet only won by men in particular, it follows that the crucial connection in any particular case is human or individual endeavor.

The project of "forming the mind at the West" is based on the conviction of the efficacy of individual effort. So, too, is the opposition to oppression.

And the whole is bottomed on the refutation of the utter "selfishness" of *modern* theories. Respecting "the Hegelian philosophy," Calvin taught that

> there is no disinterestedness in this philosophy, there is no veneration, and there is no love. Each being is all-sufficient to itself, and each revolves around itself as its own center, and each is at the same time both planet and sun, both axis and orbit. And what can come of such kind of principles, but selfishness, and animalism, and every evil work?[34]

The facile identification of form and principle is rejected as narrowing violently the realm of moral agency and leading to reasoning from results or forms instead of principles. The question Calvin seeks to answer concerns the dissimilarity between self-interest and goodness or virtue. Abstracting from the theological element, the question is best posed for our purposes in the form suggested by one of my students:

> If men do not desire freedom naturally [in fact], is it natural for them to be free? If men do not desire freedom naturally [in fact], can there be such things as inalienable rights? Do men need to be educated before they can desire freedom?[35]

If the enjoyment of and desire for freedom depend upon a level of civilization, education, and pre-existent political forms, it is a matter of great consequence to learn how human principles can be separated far enough from human practice to permit a judgment of men and what is due to them in every case. Fiedler misunderstands, however profoundly, when he contrasts the "Rousseauistic myth" with the "Gothic myth" and imagines that Stowe saw only possibilities of the identity either of the good and the natural or of the evil and the natural but nothing else. "Is the 'natural' a source of spontaneous goodness, instinctive nobility, untutored piety?"[36] As Calvin's view makes clear, the good is opposed to the natural not as evil but as that out of which articulation of the good became possible. Neither then is the "natural" simply good. One may at most say that it is an opportunity.[37]

It is of *great* significance that Calvin turned, not to the savage state but to "general literature" to find "human nature." While yet a student at Bowdoin and outlining a plan of study, he stated, in what is in effect an intellectual diary, the range and rationale of his studies. He began the diary in 1829.

> During my whole course of study, I intend to try to enlarge and liberalise my mind as much as possible, by making occasional incursions into the wide field of general literature, paying particular attention to the kind of literature, which will show me human nature as it is. Of this kind are memoirs of their own time by the most ancient men, good biography, and history, and the works of the best poets, dramatists, and novelists.[38]

There is great temptation to think that this unique modern abandonment of hypothetical reasoning in the quest of nature is responsible for the singular view of nature Calvin presents.

If Calvin had preached the efficacy of individual effort, Stowe practiced it with great energy.

> I wrote what I did because, as a woman, as a mother I was oppressed and broken hearted with the sorrows and injustice I saw; because, as a Christian, I felt the dishonor to Christianity; because, as a lover of my country, I trembled at the coming day of wrath.[39]

This passage from a letter to an unidentified addressee in England was written before Stowe embarked on a campaign to Great Britain. Just after Calvin's solo return from that campaign, he wrote to her in terms which revealed him no less convinced of the necessity of effort. He quoted an imitation of himself by his young son.

> "O Lord, bless all the absent members of the family and deliver all the oppressed and, I, Jesus sake, Amen." Do you see what the burdens of my prayers must have been of late [?] Those two petitions include my most earnest feelings.[40]

Both are as intensely committed to the relief of the slaves as we had prepared to see them committed to "forming the mind at the West." The projects are not unrelated, but we may still suspect a distinct change in emphasis.

E. B. Kirkham has contributed much to Uncle Tom scholarship. In clarifying many myths and illusions of the past, he has made it easier for us to see the likely circumstances for the composition of *Uncle Tom's Cabin*. In particular, he has shown that a frequently misquoted Stowe letter may be related to a seldom quoted Stowe letter. The seldom quoted letter is one in which Stowe announces to her husband that she will try her hand at a few sketches of ex-slaves demonstrating their capacities for useful and productive lives as freemen.[41] In short, the original aim of *Uncle Tom's Cabin* differed from the final product. We have never known how to account for the change, partly because a second letter—indeed, only a note—was always quoted as showing "dynamic . . . purpose and single-mindedness" on Stowe's part. What Kirkham has done is to reveal that this note, so far from dynamic, was almost a casual reference to a purpose not at all clearly spelled out yet.[42] Kirkham does not explicitly state that Stowe's "I shall write that thing if I live" is a clear reference to something previously defined. But the original plan could not have included an attack on the "fugitive slave law" or the rising of some "Martyn Luther . . . to set this community [Boston] right," because these are mentioned in the note outside the context of the pledge to write and are accompanied by much doubt and irresolution as to how to approach them.[43] The only trace of the novel's original purpose remains in its final pages [added after serialization] where the author offers, on the authority of "Professor C. E. Stowe of Lane Seminary" a laundry list of emancipated blacks faring well. We cannot account for this radical change. But I suggest that Calvin Stowe had much to do with it, finding the original purpose too narrow both in terms of his "project" and in terms of the need to defend himself that had arisen since then. Accordingly, I will provide a complete account, first, of Calvin's reflections on the Western project, then, of his becoming involved in the anti-slavery dispute and its subsequent emergence to the forefront.

NOTES

1. "By the bye a reviewer of *Dred* amuses me—He admits that all the trifling parts are by me—but says that some parts are so far above the ordinary usages of us women that some of the earnest *men* spirits of America must have chosen me as the Pythoress to hand their oracles out to the public. Think of my being made a myth while alive and walking. I really begin to think of pluming myself on this." ALS, H.B. Stowe to Duchess of Sutherland, Sept. 15, 1856 (Univ. of Virginia Library, copy at Stowe-Day Library).

2. The sources of *Uncle Tom's Cabin* have long been obscured by the conflicting claims of presumed models of inspiration. By way of models, there are the novel, *Memoirs of Archy Moore* (by Richard Hildreth, Boston: 1840), and the autobiography of Josiah Henson (*The Life of Josiah Henson, Formerly a Slave, Now an Inhabitant of Canada, as Narrated by Himself*, Boston: 1849). By way of ideas there are the tales of Orestes Brownson ("Laboring Classes," *Boston Quarterly Review*, 1840, pp. 358–95, 420–510) and the sermons of Theodore Dwight Weld (*American Slavery As It Is*, New York: 1839). In these cases as in many other cited influences upon Harriet Stowe's novel, claims have turned upon the application of a specific dramatic example or idea to a specific portion of the novel's text. In the case of "Archy Moore," the leading claim is pegged to the religiosity of Thomas in that novel and compared with the scenes of Uncle Tom's protestations of faith. With Josiah Henson the leading claim is based on the parallel between the trust Henson's master reposed in his honesty and the trust "Mas'r Shelby" particularly reposed in Tom. The chief contribution of Brownson is thought to be the considerations introduced in chapter 19 of *Uncle Tom's Cabin*, effecting a comparison between laboring classes in general and slave labor in particular. Weld's contributions are generally and more validly posed as extensive, but they are still confined to the narrative accounts of the abuses of slavery.

Superficial examination of these partial claims to credit for the origins of the famous novel reveals the chief defect of these claims. All are based on partial readings of the novel, treating it as a series of vignettes rather than as an organic unity. And it is precisely this latter possibility that opens at last a window to the sources of *Uncle Tom's Cabin*. Harriet Stowe may well have made use of all these sources as well as of her personal experiences, of which she certainly made extensive use [cf., Kirkham,

Building; this is a definitive account of the elements which entered into the architecture of the novel.] If the novel is indeed an organic unity, however, each of these constituent elements must be subordinated to the purpose—we may say teaching—of the novel. And as such they gain their meaning rather from the novel as a whole.

Stowe herself denied specific forebearers in a letter to the editor of the *Brooklyn Magazine*: "In reply to your inquiry I would say that none of the characters in *Uncle Tom's Cabin* are portraits—I knew of several colored men who showed the piety, honesty & faithfulness of Uncle Tom—but none of them had a history like that I have created for him. . . . It is not surprising therefore that your informant cannot tell you where the originals of Uncle Tom & George Harris are. I know of no such persons." ALS, H. B. Stowe to the "Editor of the Brooklyn Magazine," April 2, 1885 (Univ. of Virginia Library).

3. "Uncle Tomitudes," *Putnam's Monthly Magazine,* vol. 1 (Jan. 1853), pp. 97–102: "Not the least remarkable among the phenomena that have attended the publication of Uncle Tom has been the numerous works written expressly to counteract the impression which the book was supposed likely to make. This is something entirely new in literature, though not in philosophy. . . ."

4. A handful of recent Stowe scholars *do* argue for a systematic moral philosophy in her work. Camfield demonstrates how Stowe incorporates the thought of the Scottish Common Sense philosophers, in general, and Archibald Alison and Hugh Blair, in particular, in her writing. He astutely notes that "Stowe seems to be engaged in a serious intellectual defense of the sentimental ideal; she is trying to explain how naturally good human beings can lose their sensitivities to goodness. In other words, she is trying to explain the existence of evil in the best of all possible worlds." Camfield, "Moral Aesthetics."1988. 327–28. Lee argues that "the best philosophical thought of the antebellum period appears in the 'metaphysical riot of its greatest literature'" and, while acknowledging that " . . . few critics view Stowe as a philosopher . . . ," he portrays Stowe as "a systematic thinker who pursues a coherent theory of reform." Maurice Sherwood Lee, "Quarreling with Politics: Antebellum Literature and the Limits of the Slavery Debate" (Ph.D. diss., University of California, Los Angeles, 2000), p. 5, 9, 16–17. Ryan expounds the centrality of "the antebellum discourse of benevolence" (p. 752) to Stowe's fiction, especially in *Uncle Tom's Cabin* and *Dred,* which she sees as "meditations on benevolent citizenship and on the ideological construction of the homes where charity might begin" (p. 753). Ryan, *Charity Begins at Home,* pp. 752, 753 (hereafter cited as "Quarreling with Politics"). Shipp uses Bruno Bettleheim's concept of "the informed heart" as a framework for discussing the role of feelings within Stowe's understanding of human relations. Through Tom's trials and suffering Stowe shows how to remain "an integrated personality, beneficial to oneself and others" in dehumanizing circumstances. Shipp, "*UTC* and the Ethos of Melodrama," pp. 23–24. West comments: "As a political scientist, I was intrigued by Stowe's multi-layered exploration of such themes as civil disobedience, human equality, and the role of religion in politics." John West, "Going Back to *Uncle Tom's Cabin,*" *Books & Culture* 26 (2003): 26.

5. See below, Ch. 18.

6. Calvin Ellis Stowe, "Dissertation on the Use of Wit in Matters of Religion," June 7, 1823, the unpublished, uncorrected manuscript, in the collection, Stowe-Day Library.

7. ALS, C. E. Stowe to H. B. Stowe, Feb. 8, 1857, Andover, Massachusetts (Stowe-Day Library). (Particular thanks to Miss Scofield for assistance in reading the manuscript.) Stowe seems to echo Calvin's words when she writes in *The Pearl of Orr Island*: " . . . works of fiction, as we all know, if only gotten up, have always their advantages in the hearts of listeners over plain, homely truth . . . " (p. 29 quoted in Daniel James Weinstein, "Educating Sympathy: Imagination and Convention in Works by Harriet Beecher Stowe, Sarah Orne Jewett and Mary E. Wilkins Freeman" (Ph.D. diss., State University of New York at Buffalo, 2000), p. 34 (hereafter cited as "Educating Sympathy").

8. ALS LI4381, Francis Lieber to George Ticknor, Mar. 14, 1853 (Huntington Library).

9. Cf. *My Wife and I*, pp. 3–4, where Stowe characterizes *every* romance that has "ever been written."

10. Robert Forrest Wilson, *Crusader in Crinoline* (Philadelphia: J. B. Lippincott, 1941), p. 263 (hereafter cited as *Crusader in Crinoline*).

11. See book I, part I, chapter 7.

12. Although he misses much of the political import of the novel, Shipp comes close to discerning Stowe's deep intent in saying "she shapes her material with one overriding purpose in mind: persuading her readers to begin the arduous task of creating and maintaining informed hearts." Shipp, "*UTC* and the Ethos of Melodrama," p. 51. Fisher also glimpses something of the novel's profundity in describing it as "an imaginative refounding of democracy." Fisher, *Hard Facts*, p. 88.

13. Although scarcely the first or only Stowe critic to point out the parallels between George Harris and Uncle Tom, Bellin captures it well: "The contrast with Uncle Tom is pointed and persistent; the escalating mayhem of George Harris's escape finds its counterpart in the increasing purity and power of Uncle Tom's pacifism . . . Uncle Tom's nonresistance, that is, assumes a cosmic force which Stowe will not grant George Harris's merely temporal rebellion." Bellin, "Up to Heaven's Gate," p. 279–80.

14. Calvin E. Stowe, "The Advantages and Defects of the Social Condition in the United States of America," *American Biblical Repository* 2nd ser., vol. 1 (1839 hereafter cited as "The Advantages and Defects").

15. Cf. *Crusader.*

16. See Rourke ("Out of [Stowe's] descriptions [in correspondence] emerged likewise the figure of Professor Stowe—clumsy, middle-aged, and absurdly incapable of meeting the tedious and sometimes tragic episodes of their common life, and quite unfitted to care for his family"); Venet ("Absent-minded and hypochondriacal, Calvin Stowe began by admonishing his wife in the 1850s that she bore primary responsibility for supporting the family and managing its financial resources"); and Brommell ("Her husband, Calvin, a moody hypochondriac, left Harriet alone to look after their children . . ."). Constance Rourke, *Trumpets of Jubilee* (New York: Harcourt, Brace and World, Inc., 1963), p. 74. Wendy Hamand Venet, *Neither Ballots nor Bullets: Women Abolitionists and the Civil War* (Charlottesville: University Press of Virginia, 1991), p. 67. Brommell, *By the Sweat of the Brow*, p. 153. Even Lyman Beecher Stowe characterized his grandfather as "a highly emotional child of Nature who seesawed between moods of exaltation and in-

tense depression." Lyman Beecher Stowe, *Saints, Sinners and Beechers* (New York: Blue Ribbon Books, Inc., 1934), p. 164.

17. Edward Wagenknecht, *Harriet Beecher Stowe: The Known and the Unknown* (New York: Oxford University Press, 1965; hereafter cited as *Harriet Beecher Stowe*).

18. Gossett, *UTC and American Culture*, pp. 38, 49, 50.

19. Hedrick, *Harriet Beecher* Stowe. Others who focus on the positive nature of their relationship include Petersen ("Though they frequently criticized each other, their deep love for one another was obvious"); Caskey (" . . . Harriet drew great strength from her husband, whose profound influence on her has been ignored or belittled by her biographers, even including their son Charles E. Stowe"); and May ("One major remaining source both for Mrs. Stowe's opinions and her facts, and one whose importance is often minimized, was the author's husband. Professor Calvin Stowe, by no means the hen-pecked mediocrity he is sometimes turned into (even by his wife), accepted with a good deal of grace the difficult role of attendant to a literary lioness") William J. Petersen, "Naturally Different: Calvin and Harriet Beecher Stowe," in *Twenty-Five Surprising Marriages: Faith-Building Stories from the Lives of Famous Christians* (Grand Rapids, MI: Baker Books, 1997), p. 180. Caskey, *Chariots of Fire*,. May, "Introduction," p. 30.

20. Charles Edward Stowe, *The Life of Harriet Beecher Stowe* (Boston: Houghton, Mifflin, 1889), p. 291.

21. October 26, 1836 (Stowe-Day).

22. ALS, C. E. Stowe to H. B. Stowe, July 20, 1836, London (Stowe-Day).

23. See chapter 3.

24. ALS, Stowe-Day.

25. The theologians he discusses all appear, under Stowe's own name, in *Sunny Memories* a decade later. Compare Calvin's early reaction:

> I am reeling with great admiration in connection with Tholuck's Hours of devotion, DeWette's new translation of the whole Bible. It is altogether the best translation that has ever been made(,) very faithful, severe, idiomatic, perfectly clear, and in the very best taste . . . Long and faithfully as I have studied the originals, I find him a wonderful breath at almost every page. I begin to think that DeWette must be a Christian.

with Stowe's later reaction, in, book II, part I, chapter 23.

26. April, 1842 (Stowe-Day).

27. May 19, 1842 (Stowe-Day).

28. Ibid. Note that Hedrick also cites this letter in her discussion of Calvin's encouraging Stowe to write and comments, "But Calvin Stowe's main concern was not with money but with the influence she could wield over the culture; it was the same Beecheresque plan that had drawn him into Lyman Beecher's wake to the West: Beecher's vehicle was the pulpit and the schools; hers would be the periodical press." Hedrick, *Harriet Beecher Stowe*, pp. 139–40.

29. See the "Defense of Melodrama," book II, part I, chapter 24.

30. See book II, part I, chapter 22.

31. Edward Beecher, *Narrative of Riots at Alton, in Connection with the Death of Reverend Elijah P. Lovejoy* (Philadelphia: George Holton, 1838), p. 6.

32. "Life is the joyless quest for joy." Leo Strauss, *Natural Right and History* (Chicago: University of Chicago, 1993), p. 251.

33. Cf. Calvin E. Stowe, "Remarks Made While Pursuing a Course in Theological Studies," in *Library Archives, Hartford Seminary* (Hartford, CT: 1829), Secs. IX and X (hereafter cited as "Remarks Made . . .").

34. Calvin Stowe, *Origin and History*, op. cit., p. 264. This entire work, in one respect, may be read as a dialogue with Hegel, though Hegel will seldom be mentioned explicitly. Its principal argument is that it is necessary to replace a general appeal to consciousness with an appeal to reason or nature, in order to comprehend human moral development. That is, the reason in history, which Hegel purports to find, is undermined from the moment men discover that they can appeal to reason as a foundation for understanding history. This is what one would expect of a devotee of Butler's *Analogy*. But compare the untitled MS. in the "Beecher-Scoville" collection at Yale's Sterling Library, which describes a philosophy *with* love in it in terms indistinguishable from religious illumination. The reader is hard pressed to say which it is. This MS. is attributed to H. B. Stowe erroneously. It is not in her hand, and it is assigned to her only on the strength of its being bound with a MS. which is her's ("The Silence of Jesus") and, in addition, its direct address to her brother, Henry Ward Beecher. Might it be Calvin's? The hand is not too dissimilar from his *deliberate* hand.

35. Mr. Matthew McClelland, January 16, 1976, for the course, Government 151.

36. Fiedler, *Love and Death*. p. 196. Citations refer to the reprint edition.

37. See book II, part I, chapter 24.

38. "Remarks Made . . ."

39. ALS, H. B. Stowe to "My Lord __________," Jan. 20, 1853 (Huntington Library).

40. ALS, C. E. Stowe to H. B. Stowe, July 11, 1853, Andover (Stowe-Day).

41. H. B. Stowe to C. E. Stowe, 1851, Andover (Stowe-Day). Gossett, Sundquist, and Hedrick do cite this letter, but without drawing this conclusion. Gossett, *UTC and American Culture*, p. 91; Sundquist, *New Essays*, p. 7; Hedrick, *Harriet Beecher Stowe*, p. 206.

42. E. Bruce Kirkham, "Harriet Beecher Stowe: Autobiography and Legend," in *Portraits of a Nineteenth Century Family*, ed. Earl French and Diana Royce (Hartford, CT: Stowe-Day Foundation, 1976), p. 61.

43. Ibid., p. 60.

16

Calvin's Ideas

It must not be thought that Calvin Stowe's work is presently neglected because it cannot stand on its own. Besides the notice he received in encyclopedias and other standard references of his own time, and besides the fact that his work long stood as a standard curricular item in theology seminaries, standard histories of public education have often credited him with nearly as much influence in the American public education revolution as Horace Mann and Henry Barnard. Indeed, the difference between Mann and Calvin, for example, was rather that Mann entered upon systematic campaigns to affect the reform of education, while Calvin always remained essentially a teacher. It is not uncommon in intellectual history that the influence of teachers must be recovered from the shadows of the deeds of practitioners. As Harker comments in his definitive dissertation on Calvin, Mann was still a practicing lawyer while Stowe was helping to launch the common schools movement.[1]

In light of the historical influence of *Uncle Tom's Cabin,* it is no longer possible to make a neat and simple division between the ideas of Calvin Stowe and the ideas of H. B. Stowe. It may be said of them as truly as of anyone that they were collaborators. Nonetheless, to form the "mind at the West" was Calvin's own project—articulated as it was in implicit opposition to Lyman Beecher's "anti-papist" *Plea for the West.*[2] That this was his own project we learn from the essay that Calvin Stowe alone wrote in 1838. The essay, "Advantages and Defects. . . ," was originally a lecture addressed to the young men in the Colleges of Marietta and Hudson, Ohio. The lecture ended with a ringing appeal to the young men of the West to secure the "destinies of a world for ages yet to come . . ."

> a world beyond comparison greater than past ages ever witnessed, and destined to a glory *or* a wretchedness, which will throw all past history in the shade, according as you lay the forming hand on the fused and gushing tide of human nature which is billowing around you.[3]

In this article—written four or five years *before* Calvin called his wife to join him—he widens his audience to include the entire country, revealing thereby that the project of "forming the mind at the West" was none other than the attempt to account for or provide an American morality.

An earlier essay, "Importance of Studying the Bible in Connexion with the Classics," briefly laid the foundation for the formation of the mind in the West; that is, for education. Calvin answered Mr. McClelland's question: "Yes, education is necessary to desire freedom in any proper sense." Education he defined as nothing less than development of "intellectual and moral" power sufficient, in each, to "entire control over all his faculties" and employing those faculties in "the various purposes for which they were designed." The education that grants such liberty varies with the "character in the learners" but may be measured to the circumstances. The chief circumstance is consciousness of universal obligation—"ties of brotherhood"—and the chief purposes to which human faculties are adapted are adding to the happiness of mankind, on the one hand, and "governing of one's own passions," on the other hand. The "common sense" teaching of the Bible conveys the fundamental condition of freedom, and heightened intellectual powers provide for the realization or achievement of freedom to the degree possible. The combination of "a free representative government," recognizing "the rights of men, as men," and not as nations,[4] and the determination to preserve the "simplicity and life and vigorous freshness" of human intellect is the objective of Calvin's project.[5] In a series of articles done for the *Christian Watchman* starting in 1840, Calvin repeatedly cited Paley's epigram: "To send an uneducated child into the world, is little better than to turn a wild beast or mad dog into the streets." Some preparation was required to move from the "savage state" to the civil state. Freedom does not come to men without effort, *naturally*. And the great problem is to provide in advance for that effort which would preserve it. In the third of the *Watchman* series Calvin reflected on the need to eliminate the chief defect of the very necessary political representation; that is, how to eliminate subordination of intelligence to ignorance. To Calvin, the "civil" subordination of intelligence was not to be distinguished from the disharmony of the savage state.[6] H. B. Stowe provides an analogous account in *Dred*, where we see life springing forth in odd, dangerous shapes because an "unnatural pressure hinders it" in its development.[7] In the essay on the "Advantages and Defects of the Social Condition of the United

States," Calvin demonstrates to America's most trenchant critic that the life of freedom *and* excellence is possible.

The essay is called forth by Tocqueville's *Democracy in America*. It is a response to—though it does not entirely disagree with Tocqueville—two elements of *Democracy in America*. The first is Tocqueville's account of American mediocrity, and the second is his account of equality. In Tocqueville, the first is really a consequence of the particular form of the latter. Calvin however, finds it necessary to advance the problem of slavery as the decisive ground upon which equality has to be comprehended in America. Thus, the problem of mediocrity is referred exclusively to the role of aristocracy in the modern regime as contrasted with its role in the *ancien régime*. To Calvin, mediocrity becomes a consideration only to the extent that the political system seems to withhold occasion for the display of human excellence or, to deny the efficacy of individual effort. That is not a necessary consequence of the principle of equality, though it may be a consequence of democracy understood as merely anti-aristocratic.

To reveal the nature of Calvin's project it is necessary to consider his essay in some detail. To begin, Calvin effusively praised his country and countrymen. We have the greatest capacities of any people yet formed. These capacities "ought" to produce a "society far superior" to all other human efforts. He applies a teaching from the passages of Tocqueville, of which particular teaching he gives extensive citation in the body of his essay: that is, the necessity to flatter the democracy in order to gain its ear. The flattery, however, is quickly qualified by introduction of the idea that the Americans do not live up to their full capacities. In that, Calvin follows his own teaching, derived from the "Dissertation on the Use of Wit." One section exhibits the use of wit in reproof of those who are "generally too conscious of their own superiority to listen to a plain statement of their failings." Wit is employed to avoid producing "anger and contempt instead of reformation." It "conceals the harshness" of reproof under a pleasant garb.

> By such means it is possible for the virtuous to bring fashion over to their own side, and thus to secure the outward reformation at least of a host of imitators, who will neither be drawn by reason nor driven by ridicule from treading in the steps of the great.[8]

The example of this serious wit, as distinguished from the other forms Calvin discussed, is found in a sermon preached before the sovereign, Louis XIV. The preacher apparently concluded his sermon with an apology: "I know it is customary for those preaching before you to pay you a compliment; but I hope you will excuse me, for I have been searching the Bible through to find one and am sorry to tell you, that I have not succeeded."[9]

The sovereign democracy is inferentially still more imperious than was Louis XIV, as Tocqueville argued. For Calvin paid it its compliment and spoke of its "providential advantages," and though he searched, could find in the Bible only reproofs to his nation. The essay was headed by two biblical epigrams. The first was ambiguous, "He hath not dealt so with any nation," from *Psalm* 147.[10] The second epigram was the unambiguous and direful lament, "What could have been done more to my vineyard, that I have not done in it? Wherefore, when I looked that it should bring forth grapes, brought it forth wild grapes," from *Isaiah* 5.

Tocqueville's teaching found the flattery and self-deprecation essential to American democracy the necessary means of self-aggrandizement and civil peace for individuals. He did not consider it an instrument for the moral reformation of the people. Calvin quoted the following passage from *Democracy in America*:

> The ruling power in the United States . . . must not be jested with; the smallest reproach irritates its sensibility; the slightest joke, which has any foundation in truth, renders it indignant; everything must be made the subject of encomium, from the very structure of their language to their more solid virtues. No writer, whatever his eminence, can escape from this tribute of adulation to his fellow citizens. The majority lives in the perpetual practice of self-applause, and it is only from strangers or from actual experience, that the Americans have any chance of learning some truths.[11]

Though Calvin accepts the cogency and truth of this argument—as his flattery shows—he says, flattering further, that it is exaggerated. But at that point his own speaking truly and in flattery coincide, for he insists that it would be disastrous to repose the entire fate of a nation on chance (deriving truth from an intelligent foreigner is also a matter of chance). Consequently, he sets about reconstructing Tocqueville's account of America in a way that is designed to reveal and encourage an indigenous concern for the preservation of truth and goodness.

Calvin's point of departure is Tocqueville's chapter 3, in the first volume, which was simply entitled the "Social Condition of the Anglo-Americans." The purpose of that chapter was to describe the social conditions of the regime of equality in such a way as to reveal the political practices required of the regime. By titling his own essay the "Advantages and Defects of the Social Condition," Calvin indicates a greater range of choice as to the moral and political forms that derive from the social condition. And this greater range of choice is opposed to the irresistible development of majoritarian democracy operating tolerably only insofar as it preserves the tendency to consult rational self-interest.

The fact that Tocqueville's chapter 3 is Calvin's point of departure suggests that Calvin accepts the theoretical foundation of *Democracy in America* laid out in chapters 1–3. But, in order to make the case for the regime of equality's openness to moral guidance, his version of chapter 3 must return to Tocqueville's notion of the irresistible advance of equality. He must provide a substitute version that leaves greater choice.

This is accomplished, first, by the insistence that the advance of equality is inevitable—not just irresistible—but that it advances by way of moral precept and as a source of moral distinctions. Secondly, he argues that the development of rational self-interest is not a consequence of the advance of equality and, in fact, attempts to resist that motion.

Primarily, then, he reconstructs the principle of equality and only then accepts Tocqueville's argument. And, in the process, he blames not this reconstructed equality for the threatening elements of democracy but the temptations of self-interest which reliance upon rational self-interest as opposed to moral precept makes possible.

What reveals the flaw of Tocqueville's view of equality is the fact that he sees equality as complete among the citizens and not, in itself, compromised by the existence of slavery and the treatment of the Indians. Tocqueville's reflections upon these oppressions are no less severe than Calvin's, but Tocqueville's political vision permits him to separate the condition of a particular polity from its external relationships. A nation's relationships with those who are not its own citizens are essentially on the same footing as its relationships with other nations. While Calvin accepts the necessity of the particularity of regimes, he insists, on the other hand, that the particular polity founded on the basis of equality can maintain the efficacy of that moral principle only insofar as it understands its justification to be derived from its own universal and historical necessity. That is, the principle of equality can be justly applied to a nation only when any human beings who may fall within that nation's jurisdiction are comprehended in the form and requirements of the principle. On that basis he corrects Tocqueville. One finds, he says, an almost complete equality in *the free states*, where Tocqueville spoke of the nation generally.

It is true that Tocqueville provides a moving account of the differences between slave and free states on opposite sides of the Ohio River (an account which is imitated in the dramatic account of Eliza's and George Harris's escapes and the parallel descent of Uncle Tom aboard *La Belle Rivière*).[12] But Calvin finds the charge that America is untrue to itself weaker and less profound than the charge that it is negligent in its moral duty. And it is this that is the decisive defect of her social condition, since attention to moral duty is *the* condition of exploiting the advantage of that social condition.

Let us take a quick look at the summation of those advantages and defects that contain the reconstructed account of equality. The chief advantage of their social condition, Calvin says, consists in the fact that Americans *began* from the highest point of civilization ever reached by man. That high civilization does not consist in undifferentiated advance on every point. The oldest civilizations—the "great Egyptian and Oriental monarchies"—remain unexcelled in their achievements in both the heavier and lighter arts. Nonetheless, their success was tainted by the fact that an unjustly small proportion of the people shared in the progress.

> Not one man in a hundred thousand of that ancient era enjoyed the benefit of its advancement. . . . A very few were hereditary lords, the many, the vast majority, were hereditary, hopeless slaves.[13]

It was this oppression of the many—burdening "human nature" beyond what it could endure and beyond what God would permit—that led to the bloody dissolution of those empires. They were succeeded by Greece and Rome, which diffused the refinements of civilization more widely. Then, one in every three persons benefited. Again, the blood flowed. This process continued through the successive ages of man, until, at length, "England had made the farthest advances in everything calculated to elevate the intellect and the morals of the whole people . . ."

> It was from the best portion of this most advanced of the nations of the earth, from that very class of the population which had made her what she was . . . that our nation took its origin.[14]

It is a singular fact that this Christian theologian derives his inevitable moral history from pre-Judeo-Christian roots, while Tocqueville, relating for the most part the same events, commences his irresistible history in the Christian era. Calvin asserts the providential character of this history, but emphasizes its pagan or secular roots. He thinks it a decree of heaven but *because* the "analogy of providence shows it." Now, the "analogy of providence" is a determined history. It is an analogy only because it works as providence *would* work except—"it cannot be reversed." Calvin united evangelical millennialism and German idealism by substituting the political or moral art for miracle, thereby altering both. From this perspective Christianity need no longer be a political problem, and the foundation of German idealism—what Calvin calls "egoism" as distinguished from "egotism"[15]—is no longer the atom of human association.

Because of this historical advance and the change in human circumstances, the origin of American society differs radically from the origins of all previous societies.

> The history of nations [as such] has generally commenced in rude barbarianism, in savage and plundering wars, in ambition and selfishness and violence.[16]

But in America we have the example of men establishing from already developed motives of civilization a new type of nation. These men possessed "an enlightened conscience" and they abandoned the quest for comfort for something higher. Thus, they were in a position to set a term to that inevitable historical development. We noted that as more and more people were comprehended in the benefits of society, the quality of the refinements of civilization had diminished. The benefits must have been essentially material. In England, where the "whole people" were finally comprehended, we must have had at the same time the prospect of comfortable preservation for all and the threat of an utter loss of the refinements of civilization. It is in this context that we find some, "the best portion" of that population, consciously formulating the principle of a life dedicated to the refinements—particularly, the moral refinements—of civilization.

> They were truly men of principle; they not only held to the principle [the necessity to transmit to posterity certain great moral principles] distinctly and decidedly in theory, but uniformly acted on principle, and reckoned no sacrifice too costly, when called upon to make it for the sustaining of principle.[17]

Now the circumstances of this undertaking were such that they required the recognition and acceptance of *all* the achievements of the historical advance.

So the American fathers had to pursue their objectives—the empire of goodness, we might say—on the basis of complete equality, or, participation by all in the progress of society. With their principles, therefore, they transmitted to their descendants democratic institutions. The charge to their descendants was to realize the distinctive excellence of human life without endangering the conditions of human liberty. They who can become good—the best men—must do so without a privileged position in the laws and they must in their goodness advance the level of the many so far as they can—nay, so far as they rely on no artificial distinctions, they cannot avoid advancing the level of the many as they advance themselves.

Calvin next noticed that what Tocqueville first encountered in America was the "perfect equality of rank that obtains in our free states." But Calvin argued that this resulted from the *final* victory of the many over the few, rather than a continuing battle. Every person now is to make his own rank for himself. And it is in this freedom that the opportunity for the good is discovered. "If one is disposed to do good . . . no law and no governmental authority [may] prevent him" (135). The same advantage is derived from the separation of religion and politics which, permitting religious baseness, nonetheless permits religion that is "comparatively pure, moral, and free." Coupled with the further advantages of "abundance," the intentional construction of a polity "designed to secure the greatest happiness of the greatest number," and the identification of the individual's interest with the "intellectual and moral advancement" of his fellows, these elements of the American social condition provide a blueprint for the actions of the good. His specific addressees are those who, in other times and nations, may have deserved to be included in an aristocratic party. The decline and vulgarity of the many, he insists, is the responsibility of the few for so long as changes in the form of society do not diminish the power and effectiveness of rhetoric and moral example. He seems not to notice the connection between aristocratic virtues and the forms and honors of aristocratic life. These latter seem to constitute a form of education without which aristocratic virtue may not be possible. But, in the list of "Our Defects," the suggestion is made that religious and academic instruction, if rightly managed, can supply the absence.

The first of the defects is a "vast amount of vulgar and obtrusive vice" (142). This defect derives in part from the same source as all the other defects: that is, the extensive development of material well-being in the absence of submission to a moral principle. The reliance upon rational self-interest to govern the souls of a prosperous people is insufficient.[18]

> What a sad want of knowledge and of conscience in regard to moral principle is manifested even by many who are communicants in Christian churches! Whose conscience reproaches him for making what is called a good bargain! that is, taking more for a thing than it is worth, or buying a piece of property at half its known value? On whose word can you rely to keep a contract, when breaking it will bring more money? A man who uniformly keeps his word, is a prodigy and a wonder. (150)

This characterization is followed by the account of American egoism and the imperiousness of majority opinion. Because this opinion allies itself with rational self-interest and not with the refinements of civilization, American politics is said to suffer. This is evident in the "disgusting airs and intolerable assumptions of the ignorant and noisy though successful aspirant, for wealth or popular favor" (150). The entire process supplants the judgment and "authority of an elevated few" with the "uncompromising discipline" of a party. And party principles become the means for the pursuit of self-interest.

Throughout the discussion of defects, the theme is the *moral inconsistency* that attachment to rational self-interest produces. The *most frequent illustrations involve slavery*, and the *fifth defect* is said to be *the existence of slavery*. The earlier illustrations are balanced, showing moral inconsistency on both sides. Then the account of slavery shows the inconsistency peculiar to itself. That account is again of a decline from the founding generations. "The making of money now became the ruling passion . . . and by degrees the whole nation was becoming tolerant towards slavery" (155). And the very struggle over slavery—borrowing its tone from the prevailing social condition—involves mutual recrimination and abuse. But "it is all wrong, and shows a state of public conscience that must be anything but pleasing to a God of purity or love" (p. 156). It is this shift from *"public sense,"* used throughout the essay until the end, to *"public conscience,"* that reveals the nature of the defect understood generally. *Rational self-interest produces a public sense but not a public conscience.* It takes an issue like slavery to reveal the presence or absence of public conscience. There is in the nation, he says, "a want of shame."

Calvin's particular response to the difficulty is to call on "men of principle and piety" to involve themselves in political affairs. God, he suggests, would "not have permitted such a form of government to be established" except to give "men of principle an entire and unobstructed field for the exertion of their influence [?]" (157). This seems somewhat less chimerical in light of his perspective of an inevitable advance. In all prior regimes, the best men retained some privileged position from which to affect the moral formation or reformation of society. And the question Calvin is dealing with is whether that is not possible in this country. But if it is so, and the principle of the regime will be retained, it must result from extreme disinterestedness.

The second proposition for reform is that "men of principle and piety unite" in their endeavor to impart a higher tone to democracy. In short, he demands the formation of an aristocratic party without aristocratic interests. But he does not expect it to rule so much as influence the tenor of democratic rule.

> If the democracy[19] is to rule, as it surely must in this country, then the democracy must be enlightened and well principled, or it will speedily run into reckless anarchy, and end in military despotism, as it did in France. (158)

The achievement of this objective will depend upon the union of men of influence—disinterested and able men. But they are not unqualifiedly disinterested. For, they are to preserve not only the nation but also the moral refinements of civilization. Their refusal to work in this effort is likened to a man who disdained a turn at the pump of a leaking ship, "because he was a passenger, forsooth, and not a sailor."[20]

Calvin closes the essay by revealing that he gained a sense of the "immense importance" of this work as he traveled abroad studying European institutions. He is a Tocqueville in reverse. His understanding has prepared him to participate in the formation of "our national character." On this depends the "decision of the great question of coercion or self-government, of physical force, or moral power" (159). The expressions are derived almost literally from Tocqueville. This project is to be undertaken first "at the

West"—where he happens to be a professor, at Lane Seminary in Cincinnati—rather than in New England. The reason is that society in the West is more "peculiarly democratic"—unaffected by the "influence of the old world." And the feeling of citizenship is more intense in the West, with "more jealous pride in being American, more of the distinctive features of nationality" (160). In other words, Calvin intends to build upon that same unstable material which Tocqueville cites as responsible for President Andrew Jackson.

The argument is not simply anti-Tocquevillean. This is manifest in Calvin's call for an aristocratic party. Rather, his reconstruction of equality is more connected with the requirements of applying Tocqueville in America. The difficulty of the initial formulation derives from *Democracy in America's* direct address to identifiable aristocrats and the attempt to persuade them to guide democracy, the condition of which was abandoning defense of aristocratic forms and turning to the defense of principle. The application of Tocqueville in America, on the other hand, seemed to call for the discovery of a specific endeavor, the undertaking of which could lead men of principle to discover the necessity of their guiding democracy indirectly. Slavery comes to the center precisely because in America the situation is the reverse of that in France. But slavery can come to the center only on the basis of a reconstructed view of equality.[21] Calvin has indeed learned from Tocqueville. This fact is indicated in the text by the reference to an "intelligent foreigner," which introduces the quoted passage that speaks of the Americans' incapacity to learn from each other. Having learned from Tocqueville, however, he begins the elaboration of a project that is intended to negate or overcome that sad truth. This required recurrence to the historical account of the struggles between the few and the many. The lesson to be learned from this new inevitable history, however, is not that the meaning of democracy is derived from its continual opposition to aristocracy. For that would condemn the historical process and refined understanding to come to an end with the achievement of majority rule. What this history reveals is that democracy derives its meaning not from the circumstances of its birth but from the implicit promise to realize universal moral equality. For a social-political movement to properly reflect the expansiveness of history, we must witness a gradual extension of civil participation to the point of universality without requiring any particular disenfranchisements along the way. The aristocratic party that commences the process must always be comprehended by it. Where that obtains democratic tyranny is avoided, at least against the few rich or best, and may be averted from hated minorities in general.

The project of forming the "mind at the West" is an attempt to form the American mind—a project that balances and legitimizes concern for moral principles on the foundation of the democratic regime, and the achievement that permits the ringing appeal to the young men in the West at the conclusion of the essay.

> You, I say, hold in your hands the destinies of a world for ages yet to come, of a world beyond comparison greater than past ages have ever witnessed, and destined to a glory or a wretchedness, which will throw all past history in the shade, according as you lay the forming hand on the fused and gushing tide of human nature which is billowing around you. Men to whom such responsibilities are entrusted should be men of thoughtful, upright, thoroughly furnished minds, men at the farthest remove from rashness, selfishness and superficial views—they should have the steadiness, the religiousness, the far-reaching forecast of the pilgrim fathers . . . , united with the buoyancy, the enterprise, the sprightly, adventurous fearlessness of the pioneer of the West. (160)

Now I contend that it is *this* project with which Calvin Stowe wished to associate his wife in 1842. The "Dissertation of Wit" reveals Calvin's conviction that plain speech or academic speech is inappropriate to the work of moral reformation. Because he cannot address identifiable aristocrats, as can Tocqueville, he must speak to men of principle at the same time he speaks to all Americans. The "Preface" to *Sunny Memories of Foreign Lands* (written by H. B. Stowe) offers the most concise statement of the situation. For that book, it is there said, is addressed only to "really excellent and honest" Americans. And *both* of the Stowes undertook the task of explaining to such minds what really happened on their English anti-slavery campaign *and* the true meaning of *Uncle Tom's Cabin*.

NOTES

1. John Stanley Harker, "The Life and Contributions of Calvin Ellis Stowe" (Ph.D. diss., 1951; hereafter cited as "The Life and Contributions").
2. Lyman Beecher, *A Plea for the West* (Cincinnati: Truman & Smith, 1835).
3. Stowe, "The Advantages and Defects," p. 160.
4. Cf. Harriet Beecher Stowe, *Dred: A Tale of the Great Dismal Swamp* (Boston: Sampson and Company, 1856).
5. Calvin E. Stowe, "Importance of Studying the Bible in Connexion with the Classics," in *American Biblical Repository* (1832).
6. Compare the discussion of Carlyle in, book I, part I, chapter 11.
7. *Dred*, vol. II, Ch. 28, "Engedi," pp. 274–275.
8. Calvin E. Stowe, "Dissertation on the Use of Wit in Matters of Religion," Stowe-Day Library (Hartford, CT, 1823).
9. Ibid.
10. The import of the passage as a whole is positive, but as yet God has withheld his judgment.

11. Stowe, "The Advantages and Defects," p. 151.
12. See book I, part I, chapter 10.
13. Stowe, "Dissertation on the Uses of Wit," p. 131.
14. Ibid., p. 132.
15. That is, giving prominence to oneself in deed as opposed to giving prominence to oneself in speech.
16. Stowe, "Dissertation on the Use of Wit," p. 133.
17. Ibid., p. 133.
18. Calvin Stowe returns to a discussion of the inadequacy of self-interest to govern in an 1844 essay. Calvin E. Stowe, "The Religious Element in Education," in *An Address Delivered before the American Institute of Instruction at Portland, Maine, August 30, 1844* (Boston: William D. Ticknor & Co., 1844; hereafter cited as "The Religious Element in Education").
19. This is the first use of "democracy" in this sense—a specific reference to the class of the untutored many.
20. Though no attribution is given by Calvin in the essay, this appears to be a version of a "joke," found in the *Joe Miller's Book of Jests* (1739):

> Not much unlike this Story, is one a Midshipman told one Night, who said, that being once in great *Danger* at *Sea*, everybody was observed to be upon their Knees, but one Man, who being called upon to come up with the rest of the Hands to Prayers, not I, said he, it is your Business to take Care of the Ship, I am but a passenger.

I thank Professor Murray Projector of Claremont McKenna College for bringing this passage to my attention.
21. See chapter 1, p. 5, "The Question of Equality."

17

The Central Problem: Slavery

Calvin Stowe was convinced that poetic charm had to be the medium of that address to the many that could also instruct the few.[1] He wished most of all to associate his wife in his project because he conceded her capacity to clothe naked ideas in the bright garb of poetry. The first example of the closeness between her capacities and his project is seen in the years following his effort to enlist her aid. In 1844–1845, he was engaged in a heated controversy over slavery within the American Board of Foreign Missions. The controversy led to extensive publication of essays by Calvin, Lyman Beecher, and Leonard Bacon and their allies. Their essays called forth extensive rebuttals, in particular, a book by Amos Phelps. Phelps's work, published posthumously in 1848, was titled *Letters to Professor Stowe and Dr. Bacon on God's Real Method with Great Social Wrongs . . .*[2] We are not much concerned with the details of that debate.[3] But the question in dispute is important. At stake was a judgment as to whether slavery (and slaveholders) should be condemned on the basis of absolute and transcendent biblical principles or on the basis of its incompatibility with the principles of American institutions. Calvin apparently concedes the justice of a general condemnation of slavery as a system, but insists that particular remonstration be generated by a concern for healthy political principle.

In September, 1845, Calvin Stowe delivered a speech at Brooklyn, subsequently revised and printed in the *Boston Recorder*, "on the subject of organic sin."[4] This speech was a high point in a great controversy engulfing the American Board of Foreign Missions and the New School Presbyterians. The controversy stemmed, most directly, from the discovery that some of the missionary churches among the Indians had tolerated the institution of slavery. New School Presbyterianism had come into being partially over the subject of slavery. The discovery of the practice of slavery in the Indian churches was a particular difficulty that only highlighted a general problem that had been simmering since 1836. In that year the "Oberlin group" departed Lyman Beecher's and Calvin Stowe's Lane Theological Seminary, in a demand for a more absolute anti-slavery position. The general question, which had matured by 1845—along with the maturation of Theodore Dwight Weld and others into full-fledged abolitionists—was how should the church regard the slaveholder? Could he be included in the fellowship, even though owning slaves? Or, must fellowship be made to depend—as Quakers had done before—on emancipation?

Calvin's speech on "organic sin" was the apogee in the attempt to distinguish slaveholding and the slaveholder, the regime (citizen) and the man. With it he bought himself considerable problem. A member of the Board of Missions, Amos Phelps, attacked the speech. Phelps had shortly before assumed office in the American Anti-Slavery Society. Phelps's attack is of great interest because it reveals the problem Calvin had to deal with—the problem inherent in the ideas he was developing. I will concentrate rather on Phelps's attack—the case for Phelps—than Calvin's speech, for the burden is to show ultimately that Phelps's breached a weak point which is not shored up until *Uncle Tom's Cabin* appears to broad acclaim for its true biblical principles.

Calvin Stowe was associated in this struggle with his father-in-law and employer, Lyman Beecher, and also his friend, associate, and coeditor of the *American Biblical Repository*, Leonard Bacon. Phelps attacked all three, suggesting that they had deliberately undermined a strong, uncompromising abolitionist stand against the admission of slavery into the church even as a necessary evil. With historical precedent apparently on his side, Phelps set out to establish a solid biblical argument as well. This made Calvin Stowe, the scholar of the trio, the chief object of the attack. Phelps distinguished three ways of viewing slavery, according as it is (1) sinful simply,[5] (2) an innocent practice and rightful system except as abused,[6] and (3) "that of the wrongfulness of slavery as a system, but the innocence of the individual slaveholder, though part of a bad system." Phelps attributed this last to Calvin Stowe, the first to himself and the American Anti-Slavery Society. His purpose, thus, is to prove against Calvin that "slaveholding (saying nothing of personal treatment either way) is a sin, and always a sin" and thus to rebut the "last entrenchment of slavery in the free states."

Phelps maintained that Calvin Stowe, as a defender of the view that a human being may be at once a "sincere Christian" and a slaveholder, was a defender of slavery itself. Phelps rejected the distinction based on regime—or system—characteristics that he acknowledged to be the intent of the term "organic sin." He quotes Calvin that "war, polygamy, slavery, and such like wrongs, all stand on the same ground . . . different from theft and drunkenness and other individual, personal sins . . ."[7] But he believed the argument from the regime to go further than it did. Where Calvin would maintain that those institutions and habits, for which personal responsibility alone cannot account, ought not to be made the basis of personal guilt, Phelps sees only *diverse* standards of right. He could not imagine that "civil government is an organic sin" itself, within the context of which individuals may be wholly Christian. Accordingly, he rejected the definition as "a jingle of words,"[8]

> which denies that [moral distinctions] have their foundation in the nature and relation of things as God constituted them; which makes that wrong today which was right yesterday, and that right in South Carolina which is at the same moment wrong in Massachusetts. . . . Such a doctrine, I admit, will save the world from fanaticism. It will save it from persecution too . . . avoiding direct conflict with the baptized and organic superstitions and vice that prevail . . .[9]

It should be clear that, whether correct in the main, Phelps attacked a great weakness in Calvin's conception. Calvin attempted to develop conditions by which principles of political attachment and Christianity could be simultaneously developed without either undermining the other. Phelps is correct to point to the contempt that Christianity's universal impulse bears toward politics.

We should note the complete title of Phelps's argument: *Letters to Professor Stowe and Dr. Bacon on God's Real Method with Great Social Wrongs in which the Bible is Vindicated from Grossly Erroneous Interpretations.* What is the leading element of these erroneous interpretations? The leading element is secularization, the dependence upon chains of social relationship:

> those poor "organs of government," acting from "organic necessity," and unable to get out of their "organic relations" without the double consent of themselves *and* the "body politic" . . .[10]

Phelps reminded Calvin that the thrust of the separation of church and state breaks the chains of social obligation rather than the chains of religion. The next leading element is dependence on "the doubtful and contradictory testimony of mutilated fathers" in the place of the immediate interpretation of gospel and prophecy.[11] And the last leading element is "German rationalism," whose imposing edifices create a successful imposture of advance over the first ages of the church, the age of covenant.

> It has this effect I suppose, because the general mind, by mistranslations, misinterpretations and philosophies, of long standing and doubtful origin, has been drilled to the belief, that the race did begin in barbarism, that Judaism was but an improved barbarism, and that, by consequence, blood-revenge, polygamy, and nameless other abominations did have the legal allowance in

> Mosaic economy, which you allege. Now, for me, I hold no such view. I will not consent to take my theories of the race, or my translations and interpretations of the Bible, unquestioned, at the hands of Rabbinical "tradition" or mutilated fathers, or Papal apostasy, or unregenerate and proud German rationalism, transferred though they may be to the current theological interpretations of our land and day.[12]

Phelps was no mere evangelical—any more than Calvin himself was—and Phelps acknowledged Calvin as an evangelical. The heresies of which Calvin stands accused, therefore, must have their origin rather in his peculiar approach to the common objective than in alienation from militant protestantism.

The explicit argument against Calvin is entirely biblical, and the implicit philosophical argument is scarcely noticeable. Hence, when Phelps hypothesizes the need for a model of the righteous wrongdoer in order to test Calvin's theory, he does not carry on with speculation but, instead, adapts Abraham to the test. This results in reducing the outstanding questions to judgments about Abraham's behavior. But the hypothesis was stronger. It sought one who would "be guilty both of individual transgressions and social wrongs," under the most exiguous circumstances, and with the highest of motives. The question Phelps posed, How might God judge such a man?, was to be but anticipatory of the immediate question, How ought *we* to judge such a man?

The implicit philosophic claim made by Phelps—permitting him to ignore the secular application of his model—is a perfect compatibility of individual responsibilities and social responsibility, such that whatever is wrong individually *must* be wrong for the group or state, whether commanded or not. Phelps discovers the higher law foundation of political life in perfect mastery of individual responsibilities. This is true even though the state is not ordinarily so pure, in its constituent elements, as the church is required to be.[13]

In all justice to Phelps I must add that he disclaims any interest in a utopia. The implicit status of his philosophic claim may be a measure of his concern with the immediate question, which he would phrase quite moderately as the demand that no Christian, having been instructed and warned, should *continue* to hold any man as a slave. He sees not that this demand might pose a problem.

> Messrs. Birney, Brisbane and others, whose hearts were really in it, have found no difficulty in detaching themselves from the system, and securing freedom to their bondsmen. And in the face of such facts, *until you can find a wiser and better man than Abraham, and can show in the path of duty, greater sacrifices of houses, lands and kindred behind, with more frightful exile and dangers among strangers than before, tell me not of the good slaveholder who cannot manumit his*

> *slaves, and holds them only for their good, and in all this walks orderly in Christ.*[14] (emphasis added)

Precisely to provide the Phelps's abolitionists the model beyond Abraham were Uncle Tom and Augustine St. Clare devised. This challenge could have been answered more easily and expediently. Calvin could have reminded Phelps that the slaveholder was—for the time—the gateway to the slave. To eschew commerce with the one until he repented was to consign the other to life without instruction. At that level neither Phelps nor Calvin is utopian.

Calvin's argument indeed goes farther and is not merely expedient. His claim, as Phelps suspected but did not wholly appreciate, is the greater claim that, to deny fellowship on the basis of participation in "organic sin" is to deny the church to humankind as such! On the slavery issue, Phelps is correct to see Calvin as a defender of slavery. For, indeed, Phelps too defends slavery to the precise degree that he defends or contributes to that regime or state which is tied to slavery as by an umbilical. Hence, the organic status of the sin. What sustains the life of slavery also sustains the life of those whose hearts are set against slavery and is, in turn, sustained by both supporters and opponents. To eject the slaveholder from the church, *prima facie*, is unjust so long as the other "defenders" of slavery remain in the church—indeed, themselves do the ejecting. To regard the institution as a sin, without regarding the individual *prima facie* as a sinner makes it necessary to shake off the "incubus" or "cancer" as the *only* recourse for the righteous. Setting one's heart against slavery is a necessary but not sufficient condition of righteousness.

Calvin's challenge tells on Phelps's insistence that Phelps really does separate church and state but yet is able, unlike Calvin, to identify the true state as effectively as he identifies the true church. To Phelps, one judges in the latter case by the state of the heart and in the other by the results, and Calvin's obtuseness is suspect.

> How then can you speak of such legal relations, so administered, as one with those of slavery? Are slaveholding and civil magistracy identical? Is civil government, as a system, equally with slavery, an organic sin? Why then confound what God and nature, common sense, and truth never put together?[15]

Rigid as is this insistence, Calvin's argument was its Achilles' heel driven home. By permitting *some* war, *some* "military arrangements," *some* "civil governments," and *some* "physical control of one human being over another" Phelps encounters the necessity to distinguish the legitimate forms of war from the illegitimate forms. His reduction of slavery to a "banditti" arrangement, "an impious social conspiracy" of "systematic and wholesale plunder" may be accurate and especially so when contrasted with the

"God-given" and by "nature" righteous defense "in the last resort" of a government's own "life." But, although men may judge of the one or the other state by the form that the ensuing "control" assumes, Phelps gives no indication as to how one may judge the incitement and motivation to war in any given case. The legitimate and illegitimate social forms are distinguishable only by their results in this argument. In addition, legitimate government is made to depend on purity of heart. Though following John Locke in declaring that "slavery is a state of war," Phelps departs from that course in imagining that it is easy to distinguish one state of war, which is slavery, from the state of war which is an attempt by a people to establish such forms of government as conduce to their safety and happiness. To judge by results alone is treacherous where the polls never close. Calvin Stowe accordingly demands a formulation of legitimacy expressed in more directly political terms relying less upon though answering the wish for purity of heart.

Calvin Stowe's principles are made clear through Phelps's attack. So too is the problem Calvin bought for himself. The problem is the need to defend efficacious indignation and righteousness, having denied the use of the most ready instrument for the expression of modern righteousness, the attack on politics itself in the name of higher law. Phelps sees the general problem as well as the defense of slavery. He thinks it insoluble. I quote at length.

> No, brother, in God's method, individual existence and responsibility are not so merged in those of the mass. The social or governmental wrong-doer, be he oppressor, extortioner, persecutor, spoiler, sabbath breaker, or warrior, God holds to as rigid a responsibility and as deep or deeper guilt, as if he did any or all of these by the spontaneity of his own will and the might of his own right arm. Any other doctrine turns civil government and its officers away from their God-appointed mission of the prevention and award of crime, and makes *it* the hiding place and sanctification thereof, and *them* its licensed and innocent perpetrators. *That,* which has no rightful existence and exercise, and *they,* who have no rightful prerogatives and functions, except as they are the representative and incarnation of the divine government and governor, are changed at once to sheer rebellion, . . . provided only that the abominations done are of the nature of social wrongs, perpetrated under the decencies and forms of law, and in deference to organic and social necessities![16]

The present work in large measure responds to that general criticism of Calvin Stowe. It is my good fortune to have come to the awareness of a need to defend Calvin and the writing of this section last of all. The result is that this work neither loses sight of its primary subject to pursue Calvin's theory in detail—a different work is that[17]—nor quails before the enormous burden Phelps has imposed on this enterprise.

It is a matter of great surprise to conclude upon reading Phelps that he was nearly seduced by Calvin's argument. He treats the professor with the greatest respect and deference. The criticism is wholly unmarked by the animosities of which the fiery Phelps was more than capable, unless denying to Calvin's principles the status of "divine truth" and dubbing them "human wisdom" be thought bitter recrimination. Throughout, he addresses his "Brother Stowe" as indeed a brother in Christ. The same cannot be said of the short review of "Dr. Bacon's" opinions, appended at the end of Phelps's volume. Neither does Phelps bring a biblical or theoretical argument to bear against Bacon. That exchange is entirely historical and polemical. It bears on Calvin by revealing, further, the political circumstance in which he and his associates assumed for themselves the task of providing the nation with guidance on the question of slavery. Though Phelps never attacks Calvin Stowe in connection with Bacon, he does make explicit mention of Lyman Beecher and Lane Theological Seminary, as well as Dr. Bacon's "associates." Phelps knows where Calvin stands, even if he cannot help liking him!

I refer the reader to Phelps's account of the controversy with the American Board in the work itself and in the issues of the *Boston Recorder* from September through October, 1845. I shall present here only the barest summary of the rejoinder to Bacon's account of that controversy. Leonard Bacon has argued, essentially, that the rigid demands of abolitionists were imposing barriers in the way of the church's efforts to incline its influence toward emancipation and instruction.

Phelps defended the anti-slavery society against the charge that it had agitated the question of slavery before the Board. Where Bacon referred to "memorials" presented over the years, Phelps retorted that, beginning in 1836, these were rare in themselves and none of them generated by the Society. The occasion for the charge and defense was the debate over the mission church problem. The Board had conducted its own inquiry in 1844, and acknowledged the existence of the situation. It decided against action for the moment, continuing the question in the care of a committee for the next year. Phelps, a board member, sought to bring the matter to public light. But he disclaimed notoriety on that score by pointing out that the 1836 memorial had already created much debate on a similar question—the Board had been *buying* slaves in order to free them—which had been brought to the attention of the Board by "certain students at Oberlin." Doubtless these were yet the remnant of Lane Theological Seminary's Anti-Slavery Society, led by Theodore Weld and removed to the new Oberlin College only the year before in the aftermath of a nation-rocking "free speech" movement at Lane. That small anti-slavery crisis has often been considered the beginning of the juggernaut that ran aground at Sumter. Hence, Phelps could claim neither to have heightened the sense of urgency at the Board nor to have originated the challenge.

The Board's committee despaired of any change that would not "be fraught with disastrous consequences to the mission, the Indians, and African race among them." But the question had become too large to be left in shadows. The question became, "What has the Christian church to do with slavery?" The Board, led by Bacon, moved relentlessly toward a resolution, its eye fixed on 1836 as much as on 1844, that the communicant "who buys and sells human beings as merchandise for gain" would undergo church discipline. Phelps asked for "holds" to be inserted between "who" and "buys"—his eye fixed on 1844. Lyman Beecher and Bacon agreed to the change, the resolution returned to committee, and a most unattended result produced the turmoil. Inexplicably, to Phelps, the initial committee report became the Board report, as Bacon's resolution and Phelps's amendment were both lost sight of. In the aftermath, however, Bacon defended the Board—as did Calvin Stowe—and Phelps attacked.

Where Bacon turned to disciplining "specific abuses," Phelps took aim "specially and chiefly, though not exclusively, against slaveholding itself, as the generic and comprehensive abuse . . ." Abandoning the "metaphysics of the question," Phelps argued that Bacon's approach had been discredited over the nearly sixty year period since 1787, when the Church first spoke forthrightly against slavery but did not deny fellowship to slaveholders. The struggle with Bacon remains the argument against Calvin.

> The sincere and earnest friends of religion and of the slave, everywhere and of every name, are fast coming to the conclusion that Christianity and slavery cannot coexist; That there is an utter incompatibility between them; and that *no teaching or discipline of the one can have any substantial, practical efficacy against the other,* which is not directed primarily, mainly, and rigidly against the thing itself, rather than its abuse.[18] (My emphasis)

When Phelps says "the thing itself," he means the human being actually holding the slave—not the institution, or the legal relation, or the violence, etc. He means that it must be a doctrinal requirement of the Christian church that individuals may be disciplined simply for holding a slave.

> Are you the men . . . to tell the world that all men are created free and equal, but that slaveholding is not as bad as dancing [disciplinable], or marrying a deceased wife's sister [disciplinable]? And when these good brethren set themselves to answer this question satisfactorily to a British audience—may I be there to see![19]

He did not survive to hear Calvin Stowe's and H. B. Stowe's answer, five years later. But answer they did, and before a British audience, that that same America on whose breast slavery suckled was *the* condition of human decency and goodness in this world—that is, of the consummation of universal Christendom.

The questions posed in Phelps's attack contain every question—though not directly expressed—involved in articulating the political philosophy of H. B. Stowe. In addition, centering around that critical period of 1842–1846, as they do, they make much more clear the nature of the fire that burned in the furnace where Uncle Tom was brazed. But we have yet to do with Calvin's problem: How to demonstrate in some practical, efficacious manner the abolitionist misconception that political rights are derived from extra-political sources. [See book I, chapter 4 for the statement of that problem.] But, the fact is that Calvin *never* answers in his own name the charges made by Phelps in 1848. H. B. Stowe's works are the answer, as I have demonstrated. Her response begins in the "Two Altars . . ." and continues in *Uncle Tom's Cabin.*[20] But let us skip to the *Key's* "The American Church and Slavery," that we may put a period to this phase of the dialogue.

Does H. B. Stowe stand up for her husband or for Phelps? Does she remain neutral? With the reader's permission, I shall intermit a note in the text. As described below, H. B. Stowe completed the *Key* and handed it to her publisher practically at the same moment she and Calvin embarked for an extensive tour of Great Britain. Yet, part IV of the *Key*, led off by the chapter on the church and slavery and devoted throughout to the question of Christianity and slavery, must have been written in the rush of parting preparations. Indeed mention is explicitly made of at least one report released in "March, 1853."[21] I should think it most unseemly to imagine that Calvin did not give considerable attention to this extensive work that, in fact, reads rather like a direct if not explicit response to Phelps. As it is demonstrable that the two of them undertook the English journey as a joint political campaign, the circumstantial evidence is great that part IV of the *Key* is a joint response to Phelps. Indeed, if it were ever possible to say for a certainty that editor Calvin Stowe was either author or co-author of a series of historical essays on slavery, published under the signature of "Editor" in the *American Biblical Repository* from the late 1830s through the early 1840s and carrying slavery from the earliest records through to that present moment, it would be an almost irrebuttable presumption that he authored those very similar passages in part IV of the *Key.*

The entire argument in the *Key* directs our attention to Calvin by its studied silence on that one element of church history, in an otherwise compendious account, with which both Stowes were clearly most familiar. Hence, this account of H. B. Stowe's ideas—unlike the rest of the present work—will appear rather more to present Calvin's views than Stowe's views. That results from our turning to the *Key* out of order merely because it is the only direct response to Phelps. It is true, however, that Stowe's first responses are the "Two Altars" and *Uncle Tom's Cabin,* and those both speak with her voice. Hence, we must still be aware that it is Stowe we seek ultimately to understand.

The heart of the argument, developed in the *Key*, lies in the history Stowe opposed to Phelps's history. While she outlines, under the sting of Bacon's charge of agitation, only those events the American Board confronted between 1835 and 1845 and the general resolutions of the Presbyterian Church dating back to 1787, Stowe gives a "full" account touching on several denominations and political events, stretching from 1780 up to 1853. Phelps is certainly justified in the circumstances in confining his account to facts that seem to exculpate himself. The occasional and singular memorials and petitions had nothing to do with him; he addressed them *in the end* only as a responsible member of the Board, and only the surprising refusal on the part of his brethren to condemn slaveholding itself produced the principled debate over organic and personal sins. Indeed, Phelps asserts, the Cincinnati Synod (the "Lane Seminary Synod") itself protested the Board report as giving "sanction" to slavery in the missions in opposition to Calvin Stowe and Lyman Beecher. Finally, it must be recalled that, while this controversy was alive in 1845, Phelps's publication of the arguments in book form was three years later.

On her side Stowe accomplishes two important arguments. First, the wider perspective of pro- and anti-slavery activities demonstrates the crisis to be isolated neither to the American Board nor to the New School Presbyterians. It is seen to engulf every denomination, Quakers excepted, and with parallel events. Hence, from 1780 to about 1818 a consistent anti-slavery position characterizes Methodist and Presbyterian general assemblies, for example. But starting about 1835, there is equally manifest a consistent decline from the earlier, strong anti-slavery position. From the late 1830s through the late 1840s all denominations are subject to separations, the development of distinct, sectional churches. In the midst of this history is the notable evidence—not emphasized—of increasing southern resistance, beginning in the early 1830s. This resistance is manifested, among other ways, in a rash of bounty offers for the heads of renowned or infamous abolitionists. In 1836 such a reward was placed on the head of Amos A. Phelps.

The lone specific mention of Phelps, in the year 1836, leads to the second achievement of Stowe's argument (and parallels Phelps's implicit mention of Lane Seminary's anti-slavery weakness in 1836). She refused any place in her chronology to any of the events listed by Phelps from 1835 on, with evidence conceded of an awareness of the same events, and thereby demonstrates a determination to place the dispute on new ground. The undermining of Phelps's claim to innocence is counter-balanced by a refusal to blame him and abolitionists for the heat of their reaction to a worsening situation. On the other hand, while Phelps had implicitly blamed Lane

Seminary, Stowe just as implicitly builds the reputation of Lane, beginning with an 1835 incident in which a Lane student who was selling Bibles in Tennessee was unceremoniously striped on suspicion of abolitionism. Mentioned near this, and repeated later, was the undated fact of a refusal by Lane professors to countenance pro-slavery sentiments in the clergy of the Cincinnati Synod, the only "instance of this sort" produced by a "somewhat extended examination."

The formation of the New School General Assembly in 1838, including the Cincinnati Synod, is next presented as an express response to the old Presbyterian national assembly's attempt to expel four activist anti-slavery churches. Although the schools of thought, Old and New, existed previously and independently of slavery, Stowe suggests that the actual formation of distinct ecclesiastical bodies resulted from the slavery dispute. There followed the New School General Assembly's own mixed record on slavery but one which eventuates in adopting and maintaining a policy of allowing local churches to establish policy on slaveholding. To this opportunity, Cincinnati Synod and certain "professors of Lane Seminary" responded with the expulsion of a pro-slavery minister. The repetition of this tale also fails to date the event, but so strongly places it in the context of measures taken from 1846 to 1849 as to invite an assumption of similitude.

It is not in fact relevant here when the expulsion occurred, because the dispute of '45 is not mentioned, nor is Phelps's book of '48. It is the use Stowe makes of the event that constitutes it a response, not its own evidence. The American Board of Foreign Missions was Congregational as well as Presbyterian, Methodist, etc. Unlike the first histories, that of the Congregational churches (Dr. Bacon's church) offers no dates. But the entire narrative closes by noting two facts of some significance. The Home Mission Society—the new organ of New School Presbyterians and Congregationalists—in a report of March, 1853, instructs its missionaries to make no compromise with slavery. Busily at work wherever slave societies will receive them, these missionaries "discharge their consciences" and are "awakening the consciences of the people."[22] In 1850 this same Society rejected a plea for missionaries who would not discuss slavery, since that would render vain the desire to establish churches in slave states (a problem dramatically represented in the novel *Dred*).

From the mere historical account we can see evidence of Stowe's search for means to oppose slavery without *prima facie* condemning individuals—that is, a means of preserving the advantage of the "necessary evil" perspective without conceding the "necessity" of slavery. The political events mentioned by Stowe are two: the admission of Missouri in 1820[23] and the "Fugitive Slave Law" of 1850. These are mediated by mention of a fact: in 1836—the year in which Methodists oppose abolition, Presbyterians divide over slavery, and rewards are offered for A. Phelps and Arthur Tappan—in

1836 the interstate slave trade is *reported* to be increasing. Stowe's history is more comprehensive than Phelps's because her own identifies church history with American history, allowing only the concessions that Presbyterians, New School Presbyterians, the Cincinnati Synod, and Lane Seminary have made somewhat more of a most dismal situation than nearly anyone else save the Quakers (whose principles may or may not be correct). Stowe's historical outline conforms to her judgment.

> The history of this Presbyterian Church and the history of our United States have strong points of similarity . . . both made a concession, the smallest which could possibly be imagined. . . . The little point of concession spread, and absorbed, and increased, from year to year, till the United States and the Presbyterian Church stand *just where they do.* Worse has been the history of the Methodist Church. The history of the Baptist Church shows the same principle; and as to the Episcopal Church, it has never done anything *but* comply, either North or South.[24] (My emphasis)

The disease, we might say, seems to be organic. As such it should require not isolated but systematic and global treatment. The question is whether it is possible to sustain the American regime *and* slavery, assuming the preferability of the former. It has by this point become a clear-cut regime question.

In addition to the historical outline, Stowe explicitly discussed the *principles* of the '45 debate. She began with a two-fold assertion. The church in the United States is a vast social and political power, in spite of formal separation. And the republican nature of the regime—its dependence on opinion[25]—implicates every republican citizen in the practical defense of slavery, whatever the actual status of his conscience. From this fundamental ground she constructed both the concrete response to Phelps's desire to part wheat from chaff and the formulation of a preferred alternative.

The argument from the power of the church is constructed around a simple syllogism. The American clergy exercise great power—as a body, perhaps more than any other men in the country. American clergy are usually elected by the "church," the congregation. "The clergyman is the very ideal and expression of the church." There is identity of opinion between clergyman and the church, else clergyman does not remain. The power of the clergyman is the power of the church, over which the clergyman, "free minister," has considerable influence. The church prepares minds to meet important questions.

From this perspective it is manifest that public opinion in the nation—the source of law—is moved to support slavery. The history of the church becomes a history of public opinion on the question. If the church is vitiated by either acceptance of slavery or compromise with it, it is idle to speak of purifying the church by removing the sinners. Instead, one must inquire what the church really believes of slavery and how to correct that opinion.

> Do these Christians merely recognize the relation of slavery in the abstract, as one that, under proper legislation, might be a good one, or do they justify it *as it actually exists* in America?[26]

Not only did Stowe consider the latter statement true of many southern churches, but she regarded the former statement as widely held even outside the South. Accordingly, she slices through all the quibbling about buying, selling, and holding men "for gain" with the notion that the "essence" of trade is gain—"the mere purposes of gain." Whatever upholds trading to any degree furthers gain.

The question is whether any incidental act of trade—such as Henry Ward Beecher's slave-auctions, necessarily furthering such gain—is also morally culpable. The answer is that the act is not morally culpable, while the necessity is morally heinous.[27] That is, the condition that makes such an action a virtue is an instance of the organic effect. Unfortunately, "the practical organic workings of the large bodies of the church, are all gone one way."[28] It must also be the case, then, that slaveholders themselves are subject to this organic effect—the "blinding power of custom" in its worst expression. Even the sincerely religious will have difficulty "elevating" themselves under the influence of slavery.

> After the Reformation, the best of men being educated under a system of despotism and force, and accustomed from childhood to have force, and not argument made the test of opinion, came to look upon all controversies very much in a Smithfield light, the question being not as to the propriety of burning heretics, but as to which party ought to be burned.[29]

We ordinarily expect to encounter many "sincere" and pious men, with respect to their particular circumstances and with little respect to the barbarity of their particular practices. When we make sincerity a test of the slaveholders' Christianity, however, we give up the struggle for right—unless we expect also to teach.

> There is something in conscientious conviction, even in case of the worst kind of opinions, which is not without respectability . . . that there may be very sincere Christians under this system of religion, with all its false principles and all its disadvantageous influences, liberality must concede . . . it is the deepest grief, in attacking the dreadful system under which they have been born and brought up, that violence must be done to their cherished feelings and associations.[30]

These sad reflections were drawn chiefly from a portrait of the southern churches. But a canvas of northern churches produced a conviction that the identical effect derived from commerce and temporizing with "an acknowledged sin."

The problem is clear: Christianity affords to the Christian neither the option to turn toward nor the option to turn away from the sinner, however abhorrent the sin. On the occasion when the New School General Assembly was petitioned to expel three slaveholding congregations, that body was besieged by the pitiful plea that it not spurn brethren who had stood by them and ultimately hoped to stand at their level. What, then, is to be done but to grind out compromise "between upper and nether millstone of two contending parties?" This standard were wonted in ordinary circumstances, but not in a great crisis.

> The Church of Christ since 1818 had done nothing but express regret and hold grave metaphysical discussions as to whether slavery was an "evil *per se*," and censure the rash action of men who, in utter despair of stopping the evil any other way, tried to stop it by excluding slaveholders from the church.[31]

To the rhetorical question, whether a little injustice were not worth it in order to do *something*, Stowe makes no direct reply. She only asks another question, "ought not something to be done . . . stopping the evil?"[32]

Before answering the query, Stowe notes an "ever-increasing" hostility to slavery in a decided majority of ministers and church-members, taken as individuals. What then impedes the crusade? First,

> the sincere opponents of slavery have been unhappily divided among themselves as to principles and measures, the extreme principles and measures of some causing a hurtful reaction in others. Besides this, other great plans of benevolence have occupied their time and attention and the result has been that they have formed altogether inadequate conceptions of the extent to which the cause of God on earth is imperiled by American slavery, and of the duty of Christians in such a crisis.[33]

It is no exaggeration to say that the latter cause is still weightier to Stowe than the former. The failure to see the centrality of America in the attack on slavery largely contributed to the disagreement among anti-slavery men. To mean well and "wreck the ship" or "lose the battle," she said, is to be lamented. When she declared that "we *are* wrecking the ship," she meant America. When she declared that "we *are* losing the battle," she meant the particular achievement of principles of right.

What it means to say that the battle is lost is that "everyone does as much for slavery as would be expedient, considering the latitude they live in."[34] This is the foundation for conjoining the republican and Christian attack.

But before that is made plain Stowe clearly spurns her brethren of lower latitude once and for all.[35] She inverts the plea for brotherly love: "We love his better self, and we will have no fellowship with his betrayer."[36] This is achieved in a passage that lauds the virtue which was possible for southerners. This means that it *is* appropriate to expel slaveholders from churches and slaveholding churches from general fellowship—Phelps has won the chief concession—*if* it is also true that the way to cure the patient's "disease" is through an attack on southern brethren, as it clearly does not lie in defending them.

> But it is clear who should be attacked: the sinner. Who sins? the whole power of government, and the whole power of wealth, and the whole power of the fashion, and the practical organic workings of the large bodies of the church . . .[37]

And it is the peculiar nature of the government that makes the sin peculiar. Clergymen who cite Paul's counsel to the bondmen—"bear with patience your thralldom"—neglect the fact that Paul was "only a fellow-sufferer" with them, not a "republican clergyman" with the right to make and sustain "those laws."

> What is this Church of our Lord Jesus Christ that they speak of? Is it not [in America] a collection of republican men, who have a constitutional power to alter these laws, *and* whose duty it is to alter them, and who are disobeying the apostle's directions every day till they do alter them?

Stowe made it clear in the beginning of part IV of *Key* that where she says church she also means clergymen, and *vice versa*, and indeed where she says clergymen, she means someone formed to the opinions of the many.

> Every law to which the majority of the community does not assent is, in this country, immediately torn down. Why, then, does this monstrous system stand from age to age? Because the community CONSENT TO IT.[38]

The majority rules! It favors slavery. It rules by right—consent of the governed. It is this that Phelps did not conceive. The expulsion of "the majority" from one's fellowship is nothing but self-exile. Slavery is indeed to be attacked, but not those sinful brethren whose opinions—consent—are necessary to remove slavery. They are northerners as well as southerners, who must be memorialized as better than they are—with brotherly love, even if inverted.

What is said of "every Christian at the South" who sustains slave law "as a republican citizen," is equally true of "every Christian at the North" with respect to prejudice and other horrors besides slavery. If men cannot so readily sight their enemies—as a guide to practice—might they achieve the same result by focusing on the objects of their mercy?

> Alas for the poor slave! What church befriends him? In what house of prayer can he take sanctuary? What holy men stand forward to rebuke the wicked law that denies him legal marriage? What pious bishops visit slave-coffles to redeem men, women, and children to liberty? What holy exhortations in churches to buy the freedom of wretched captives? When have church velvets been sold, and communion cups melted down, to liberate the slave? Where are the pastors, inflamed with the love of Jesus, who have sold themselves into slavery to restore separated families? Where are those honorable complaints of the world that the church is always on the side of the oppressed?—that the slaves feel the beatings of her generous heart, and long to throw themselves into her arms? Love of brethren, holy charities, love of Jesus—where are ye? Are ye fled for ever?[39]

Even *radical* abolitionists appear moderate indeed when judged against some of the standards of antiquity. But these standards all derive from the attempt to form practice around the necessity of salvation for some particular soul or souls.

That this is Stowe's intent, and response to Phelps, is revealed when, in relating the six conditions or means for the abolition of slavery, Stowe listed the first as consisting of three elements intended to "purify" the Christian from "complicity" with slavery. First is the elimination of prejudice. Second is to provide direct protection to black congregations. And third, the most important, is abstention from all "*trading in slaves*. . . . It is not necessary to expand this point. It speaks for itself" (my emphasis). This point speaks most volubly by cutting through the confusion over "buying, selling and holding." As the example of early martyrs revealed, it may be an act of mercy to buy or sell or hold a slave in some circumstances—perhaps the means to secure freedom to a slave. "Trading," on the other hand, can be entered only for profit. The test of Christianity will not be Phelps's "slaveholding" but rather profiting from slaves.

Having achieved this point—Calvin's victory over Phelps's argument on the strongest possible anti-slavery grounds—Stowe is then free to speak of gentle methods of persuasion and influence: not to "reject the good there is in any, because of some remaining defect." The conclusion, accordingly, is *all* Calvin. We find that an "irresistible influence is pervading the human race" and inclining it toward good.

> Worldly men read the signs of the times, and call this power the Spirit of the Age—but should not the Church acknowledge it as the Spirit of God?[40]

This is a complete merger. Tocqueville's irresistible force of equality and Hegel's world *geist* become the word of God. And the prophet of the Lord applies it to the "moral conflicts" of the hour, which conflicts are always won by "the party who can preserve, through every degree of opposition and persecution, a divine, unprovokable spirit of love." Mere indignation—"anger, wrath, selfishness, jealousy"—is vitiated by inherent weakness or defect. "Love and love only, is immortal."

> In undertaking this work, we must love both the slaveholder and the slave. . . .
> This holy controversy must be one of principle, and not of sectional bitterness.[41]

This means distinguishing the principles from the men—the citizen from the man—the "organic sin" from the personal sin.

> Some have supposed it an absurd refinement to talk about separating principles and persons, or to admit that he who upholds a bad system can be a good man. *All experience proves the contrary*. Systems most unjust and despotic have been defended by men personally just and humane. It is a melancholy consideration, but no less true, that there is almost no absurdity and no injustice that has not, at some period of the world's history, had the advantage of some good man's virtue in its support.[42]

Not merely general human limitations bear anti-utopian implications, but the connection between individual virtues and organic necessities bear such implications as well. The abolitionists, who *did not understand Uncle Tom's Cabin*, must surely have understood this. Yet, Lewis Tappan praises the first work and the *Key*'s defense of it throughout his correspondence, never questioning Stowe's *bona fides*.[43] Surely, conceding the right to revile the slave*trader* was not enough to win so major a concession. Might it be that the Phelps school was *persuaded* by the argument, just as Frederick Douglass's 1848 "What Country Have I?" was answered—apparently persuasively—in the debate Stowe staged with George Harris?

Though Calvin Stowe's argument is successful against Phelps's particular attack, it is not completely clear there are conditions of Christianity and political attachment that can be developed simultaneously, neither serving to undermine the other. The answer to that profound difficulty is suggested in all the works we have to consider. But we deal with it in this study only in the discussion of "Sunny Memories," which is specifically given to that task.[44] Paradoxically, however, it has been demonstrated, through the practical necessity of appealing to the majority and relying on consent, that radical abolitionists despise politics as such and appeal beyond the condition of political life—consent—in the attempt to defend individual rights. The picture of their self-exile—their willingness to refrain from commerce with all—even the majority who hold pure opinion—is comical to be sure but a matter of the gravest import.

There is no known explicit response from Calvin to Phelps's 1848 reprise. I invited the reader to consider Stowe's work, which shortly followed, the direct response. We have seen the form that it takes in the *Key*. But the earlier works are still more important, especially "The Two Altars." In addition, I would note that the fact that Stowe may be thought to respond to Phelps is no suggestion that she "had no ideas of her own." Calvin may have deferred not only to a superior pen, but also to a superior mind. There is certainly evidence enough of independence of mind on her part. The very opinion with which she begins in 1836—clouded only by Calvin's "views expressed" we know not how—shows a great strength and independence if a somewhat different view than emerges in 1849–1850. In 1836 she wrote her "Franklin" (the pseudonym she employed) attack on the Alton rioters, manfully calling on "every man to stand sternly up for"[45] law and order. But even then she was doubtlessly aware of her brother Edward's more fulsome account of the riots and slavery and was probably not spared the kind of opinion matured in Charles Beecher's—yet another brother—*The God of the Bible against Slavery*. That tract among other things describes the "legal relation existing" between master and slave as "intrinsically and unchangeably selfish."[46] Charles underscores what Stowe called "our question" in 1862.[47] The question was what would be the fate of America when God redeemed the slave—the question upon which Calvin insisted. And Stowe had not hesitated to emphasize the same question to Frederick Douglass more than ten years earlier—all the time affirming unbending hostility to slavery.[48] By the time Stowe joined forces in Phelps's debate, her defense of law and order had matured beyond protection of the "rights of property and free opinion." Stowe was prepared for the battle.

As that rather desultory debate had died down, the issue of slavery had heated up. The Fugitive Slave Law of 1850 focused attention. This excitement produced Stowe's first *serious* anti-slavery piece—not *Uncle Tom's Cabin* but a piece called "The Two Altars, or Two Pictures in One."[49] What especially distinguishes this piece—in view of her later work—is the attempt to relate the American founding and the character of slavery without a single invocation of scripture as precept. Indeed, the now-free-former-slave about to be captured as a "fugitive" is shown being taken immediately as he concludes a prayer of thanks for his prosperity. The piece consists of two short cameos. The first is subtitled "The Altar of Liberty, or 1776." The second is subtitled "The Altar of ______, or 1850." The blank in the title is supplied in the text, when the fugitive is said to be "sacrificed—on the altar of the Union." The object of attack is the "Compromise of 1850"—and its Whig defenders. In that, moderate and radical abolitionists could join. Hence, we see Stowe, previously unpublished on the controversy, being published by the American Anti-Slavery Society as Phelps had been earlier in his refutation of Calvin.

The original dispute was not lost in this camaraderie, however. We have noted that Stowe avoided the use of biblical precept and revealed mistaken political principles, blithely ignoring Christian brotherhood. Both these circumstances are reflected in the absence of the minister as such from *Uncle Tom's Cabin*. But Stowe's defense of the position identical to Calvin's is more fundamentally reflected in opposing slavery to liberty. That device permits her to argue silently that the question of which altar is the right political altar is prior, practically speaking, to the question of whether men will be granted access to a religious altar.[50] Her appropriation of a religious usage is also an appropriation of its substance. The same argument is presented at greater length and much more substantively in that section of *Uncle Tom's Cabin* where the minister *does* appear—though not in his function as minister. In the "Two Altars," then, we have the first evidence of the manner in which Calvin's naked ideas could be wafted poetically across the many, and at the same time, a specific cause be furthered, giving concrete expression to the import of those ideas.

It would be a mistake to think of this merely as Calvin's project, however. In Stowe's hands it becomes transformed. She explains the relationship in these words:

> My old rabbi and I here set up our tent, he with German, and Greek, and Hebrew, devouring all sorts of black-letter books, and I spinning ideal webs out of bits that he lets fall here and there.[51]

Thus it is that *Uncle Tom's Cabin*, in her hands, becomes something more than a demonstration of the possibility of goodness in the absence of protective social forms—the deepening or Americanization of the Tocquevillean project—but it becomes a rousing attack on the modern humanism which resulted in the paralysis of the practical good and a substitution of an ideal version. It takes an ordinary discussion of the master-slave relationship and, through inversion and dematerialization, deepens it, in the end producing an ethics necessary to accompany Calvin's project of providing guidance for democracy.

Clearly then, those literary traditions that pursued researches into various literary or historical models for the origins of *Uncle Tom's Cabin* misplaced their emphasis.[52] For literary and historical models at most could provide the material upon which Stowe had to work. The genesis of *Uncle Tom's Cabin* is rather to be found in the development of that project at the center of the work. And with this is to be sought the perception that certain abstruse reasonings on the nature of political association—such as those in Tocqueville or in Carlyle's "Occasional Discourse on the Nigger Question"—required a specific American response or formulation. These considerations lead us straight back to Professor Stowe[53]—that same Stowe who at the center of his own life-work found it necessary to construct a refutation of Hegelianism (the materialization of the master-slave relationship) and what he considered the all-prevailing egoism of its historical understanding. Calvin's "life-work" indeed contains a passage which is echoed in *Uncle Tom's Cabin,* suggesting such a height of association and mutual instruction as to reveal Calvin and Stowe to be entirely fused—or confused—in the development of those principles and reflections to which they devoted the endeavors of their life. (See book I, part I, chapter 14, pp. 235–40, and also chapter 10, p. 158, and chapter 12, pp. 185–99)

In his work, Calvin discussed the effects of Hegel on some men of reflection. And he mentions one Goeschel,

> a truly pious and eminent jurist; but inasmuch as he could find in Goethe an apostle of Christianity, and in the Faust a high development of the Christian spirit, it is not so surprising that he can see in Hegel the Christian philosopher.[54]

In a similar circumstance in *Uncle Tom's Cabin*—the attack on modern humanism—Stowe reflects on the implications of this judgment.

> The Gift to appreciate and the sense to feel the finer shades and reflections on moral things, often seems an attribute of those whose whole life shows careless disregard of them. Hence, Moore, Byron, Goethe, often speak words more wisely descriptive of true religious sentiment, than another man, whose whole life is governed by it. In such minds, disregard of religion is a more fearful treason—a more deadly sin. (*UTC*, 348)

Nietzsche, it seems, is right in placing Stowe squarely in the stream of the development of Western political philosophy—if only as an epigone. It is not clear, however, whether Nietzsche understood that the attack on slavery was to be subordinated to the aim of defeating "atheistic liberty." The abolition of slavery was the necessary condition of Stowe's project. It was not, however, the sufficient condition for undertaking the project.

NOTES

1. "Remarks Made . . ." "A serious argumentative writer, who is labouring to establish an important point by solid argument, is perfectly justified in introducing a brilliant metaphor or a sarcastic remark for, if it be really appropriate, it communicates a peculiar zest and energy to his reasoning. But if he attempts to use wit or brilliancy, let it be that, which is above the reach of vulgar capacity, and let him by all means avoid all childish play upon words, and commonplace raillery. Otherwise he will be suspected to want resources as well as honesty, for no man would load his gun with gravel stone, if he had plenty of shot." Sec. VI.

2. Amos A. Phelps, *Letters to Professor Stowe and Dr. Bacon on God's Real Method with Great Social Wrongs in Which the Bible is Vindicated from Grossly Erroneous Interpretations* (New York: William Harned, for American Anti-Slavery Society, 1848).

3. For which the reader should consult Harker [and other citations discussing this debate].

4. *Boston Recorder* [July 1830–May 11, 1849].

5. ". . . in the same sense in which gaming, drunkenness, falsehood, adultery, idolatry and the like are so . . ."

6. The Calhoun and Hammond School.

7. Phelps, *Letters to Professor Stowe and Dr. Bacon.*

8. Ibid.

9. Ibid.

10. Ibid., p. 37.

11. Ibid., p. 39.

12. Ibid., p. 46.

13. Ibid., p. 102.

14. Ibid., p. 107.

15. Ibid., p. 20.

16. Ibid.

17. I would note that the predicates for the more detailed work have been laid in the Harker dissertation. Moreover, the account provided here indicates the pathways for the perfection of Harker's work.

18. Phelps, *Letters to Professor Stowe and Dr. Bacon*, p. 163.

19. Ibid., p. 169.

20. Berghorn dates Stowe's public response to this question as emerging first in her 1845 article, "Immediate Emancipation" (as does Gossett); however, Graham cites "Two Altars" as her "first anti-slavery story." Berghorn, "'The Mother's Struggle.'" Gossett, *UTC and American Culture*, p. 88. Graham, "HBS and the Question of Race," p. 614. Hartshorne attributes her affirmation of the concept of slavery as "organic sin" to her brother, Edward; nevertheless, they agree as do a number of other Stowe scholars that, as Ipema puts it, "Stowe's is a protest against the system of slavery—she believed that the system is at fault." Sarah Dickson Hartshorne, "'Without Divine Intervention': Three Novels by Harriet Beecher Stowe 'Herself'" (Ph.D. diss., Brown University, 1990; hereafter cited as "Without Divine Intervention"). Ipema, "The Voice of Protest," p. 46.

21. Harriet Beecher Stowe, *The Key to Uncle Tom's Cabin* (Boston: John P. Jewett & Co., 1853; reprint, Port Washington, NY: Kennikat Press, 1968), p. 430 (hereafter cited as *Key;* citation pagination refers to the Kennikat Press edition.)

22. Sec. IV of *Key*.

23. She consistently cited the "Missouri Compromise" as barring emancipation—until "Sunny Memories," that is, and the fight over Nebraska—not because cotton and rice demanded slaves, but because new markets made the property too valuable. Old states became breeders to the new. After Nebraska she would always cite the Louisiana Purchase!

24. *Key*, p. 426.

25. Stowe's awareness of the power of opinion is revealed early on in a letter she wrote while teaching in her sister's academy in Litchfield: "'When the girls [i.e., her

students at Catharine's school] wish what is against my opinion they say, 'Do, Miss Beecher, allow just this.' '*Allow* you?' I say. 'I have not the power; you can do so if you think best.' Now, they cannot ask me to give up my opinion and belief of right and wrong, and they are unwilling to act against it. . . . Ere long they will find that under the dominion of conscience and a correct public sentiment they have rulers they cannot sway like teachers of flesh and blood." HBS to Catharine Beecher, December 16, 1829 quoted in Hedrick's biography, p. 60.

26. *Key*, p. 387.

27. Stowe touches on this question again in *The Minister's Wooing*, with Dr. Samuel Hopkins's purchase of slaves. Pierson comments: "On balance, Hopkins receives praise for his charity work, but as Stowe's contemporaries knew, the purchase of slaves, even for the purpose of immediately liberating them, was not without problems. The purchase casts him as a slave buyer and, however briefly, a slave owner." Michael D. Pierson, "Antislavery Politics in Harriet Beecher Stowe's *The Minister's Wooing* and *The Pearl of Orr Island*," *American Nineteenth Century History* 3, no. 2 (2002): 11.

28. *Key*, p. 432.

29. Ibid., p. 401.

30. Ibid., p. 402.

31. Ibid., pp. 421–22.

32. Ibid., p. 433.

33. Ibid., p. 427.

34. Ibid., p. 433.

35. Stowe's *Geography*, in its various editions, reflects this maturing sentiment. See book II, part II, Coda.

36. Op. cit.

37. Ibid., p. 432.

38. Ibid., p. 479.

39. Ibid., p. 473.

40. Ibid., p. 499.

41. Ibid.

42. Ibid.

43. One example is Tappan's dispatch to the British & Foreign Anti-Slavery Society's *Reporter*, as reported in Annie Heloise Abel and Frank J. Klingberg, eds., *A Side-Light on Anglo-American Relations, 1838–1858* (Lancaster, PA: The Association for the Study of Negro Life and History, 1927), p. 309 (hereafter cited as *A Side-Light on Anglo-American Relations*).

44. It is worth noting here that, using Catherine Gilbertson as his authority, Harker states that "Professor Stowe insisted upon the publication of ["Sunny Memories"] . . . " Harker, "The Life and Contributions," p. 66.

45. Harriet Beecher Stowe, "To the Editor of the *Cincinnati Journal and Luminary*," *Cincinnati Journal and Luminary* (1836).

46. Charles Beecher, *Anti-Slavery Tract No. 17* (New York: American Anti-Slavery Society, n.d.).

47. H. B. Stowe to Duchess of Argyle, July 31, 1862, in Annie Fields, *Life and Letters of Harriet Beecher Stowe* (Boston: Houghton, Mifflin and Co., 1897), p. 271–272.

48. H. B. Stowe to Frederick Douglass, July 9, 1851, in Stowe, *The Life of Harriet Beecher Stowe*, pp. 150ff.

49. Harriet Beecher Stowe, "The Two Altars: or, Two Pictures in One," *New York Evangelist* (1851).

50. Cf. *Dred*, Ch. 32, "Lynch Law Again," pp. 320–321.

51. Quoted in Wagenknecht, *Harriet Beecher Stowe*, p. 59.

52. "In the progeny of books as in that of princely houses, genealogies are sometimes to be reckoned not in the descent of a classic but through barely mentionable by-blows." Moses Hadas, "Paganism at Bay," in *A History of Latin Literature* (New York: Columbia University Press, 1950), p. 379.

53. That same professor whom student R. W. Patterson recalls as "'especially fond of Milton and Carlyle.'" Harker, "The Life and Contributions," p. 181.

54. Calvin E. Stowe, "The Four Gospels as We Now Have Them in the New Testament and the Hegelian Assaults on Them," *Bibliotheca sacra* 8 (1851): 507, and Stowe, *Origin and History*, p. 258.

18

The General Significance of *Uncle Tom's Cabin*

The particular significance of *Uncle Tom's Cabin* was discussed at the opening of book I. Yet, it is necessary here to give a further view of the subject in order to appreciate the account of Calvin's ideas and problems that I have presented as an introduction. We noted above the charge which Nietzsche hurled at Stowe and—unknowingly—at Calvin. Let's consider it more closely.

> In La Rochefoucauld we find consciousness of the true motive springs of the mind—and a view of these motive springs that is darkened by Christianity. The French revolution as the continuation of Christianity. Rousseau is the seducer: he unfetters woman who is henceforth represented in an ever more interesting manner—as suffering. Then the slaves and Mrs. Beecher-Stowe . . . (even to develop sympathy for the genius one no longer knows any other way for the past five hundred years than to represent him as the bearer of great suffering![1]). Next comes the curse on voluptuousness (Baudelaire and Schopenhauer); the most decided conviction that the lust to rule is the greatest vice; the perfect certainty that morality and disinterestedness are identical concepts and that the "happiness of all" is a goal worth striving for (i.e., the kingdom of heaven of Christ).[2]

Never was there more profound appreciation of the significance of *Uncle Tom's Cabin* than Nietzsche's. He traced the genesis of that work to sources we are now exploring for the first time. But I am not convinced that Stowe's work bears the full weight of the tradition to which Nietzsche adverted. That is why I sought anew the genesis of the novel.

I have already suggested that the genesis or significance of the novel lay in the creation of the human model of surpassing excellence as a democratic standard. But we should be mindful of the immediate circumstances of the novel's appearance. This is perhaps more important for Americans than any other human beings, since Americans, as it seems, have only recently regarded the work as an example of profound interpretation. We know what immediately prior generations long thought: The memory of Uncle Tom has not fared well. But that is trivial. For what counts—perhaps even to Stowe—is the fact that Uncle Tom's own generation of Americans, though granting him much indeed, granted him less than he deserved. There were numerous examples of intelligent people taking the work seriously. But, with one significant quasi-exception, they were all Europeans. Heinrich Heine, George Eliot, George Sand—all hailed the work as immensely significant, as did countless lesser-known publicists. Stowe, herself, was even moved to note in 1856 that the French, for example, seemed far more adept at penetrating her subtle shades of meaning.[3] But, giving due credit to her judgment and feelings, we may nonetheless argue that what occurred was fitting.

For one thing, the European was still close enough to a past in which excellence was central to the principles of civilization. And, at that, it is very difficult to find any European commentary which went beyond the sincerely felt but limited conviction of the wrongfulness of slavery and the holiness of Christian purity. One imagines that Stowe must surely have recognized how inherently limited was the American capacity to respond to her teaching. No American could attain that clarity of conviction open to the European without reflecting it in his opinion and actions upon the question of the day. Circumstances, therefore, were more compelling than reflection in itself. And, in those terms, the American reaction was fully as understanding as the European. For, Americans could do neither more nor less than oppose or defend slavery. And it is precisely of this character that the American reactions were formed.[4] It is but infrequently noted that each of Stowe's three principle anti-slavery novels appeared in the wake of and simultaneously with the three crises of the 1850s that preceded the ultimate crisis: the election of Lincoln. *Uncle Tom's Cabin* was "called forth" by the Compromise of 1850, the "Fugitive Slave Law." The central work—a thoughtful analysis of the principles of *Uncle Tom's Cabin—Sunny Memories of Foreign Lands,* appeared at the height of the Kansas-Nebraska crisis in 1854. And the final work, the apocalyptic *Dred: A Tale of the Great Dismal Swamp,* foreshadowed the election of Buchanan—an event anticipated as a crisis by Free-soilers—and the "Dred Scott Decision." In each of these crises her works constituted a portion of the arsenals of the combatants. Because her teachings always had to make their way among many contending convictions in America, Stowe's American readers were not at liberty to profound her deeper and more settled principles.

There is, as I indicated initially, one decisive exception to this consideration. Francis Lieber was a naturalized American and among the first American political philosophers as such. From 1835 to 1856 he held a chair in political economy at South Carolina College in Columbia. This adopted South Carolinian has suggested a greater importance to *Uncle Tom's Cabin* than could be realized in the event. According to his account, exaggerated perhaps, its appearance marked the commencement of a new era in the world. For Lieber, the importance of the work goes beyond its attack on slavery, though arriving at the conviction that slavery must be abolished was necessarily incident to that perception. His review essay, through a series of turns, quickly penetrates to the problem of *Uncle Tom's Cabin*. First, the direct question is put in the opening of the third paragraph:

> Is a saint like Uncle Tom possible? . . . That Christianity has produced such saints—so pure, lowly, forbearing, so ignorant except in the knowledge of Christ, so lamb-like, we know from the first centuries, and (it) only remains a question whether Christianity may not present itself to the soul of a *peculiarly favored* negro with all the freshness, fervor, singleness and excellence of the first centuries?[5]

This is a slight misunderstanding—but only slight—since the crucial problem is in Tom's slavery rather more than his being negro, as Nietzsche noted. But Lieber returns, indirectly, to show this.

He cited the absence of the minister to underscore the purity of the novel's Christianity but also its anomalous character and presence. The anomaly is human, and to that problem he turns in the ninth paragraph:

> There can be no doubt that slavery appears so frequently doubly hideous *because* brought into such close contact with Christianity, civilization. . . . Where slaves do not partake of our civilization, . . . no Uncle Tom, no almost white mother torn from her children, no learned black minister sold for a price can appear. Where the whites are not free republicans, the contrasts and all the fugitive baseness cannot appear so staggering to our souls. It is always [so] when an institution draws nigh to end, when it is in a transition period. Paganism at the time of Socrates and in Socrates was not so hideous as in Julian the Apostate nor said Socrates such nonsense about it as Julian . . .[6]

The anomaly consists largely in the pain given to the civilized when they must witness and indeed participate in the denial of justice to those possessing the very excellences of civilization. Nonetheless, that cannot provide a complete account of Lieber's reaction, for as yet there is no indication that either his philosophic or patriotic life must suffer as a consequence of this discovery.

He may be moved to benevolence but neither to lament nor correction for himself. The principles discovered are consistent with the "whole tenor of the modern spirit," if more demanding. He does not shrink from the final affirmation, though he expresses disbelief:

> The character of Saint Clair (*sic*) seems to me psychologically false from the moment of Evangeline's death or rather from the moment of [his] last long conversation with her. This going on "reading the papers" as before is unnatural *with all those conversations with Tom*. And, then, why the "At last! at last!" Does such a character become converted by a [stab/slave] and at that moment (?)[7] (My emphasis)

It is clear that what Lieber finds psychologically false is what he admits that the book demands: that a free republican, however assured of his particular education and status, be open to the example and guidance of excellence, whatever its source. Under those terms it is insufficient to be repulsed by the anomaly of slavery, for it may even be necessary to recognize the standard of one's own actions and morality in some particular slave—in effect, to become pupil to a master who is a slave.

We may see, then, why it is a necessary incident to understanding the novel that one must arrive at the conviction that slavery must be abolished. It does not befit free men to be ruled by slaves. And to the extent that such non-coercive, officeless rule is possible, no free man who is open to its teaching of excellence can assure himself that such will not be the circumstance in which he finds himself. Lieber, at least, seems to see this. His rejection of the model as psychologically false is weak—founded on a "seems to me." His hesitation is however genuine. He is perplexed but still, as I said, the only American at the time to consider the novel at leisure. But his review, which at least discloses the possibility of a profound understanding of *Uncle Tom's Cabin*, was never published—so far as I know. The unique copy of it reposes in the Huntington Library—a rough draft in his own hand.

This original profound reaction to *Uncle Tom's Cabin* neither responds to Nietzsche nor clarifies our modern ideas about the novel's significance. The debate over the novel's significance is, if anything, as wide as that over its sources. I have eschewed the task of criticizing much earlier Stowe scholarship. Not only has it been thoroughly canvassed by scholarship at the end of the twentieth century, but the more of it I read, the more convinced I became that such errors as plague it are best revealed by new and innocent demonstrations of the novel's teaching. To take but one example, I will make no further mention of Furnas's *Good-bye to Uncle Tom*. Much useful and important work has been done, and I will refer to it as required. But all else I defer to footnotes, bibliography, or silence, pleading the already burdensome length of this work.

The significance of the novel might be shown in terms of the author's expectations, the novel's actual effect (a task largely fulfilled in other works[8]), and the judgments of scholars of some understanding. But it were well to construct a foundation from which Stowe might speak to Nietzsche in order to effect this comparison. I quote at length:

> There is a twilight-ground between the boundaries of the sane and the insane, which the old Greeks and Romans regarded with a peculiar veneration. They held a person whose faculties were thus darkened as walking under the awful shadow of a supernatural presence; and, as the mysterious secrets of the stars only became visible in the night, so in these eclipses of the more material faculties they held there was often an awakening of supernatural perceptions. The hot and positive light of our modern materialism, which exhales from the growth of our existence every dewdrop, which searches out and dries every rivulet of romance, which sends an unsparing beam into every cool grotto of poetic possibility . . . this spirit, so remorseless, allows us no such indefinite land. There are but two worlds in the whole department of modern anthropology—the sane and the insane; the latter dismissed from human reckoning almost with contempt.[9]

The spirit of modernity is an unsparing, choking presence; *Uncle Tom's Cabin* is an expression of *ressentiment.* Nietzsche's genius is a suffering genius not from virtue but from necessity. The significance of the novel lies in the claim that the inexorable advance of modernity—sanity—is not identical with moral advance. To Stowe this resulted from the simple reflection that sanity was only gain. It was modern progress that perpetuated slavery; that is, the increasing value of the property due to expansion.[10]

What *Uncle Tom's Cabin* accomplished was the demonstration, yes, of the "identity of disinterestedness and morality." It expanded the range of moral possibilities, raised consciences. The famous *Suppressed Book About Slavery,* in 1856, was already citing Tom's example to prove that "the weak" could become strong and the "meanest," honorable.[11] This it was that offended Nietzsche—this romance, this impossible dream. There were none who saw the necessity that the absurdity point beyond itself.

> The coarse, the low, the mean, the vulgar, is ever thrusting itself before the higher and more delicate nature, and claiming, in virtue of its very brute strength, to be the true reality.[12]

Forrest Wilson cited the *London Times* review of *Uncle Tom's Cabin* to indicate one barrier to understanding. He implied that the "Catholic" prejudice of that paper prescribed rejection of the "audacious trash" of "the miraculous conversions of those who came into contact with saintly Uncle Tom." Accordingly they saw no connections among the various sketches and characters, each executed singly with considerable skill.[13]

Duvall made a similar remark in his review of responses to the novel. Some critics could not see the book as a whole, "its organic and imaginative sufficiency." Consequently, they only analyzed "the 'arguments' of the book, to challenge the propositional logic of its thesis."[14] The inverted commas he assigned to "arguments" revealed his judgment of this process, a judgment he makes express seven pages later. Hence, we find an impassable gulf erected between Stowe's fiction—her romance—on one side and her logic on the other. She who appealed from the sane-insane dichotomy was mated to it forcibly. Criticism only recently broke away from this crusty mold.[15] Previously, the occasional threat to do so always ended in a strange withdrawal from the opportunity presented. I have Edmund Wilson and Leslie Fiedler especially in mind, as well as Duvall's ignoring the evidence in front of his nose so to speak. I discuss Fiedler's original perplexity elsewhere.[16] For whatever reason, he saw "an astonishingly various and complex book, simplified in the folk mind," and chose originally to treat the simplified version![17] Wilson, however, is both more perplexing and easier to explain. He had little respect for the literary character of the novel—the "ineptitude of its prose." Still, it captured him.

> What is most unexpected is that, the farther one reads in *Uncle Tom, the more one becomes aware that a critical mind is at work,* which has the complex situation in a very firm grip and which, no matter how vehement the characters become, is controlling and co-ordinating their interrelations.[18]

From this it was but a short glance to the principle by which and for which all this power was coordinated. But Wilson did not pose to Stowe the question, Where are you going? He knew in advance. He set out in his work to dislodge "pretensions to moral superiority" from any and every effort to explain moral-political endeavors. Wilson recognized that people made moral arguments, but he regarded them as fundamentally irrational—at least when claims of superiority were made.[19]

It was accordingly sufficient for Wilson to find that Stowe's preoccupation was not with slavery but with Christian morals (which we "*began* to see in *Dred*"), to rebut any need for analysis of her argument.[20] That this is erroneous is all too obvious from the above account of the Phelps debate and the contribution of the *Key*. But it is revealing to note that the religious argument of *Dred* is given almost entirely in expository form in the *Key* already! The same is true of other arguments in *Dred,* save those from "nature." Through analysis the whole argument could have been derived from *Uncle Tom's Cabin,* or at least its *Key*. On the lowest level, then, we show that Wilson needed to analyze Stowe's argument. In addition nothing is so necessary to discerning the significance of the novel than to take seriously its argument from moral superiority. Wilson in effect treated Stowe as Nietzsche had done, but with far less awareness of what was at stake. Though he found himself in the grasp of a strong argument, he was unable to query it.

His was a neophytish moral or cultural relativism. Like the Patriarch, Jacob, he did not know the angel with whom he imagined to wrestle. Unlike Patriarch Jacob, his ladder did not ascend to heaven, but merely down through the generations. It shows up in images of the same naiveté, produced by those who describe Stowe's "feminizing" of American culture without ever recognizing the significance of the absence of the mother as such and the woman as distinct from Stowe's "Cloudland" utopia.[21] To judge the significance of *Uncle Tom's Cabin* in particular and Stowe's work in general, we must rethink the work itself and consider Stowe's own standards of effectiveness.

As early as 1844—in the midst of Calvin's lobbying for his project—Stowe wrote an introduction to *The Works of Charlotte Elizabeth,* in which introduction she favorably compared this author to the great Dickens only to add honestly that "the present question is not which evince the most talent, but which are the best adapted to practical purposes."[22] Unquestionably, Stowe wrote much to practical purposes. No attempt to explain her writing can abstract long from "practical" endeavors. She found herself in 1853–1854 in the midst of an "association of individuals" dedicated to advancing anti-slavery discussion in Boston at her expense.[23] She considered even association with "ultras" to advance the purpose of her book. Similarly, she self-consciously undertook a campaign to England in 1853 to further the purpose of the book.

> It certainly cannot be agreeable to have such things brought out about one's country, and I, as an American, expect to feel very unpleasant about it, when I get to Europe, but then I do not see any way that a cancer can be cut out without giving pain. . . .
>
> . . . the city of Charleston is in a perfect state of blockade as to admission of any discussion from the northern free States, and yet I saw advertised by a book-seller there, all the leading English Reviews, each one of which has, within a few months, a very decided article upon slavery. The one in Blackwood I think has a good many statistics. . . . There is besides all this, in England, some considerable well meaning but ill guided enthusiasm on this subject . . .[24]

A concrete, practical assault on slavery itself could not be better thought out. And anyone may consult Forrest Wilson's account of Stowe's anxiety in the early phases of the Civil War.[25] The practical purpose was indeed the elimination of slavery. But it is not obvious that an account of "Christian morality" or morality in general is not the, or at least a, means of achieving that end. The significance of the novel lies in its successful adaptation of the specific means—the didactic novel—to the specific end envisioned—moral persuasion.

The significance of Stowe's novel lay in its being dedicated to the work of moral reclamation and preaching. Before the close of her life she penned a preface to her "official biography." She closed her preface by handing on the torch—halfway—in Bunyan's words:

> My sword I give to him that shall succeed me in my pilgrimage and my courage and skill to him that can get it.[26]

She was not embarrassed to have been a preacher and did not quail before the sight of what she had done. With her very own boldness and courage must she be approached if once and for all her heirs are to possess a sure sense of where she stood. Undertaking this task constitutes a slight embarrassment for me. All of my researches, publications, and teachings heretofore have set forth the implicit principle that legislation is a fundamentally sounder progenitor of morals than preaching. Undeniably, Stowe was, if anything, a preacher.[27] Calvin Stowe, besides all else, was a preacher. And my conscience ought reprove me for dilating—preacher-fashion—on their long-range sermon. But I find slight solace in the possibility that, though preaching may be inefficacious for most, it may be a source of reflection for the legislator or would-be legislator. And if a critical analysis of some preaching may form the basis of legislative art, then perhaps a scholar may be forgiven for devoting due attention to this particular preaching—easily the most significant preaching of the entire American past.

We are less moved to remonstrance upon reading Edmund Wilson's characterization of diaphanous spirits in the place of the human beings and human problems offered by the novel because we remain indebted to his initial willingness to resist literary embarrassment and to confess Stowe's power.[28] In addition, his ghoulishness suits the atmosphere. Harriet Stowe maintained, to the end, that the story of Uncle Tom began to form itself in her mind with a vision of his death. By the time *Uncle Tom's Cabin* appeared, Uncle Tom had already assumed the form of a ghostly spirit.[29]

NOTES

1. See chapter 1.
2. Friedrich Nietzsche, *The Will to Power* (New York: Random House, 1967), aphorism 94.
3. Ellis contends that the French were but briefly enthralled with Uncle Tom and saw the work mainly as escapist and as reinforcing widely held notions of romantic racialism. Lisa A. Ellis, "The Popularity of *Uncle Tom's Cabin*: Escapism and Ethnocentrism in Mid-Nineteenth Century France" (master's thesis, Hunter College of the City University of New York, 1999).

4. This is captured most completely in Gossett, whose work interprets *UTC* and related works as though they had only the goal of confronting slavery and estimates of racial capacities.

5. Op. cit. Lieber, "Uncle Tom."

6. Ibid.

7. Ibid. The account of Lieber's reaction is strengthened by the remarks cited from his correspondence in works such as Gossett. His reaction differs substantially from his reports of reactions by other southerners, except those going to the fact that it was widely noticed and evidently important.

8. It is highly controversial whether anyone can ever actually ascribe some worldly but not merely literary effect to a novel. Nonetheless, Stowe's novel has been subject to considerable speculation on that score. Accordingly, the bibliography appended at the end of this volume offers a partial listing of works in this genre. In addition, one were wise to remind himself of the not very distant judgments of black American poets, Frances Ellen Watkins Harper, Langston Hughes, and Paul Laurence Dunbar. They accorded Stowe great responsibility for the emancipation of the slaves.

9. *Dred,* Ch. 1, "Life in the Swamps," p. 5.

10. *Dred,* p. 323. Stowe blamed the Louisiana Purchase.

11. George Washington Carleton, *Suppressed Book About Slavery* (New York: Carleton, 1864; reprint, New York: Arno Press, 1968), Pt. 3, Ch. 1, p. 120. Citation pagination refers to the Arno edition.

12. Stowe, *Poganuc People,* Ch. 23, p. 251.

13. Robert Forrest Wilson, *Crusader in Crinoline,* Pt. 2, Ch. 2, p. 326.

14. Severn Duvall, "*Uncle Tom's Cabin*: The Sinister Side of the Patriarchy," *New England Quarterly* (1963). Reprinted in *Images of the Negro in American Literature,* ed. Seymour L. Gross and John Edward Hardy (Chicago: University of Chicago Press, 1966), p. 13.

15. Recent exemplars would include: Sachs, who finds in *Uncle Tom's Cabin,* "a coherent stylistic scheme" and notes that many critics have entirely overlooked the strategic and self-conscious element that is integral to all of Stowe's work . . ."; Donovan, who compares "Stowe's surface style" to a "'verbal quilt,'" adding that "events are set side by side so as to comment silently on one another" or "to change the mood or the aesthetic effect"; Camfield, who points out that "the antirationalism of Stowe's work . . . has in part kept most twentieth-century critics from seeing the fully elaborated philosophical basis of her work"; and Shipp: "Once we recognize the presence of the author's genuine thematic concerns, we may begin to suspect that none of her choices are arbitrary or accidental." Sachs, "Describing a Sphere" pp. 65, 132. Donovan, *UTC: Evil, Affliction, and Redemptive Love,* p. 30. Camfield, "Moral Aesthetics," p. 335. Shipp, "*UTC* and the Ethos of Melodrama," p. 28.

Weinstein proposes an underlying rationale for the approach taken by Stowe and her contemporary colleagues, suggesting that "in order to present themselves as active social agents, female authors had to present themselves as artists capable of projecting visions of the world worthy of both ethical and artistic genius." Weinstein, "Educating Sympathy," p. 28. Sundquist's assessment is that "the triangular entanglements among the role of women, the place of blacks in American history and society, and the radical powers of Christianity cannot be pulled apart or reduced to easy schematic interpretations. Precisely their knotted complexity reveals how inadequately *Uncle Tom's Cabin* has been understood and how central it is, as a literary and political document, to the American experience." Sundquist, *New Essays*, p. 7. Also noteworthy and usual for the time at which he wrote are Levin's comments: "It seems to me likely that the extraordinary popular success of *Uncle Tom's Cabin* may owe as much to the book's intellectual power as to its strong sentiment" and "To see the richness of the historical evidence in *Uncle Tom's Cabin*, . . . we must study the complex reality of the whole book." Levin, "American Fiction as Historical Evidence," pp. 133, 154.

16. See chapter 1.

17. In fairness, Fiedler subsequently explained this dichotomy, in his "Home as Heaven, Home as Hell: *Uncle Tom's Cabin*," in *Rewriting the Dream: Reflections on the Changing American Literary Canon*, ed. W. M. Vehovoeven (Amsterdam: Rodopi, 1992).

18. Edmund Wilson, *Patriotic Gore: Studies in the Literature of the American Civil War* (New York: Oxford University Press, 1962), Ch. 1, p. 6 (hereafter cited as *Patriot Gore*). Emphasis added.

19. Ibid., pp. xxxi–xxxii.

20. Ibid., p. 37.

21. See book II, part II.

22. Harriet Beecher Stowe, ed., *The Works of Charlotte Elizabeth*, 2nd ed. (New York: M. W. Dodd, 1845), "Introduction," pp. v–vii, dated May 22, 1844. Cf. Stowe's article "Literary Epidemics (part 2)" in the July 13, 1843 edition of the *New-York Evangelist* in which she writes, "We think, however, that the time of Dickens' popularity . . . is drawing towards its close . . . apart from his character as a story-teller, Dickens appears to have very little cultivation or mental resource to fall back upon . . . " and "as to the influence, in this respect [i.e., morals], of his individual writings on young minds, every Christian parent and guardian must use his own judgment . . ." and "If this age be *par excellence* a temperance age, we think that the writings of Dickens are as much *par excellence* anti-temperance tracts" (p. 1).

23. Garrison, Phillips, May, Calvin Stowe, and H. B. Stowe were the association. ALS, H. B. Stowe to H. W. Beecher, Jan. 13, 1854 (Stowe-Day).

24. Harriet Beecher Stowe to Daniel R. Goodloe, Feb. 9, 1853, Andover, in Stephen B. Weeks, "Anti-Slavery in the South. . .," *Southern History Association* 2, no. 2 (April, 1898).

25. Forrest Wilson, op. cit., pp. 478–79.

26. Charles E. Stowe, op. cit.

27. Hartshorne describes Stowe's writing as "a secular sermon." Hartshorne, "Without Divine Intervention," p. 148. Weinstein comments that "Stowe . . . wrote her sermons as fiction." Weinstein, "Educating Sympathy," p. 25. Kimball calls *Uncle Tom's Cabin* "an extended sermon." Gayle Kimball, "Harriet Beecher Stowe's Revision of New England Theology," *Journal of Presbyterian History* 58, no. 1 (1980): 64 (hereafter cited as "HBS's Revision of New England Theology"). Ammons writes: "Essentially a theologian and preacher, she foresaw change resulting from spiritual reorientation." Ammons, "Stowe's Dream," p. 170. Stowe so designated herself in a letter to one of her brothers: "You see my dear George that I was made for a

preacher—indeed I can scarcely keep my letters from turning into sermons . . . " (HBS to George Beecher, February 20 [1830?]—quoted in Hedrick, *Harriet Beecher Stowe*, p. 64.) To Lewis, *Uncle Tom's Cabin* "performs as one huge sermon," with "the nation as [Stowe's] congregation," into which the author incorporates what "she had learned from babyhood," namely, "the Puritan habit of thinking in pairs of opposites by means of which any proposition could be tested by common sense." Lewis, "Message, Messenger, and Response," pp. 5, 22, 24. Lewis analyzes in great detail the manner in which Stowe based the novel on the standard conventions of Calvinist sermonology.

28. Cf. Gossett: "More than anyone else, it was probably Edmund Wilson who led other critics to take another look at the novel . . . " Gossett, *UTC and American Culture*, p. 398.

29. Although there is much one might argue with in her overall treatment of *Uncle Tom's Cabin*, Roberts' evocation of its ghostly aspects is powerful: "In Stowe's fiction, the South is populated by insistent, clamorous bodies who, like poltergeists, are more felt than seen. The masses of slaves are 'invisible' as ghosts compared to the dominant, visible whites who own them. It is as if Stowe is determined to utter the spell that will force these shades into visibility, to assert their physical being . . . Stowe defies their official subterranean status and focuses on the harms done to their bodies as well as to their minds." Diane Roberts, *The Myth of Aunt Jemima: Representations of Race and Region* (New York: Routledge, 1994), p. 26.

Book II

NON-UTOPIAN OPTIMISM: HARRIET STOWE'S EVANGELICAL LIBERALISM

I

THE MIDDLE PASSAGE: SUNNY MEMORIES

19

An American Campaign Abroad

> What, one would think, doth seek to slay outright,
> Oftimes, delivers from the saddest plight,
> That very Providence, whose Face is death,
> Doth oftimes, to the lowly, Life bequeath.
> I taken was, he did escape and flee,
> Hands Crost, gives Death to him, and life to me.
>
> —*Pilgrim's Progress*, 2nd pt., p. 362

Stowe's only explicitly American book is a book primarily about England—a collection of letters written to relatives and friends during her travels abroad in 1853. It is doubly American, addressed and sent to Americans in America. Yet, it is somehow about Europe, for she spoke of European sights and images. But, these descriptions were intended for American eyes. Indeed, she took advantage of a preface to warn England, specifically, "that the book has not been prepared in reference to an English but an American public, and (to) make due allowance for that fact" (*SM*, iv). She would have wished to keep it from English eyes altogether, to have never permitted its publication there. A book about England but relevant only to Americans reminds us of a predecessor of Stowe, with whom she was not unfamiliar: Tocqueville.[1] We must be aware then, that what may be merely a precaution against serious criticism from Englishmen for her misunderstanding, may also be an intended invitation to Americans to consider the work more than a travelogue.[2] The discussion of England claims our particular attention both because England alone is cautioned against misunderstanding and because the discussion occupies more than two-thirds of the book.

The book is entitled *Sunny Memories of Foreign Lands.*[3] The author refers to it, in the preface, as "Sunny Memories." It is a book of recollections, a history of sorts. It has been given "*couleur de rose.*" Some of the characters and scenes may be "drawn with too bright a pencil," but there are faults greater than those induced by "admiration and love." It may be useful for "America and England" to speak to each other in other terms than those of "illiberal criticism." And since "Sunny Memories" speaks *only* to Americans it must be designed to demonstrate how liberal criticism should manifest itself, coming from Americans. This kind of history is a form of magnanimity or, at least, liberality. It is designed to have a "useful influence" and primarily on those, not of whom the history is written, but to whom the history is addressed. The meaning and content of liberal history are developed below. But the closest model to this form of history in the literature we possess follows it in history. That is Nietzsche's "monumental history."[4] For Nietzsche there is a clear distinction between critical history and monumental history, while the history we are offered here seeks to combine the two. The liberality of liberal history is for England; the instruction or criticism is for America.

This work would not have been published even in America, but for the fact that the circumstances of Stowe's journey had been misrepresented there. Hence, the liberality is strictly subordinate to the usefulness of this history for Americans. In America, misrepresentations were effected not just among those "predetermined to believe unfavourably," but also among "really excellent and honest people." For this reason, the *truth* must be spoken. It need be spoken only to the "really excellent and honest." Stowe considers such people "a wide circle of friends, between whose hearts and her own there has been an acquaintance and sympathy for years, and who, loving excellence, and feeling the reality of it in themselves, are sincerely pleased to have their sphere of hopefulness and charity enlarged" (*SM*, iv). She wrote the book only for them, and all others, perchance stumbling across it, are entreated to close it immediately upon the discovery that they are reading private letters. Unlike *Uncle Tom's Cabin,* which seeks to persuade the slaveholder of the evil of slavery, "Sunny Memories" seeks to teach the opponent of slavery the true grounds of his opposition.

"Sunny Memories" *is* a book. It was published. It was available to the many. The letters of which it consists were "compiled from what was written at the time and on the spot," for the most part, but "some few" were composed after the return to American shores (*SM*, v). They were, in other words, written for inclusion in the book. Nonetheless, every letter bears the postmark of a foreign city. The reader cannot distinguish those written for a private purpose and those written for a public purpose. As they are all private letters, they are all also public. As they are addressed to a limited public they remain private. As a book, "Sunny Memories" is the very opposite of *Uncle Tom's Cabin*. And it is upon this fact that *this* analysis must turn, though the achievement of this requires a reading of "Sunny Memories" that is not immediately available. The very distinctions that are hidden from the ordinary reader become the basis of discovering the teaching of "Sunny Memories." This is facilitated by the felicitous accident, if accident it were, by which the author instructs the reader in the labor required to disclose that teaching. In a paragraph that falls almost exactly in the center of the first volume, both by page and by letter number, the author paraphrases a description of Gothic architecture from an architectural critic in the following words:

> One remark on this building, in Billing's architectural account of it, interested me; and that is, that it is finished with *the most circumstantial elegance* and minuteness in those concealed portions which are excluded from public view, and which can only be inspected by laborious climbing *or* groping; and he accounts for this by the idea that the whole carving and execution was considered as an act of solemn worship and adoration, in which the artist offered up his best faculties to praise the Creator. (*SM*, 160)

Since, as will be seen below, the borrowed architectural account is in fact the author's own account, arranged in a manner to suit her purposes, the paraphrase becomes a statement of her work and purpose. It becomes necessary, then, to take the preface most seriously, and seek what is private in "Sunny Memories" in order to reveal its teaching. What is hidden is precisely the distinction between the private and the public content of the work. The task of analysis requires bringing those distinctions to light.

Tangible evidence of Stowe's artfulness is of greatest significance. The analysis of *Uncle Tom's Cabin* has already proved how such evidence may be revealed through textual analysis. "Sunny Memories" is no less distinguished in the artfulness of its construction. But beyond the evidence external to textual analysis, we have evidence in the text, which justifies the emphasis on interpretation in the present case. The evidence will be presented as the interpretation is developed. But we may mention the most dramatic case now, both for its conclusiveness and its comprehensiveness.

Stowe opens her account of her journey with the declaration that she sailed in the ship *Niagara*. This is a lie. It was not a mistake. While she may well have neglected the *Times of London's* accurate notices of April 11th and 12th, she could not have neglected her own diary entry, which correctly identified the "Royal mail steamer *Canada*." Stowe relied on her diary (written with and for the most part by her brother, Charles Beecher) to compose "Sunny Memories." The diary was only uncovered late in the twentieth century, revealing conclusively that the "error" in naming the vessel was intentional.[5] The reader is at a loss to account for such a turn, until he recognizes the artfulness of the work as a whole. That minor detail emphasized Stowe's determination to speak about America through an ostensible discussion of things English. While Canada is wholly English, Niagara is ambiguously English and American and thus better suited to Stowe's purpose. It is then no accident, as we see below, when she concludes her account of this journey with a re-introduction of Niagara—here the real thing—as a symbolic expression of the sublime truths concerning things American which she has presented in her book.

"Sunny Memories" is not a special book; it is a travelogue. It is occasion for memories of a journey. The journey, however, was itself occasion for memories, memories of a past and an especially Scottish-English past. "Sunny Memories" are, therefore, the memories of memories as well as the memories of immediately present experiences. It is with respect to the influence of the ancientest on the most recent memories that "Sunny Memories" is instructive. Of immediate experiences, one stands out as most significant and indeed the occasion of the journey. That is the publication of *Uncle Tom's Cabin*. The journey was particularly the journey of the author of that death knell for American slavery, and the organized as well as the spontaneous receptions of the journey were particularly anti-slavery receptions. It was, indeed, the reported anti-American flavor of these foreign demonstrations that Stowe considered a misrepresentation of the circumstances of her journey. Her response is a defense of her view of America, but not explicitly so.

The book begins by ceding to modesty and the retired, private character of a woman's life the same rights those principles had ceded during the journey itself. In each circumstance of public welcome and address, the role of responding fell to Calvin Stowe, Mrs. Stowe's husband. Unlike the journey, however, where Stowe remained silent in public and spoke only through the privacy of letters, in "Sunny Memories" she comes *before* Calvin in a preface. The preface, as we have shown, raises the problem of the distinction between the public and the private as requiring solution before the book can be understood. In the sense that the book is for American eyes only, the problem is an American problem. Only this irony permits us to raise the two-fold problem of Stowe's immodestly preceding Calvin in a public utterance, while yet consigning to Calvin the task of formulating—as he did on the journey—the public challenge which is the occasion of the work itself.[6] How far Calvin's sentiments are his and only his we cannot wholly ascertain, and in any event must defer for judgment until we have reflected those public views in the private views, which follow. But Calvin's views are public, and we may listen yet:

> I went to Europe without the least anticipation of the kind of reception which awaited us; it was all a surprise and an embarrassment to me. I went with the strongest love of my country, and the highest veneration for her institutions; I

> everywhere in Britain found the most cordial sympathy with this love and veneration; and I returned with both greatly increased. But slavery I do not recognize as an institution of my country; it is an excrescence, a vile usurpation, hated of God, and abhorred by man; I am under no obligation either to love or respect it. He is the traitor to America, and American institutions, who reckons slavery as one of them, and, as such, screens it from assault. Slavery is a blight, a canker, a poison, in the very heart of our republic; and unless the nation, as such, disengages itself from it, it will most assuredly be our ruin. The patriot, the philanthropist, the Christian, truly enlightened, sees no other alternative. The developments of the present session of our national Congress[7] are making this great truth clearly perceptible even to the dullest apprehension.[8]

The problem of interpreting "Sunny Memories" thus turns on the possibility of understanding why a "private" response to this "public" challenge becomes necessary.

Some guidance is found in the manner in which the book is organized. The introductory chapter, in which this challenge is found, attempts to clarify the public record concerning the outpouring of British sentiments during the journey. Accordingly the private letters, which offer Stowe's sentiments and appraisals of these events as they occurred, are distinct from the portrayal of the events themselves. The introduction offers a selection of the public addresses as they appeared in journals and Calvin Stowe's own addresses in response. Though not all the addresses could be given (she mentions in her letters some he does not and, of those he does mention, gives some facts he does not), those that are, are given in their *entirety.* As to his own remarks, Calvin has corrected the public record from his own notes and memory, abridging his remarks "without changing the sentiment." The work begins, therefore, with an explicitly public record, and, although the private letters parallel the occasions of the public addresses, they are distinguished from them by a form of expression intended only for a few.

That Calvin's public remarks have been, to some extent, recast only emphasizes the necessity of further distinguishing private and public speech. The latter constitutes that for which he was "willing to be held responsible." Calvin, in other words, admits that some of the words and deeds of a citizen abroad may be judged culpable in a public sense. In defending the freedom of the citizen to speak as he wishes anywhere, Calvin does not envision a license that would permit the citizen a *right* to engage in activities and speeches that might border on the treasonable or at least compromise the national integrity of his polity. It is the burden of "Sunny Memories," therefore, to prove that the Stowes' activities in England were wholly consistent with that freedom granted to the American citizen in the context of his own regime and, further, that they were not sloth in defending the principles of that regime while being entertained *as public persons* by foreigners possibly hostile to those very principles. One must consider first the nature of those remarks for which Stowe explicitly may be held responsible, but reserving always the question that must follow: What happens to that private speech which is published, i.e., which is made public? And, does it, too, accord with the responsibility of the citizen to the polity?

The public record represents the outpouring of warm emotion.[9] At stops along the journey through England—from Liverpool to London via Glasgow and Edinburgh with stops along the way—Stowe was feted in public ceremonies attended, at each instance, by anywhere from several hundred to several thousand persons—offering warm friendship for her and warm indignation directed toward the American slaveholder. Between April 11th and May 25th, 1853, approximately fifteen such unsolicited demonstrations were held and penny subscriptions amounting to some twenty thousands of dollars were placed into the hands of the crusader for the sake of American slaves. As many more informal gatherings, parades, and "visits" were held during this same time, the uproar in the press—American and British—was but the reflection of the feverish activity of the tour.

The initial address was delivered at a Liverpool breakfast, and both it and the response are notable for their great political moderation. The chief sentiment expressed by Rev. Dr. McNeile in the welcome was a deep gratitude for the religious character of *Uncle Tom's Cabin,*

> the thorough legitimacy of the application of Scripture,—no wresting, no mere verbal adaptation, but in every instance the passage cited is made to illustrate something in the narrative, or in the development of character, in strictest accordance with the design of the passage in its original sacred context. (*SM*, xiv–xv)

Calvin appropriately responded with gratitude for this judgment, explaining that *Uncle Tom's Cabin* was threatened with the prospect of being labeled "anti-Christian" by some American religious newspapers. The report of this first meeting, then, served to deflect the most important argument against Stowe's novel. Its moderation not to say mildness serves to underscore the specific importance of that argument. It is a fact that, by and large, as time passed the meetings became more strident, and the authenticity of *Uncle Tom's Cabin* was adverted to with far less frequency. Perhaps the central issues at stake became more important.

I will summarize the chief issues and the character of these meetings as the basis of an interpretation. The moderation of the initial reception served to permit chastising without enraging Stowe's American critics. This was followed by a meeting, still at Liverpool,[10] in which the hosts to Mrs.

Stowe felt constrained to reject a charge of meddling in American affairs. The apology, such as it was, admitted the truth of the argument that there existed English problems requiring attention, but insisted that attention to ills abroad is least of all a sign of indolence at home. Next, Calvin read a note from Stowe herself, the first of only two notes during this series of appearances. Wishing to speak in her own name, she presented a short response of thankfulness, which afforded a moment to argue the universal nature of the struggle against slavery. She would not permit it to be particularized and suggested further that the effort was in behalf of a humanity wider than slaves, conceivably including British factory workers. Her note, then, dealt with the same criticism by advancing the argument to another plane. It is something of a surprise, therefore, that Calvin, concluding the note, continued with a strident defense of British interest in American ills. He even judged as between the two, summarily pronouncing differences in character that amount to moral superiority versus moral inferiority: "England repents and reforms. America requires to repent and reform" (*SM*, xx). One is tempted—viewing the events of these first days—to conclude that all the parties involved were simply following the headlines. To some extent that is surely true. Yet, the fact that the meetings progressively brought out new concerns and greater intensity of concern also suggests a conscious attempt to formulate a public understanding of these matters. Such is the case with the apparent disagreement between Mr. and Mrs. Stowe, eventually to be supplanted with obvious agreement as to a yet more daring formulation.

Leaving Liverpool, the Stowe party traveled to Glasgow, and, as it would be the rest of the trip, their approach was heralded. Not only were itineraries published but so was discussion of the Liverpool meetings. It had become a matter of great concern that this "tour" not be the occasion for an outpouring of anti-American sentiment. Thus, a masterful effort was made at the Glasgow public meeting of April 15th to discover the narrow ground of an equally warm love for the critic and the criticized. The address offered immoderate praise of the work and the author, hailing *Uncle Tom's Cabin* as a "consummate work of art and of nature." That the novel should have the effect it did was regrettable though defensible. It was producing a "stir," and "irritation," but this was preferable to a lack of movement. The evidence for the necessity of movement is that blush—that rightly generated "blush of patriotism"—to be seen in the cheeks of those caught inconsistently defending liberty and maintaining slavery. This amounts to criticism, to be sure, but of a modest character. Indeed, the Glasgow hosts almost treat the "American error" as but a minor lapse of attention. That such mild criticism coupled with extreme praise of Stowe suggests a form—which may well work—for avoiding the trap of anti-American sentiment (*SM*, xxii).

Almost predictably, Calvin failed to follow suit. His response consists of two elements that are united in their purpose. First, he established that their (the hosts') judgment of the novel was a function, not of their aesthetic taste but of their political sentiment. Part of his argument includes the suggestion that the book is not a work of art but a political necessity, "forced" into being by the Fugitive Slave Law. Hence, there is a necessary dissimilarity between American and Scottish public sentiment with respect to freedom. This converts their praise of Stowe into self-praise, effectively reducing the masterful address to a single argument: modest admonition of Americans seen from the light of Scottish superiority.[11] And the same sense of moral superiority that issues in contempt can issue in profound indignation. Secondly, there is a strong denunciation of American "Law" and sentiment, which is coupled with a cautious denunciation of British support for slavery through cotton purchases. The second argument, then, foreshadowed an English inconsistency and was meant to bring a blush into the cheeks of Scottish "lovers of freedom" sufficient to convert modest admonition into chastening reproach (*SM*, xxiv–xxv).

Whether Calvin, the professor, was successful at the Glasgow meeting cannot be judged. We have no further report of the sentiments of those present. But if the Edinburgh meeting five days later—its abrupt change of tone—and the necessity of a second and final note from Stowe are any indication, he succeeded beyond measure. In this meeting, the tone of address was openly admonitory—indeed, reproachful—for the first time. It issued in an open avowal of the abolitionists' cause and a declaration that mere reform is unacceptable.[12] Harking back to their own history, in the same hall the Edinburghians had once before rejected half measures, declaring for total abolition in Edinburgh and England, and they pressed their condemnation with a strong sense of righteousness (final and full emancipation in England came in 1832). Stowe, in a note read by Professor Stowe, responded by again seeking to advance the plane of criticism to the universal. Following Calvin's Glasgow appeal, in her own name she disclaimed personal merit and insisted on accepting congratulations and charges alike "in the name of oppressed and suffering humanity." Unlike Calvin, she did not speak to the measures her audience might take to be consistent in their reproach. She rather appealed to the contrast between human and divine views—in light of the universal element involved—to encourage hopefulness and action. In the human view the cause may appear without hope. But just as its predecessor, the cause of Scottish freedom (a reference to the struggle for religious liberty by "covenanters," Scottish Presbyterians), succeeded with divine assistance, so might the present cause succeed. What is the divine view? The necessity of the change proposed. The ineluctable force of *present* history represents divine will. It is this force that constitutes—or, is in fact constituted by—a "universal sighing of humanity in all countries," which anticipates "divine judgment." And it is to "human judgment" to assist this "sacred cause." What the universal elements amount to, then, is the political identity—an identity that "Law" cannot be permitted to mask—of all modern movements of human improvement (*SM*, xxix–xxx).

Professor Stowe followed the reading of Stowe's note with a rather extended lecture, in which he depicted an emerging sense of collective responsibility for human suffering. This sense is transmitted through the medium of universal Christianity, and improved "facilities of communication" enlarge its power most significantly—permitting Christians in diverse polities to serve to discover through others the essential defects of their own regimes. But for this, such defects go unnoticed because of the effect of proximity. All the defects of modern regimes are "relics of paganism"—so must slavery be understood—and, in consequence, are objects of missionary care. The particular corollary to this general understanding of Christianity in diverse polities (though not necessarily in the Christian Republic and, perhaps, applying specifically to defects and not to principles) is the premise that there resides no legislative power in the states to remove the evil itself. Thus, argued Calvin, we find that no national power controls slavery but only the legislative power of the slaveholder himself. Bizarre as this view may seem in the light of the slave codes, it will later come to light as, in fact, a blow at the power of slave states to legislate on behalf of slavery through a national legislative power. In this manner it ultimately leads to arguing the unconstitutionality of any national "Act" with respect to slavery, under circumstances in which all such acts were considered pro-slavery. This avoids the self-contradiction of both abolitionist and secessionist, of course, each of whom wished to grant but half of the corollary power to establish and/or prohibit.[13] But in this context—and provisionally—the view serves to separate the regime from its defect, such that opposition to slavery may be maintained as not only not treasonous but a form of ministering to the "consciences" of the people (*SM*, xxxi).

To see slavery as a pagan relic is almost identical—in terms of the regime—with considering it an accident, though not without cause: "Our fathers never intended slavery to be identified with the government of the United States; but in the *temptations of commerce* the evil was overlooked" (*SM*, xxxi, emphasis supplied). This initial accident is the necessary condition for the continued existence of slavery. But it was not sufficient. The sufficient condition was that the cause of the accident should continue to operate and then only in circumstances of drastically revised opinions. What caused opinions to change, however, was the continued operation of the cause—temptations of commerce. To Calvin this explained why public sentiment of the last generation had changed for the worse. The profitability of cotton in the absence of the restraining opinion of the founding era perpetuated slavery. The profitability of cotton—caused unfettered self-interest. The formula seems to suggest the necessity of an attack on public sentiment sufficient to render it the manacle of interest. Calvin proposed, however, entering into competition with slave cotton by producing free cotton, especially employing Chinese immigrant labor in the American West, but also in British territory where climate permits.[14] The suggestion is founded on the notion that one can best "minister to conscience" by co-opting the mead of conscience, the temptations of commerce. But this is only half true.

Calvin's Edinburgh dive into history, theory, and political economy was directly related to his Glasgow challenge to English consistency. By proposing the cultivation of free cotton he provided a means of compliance with his challenge that his audience free itself of the stain of slave cotton. Of course, he also showed himself to be aware of the temptations of commerce in a broader sphere than the national context of slavery. Looked at in its most general aspect, Calvin's characterization of the defect of the American regime, however possessed of truth, has more to do with his characterization of the English defect—a fact to which, in later meetings, he returned with vehemence and still more explicit proposals, as the force of proximity began to seem a near over-match for disinterested Christianity. Indeed, in this very meeting, Calvin's response was followed by further remarks from the hosts, constructed of acerbic denunciation of the degradation that is slavery and praise of that *American* ingenuity which can surely succeed in eliminating it.

The Edinburgh meeting represented a turning point in the tour. From this meeting arose a false report that an American flag had been burned. Though the report was false, it was certainly true that, if vehemence of speech could burn, Old Glory received a grand roasting. Hence, the situation was fraught with potential embarrassment both for hosts and guests. The very publication of "Sunny Memories" was evidence that embarrassment could not be altogether avoided. Little wonder the American ambassador, the recently appointed Joseph Ingersoll, busied himself during these days seeking to minimize any possible damage and especially to ward off any fatal blow that might have been delivered during the grand culmination at London just ten days hence.[15] From all *appearances*, some caution certainly came to rule. The meetings immediately following—at Aberdeen on April 21st and at Dundee on April 22nd—show no responses by the Stowes to addresses decidedly calmer—though emphatic—in tone. Both meetings produced far more encomium for Stowe than reflection on slavery. At the Aberdeen meeting, in fact, the encomium was followed only by a terse announcement that Aberdeenians were actively engaged in assisting fugitive slaves—an important enough announcement but shorn of denunciatory rhetoric. The Dundee address hailed the "salvation" of American literature and offered prayers of thanks that "the waters of skepticism" were waning in America. In its directest address to slavery, it was thankful "that genuine liberty and evangelical religion are soon to clasp hands, and to smile in unison on the ransomed, regenerated and truly 'United States'" (*SM*, xxxviii). Both addresses reflect in a profound manner part of the essential concern of *Uncle Tom's Cabin*; both were also extraordinarily temperate. This is at least the "public" record. As we shall see in the private letters, Calvin does not tell the full story of those last days in April. But the public record served its purpose, and that is what we seek to record here.

The next address in this volume—prior to the opening of the London season—came from the Glasgow University Abstainer's Society. This offered a pledge of fidelity to the cause of the oppressed but evinced equal if not greater concern for those enslaved by drink than those enslaved by man. Temperance, in more ways than one, seemed to have settled down around this tour. For one week, between April 25th—the date of the Glasgow University Address—and May 2nd—the opening at London—the party appeared to have engaged in all the ordinary delights of tourists as they prepared for the journey to London. "Sunny Memories" records no public meetings or addresses in this introduction. The letters, however, disclosed that there were further meetings in and about Edinburgh, primarily temperance meetings, at which speeches were made. There was also at least one abolition meeting, in Coventry, with members of a Birmingham Society. On this occasion an address was read and Calvin replied. Nonetheless, the "Introduction" brings us directly to London, and that upon the opening of the annual season of Congregational revivals or "May Anniversaries." The stay in London began with the same tenor as the Aberdeen and Dundee meetings. On May 2nd, Stowe was praised, in a company of notables, for a task performed in the interest of humanity. On May 7th, the hosts at a second public meeting spoke mildly on behalf of the slaves, admonishing America to adopt ameliorative efforts.[16] And on May 13th—after eleven days in London—there was a return to the form of address that commenced the tour in Liverpool.

Just as his host had raised the image of the tour's start—praising the scriptural fidelity of *Uncle Tom's Cabin*—Calvin Stowe, too, replied as beginning anew. But his new beginning was not a mere repeating. Speaking in his own name, he drew together all the essential arguments of the first half of the tour. But he did so only after expressing a great reluctance to speak at all, invoking the Union of English and American Congregational churches and appealing to a right of birth—through ancestors who had fled London seeking freedom of conscience. After this lengthy apology he delivered an address of five parts: statement of the current status of slavery; an interpretation of American history with respect to slavery; the Christian Republic with respect to slavery; the profitability of slavery; and the Christian challenge to slavery.

In opening his address, Calvin said he was reluctant to speak of slavery, not simply, but only while away from America. He suggested, therefore, that the question of a defect in one's own regime is properly addressed only to a fellow citizen—and then perhaps only to a few. That is true as far as it goes. But Calvin went farther. In seeing the ancestry both of his polity and of himself in England, and at the same time maintaining the pre-eminence of universal elements in the form of that citizenship, he widened the notion of the citizen sufficiently to make himself at home in London. Add to this that the defect was not *in* the polity, properly—in its principles—but rather was an accident, an "excrescence," and his reluctance was finally overcome.

He commenced his substantive address with a declaration before a London audience as to the constitutionality of an American law, the boldness of which enterprise is effaced by the reflections in the paragraph immediately above. In the decisive sense, the members of his audience are no more restrained by unconstitutional American laws than himself. He laid at the beginning the groundwork for his appeal at the end. That groundwork consists of the argument that Congress possesses no power over slavery. Neither, then, can the states, which can place no such power in Congress. Since the slaveholder alone may legislate for the slave, the Fugitive Slave Law is unconstitutional. This means, of course, that the "Compromise Measures" of 1850 were illegitimate in the extreme, as, indeed, the "Missouri Compromise" was by further implication. It was within the power of the government—and all that that implies—neither to assist the slaveholder in recapturing his slaves, nor to forbid or permit the extension of slavery into any territory. Calvin mentions only the Fugitive Slave Law, here. But his earlier mention of the Kansas-Nebraska debate and its repeal—indeed, rejection of the constitutionality—of the Missouri Compromise, permit us to draw out the further implications. Calvin had yielded to the repeal of the Missouri Compromise and accepted its principles, but in their most extreme form. He had opened the entire nation both to the agitation of abolitionists and those who would aid the slave in his escape, and to the extension of slavery throughout the entire United States. That this was done in order to eliminate slavery once and for all is remarkable. We must ask what induced him to anticipate any happy result from such dangerous means.

From the time of the Revolution, the history of slavery was of a progressive and voluntary abolition. The "Bill of Rights"—Massachusetts', that is—was, among the fathers, taken to heart, and slavery was generally condemned. Everyone expected it to "melt away before the advancing light of truth." And, although full social equality was not instituted among free blacks and whites, some changes were made and must yet be pushed. But sentiment seemed rather to have hardened in these matters. The "Christian Republic" in 1853 was upholding slavery, and in this the church largely acquiesced. Calvin characterized contemporary slavery much after the manner of the *Key to Uncle Tom's Cabin*: he referred his auditors to current journals, and especially their advertisements. He read the lament of the Paris Correspondent of a New York journal, in which it is protested that he could defuse sentiment created by *Uncle Tom's Cabin* by calling it a "romance."[17] But, the blatant advertising of sales, auctions, trackers, drivers, and dog teams continually gave the lie to his every effort. That the church should defend such slavery is but the result of power—the power of interest. The power of the system to control the clergy was derived from its commercial power, for cotton—having become principal—became intimately connected with commercial affairs of the entire country. As it turned out, the power of more than the American clergy was at stake. American and Englishman were united by interest. The growth of pro-slavery sentiment in America paralleled the growth of British use of cotton.

Britain, Calvin argued, purchased two-thirds[18] of American cotton. And this alone would have made the extension of slavery necessary. In response, therefore, the Chinese ought to be employed to grow free cotton:

> If Christians will investigate this subject, and if philanthropists generally will pursue these inquiries in an honest spirit, it is not long before we shall see a movement throughout the civilized world, and the upholders of slavery will feel, where they feel most acutely—in their pockets. (*SM*, xlix)

This challenge, unlike its original, but begins his peroration. It is, in fact, the statement of the moderate Whig, pro-compromise position. And, as we saw, the opening of this address embraced the radical rejection of the 1850 measures and the other compromises with which it was allied. Hence, he carried the argument a step further. As before, the pain others will materially experience is but the converse of the pain the crusaders will not have to experience materially. When first enunciated, this seemed a virtual abandonment of "ministering to people's consciences," and so it does now but with an important codicil. Calvin frankly acknowledged that he despaired of *simple* appeals to conscience and right principles. In abolitionist terminology, he had abandoned the appeal to "Higher Law." He noted that few really defend slavery so much as many "shield it from aggression" with the cry, "It is the law of the land." How forceful is such an assertion to an alien! This he had gotten his audience over or at least prepared them to ignore. But, that it reappears in the context of a discussion of right and self-interest suggests a further meaning. That interest does not bow to the regime is evident. But the case of right is not so clear, and the question of despairing of the appeal to conscience raises itself as *right* bowing to the *law of the land*. The Whig compromise position seemed to be the abandonment of right. The "Higher Law" was not abandoned by Calvin; he understood it to have lost dignity, a dignity somehow requiring to be imparted by the law of the land.

That all important qualifier, "simple," formulates the response. The simple appeal to conscience will indeed fail, but a mixed appeal may be *blessed* with success. The first element of mixture is interest, and it has been taken over from the compromise position. The second element is a public sense of right steeled for resisting law—albeit unconstitutional law. Calvin returned with the example of the missionary, this time, the Bible missionary. These children of the Puritans distributed the Bible itself where it was illegal, with the exception of the American South. Should the law of Rome be accorded so little respect and that of South Carolina so much? The church had a duty to treat the case of the slave as one with the Hindu native. The duty is never to cease from admonition until a favorable influence is produced. But he who was most to be influenced, in the South, was not, as it were, the native, but the Christian. Calvin did not point this out. He was aware that a justification of missionary work among slaves is an attack on slavery, but he was equally aware that the only alternative is to forswear the missionary claim; i.e., the universal claims of Christianity and the prospect for a Christian Republic. In effect, he denied that it is necessary to choose between revolution and the church. For, to keep the church, it was necessary to cause revolution.

That right which must resist the law is the right of Christianity to rule men wherever they be found. It is a right which is not found in law, but which nonetheless founds universal law. In the contemplation of this universal aspect, the political identity of all genuine modern movements of human improvement, Calvin sanguinely reflected on the particular benefit to be derived from such an understanding.

> In due time God will prosper the right, and in due time the fetters will fall from every slave, and the black man will have the same *privileges* as the white. (*SM*, li)

In this manner does he conclude his strongest call for intervention; and that followed the strongest hesitation yet to speak at all. That it should occur in this manner is made to seem all the more artful by the complete absence of direct challenge or affront in the remarks of the hosts. Only two addresses of equal importance remain to be considered. But this is the first of a triad. So structured and artful as it may be, it is but an introduction to the resolution of the difficulties it harbors. It is, in a manner of speaking, the opening gun in Stowe's attempt to wrest complete control of the conditions of what is essentially a radical critique of America.[19]

The very next day, May 14th, in a quiet meeting the host expressed the proper sentiments (there is a "union of sentiment" which respects no borders) but, withal, was restrained in his advocacy. On behalf of his wife and himself Calvin disclaimed all credit for movement in the cause and warmly thanked his hosts. But, following this meeting—in the space of the next few days—they clearly reflected on the next step to take and concluded on offering a formal resolution at the Exeter Hall demonstration, largest of the tour, on the evening of the 16th. That such concert existed is indicated by the divergences between the account in Letter XXI and that in the "Introduction." All that is noted in the letter is that Calvin "spoke on this point, that the cotton trade of Great Britain is the principal support to slavery, and read extracts from Charleston papers . . ."[20] No mention of a formal resolution is made, and no report of the crowd's reaction is given. The brouhaha is only mentioned in subsequent letters considered only in the light of *ex post facto* discussions. Clearly, the letters sought to minimize what was boldly confessed in the "Introduction," and they create an image or claim of innocence, which seems to have no public purpose. Indeed, since the letter's description more nearly matches the address of the 13th, just described, it tends to divest the series of its progressive character But the "Introduction" shows the affair in all its boldness, and suggests that no such general reflection as claimed was made. That the public record, given in its "entirety" when given, is intentionally at odds with the private record requires an account that describes the intention entertained both in the preparation of the book and in the Exeter Hall meeting itself. At first glance, it may seem that they were emboldened by the host's opening declaration. But that does not account for forethought, which the resolution implies. What is more likely is that they felt some necessity—still—to press the task of forging proper sentiments in the smithy of the British conscience.

The abolition rally at Exeter Hall exceeded all others. It was vituperative and jaunty. The gentle mood of the prior meeting was but a lull. Exeter Hall's denunciations of slavery and the society that practiced it were immoderate and included an attack on President Franklin Pierce's inaugural "defense" of slavery. The address cited the decision of Judge Ruffin, again made available in the *Key to Uncle Tom's Cabin*, and concluded with a call for action. This was the first call to action, *per se*, to emanate from any of the hosts during the tour. It called upon the English and American Protestants ("sole depositories of the Protestant truth and of civil law and religious liberty")[21] to act as a single body for the overthrow of slavery. And it projected the rule—indeed, the empire—of a Christian Republic.

Calvin responded to this rousing appeal without the least reluctance. He offered no apologies and, ever one step ahead of his host, raised a direct challenge in the form of a resolution—not even pausing for the usual word of thanks. He appealed for a "union of sentiment" but cautioned that sentiment must be purified to be effective. His starting point, it can be seen, was response to the harmless address of the 14th. Of what does purification consist? Consistency! Every condemnation uttered must be accompanied by an expiative act in demonstration of consistency. This is a retreat from the call for free cotton and a return to the demand for a boycott of slave cotton. Yet, he still included a nod toward the need to minimize the pain. An American history was given, but on this occasion the "fathers" were named. They are Jefferson, Madison, Franklin, and Jonathan Edwards. Taken in descending order, this yields a picture of historical development that also discloses the one thing presently needful: equality. And of the whole chain (equality founded in commerce founded in machines and industry founded in protestantism renewed American style) the originating source was taken to be an advanced strain of American protestantism. This is the path or history that must be followed for an effective condemnation of slavery. Because Britain purchased four-fifths of the United States' cotton she sustained slavery. But she also purchased thereby a right to interfere. There are three choices—three ways to abolish slavery: (1) bloody revolution; (2) moral suasion; (3) making slave labor unprofitable.

It remains to answer how the fathers would choose, but, thus abruptly, coupling direction with a call to action, Calvin ended. That his purpose was something more than stir is suggested by the alternative offered in the end, although that is seen clearly only in the final meeting a week later. Yet, stir he did, to the point of bringing forth catcalls and angry responses from the audience. The tour had come full circle, from suspicion of anti-American sentiment to suspicion of anti-British sentiment. Indeed, to some this direct challenge seemed pro-slavery in intent. Thus, the presentation of the public record is followed by an explanation—as was the case of the Edinburgh meeting upon which it was necessary to deny flag-burning—in which Calvin reaffirmed his position, claiming consistency, and closed with a statement from Charles Dickens which had been published in the abolitionist *National Era* at Washington and which echoed a similar sentiment.

Calvin may well have been consistent, and it might yet not be unfair to see the abrupt commencement and end, the absence of formal acknowledgments, and the specific form of challenge as directed toward an end consistent with a defense of America. This Exeter Hall meeting was by far the most anti-American in sentiment and went so far as to call into question the genuineness of her love of liberty. That Jefferson, Madison, Franklin, and Edwards were chosen as "fathers" would alone suggest that Calvin was never in doubt as to whether American liberty was defensible. If we consider again the Edinburgh meeting, we note the primary emphasis on the function of a universal Christian community to discover, one to another, the defects of their respective regimes. This process of discovery takes place only on the ground of that very necessary condition, the intention of the regime. America is defensible precisely to the extent that—the very Christian Republic itself—no defect exists which can be discovered to her except on the basis of her own principles. To play the game, the Briton must become to some extent American. The reverse is not possible despite Calvin's appeal to ancestry and purpose in the opening of this chapter. His remarks here amount to a rigorous insistence on American principles as precondition for condemnation. Insofar as those American, those universal principles are not British, it is certainly an anti-British sentiment. And in the decisive analysis, as the May 13th address shows, it is America rather than her protestantism which is the condition of human improvement.

But for one fact, then, we would have dealt with the difficulty posed by this meeting of May 16th. That fact is Calvin's advance preparation. He had not heard the attack, presumably, when he drafted the resolution and could only have anticipated it in a general sense. It is possible he would have more greatly enveloped the resolution, *extempore*, had the attack been less strident. Or, perhaps he knew from the Earl of Shaftesbury, in advance, the content of his remarks.[22] Or, again, perhaps the resolution was drafted with reference to something other than the address, one of several, that evening. That the latter is at least a likely possibility is suggested both by what we have considered and the last address to be considered. The question then becomes: Can we take as matter of chance the anti-American sentiment of the Exeter Hall meeting, and yet see the necessity for discovering the ground of a defense of America?

In beginning the Exeter Hall address by advancing the necessity of a purification of sentiment, Calvin identified the strongest chord that ran through each of the last three major addresses. On May 13th he despaired of a simple appeal to conscience but concluded by invoking a mixed appeal to conscience. There he established that "right principle" was intimately connected with right opinion, and the mixed appeal sought to secure right opinion. The address had begun by raising the question of the relationship of the principle of a polity to its law. Between its beginning and its end there lay an implicit question: What is the relationship of the principle of a polity and public opinion or sentiment? It was seen that an accidental cause could undermine the *opinion* necessary to sustain the regime. But is it the same to undermine the *principle*? Might an accidental cause, or specifically, that same accidental cause have undermined the principle of the American polity as well?

The opening of the address of the 16th yields Calvin's answer: Principle is independent of sentiment. Though sentiment is necessary to actuate principle, its loss is not the loss of principle. Hence, sentiment is susceptible of being brought back into line with principle. That is, sentiment can be corrupted. But principle may only be abandoned. To choose to purify sentiment is to choose to sustain principle. To sustain the principle of a polity under attack requires defense, and especially in the case when the attack is mustered by one's nominal friends. It is well noted that abolitionists often failed to distinguish in their attacks between slavery as an evil in America and the American polity itself. The address of the 16th provided the counter attack, as Calvin saw it. There remained but the completion of the task of purifying opinion.

The denunciatory appeals at Exeter Hall followed Professor Stowe's unprovoked call for intervention on the 13th of May. So, too, does the address—the host's address—on the 25th of May seem to have been called forth by Calvin's demand for a purity of sentiment at Exeter Hall. In this address, the hosts recognized the pre-eminency of opinion and avowed some *guilt* on their own part. The achievement of great objects was said to require the working of change in public opinion and *Uncle Tom's Cabin* was lauded for such an achievement. Its substantive content was taken to be Christian precept, but its mode of teaching was the decisive element. With respect to their guilt, the welcoming address confessed a responsibility to "wash our hands" of the iniquity but concluded that they were unsure how this was to be done.

The process of purification, it seems, had begun. The last three major addresses, in that sense, represent a dialogue or dialectic through which Calvin sought to bring about a restrained sense of indignation, which, because of its restraint, can be given a wider scope. Thus, the moderation with which the tour ends eclipsed that with which it began. That this result be obtained and the dialogue successfully reach a resolution, the last speech would have to have the character of a conclusion. That is the same as to say that it will be possessed of extraordinary self-consciousness. Hence, it seems less than accidental that Calvin's last response calls itself the "last address," though it is *literally* the last *he* must give before embarking for the return to America.[23]

The self-consciousness of these concluding remarks is expressed in dual fashion. At the surface, they explicitly convey the complete outline of the plan of attack on slavery as that plan had been developed *during the tour*. On the other hand, this last address is explicitly the speech of Harriet Stowe. Within it, therefore, one can trace the lines of all previous speeches to discern how far Calvin spoke only for himself and how far he spoke for Stowe. That is made unnecessary, at least in appearance, only by the opening declaration that Mrs. Stowe and he "are perfectly agreed in every point with regard to the nature of slavery, and the best means of getting rid of it" (*SM*, xli). Thus, the jointly owned conclusion is in fact a conclusion of jointly owned prior remarks. Thus, Calvin proceeded to deliver himself of a final address distinguished from all the previous addresses by strategically flaunting the first person plural.

Calvin began by admiring the address "just heard" as that, of all in the journey, which may best have "expressed the sympathies and feelings of our own hearts." That pre-eminence it awarded the task of changing opinions is the light in which any despairing of simple appeals to consciences must be seen. *Uncle Tom's Cabin*, or a sense of right steeled to resist law, is the necessary condition of *Dred,* yet to be written. In the absence of that apocalyptic attack on corrupt sentiment, the appeal to self-interest, must be couched in terms of the provisional appeal already suggested, the temptations of commerce. But even that provisional appeal bespeaks the principle enunciated in *Dred*: the avoidance of pain. This, the *real* temptation of commerce, must be subsidiary, but present. The complete outline of "our view," therefore, reveals the true order and rank of the elements in this attack.

It is first necessary to show the utter wrongfulness of the system of slavery. Doing so establishes "the great moral ground" on which the crusader must always first insist. The moral excellence of *Uncle Tom's Cabin* (the first claim of excellence during the tour) consists precisely in this demonstration of wrongfulness coupled with a simultaneous showing of the Christian spirit of forgiveness to those involved.[24] It derives its "great power" from these two characteristics. The latter seems the corollary to the view that the wrongdoer is merely ignorant and therefore involuntarily unjust.[25] Establishment of the great moral ground, then, seems to depend on the cultivation of an awareness that there are all kinds of men "of differing levels of moral development"—men whose consciences need to be awakened. It is an argument addressed to friends and enemies but especially to friends. Still, it is only half of an argument. *Uncle Tom's Cabin* is, alone, a simple appeal to conscience, and the mixed appeal requires a sequel. Once the "great moral ground" is secure, the other shoe must fall. She proceeds as if addressing Ophelia St. Clare (see book I, part I, chapter 11, pp. 135–37:

> One would believe that when they saw a thing to be wrong, they would at once do right, but prejudice, habit, interest, education and a variety of influences check their aspiration to what is right. (*SM,* lxii)

It is through the restructuring of public sentiment that one succeeds in altering such error. Before force, public sentiment is the crucial nexus. They judged it the role of the churches—"dormant" some years—to begin the construction of a suitable universal sentiment. This sentiment of right is, for some, a consciousness of right undone. As with a child, consciousness of right undone is indistinguishable from consciousness of a spanking yet to come. Hence, the attack on interest must also be waged.

In the second place, they reaffirmed the Exeter Hall proposal, though in modified form. And all the modifications seem to acknowledge that its extreme formulation was but an attack on inconsistent British sentiment. Given purer sentiment, they called, first, for a demonstration of the *feasibility* of competition with slave cotton. And, as to a boycott of slave products, it was accepted that "the state of society is such that we cannot at once dispense with all the products of slave labor" (*SM,* lxiii). But, no one conscious of this imperfection in his regime can reject the notion in principle. That is all that is required for pure sentiment, and there should be no objection to the expiative act of avoiding products of slave labor *as much as possible.* For emphasis, Calvin offered two examples—one of avoidable and the other of "unavoidable" inconsistency. The principle may legitimately be compromised for the sake of interest or avoiding pain. But, we must not overlook the fact that this can be admitted only after indignation had been, first, given basis and then restrained. In that light, insistence on purity of principle becomes an instrument of defense against unrestrained indignation based on a premise of the necessary opposition of self-interest to principle. Again, a distinction between good sentiments and good principles emerges but this time in a manner that raises the question as to how far interest may compromise principle. In other words, the true problem concerns the difference between those temptations of commerce which, *because* they *only* compromise or obscure principle, permit the rule of principle through sentiment and those temptations of commerce which in fact do not compromise but rather abandon principles.

The third and last element of the attack on slavery is prayer to God. It is explained with the single statement: "This ought to be, and must be, a religious enterprise" (*SM*, lxiii). Whether this suggests the possibility of justifying the enterprise on non-religious ground, it surely connotes the instrumental—though not necessarily simply instrumental—role of religion in the struggle.

Calvin next mentioned "one more subject," and it is unclear whether it is actually a fourth method or element. He called for unity among the opponents to slavery. That such unity would serve an instrumental role in consummating the struggle is clear. It would seem, then, to be a fourth element. But the condition of unity is not fully spelled out. In each of the prior addresses, that condition had always been identified, when mentioned, as British and American protestantism. But if that were so, the third element would be but the condition of the fourth, and they would be but one element, actually. And insofar as unity with respect to the struggle could be purely secular in terms of its objective, the religious character of the enterprise would be incidental—it might be a necessary but could not be a sufficient condition of success. This was hinted at in Edinburgh, where Calvin contrasted the unity among slavery's supporters with their differences as to every other subject.[26] He suggested, there, that slavery's opponents could follow the example. This "Introduction" does not answer the question. It answers only the questions that must be answered for British abolitionists. But the question for American abolitionists—what is the principle of the polity, or more specifically, how far need it be compromised to permit its rule—remains to be answered.

As newspaper reports of the day and the Charles Beecher *Diary* make abundantly clear the progressive character of this "Introduction" is completely fiction. The Stowes did not labor to correct the deficiencies of public opinion in England. Everything that was said at the conclusion of the campaign had already been said at the beginning. It is therefore reasonable to conclude that the fictionalized account is related to the fact that this book was written for American eyes only. The end in view was to lay a foundation for a broader consideration of the characteristics of American democracy than a focus on slavery would permit. One way to achieve this without abandoning the goal of abolishing slavery is to introduce contrasts between America and England revolving around differing approaches to that question. In reality, the contrasts relate exclusively to the alternatives Americans faced in deciding what to do about slavery.

The fictionalized account, in short, was a means of constructing grounds for public debate without alienating any important segment of opinion at the outset of the debate. Calvin closed his introduction with a personal note, which emphasized just that intention. Altogether he had posed the question as to just how Americans can manage to salvage their liberty, and what will be the consequences of such efforts for their happiness? The response to this question requires that our focus be removed from the immediate problem of slavery (though never neglecting it) and reconsidering what it is that America was and is expected to become. The letters supply that, using the cover of privacy to abstract from slavery and to describe a "sunny future" through reflections on "Sunny Memories."

NOTES

1. In addition to the extensive notice, above, of Calvin's and Stowe's direct and indirect commentaries on *Democracy in America*, Stowe included extensive direct application of Tocqueville in the chapter "Domestic Manners," of her last work, *American Women's Home*, co-authored with her sister, Catharine Beecher. Brown notes that Catharine Beecher quotes Tocqueville in her 1841 *Treatise on Domestic Economy*. Brown, *Domestic Individualism*, p. 22.

2. Even to this date, however, there is little or no evidence that Stowe scholars have discerned her intent, as the minimal commentary on "Sunny Memories" that exists does, in fact, regard the work as primarily a travelogue. Hedrick is but one example of this trend: "Stowe also used the pages of her travel book to impart useful information and to instruct her readers in the etiquette of travel." Hedrick, *Harriet Beecher Stowe*, p. 267. Baym is rare in noting Stowe's deliberate use of artifice in the book, but does not explicate the full meaning behind the artifice. Nina Baym, *American Women Writers and the Work of History, 1790–1860* (New Brunswick: Rutgers University Press, 1995). Lee recognizes the philosophical underpinnings of much of Stowe's *oeuvre*, but nevertheless views "Sunny Memories" as "a mix of political agitation, aesthetic speculation, and travel-narrative pleasure," thus also overlooking its broad philosophical message. Lee, "Quarreling with Politics," p. 66. Newman sees

that "*Sunny Memories* . . . is not so much a travel book as a work of polemic"; however, her article on Stowe's apparent defense of the Highland clearances addresses but one small portion of the extensive meaning lurking beneath the surface of this work. Judie Newman, "Stowe's Sunny Memories of Highland Slavery," in *Special Relationships: Anglo-American Antagonism and Affinities, 1854–1936*, ed. Janet Beer (Manchester: Manchester University Press, 2002), p. 32 (hereafter cited as "Stowe's Sunny Memories"). Cotugno discerns that Stowe has a message for Americans in this work, but develops a somewhat different explication of that message than the one offered here. "Trollope and Martineau, Sedgwick and Stowe each also published volumes of travel sketches, and here again a reforming national agenda prevails. Couched in these accounts of far-away places (and sometimes baldly on the surface) are deliberate commentaries on the condition of life at home." Cotugno, "Form and Reform," p. 14.

3. The full citation for "Sunny Memories" is *Sunny Memories of Foreign Lands*, 2 vols. (Boston: Phillips, Sampson, and Company, 1854). I refer to it throughout as "Sunny Memories" in the text, *SM* in notation.

4. Friedrich Nietzsche, *The Use and Abuse of History* (Indianapolis: Bobbs Merrill, 1957), pp. 11–13. The wish for such a history was, however, elegantly conveyed by Rufus Choate in his 1833 address on "The Importance of Illustrating New England History by a Series of Romances Like the Waverly Novels," in which he urges the writing of historical novels not as "substitutes *for* history, but supplements to it," in which history might be shown "from a different point of view, and through a brighter, more lustrous medium, and by a more powerful optical instrument"—by means of which "you see the best of everything,—all that is grand and beautiful of nature, all that is brilliant in achievement, all that is magnanimous in virtue, all that is sublime in self-sacrifice; and you see a great deal more of which history shows you nothing." Rufus Choate, "The Importance of Illustrating New England History by a Series of Romances Like the Waverly Novels," in *The Works of Rufus Choate, with a Memoir of His Life*, ed. Samuel Gilman Brown (Boston: Little, Brown and Company, 1862), pp. 323, 341.

5. "By the Royal mail steamer Canada we have advices from New York to the 29th, and from Boston to the 30th ult. She brought fifty-four passengers, among whom is Mrs. Harriet Beecher Stowe, authoress of *Uncle Tom's Cabin*, but no specie." *Times of London* (April 11, 1853, Monday). An almost identical notice was repeated on the following day. "Diary, Friday Ap. 1, Canada." Heading from first page of Charles Beecher's *Diary*. I have used a typescript copy, generously lent by the Stowe-Day Library, where the original is preserved (hereafter cited as *Diary*). The entire *Diary* has been published as Charles Beecher, *Harriet Beecher Stowe in Europe: The Journal of Charles Beecher* (Hartford, CT: Stowe-Day Foundation, 1986).

6. Hedrick detects some of the subtlety and complexity here; writing about the Stowe's 1853 tour of Britain, she says: "Acting privately properly, she was nevertheless speaking publicly. Stowe was careful in her outward behavior to do nothing that would upset this delicate standoff between ideology and reality, for it allowed her to move back and forth between the private and the public realms and to have an influence in both." Hedrick, *Harriet Beecher Stowe*, p. 238.

7. May, 1854. The reference is to the impending Kansas-Nebraska Bill, and the threatened extension of slavery into western territories. As the Compromise of 1850

and its Fugitive Slave provisions gave birth to *Uncle Tom's Cabin*, the Kansas-Nebraska debate issued in "Sunny Memories." See Jaffa's *Crisis of the House Divided*, for the best account of these debates.

8. *SM*, pp. xii–xiii. The question of the relationship between Stowe's ideas and Calvin's ideas, as well as questions about the purpose of the journey and the use Stowe made of the thousands of dollars placed at her disposal on behalf of the slaves (the placing of a thousand copies each of *UTC* and the *Key* is but one example only), may be answered by consulting Stowe's "Letter to the Ladies' New Anti-Slavery Society of Glasgow, the Contents of Which are Designed Equally for the Anti-Slavery Societies of England and Scotland." The pamphlet, dated 18th November 1853, offers a succinct account of the "demonstration" intended. Harriet Beecher Stowe, *Letter to the Ladies' New Anti-Slavery Society of Glasgow, the Contents of Which are Designed Equally for the Anti-Slavery Societies of England and Scotland* (Glasgow: John Maclay, 1853).

9. A partial account of the public record is found in Horace Perry Jones, "The Southern Press Follows Harriet Beecher Stowe Abroad," *The McNeese Review* 27 (1980).

10. The last recorded in this "Introduction." At the conclusion of the Exeter Hall address (given on April 13), Calvin Stowe claimed to have raised his free cotton plan at Liverpool; so, too, does Harriet Stowe in her letters. Yet, no record of it is given here; which is all the more anomalous since that plan comes to play the central role in both accounts of the proceedings of the journey. Neither does Charles Beecher's *Diary* record such a plan. He does, however, say that Mr. Stowe is a most effective speaker whose words are "like red hot steel." He expected the final Liverpool speech to "create some sensation in the U.S." and added, significantly, "I do not forget nor does he, nor Hatty that every word we say here, we must meet at home" (Beecher, p. 33).

11. The April 18 *Times of London* report of this speech shows that Calvin made this claim even more emphatically than his American version reveals. Nevertheless, the actual version also shows a vigorous defense of the "American Mind," which was likewise absent from the American version.

12. Actually, according to the *Times*, Calvin had already narrowed the alternatives to two at Glasgow. Either slaveholders had to be "persuaded" to abolition, or "bloody revolution" would be necessary.

13. Cf. Jaffa, *Crisis of the House Divided*, p. 199.

14. Here Calvin follows the example of West Indian planters who turned to Indians of the sub-continent to replace the ex-slaves about whose habits Carlyle was so exercised.

15. Forrest Wilson, *Crusader in Crinoline*. This is discussed in particular below.

16. May 7, according to the *London Times*, was the date of the "Stafford House Reception." This is what Calvin reports. He gave no response. But he fails to note that Charles Beecher responded and read a letter from the abolitionist Cassius Clay. In addition, Stowe specifically and intentionally conveys the idea that there was no response. See the discussion of "Letter XIII" below.

17. Saunders provides an instructive account of the many attempts to discredit the novel by calling it a "romance" and also critiques the limitations of that effort. Saunders, "Houses Divided."

18. He elsewhere says four-fifths.

19. Hedrick misses the art and the message when she attributes Calvin Stowe's articulation of a "free-cotton" position to the chance meeting of the Stowe party with Joseph Sturge of Birmingham, "a strong proponent of the view that if the markets for slave cotton disappeared, so too would slavery." She then adds, "Not having any formulated antislavery platform to stand on, the Beechers were readily susceptible to the plan presented to them by their Birmingham hosts. After a meeting arranged by Sturge and Elihu Burritt, Harriet's party agreed to work with the Quakers in promoting 'free-labour.'" Hedrick, *Harriet Beecher Stowe*, p. 241.

20. *SM*, vol. II, p. 34.

21. A *New York Weekly Times* account of Shaftesbury's protestantism, July 10, 1852, 1:42, p. 6. "We are feeble, if hostile; but, if united, we are the arbiters of the world. Let us join together for the temporal and spiritual good of our race."

22. In Letter XXI, Stowe asserts that she entered late and missed "a very able speech" by the Earl. From this it is unclear whether she is referring to what she knows from report, or from the next morning's paper, or from advance knowledge of the contents. But each is fully a possibility.

23. In reality, he did not *have* to give it. Charles Beecher's *Diary* entry for May 24 reveals that Calvin had been scheduled to depart on the 25th and Charles had been scheduled to speak at Willis's Rooms. Without explanation Calvin postponed his departure to make the speech. "When he came down Stowe, whose trunks were all packed, and who had announced his absolute determination to start tomorrow, spoke up and said—'Well I've concluded to stop tomorrow and make a speech.'" Cf. p. 168.

24. As Smiley recently wrote: "The power of *Uncle Tom's Cabin* is the power of brilliant analysis married to great wisdom of feeling." Jane Smiley, "Say It Ain't So, Huck," *Harper's Magazine* 292 (1996): 65.

25. Cf. Aristotle, *Nichomachean Ethics.*

26. Actually, according to the *Times of London*, he had already done this at Glasgow in one of the *first* speeches of the campaign.

20

A Cause Célèbre

Before we consider the letters, in some sense as a treatise, we must first acquaint ourselves with further examples of the reporting of these events and the public atmosphere that surrounded them. As has already been remarked, in consideration of the "The Ghostly Cry," *Uncle Tom's Cabin* blew in a blizzard of controversy in 1852. And it did not cease there. The very challenges to the work inspired *The Key to Uncle Tom's Cabin*, which Stowe completed and placed in her publisher's hands as she departed for England. Yet, it would be misleading to suggest that there were no other public questions of more pressing concern. Though papers might lament the increasing tendency of public discussion to ground every argument in the "negro question,"[1] it was nonetheless the case that many papers succeeded in showing a studied indifference to *Uncle Tom's Cabin* and abolitionism in general. And this was true of papers of all stripes. Though none could escape the claims of the building warfare altogether, they did their best to resist hewing the timbers destined to burn. An example of this is the *New York Journal of Commerce*, whose editorial determination to avoid giving exposure to the railing happily coincided with its special editorial orientation to commercial affairs. Yet, the single issue in which the *Commerce* reports Stowe's movements at Stafford House also contains a note of an "aborted" slave uprising in New Orleans, the happy announcement that Lydia Baisley had succeeded in raising half the price of her son and that his owner had voluntarily relinquished the other half, and a comment on one Trainor, ex-slave, petitioning for assistance in procuring the freedom of his wife. The *Commerce* adjudges that she is probably better off where she is than with "her lazy, lecherous, runaway husband."[2] Its determination to avoid encouraging discord was, however, sincere. It is further true that there was substantial pressure for men of all stripes to consider the "Compromise Measures of 1850" as ending the discussion—a pressure that intruded itself upon and determined the outcome of the 1852 presidential nomination.

Through all this, the winds generated by *Uncle Tom's Cabin* raged about unpredictably. When they burst forth from aristocratic quarters in England no one could remain indifferent. An address to the "Women of America" sailed across the Atlantic at the end of 1852, carrying the message that half a million British women expected America's women to put an end to slavery. This "Affectionate Address"[3] did indeed address American women in tones of sisterly affection and even assigned a not inconsiderable portion of guilt for the existence of slavery to old John Bull. The address was not drafted, however, by the Duchess of Sutherland, its chief sponsor. It was drafted by the Earl of Shaftesbury. He conceived the idea, drafted the address, and suggested to the ladies that they set about procuring the signatures, which *they* succeeded all too well in doing. Shaftesbury's role was never concealed, and the ladies who owned the address unhesitatingly affirmed their concurrence in his opinion. Yet, his role added to this feminine dialogue the threat of the intervention of real politics—of men talking to men, even if behind the skirts of the women.

To this address a reply was drafted, in late January, 1853, by the wife of the recent President, John Tyler. The author found herself under the unfortunate necessity of having to write from Sherwood Forest, Virginia, but abated no ardor in her enterprise on that account. The suspicion was common, though the fact never established, that this "Robin Hood of Sherwood Forest" was in fact more than seconded by "Little John."[4] The author rejected the admonitions of the English ladies as unnecessary and ill-tempered. In reporting these events, newspapers gave full vent to the role that *Uncle Tom's Cabin* played in inspiring the original dart. The novel threatened to become an instrument of real politics rather than a mere romance. It is, therefore, a virtual declaration of war when Stowe announces, on January 1st in the *New York Weekly Times* (picking up a *Boston Traveller* lead), that she is preparing a trip to the United Kingdom, as the guest and at the expense of abolitionists there.[5]

The reaction of the American press to the "Affectionate Address" was measured and limited. They considered it an inappropriate source for extended discussion of great public issues. The most serious, though at first essentially muted, reflection to which the address gave rise was the aim of British policy in engendering a rift between North and South. At a time when it was conceived that England yet had designs on Oregon and might enter into some arrangement with Mexico, it was not assumed that she would abstain from seeking to check rising American influence by sowing discord. The matured version of this fear was given expression and gained the color of credence as Stowe approached London and it became clear how widespread was the "enthusiasm" of British notables for her crusade. The *New York Observer*, in an article entitled "Hatred of America," formulated the uneasiness.

> Mrs. Stowe's book has called out Lord Denman, the venerable ex-Lord Chief Justice, and a host of other writers, both aristocratic and plebian, and the whole country rings with the transcendent selfishness and iniquity of the American nation. Unfortunately, this book has revived the old animosities, and contributed to nullify that friendly feeling to which the Peace Congress, and Industrial Exhibition, and increased intercourse, and all the movements of civilization had so wonderfully contributed. This may be no evil in the eyes of many philanthropists on both sides of the Atlantic, as it calls attention once again to that unfortunate calamity which afflicts our country; and I verily believe that if the agitation were to lead to a disruption of the Union, and to all the horrors of a servile war, they would be less evils in the eyes of the English than the least of the misfortunes which slavery entails. . . . But we in America have more cause to love England, than England to love us, as the old mother of our civilization, the parent of our best institutions, and hence, on reflection, (we) will I hope palliate the folly which is about to emanate from Stafford House.[6]

That the view implicit in this article was not limited to the staunch anti-abolitionists is made clear after the Stafford House reception, by the in fact pro-free soil though moderate *New York Weekly Times*.

> The motive which prompted (the Stafford House affair) is not to be mistaken. The great ministers of state, who attended the distinguished levee, were moved by no ordinary sentiment, and it was, we dare venture, quite as hostile to this country and its institutions, as it was adverse to the existence of involuntary servitude. They would heap reproach upon us, whenever permitted to do so, with impunity. . . . The same feeling that prompts your men of Manchester to look abroad the world over for new cotton fields, that they may be in fact, as they would feel in national sentiment, wholly independent of the United States, was probably the controlling motive that induced Lords Russell and Palmerston, and Mr. Chancellor Gladstone to give countenance to the Anti-Slavery Address. . . . They would wound the sensibility of a rival power by lavishing honors on one who is supposed by her writing to have brought opprobrium on its social and domestic relations.[7]

We would find similar sentiment expressed in other journals, as will be noted below. At this point it is sufficient to note that the discussion of patriotism in Calvin Stowe's introduction is not uncalled for. Yet, it comes after the fact. And all of these reservations were expressed, in some form, before and during the Stowe's journey. To understand the choices they faced we must look more closely at the journalistic exchanges.

The *Observer* gives great credence to Mrs. Tyler's reply to the "Affectionate Address."[8] Indeed, they tendentiously denominate her "a Northern lady" in order to fix her claim of disinterested nationalism, despite the fact she married Tyler in 1844 and lived in Virginia—once they left the White House—ever after. But what did this "specially worthy" letter assert? Mrs. Tyler tasks the Duchess of Sutherland for abandoning her station, both as a woman and as of high birth. And, again, the letter justifies indignation that Sutherland should dare to presume upon the amity that subsists or should subsist between America and England to interfere with domestic problems. The letter threatens and reviles, questioning not only the motives of the author but also the virtue of Britain herself. And it denies to aristocracy a perspective from which it may judge the demands of justice.

> I pray you to bear in mind that the golden rule of life is for each to attend to his own business,[9] and let his neighbors alone! *This means* peace, love, friendship. The opposite means hatred, ill-will, contention—it destroys the peace of neighborhoods, and is the fruitful cause of discord among nations.

This morality would be ironic if intended to be universally *enforced*: teaching as it does the necessity of slave rebellion as the *only* means of attaining self-respect. *The* condition of peace is force sufficient to secure it. But Mrs. Tyler addressed only Britain, and did not include "all men" in this declaration of independence. She earlier forswore the resort to the sword as her intent. And we may take her at her word without pursuing the theoretical line that if British power results from the sword, as she maintained, then the American power that exceeds it must exceed in force, even if it self-consciously forswears the use. But whether through steel or oratory, the British lion is made to tremble.

> I allude to a power more resistless, and more certain in its results—the power of example—the example of a free, prosperous and great people, *among whom all artificial distinctions of society are unknown* . . .[10]

Treating her response with no greater rigor than it demands, we must conclude that Mrs. Tyler's reply to the "Affectionate Address" is not just a spiteful "mind your own business" but a notice that age has overtaken the possibility of aristocratic disinterestedness. Hence, there is no longer *any* business for an *aristoi* to mind. The problems of slavery, therefore, will be resolved with resort to other supports.

The *Times* also spoke in positive terms of Mrs. Tyler's reply, though not so glowingly as the *Observer*. But it did so reluctantly, preferring to avoid the subject altogether.[11] The intensity of concern, however, overcame editorial resistance. To the *Times*, the reply was a complete and final response, if unnecessary. In its eyes, the ladies of England did no more than make a good-natured error. "Proceeding with the light before them, of which the dark lantern of Mrs. H. B. Stowe furnished the larger proportion, they may have magnified the evil of slavery and their influence in repressing it, to unjustifiable dimensions." And, with true Socratic magnanimity, it is proposed that the proper response to good-natured error is correction, not rebuke. Indeed, the *Times'* sympathy with the motives of the "West End ladies" finally induces the confession that it had praised the Tyler letter more highly than it perhaps deserved, "in our longing to have the '*regne feminie*' content . . . ," and—we might add—to leave the matter as a question of etiquette.

> That *tu quoque* argument is, however, unfortunate. All the effect of a judicious moderate reply is lost in the ill-natured recrimination of the "look at home," the *nosce teipsium* injunction.[12]

But, in fact, the philanthropists who forged the first link in this chain had been busy at home, and that for many years. Thus, the attempt to throw the dust of modern progress into the eyes of ancient aristocracy with a *nosce teipsium* reveals only a niggardly spirit that confirms the necessity of the very missionary spirit upon which it had embarked. The *Times* closed its article by again insisting it would no longer continue the dialogue—a pledge it kept. But there was also an invitation for the vengeful-minded to find an analogous case of charity in England, about which some article could be printed.[13] The door was left ajar.

The argument continued in this desultory fashion up until the very point of Stowe's arrival in England in mid-April. But during this warm-up the Earl of Shaftesbury had penned his own defense, upholding the address, and seriously questioning Mrs. Tyler's reply.[14] Indeed, some question even of the lady's character was implied, in that Shaftesbury doubted her authorship on no further evidence than the tone and quality of the sentiments. Since she signed her own name, gave no indication that she had had assistance, and had made an issue of Shaftesbury's admitted authorship of the British address, his questioning of the reply's true origin suggested a feigning inappropriate in a lady. That patriotism should become still more heatedly involved at this point is not surprising. Well more than a month after the report of Shaftesbury's initial retort, the *Observer* was still fulminating—meticulously questioning his defense and pointing an accusing finger at Britain for her treatment of the Dissenters and her denying the "most sacred right of man," freedom of conscience.[15] It hurled again the response it opened in February:

> However, the Earl of Shaftesbury may affect to despise the righteous retort of Americans, "Physician, heal thyself," it is infinitely true, that America is far in advance of England in all rational and disinterested philanthropy.[16]

The *Times* was less certain that the retort was justified but found it nonetheless necessary that Shaftesbury understand the biblical injunction.

> His argument, that one charge is not answered by another is undeniable. But, in truth, slavery is an evil *sui generis,* and must be dealt with on its own special grounds.[17]

That the exchange had become a dialogue among men, and hence a matter of real politics is the inescapable conclusion. It is a matter of paradox, then, that Stowe's affected modesty of keeping silence in public and permitting her husband or brother to make all response, in the name of observing (and restoring) proper etiquette, but further gave occasion for this dialogue among men. Thus, Stowe must be found guilty of endangering the well-being of her nation in either account. And this does not even touch the question whether complicity with the ulterior motives of them who wish Americans harm might not be treasonous. The South may have exaggerated its claims to protection when it sought to deny the northerners the right to agitate the slavery question in America. But how far could it legitimately claim to interfere with a planned trip amidst expressedly hostile foreigners for the same kind of agitation? As the *London Morning Chronicle* put it, "the lady might have done better than to parade abroad 'her own merits and her country's shame.'"[18]

In London, the two events that stood out were the Stafford House gathering and the Exeter Hall rally. Each was viewed with alarm in some quarters. Whether Mrs. Stowe could have done better than "parade her country's shame" abroad the *Times* did not say. But we have already cited its suspicions of the leading men there. Those suspicions loom even more largely in the full article. In the paragraph immediately preceding that in which Russell, Palmerston, and Gladstone were guarded against, the *Times* reported that the abolition "Anniversaries" were being held in New York and presented a "striking contrast to the Stafford House demonstration." The leading men at New York were "William Lloyd Garrison, Abby Folsom, Lucy Stone, and Frederick Douglas (sic)." They were

> a compound of semi-infidelity, Woman's Rights, and run mad fanaticism and amalgamation, without practical aim, and *wholly impotent for political mischief.* Their doings in this metropolis were as *utterly contemptible* in popular estimation, as their social influence is *unworthy of serious consideration.* (Emphasis supplied)[19]

Now, if Harriet Stowe's efforts were possessed of all that the assembled abolitionists were not, they would have had a clear, practical aim, have had power to do political mischief, and have been worthy of respect and serious consideration. But that is the point of the second paragraph. According to the *Times*, the meeting was assembled for not her purposes but those of the British ministers. It could only have been a rather comical pretension on her part that her ends were being served. Or, her ends bordered on the treasonous.

Yet, from every report, she took herself in all seriousness. At Stafford House, seated between the Duchesses of Sutherland and Argyll, Stowe freely canvassed the whole subject of slavery, making practical proposals as she went along.[20] She claimed a "deep sympathy" for *Uncle Tom's Cabin* to exist in America and refuted the claim that it was forgotten by pointing to a sale in the first three days of sixty thousand copies of the *Key*, only just published. Among practical proposals, she spoke of the use of free-grown cotton, and called for the education of "British subjects in Canada." The article does not indicate what it may be to which they will be educated, but Canada was, of course, the terminus of the "underground railway." It is also the case that, after Lord Shaftesbury read a short address designed only to acknowledge her presence and the existence of the "Affectionate Address," Stowe's brother, Charles Beecher, responded with thanks and read a letter, from the abolitionist Cassius Clay, which described "the progress of emancipation in Kentucky," giving much credit to *Uncle Tom's Cabin*. Thus, to the Stowe eye, so far as the world could see, all was abolition.

The Exeter Hall rally, nine days later, was a much noisier affair and, perhaps for that reason, all the more open to the same kind of charges. It eventuated in a resolution which induced the *London Economist* to cry, "Where is this sort of moral crusade to stop?"[21] By now, the familiar chants of this six to seven week campaign swing had begun to ring hollow to some of the press—that is, they no longer heard the speeches; they only heard the speakers. The French correspondent for the *Commerce* gives this ill-tempered but informative description.

> We may presume that Mrs. Beecher Stowe's appearance at the soiree given to her by the British and Foreign Anti-slavery Society was her valedictory public display in London. The convocation of professional emancipation—cosmopolitan philanthropists, was *au complet*—according to the label hung out for our omnibuses when they are full. The report says that the presence of several gentlemen of color, on a mission to England from America, along with Quakers, dissenting ministers, and richly dressed ladies lent *picturesqueness* to the company: black and white—like the keys of a piano. As Mrs. Stowe's health did not allow her to shake hands with each individual, the host of worshippers passed by the platform in *groups* bowing to her in rotation: this was as scenic as when troops defile before an illustrious commander. The address of the Committee of the Society is prolix and trite; but Professor Stowe, in returning thanks for spouse and himself, pronounced it to be matchless in condensed argument and phrases; the Professor might be reproached with tediousness and tautology; he repeated his old tirade against the products of slave-labor, and

> complained of the apathy of the *churches* of the United States; they do not excommunicate all except abolitionists.[22]

It was not the Stowes' "valedictory appearance." But it was that longest remembered. This rally elevated what had been admonitions to demands and formally adopted resolutions in which to frame them. It also turned attention toward Britain. And in doing so, it returned the abolitionists to the ranks of the impracticable. The long article in which the *London Economist* voiced its plaintive cry provides two such resolutions:

1. "the principle of immediate and unconditional emancipation is the only one that is consistent with the rights of the slave and the duties of the master."
2. "those who are in earnest in condemnation of slavery should observe consistency; and, therefore, it is their duty to encourage the development of the natural resources of countries where slavery does not exist"; and the "meeting earnestly recommended that, in all cases *where it is practicable*, a decided preference should be given to the products of free labor by all who enter their protest against slavery, so that at least they themselves may be clear of any participation in the guilt of the system, and be thus morally strengthened in their condemnation." (Emphasis supplied)[23]

Of the three categories of men addressed, rights were assigned to only one, the slave, while duties are assigned to the master and the protestant. That is, he who is not comprehended in the civil polity can only have rights; and they who are comprehended in the polity have corresponding duties. In the first case of duty, however, is a problem, if we view the master as owing the slave's emancipation to the slave himself. For we have not been told what united men within with those without the polity. The difficulty is not removed by considering the master's duty as to the polity, for that only removes the question to the level of what unites a polity, of necessity, with those men without. To resolve the problem, it is necessary to see this other-regarding duty as manifest in the very condition of civil life, and hence requiring, for the fullness thereof, some form of transcendent expression.

But these were not the reflections that concerned the *Economist,* which saw in the two resolutions only an *inconsistency* with the requirements of civil intercourse. As to the last resolution, the *Economist* considered it impossible; and as to the first, it "is not to be surpassed for impracticality by any project hatched in the world either inside or outside of Bedlam." Such a demonstration, therefore, is as good as—that is, no better than—no demonstration. The *Economist* is not concerned with the noble men, who were for the most part absent this democratic effervescence. But there is good question whether the Stowes, by pursuing such inquiries, may not compromise British politics.

> Unfortunately, however, this proceeding has a moral and a political aspect which is not pleasant. Parties in the United States are contending fiercely against one another. The question of slavery there is one of political party. . . . Their politicians promulgate resolutions hostile to our influence in America, and the proceedings in Exeter Hall will appear to them under a political aspect.[24]

The press reaction to the Stowe campaign, then, was largely divided between that which looked to its effect on public opinion for good or ill and that which considered its effect on the opinion of lawmakers. When we consider the controversy surrounding the "Affectionate Address," we realize that what Stowe does is to undermine *that* controversy and not very real threat with a threat that is real indeed. Somehow, the women shouting at women had been converted to men fearing the designs of men—academic politics was supplanted by real politics.[25]

"Sunny Memories" was published in 1854. The campaign effectively ended in early June, 1853. Thus the task of sustaining the opinion and concern initially generated by *Uncle Tom's Cabin* was not completed by the appeal to Britain and, perhaps, could not be. But that appeal did successfully convert *Uncle Tom's Cabin* from a mere woman's romance into an instrument of political warfare; that is, a weapon fit to be wielded by men. "Sunny Memories," as an analysis of *Uncle Tom's Cabin,* is an elaboration of the end for which the tool is designed as well as a means of responding to the debate of the tour. Indeed, it almost had to be written, without respect to press reaction, in order that the fulfillment of *Uncle Tom's Cabin* become possible. The *Times'* correspondent had less in mind, but came close to the truth in his instinctive judgment that Stowe would write further.

> Mrs. Stowe is now the honored guest at Stafford House and, fairly installed among the fashionables of the West End. On Saturday there is to be a grand gathering of her aristocratic "sympathisers" and admirers, and the occasion will doubtless be very interesting and worthy to be reproduced, probably by the pen of the talented and estimable lady in whose honor it takes place.[26]

What she did write was more than a characterization of the fashionables. It was more than a discussion of slavery. And it was more than a collection of fugitive sentiments on love and death. As the "Introduction" has shown, the important question was, what is the principle of the American regime and how can it be preserved? Although the discussion of slavery *can* permit one to transcend the limits of his regime, it cannot of itself yield that transcendent expression which is required to lay bare the conditions of civil life. In

"Sunny Memories" we are not permitted to forget slavery—it can always serve to jar our prejudices—but we are introduced to a far broader range of considerations.

NOTES

1. *New York Weekly Times,* 2, 67 (January 1, 1853), p. 2.
2. *New York Journal of Commerce,* xxiiv, 8, 56 (June 19, 1853), p. 1.
3. "An Affectionate and Christian Address from the Ladies of England to the Ladies of America." Copies are found in the Stowe-Day Library, The Connecticut Historical Society, and the Huntington Library, as well as elsewhere.
4. *Weekly Times,* 2, 72 (February 5, 1853), p. 3.
5. Ibid., 2, 67 (January 1, 1853), p. 7.
6. *New York Observer,* 31, 13 (March 31, 1853), p. 102.
7. *Weekly Times,* 2, 89 (June 4, 1853), p. 2.
8. *Observer,* 31, 7 (February 17, 1853), p. 54.
9. Stowe is, in fact, quite aware of both this precept and its limits, as is shown in her short story "Let Every Man Mind His Own Business." Harriet Beecher Stowe, "Let Every Man Mind His Own Business," in *The Christian Keepsake and Missionary Annual* (Philadelphia: W. Marshall and Company, 1839).
10. *Observer,* op. cit., p. 56. Emphasis supplied.
11. *Weekly Times,* 2, 73 (February 12, 1853), p. 2.
12. Ibid., 2, 74 (February 19, 1853), pp. 2 & 6.
13. See the account of the London seamstress and the millinery business, in book part I, chapter 23, pp. 371 ff.
14. *Weekly Times,* 2, 74 (February 19, 1853), p. 3.
15. *Observer,* 31, 13 (March 31, 1853), p. 101.
16. Ibid., 31, 7 (February 17, 1853), p. 54.
17. *Weekly Times,* 2, 89 (June 4, 1853), p. 2.
18. Cited in *Journal of Commerce,* xxiiv, 8, 56 (June 8, 1853), p. 1.
19. *Weekly Times,* 2, 89 (June 4, 1853), p. 2.
20. Ibid., 2, 88 (May 28, 1853), p. 5.
21. Cited in *Journal of Commerce,* xxiiv, 8, 56 (June 8, 1853), backpage.
22. Ibid., p. 1 and *Weekly Times,* 2, 89 (June 4, 1853), p. 1.
23. Ibid., backpage.
24. Ibid.
25. Although Hedrick frequently slights Stowe's political astuteness, she does, in her biography acknowledge that "early on [Stowe] learned ways to speak both from the women's sphere and from men's." Hedrick, *Harriet Beecher Stowe,* p. 108.
26. *Weekly Times,* 2, 88 (May 28, 1853), p. 6.

21

Seasickness; or, the Way Things Really Look

We may now turn to the heart of "Sunny Memories," the "Letters" themselves. We will discuss in detail only the first letter, Letter XXII, and the final letters. The remaining letters will be summarized, as we draw forth the principles Stowe has rather sculpted into her work than expressly declared. We take this path as a compromise with the problem of space. As for the letters treated in detail, the reason is that in Letter XXII, on the one hand, Stowe articulates a completely reasoned account and defense of "melodrama" and it has not heretofore been rightly noticed. On the other hand, the first letter and the final letters are characterized by the highly important symbolic usage of "Niagara," explained earlier. As such they represent the comprehensive statement of the purpose of "Sunny Memories" and Stowe's political philosophy.

In the first letter metaphor and construction are used to reveal the breadth if not the order of the considerations in the letters as a whole. While the readily accessible ship of life metaphor presents danger as well as charm, it is fundamental in this letter. Hereafter, however, we guard—perhaps overmuch—against the use of metaphor as a *basis* of analysis. Indeed, we will stay the pen even when the suggestive power of some literal construction seems beyond the capacity of accident. This we will do explicitly to emphasize the character of the literal construction and hence the purpose of the author. But in the first letter, where we are afforded a view of life at sea, of which the elements are ever likened to human life, and where the author's intention has been revealed, no such moderation need prevail.

Stowe wrote the account of the voyage after the completion of the voyage. Her judgments of the voyage are mature and comprehensive. The most important judgment—that for which the remainder serves as explanation—is that which regards as temporary illusion the pre-voyage view of a voyage as the fulfillment of dreams of poetry and romance, "our highest conceptions of free, joyous existence." That view quickly yields to "disgust of existence." The familiar seasickness that is literally intended by this disgust is resisted by all men, even the best, but only as they gradually yield. The effects are manifested in differing manners. The humanists (poet and skeptic)—mere passengers—respectively paint the cause of the distress in terms quite unfitting its consequences and deny the existence of cause and consequence before yielding, respectively, in surrender and precipitous withdrawal. The seat of stability is in the bowels of the ship, and there the "philosophic cook" resides. For him, the ship of life is endured, for without him it cannot be. But he draws no great joy or pride from this circumstance. He is rather a melancholy, dejected creature who, like the passengers themselves, or at least the best of them, must box in his soul to withstand this trial. Most of his efforts are cosmetic and performed with indifference. Only on rare occasions are his powers summoned forth.

The difference between the passengers and the artificers of this voyage seems to consist entirely in the placidity with which the artificers view the generally disgusting circumstances. Their placidity stems not so much from their transcendence, for in truth they seem not to transcend. But it derives rather from their certainty both as to the necessity of the voyage and the impossibility of its being otherwise. The author avows no consciousness of any flaw in such fatalism. But two factors suggest such a flaw. The first is the radically untraditional location of the philosopher in the bowels of the ship rather than at the helm—and that, not under duress but resignation. The second factor is the nature of the voyage for the other—"ordinary"—passengers, who are distinguished from the poet and the skeptic by a diverse and lively concern for things just as they have found them and either liking or not liking them.

As our poet discourses "magnificently on the color of the waves and the glory of the clouds," and our stoic counsels "a little self-control and resolution," there are countless young ladies who are going to die in ten minutes and "don't care" if they do. And there are the charmed few who "escape all these evils. They are not sick . . . and always meet you with 'What a charming run we are having!'" There are others, of a disinterested turn, who can console themselves by watching the charmed few. And there was the author, too unfortunate to be among the last and too determined to yield. She embarked prepared to sit, read, sew, sketch, and chat.

> Let me warn you, if you ever go to sea, you may as well omit all such preparations. . . . For be sure that in half hour after sailing an infinite desperation will seize you. . . . Nevertheless, your fate for the whole voyage depends upon your rousing yourself to get upon deck at first; to give up, then, is to be condemned

> to the Avernus, the Hades of the lower regions, *for the rest of the voyage. . . .* I could not and would not give up and become one of the ghosts below . . . (Emphasis supplied)

For Stowe, seasickness requires doing something. It is a thing that can neither be accepted nor endured. Her biographer, Forrest Wilson, takes the "infinite desperation" of this passage as her confession of common weakness.[1] It is rather the motive or source of those uncommon exertions to avoid surrender to fate. Wilson was misled, perhaps, because she does not directly avow such exertions and, to the contrary, sympathetically portrays the seasick perspective.

> Where in the world the soul goes to under such influence nobody knows; one would really think the sea tipped it all out of a man. . . . The soul seems to be like one of the genii enclosed in a vase, in the Arabian nights, now it rises, . . . again, it goes down. . . . *A sea voyage is the best device for getting the soul back into its vase that I know of.* (Emphasis supplied)

It is certainly pardonable, but it seems that Wilson's mistake was none other than reading metaphorically what makes perfect sense literally, provided the essay as a whole is understood metaphorically. It is true that the soul gets "tipped out," but it is equally true that the sea voyage gets it *back in*.[2] Far from being disgusted for the "rest of the voyage" she claims a self-possession unmatched by any of her fellow passengers and rivaled only by the "philosophic cook." This leads us to some doubt respecting the fatedness of the voyage.

We could perhaps explain the "philosophic cook's" untraditional location by adverting to Stowe's inherited Puritanism. If God is at the helm, our cook is in fact our chieftain, having nothing more to do than arrange the items of an established menu. Being in the service of what is transcendent, he is, himself, under no necessity to transcend. If he is indeed melancholic, it may be because he is philosophic but to no end. His virtue is his sadness. But Stowe's position in this little drama renders such an analysis untenable. She is but a passenger, yet she arrives at the cook's understanding of the voyage—at least as to its necessity if not its predestined end. She is not melancholic. If in its vase the soul must be, there is no better way. Further, with such self-possession it becomes possible to rise from the lower levels.[3] Stowe's understanding is independent of the cook's. Because her understanding is not melancholic, her understanding in some sense transcends the voyage itself. But if this were true, it would be the case that there was in fact *no* one at the helm, and the cook's dejection is the result of his own "wisdom," or, the captain is wholly unconcerned with the circumstances of the voyage. (The captain of the ship is never mentioned in this letter, but the crew is assembled for Sunday morning worship, though this may be only a "form.") The inferences from both of these views are treated as impiety in Plato's *Laws*.[4] But it is also the case that Socrates, in the *Laws*, recommends constant motion for infants to encourage their development,[5] and Stowe here brands this gratuitous rocking as the cause of their being "so many stupid people in this world."

As yet, this is too cryptic. We must consider at length her concern with cooking to determine what is meant. She manages to succeed in mastering the evils of the sea partly by watching the cook for hours at a time. In him she finds a "tall, slender, melancholy man, with a watery blue eye, a patient, dejected visage, like an individual weary of the storms and commotions of life." All his duties are performed in this "sad composure."

> All is done under an evident sense that it is of no use trying. Many have been the complaints made of our coffee . . . , which, to say the truth, has been as unsettled as most of the social questions of the day, and, perhaps, for that reason quite as generally unpalatable; but since I have seen our cook, I am quite persuaded that the coffee, like other works of great artists, has borrowed the hues of its maker's mind. I think I hear him soliloquize . . . "To what purpose is coffee?—of what avail tea?—thick or clear?—All is passing away—a little egg, or fish skin, more or less, what are they?" and so we get melancholy coffee and tea, owing to our philosophic cook. . . . I can see how these daily trials, this performing of most delicate and complicated gastronomic operations in the midst of such unsteady, unsettled circumstances, have gradually brought him into this state of philosophic melancholy. Just as Xantippe made a sage of Socrates, this whisky, frisky stormy ship life has made a sage of our cook. Meanwhile, not to do him injustice, let it be recorded, that in all the dishes which require grave conviction and steady perseverance, rather than hope and inspiration, he is eminently successful. (*SM*, I, 10)

It is, perhaps, clearer now that the reflections engendered by the character and deeds of our cook lead to a general conception of the causes of social melancholia and prepare us to consider why "hope and inspiration"—those sisters of revelation—are insufficient instruments in the weightiest tasks. Unsettled social questions are oft times like the most cosmetic culinary achievements: matters which, properly arranged or seasoned, delight our taste but do not necessarily answer to the requirements of a healthful diet. The unsettled social question of 1854 was slavery and, as such, is to be understood in the light of the cosmetic constitutional and legislative compromises that served to palliate but not to resolve the question. The resolution of that difficulty was required to permit enjoyment of the greater blessings of civil life but would not produce of itself such enjoyment. We may be forgiven the liberty of this paraphrase of our cook:

> To what purpose is liberty?—of what avail equality?—much or little?—all is passing away—a little slavery or oppression, more or less, what is that? and so we get diluted liberty and equality, owing to our philosophic chieftain.

Though such reflections may not be required by the diet of the healthy man or citizenry, we see they nonetheless can result in a kind of wisdom that succeeds "eminently" in its care for true health.

Stowe's understanding, we have said, was not that of the cook. She was withal happier. We do not know if her happiness was the result of some knowledge of other possibilities for the voyage or only the result of her own victory over its nausea. That is, we know not whether she is happy because she finds reason within the unsettled human condition to be content with human prospects just as they are, or because she has not indulged in utopian philosophical speculation and thus has not been disappointed by the real world. But we know that she is writing a liberal history, chiefly contained in the Letters II–XXX. That liberal history may be like Nietzsche's unseasonable history—contrary to its time but with an influence on it for the benefit of the future. The singularity of her social history may be the analogy of her personal history during this voyage. She says of herself that she has a strong head and demonstrates it in precisely those passages devoted to our melancholy cook. The specific shipboard events of Letter I are narrated in the past tense predominantly, until just after midway through the letter, where, Stowe writes, "There is no place where killing time is so much of a systematic and avowed object as in one of these short runs, . . . People with strong heads, who can stand the incessant swing of the boat, may read or write" (*SM*, I, 8). Then, for four paragraphs, she narrates a series of specific events entirely in the present and present perfect tense, as if to say, "I am writing at this moment." After, she returns to the predominance of the past tense. We do not know if in fact she withstood the incessant swinging.

Stowe says in Letter II that she had been "withered" by seasickness, but it is the *claim* that she was one who could write that is important in "Sunny Memories." Of further importance is the fact that those paragraphs are all the "cooking" paragraphs, where surely a strong head was needed. Moreover, it would be the necessity of the voyage that brings her to write, since she embarked expecting to "sit, read, sew, sketch, and chat." If these passages were written during the voyage, and they spent "hours at a time" during this "short run" observing the cook and ruminating in this fashion, her claim has basis enough to be taken seriously. That they actually did watch and ruminate we have collaborative evidence in a heretofore unpublished letter written by Calvin, embarked in the actual ship *Niagara* for his return. In privately reporting the voyage to her, he mentions the various persons and stockyard animals either returning or not. One of those not returning is "our lemancholy" cook.[6] From the evidence of this statement we can see not only that they watched him—though not for how long—but that they enjoyed quite a good laugh or two in pondering a character who resembles at least in bitterness the portrait of "Sunny Memories."

Has not even the unwary reader paused here to chuckle, exclaiming to himself, "How hypercritical? Why Harriet Beecher Stowe never *could* have meant *all* that is asserted here, and even if she did, how could no one save yourself, in a hundred and fifty years have noticed it?" To the last question I have no response. To the former question a response is ready: Stowe meant not only this but far more, as this analysis will continue to show. But pause again. Do we not recall how explicitly in *Uncle Tom's Cabin* Augustine St. Clare was made a satire—if positive—of Thomas Jefferson, up to and including the parody of the Declaration of Independence which many considered Jefferson to have rescinded if not in words at least by the wavering deeds of his life?[7] Is not the so well-named "lemancholy cook," again, the perfect parody of the character, St. Clare, with the *mere* addition to his Hamlet-like resignation of the stewardship of affairs? Could Stowe have meant all this? I suggest that the reader who doubts may reconsider the analysis of "Miss Ophelia's Opinions."

NOTES

1. Forrest Wilson, *Crusader in Crinoline*, p. 344.
2. See book, part I, chapter 25.
3. As the *Diary* recorded, while others had succumbed, "Hatty however was brave as a lion. Mr. Stowe in his glory."
4. *Laws*, Book X.
5. *Laws*, Book VII.
6. C. E. Stowe to H. B. Stowe, June 4, 1853, S. S. *Niagara*. Also, Charles Beecher's *Diary* confirms the account.
7. Cf. Allen, "The Manners of Liberalism."

22

The Scotland Campaign

A Beginning and End of Liberal History

I. A NEW HISTORY FOR A NEW ENTHUSIASM

The disinterested enthusiasm with which Stowe surveyed the cook is not unlike that she attributed to the Irish, who received nothing in return for their ardent enthusiasm for the rebellious Daniel O'Connell.[1] She considered such capacity, "on the whole, a nobler property of a human being than shrewd self-interest." But it is not a matter of indifference how such enthusiasm is expressed, as we have seen. The morality that follows upon the moral armament of ardent enthusiasm may be destructive of the possibility of morality altogether or, at best, result in an oppression not to be distinguished from the reign of shrewd self-interest alone. Disinterested enthusiasm—that is, evangelical fervor—is, "on the whole," nobler. But the qualifier reveals its danger as much as its promise. The distance is not so great between Aristotle's man who lives without the *polis* and must be a beast or a god,[2] and the American founders' city without laws. The latter took the absence of law to be identical with the felicity of the cherubim but could do so only so long as law was denied all participation in the transcendent.[3] From the moment law *can* come to be seen as participating at all in the transcendent—even as did the philosophic cook—it must follow that a lawless city, an unjust or beastly city, is fully as possible as the city of angels, and no more. And only the possible necessity to attain the justice of the angels in the city of man can incline men away from the lawless realm.

The *Niagara*'s passage through dangerous shoals in its approach to Liverpool called to Stowe's mind tragic shipwrecks and led to direct application of the ship of life metaphor to the theme of "Sunny Memories."[4]

> What an infinite deal of misery results from nature's inflexibility in this one matter of crossing the ocean. . . . Surely, without the revelation of God in Jesus, who could believe in the divine goodness? I do not wonder the old Greeks so often spoke of their gods as cruel, and believed the universe was governed by a remorseless and inexorable fate. Who could come to any other conclusion except from the pages of the Bible? (*SM*, II, 16)

Job alone could come to another conclusion in the face of "nature's inflexibility." To Stowe, human psychology rested entirely on the articulation of human aspirations or desires in a transcendent logic or theology. And it is especially against this psychology that nature herself wages war in civil life, particularly modern civil life.[5]

As the steamer drew into Liverpool, Stowe thought the city "a real New Yorkish place"—a thoroughly modern place—the center of meeting for "ships of all nations." The American stars and stripes were floated out, only to join that "forest of ships," with "masts bristling like the tall pines in Maine; their many colored flags streaming like the forest leaves in autumn" (*SM*, II, 16). This cosmopolitanism—universalism—is one of the central themes of "Sunny Memories" but so, as we shall see, is nationalism—its corrective. There is danger in universalism, it seems, for the work of nature is to mingle rather than to distinguish. And for purposes of civil life, distinction is a necessary principle. Civil life requires that men remember, that they save distinctions.[6] Nature gives men especially the power of forgetfulness—self-forgetfulness so far as the civil self is concerned. Distant chimes are required to remind one. "I had quite forgotten it was Sunday." The cosmopolitanism was a momentary vision, which receded before the appearance of England and English religion.

> An American, particularly a New Englander, can never approach the old country without a kind of thrill and pulsation of kindred. Its history for two centuries was our history . . . Spenser, Shakespeare, Bacon, Milton. . . . It is Anglo Saxon vigor that is spreading our country from Atlantic to Pacific, and leading to a new era in the world's development. America is a tall, sightly young shoot, that has grown from the old royal oak of England; divided from its parent root, it has shot up in new, rich soil, and under genial brilliant skies, and therefore takes on a new type of growth and foliage, but the sap in it is the same. (*SM*, II, 18)

Mrs. Tyler was not in error to presage the rise of American greatness as the commencement of a new era. But she failed to understand that the roots cannot be cut. Because the "old royal oak" is at the source, a perspective of aristocratic judgment will or at least *can* always exist. Nature is indifferent to this new growth so far as its character is concerned. If America is to be boundaried by the two oceans, nature will not decide whether she grows from slavery or freedom. The settlement of the Nebraska question will solve the problem, and one basis for settlement will be the cultivation of a memory that can combat the shrewd self-interest that is always present-oriented.[7]

Stowe was met by a great crowd, of which the "air of health"[8] but made her feel "more withered and forlorn." But their great kindness convinced her that she had "touched the English heart" as well as the land. She was beginning to feel at home, and as the party finally reached its residence, a "cottage, whose porch was overgrown with Ivy," she ceased altogether to feel a stranger. She commenced immediately the construction of her history.

Starting with the old "Cock Robin" nursery rhyme, Stowe distinguished the English robin from his bigger, American "fourth cousin." Both were implicated in the injustice portrayed in the nursery rhyme. But the English cock robin, Sir Robert Walpole, succumbed to the might of royal wrath. The great are never justly felled by insignificant ones.[9] A still more apt display of the wisdom of the ancient rhyme,[10] however, is the vivid relief of Charles I's death. That was an unjust murder, the great felled by the little. The American heirs of Charles's assailant may take no pride in their ancestor, Cromwell or, more particularly, enthusiastic protestantism. The new view of their tradition, therefore, must replace the unjust history with a just or liberal history. Poor Charles, however, was rescued from opprobrium only temporarily. The reader thereby notes that liberal history is for the reader's sake, Charles's for England's.

The positive result of liberal or rosy history, in this case, is only to lay a foundation to supplant intolerant protestantism. We can develop this argument at length only later, but we may anticipate it and capture those passages through which the transition is effected. The rewriting of this rhyme led naturally to Letter XI and the tour of Warwick Castle—the representative feudal establishment. There, Charles and Cromwell confronted each other without the disguise of rhyme. They were shrouded only by the "historical mist" that filled Stowe's head as she reflected on the wars of Warwicks—all for justice! In a long hall at Warwick were at opposite ends a cast of the face of Cromwell and a painting of Charles on horseback. Cromwell she must own as an ancestor (*SM*, 243–244), but she need not take joy in it. It was Cromwell who destroyed the glorious Kenilworth and, indeed, "seems literally to have left his mark" on every ruin she saw in England. Poor Charles was as duplicitous as ever a kingly spirit was, but he did not thereby break with any tradition. In the presence of the ruins of feudalism, royalty—even duplicitous royalty—is preferable to Cromwell.

Cromwell's "Puritans arrayed against them all the aesthetic principles of our nature" and justly incurred the prejudice of a world which looked no deeper. She will yet be a Puritan, but she will be more sympathetic to Charles than to Cromwell ("Poor Charles had rather hard measure, it always seemed so to me. . . . So I intend to cherish a little partiality for the gentlemanly, magnificent Charles I" [*SM*, 234–35]), and must labor to show the compatibility of the age of past glory with the remembrances that must form part of the Christian Republic.

In this same letter she announced the "new state of society which we are trying to found in America." And this correction of our historical view is part of the founding effort. The success of the founding depends on our opinions of our history, and in the presence of feudal ruins we must seek the models of justice that most accord with the justice we seek.[11] Hence, Charles is preferred. In the presence of the representative royal estate, however, bad princes have not so much charm. At Windsor the "same picture" of Charles hangs. But there, no longer opposing Cromwell, its charms and special status are gone. Indeed, there were many other views of Charles and even of his family, but the charm did not return. In the presence of Cromwell the aristocratic perspective holds its sway without effort. In the presence of royalty, the aristocratic perspective must make special efforts for the sake of justice in order to rule. It seems to define itself, in its truest sense, by its distance from royalty—counted as a continuous line.

What this means is that the one circumstance in which the aristocratic perspective is of obvious value is the democratic, and as we recede from democracy, aristocracy is put to greater need to defend itself. Where the governed lose the power of consent, they who govern lose—by that much—the advantage of unquestioned obedience. The virtue of democracy is magnanimity; the virtue of monarchy is good grace. We may defend the American fourth cousin of Charles against the ardent enthusiasm of William Lloyd Garrison, but we cannot submit to conservative rule under happier circumstance. Stowe's rewritten history demonstrated the role of historical understanding. It resembles Winston Churchill's consistency.[12] Because it is expressed in a transcendent logic, it seeks to nest in the most propitious grounds in each case. She may not prefer Cromwell, but she will remain a Puritan.[13] In the heavenly scale, the destruction of monuments of past glory is not so great a crime. The "ceaseless singing and rejoicing of the birds" amidst the "old gray ruins" was itself the evidence of the proper detachment with which to view the ruins. A tolerant protestantism would possess a kind of memory which would stay the axe from such monuments. But it would also possess the kind of memory which would save the protestantism from among the ruins.

Stowe found Britons just like Americans, with an identity of "sentiment and feeling"—save on the question of slavery. "That question has, from the very first, been, in England, a deeply religious movement." Its analogue in America is the work of foreign missionaries, and that, too, is resisted by "men of worldly habits and principles." These abolitionists remembered their own struggles and sympathized with America. They were not, as she had heard, intolerant on the subject. They saw or could be made to see the "peculiar difficulties" besetting the subject in America. Their censure was moderate and understanding. The first full day was filled with such warm sentiment and only occasionally a touch of English pride. The pressure of moral responsibility eventually gave way to dinner and a stroll about the grounds of her residence. But even this liberty led to indirect reflection on American slavery, vitiating the view of its harshness. *Uncle Tom's Cabin* made much of the separation of families. The very opposite was here witnessed. Among the English,

> there is more idea of home permanence connected with the dwelling place than with us, where the country is so wide, and causes of change and removal so frequent. . . . We shed our houses in America as easily as a snail does his shell. *We live a while in Boston, and then, perhaps, turn up at Cincinnati.* Scarcely any body with us is living where they expect to live and die. . . . All which is a propos to our having finished our walk, and got back to the ivy-covered porch again. (*SM*, II, 31; emphasis added)

This does not make the slave's involuntary move any the more "wished for" by the slave. But it does palliate the evil in a relative sense, insofar as "Everybody's doin' it." Still, Stowe had much fire left to breathe about the slave's plight, however ambiguous the word "involuntary" might become when viewed in this light. Using her own biographical migration, which we emphasized in the passage, and ending her life short of the last two moves—the most recent to Andover and that before to Brunswick, Maine, where *Uncle Tom's Cabin* was written—but indicating that the purpose (propos) of the discourse is to return us to the "ivy-covered porch" and hence, Uncle Tom's vine covered cottage, she reminds that these narratives will often wander but are, in fact, intended to revolve around *Uncle Tom's Cabin.*

The anti-slavery "parties" continued. Calvin was asked to speak at an evening meeting and, "among other things," questioned the free world's support of slavery through cotton purchases. He thought it worthy of "inquiry whether this cannot be avoided."

> It is probable that the cotton trade of Great Britain is the great essential item which supports slavery, and such considerations ought not, therefore, to be without their results. (*SM*, II, 37)

As noted above, this meeting and speech went unreported by Calvin. Had they been so, the progressive character of the "Introduction" would doubtlessly have been impaired. It is of good question why she includes it and fails, elsewhere, to include others. But these reflections will be taken up at the conclusion of this book. In these premises, it is of worth to note that it is reported as the *first* public expression on their part. As the first, the emphasis on free cotton is crucial, but the more important is the fact that, as reported, this speech bears the stance of the moderate reformer seeking to ignite a movement.

As the Liverpool stay ended, a general placidity reigned fully agreeing with Calvin's portrait. The meetings widened their scope as the general movement of reform in England responded to it. In a discussion of the "female philanthropist," Mrs. Chisolm, the Stowes gave their approval to a reform movement generated by a pious Catholic despite the doubts of some men. The discussion ended with all agreed "that the *great humanities of the present age* are a proper ground on which all sects can unite."

Again, the "style of feeling expressed was *tempered*" (emphasis supplied). Stowe sought to encourage a general "enthusiasm for freedom and humanity," and every emphasis was on its moderation. She closes this letter with a defense of the English in this regard, in which she argues that their own social ills do not disqualify them to recognize ours. She would prefer "inconsistent and imperfect" enthusiasm to none at all. And the English, because of their great moderation, are much better. Their hearts have been "enlarged by the love of all mankind," and this fits them to works of benevolence at home.

II. HABITS OF THE HEART

Letter II approached the project of renewing the memory of America through a view of Old England. It demonstrated the operation of the principles of Old England by discussing the English concern for American slavery. The latter part of the enterprise exists under a cloud, for we know already that Charles I does not retain our preference for long. Whether "imperfect and inconsistent" enthusiasm shall do so is not made clear. But we were told that disinterested enthusiasm is always noble. Hence, we should expect that "imperfect and inconsistent" enthusiasm shall continue to be preferable for only so long as it remains disinterested. From this point, the letters commence the articulation of the memory, primarily. The characterization of moral enthusiasm was deferred. But the approach we shall take is to complete at least a summary of moral enthusiasm. Then we may trace the development of the new history. The two lines of thought will next be set in the context of the campaign and we will thence draw appropriate conclusions.

We may justify this neglect of chronology by the demands the creation of a new history imposes. To reach its proper end, history, itself, must be unhistorical. It otherwise exists only to expire with the circumstances that bring it into being. But if history be anything of importance in itself, it is so by virtue of its eternity. Its creation, therefore, must take place in the interstices of time—in those eternal moments that set the pulse of humanity. Such were the moments of the Lincoln-Douglas Debates, in which those great warriors canvassed thousands of years in preparation for the work of a few. Those passages of "Sunny Memories" we need to consider occur at just such points—where time stands still. If we have recourse to the chronology in the following table compiled from "Sunny Memories" and the official biography which "rectifies" "Sunny Memories,"[14] we will see that, historically speaking, everything that is said to have happened could not have happened at the time in which it had to occur, save that time stood still. And not the least of those things that occurred was the writing of well over two hundred pages of carefully researched letters (which puts the lie to the orthodox interpretation that Stowe wrote hastily and sloppily). We elsewhere raise the suggestion that difficulties such as these are not unintentional. But here, as time stands still for Stowe, we may take advantage of it to abandon temporarily our chronology.

In Letter IV Stowe described a day in Glasgow in a manner that became routine. There were calls to make and blessings to be exchanged. She found herself under an immense and constant pressure with "invitations of all descriptions to go everywhere, and to see everything, and to stay in so many places." It was a popular enthusiasm the intensity of which bespoke a crushing truth. Her portrait of slavery was, after all, a portrait of bleakness and its success but a testimony to the existence of that profound evil, as she saw it. She was withal "oppressed with an unutterable sadness" by this apparent eagerness to follow her crusade. Still, it is the picture of that eagerness or enthusiasm she wished to have in America and perhaps, after all, she is sad only because this is Glasgow and not Richmond or Cincinnati.

> To me there is always something interesting and beautiful about a universal popular excitement of a generous character, the object be what it may. The great, desiring heart of man, surging with one strong, sympathetic swell, even though it be to break on the beach of life and fall backwards . . . has yet a meaning and a power in its restlessness, with which I must deeply sympathize. . . . I do not regard it as anything against our American nation, that we are capable, to a very great extent, of these sudden personal enthusiasms, because I think that . . . the capability of being exalted into a temporary enthusiasm of self-forgetfulness, so far from being a fault, has in it a quality of something divine. Of course, about all such things there is a great deal which a cool critic could make ridiculous, but I hold my opinion . . . (*SM*, IV, 54)

The first such "temporary" excitement was, perhaps, the French Revolution, and there the mania of the mob demonstrated its full capacity. Nonetheless, this mania has something of the divine in it. Stowe is willing to flirt with this whimsical god, though fully yielding to the weight of the argument against him.[15] Her endorsement is not blanket; she sympathizes

Table 22.1. Chronology of the Passage

	Calvin's Account	*Letters' Account*	*Official Biography*
Apr. Sun. 10		Arrive Liverpool	Arrive Liverpool
Apr. Mon. 11	Liverpool Breakfast Party	Liverpool Breakfast Party	Liverpool Breakfast/ Night rally
Apr. Tues. 12		Evening rally/ visit Speke Hall	Leave Liverpool/ arrive Glasgow
Apr. Wed. 13	Rally-Liverpool Association	Rally-Negroes Friend Society/ leave Liverpool/ arrive Glasgow midnight	Morning breakfast/ tour cathedral in afternoon
Apr. Thurs. 14		Receive deputations/ visit cathedral	Ill in morning/ "Tea Party" in evening
Apr. Fri. 15	Glasgow Rally	Ill all day/ "Tea Party" in evening	
Apr. Sat. 16		Visit Bothwell Castle/ Glasgow Rally/ "tomorrow we sail Clyde"	
Apr. Sun. 17		Sail the Clyde/ "tomorrow is Sunday"	Sail the Clyde
Apr. Mon. 18		Kept bed all "Sunday"/ To Edinburgh "tomorrow"	Kept bed all day
Apr. Tues. 19		Left Glasgow/ arrive Edinburgh	
Apr. Wed. 20	Edinburgh Rally		Left Glasgow/ arrive Edinburgh
Apr. Thurs. 21	Aberdeen Rally	Arrive Aberdeen/ evening rally & reception	"Great Tea Party" at Edinburgh
Apr. Fri. 22	Dundee Rally	Leave Aberdeen—arrive Dundee/ Dundee Rally	

Apr. Sat. 23		Breakfast party/ return to Edinburgh/ Workingmen Rally	
Apr. Sun. 24			
Apr. Mon. 25	To Glasgow Temperance Meeting	"Great Tea Party"/ Rally	Rally/ "next day felt miserable"
Apr. Tues. 26		To Glasgow Temperance Meeting/ Tour Melrose Abbey	Arrive Aberdeen/ evening rally
Apr. Wed. 27		Rest/ private party in evening followed by Temperance soiree	Arrive Dundee/ dinner party/ rally
Apr. Thurs. 28		(Travel to Birmingham) "Few calls to make"	Return to Edinburgh/ Workingmen soiree
Apr. Fri. 29		(Drive to Stratford-on-Avon)	"Few calls to make"
Apr. Sat. 30		Visit Warwick, Kenilworth, Coventry/ "next day Sunday"	Travel to Birmingham
May Sun. 1		Birmingham Abolition Society/ Depart for London/ Dinner at Lord Mayor's	Birmingham Abolition Society/ to London
May Mon. 2	Lord Mayor's Dinner	Dinner at Lord Carlisle's	Dinner at Lord Carlisle's
May Tues. 3			
May Wed. 4			

but in "unutterable sadness." The quadrennial experience of the American presidential election may come to mind. But there the "personal enthusiasms" tend not to be "self-forgetful." The self-interest of the voter looms so largely that then he is less than ever likely to remember anything other than himself. Hence arises the necessity of some personal enthusiasm in which the forgetfulness is limited to egotism and in which men—if only temporarily—don an other-regarding vestment.

As suggested previously, the effectiveness of moral enthusiasm hinged on its taking root in the breasts of "working men." While Stowe identified with them, and while she claimed most to be interested in them, she nevertheless recognized their great weakness. The great nationalism of the workingmen made it especially difficult to implant disinterestedness or universal enthusiasm in their breasts.

III. CONSTRUCTING MORAL ENTHUSIASM

Letter V made clear that the agent of excitation is just such a work as *Uncle Tom's Cabin*, though we must always add, in Stowe's silence, this campaign as well. When Stowe sailed the River Clyde she passed through many villages and met with the common people. She summed the experience.

> I have seen how *capable* they are of a generous excitement and enthusiasm, and how much may be done by a work of fiction, so written as to *enlist* those sympathies which are common to all classes. . . . Certainly, a great deal may be effected in this way, if God gives to anyone the power, as I hope he will to many. The power of fictitious writing, for good as well as evil, is a thing which ought most seriously to be reflected on. (*SM*, V, 76)

It is a matter of grave concern to the theologian to question why this traditionally Christian virtue is to be imparted by a work of fiction—however inspired—rather than the inspired pages of the *Bible*. This enterprise is undertaken in the full awareness of the justified Puritan fears of the evil that may be produced by romance. It is, indeed, only in the nineteenth century that American Puritans began to relax their fear of the novel. Stowe's invocation of the novel as an agent of moral education is a questionable enterprise even in her own eyes.[16] Yet, she cannot resist the capacity she finds in the vulgar to respond to such an education, though its very success but trains them to respond to evil lessons that follow in the mode of the good.[17]

One reason for her sanguine expectations of a good result must surely be the fact that she considers herself one who has been given the power to do good in this way. But the power God gives is indifferent—"for good as well as evil." Hence, her expectations must be based in some unclaimed notion of good, which she expects to prevail. She was well pleased that a "penny offering" presented at an Edinburgh rally came from the "slender store" of the poor. It is an indication of a spirit of generosity, which necessarily results from moral education and is not subject to the ambiguities attending the generosity of the rich. She opens the door to the possibility of magnanimity as a virtue accessible to the many and, hence, compatible with democracy in the fullest sense. Prior to this discussion she described this Edinburgh rally as one in which Scotland and England were defended against the charge of neglecting their poor. The profoundest defense against this calumny is that which shows the existence of a regime in which the poor can yet exercise the highest virtues. That their poverty is not incompatible with their virtue is possible, finally, only if their poverty is not their necessary condition. And if the latter be not the case, it can only be the result of those things that place that poverty in way of ultimate relief. Thus, through all the arguments of "Sunny Memories" with regard to "liberal movements" in England, she goes no further than the demonstration of just this case. It is important to note its role in justifying a disinterested enthusiasm among the poor. The only bar to the practice of virtue—including virtue as a momentary enthusiasm—is the denial of the humanity of men. Poverty in itself is not a denial of humanity.

IV. THE WORK OF MORAL ENTHUSIASM

In Letter VI Stowe reported an Aberdeen rally. Here can be seen the consummation of Stowe's argument—which is, as yet, identical with the children's happy ejaculation in Letter I that they are blessed English children, born where no child could be bought or sold. The Aberdeen rally aroused Stowe's enthusiasm.

> The speakers contrived to blend enthusiastic admiration for American with detestation of slavery. . . . One of the speakers concluded his address by saying that John Bull and Brother Jonathan [Edwards], with Paddy and Sandy Scott, should they clasp hands, might stand against the world. (*SM*, VI, 99–100)

In this celebration of the rites of humanity or the recognition of natural rights or of Saxon-Celtic superiority is only the reservation that Brother Jonathan's temporary oversight prevents the handclasp. The "enthusiastic admiration for America" is thus qualified by a preference for the United Kingdom. Nonetheless, there is a consciousness that that for which England is loved is yet expected to have fullest manifestation in America. This becomes clear once we realize that the obvious racial identity intended is but the vehicle for the expression of a deeper identity. The racial identity is seriously undermined by "Paddy's" inclusion in the family, thus subordinating difficulties in the English-Irish relationship fully as weighty as those separating North and South. This is a demonstration of the universalizing influence of this momentary enthusiasm.

But, if that be true, it must also be true that English claims to the rewards that follow enlightened acceptance of the laws of nature is tenuous, more in the way of promise than accomplishment. In which case, the only real practical defense of the principles of natural rights lies with that polity which first instituted a regime on that basis rather than that which first preached it. Cromwell's despotism was ultimately succeeded by emergence of the doctrine of natural rights but not by a regime *explicitly* dedicated to those principles. To emphasize this aspect of English history is to disqualify them for giving lessons to America. To obscure it is to pretend an English superiority from which their admonitions derive their force. The latter course justly incurs American indignation in the face of haughty and unmerited pretense. The only ground from which English criticism of America can be seen as just, therefore, is that which sees the source of that criticism in American principles. This requires that the defects of the English regime be admitted at the same time that their participation in the defense of natural rights be established. The formula was manifested in our analysis of the enthusiastic call for a natural rights front. Stowe follows this at once with a more serious statement of the difficulty and the response to it.

Even more damaging than the recognition of the continuing oppression of the Irish is the argument that there is a continuing oppression of the Scottish people. Throughout "Sunny Memories" Stowe speaks of the oppression of Scotland as a thing of the past. But, opening Letter VII, she does not speak in her own name. For there Scotland's *present* ills are presented for *spiering* [inquiry]. She reverts to an "Old Scotch Bachelor" who sent a letter to her at Aberdeen, and which she received there. We give the letter in its entirety before commenting:

Stonehaven, N.B., Kincardineshire,
57 ° N.W. This 21st April, 1853

To Mrs. Harriet B. Stowe:—

My dear Madam: By the time that this gets your length, the fouk o' Aberdeen will be shewin ye off as a rare animal, just arrived frae America; the wife that writ Uncle Tom's Cabin.

I was like to see ye mysel, but I canna win for want o' siller, and as I thought ye might be writin a buke about the Scotch when ye get hame, I hae just sent ye this bit auld key to Sawney's Cabin.

Well then, dinna forget to speer at the Aberdeenians if it be true they ance kidnappet little laddies, and selt them for slaves; that they dang down the Quaker's kirkyard dyke, and houket up dead Quakers out o' thei graves; that the young boys at the college printed a buke, a maist naebody wad buy it, and them cam out to Ury, near Stonehaven, and took twelve stots frae Davie Barclay to pay the printer.

Dinna forget to speer at ________, if it was true that he flogget three laddies in the beginning o' last year, for the three following crimes: first, for the crime of being born of puir, ignorant parents; second, for the crime of being left in ignorance; and, third, for the crime of having nothing to eat.

Dinna be telling when ye gang hame that ye rode on the Aberdeen railway, made by a hundred men, who were all in the Stonehaven prison for drunkenness; nor above five could sign their names.

If the Scotch kill ye with ower feeding and making speeches, be sure to send this hame to tell your fouk, that it was Queen Elizabeth who made the first European law to buy and sell human beings like brute beasts. She was England's glory as a Protestant, and Scotland's shame as the murderer of their bonnie Mary. The auld hag skulked away like a coward in the hour of death. Mary, on the other hand, with calmness and dignity, repeated a Latin prayer to the Great Spirit and Author of her being, and calmly resigned herself into the hands of her murderers.

In the capital of her ancient kingdom, when ye are in our country, there are eight hundred women sent to prison every year for the first time. Of fifteen thousand prisoners examined in Scotland in the year 1845, eight thousand could not write at all, and three thousand could not read.

At present there are about twenty thousand prisoners in Scotland. In Stonehaven they are fed at about seventeen pounds each, annually. The honest poor, outside the prison upon the parish roll, are fed at the rate of five farthings a day, or two pounds a year. The employment of prisoners is grinding the wind, we ca' it; turning the crank, in plain English. The latest improvement is the streekin board; it's a whig improvement o' Lord Jonnie Russel's.

I ken brawly ye are a curious wife, and would like to ken a' about the Scotch bodies. Weel, they are a gay, ignorant, proud, drunken pack; they manage to pay ilka year for whuskey one million three hundred and forty-eight thousand pounds. But then their piety, their piety; weel, let's luke at it; hing it up by the nape o' the neck, and turn it round atween our finger and thumb on all sides.

Is there one school in all Scotland where the helpless, homeless poor are fed and clothed at the public expense? None.

Is there a hame in all Scotland for the cleanly but sick servant maid to go till, until health be restored? Alas! there is none.

Is there a school in all Scotland for training ladies in the higher branches of learning? None. What then is there for the women of Scotland?

A weel, be sure and try a cupful of Scottish Kail Broase. See, and get a cup Scotch lang milk

Hand this bit line yout to Rev. Mr. ________. Tell him to skore out fats nae true.

God bless you, and set you safe hame, is the prayer of the Old Scotch Bachelor. (*SM*, VII, 107–9)

If Stowe followed the instructions of her correspondent, the facts of this letter are *all* true. Since she states, before offering it, that she has omitted the parts "more expressive than agreeable" and mentions no other excision, we may imagine that the facts *are* true. The parts omitted were indicated in the text by an interlinear sign of elision. We cannot know entirely, but since they follow the question, "What then is there for the women of Scotland?" we may imagine that those parts answered the question. In that case they were omitted for reasons of propriety or agreeableness. It is further the result of that intention to deny the necessity of further elision for either of the two reasons given. Stowe refers to the bachelor as "some Christopher in his cave, or Timon of Athens." That is, we are at liberty to consider him, in his isolation, as either bearing the heavy burden of English sins or wandering misanthropically in a just condemnation of the infidelity of his fellow men. Though our choice will determine whether there is hope for Scotland's relief, it will not affect the necessity of considering the bachelor's censure just.

Stowe presents the bachelor as a misanthropic curiosity. His aspirations, in appearance moved by love of his fellows, are in fact grounded in a rejection of their humanity and thus doomed to failure. She answers him by both denying the necessity of undertaking such inquiries and arguing that there have been attempts at reform to which he is blind. The attempts at reform in Scotland are said to contain a lesson for America; she too can feed and teach her poor. But, taking America at her very best, the inquiry proposed would "bring but an indifferent answer." We may be entitled to wonder, however, whether the inquiry is doomed in America only because America is so far in advance of the situation described by the bachelor? Indeed, we must conclude that the true "fats" about Scotland are facts that cannot be said to be true, generally, of America.

Now, what becomes of that claim if the "old Scotch Bachelor" is none but the pseudonymous American crusader?[18] Can the principle have an application in the presence of such true facts and absent expressed concern? Stowe has already indicated that some reform efforts were underway, and these presumably placed matters in the way of ultimate relief. But the recognition of American superiority complicated that. If we take away the bachelor, we must seek to bolster the argument in some other way. That the letter may have been penned by Stowe is suggested by the unnatural dialect—especially the common nineteenth-century English and American but uncommon Scottish use of "Scotch" for bodies rather than spirits.[19] But more revealing still is the clearly intended parody of the *Key to Uncle Tom's Cabin* in the expression "key to Sawney's Cabin." Besides definitively establishing the literary character of the bachelor's letter,[20] this fact suggests Stowe's own authorship.

The *Key* had indeed been published recently. But our Timon is isolated, and like the other workingmen Stowe has met, cannot likely afford newspapers. We know he cannot afford to travel the short distance (a scant fifty kilometers) from Stonehaven (where she stops on her way from Aberdeen to Dundee) to Aberdeen, "for want o' siller."

Thus, we take the "old Scotch Bachelor" to be Stowe herself, establishing in strong terms the English defects under a name other than her own because of the stringently anti-English sentiment enunciated.[21] We may add by way of parenthesis the circumstantial though not conclusive evidence that the Rev. Mr. ________ to whom the bachelor's letter was referred for authentication may well have been the Rev. Mr. Stowe. His status as expert was derived from the "official" report on European education in its relation to the state of society that he compiled while on a journey that included Scotland in 1836 and which he submitted to the Ohio legislature. The latter had commissioned the study.[22] The indictment of England that *he* penned would constitute the reservation against British republicanism. Stowe's notice of efforts toward reform would constitute a latter day judgment of that indictment.

By these standards England was "retrograde" in the natural rights movement. If England is justly to aid in the fight against slavery, it must also become more strongly wedded to those American principles that are responsible for the struggle. The entire history of English reform, it would seem, must be subordinated to this one great reform once and for all establishing the recognition of universal natural rights. The key to this change is the encouragement of these universal enthusiasms in the workingmen. The implicit argument is that past reforms were deficient as the work of English nobility. The deficiency stems not from their nobility but solely from their having undertaken the reform without *first* having rendered the workingmen the base of the regime. Julia Tyler's cry, "artificial distinctions," returns for further yeomanry.

> Working men, *as a class*, . . . are to form, more and more, a *new power* in society, greater than the old power of helmet and sword, and I rejoice in every indication that they are learning to understand themselves . . . (*SM*, VII, 127)

They were, in other words, responding to her call—having their *consciences raised*. It is for them, however, a matter of interest. "No other class" is so "vitally interested" in the defeat of slavery. Its principle affects their interests. And what is that principle but for *one half* of the community to deprive the other of "education," "opportunity to rise in the world," "property rights," and "family ties," in order to make them "convenient tools" for the "profit and luxury" of slave holders. The expression "one half" is given emphasis to demonstrate that this principle of slavery is not founded on the traditional battle of the few and the many. It is a democratic principle, which arises when democracy is conceived to be but the civil operation of the right of the stronger.[23]

In this sense, the workingman's interest is in a view of natural rights that transcends mere interest. The principle of slavery, we may say, is the principle of a morally indifferent democracy. If further evidence were required, we could return to the "Scotch Bachelor" who commenced the letter, which this discussion ends. Those things to be denied the slave on principle all have correspondence in the bachelor's letter—including the interlinear section—save the element of religious tolerance or freedom of conscience. It is surely a surprise to see that the "principle of slavery" does not include the deprivation of freedom of conscience. But freedom of conscience can only be endangered conscientiously. That is, only the claim of a superior or precedent morality can impair freedom of conscience. Obligatory observation of established liturgies or doctrines presupposes superior moral claims. If the principle of slavery is in itself the denial of morality—a kind of morality, to be sure—it can strictly speaking neither permit nor deny freedom of conscience. Stowe was always careful, in fighting slavery, to condemn the South for not permitting slaves to read the *Bible themselves* rather than for denying them religion. The cause of the slaveholder's deeds was taken to be motive in the narrow sense of profit. On such principles, of course, one-half (rather than 50 percent plus one) of the community would always enslave the other half.

Clearly, aristocracy never amounts to one-half the community. Hence, in itself, aristocracy is not slaveholding. Indeed, it is partly because aristocracy's numbers are originally few that it cannot be the basis of the regime that refutes the principle of slavery. The working class will always be large. If it can be awakened to its interest as a class—that is, its interest beyond narrow self-interests—it can *acquire* the universal concern required to sustain the *recognition* of natural rights.[24] The principle of slavery is the exercise without the recognition of natural rights. Stowe prepares recognition as the condition not of exercising rights simply but sustaining them. This recognition is manifested in bursts of momentary enthusiasm.

V. CITIZENSHIP RECONSTRUCTED

To sustain the recognition of natural rights requires a more comprehensive citizenship than momentary enthusiasm seems to convey. Yet, it is this great moment that creates the basis for comprehensive citizenship. What is required is the moral horizon that saves natural rights, a conscientious commitment that does no harm to conscience itself. It is in the moment of momentary enthusiasm that the articulation of such a morality is to be wished, but it may follow if necessary. In any case, what springs to life in a moment must be rooted in a near eternity to preserve the "moral purity" of a people. The regime so constructed will always be under the test of consistency to its principles—in large measure *because* they were imparted in a momentary enthusiasm which fact heightened the prospect of their being heedlessly abandoned. The efforts required for preservation may well be wholly unlike those required for founding, if an attempt to transcend the momentary enthusiasm in search of what is more permanent is to be made.

What Stowe proposes as a provisional reply is that we consider not whether a nation's morality is intact, but how to keep it so. The task of preservation cannot in itself prepare the task of overcoming the crisis. But where preservation is possible, the decline from the standards of a momentary enthusiasm can perhaps be averted. In this we can recognize an origin of contemporary liberalism's concern with the "conditions of life" as *the* means of manifesting a concern for the principle of equality. Stowe does not confuse equality of opportunity with equality of condition, but she does raise the possibility of such an error through her approach. As the workingmen were made the basis of future movements of improvement, so must the conditions of their life be secured to guard their "moral purity." Letter X records travels through industrial areas as the Stowe party headed toward Birmingham *in cognito*. She found prodigious manufacturing and described the effect on the air of chimneys belching forth "smoke, smut, and gloom." Everything is given a grimy and sooty appearance:

> It is true that people with immense wealth can live in such regions in cleanliness and elegance; but how must it be with the poor? I know of no one circumstance more unfavorable to moral purity than the necessity of being physically dirty. Our nature is so intensely symbolical, that where the outward sign of defilement becomes habitual, the inner is too apt to correspond. I am quite sure that before there can be a universal millennium, trade must be pursued in such a way as to enable the working classes to realize something of beauty and purity in the circumstances of their outward life.[25] (*SM*, X, 192)

Hence, unlike Karl Marx (exiled in London at this time), who expected the millennium to be a great spring-cleaning and efflorescence, Stowe sees the liberation of mankind from drudgery as the condition of the millennium. Thus, she more nearly resembles classical liberals. The struggle against the savage state includes a conscious effort to remove memory-invoking symbols of that state's existence. The notion seems simplistic at best. Can we really imagine that all it requires to make a "white collar" job is to give the worker a white collar and keep it clean? Or, to give to a worker a title less suggestive of the origins of the matter with which he labors?

A. Utopian Dreams

Stowe presents her formulation in all seriousness. The invocation of "beauty and purity"—though not in an unqualified sense—is an appeal to elements especially required in the "bustle of modern progress." She explains herself by adverting once again to the white-black contrast—the art of the melodrama, of which she was the unquestioned master. After the journey through the grime and soot of modern industry, they journeyed through "peculiarly old English" country—that which is being submerged beneath the tide of the "regenerating force of modern progress"—to Stratford-on-Avon. Here is clear air and light. But this old England is old in a sense other than its aloofness from the modern bustle. Beneath the surface—as below its clear skies—they returned to the "hours of national childhood, when popular ideas had the confiding credulity, poetic vivacity, and versatile life, which distinguish children from grown people." It was an age of darkness of mind or spirit—pre-Enlightenment. The beauty and purity of the lives of these old Englishmen was shrouded by the darkness in which they lived, just as the bright light in which modern men live is compromised by the grime or darkness of their lives. Shakespeare lived in such an age. It would have been beyond his reach to build "those quaint, Gothic structures of imagination" had he been born "in the daylight of this century." In that age of darkness, beauty and purity were not subjoined to considerations of human improvement. And the level of maturity they attained resulted partly from the absence of these moral fetters. Thus, Stowe's four-level contrast offers the paradox of a clean but morally credulous, unenlightened but aesthetically sophisticated past, as a rival of the dirty but skeptical, enlightened but *jejune* present. The workingmen might seem to have gained little in the exchange—unless Shakespeare's fellows had lost more than they need have lost.

Stowe maintained that the circumstances of Elizabethan England had circumscribed Shakespeare's art: "Both Gothic architecture and Gothic poetry were the springing and efflorescence of that age, impossible to grow again." But unless matters might have been otherwise, there can be no basis to lament either dirty philistinism or innocent stupidity. Thus, she held that Shakespeare, the man, was not limited by his regime in the same manner that his art was limited. He penetrated to the basis of those questions that, for us, are at the surface.

> Our ride along was a singular commixture of an upper and under current of thought. . . . So, as we rode along, our speculations and thoughts in the under current were back in the old world tradition. While, on the other hand, for the upper current, we were keeping up a brisk conversation on the peace question, on the abolition of slavery, on the possibility of ignoring slave-grown produce . . . and, in fact, on all the most wide-awake topics of the present day. (*SM*, X, 195)

The reconciliation of these contrary currents comes through reflection on the question of whether Shakespeare would have concerned himself with the upper current. He would have understood, but he need not for that reason be understood as forming an approach to these questions. Choice as opposed to circumstance is the limiting factor in the individual case. Moral purity is a hedge against the exercise of the faculty of choice, at least in the case of most men.

> That [Shakespeare] did have thoughts whose roots ran far beyond the depth of the age in which he lived, is plain enough from numberless indications in his plays; but whether he would have taken any practical interest in the world's movements is a fair question. The poetic mind is not always the progressive one; it has, like moss and ivy, a need for something old to cling to and germinate upon. The artistic temperament, too, is soft and sensitive; so there are all these reasons for thinking that perhaps he would have been for keeping out of the way of the heat and dust of modern progress. It does not follow because a man has penetration to see an evil, he has energy to reform it. (*SM*, X, 197)

One is tempted to justify the simplistic notion that workingmen require beauty and purity on this discovery that knowledge is not virtue. Where a people's morality is suspended by the tenuous thread of a momentary enthusiasm, renewed through symbols of perfection, there seems no task for political philosophy, which is ever attentive to what morality requires.

Stowe emphasized the argument by invoking Erasmus—who saw as much as Luther but preferred the peace of his study to truth itself. Truth seems destined to decline from the status Aristotle accorded it—being preferable to friendship—until Stowe introduces Milton. That this poet, not long after Shakespeare, was a reformer makes it "not quite certain" that the latter would not be a reformer *in this age*. But does this make sense? In what way does the choice of any one poet create a presumption as to the choice of another? Stowe demonstrates the difficulty herself when she suggests that Milton's defense of truth may be modeled, like his art, on Greek forms. Thus, we are no further informed as to Shakespeare's choice and have the added difficulty of having raised a potential ideological barrier to the appreciation of art. Are workingmen to obtain their beauty and purity from party manuals? Or, is it suggested that the peculiar beauty and purity required by the modern working class awaits articulation at the hands of a poet?

Milton and Shakespeare are related by more than English blood. Indeed, Milton began his career trying to reproduce the effects of Shakespeare. Yet, he soon enough gave that over and built afterwards exclusively on Greek models. "Had he known as little Latin and Greek as Shakespeare, the world, instead of seeing a well-arranged imitation of the ancient epics from his pen, would have seen inaugurated a new order of poetry." That was the special merit of Shakespeare—the forging of a new order from the chains of tradition. "He was a superb Gothic poet; Milton, a magnificent imitator of old forms, which by his genius were wrought *almost* into the energy of new productions." Between Shakespeare and Milton there is the relation of

Gothic to Greek architecture. In the latter, there "is a cold unity of expression, that calls into exercise only the very highest range of our faculties." If the spirit of the reformer in Milton is allied to the limitation of this cold rationalism, it may be that Shakespeare's grandeur placed him beyond the role of reformer—or, at least the ability to see *all* the nuances of life made reform much more problematic for him. The modern poet who would be his equal would be she who could invest modernity with the charm of poetry and yet remain anti-utopian, the poet of anutopia.[26]

B. The Poetry of Anutopia

Such chastening reflection as this prepares the end of this section of upper and under currents. Momentary enthusiasms are grand—and even noble when disinterested—and in them lasting regimes may be founded, but they are momentary *because* they are human. The beauty and purity that the morality of workingmen requires is none other than that which recognizes and provides for their weaknesses. The elimination of weakness itself is not possible. The utopianism of modernity must then come to terms with the necessity of political choices as distinguished from merely rational choices. The section ends by reporting a visit to an elderly invalid, who had requested to see Mrs. Stowe. They heard the old lady prophesy "the final extinction of slavery" the world over. The prophecy saddened and pleased Stowe, for she knew that if every "true Christian in America had the same expectation, then slavery should no longer exist." *Vox populi, vox dei*; and that god is much less subject to the mantic speech than to the manic cry.

In an age of universal principles, utopianism is more than a gratuitous diversion. Ignoring the necessity of political choices sometimes constitutes an attack on nationalism that undermines all possibility to sustain genuinely cosmopolitan principles. The pretense that the only barrier to universal morality is the existence of mundane or parochial morality constitutes an attempt to revoke the founding agreement by which it became possible to subject politics to a transcendent logic, that is the consent founded in natural rights. It is an ahistorical view of political life. Thus, in the name of a transcendent logic, some reformers would dismantle national systems, and ultimately political systems generally. In Letter XII, just after the conclusion of an eternal moment, Stowe presented a summary of a discussion with the leader of Europe's peace movement, Elihu Burritt. That discussion is the basis of the foregoing reflections.

The proposal had been made that all standing armies be disbanded, and that a "national arbitration" system be established. Stowe presented these ideas as sympathetically as a true believer, and seemed almost enthusiastic. But she takes them to go only so far, which she demonstrates first, by giving them a wider application than would their partisans.

> These ideas were not *entirely* chimerical, if we reflect that commerce and trade are as essentially opposed to war as is Christianity. . . . The whole current of modern society is *as much* against war as slavery . . . (*SM*, XII, 249; emphasis supplied)

Thus, Stowe agrees with Calvin Stowe who, citing Carlyle,[27] would consider it the addition of substantial beauty and purity to the workingman's life had he not so frequently to go to war. In his article, Calvin argued that modern progress greatly narrows the "just" causes of war but does not suggest that there is never a just cause. Similarly, Stowe's emphasis here is on "entirely" rather than chimerical, for—although the principle refuting slavery equally refutes war—the principle, limited in its application to "national difficulties," cannot take precedence over those difficulties which must be resolved as a condition of nationality. Hence:

> When we ask these reformers how people are to be freed from the yoke of despotism without war, they answer, "By the diffusion of ideas among the masses—by teaching the bayonets to think." (*SM, XII, 249)*

Thus, the reformers seek to continue the pursuit of the goal of universal Enlightenment.

In this resides their utopianism. They expect success *only* when the momentary enthusiasm becomes eternal universal enthusiasm—at the end of all history. They deny, therefore, the possibility of a cosmopolitan morality, established in a momentary enthusiasm and perpetuated by the care taken to preserve favorable circumstance. The utopian suggests that it is necessary to convince the despot's soldier to defend no longer the despot's will, at which point the subjugated will go free. He attacks despotism, therefore, through the attack on nationhood itself—and all that means. Stowe makes no direct comment but shows the anticipated fate of such an approach by linking it with ends traditionally understood to be impossible of achievement, even in the Bible.

> The object that they are aiming at is one most certain to be accomplished, *infallible as the prediction that swords are to be beaten into plowshares, and spears into pruning-hooks, and that nations shall learn war no more.* (*SM*, XII, 250)

This is the same as to say that these things will come to pass in the judgment day. As such, they can have no place in human political calculations per se.

Stowe cannot reject the Quaker utopian, however much in error, for his opinion constitutes part of the movement of momentary enthusiasm, which shall bring a permanent end to slavery. As matters stood in 1853, they *also* abstained from slave-grown produce and thus already formed a "market" that, if it could have been widened, would have opened the field for free enterprise to deal a death blow to slavery. "All the forces of nature go with free labor; and all the forces of nature resist slave labor." This can at least appear the case if workingmen are brought to see their salvation in their freedom and the only threat to it in slavery. Morally armed democracy is the alternative to morally indifferent democracy, so long as morally armed democracy can save its foundation in the working classes *and* does not succumb to the temptations of self-denying utopianism.

Moral enthusiasm is not an unmixed blessing. Properly moderated it is the only legitimate foundation of movements of human improvement—erecting a defense equally against cold rationalism and despotic self-interest. Its task is to defend against the two prime sources of human motivation (reason and passion). Only the elaboration and succoring of a derivative self-interest that is other-regarding stands a chance of competing with the other forces. This task requires a tradition—something old to which to cling—and poetic art as its foundation. The inculcation of an aesthetic sense, reverent regard for beauty and purity, ensures a measure of abstraction or disinterestedness which will permit the indulgence of self-interest. It is, therefore, the expression of human aspirations or desires in the form of a transcendent logic that constitutes morally armed democracy. If that democracy is not just another species of moral despotism, it is not so only by virtue of that logic in which it is rooted. I will try to formulate that logic in its own terms, after we have discovered the mythopoetic structure that enfolds it.

VI. RECONSTRUCTING NATIONAL MEMORY

Underlying the account of enthusiasm was the reconstruction of a national memory. Liberal history is the foundation for legitimating the political influence of moral enthusiasm. The effort of renewing the memory of America had for its immediate goal the construction of a moral foundation for the total abolition of slavery. But it is also just to say that it was an attempt to reinterpret the American founding in a manner capable of perpetuating the regime that could successfully abolish slavery. Thus, the discussion of Old England is foremost an anticipation of New America.

Referring American principles to roots in a distant past is calculated to increase veneration for those principles. But that matter were not so simple, since not all of the past is suitable medium for the communication of these principles. What is especially striking is that primary emphasis is to be placed on writers-poets. As has been suggested, Stowe began American history in the age of Elizabeth, the age of Shakespeare. That was not only the era of settlement and exploration but also the era in which slavery was introduced. But that most distant relation was not the earliest subject of Stowe's historical musing. It is rather the more nearly related Walter Scott. This chronological promiscuity was imposed by geographical necessity, but it was reflected in a more serious mingling of the old and new in a capricious and arbitrary fashion. In Letter II growing things were taken as contemporaneous things, the new. The old things were roots, at the depths. Such clarity was not continued once the history began.

In Letter III our attention is detained, as we parse the narrative, by the continued notice of the natural vegetation—of growing and living things. But here we find the living conjoined with the very old. In this letter the remembering begins in earnest. The party embarked for Scotland by rail, and Stowe "dimly" recalls the "views of Scotland" from Burns's songs and the "enchantments of Scott." These poets had filled her childhood hours.

> And, by the by, that puts me in mind of one thing; and that is, how much of our pleasure in literature results from the reflection on us of other minds. . . . The literature which has charmed us in the circle of our friends becomes endeared to us from the reflected remembrance of them . . . so that our memory of it is a many-colored cord, drawn from many minds. (*SM*, III, 41)

Rather the associations they produce than the truths they convey measure the importance of those memories drawn from poetry. But, what is perhaps more important still is the fact that the memories are of a community—a circle of friends who are surely fellow citizens and perhaps even parents. They are also those with whom Stowe has never shared more than a common sentiment, as she introduced them in her preface.

The specific structure of these memories is personal; but they are personal recollections of essentially public concerns. This includes even the reflection on the relative worth of the poets, Scott and Shakespeare. The memories serve the purpose of demonstrating their respective powers and the places to be accorded them in our own history as we consider its weightier themes, the fate of the martyrs and their meaning for us.

Walter Scott is not only the link between our present and our past but he, more than any other author, has hallowed "every foot" of the countryside of Scotland. He introduced us to the very old Castle Lancaster, which "looks as fresh as if it had been built yesterday." But it was old—and every bit as much as the real old Carlisle that quickly succeeds it. Now the wall and castle of Carlisle are fit for working a theme. Thus, it is made certain that this is the very Carlisle from the "Song of Albert Graeme."[28] That is the song, remember, "which has something about Carlisle's wall in every verse [?]" What the song has, that is not identified, is a sun that shines continuously on Carlisle's wall through an entire dream of love, marriage, murder, revenge, and suicide. That sun will still be shining when we close this memory of "old castles and ivy" in Letter XI. It is the agent that will foster the germination of the seeds planted in these feudal ruins. The sun shone on its walls then and shines now on Carlisle's walls, though the castle "stands only for a curiosity, and the cotton factory has come up in its place."

> So goes the world,—the lively vigorous shoots of the present springing out of the old mouldering trunk of the past. (*SM*, III, 47)

But the bright glare of sunlight—like nature's indifference—nurtures defect as well as health. The Cathedral of Glasgow is a stout, splendid example of old architecture. The cathedral was defended by the people during the iconoclasms. But one casualty reveals a flaw: all the stained glass is gone. Thus, raw sunlight streams "through the immense windows" with a brightness that reveals "defect and rudeness in the architecture." The "colored rays of painted glass served to conceal the defects"—the very opposite "of the cold, definite, intellectual rationalism, which has taken the place of the many-colored gorgeous mysticism of former times." Hence, the need for "sunny memories."

The great difficulty is to judge what things should be colored and what left in the raw sunlight. That the present should always be exposed and the past always enshrouded in a mist is impossible, save on the principle of Thomas Jefferson's revolution every generation. What is more likely is that the light that exposes present defect must be reflected off memories that have been colored. Some memories, of course, must remain uncolored for their instructive power or receive a coloring that creates aversion rather than charm.

Not all of former times is to be praised—least of all by them that best know them. But Stowe cannot resist the impulse to visit

> the mouldering remains of a state of society which one's reason wholly disapproves, and which one's calm sense of right would think it the greatest misfortune to have recalled . . . (*SM*, IV, 60)

Since she can, but three pages later, explain the nature and source of the admiration, what she cannot "understand nor explain" must be only the connection of those admirable principles with this particular "state of society"—the feudal regime. But the very appearance of ancient majesty stifles any attempt at democratic protest. The ruins of Bothwell Castle capture one's soul; its many ways and views raise before one the "special phantasmagoria of chivalry and feudalism." Battle cries alert us on the one hand, and on the other, a "deep stillness, that green, clinging ivy, [and] the gentle, rippling river" describe "something more imperishable than brute force." The principle of ivy is "clinging and tenacity," which induces some poets to consider it womanly, hence commonly resulting in the "appropriate" considerations of "fidelity, friendship, and woman's love." But it may describe a "higher love" which is "unconquerable and unconquered" and "has embraced this ruined world from age to age, silently spreading its green over the rents and fissures of our fallen nature . . ." The ivy cannot have been called forth by feudalism and chivalry, and it is that we are remembering, even if these reflections do chasten or color our memory.

Our appreciation of feudal glory is heightened by Scott's detailed preservation of that glory. But to the Scot those are tales of days well gone by. "Our enthusiasm . . . does not meet a response in the popular breast." Scott glorified the very institutions that oppressed these people. Thus, he is lost to the Scot and, perhaps, justly so. Nonetheless, there is in his work much that a disinterested view can appreciate.[29] For Americans, the prospect of feudalism is so distant—"a thing so much of mere story and song"—that there is liberty to depict it in romantic hues.

> I have often been dissatisfied with the admiration, which a poetic *education* has woven into my nature, for chivalry and feudalism. (*SM*, IV, 62; emphasis added)

But upon closer inspection she discovered some foundation in right for that poetic education not "inconsistent with the spirit of Christ." The Black Douglas family was not admired for hardness and cruelty, hastiness to take offense, nor fondness for blood and murder. Rather, admiration looks to "their *courage*, their *fortitude*, their *scorn of lying and dissimulation*, their high sense of *personal honor*, which led them to feel themselves *protectors of the weak*, and to *disdain to take advantage of unequal odds* against an enemy." Any "reliable character" must be based on these qualities. "The beautiful must ever rest in the arms of the sublime. The gentle needs the strong to sustain it, as much as . . . yonder ivy" needs a rugged wall. "When we are admiring these things therefore, we are only admiring some sparkles of that which is divine" (*SM*, IV, 63; emphasis added).

This is not a latter day version of deism. These divine sparks ignited human political fires. And Stowe asks, in effect, that they who know from experience what accompanies Scott's landscapes be brought to know the beauty that lies beneath the torture chamber. She may not succeed, nor even expect to, but if Stowe persuades Americans to make the effort to convince the Scot, she would have formed the Americans' view as intended.

> Since there are two worlds in man, the real and the ideal, and both have indisputably the right to be, since God made the faculties of both, we must feel that it is a benefaction to mankind, that *Scott was raised up as the link between the present and past.* It is a loss to universal humanity to have the imprint of any phase of human life and experience entirely blotted out. (*SM*, IV, 70; emphasis supplied)

We must remember, and our best memories form the walls within which our worst memories decay. The eternal sunshine that illumines our best memory also imparts new life to our decaying memories. Whether a cotton factory describes less injustice than ancient dungeons is perhaps less important than the fact that the cotton factory, too, will be a decayed memory.

> Scott's fictions are like this beautiful ivy, with which all the ruins here are overgrown; they not only adorn, but, in many cases, they actually hold together, and prevent the crumbling mass from falling into the ruins. (*SM*, IV, 70)

Scott's fictions perform the task that Scottish memory cannot perform, because the stark picture of oppression dominates Scottish memory. To the possessors of the ruins of Bothwell Castle, the ruins are "objects of taste." And if they cannot escape the dark memories of pain and injustice to appreciate the more sublime nature of the structures, they can perhaps be excused. They live in a country in which a continuing sensibility to oppression is to their advantage.

But Stowe abstracted from far more than the Scottish memory of oppression. Her architectural guide, Billings, had argued forcefully in his "Introduction" that Scottish indifference to the ruins resulted rather more from the modern pursuit of gain than the ancient religious wars. The depredations caused by John Knox and the Scottish reformation, for example, were minor when compared to those caused by the pursuit of gain in the "last hundred years." Old cathedrals, abbeys, and castles alike had become virtual rock quarries—the corporate nobles setting the example and being followed down to the last peasant. The ruins are left always seeming newly destroyed.

> Examine any of the great ruins in the ancient burghs. Do they present any masses of fallen or ivy-covered ruins? We answer, No. There they are—fresh-made, clean-picked, and naked skeletons—standing rugged against the sky; having *all* the hideousness of destruction, instead of the *picturesque beauty which invariably accompanies natural decay.* (Billings, 4; emphasis supplied)[30]

Stowe's "poetic education" has enabled her to reinvent Scottish ruins with beauty. As such, she silently criticizes the Scot's philistinism. Yet, she also shows that the evils caused by the pursuit of gain are problematic. This modern principle is condemned as it gives rise to slavery but not as it substitutes a cotton factory for a feudal castle. When Stowe announces—against the advice of her authority—that "all the ruins here are overgrown" with ivy, she establishes for the Scot a reputation he does not merit. That this were not unjust or overly generous, we must decide either that the fault which is overlooked—nay, colored—is trivial or that it is qualified by something which produces an effect the equal or better than the sensitivity to beauty.

Hence, the pursuit of gain must be permitted to the Scot *because* he is improved rather than harmed by it. What accompanies the pursuit of gain in Scotland may be expressed negatively: the absence of slavery.

So unlike the regime of slavery, their own regime awakens in them "a spirit of independence and resistance." In the working classes of Scotland and England, there is a strong sense of nationality—a thing always more true of the middle and laboring classes than the higher. Their nationalism substitutes for the absence of rosy memories.

VII. A NATIONALIST DEFENSE OF COSMOPOLITAN FREEDOM

It were well to pause here and state candidly the subject of these reflections: religious intolerance. Feudalism carried other forms of oppression in its breast, to be sure, but the one of greatest significance was and is religious intolerance. The very birth of America was a response to such despotism. Is it not the case, therefore, that any American romanticizing about feudalism will tend to undermine the fear of intolerance that is the soul of freedom of conscience? Stowe's answer is no. To her, the Covenanter and Dissenter overreacted in identifying everything feudal as bigoted. Similarly, it is a mistake for a republic to reject legitimate standards of virtue in the attempt to guard against intolerance. Those standards can be resurrected, if the memory of those blighted ages can be resurrected without the threat to freedom as its principal character. This is the heart of Stowe's project.

At Edinburgh and Aberdeen Stowe makes to herself the strongest case for the virtues of feudalism. Stowe opened her reflections on Scottish tragedy and greatness with the memory of Mary's lamentation, but she developed them with the memory of "Scots wha ha wi' Wallace bled." Letter VI, however, will depend not on the poet through whom we recall the Battle of Bannockburn but the real scene. The historical narration of Bruce's address was accounted to convey as much moral grandeur as the poem.

> Its power lies not in appeal to brute force, but to the highest elements of our nature, the love of justice, the sense of honor, and to disinterestedness, self-sacrifice, courage unto death.
>
> These things will live and form high and imperishable elements of our nature, when mankind have learned to develop them in other spheres than that of physical force. Burns's lyric, therefore, has in it an element which may rouse the heart to noble endurance and devotion, even when the world shall learn war no more. (*SM*, VI, 90)

The very virtues which are wanted for the defense of modern freedom are these esteemed companions of war. It is supposed they can serve noble purposes in the absence of war, but it is admitted that without them war is certainly futile. It was the bloody Scottish victory as much as Bruce's address that memorialized Bannockburn. The poet was able to invest speech with the moral power of deeds.

The discussion of Burns is followed by a second discussion of Shakespeare. The analysis of Scott was interrupted in order to show what it is that is consistent with modernity in feudalism. The immediate defect of feudalism, as it appears from Stowe's contrast, was its worldliness. But this would not seem to explain its intolerance, especially since modernity's proud boast of tolerance is rooted in the choice of the worldly over the otherworldly. Stowe would readily grant this, but would maintain that in feudalism, the highest motives of the human soul served worldly ambition, while modernity pursues worldly goals with the lowest motives of the human soul. Intolerance, she thought, was more the result of the disproportion—placing the high in service of the low. This disproportion is seen most clearly in Scott, and its results are seen in the Scottish Covenanters. But a case for the proper view of morality must be framed before the critique of Scott can be matured. Thus, the reader is reminded that, while Scott is the theme, the next subjects will be Shakespeare and the Covenanters.

Stowe's tour passed Glamis, which even Scott attests is truly gloomy, and of which there are even apparently true stories every bit as melancholy as "Macbeth." Stowe's circle wondered how far Shakespeare had to create the tragedy and how far "tradition and history" offered it "ready to hand."

> It seems the story is all told in Holingshed's Chronicles; but (Shakespeare's) fertile mind has added some of the most thrilling touches, such as the sleepwalking of Lady Macbeth. . . . It always seemed to me that this tragedy had more of the melancholy majesty and power of the Greek than anything modern. The striking difference is, that while fate was the radical element of those, free will is not less distinctly the basis of this. . . . The theology of Shakespeare is as remarkable as his poetry. A strong sense of man's moral responsibility and free agency, and of certain future retribution, runs through all his plays. (*SM*, VI, 94)

It is then the individual sense of moral responsibility, as opposed to either *moira* or collective moral responsibility, which is the precious element of feudalism. It is consistent with tolerance when it is expressed as a condition of the loftiest aspirations. "Every man his own pope," in its political bearings, *is* a doctrine of tolerance but only within range of acceptance of the idea that each man *requires* a pope. In short, freedom of conscience for Stowe must be so formulated as not to free men *from* conscience. Whether this goal is really attainable we will have occasion later to consider. But on the basis of these principles Stowe declared the Covenanters both the heirs of feudalism and the fathers of America.

Two views of the virtues of the human soul form the basis for a judgment of the Covenanters, not of their faith. In Letter IV we found the manly virtues to be courage, fortitude, scorn of lying and dissimulation, and the high personal honor that protects the weak and disdains unequal advantage over an enemy. The list was repeated, with a change, in Letter VI; love of justice, sense of honor, disinterestedness, self-sacrifice, courage unto death. In the first we found the stubbornly admired principles of feudalism, the avowed companions of war. In the last we found the "highest elements of our nature," the identical companions of war. The love of justice may seem identical to the disdain of unequal advantage, but it can serve as motive for peace as well as war. It animates the desire for tolerance as well as honorable victory. Through the medium of just such transformed virtues the Covenanters participated in feudal principles. Their righteousness subjected them to grave peril, but they succeeded.

The descendants of the Covenanters have yet to come to terms with the full implications of those virtues that served their fathers and now would be preserved. The town of Aberdeen reflects the wars of those holy days, the same war that, in the breast of the poet, made "L'Allegro" new, clean, and modern and made "Penseroso" old, mossy, dreamy. Milton sought to accommodate the old and the new in his defense of tolerance—the best of old and new. So has Aberdeen two parts which display a similar "sharpness and distinction" architecturally. The town "bears the mark of the hand of violence . . ." In the cathedral, where this is most manifest, one sees the images of bishops and saints, which

> seem to have been woefully maltreated and despoiled, in the fervor of those days, when people fondly thought that breaking down carved wood was getting rid of superstition. These men did not consider that . . . when human nature is denied beautiful idols, it will go after ugly ones. (*SM*, VI, 102–3)

Had they been made sufficiently aware of the origins of their virtues, they were more loath to abandon them.

Billings improperly blamed the modern pursuit of gain for these depredations. It is rather the absence of a check on than the presence of the pursuit of gain that causes the modern difficulty. And the check is absent because of the original iconoclasm, which threw off the relics of the ancient world indiscriminately. A "tradition and history" that was not all bleak would have saved a tolerance to match the poet's own. The space given the other, modern half of Aberdeen by Stowe effects the kind of reconciliation sought, "that we might not neglect the present in our zeal for the past." Of the modern world alone—a world that includes commerce or the pursuit of gain—may it be said that cosmopolitan principles fully prevail.

The virtues of the past failed to produce human happiness because they were not allied to cosmopolitan principles and did not lead to tolerance. That they may still be called virtues—the highest elements of our nature—creates a difficulty. It is possible to realize the highest elements of human nature in the absence of the truly human way of life. In the ancient world, political philosophy found human happiness, in particular as well as in general, to rely on the achievement of the specifically human end: life in the *polis*. The *polis*, understood in its true sense, was the self-sufficing community of friends. Political experience and not gain, therefore, was *the* condition of individual happiness. If there were any exception to this, it existed only as to those for whom life in the *polis* was fundamentally impossible. For the vast number of men this was not the case. Hence, the life according to virtue was foreclosed to men save as they enjoyed life in a well-ordered *polis*. But for Stowe, the highest elements of human nature are attainable for significant numbers even in the ill-ordered commonwealth. Thus, human happiness in particular, like individual wealth, is not radically dependent on human happiness in general.

One of the consequences of human happiness in particular, however, is the necessity of a preference for human happiness in general. Where once the individual practice of virtue depended on the existence of the virtuous community, now we find the existence of the virtuous community to depend on the individual practice of virtue. The difficulty then resides in the fact that this ethic is compatible with either the ill-ordered or the well-ordered regime. That is, though it may be the necessary condition of human happiness or of the regime founded on certain cosmopolitan principles, this ethic is not a sufficient condition of the latter. This notion of the order to which the human soul belongs was missing from Scott and accounts for his being forgotten by Scots.

VIII. SECULAR SALVATION

The final analysis of Scott, commenced in Letter VIII, impresses the reader with nothing if not the fact that the poet is dead. The letter is organized into sections that accommodate a tour through "Melrose, Dryburgh, and Abbotsford," but in an order that also accommodates a theme. Though the party arrived first at Melrose and contracted the services of a guide, it toured first—according to the narrative—Abbotsford. Then a skiff was hired that The Tweed may be crossed and Dryburgh toured. After returning in the skiff, Melrose was toured. This carries them to the house Scott built for himself, to the place of his burial, and to the scene of his highest poetic achievement, the description of Melrose Abbey and, hence, his epitaph. Already, the rehabilitation of Scott is suggested. In addition, some reference is made to *Uncle Tom's Cabin* at the end of each section, and, finally each section has its dominant theme. Hence, we discuss Scott at Abbotsford and the "dead and the ugly"; the family estate and burial ground at Dryburgh and the "dead and the beautiful"; and Scott's portrait of Melrose Abbey and the "beautiful and the living." As noted, each section ends with notice of *Uncle Tom's Cabin* and contains—or, more exactly, through them all runs—the refusal of the Scot to believe Scott. "To how little purpose seemed the few, short years of his life, compared with the capability of such a soul. Brilliant as his success had been, how was it passed like a dream" (*SM*, VIII, 128). All trace of Scott was gone. He wished to establish a family, but his issue failed. The evidence of artifacts was consulted. Stowe searched through relics with thoroughness. She arrived at Abbotsford—a labor of love for Scott—and pronounced it a "mistake and a failure" taken either as speculation or as architecture.

Her judgment of Abbotsford could not stand as comprehensive judgment of Scott himself, however. Thus, the building maintained its interest as an access to the poet's soul. It was entirely the work of his vision, and it stands, accordingly, as a monument of his dreams. Its growth was irregular—like marine formations—and it traduced aesthetic and utilitarian principles (i.e., it dedicated the highest elements of human nature to the pursuit of mere worldly ambition). "But by none of these rules ought" it be judged, but "rather as the poet's endeavor to render outward and visible the dream land of his thoughts" and his "refuge from the cold, dull realities of life" (*SM*, VIII, 133). Viewed in this light it is indeed a view into his soul. For this reason alone does it interest her and steel her to resist, as she tours the rooms, "a coldness, like that of death." But her interest finally fell victim to the poet's very inwardness.

> One thing disappointed me, there was not a single view from a single window I saw that was worth anything, in point of beauty; why a poet, with an eye for the beautiful, could have located a house in such an indifferent spot, on an estate where so many beautiful sites were at his command, I could not imagine. (*SM*, VIII, 135)

Scott had every reason, every inducement to consider the beautiful his guide in constructing his home and failed to do so.

Stowe cannot imagine why, but forces the reader to consider if Scott, in his soul, did indeed have an eye for the beautiful. The evidence for his capacity is found in his fidelity to the beauty of nature in his descriptions, which forms the basis of rapture at Melrose. But we were shown in Letters IV and V that that capacity is qualified. The former letter noted that Scott preserved the picturesque of Scotland because of great attention to accuracy in his descriptions. From him came advice "worth remembering by every artist—that no imagination could long support its freshness, that was not nourished by a constant and minute observation of nature." But in Letter V a visit to Roseneath discloses that charming spot to be a peninsula.

> "A peninsula!" said C_____. "Why, Walter Scott said it was an island!" Certainly he did declare most explicitly in the person of Mr. Archibald, the Duke of Argyle's serving man, to Miss Dollie Dutton, when she insisted on going to it by land, that Roseneath was an island. It shows that the most accurate may be caught tripping sometimes. (*SM*, V, 72)

If this is to be considered a genuine sign of Scott's tripping, it is also an indication of the character of his art. It proceeds less from the depths of his soul than from a laborious striving to reproduce the familiar. That this approaches the truth is revealed in the visit to Melrose. But the effect of this circumstance on our conception of Scott induces us always to make allowance for that in the familiar to him which obscures the true or the beautiful. The singular failure in the construction of his residence justifies this cautiousness.

When the party made its way from Abbotsford to Dryburgh, they engaged a skiff. Stowe found that the boatman and his entire family had read *Uncle Tom's Cabin*. She sought to know if the common people read Scott's works, but the boatman responded that "Scott was not so much a favorite with the people as Burns." Stowe created a similar situation at the end of the Dryburgh tour, as they prepared to re-cross the Tweed. They left Dryburgh with their hosts and friends accompanying them to the boat.

> As we were walking towards the Tweed, the Eildon Hill, with its three points, rose before us. . . . I thought of (Scott's) words . . .
>
> "Warrior, I could say to thee
> The words that cleft Eildon Hill in three,
> And bridled the Tweed with a curb of stone."
>
> I appealed to my friends if they knew anything about the tradition; I thought they seemed rather reluctant to speak of it. O, there was some foolish story, they believed; they did not well know what it was. The picturesque age of human childhood is gone by; men and women cannot always be so accommodating as to believe unreasonable stories for the convenience of the poets. (*SM*, VIII, 149)

At the end of the tour also, she discussed *Uncle Tom's Cabin* and modern movements, with a literate "working family." Thus, Scott is forgotten; his tales are replaced by a new kind of tale of death. If the confiding people do not believe the story of Uncle Tom for the convenience of the poet, it is only because the poet constructs this myth for the convenience of the people.

IX. WE ARE NO SLAVES

Whether contrasted with *Uncle Tom's Cabin* or Shakespeare (about whose characters one feels "as if they must have had a counterpart in real existence"), Scott loses. He can neither bear the memory of the tradition nor lead the battalions of reform. But it is still not clear why he loses. The lines that follow the passage cited above suggest a reason. Unreasonable stories will no longer be believed by a skeptical people, but immediately after Stowe's party reaches the skiff and takes farewell of its friends, she adds, "I hope we may meet again sometime." And the host responded, "I am *sure* we shall madam; if not here, *certainly* hereafter." The unreasonable story is *only* that in which a disproportion between the elements of human nature and the elements of human ambition persists. Like Abbotsford itself, such a story scorns the utilitarian but has no conception of the beautiful.

At Dryburgh Stowe found a "rich, poetic ruin," everywhere beautiful, as Abbotsford was ugly. It is memorialized in Scott's "Eve of St. Joan," in which the dead somehow live on. But here lay Scott and his wife in graves covered with flat stones—in the very region of the netherworld between life and death.

> It is strange that we turn away from the grave of this man, who achieved to himself the most brilliant destiny that ever an author did . . . obtaining all that heart could desire of riches and honor,—we turn away and say, Poor Walter Scott. (*SM*, VIII, 142)

The poet seems to be excluded even from the world of his own fancy. But in spite of his worldliness, he was withal a good man.

> It has often been remarked, that there is no particular moral purpose aimed at by Scott in his writings; he often speaks of it himself . . . although moral effect was not primarily his object, yet the influence of his writings and whole existence on earth has been decidedly good . . . He never enlists our sympathies in favor of vice, by drawing those seductive pictures, in which it comes so near the shape and form of virtue that the mind is puzzled as to the boundary line . . . (*SM*, VIII, 143)

Scott had been blamed for injustice to Covenanters and Puritans in his "Old Morality." But, in fact, he sought to be as fair as he knew. He characterized a Puritan who fully met *his* understanding of the distinction and, indeed, sought to make him perfect. The character, however, was hollow.

Scott succeeded in describing a real character when he drew the rival because it was with him that "he had full sympathy" and "put his whole life into." He presented a model of secular virtue—whether through his own life or his characters—which is admirable. But his model, without being transformed, cannot share in erecting that life which the modern Scot will live. The identical virtues, which are manifested or called forth by the "war spirit," are required for "devotional enthusiasm." But the decisive element governing the depiction of the character is not knowledge of the virtues so much as it is knowledge of the conditions of virtue—the use to which it must be put.[31] Henry Morton was a failure in just the sense that Uncle Tom succeeds.

> Henry Morton is a laborious arrangement of starch and pasteboard to produce one of those supposititious, just-right men, who are always the stupidest mortals after they are made. (*SM*, VIII, 144)

These things were becoming clear to Scott in his last days, but he had not another life in which to apply them.

After the visit to the ruins the party walked to Dryburgh village. During this walk one from among a "knot of workingmen" approached them, ascertained Stowe's identity, and invited the party to refresh itself in his cottage. To his children, she was introduced as the "mother of Topsy and Eva." Of course, everyone had read the book. They enjoyed lengthy conversation about America. Finally, someone from Stowe's party quoted, "The working classes of England and Scotland are not as well off as the slaves."

> The man's eyes flashed. "There are many things," he said, "about the working class, which are not what they should be . . . but," he added with emphasis, "we are no *slaves*." (*SM*, VIII, 148)

Stowe picked up the thread of that defense and led her friend through a series of "recent improvements." In the very cottages of the "most nationalistic" class of Scotland, she had dislodged Scott and begun instruction in a new catechism—one might also say she continued the instruction *Uncle Tom's Cabin* had begun. "Our host, before the meal, crave the blessings of him who had made of one blood all the families of the earth; a touching allusion, I thought, between Americans and Scotchmen." And, we might add, an allusion no more difficult to believe than that they were to meet again in the hereafter.

Though Walter Scott is not so well remembered by the Scot, we are finally charged to remember something of that life to which he introduced us. We must dislike Scott for his morality and the disingenuous disavowal of it, but we must recall his art. The last stop of this tour is Melrose, the ruins of Melrose Abbey. Stowe was unreserved in her praise.

> The sad, wild, sweet beauty of the thing comes down on one like a cloud; even for the sake of being original you could not, in conscience, declare you did not admire it. (*SM*, VIII, 150)

In his description of Melrose Scott's poetry most nearly and completely revealed what really exists. His descriptions are exact, and to that extent do they partake of a life beyond his own. This is Shakespearean Gothic. To Stowe such structures had a never-dying charm and variety. Everything at Melrose breathed the air of beauty and life, even the gravesites. That site reputed to be the grave of "Michael Scott" induces a strong sense of reality. And the grave of Scott's factotum, Tom Purdie, called forth images of life as well as the memory of another departed Tom.

> Here, between master and man, both freemen, is all that beauty of relation sometimes erroneously considered as the peculiar charm of slavery. (*SM*, VIII, 158)

The initial praise of Melrose Abbey slides insensibly into the eulogium of Tom Purdie and thence into the defense of freedom. And it is that that Scott portrayed most effectively. His chivalry was genuine and his characterizations of the struggles and honors of free men constitute just praise of freedom even if they are limited to the worldly view.

But Letter IX affirms that it is only the freedom and not this peculiar relation that is appropriate to America. The day after the tour, Stowe and Calvin engaged the gentry in conversations that ran mostly on the poor and servants. She reports that the "openings for profit" are so many in America that servants are few, "except as temporary expedients." The ladies wondered at the possibility of family attachments, and Stowe settled their minds that there was no such thing: "Old and attached family servants in the free states were rare exceptions." Hence, the "beauty of the relation" *is* peculiar to slavery in America, but rather because of the nature of the American regime than the nature of the service. The example of Tom Purdie can only serve the interest of slavery, since, without slavery, Tom would never remain a serving man.

> This, I know, must look to persons in old countries, like a hard and discouraging feature of democracy. I regard it, however, as only a temporary difficulty. (*SM*, IX, 173)

Eventually there will emerge a new order of "labor and industrial callings," and though the door will remain forever closed to aristocratic *forms* of service, there will be a kind of service in America fully as faithful and efficient.[32] And when it is made as "pleasant, profitable, and respectable" as industrial callings, it will be as permanent. It is for the sake of this American consummation that a spirited defense of the freeman's character must be saved.

To save this of Walter Scott, it is necessary to amend our view of his powers of observation. We must hold that he appreciated the wonders of Melrose even if we are unsure how thorough was his grasp. Billings's architectural account is cited to show that the elegance of the structure has attained a minuteness that conceals its greatest wealth from public view. Only "laborious groping" could reveal this act of worship in its fullest sense. But Billings notes only that it is as exquisitely finished where unseen as where seen. Thus, the joy one gets from making special effort to view hidden recesses "is produced by the same" care as is seen in the open.[33] Stowe's laborious groping is rather a lesson to her reader. In the present case, the lesson seems to be that Scott *must* be believed, even if wrong. Billings cites Scott's poetic description of the east window, although Scott "calls it what it is not—an Oriel." Stowe rejects the pedanticism—subordinating the truth of the account to its beauty—when she says of her party, "we looked through the east oriel . . ." By employing the proscribed term, she announces a willingness to see some things through Scott's eyes, though she knows that he did not know.

The party ended its daylight tour but formed a determination to return at night in order to verify Scott's claim that it must be seen in moonlight. In the interim, serious doubt was raised, by Scots of course, as to whether Scott had ever done so himself. They set out to see it, in spite of the near certainty that Scott had never done so himself. They went so far as to undertake this project "in the dark," despairing of a tardy moon, comforted by the reflection that "Sir Walter would think (it) rather a silly thing." Scott, however, rises to this last challenge to his credibility. His description so "exactly" corresponds to the reality of the place that, at last, she *had* to feel that "Scott must have been here in the night." The question of fact is superseded by the question of right, and a reformed Scott is rendered a suitable part of America's "traditionary lore" (*SM*, IX).

The Stowe trip to Scotland ended with "lofty but sad memories" and "sympathies and inspirations." Hence, only the foundation had been laid for the construction of those memories with a "*coleur de rose.*" Letter IX summarizes, in some respects, what has been achieved by focusing on Quakers and Covenanters—the two prime examples of Scottish reformers in the larger view. In each we view the effect of shifting the free man's chivalric sense from the defense of worldly honor to the defense of "principle." But something is missing. As to the Quakers, she wants something beyond "Doric simplicity"—"a higher development of religion still, when all the beautiful artistic faculties being wholly sanctified and offered up to God, we shall no longer shun beauty in any . . . form . . . as a temptation." So much for the praise of homely matriarchy! The defense of principle must effect its redemptive virtue in this world as well as beyond. The transcendent logic is for the sake of a just regime. Stowe cites the testimony of Christ as authority for this tentative construction:

> There is no man that hath left houses or lands for my sake and the gospel's but he shall receive manifold more *in this life.* (*SM*, IX, 187)

Then she renders the formulation still more radical.[34]

Standing over the graves of Covenanters, she concluded that they died for truth and right. Their errors—such as the defacing of carved images—were as nothing to their defense of a sacred principle that was "vital to their country's existence." As with Scott, are we to learn of the Covenanters and Quakers that it is not their faiths we are tasked to recall, but their characters? To Stowe these were the peculiar qualities of liberty, and the millennium is the efflorescence of these qualities. The struggle of the Covenanters gave birth to a national literature:

> A vigorous and original literature is impossible, except to a strong, free, self-respecting people. The literature of a people must spring from the sense of nationality;[35] and is impossible without self-respect, and self-respect is impossible without liberty. (*SM*, IX, 189)

Covenanters would consider their cause cheapened to find it reduced to the generation of a literature. The heavenly salvation they sought justified itself without respect to the success or failure of human political experiments. Or, their refusal to repeat the simple words, "God save the King," would be ludicrous. And, too, they would not have considered the purpose of their faith the generation of a nationality, though they would happily and readily concede it the basis of a community. They could not concern themselves with nationality because they could not conceive the task of the community to be the binding of the "highest class of mind" to the service of the lower classes.

But as we learned in Letter IV, nationality is more particular to middle and laboring classes. Indeed, it was added there that "the highest class of mind in all countries loses nationality, and becomes universal; it is a great pity, too . . ." (*SM*, IV, 69). At least one reason it must be a great pity stems from the necessity of nationalism to generate a literature, and the presumption that the highest class of mind is the literary mind. It must be bent to its task since it does not approach it willingly.[36] The life of the Quakers and struggles of the Covenanters are seen by Stowe as effecting this result. The free man's chivalric defense of freedom not only protects a democratic liberty, but also preserves the role of aristocracy in the absence of aristocratic forms.

We have posed a difficulty which we can only see resolved when we see the use to which this new memory is placed. The principles of moderation are universal—the recognition that all men have an equal right to justice and the possibility of attaining it. The practical embodiment of those principles is democracy, since the only legitimate alternative risks more than man can rightly be asked to dare. But democratic liberty—the investiture of the laboring and middle classes—is manifested in a nationalism which combats the natural cosmopolitanism of aristocracy. How, then, can the principles of modernity be expected to survive their only practical embodiment?

X. AN ETHICS FOR MODERNITY

The report of the visit to Stratford-on-Avon in Letter X reveals that Shakespeare is all that Scott was not. Stowe visited the home of Shakespeare's birth and from its liveliness divined the inspirations of his writings. She conceived that it must have been from his mother that he derived "those models of lily-like purity, women so chaste and pure in language that they could not even bring their lips to utter a word of shame" (*SM*, X, 202). The age of Elizabeth was an age of grossness and coarseness better served in the "Merry Wives of Windsor," addressed to the taste of the virgin queen, than in the purity of a Desdemona. "In order to appreciate Shakespeare's mind from his plays, we must discriminate what expressed the gross taste of his age, and what he wrote to please himself. . . . The 'Midsummer Night's Dream' he wrote from his own inner dream world." Were the analogy applicable to Stowe's own work, we would say that she created George Harris to satisfy the taste of her age, while Uncle Tom was created to satisfy her dreams. Hence, her adaptation of the melodrama would be akin to the form of esoteric-exoteric writing. We discover in this a principle of discrimination: the assignment of the higher of alternative standards to the man who expressed them both.

That Shakespeare's home should incline Stowe to images of life and beauty or high standards prepares us to discover in Shakespeare a much more accessible source of "Sunny Memories" than in Scott. Even the very picture of death raises the presence of life when we consider Shakespeare. We must quote at length to emphasize the contrast. In the streets of Stratford she saw a funeral train, which led her to reflect.

> That loving heart, that active heart, that subtle, elastic power of appreciating and expressing all phases of humanity, are they breathed out on the wind? . . . or are they still living, still active? and if so, where and how? Is it reserved for us in that "undiscovered country" he spoke of, ever to meet the great souls whose breath has kindled our souls?
>
> I think we forget the consequences of our own belief in immortality, and look on the ranks of prostrate dead as a mower in the fields of prostrate flowers, forgetting that activity is an essential of souls. . . . We speak of the glory of God as exhibited in natural landscape making; what is it; compared with . . . the mak-

ing of souls, *especially those souls which seem to be endowed with a creative power like his own?*

There seems, strictly speaking, to be only two classes of souls—the creative and the receptive. Now, these creators *seem to me* to have a beauty and worth . . . *entirely independent of their moral character.* That ethereal power which shows itself in Greek sculpture and Gothic architecture, in Rubens, Shakespeare, and Mozart, has a quality to me inexpressibly admirable and lovable. *We may say it is true, that there is no moral excellence in it; but none the less do we admire it.* God has made us so that we cannot help loving it; our souls go forth to it with an infinite longing, *nor can that longing be condemned.*

That mystic quality that exists in these souls is a glimpse and intimation of what exists in him in full perfection. *If we remember this* we shall not lose ourselves in admiration of worldly genius, but be led by it to a better understanding of what he is to whom all the glories of poetry and art are but symbols and shadows.[37] (*SM*, X, 222–23; emphasis supplied)

Now, it is true that this thoroughgoing humanism is qualified by the invocation of piety in the end. But that piety is conditional. God is honored not for what he is in himself, but for what we may see of him in man. We cannot forget that it is ambiguous whether the creator of the creative soul is *the* Creator, or he "whose breath has kindled our souls." If the Creator creates both souls indifferently, it is the great-souled man who is at least the efficient cause of the possible attainment of the soul's highest nature. It is further the case that the Creator creates *all* things, but our interest properly is held *only* by the one thing.

The meaning of this is made clear in Letter XI, where Stowe argues that the merely natural "gems and lapis lazuli" hold no interest for her. But the "canvas, made vivid by the soul of an inspired artist," holds her attention *specifically* because God created the soul that created the canvas image. The gem, she avers, interests her only "so far as it is pretty in itself." Hence, the imitation of the work of God may, because of the possibility of imitation, possess a higher status than the work of God in itself. It is for this reason that the creative soul is beautiful, even when it is not morally excellent.

According to this doctrine, morality operates especially on the receptive soul, and the excellence that attaches to it is a specifically mundane excellence. The longing for the transcendent, therefore, is imperious precisely because it longs for a realm beyond morality. This doctrine undermines every notion of a human excellence that is rooted in the habits of virtue. Indeed, on the basis of this doctrine we discover that Scott *did* pursue a moral purpose. We are taught to dislike him for his very morality. His disclaimer was disingenuous—an attempt to emulate what was beyond his powers. Thus, there are two kinds of poets: they who are the purveyors of a regnant morality are one kind; they who can successfully fly before a regnant morality are another. Of this latter, there are again two kinds. They who are beyond morality and show no moral excellence are one kind; they who can exercise their powers in the language of morality are another kind. The invocation of piety at the end of this passage is conditional, but it is not without significance.

One forms no image of Shakespeare dead—only living, active. This is true in spite of the singular disadvantage that he is buried beneath flat stone in the chancel of the village church. And, too, like Scott, he sought to save his name through a family. Thus, having only a daughter survive him, he entailed his estate through her. But she proved unfruitful, and there ended the line. That fate produced a lament for "Poor Walter Scott." For Shakespeare, there is but one rebuke, "Genius must be its own monument." Unlike Scott, of Shakespeare there are virtually no relics left, by which some estimation of his character may be formed.

> The only means left us for forming an opinion of what he was personally are inference of the most delicate kind from the slightest premises. (*SM*, X, 216)

The slender evidence of his will divulged his hope for a continued genealogy. There was also a profession of faith—of things incidental to his life almost the only testimony of his piety. Yet, coupled with evidence "scattered through his plays," it is "probable . . . that, in the latter, thoughtful and tranquil years of his life, devotional impulses might have settled into habits, and that the solemn language of his will . . . was not a mere form." Shakespeare, then, closed his life in piety and was again unlike Scott who closed his life with the humble avowal he aimed at no moral purpose.

We are not permitted to close this portrait of Shakespeare's character without bringing forward from Letter XIX a correction for one of its elements. That letter corrects much that preceded it, but for this particular correction we cannot wait. Of a conversation with Macaulay Stowe reports that he—like all men—saw no characteristic difference in Shakespeare's women. Men, she maintained, will never see the light of that matter—"so long as men are not women." To them, "Miranda, Juliet, Desdemona, and Viola" are all the same.

> As matter too soft a lasting mark to bear, And best distinguished as black, brown, or fair. (*SM*, XIX, 7)

"Mrs. Jameson," in the "Characteristics of Shakespeare's Women," presented the essential arguments for the opposite view, of which Stowe observed,

> A book for which Shakespeare, if he could get it, ought to make her his best bow, especially as there are fine things ascribed to him there, which, I dare say, he never thought of, careless fellow that he was!
>
> But I take it that every true painter, poet, artist is in some sense so far a prophet that his utterances convey more to other minds than he himself knows; so that, doubtless, should all the old masters rise from the dead, they might be *edified* by what posterity has found in their works. (*SM*, XIX, 8)

"Delicate inferences" from the "slightest premises" may fall wide of the mark with regard to the character they are said to portray as it actually existed. But this portrait was intended for Stowe's contemporaries rather than Shakespeare's. That Stowe would so openly avow her purpose as this analysis seems to suggest is but the illusion created by a close reading and exegesis to which "Sunny Memories" cannot be expected generally to be exposed. It may be fairer to note that the final standard by which we judge Shakespeare's character was his moral success.[38] He was loved in his own day, as well as after, forming rather than falling victim to the tastes of subsequent ages.

We do not wish to argue that Stowe considered herself a Shakespeare or even that the salvation of modernity depended on the reappearance of a Shakespeare. That would certainly be a curious argument, that neglected the weighty considerations of political philosophy and especially the humanist labors of the eighteenth century and sought to derive ethical norms from the diverse materials of distant poets. Even exponents of the "Bible as literature" will confess that it gains its moral force from the weight of that legislative tradition founded by Moses. The example of Shakespeare does not contain an ethics for the many. Shakespeare's example is rather to elaborate the ground on which or manner in which such an ethics is to be articulated, consistent with the establishment of genuine civilization. But it is implicit in Stowe's premise that the proper coloring of a tradition will yield a desirable civilization. The requirements of establishing piety or ethical norms are even more universal than the principles of modernity, standing outside history as they do.

XI. DEMOCRATIC ETHICS

In Letter XI Stowe dove to the bottom of her history—the history of those "old war times" which have passed. She returned to the great estates of the past, those "perfect models," to seize the ideas which will be consummated in the "new state of society we are founding in America." Though perfect models, those great estates were as Plato's *Republic*, impractical. But as models they describe the lineaments of the structure that will succeed them. Modern man must worship the ancient heroes, the glorious past in which men were demi-gods, in order to achieve a *new* form of civilization. Thus they achieve practically the theoretical promise held forth in the ancient vision. Oddly enough, that theoretical vision manifested itself in the shape of real, solid forms—aristocratic and chivalrous forms. And the consummation of that vision will be the advance beyond those real, practical forms. The consummation will achieve the rule of aristocracy and chivalry without the appearance or image of that rule.

Letter XI reports the visit to Warwick—the "representative feudal estate." Stowe authenticates its date from four years after the birth of Christ and notes that it is still maintained in elegance by Warwicks. It was spared the hand of Cromwell, which lay waste to Kenilworth, once equally extensive. She suggests no cause for this, but does note that a Warwick led the navy of the Commonwealth. Warwick invokes the memory of war and the dream of peace at once.

> With my head in a kind of historical mist, full of images of York and Lancaster, and red and white roses, and Warwick the king maker, I looked up to the towers and battlements. . . . We went in through a passage way cut in solid rock. . . . These walls were entirely covered with ivy, hanging down like green streamers; gentle and peaceable pennons these are, waving and whispering that the old war times are gone.

The time of peace had come, but it was the wars of Warwick—always for justice—and their legacy that contributed to spawn this era.

The Earls of Warwick always stood near the head of the most stirring movements of the world though eighteen centuries. From the slaying of dragons and mastodon cows, to king making and scholar making, to disinterested support of the Puritan experiment, they were, above all, public men. She recounts their sagas of war and intrigue, bringing them to the edge of American history and the disposition of the "present Earl" to isolate himself from "public or political life." The Warwick sword was sheathed when peace descended. When Stowe became satiated with the things to be seen, she concluded her "exposé" and paused to reflect. First, these feudal estates were beloved by the English and appear, thus, in no danger of going under in the democratic onrush. Second, the complete absence of such an "institution" in America can only give rise to the wonder of what replaces it? The first reflection is, in fact, an affirmation that the danger of Cromwell is past, as we shall see again. The second reflection is, in fact, a question which is answered in Letter XIV. There is reported a drawing-room conversation at Lord Carlisle's estate, in which conversation America's distinguished men are panegyrized—"particularly of Emerson, Longfellow, Hawthorne; also of Prescott." Stowe believed that intelligent foreigners could heighten American appreciation of "our literary men."[39] This was an especial need of Americans

> because we have nothing to glory in—no court, no nobles, no castles, no cathedral; except we produce distinguished specimens of humanity, we are nothing.

To the solid institutions of the past America must add perfected specimens of man worthy, if constitutionally forbidden, to inhabit those temples.

The inculcation of an appreciation of our "literary men" is intended to produce an effect similar to that of the great estates on the Briton. But the worship of men—indeed, the human soul—is calculated to produce a decided advantage for America and, hence, modernity. We will quote at length.

> The influence of these estates on the community cannot but be in many respects beneficial, and should go some way to qualify the prejudice with which republicans are apt to contemplate any thing aristocratic . . . in a very important sense these things belong to the whole community, indeed, to universal humanity. It may be undesirable and unwise to wish to imitate these institutions in America, and yet it may be illiberal to undervalue them as they stand in England . . . antique grace might plead somewhat in its favor, and it may be better to accommodate it to modern uses, than to level it, and erect a modern mansion in its place. Nor, since the world is wide, and now being rapidly united by steam into one country, does the objection to these things, on account of the room they take up, seem so great as formerly. . . . With such reflections the lover of the picturesque may comfort himself, hoping that he is not sinning against the useful in his admiration of the beautiful.

It is necessary to interrupt the flow of this argument by way of anticipating the conclusion. The argument that the feudal estates now take up less space than they once did is spurious or, perhaps, specious is more exact. If indeed steam is uniting the world into one country or empire, it surely increases the possibility that citizens from far-flung regions can transport themselves to preferred residences in a fairer portion of the empire. In that case, while the wide earth shrinks, men become more not less crowded. In another sense, however, the argument is meaningful. We have already identified ancient aristocratic structures as the symbols of true aristocracy. In Aristotle's *Politics* we learn that in some measure the truly great man takes up too much space in the republic. His fellow citizens are constrained either to bow down to him or to ostracize him. But that was a republic which, in the modern view, had to be small because of the limitations of the earth's resources and method of exploiting them. The liberation of the earth's resources for human use made possible the large republic. Now, in the large republic, the man of extraordinary goodness has room in which to live without threatening his fellow citizens. Hence, they may save their republican institutions and still keep him in their midst.

But one limitation is imposed on the man of extraordinary goodness. As suggested at the conclusion of the above passage, he must be willing to consider the love of the beautiful as irrational. What is rational—the standard of utility—is the service of the passions. It is Stowe's hope that even this inconvenience may be eliminated.

> One Great Achievement of the millennium, I trust, will be in uniting these two elements, which have *ever* been contending. There was great significance in the old Greek fable which represented Venus as the divinely-appointed helpmeet of Vulcan [Hephaistos], and yet always quarreling with him.
>
> We can scarce look at the struggling, earth-bound condition of useful labor through the world without joining in the beautiful aspirations of our American poet,—
>
> "Surely, the wiser time shall come
> When this fine overplus of might,
> No longer sullen, slow, and dumb,
> Shall leap to music and to light,
> In that new childhood of the world
> Life of itself shall dance and play.
> Fresh blood through time's shrunk veins be hurled,
> And labor meet delight half way."[40]
>
> In the new state of society which we are trying to found in America, it must be our effort to *hasten* the consummation. These great estates of old countries may keep it for their share of matters to work out perfect models, while we will seize the ideas thus elaborated, and make them the property of the million. (SM, XI)

Stowe, following Bacon, reads the ancient myth divested of its theogony and dedicated to the singular task of relieving man's estate. But, by connecting the ancient myth with Lowell's millennialism, she also calls into question the adequacy of anticipating a perfect synergy between man and the things of nature. Her alteration of "Earth" to "World" and of the passive, "blood in time's veins making mirth," to the forceful and active, "hurling of blood through time's veins," reaffirms man's control of nature and lays the groundwork for his "making history," his "will to power."[41]

Bacon's conquest of nature in Stowe's hands becomes, however, the conquest of human nature. When Stowe argues that the useful and the beautiful have "ever" been contending, she supplants the traditional understanding with a new version. Traditionally, passion and reason contended for rule of the human soul. The attainment of excellence was conditioned on the submission of passion not to say spiritedness to the dictate of reason. This formula was the formula of rationality. Bacon's rationality upset that formula and reduced reason to the calculative faculty.[42] Stowe, therefore, takes rationality already formed as the calculated pursuit of the goals of passions. But, where Bacon had resolved the tension between reason and passion by reducing reason to passion, Stowe resurrects that tension in the name of the objects of passion and reason traditionally understood; viz, the necessaries of life (pleasant or useful things) and the excellent or beautiful things. But she does not resurrect the rational as the excellent or the irrational as merely the comfortable preservation of life. This is surely a result of the awareness of a connection between the necessaries of life and the excellent things. But this cannot explain why she apparently accepts the hierarchical reversal. It is crucial to raise this question because we must know if Stowe—an artist—intends ultimately to reduce political philosophy to a mere aestheticism.

The inheritance with which Stowe struggled is the enlightenment as much as it is Puritan millennialism. Indeed, the universal principles of modern politics are Enlightenment principles, if also Christian. The earthly salvation those principles presaged was conditioned on a successful popularization of philosophy or science, to put it crudely. Ultimately, it was thought that morality itself could be done away, as rational self-interest would answer to every requirement of human intercourse. But we see from the "American poet" that the many are "sullen, slow, and dumb." What they require is not the wisdom of age but a "new childhood." In keeping with the millennial expectation of a regeneration of mankind, the call is not so much for a wiser man as for a new man—a man of new piety. Thus, in spite of the similar appearance of historicism, that nineteenth-century child of the enlightenment, to millennialism, they are fundamentally opposed. To the historicist it does not matter what men believe, and all accounts of differences that remain after interest has been served will be traced to belief. Lowell's millennialism prophesies the complete effacing of difference. But, for Stowe, the effort in America seeks specifically to generate new principles and those of such a nature as to accommodate the differences in men. If the new piety must accommodate differences—at least until the disadvantage of number is removed for the lover of the beautiful—it must be also possible for the lover of the useful to sin against the beautiful. This is suggested in the "illiberal" undervaluing of aristocratic institutions, and morally indifferent democracy comes to resemble nothing so strongly as it resembles intolerant protestantism. This tenet separates Stowe from the Enlightenment as well as from Lowell's millennialism.

We may see in this a conscious attempt to free America—hence, the world—from the eighteenth-century enlightenment and from historicism. Or, it may be thought the re-incarnation of New England Federalism's railing against Jeffersonian republicanism. The attempt, in itself, however, both transcends the eighteenth century—by re-reading prior history, "Sunny Memories" of noble efforts—and exceeds the optimism of that century by creating a hope for *earthly* salvation which is not merely grounded in the useful—hence, rationalistic. If the revolution of the eighteenth century was on behalf of reason, but launched the regime which takes the useful as ultimate, the standards of reason have been corrupted and the rational must be considered that which satisfies the passions, simply. To the extent that is true, the sublimely beautiful (nay, wisdom itself)—satisfying no passion, simply—must emerge from the sphere of the irrational or miraculous. The things of nature, understood in this light, are indeed unrelated to the divine things. Yet, it is the same human soul that communes with the things of nature and things divine. Thus, this division of the objects of human affection into useful and beautiful corresponds to the division of kinds of soul into receptive and active. That raises the question whether the two kinds of soul can exist in any one individual, or whether for each individual only one is possible, and, if the latter, how the millennium will resolve the tension between the men superior and inferior, especially if the inferior are the rational who control the useful and productive forces, and the superior are the irrational who control only themselves.[43]

Stowe anticipated the reader's suspicion that the tales of the sagas of Guy of Warwick and the reflections to which they gave rise might be "a sheer fabrication, or, to use a convenient modern term, a myth," at page 241 of Letter XI. Her response is that his "identical armor," along with pots, fork, and a sword—all of enormous size—still hang there. Those ancient heroes, like the first men Socrates cites in the *Laws*, were of a stature that would astound the ingénue or newcomer. Their deeds were of the same stature. ". . . there is a rib of the mastodon cow which he killed, hung up for the terror of all refractory beasts of that name in modern days." There are also "authentic documents" dating the family from four years after the birth of Christ[44] and revealing their exploits and enchantments. A "scarce book" by "Dr. John Kay, or Caius," written in 1522, described the "rare and peculiar animals that roamed those grounds when England was full of woods and forests." And, lastly, the chronicler of Sir Guy adds that, after much labor to win his wife, Sir Guy left her "to spend the other part of his life for God's sake, and so departed from his lady in Pilgrim weeds . . ." The story of Sir Guy is the story of a pre-Christian ascetic or martyr—a soldier before the cross. If the documentary and testamentary evidence fails to persuade us to the myth, there remain but the exertions of latter day soldiers of the cross wielding the identical pre-Christian armor.

Cromwell was a candidate for that office, but an inappropriate candidate. The Christian Republic will not be erected until its friends are reclaimed. The ruin that Cromwell made of old castles is but a sign of the ruin and "desolation" that is yet in man. We need call upon the myth of Sir Guy only when we have commenced the restoration of these ruins. The ruined columns of Kenilworth are now supported by the ivy which, itself, was supported by the walls of Kenilworth. There is, perhaps, some ivy which can be planted about the human soul to hold it up until the time comes to celebrate its freedom. With this Stowe closes her new history and concludes, "Thus much of old castles and ivy." Now, it is important to note that, everywhere in Scotland, as in England, Stowe found ivy carrying on the traditions of forgotten heroes, though her architectural authority, in Scotland, completing and publishing an account of his journey just before her arrival, could find ivy practically nowhere due to the depredations of an insatiable modernity. It is fair to say, then, that "Sunny Memories" are wrapped in ivy that supports a tradition which would otherwise go unseen.

XII. DEMOCRATIC MAGNANIMITY

The last fact to be established in this new history is the necessity for the American Puritan to prefer Charles I to Cromwell. This indirectly reveals the status of Stowe's history in her political philosophy, by emphasizing the nature of Warwick justice. The Puritan's debt to Cromwell is less compelling than his debt to the Warwick, Robert Grenville, a high Episcopalian who supported the Puritan colony. The standard of disinterestedness in Grenville's action—moved by a "chivalric sense of justice"—transcends the requirements of faith. But disinterestedness has been the peculiar property of aristocracy rather than republicanism.[45] The preference of Charles I to Cromwell does not carry over to the other Warwick who defended Cromwell, and who more nearly resembles the successor Warwick among that company of lords that restored Charles I's successor.

As Charles I is preferable to Cromwell, both Warwicks are preferable to Charles I. We begin to fathom this Warwick sense of justice, which triumphs through eighteen centuries of political warfare. Its tolerance for diverse faiths ensures a steady line of supplicants and a steady line of Warwicks. Its disinterestedness or openness is the one kind of self-regard that requires a freedom from concern with mere self-interest or the requirements of a regnant morality. That Puritans should owe a greater debt to British aristocracy than to Puritan republicanism establishes the incapacity of moral enthusiasm and demonstrates the necessity of the disinterested defense of universal principle at the same time as it undermines the foundation, exclusivity, of moral enthusiasm. We are compelled to believe not the myth of Sir Guy's faith, but that he could not voluntarily refuse the consummation of that passion for which he had so long labored. It is similarly a political requirement that the abolition of slavery be seen as the conscious rejection of a powerful passion, if the regime is to be understood as properly grounded on principle as opposed to interest. We may urge that without his religious faith Sir Guy had no *cause* to forego the indulgence of his passion; that it were irrational and certainly not undertaken for the fun of it. Stowe cannot respond to this objection. The admiration of greatness evokes its own defense.

Liberal history is designed to give to the regime based on moral enthusiasm a memory that can give the institutions of that regime a hallowed tradition. Its purpose, therefore, is practical rather than theoretical. Liberal history defends rather than establishes the principles of the regime based on natural rights. It were more exact to say that it provides *a* mode of defense. That this mode is preferable to alternatives can only be established by the kind of argument that will reveal the ends of the regime and their consistency with the mode preferred.

At the center of liberal history is the double requirement that the modern regime relieve man's estate *and* secure the pre-eminence of the excellent. This is a goal, it may safely be said, that was never seriously thought possible by any weightier thinker. When modernity abandoned the ancient preference for the regime of virtue, it considered the ancient world too sanguine in the expectation that large numbers of men must always live in a relative state of privation. But modernity—at least its better thinkers—understood that the elimination of privation as a condition of human life required that man *qua* man forego the worship of human excellence. The general elevation of the race was thought adequate recompense for any specific decline that might occur. And certain individuals—though bereft of the concerns of the ancients (dare we say liberated?)—might still pursue that elusive goal of divine excellence. The thought that *all* men might actually achieve the specific elevation available to the best of men was always consigned to the realm of the visionary and the utopian. Though the contemporary world has come more and more to be dominated by utopians, the founders of modernity never expected even so much as the simultaneous material elevation of the many in the presence of the encouragement and attainment of excellence of the few. In one sense, Stowe's vision of liberal history is thought utopian by the very utopians themselves: They settled on the belief that total elevation was required as a result of their belief that justice was impossible in the presence of serious differences between the few and the many.

At the center of the defense of moral enthusiasm was the requirement that the wills of the best of men—*qua* best—be bent to the purposes of the modern regime. At the center of liberal history is the requirement that the best of men—*qua* best—be independent of the regnant morality. We are reminded of Plato's dictum that philosophers be forced to be kings. That was considered impossible, until modernity upset the meaning of reason and philosophy, and philosophers were found eager to be kings. But how much more impossible again, when philosophers must be forced to be kings under the condition that they be irrational—genuinely philosophical? Just this or something like it is proposed by Stowe as the necessary politics of the modern regime. And it is given the color of possibility only by the fact that, in a democracy (where opinion rules), every man is king. Since, that is, no one denies that a philosopher must be a citizen in some city, a philosopher can be forced to rule wherever citizenship in the best case is made dependent on ruling. Socrates, the "best citizen of Athens," avoids this trap only by abandoning such a city or abandoning philosophy. That he knows he knows nothing not only cannot excuse him; it is his best recommendation. Now, the good ruler and good citizen are of necessity identical, and we need only wonder whether the good man and the good ruler are identical. What? If every man is king, then every man rules—eligibility for rule becomes identical to eligibility for citizenship, which is little more than being born. How can you admit, in that case, a distinction between good rulers and bad rulers without also distinguishing good and bad citizens? Are men to be distinguished in their humanity as good or bad, and extended or denied citizenship on that basis? What? Is the polity to be a union only for the good? Is it not, itself, the condition and inculcator of goodness? If the polity is not the condition of good, then what is?

NOTES

1. Called "the Liberator," O'Connell was an Irish reformer of the early to mid-nineteenth-century era. He espoused Catholic Emancipation and led the Irish separatist forces.
2. *Politics*, Book I.
3. Alexander Hamilton, et al., *The Federalist Papers*, #51. "If men were angels . . ."
4. See book, part I, chapter 25 for a parallel to this "Niagara" experience.
5. This perspective is subsequently made entirely clear in the lengthy critique of modern utilitarianism as a foundation for free government that runs throughout the novel *Dred*.
6. Beecher and Stowe, *The American Woman's Home*.
7. See book I, part I, chapter 8, and note 67.
8. She had been prepared to meet this robustness by the claims of Lord Carlisle (The Right Honorable The Earl of Carlisle [Lord Morpeth]). George William Frederick Howard Carlisle, Earl of, *Travels in America* (New York: G. P. Putnam, 1851; hereafter cited as *Travels in America*). Stowe cites this work in "Sunny Memories" as the only *sensitive* account of America by a foreigner.
9. The former French President, Charles DeGaulle, at least, could not dare to think this true. Cf. Andre Malraux, *Les Chenes Qu'on Abat* (Paris: Gallimard, 1971). Sir Robert Walpole's triumph over the accusations of personal corruption to which his political zeal exposed him demonstrated that the celebration of his fall was premature. The insignificant ones who claimed his destruction could startle themselves upon his arising from the ashes and returning to power ever more grandly, to fall, finally, only three decades later. The injustice of his first, temporary fall is measured

by the same standard according to which his last fall—the fall of "Robinocracy"—is just. The rhymer fails, therefore, to show the justice of Cock Robin's death, as childhood remembrance and folkloric emendation suggest when we recite, in answer to the theme, "I, said the sparrow, with my *little* bow and arrow." The addition of the diminutive in application to the weapon reflects also upon him who wields the weapon. Surely, the great ones are never justly felled by the petty carping of the insignificant ones. Walpole, in the period leading to his 1742 defeat, had incurred the royal wrath. To show fully the justice of his fall, the rhymer must indicate this presence.

10. William S. and Cecil Baring-Gould, *The Annotated Mother Goose* (New York: Branhall House, 1962), p. 36, note 50.

11. Cf. Cotugno, who detects something of Stowe's intention here, when she says that Stowe and the several other nineteenth-century women writers who are the subjects of her dissertation were attempting both to form and reform national identity during what they perceived to be a period of tremendous upheaval." Cotugno, "Form and Reform," p. 2.

12. Cf. Winston Churchill, *Thoughts and Adventures* as cited in Jaffa, *Crisis of the House Divided*, pp. 45–46.

13. Scholarly speculation on whether Stowe remained a Puritan arrives at differing judgments. For example, whereas Hartshorne concludes that "Stowe's later novels all affirm the ideals and optimism of the early Puritans . . . ," Strout holds that "Mrs. Stowe was no Calvinist. . . . [*Uncle Tom's Cabin*] was in large part a protest against the Calvinist doctrine of human inability to merit salvation." Hartshorne, "'Without Divine Intervention,'" p. 54. Strout, "*UTC* and the Portent of the Millenium," pp. 379–80. Tang astutely recognizes that for Stowe "throughout history, Puritan temperament supplied the moral certainty and stability that a society required for moderate reform rather than drastic upheavals." Edward Tang, "Revolutionary Legacies: History, Literature and Memory in Nineteenth-Century America" (Ph.D. diss., New York University, 1996), p. 236 hereafter cited as "Revolutionary Legacies"). Cox asserts that in *Uncle Tom's Cabin* and *Dred*, Stowe had "transformed the spirit of Calvinism into secular melodrama," but that in her later New England novels "what had been Puritanism converted into melodrama suddenly becomes Puritanism converted into history." James M. Cox, "Harriet Beecher Stowe: From Sectionalism to Regionalism," *Nineteenth Century Fiction* 38, no. 4 (1984): 463, 464. An insightful account of the "complexity and ambivalence of Harriet's attitude toward 'Calvinistic Puritanism' . . . " is found in Caskey. Caskey, *Chariots of Fire*. Kimball also provides an in-depth account of Stowe's attitude toward Puritanism, emphasizing its complexity and highlighting Calvinism's strong influence on Stowe even while concluding that ultimately Stowe turned away from it. Kimball, "HBS's Revision of New England Theology." May likewise captures the complexity of Stowe's intellectual and emotional involvement with Calvinism: "In her mature life Harriet Beecher was to see clearly . . . that Edwardsian Calvinism . . . drove the majority into religious indifference, the most courageous minority into active hostility, and the most sensitive minority into hell on earth. Yet she was far too close to her father and his religion, and too deeply convinced about the faithfulness of Calvinist pessimism to actual life, to abandon the inherited doctrine soon, easily, or ever completely." May, "Introduction," p. 20. Likewise, Buell's assessment is on the mark: "For Stowe,

'Puritanism' means, finally, a delicate, complicated, precisely articulated, constraining yet also nourishing and protective social/religious order which is the direct precursor of our more enlightened yet also more diminished one." Lawrence Buell, "Rival Romantic Interpretations of New England Puritanism: Hawthorne Versus Stowe," *Texas Studies in Literature and Languages* 25, no. 1 (1983): 94.

14. Cf. Charles Edward Stowe, *Life of Harriet Beecher Stowe*, especially pp. 216, 223–24, and compared with "Sunny Memories," pp. 77 and 247–57 respectively. To take but one example: The earliest point at which the Glasgow tea party could have been held, according to the letters, was Friday the fifteenth of April (the actual date). Stowe was in ill health, but roused herself for the tea party—a mammoth affair of two-thousand people. The next day, she spent most of the day touring Bothwell Castle and attending a big abolition rally in the evening. That day would have been Saturday, but describing the day on which she goes sailing on the Clyde, she refers to the following day as Sunday and says that she unfortunately remained in bed all that day because of poor health. She had much wanted to hear a sermon. That would mean she sailed the Clyde and toured the countryside during the very same time she toured Bothwell Castle and its environs! Little wonder she was ill!

15. This accounts for the curious adaptation of Edmund Burke, the great "conservative," to the role of "lead crusader." See book, part I, chapter 25.

16. Cf. her "Introduction" to *Charlotte Elizabeth*, as discussed in book I, part II, chapter 4. Stowe commented often on the novel as an agent of moral education. See also, as examples, her preface to *Library of Famous Fiction* ("Now this possession by human beings of this glorious faculty of living an unreal life, and seeing things invisible, is a sufficient answer to those who doubt the uses of fiction. This splendid capability certainly was meant for something. It is a precious gift, and one worth accepting.")Harriet Beecher Stowe, preface and introduction to *A Library of Famous Fiction, Embracing the Nine Standard Masterpieces of Imaginative Literature* (New York: J. B. Ford & Company, 1873), p. viii. See also her article on "Anti-Slavery Literature" ("The use of the novel in the great questions of moral life is coming to be one of the features of the age. Formerly, the only object of fictitious writing was to amuse. Now nothing is more common that to hear the inquiry of a work of fiction, 'What is it intended to show or prove?' A novel is now understood to be a parable—a story told in illustration of a truth of fact." Harriet Beecher Stowe, "Anti-Slavery Literature," *The Independent* (February 21, 1856).

17. Several Stowe scholars have commented on Stowe's belief in the educating potential of the novel as a genre. Henry, for example, cites the passages in *Dred* in which the reading of novels is discussed as an instance in which Stowe "emphasized explicitly" "the pedagogical power of fictional texts." Henry, "Originating Fictions," p. 115. Cotugno likewise cites these passages as evidence that "Stowe echoes Harriet Martineau's assertion that fiction is by far the most effective way to convey historical and moral lessons for women and men alike." Cotugno, "Form and Reform," p. 184. Berghorn suggests that Stowe used the novel as a means to activate emotion in the reader so that "the skeptical intellect can be . . . suspended." Berghorn, "'The Mother's Struggle,'" p. xvii. Camfield locates a possible source for Stowe's thinking on this matter in Hugh Blair's *Letters on Rhetoric and Belles Lettres* (1783), which Stowe reports in an 1863 autobiographical sketch as having read. He points out that "Blair . . . strenuously advocated the value of novels as teachers of the young" and

that he felt that "the use of fiction to develop taste in the young could help promote morality." Camfield, "Moral Aesthetics," p. 330. Smith, however, claims more than seems reasonable given Stowe's unshakable (if often tested) religious beliefs when she says that Stowe asked "whether art, in place of a conflicted Bible of waning authority, might become that ideal text which could unite America's readers across lines of creed, race, and gender." Smith, "The Sentimental Novel," p. 237. Marotta likewise attributes to Stowe an heresy that seems improbable when he says that Stowe, along with George Eliot, offers readers "not the eternal consolations of religion, but the temporary consolations of art" and that "the replacement of Providence by the author's providence—an acknowledged replacement, not a sleight-of-hand—also suggest the identity of the two providences." Kenny Ralph Marotta, "The Literary Relationship of George Eliot and Harriet Beecher Stowe" (Ph.D. diss., Johns Hopkins University, 1974), p. 165; (hereafter cited as "The Literary Relationship of George Eliot and HBS").

18. I am indebted, in the following section, to two ex-Scots for assistance in translating and interpreting this remarkable letter: Dr. Frances McFarlane of the Université de Rouen, Faculté des Letters et Sciences Humaines; the late Dr. John B. Rae, Emeritus Professor of History, Harvey Mudd College. I have written responses from each, discussing the possible authenticity of the letter. It is most notable that Charles Beecher, who read and answered the bulk of Stowe's correspondence during the journey, makes no mention of an "Old Scotch Bachelor," nor of such a letter.

19. Dr. Rae, letter of July 17, 1975.

20. Dr. McFarlane, letter of September 8, 1975. On the subject of the availability of the *Key*, Lewis Tappan, correspondent to the British and Foreign Anti-Slavery Society, still notes in the April 1, 1853 *Reporter*, that the "'Key,' of which I spoke in my last, will be published this month . . ." This is reprinted in Abel and Klingberg, *A Side-Light on Anglo-American Relaitons*, p. 319.

21. Cf. Newman: " . . . Stowe's strategy was not focused upon the *contrast* between the slave and the wage labourer, but upon the strikingly close *parallels* between the slave and the Highlander." Newman, "Stowe's Sunny Memories," p. 31.

22. Calvin E. Stowe, *Report on Elementary Public Instruction in Europe, Made to the Thirty-Sixth General Assembly of the State of Ohio* (Harrisburg: Packer, Barrett and Parke, 1838).

23. See book I, part I, especially chapter 11.

24. Though she does not explore the philosophical underpinning of such regime change, Cotugno does recognize Stowe's concern with a new place for the working class in liberal democracy: "If the abstract notion of the 'citizen' was to be extended beyond the white, male, and in Britain, upper-class person, then writers were going to have to embody the disenfranchised in their texts . . . " Cotugno, "Form and Reform," p. 209.

25. Stowe's ideas on the correlation between the cleanliness and order of the home and the spiritual condition of the homes occupants are elaborated in *The American Woman's Home* and in *Household Papers and Stories*, as well as elsewhere in her writing. Harriet Beecher Stowe, *Household Papers and Stories* (Boston: Houghton, Mifflin and Co., 1896; reprint, New York: AMS Press Inc., 1967; (hereafter cited as *Household Papers and Stories*). Citations refer to AMS Press edition. Further, this aspect of her thought has attracted attention in recent Stowe scholarship. Weinstein,

for example, states that "the governing philosophy in these works is that a properly ordered home environment can influence others as well as if not better than a well ordered sermon." Weinstein, "Educating Sympathy," pp. 19–20. Sachs finds that to Stowe, "keeping a home may be premised upon the literal sphere of the house, but from here the process also expands to incorporate progressively larger and loftier realms; and finally, it swells to assimilate eternity." Sachs, "Describing a Sphere," p. 1.

26. "There is . . . that wreathed involution of smiles and tears, of solemn earnestness and quaint conceits; those sudden uprushings of grand and magnificent sentiments, like the flame-pointed arches of cathedrals; those ranges of fancy, half goblin, half human; those complications of dizzy magnificence with fairy lightness; those streamings of many-colored light; those carvings wherein every natural object is faithfully reproduced, yet combined into a kind of enchantment: the union of all these is in Shakespeare. . . . Milton had one glorious phase of humanity in its perfection; Shakespeare had all united; from the 'deep and dreadful' sub-bass of the organ to the most aerial warbling of its highest key, not a stop or pipe was wanting." *SM*, Letter X, 207.

27. In the essay, "Advantages and Defects," Calvin cites *Sartor Resartus, on Heroes, Hero-Worship, and the Heroic in History.*

28. Walter Scott. "Lay of the Last Minstrel," Canto vi, xi.

29. As Martineau elaborates in her essay. Harriet Martineau, "Achievements of the Genius of Scott," in *Miscellanies by Harriet Martineau* (Boston: Hilliard, Gray & Co., 1836).

30. A finely preserved copy of Robert William Billings's *The Baronial and Ecclesiastical Antiquities of Scotland* (Edinburgh and London, 1848–1852) is available at the Henry Huntington Library.

31. Or, as Montesquieu might say, it is easier for one to do good than it is to do it well. Charles de Montesquieu, *De L'*Esprit des Lois, ed. R. DeRathé (Paris: Garnier, 1973), Bk. XXVIII, ch. 41.

32. Stowe elaborated a plan for effective domestic service in her later years, in *Household Papers and Stories.*

33. "Another feature of the more legitimate types of Gothic, which may be found in a very interesting form at Melrose, is wanting at Rosslyn. This is the cryptic decoration—the carrying out of the plan of ornamentation as well where it is unseen as where the effect is conspicuous; a system deemed to embody the architect's silent homage to him to whom the temple was reared." Billings, op. cit., "Rosslyn Chapel."

34. Indeed, we shall do more, as she attests in Letter XI. Men, in the end, will forcibly submit themselves to beauty. See the discussion of "Beaver Brook" below and note 40.

35. Sawaya suggests that in *Old Town Folks* Stowe works to forge a renewed sense of national identity for Americans; he says she "combines contemporary ideas about domesticity with ideas about education in order to create a stable basis for a homogenous national identity." Sawaya, "The Home Front," p. 12. Henry focuses on Stowe's use of fiction to shape national identity: "What is striking is Stowe's self-consciousness about how accounts of cultural origins belong as much to the discourse of romance and fiction as to the discourse of objective fact and history, and how these accounts of 'our' origins . . . are no less powerful for being, in some sense, fictional." Henry,

"Originating Fictions," p. 109. Writing specifically about "Sunny Memories," Henry asserts that "Stowe's need to interpret American history as continuous with what was most admirable to her about English history meant that she worked out for herself a coherent historical narrative, at times in the face of empirical evidence of working conditions in England. This act of will on her part parallels her own stated beliefs about the dictates of artistic and narrative coherence over the available empirical data." Ibid., p. 122. Cotugno also sees in "Sunny Memories" an attempt to "form and reform national identity." Cotugno, "Form and Reform," p. 2.

36. Edmund Wilson's *Patriotic Gore* was ironically on the mark, even in its erroneous reading of *Uncle Tom's Cabin.* Edmund Wilson, *Patriotic Gore.*

37. Thus does Stowe herself defend against the heresy in Marotta's charge that she sets up works of fiction, including her own, as creations that rival God's creation.

38. Unlike the fate Stowe predicted for Dickens, whom she faulted for his insufficiency as a "moral writer." ("We think, however, that the time of Dickens' popularity . . . is drawing towards its close . . . ") Harriet Beecher Stowe, "Literary Epidemics (Part 2)," *New-York Evangelist* (July 13, 1843).

39. See book I, part II, chapter 16.

40. James Russell Lowell, "Beaver Brook." Stowe *corrects* Lowell in order to emphasize man—"world" instead of "Earth"—and his power—blood "hurled" through time's constricted veins; i.e., finite time or history. The original read:

> In that new childhood of the *Earth*
>
> — — —
>
> Fresh blood *in* Time's shrunk veins *make mirth.*

Compare this with Letter XXXIII in which Stowe muses about future human power over nature.

41. Francis Bacon, *The Wisdom of the Ancients.* But, note that Hephaistos was cast from heaven for interfering in his parents' quarrels.

42. For a good account of this subject, see Howard B. White, *Peace among the Willows* (The Hague: Martinus Nijhoff, 1968).

43. Compare the metaphysics of Uncle Tom at book I, part I, chapter 13. Also, see part II, chapter 18.

44. Actually, the year of the birth of Christ, if modern criticism (already attained by Stowe's era) is to be accepted.

45. Note Stowe's attribution to the slaves in her "preface" to *Colored Patriots* of not just disinterestedness but magnanimity. "In considering the services of the Colored Patriots of the Revolution, we are to reflect upon them as far more magnanimous, because rendered to a nation which did not acknowledge them as citizens and equals, and in whose interests and prosperity they had less at stake. It was not for their own land they fought, not even for a land which had adopted them, but for a land which had enslaved them, and whose laws, even in freedom, oftener oppressed than protected." Stowe, introduction to *The Colored Patriots,* p. 5.

23

The Practical Politics of the Matter

Since "Sunny Memories" is a practical work and not a theoretical work, we can understand the principles of its political philosophy only from the form of its politics. For this we must consider the political objective, the abolition of slavery, both as it is articulated and as it is pursued in Stowe's campaign. While the history was completed just before the campaign entered the London season and the earnest work of reform, we must not forget that the campaign had been underway throughout all the passages that we have considered already. Stowe's view of the wished for nature of democratic politics is most fully displayed in her account of her own political activities.

The campaign is divided into two phases. The Scottish phase emphasized the role of "workingmen." The London phase emphasized the role of the "aristocracy." That tension is not odd since Stowe's mission required her to speak to both sides. If, as a contemporary critic exclaimed, *Uncle Tom's Cabin* was the *Iliad* of the blacks, then "Sunny Memories" is surely the *Odyssey* of their avenger. The *Edinburgh Review* considered *Uncle Tom's Cabin* to have repealed the Fugitive Slave Law.[1] It at least cultivated a widespread sentiment, which made the compromise of 1850 impracticable. That the novel had such a practical effect may be undeniable at the same time we discover that no manifest practical political guidance can be gleaned from its pages. It is surely some such reason as this that makes an elaborate analysis of the novel itself necessary. Through the analysis we achieve a clear understanding of the political practices that would be consistent with decent opinion. In that sense, Stowe's progress through Scotland and England presents a tangible example of what was to be wished in America. And the emphasis on "working men" on the one hand and "aristocrats" on the other hand demonstrates the nature of that alliance which must be pursued and maintained if decent opinion is to reign.

Stowe actually opened the campaign on British soil, landing at the seat of the English anti-slavery campaign, Liverpool.[2] She made use of the enthusiastic crowds which greeted her, and the whirl of anti-slavery meetings, to lay the framework of the two phases of her campaign. That framework consisted chiefly in the discovery of a broad common ground between English and American reformers, who indulged moderate criticism of the American sin while also recalling the English original sin. English paternity of American slavery was considered as placing a heavy responsibility on England to work a moral influence toward abolition. In short Stowe cleared herself of any charge of rabble-rousing. Even if she were to take some action in this circumstance, it could seem to be no more than the circumstances permit and demand.

The implicit English claim of superiority complicates this sanguine view of her campaign project, inasmuch as it heralds an English magnanimity that is hoisted at (or, flown over?) every public representation. The response to this phenomenon was to be different from the provisional public response offered by Calvin. At this point the first notable difference between the public and the private records arose. According to Stowe's report, on the evening of the first day, Professor Stowe was called upon to speak. "Among other things," he questioned the free world's support of slavery through cotton purchases. In fact, he went so far as to name Great Britain's cotton trade as "the great essential item which supports slavery." Calvin's report made no mention of this portion of his speech—no mention of the attempt to provoke or shame the British. But in reporting the Exeter Hall speech Calvin did claim to have made his proposal at Liverpool. Calvin and Harriet thus agree that the private account is the true account of that speech. It was suppressed in the public version to emphasize the moderation of the Stowes' political endeavor and to show them responding to British opinion rather than seeking to formulate it.

Again, the public account contained a note from Stowe, in which she disclaimed responsibility for British anti-slavery opinion and sought to discover a cosmopolitan basis for attachment to it. But the private account suppressed all mention of this endeavor. Thus, the appeal to cosmopolitanism is called into question in the private account—at least the kind of cosmopolitanism invoked in her note. The challenge to British superiority is reserved as private—"Sunny Memories" is for American eyes—while the appeal to cosmopolitanism is entirely public. This clarifies the nature of Stowe's political enterprise in its commencement. American superiority—exclusive or parochial superiority—is from the beginning the ground of the critique of slavery and injustice.

Stowe's influence in drawing contending sects of do-gooders together around "the great humanities of the present day" constitutes *the* example of this perspective. At the end of the tour, in London, she met Mrs. Chisolm again and without reference to her Catholicism. She reported to her father, concerning the various sects and social movements, that she "thinks it has been my peculiar lot to see the exhibition of more piety and loveliness of spirit in the differing sects and ranks in England than they can see in each other." The English, however, need not so much to see the ground of toleration as love its defender, America. The two phases of Stowe's campaign aimed at demonstrating this point across a broad range of issues.

What was accomplished during the Scottish phase of the campaign? Above all Stowe drew out the significance of differences of social rank in movements of modern humanitarianism. She did not hesitate to affirm the advantages of the new world over the old, and she suggested that the advantage consists, in large measure, in the shift of power to workingmen. Scotland impressed her much as Liverpool had. If anything, the color of health was "intensified" in the Scottish children she met in Glasgow. She was in as much demand, if not more, by friendly followers. In the first day she received deputations from far-flung places—Paisley, Greenock, Dundee, Aberdeen, Edinburgh, and Belfast—and "invitations of all descriptions to go everywhere, and to see everything, and to stay in so many places." She complained of too little time to award a grateful thought to the myriad impressions, as her campaign produced its desired but lamentable result. She was not bored, but "it . . . oppressed me with an unutterable sadness."

Stowe was doubtless saddened by the reflection that all the excitement was brought about by a sense of the desperation in the American situation. Nonetheless, almost the first fact she noticed about Glasgow was the disappearance of the apple orchards that were once its renown. It seemed that "the introduction of the American apple" and "its superior excellence" had undermined the marketability of Scottish apples. Stowe leaves it to her reader to draw the general application from this particular fact. But the very next subject is a soiree among workingmen, the very class she wished to see. And that at least raised the possibility of a contrast between the American and British working classes as a key to American superiority—whether it is a superiority of nature or of laws. It also disclosed, more tangibly, the effect of the "workers' paradise" on the old world. Macaulay's reflections during the Reform Bill debate of 1832, that America could withstand universal suffrage because of the elevation of her laboring class, would seem ironic if the success of America's workingmen were always to undermine the profitability of labor in Britain.

From this point until the party left Scotland for Birmingham, the public meetings and private discussions were dominated by notice of the "workingmen" or "common people." While the nature of moral enthusiasm and construction of a liberal history clearly establish the upper current of "Sunny Memories," this under current is just as clearly the dominant theme of the campaign. Indeed, even slavery receded into the mists, frequently becoming but a reflection on the conditions of labor in general. The existence of slavery in America, therefore, served primarily to qualify the superiority of the conditions of American labor and to point toward a reconciliation wherein British labor could attain the elevation of American labor and American labor could be liberated from the drag of slavery in a single cosmopolitan leap.

At Edinburgh, Stowe paused to look ahead to the class that wanted to see her. She received at Edinburgh invitations from the Duchess of Sutherland and the Earl of Carlisle and from Mr. Binney and Mr. Sherman (Congregational clergy) for London visits.[3] Surely, if anything independent of her reflections could qualify her suggestions as to the relationship between British and American labor, it would be the relationship between British labor and British aristocracy. And that, she was mindful, had no particular analogue in America. The reader is reminded, therefore, that until occasion is presented to reconcile this difference, one can only form a vague and indifferent idea of the practical application of Stowe's principles. As far, at least, as British labor is concerned, Stowe's teaching is useless until it touches British aristocracy.

The chronological order of Stowe's reports seems constrained to the development of the themes of the book.[4] Stowe considered the plight of the working class the central theme of discussions of modernity. Because of the centrality of this theme, it was necessary to correct the picture of English superiority by focusing on Scottish workers. This establishes American superiority in the decisive case. But America still wants perfection. It was necessary, therefore, to argue that the barriers to perfection in America and England differ. In England, the presence of an aristocracy is connected with the want of perfection. But it is unclear whether aristocracy is in itself bad. Thus, it remains to be shown whether England may enlist in modern progress and whether the want of aristocracy in America is connected with the want of perfection.

British aristocracy was exonerated of the charge of heartlessness. Moreover, Stowe revealed the ability of the aristocracy to impart its distinctive virtue to the democracy. To emphasize her solicitousness for workers, Stowe shows a studied indifference to the heated nature of the Edinburgh rally—report was, an American flag was burned! She ignored Calvin's complex account of moral and political responsibility and his characterization of the evils of the temptations of commerce. And she ignored her own note—the second of the tour—which was read at the rally. All of these things and the tenor of the succeeding meetings in Scotland placed American slaves and Scottish superiority at the center. Calvin's attack displayed one mode of reversing this, a public mode. The private letters show another and more conservative approach.

Insofar as the "principle of slavery" describes, in 1853, an essentially American phenomenon, then all Stowe's statements on the workers' plight were rooted in an appraisal of the American condition. And the fact that, in the Edinburgh statement, the *new* power of the workers will supplant "the old power of helmet and sword," means that the aristocracy that has been overthrown was not the source of the evil (slavery) that remained to be removed. Such ills as the English poor may suffer cannot, then, be ascribed to aristocracy itself, and the campaign's appeal to the democracy is largely an appeal for self-restraint. If it is true that Stowe "let slip the dogs of war," it is not true that she did so mindlessly. Clearly, one of the things that Stowe finds wanting to American perfection is some form of principle that will generate the kinds of attachments that characterize aristocracies.

During the second or London phase of the campaign the theme of the undercurrent shifts to the aristocracy itself, and the upper and under currents eventually converge in a single stream of thought. Pronounced blurring of the distinction between public and private meetings sharply characterized this phase of the campaign. The public meetings are related as if they were drawing room *tête-à-têtes*, and the reflections of the private meetings are given public force. There is also, on Stowe's part, a studied indifference to the public pronouncements of aristocrats, as though this were not the class she came to see. She teaches us rather to pay attention to the private deeds of aristocrats—and of herself as well. And she appears, therefore, to disclaim the need for a public justification of aristocracy, though she has led us precisely to such an expectation.

We can best discern her purpose if we separate the two strands of this final phase of didacticism in "Sunny Memories." Besides relating the events of the campaign, she extensively discusses religion, a term she seems to employ to denote moral principle. Unlike the account of the first half of the campaign, where religion is treated as a phenomenon and she discusses, particularly, Quakers and Covenanters in terms of their attachment to moral principle, the account of the second half emphasizes the substance of religion. On Sunday, May 8th, she went to hear the sermon of Baptist Noël, because she remembered his beautiful hymns. This is the first report of a sermon during the entire tour. Noël spoke, she reported, of faith, hope, and charity. "His style calm, flowing, and perfectly harmonious, delivery serene and graceful, the whole flowed over one like a calm and clear strain of music. It was a sermon after the style of Tholuck and other German sermonizers," who are so unlike American divines of the "old school." For the English divines,

> The purpose of preaching is not to rouse the soul by an antagonistic struggle with sin through reason, but to sooth the passions, quiet the will, and bring the mind into a frame in which it shall incline to follow its own conviction of duty. They take for granted that the reason why men sin is not because they are ignorant, but because they are distracted and tempted by passion.[5]

Stowe's training, on the other hand, was in "controversial theology," where preachers "guarded every religious idea by definitions" and flattened them on a "logical anvil" before applying them to "heart or conscience."

Though she enjoyed Noël "extremely," she remained in doubt about the reaction of American theology professors to such a sermon. The idea of *one* sermon on *faith, hope, and charity* would be shocking. "We should have six sermons on the nature of faith to begin with: on speculative faith; saving faith; practical faith; and the faith of miracles; then we should have the laws of faith, and the connection of faith with evidence, and the different kinds of evidence, and so on." The American manner could improve the English preaching, just as sermons like Noël's might "be useful, by way of alternative," for Americans. Under the necessity to choose only one, however, she would choose the American style. Independent of its inspirational value, Stowe thought the habit of that style "one of the strongest educational forces" in the American mind.

This is a decision of the head rather than of the heart. It is governed by the end of these reflections on religion and education. We can gain a glimpse of Stowe's sympathies from a letter earlier written by Calvin, who remained in his apartments due to illness and did not hear Noël. The letter is significant in its own right, but also because it is one of a long series written in the spring of 1842 and which included the important "you must be a literary woman letter." In this case, Calvin compared Stowe to Tholuck:

> I am reeling—with great admiration in connexion with Tholuck's hours of devotion. . . . I want you home to talk with, for since you are gone there is nobody that knows anything in the field that interests me most. Your father comes the nearest to you in this respect, but he, you know, has no opinion of any [one] that believes goodness and an enlightened regard to one's own happiness are not one and the same thing—and accordingly there is a flaw in his theological system which I hate with proper hatred—and there is nobody in this wide world (except Professor Tholuck and a few like him) with whom I can talk with such satisfaction as I can with you.[6]

If, then, we may follow Calvin's lead, the educational strength of the American style is rooted in its adamancy regarding questions about human goodness.

On the following day Stowe observed the examination of borough-school boys and found something to praise in their education. They were tested in reading and reciting poetry, arithmetic, algebra, natural philosophy and "last, and most satisfactorily, in the Bible."[7] She concluded that the boys were well learned and not crammed, but she was most astonished when the master exposed them, on the Bible, to the random questions of the gentlemen in attendance. They "were wonderfully taught." Thus, even if this were only a sample, there was at least a model of thorough education in England.[8]

The performance of the borough-school boys may be contrasted with the implications of an anecdote related by a master of Harrow some ten days later. This is reported in Letter XIX, which is interposed out of sequence, since the letters following are dated May 12th and 13th. Apparently the Queen once visited the school and charged it with over-emphasizing the ancient classics. The master responded that she may judge whether this were true by observing the public men that the school had produced. Stowe found the reply adroit but specious, since it might hold in any case whatever. She instanced Benjamin Franklin, George Washington, and Roger Sherman as men America produced without any classical education. Stowe thought it curious that "Christian nations" should begin the education of their youth with heathen literature and mythology, especially since the inspired literature of the Bible is of "confessedly superior quality."[9] But the education of the borough-school boys reminds us that we are discussing the education not of youth but of the aristocratic youth of Christian nations. The use of the classics, therefore, is seen as having limited the development of English aristocracy, as it has "lain like a dead weight on all modern art and literature . . ."[10] This procedure, she found, has thwarted "variety and originality."

Later in the week, on May 13th, Harriet and Calvin paid a private visit to the grave of the hymnodist, Dr. Watts. She had characterized the literature of Pope and Dryden as so heathenish that it admitted of no change "in the religion of the world" since the old Greeks or Romans. Here, therefore, she sought to establish Watts's "rank as a poet." He is held, in smoothness, to be the equal of Pope and, in melody and majesty, the superior of Dryden. His paraphrase of the 148th Psalm was thought the best harmonious versification in the English language. Dr. Johnson's negative appraisal of Watts was discounted, since his authority is questionable. He "thought Irene" was poetry. All things else being equal, then, Watts was to be celebrated. The *whole* source of his poems was his Christian religious fervor, and he stands, therefore, in stark contrast with virtually all poets of reputation.

The summary of these reflections seems to indicate a preference for naive belief, sharpened by diligent questioning. But the prey must not be seized too quickly. It is possible that Watts's elevation is due not to his piety, *per se*, but to the form in which it is cast. Pope and Dryden, it must be remembered, are not denied the status of poet. It is only said that their poetry is narrow. The education of the lads at Harrow is also said to be narrow. If Watts's piety is identical to that of the borough-school boys, it is more general than ancient piety. If it can be expressed in poetry, then poetry too may be general. The elevation of Watts is a function of numbers. Pope and Dryden are outpolled. Nonetheless in America the key to this general piety is radical questioning. Hence, its substance must conform to clear standards as much as ancient piety.

On Sunday, May 15th, Stowe returned to church and heard the Congregationalist, Mr. Binney, preach. That was the first sermon she had heard in England that "seemed to recognize the existence of any skeptical or rationalizing element in the minds of his hearers." And on the 19th she spoke with the Anglican, Mr. Burney, who wished to hear a comparison of English and American preaching style. She repeated her earlier reflections and instanced Baptist Noël. Then, in her turn, Stowe wondered whether skepticism had pervaded the English mind, as novels, like Kingsley's, had suggested. Mr. Burney concurred and noted that the working classes are especially susceptible. Next, she questioned the religious intolerance, which, by report, she had expected but had not met. Again, Burney concurred, but he explained that the lack of intercourse resulted rather from circumstance than intent. A court and aristocracy in an established church will necessarily carry the pressure of fashion with it. On the following afternoon, Stowe visited Lord John Russell's country estate. She found there, on a central table, "a beautiful edition of that revered friend from childhood, Dr. Watts' Divine Songs . . ." Among modern religious texts *for children,* "these divine songs" have no superior. And, finally in Lady Russell's apartments after dinner, she reflected on the "identity of feeling and opinion among the really good" in differing regimes and societies. Conceding a difference in English and American institutions, Stowe thought "a general basis of agreement in so far as radical ideas of practical morality and religion are concerned . . ." was very possible.

The resolution of this train of connections is easy. The distinct advantage of American piety is openness, of English piety, simplicity. The vehicle for combining the two is poetry. And the task of the poetry is to speak to the many (and particularly to children), not just the few. Hence, the substance of this piety must be such as to afford hope and pleasure to men of differing capacities without explicitly distinguishing men. The truth was told in the passage following the Harrow anecdote. Watts was the best *juvenile* poet, not the best poet. For the best simply a higher, if non-classical, standard exists. At that point, Stowe maintained that anyone who wished to use the English language effectively need study three models: Shakespeare, Bunyan, and Defoe. The combination of the three could produce depth of understanding of the human soul, pure piety, and refined secular taste. The substance of such a combination would produce the kind of appeal that would unite the "really good" in the pursuit of "radical ideas of practical morality and religion."

Next, Stowe considered religion with respect to form as opposed to substance. And Stowe gives an example, subsequently balanced, of the critical attitude. Reporting on a Quaker meeting, Stowe revealed her distaste for the Quaker manner of speech, "a kind of intoning somewhat similar to the manner in which church service is performed in cathedrals." She notes that religions in all ages have "inclined to this form of expression," instancing cantillations and the prayers of Covenanters and Puritans as well as cathedral service. But in Letter XXVII, she reported a service at St. Paul's.

> There is a peculiar manner of reading the service practiced in the cathedral, which is called "intoning." It is a plaintive, rhythmical chant, with as strong an unction of nasal as ever prevailed in Quaker or Methodist meeting. I cannot exactly understand why the Episcopacy threw out the slur of "nasal twang" as one of the peculiarities of the conventicle, when it is in full force in the most approved seats of church orthodoxy.[11]

But she averred that she listened uncritically and sympathetically, opening herself to whatever inspiration might be possible. The openness prevents severe criticism.

Since the two notices of intoning are contradictory, it would seem that they reveal nothing, if not confusion, about Stowe's views. But it is helpful to look at the contexts in which they are made. The first statement, made at a Quaker meeting, is followed by discussion of free labor and Quaker consistency in abstaining from slave-grown produce. Stowe is, in the end, unsympathetic with Quaker absolutism. The St. Paul appraisal is followed by a report of a conversation with Richard Cobden. That conversation was a "comparison of views," whereas, with the Quakers, she declines to state an explicit view. The conversation with Cobden ended in optimism about "the cause." The temptation is strong to find that religious tolerance is subordinated to views of policy. That is, the edge of criticism is blunted in service of right political opinion but not otherwise. An indirect criticism of St. Paul's may serve to confirm this. Stowe thought its "Italian style" of architecture inferior to the Gothic. "The very rudeness" of the Gothic suggests a struggle to express religious ideas "too vast to be fully expressed." Any pretense of absolute expression, then, is viewed as an impostor and a harbinger of intolerance. Pure or simplistic piety does not gain its character by erecting unassailable systems but by acknowledging weakness. Its defects are supplied by refined secular taste and profound psychology.

Since the first object of care for such a religion must be the many, it is doubtless no accident that the first of two summary letters for the campaign should be devoted to a view of "the religious instruction and general education of the masses." Originally there was tension between aristocratic society and democratic religion, resulting from the awe that was induced by the thought that the noble "needs be saved by the same savior" as the "ignorant and debased." But, "modern popular movements" are all founded in "the equal value of every human soul."[12] The chief consequence she cited is the re-orientation of "fashionable literature." It now caters to the working class where it once catered to the great. "*Punch* laughs at everybody but the working people," and if they do come in for a laugh contempt is not its sister.[13] From this Stowe concluded that the "great ship of the world" had tacked and set a new course. The British abolitionists, Clarkson and Wilberforce, were credited with beginning the change. Thus, it was of recent vintage, significantly, post-Enlightenment and post-American and French revolutions. This "great humanitarian movement" described society's "religious parliament" and the community.

The public measures that attest this religious awakening, based on Shaftesbury's account, are all post-emancipation and post-Reform Bill.[14] Thus, the religious democracy is distinguished from emerging democratic and radical politics in England. The measures cited are Poor law reforms; reform of insane asylums; the ten-hour factory bill; regulation of child textile labor; removing women and children from coal pits; ragged school system; The Laborers' Friend Society; repeal of the Corn Laws; reform of millinery shops; reform of lodging houses; bath and wash houses; and the public health act. These were taken to be the numerous signs of Christian endeavor. And it pleased Stowe to think that "the Lord 'has much people' in England." The many differing sects all showed "evidence of that true piety" founded on "obedience to God, and a sincere desire *to do good to man.*" Because the former, to Stowe, is fulfilled in the latter, she was happily able to report that, from "many sects and opinions," there was but "one Christianity."[15]

It was no exaggeration to say that Stowe had subordinated the substance of religion to policy. In fact, the statement is reserved. Stowe identified the content of religion with social justice, and she stands at the beginning of a long line of theologians and critics whose posture of piety is borrowed from the humble pleader. The fact that the substance of the piety she depicts coincides with the aim of her campaign suggests, therefore, that the final articulation of her teaching should emerge from her report of the conclusion of this campaign.

The London tour opened with a dinner hosted by the Lord Mayor. The evening was slow-paced, producing kind allusions to Stowe and to *Uncle Tom's Cabin.* There were also casual reflections on the differences between the English reaction to Dickens (who was present) and the American reaction to Stowe. Stowe thought the difference unusual, since "they are *by pro-*

fession conservative, and we by profession radical" (emphasis supplied). We can think the contrast itself unusual since elsewhere Stowe describes the tales of Dickens as relatively harmless. But she apparently wishes to open this phase of the campaign by emphasizing the paradox of conservative, aristocratic England responding to liberal pleas on behalf of a poor, and liberal, democratic America resisting Stowe's imprecations on behalf of the slaves. But just as the English may not have known themselves with regard to tolerance, the qualifier, "by profession," suggests they may not know the true character of their political actions. It is, however, less in the way of a surprise that the English do not know themselves, than that the liberal, democratic Americans pursue a political course that belies their profession.

It is a theme we cannot by now neglect: every phase of this campaign and substantive section of this book opens with a generosity of sentiment toward England and closes with a serious qualification of that initial generosity. This last section follows the pattern in its opening. It carries, however, the burden of an established context as well as the necessity to conclude. If the pattern were followed exactly, it would be difficult to image a strong attack on slavery following. Professor Stowe's public remarks, we noticed, reversed the procedure and concluded, after placing England on the defensive initially, with construction of a strengthened coalition to undertake the chastening of America. Accordingly, the principal objective of the campaign is at stake in Stowe's treatment of English aristocracy.

The public record and the contemporary accounts presented above reveal that the objective of stiffening resistance to American slavery remained. Notably, however, those emphasized the appeal to the democracy. And where the aristocracy was noted, it was generally to question the sincerity of their attachments. We gain further evidence of the actual nature of the campaign from the American Government's concern with these developments. Ambassador Ingersoll, who earlier busied himself in muting the effects of this parade, was in attendance at the Lord Mayor's. He probably reported to Washington, in the surmise of Forrest Wilson, the near embarrassments resulting from Stowe's pilgrimage. This much at least is reliably inferred from his successor's appraisal several months later.

> I have learned . . . that the Queen had absolutely refused to see Mrs. Stowe either at the Palace or the Duchess of Sutherland's; and that she had refused to attend the concert given at the latter place. . . , lest she might meet Mrs. Stowe there. My informant says, she remarked very sensibly that American slavery was a question with which Great Britain had nothing to do.[16]

By de-emphasizing these factors, the private letters set the stage for a general appraisal of the requirements of modern politics. And this last phase of the campaign sets forth defenses of Stowe's general appraisal on each of the critical points, climaxing with a defense of her mode of teaching, the melodrama.

First Stowe defended the aristocracy's concern with American slavery. She connected it with a defense of the May 7th Stafford House rally.[17] Defending Lord Carlisle against Americans who sneer at any sign of distinctions and especially conventional distinctions, Stowe highlighted his openness, the fact that he is not blinded by conventions.

> He is the only traveler who ever wrote notes on our country in a real spirit of appreciation. While the Halls, and Trollopes, and all the rest could see nothing but our breaking eggs on the wrong end . . .

The American press was "sneering" at the preface Carlisle had written for an English edition of *Uncle Tom's Cabin*. They considered it unsporting of an aristocrat to concern himself with degrees of social difference in another country. But he had long been a reform leader, and he had always confessed his anti-slavery sentiments.[18] His relationship to criticism of America is identical to his relationship with criticism of his own country.

There was a related criticism of Lord Shaftesbury, the central figure in the Stafford House affair. Stowe reported amusement in London over the "vivacity" of American attacks on him as a Johnny-come-lately who should devote his attention to the English poor rather than the American slaves, "as if he had been doing anything else these twenty years." They contrasted him with Lord Ashley, whose struggles in the House of Commerce were renowned. But they had been amusingly vexed by the "provoking facility in changing names which is incident to the English peerage," for Lord Ashley was none other than Lord Shaftesbury. This case of Americans breaking eggs on the wrong end served to exonerate Shaftesbury and Carlisle. Implicit in this social *faux pas* is acceptance of the very standard elicited in defense of Carlisle. And that should lead to capitulation on the crucial objection, which is that the acceptance of some social inequality justifies every social inequality or that the demand for some social equality conveys authority for a complete leveling.

Incident to escaping the miasma is recognition that nature prescribes some inequalities. The discussion of Carlisle produced the reflection that America's task is to produce some perfect specimens of humanity—examples fit to inhabit, even if constitutionally forbidden, the courts, castles, and cathedrals of the past. But Americans were to some degree confused by the fact that, where distinctions exist by convention, nature's distinctions were not so readily visible. They required to profit from Carlisle's example of openness and to refuse to permit conventional distinctions to obscure the distinctions of nature.

The path of escape for Americans is to take seriously the social task of producing "distinguished specimens of humanity." The assured existence of this untitled aristocracy would represent the full achievement of the American purpose. As the examples in Letter XIV were the "literary men" discussed with Carlisle, the characterization of openness in Letter XV turned to art. Stowe visited the Dulwich Gallery to see the old masters. Declaring herself unbound by tradition and confident in her own judgment, she freely liked and disliked the old masters according to canons never before suggested. She sought, foremost, one thing in an artist: "What kind of mind has this man? What has he to say? and then I consider, How does he say it?" She disliked Rubens intensely, but nonetheless conceded his artistry, applying her standard. She thought that he obviously possessed such facility of expression that he could have painted his subjects in "any other way (that) suited his sovereign pleasure . . ." It is this having one's "taste crossed by a clever person" that is unsettling, for the exercise of such power leaves one with "less hope" for himself.

> These are merely first ideas and impressions. Of course I do not make up my mind about any artist from what I have seen here.

And five days later, in Letter XVIII, she profited from her openness and discovered a Rubens she liked—one that satisfied her both as to conception and coloring or execution. Nonetheless, her initial radicalism, qualified by openness, serves to convey to artist and witness the nature of their relationship.[19]

This is not merely incidental to our analysis. For, as we shall see in the Stafford House account and subsequent discussion, the analysis of art is the principal vehicle through which Stowe conveys her political philosophy in this last phase of the campaign.[20] Art is here what cathedrals and castles were in the first half. And the notion that the distinguished species of humanity must so behave himself as not to impair the hope countless witnesses of his deeds have for themselves is central to the effective functioning of this untitled aristocracy amidst a people given to equality. Presumably, the witness' openness, if it produces no reward, cannot be sustained. And in America, Stowe had said in Letter XIV, unless we can glory in "our men and women," we have nothing. The defense of English aristocracy is, at bottom, a defense of distinction based on talent. Stowe then closes Letter XV, May 6th now, looking forward to the Stafford House defense. "Tomorrow at eleven o'clock comes the meeting at Stafford House. What it will amount to I do not know; but I take no thought for the morrow."

Letter XVI is dated May 8, the day following the meeting at Stafford House. Stowe opens with the following statement: "In fulfillment of my agreement, I will tell you, as nearly as I can remember, all the details of the meeting at Stafford House." Now, this promise is not recorded in any of the published letters (the *unconcern* just noted is the closest equivalent!). It was therefore either in a letter to "Dear C.," left unpublished, or given orally prior to departure from the United States. It was in any event a commitment made without respect to the controversy that was ultimately produced. Hence, its objective must have been to satisfy some curiosity about the aristocracy in these circumstances. The letter redeems a pledge to characterize the aristocracy's public bearing. The emphasis on attention to every detail should indicate that any omissions are due to the insignificance of the details.

After this opening Stowe writes a fourteen page essay, only two sentences of which are devoted to the "welcome address," and the second of which sentences refers the reader to an enclosed paper that prints it. No other fact—not applause, not congratulation, not prayers—nothing more is related. But there are, two pages after the acknowledgment of the "welcome," her own reflections in defense of the principles involved in the meeting and an interpretation of what it means to America. The bulk of the remainder of the essay is a description of the residence, and the individuals about, with reflection on the underlying meaning of the circumstances. Thus, in the fourth paragraph of the essay, in which she is passing from room to room in a state of "confusion," she noticed, upon reaching the drawing room, the "artistic, poetic air" of the room. This was held to result from the careful arrangement that created a "unity of impression." The unity stems from what painters call the "ground tone, or harmonizing tint, of a picture."

> The idea, I suppose, is to produce a mass of color of a certain tone, and not to distract the eye with the complicated pattern. Where so many objects of art and virtu are to be exhibited, without this care in regulating and simplifying the ground tints, there should be no unity in the impression. This was my philosophizing on the matter, and if it is not the reason why it is done, it ought to be. It is as good a theory as most theories, at any rate.[21]

The discovery apparently ended her confusion. And one of the things that is achieved by this liberation of aesthetic taste from the sovereign tyranny of personal whim is the subordination of aesthetic discrimination to something greater than oneself—a general theory, here called the "unity of impression."

This essay itself, like the book as a whole, has different sections that require to be harmonized. But it is sufficient that its different emphases are all subordinated to one general theory. The ground tones conveyed by workingmen and aristocrats are sufficiently distinct, considered in themselves. But if, in their distinctness, they are nonetheless founded in some principle of unity, we may come to understand them as not disharmonious.

And we may eliminate the confusion these letters only seem to evoke as they pass fitfully from subject to subject.

One of the things achieved in this essay that breathes a gentle and charitable solicitude, is a reversal of the positions of England and America. Elsewhere, it is said that they are by profession conservative, we by profession radical. But the description of the residence—so professionally arranged in accord with the demands of reason or theory—the assembled persons—who either seem magically relieved of the ravages of age,[22] or, if aging, much more youthful than they were in fact and, indeed, much younger than Americans—these descriptions at least erase the traditional prejudice of the old as conservative and the young as radical. In the very center of the essay is drawn a consequence or cause of this reversal.

> Generally speaking our working minds seem to wear out their bodies faster; perhaps our climate is more stimulating; more, perhaps, from the intenser stimulus of our political *regime*, which never leaves anything long at rest.[23]

Thus, a new cause of aging or conservatism can be found: ceaseless innovation. And, the traditional fear of change comes to be identified with the more liberal—or, at least, youthful—view, predicated on the necessity of one fundamental change: the elimination of ceaseless innovation and its causes. Whether this is compatible with modern progress is unclear; there may be a kind of humane progress which is not understood to rely on the willingness to cast aside tradition—which may be compatible with the kind of old "institutions" that render radicalism safe for English aristocrats. Stowe, we remember, looked upon the old masters unbound by any tradition. But there is perhaps a difference between the attitude which casts tradition aside and that which is not ruled by tradition itself. The kind of questions she asked—"What kind of mind has he"; "What does he say"; "How does he say it"—suggests not an openness to reject but an openness to learn from old masters. And she duly proved that she did learn. Presumably, a constitution or *regime* must emphasize the wisdom of the old masters at the same time it encourages a liberty of opinion, in order to satisfy the demand for an end to ceaseless innovation. But in this particular essay the task was to report "fully" the Stafford House meeting and thus to defend British aristocracy's concern for these American questions. That is, the task was to defend an innovation. We may see, therefore, that the final section is disharmonious or out of place only in the tones employed in its construction, not in its end. And in it, the end should be most manifest.

It were well, first, to recall the author's state of mind. In the end of Letter XV, she said, "I take no thought for the morrow." But on the morrow she is seen uneasy and apprehensive.[24] Stowe did then take thought of the morrow. But this little lapse would win only sympathy for a most polite sensitivity to differences in social form, were it not that the record in the press shows her more confident than she admits. The Duchess reportedly assured her that no response would be required when Shaftesbury, under the deputation of the Duchess of Sutherland and the ladies of the committee which oversaw the gathering of signatures for the "Affectionate Address," read a brief note of acknowledgment. And Calvin agreed, in the "Introduction," that no response was made. But the Stowe party nonetheless did respond. Stowe's brother, Charles, was tapped to prosecute the cause. It is further reported in the London *Times* that, far from being ill at ease, Stowe held regal sway—at least among the ladies. These letters do not record, what in fact occurred, that the ladies and gentlemen separated and that Stowe, seated between the Duchesses of Sutherland and Argyle, held forth on the nature of American slavery and American sentiment in regard to it.

But we cannot resolve the contradictions between Letters XV and XVI with reference to the *Times*. It is first necessary to regard these letters in the context of the letters as a whole. And that requires an understanding of what is done explicitly in the doubtful letters. To describe Stowe's state of mind as she depicts it in Letter XVI, we are permitted to recognize that she abstracted from elements among the events related. But to know her state of mind as she intends it to be understood in the letter itself, we must derive our understanding from the content given. What Stowe omits tends to de-emphasize the political or public character of the Stafford House affair and treats it as a mere social or private gathering. The full details she recalled, therefore, are primarily social details. That the explicit defense of aristocracy is a minor portion of the essay is justified by the predominance of private concerns in the essay as a whole. But, that defense is yet thought necessary, after the most egregious political dimensions have been excised and in the presence of a primarily social affair—which only heightens our appreciation of the tenuousness of the aristocracy's concern with apparently democratic principles. Stowe points, therefore, to a dimension beyond politics as the source of this concern—a source open to democrat and aristocrat alike. Still, the aristocrat's manifestation of concern is or ought to be essentially private.

By presenting the events of the Stafford House affair not as a consequence of her appeal but as matter incident to the status of the participants, Stowe defends the aristocracy's concern as a consequence of the aristocracy's station. That is certainly not a politically persuasive defense; hence her anxiety. But the letters as a whole call for a persuasive defense, and this does lay the basis for an account which may reflect the independent operation of certain political principles. She is confident of her own grasp of these principles, hence the nonchalance of Letter XV; but their dissemination requires political persuasion. In the end, then, the Stafford House affair lays the groundwork for an appropriate rhetoric—a rhetoric not offensive to equality. That such rhetoric arises from a defense of aristocracy is the key to its purpose.

Since this was a mere social gathering, Stowe taxed her memory to recall the details of household arrangements and individual character. Hence, she launched into those descriptions that led to her theorizing about the nature of harmonizing tints. She commented on everything, including paintings, remembering the subject and the artist in every case save one. But, of the one, she did remember that it was Flemish, and that it was of Christ under examination before Caiaphas. She remembered the details of light and shadow, and even the inscription the painting bore, which she quoted.

> He was wounded for our transgressions,
> He was bruised for our iniquities;
> The chastisement of our peace was upon him,
> And with his stripes we are healed.[25]

She could not recall the artist. But she related the painting directly to the Stafford House affair, citing its presence "in the midst of this scenery" as affecting her greatly. Now, it is immediately after this that she related the convening of the assembly—the chief cause of the necessity of a defense of aristocracy. It appears that this special example of the greatly superior man who eschewed all public endeavor is of special relevance to that defense. This amounts to a secular application of the example of Christ. What it conveys is a special need for the superior man humbly to submit his capacities to the service of inferior men and for the special purpose of improving human life.[26] We are yet more convinced by the coincidental existence of several more or less contemporaneous catalogues of the Stafford House collection, none of which report the presence of this painting. We cannot even attest to its existence.[27]

Perhaps stronger still is the application of the following principle. The assembly was convened and dismissed, in the text, in little more than a paragraph. Then Stowe returned to a tour of the faces and premises, only to come abruptly to an idea of the dependence of the "English future" on "the character and education of the princes and nobility." We have already seen the deficiency of the aristocracy's education in its dependence on the classics. But here something more is meant, for this reflection serves as introduction to the defense of the Stafford House meeting. And in that defense we discover that the aristocrat, Lord Shaftesbury, had further reason for his concern than his history of reform. He had been educated by the "tale of American slavery"—by *Uncle Tom's Cabin*.

Fittingly, in the defense Stowe emphasized the public dimension of the meeting. She humbled herself, considering the "Affectionate Address" not a "personal honor" but rather "the most public expression possible" of the sentiments of English women on "one of the most important questions of our day": the "religious bearing" of individual liberty.

> The most splendid of England's palaces has this day opened its doors to the slave. Its treasures of wealth and of art, its prestige of high name and historic memories, have been consecrated to the acknowledgement of Christianity in that form wherein, in our day, it is most frequently denied—the recognition of the brotherhood of the human family, and the equal religious value of every human soul.

We may suggest that the connection between "the most important question" and what is "most frequently denied" in our day is that the equal religious value of souls is the source of authority for individual liberty. And the achievement of this authorized end, in the presence of an inescapably hierarchical family, depends upon discovering the basis of collective authority in the most vulnerable members of the family. The only form in which we can understand that the palace, its art, and its memories have been consecrated to the slave is that we see the principles derived from reflection on these things as the act of consecration.

Returning to the address, Stowe found that the "most public expression" was fixed in the "most public manner" and had become part of an historical record. Yet, she denies the insinuation of American papers that it was a political movement. "Nothing can be more false." The founder of the enterprise was motivated by the same kind of religious sentiment that led him throughout his life to combat "white-labor slavery" in England. Lord Shaftsbury's "heart was overwhelmed by the tale of American slavery, and (he) could find no relief from this distress except in raising some voice to the ear of Christianity." His address to the ladies of England, inviting them to speak out to American women, was inspired by a fear "of the jealousy of political interference." Thus, it was intended as a public substitute for politics, which might nonetheless affect desired political objectives. It was, therefore, the very model of that private activity whose essential aim is public benefit. In our own time, of course, the benefit of that nineteenth-century convention circumscribing the sphere of woman to the private is not available.[28] Nevertheless, this was sufficient at the time to justify Stowe's pretense that the action was not political. And if further proof were required, it could be noted that Shaftesbury followed the example of his primer, *Uncle Tom's Cabin*, in having women speak to women rather than to men. It is almost ironic when Stowe concludes that the remonstrances in the "Affectionate Address" contain only "the mildest form (of) the sentiments of universal christendom."

Immediately afterwards Stowe gave a particular demonstration of the kind of use to which the education of noble men may be put. In an unrelated letter sandwiched between two letters dated May 8, she undertook a lengthy defense of the Duchess of Sutherland and the Sutherland estates. Again, the defense is said to be a response to criticism in American papers. The defense of Sutherland consists of two arguments. The first is a meticulous demonstration of the improved conditions of Sutherland tenants since 1811, when a "new system" was adopted, eliminating much of the feudal nature of the relationship. The second argument is a general demonstration that an intentional and careful effort to improve the morals and material conditions of a backward people can succeed in a relatively short time if pursued with the proper care. The first argument indeed serves as a showcase for the second, permitting Stowe to address one of her favorite themes indirectly, avoiding anti-negro prejudices. In Letter XXV, again to "Dear C," undated, and in which the defense of her own consistency is presented, she had preferred an emigration of slaves to Canada as opposed to Africa or Latin America.[29] Hence, when she describes the progress of reform among white—mostly Protestant—Scotsmen, we are afforded a comparison of the alternatives. The immediate effect of the Sutherland reform was likened to the disbanding of an army, producing much confusion and rootlessness. In the Sutherland case, some force was required to effect the resettlement. Eventually, however, the people moved in accord with the natural attraction of improved opportunities. But in the extreme north, "this refuge was wanting."

> Emigration to America now became the resource; and the surplus population were induced to this by means such as the Colonization Society now recommends and approves for promoting emigration to Liberia.

Stowe admitted that problems would have arisen but for the safety valve of emigration. But she considered emigration to America of far greater moral and material promise than emigration to Liberia.[30] That, in either case, emigration ought to be considered a last resort is, therefore, her considered judgment. Yet, the key to its being a last resort is the pursuit of reform activity—very largely private activity—intended to benefit society. The Sutherland system was changed in 1811–1812, and the transition was completed in 1819–1820. To Stowe this was "an almost sublime" example of benevolence. Private resources of wealth and power were marshaled specifically to shorten "the struggles of advancing civilization" and to elevate very rapidly "a whole community to a point of education and material prosperity" otherwise beyond their unassisted reach.[31]

Stowe's defense of the aristocracy is provisional. It is a defense of an aristocracy which understands its capacities and privileges "'as a ministry' which they hold for the benefit of the poor." Letter XX, in which this use of Fenelon is made, partially retracts the generosity of sentiment in Letter XVI but does not undermine the thesis that aristocrats have a right to take part in these matters. Since the defense of aristocracy was concluded in Letter XVIII, Letter XX was free to treat Shaftesbury and Sutherland as individuals rather than as representatives of a class. We are accordingly informed that the English youth and health and beauty we noted earlier do have an essential connection with English conservatism. In the first place, it is made clear that only aristocratic English men and women were being described. And their advantage is derived, in the case of women in particular, from the nature of their domestic institutions which are inescapably connected with their constitution. That they are allowed to concentrate wealth in their hands is the efficient means whereby they are liberated from many of the toils of the American wife, and hence preserve their beauty. But the decisive factor is the English regime—a perfect contrast to the intensely stimulating American regime—and it prolongs physical distinction by perpetuating an aristocracy of sign. Stowe does not defend this aristocracy of sign. Neither does she attack it. The defense of aristocracy she does offer makes it clear that one need not distinguish constitutions on formal grounds in order to distinguish the benevolent and malevolent. Consequently, she takes as the core of her theory the distinction between state and society, or public and private, as if it were the originating principle of modernity and not a mere derivative of social contract theory. And she is thus far right: the idea of a community consciously formulating a political system for itself must presuppose a prior distinction between the public and the private things, in which distinction the private things are of greatest importance.

The conclusion of the defense of aristocracy in Letter XVIII, therefore, returns to a discussion of art and to Stafford House in order to liberate the theory from its trappings. The achievement of this is the condition of the implicit criticism of aristocracy in Letter XX. The beginning of Letter XVIII contrasted British and American preaching. It then offered an example of useful instruction for English youth, and which the aristocracy had not followed. The queen had already implied a criticism of the education of aristocratic youth. Thus, in Letter XX the education afforded the royal young is instanced as more conformable to the tasks of aristocracy and a piece with the work of Shaftesbury and Sutherland. It is with these qualifications in the background that Letter XVIII, like an American theologian, guards the previous theory with definitions. The first such was Stowe's discovery that she could be satisfied by Rubens after all. She made this discovery while viewing the collection of the poet Rogers. During the visit he commented on the significance of the Stafford House affair. Hence, the very next subject is a return engagement with the Stafford House collection.

Though this revisit to Stafford House is specifically to view the paintings, Stowe "purposely delayed" the tour with a discussion of a "noble staghound" and the superiority of the real thing to all Landseer's craft of depiction. Now, this is not a recanting of her preference for the creative soul over the works of nature. But it is a recognition that the significance or truth of works of art separated from the power of their creators is diminished in the presence of the real thing. The delay prepares her to see the limitations in the art, divested now of all the significance it previously borrowed from the "affecting scenes" of the meeting.

She approached her task like a naturalist pressed for time: "Like a botanist dropped into the middle of a blooming prairie, and *only an hour* to examine and make acquaintance." But why had she delayed the tour, if she were conscious of the limited time available? It can only be that while emphasizing the care with which she viewed these works, she wished also to emphasize how readily the viewing could be accomplished. The first report demonstrates that she was not afforded such care in the previous review, when she remembered all the "details." They passed through several rooms, "filled with Titians, Murillos, Guidos, etc." In the process she noted "four Raphaels,[32] the first I had ever seen." But she must have "seen" them if the previous tour were complete, although she may not have noticed them.[33] It is safe to say that these Raphael's did not lend themselves to her purposes. In any event, she confessed that they pleased her less than she had expected though perhaps as much as necessary. What had she expected?—"a divine baptism, a celestial mesmerism."

> It is too much to ask of any earthly artist, however, to gratify the aspirations and cravings of those who have dreamed of them for years unjustified. Perhaps no earthly canvas and brush can accomplish this marvel. I think the idealist must lay aside his highest ideal, and be satisfied he shall never meet it, and then he will begin to enjoy.[34]

That enjoyment which is the opposite of realizing the highest ideal is not only a lowering of ambition or ends but a condition of lowered ends. That is, if enjoyment begins only after acceptance of the impossibility of the ideal, then enjoyment is opposed to insistence upon ideals. What then is natural to enjoyment? In this tour Stowe went on to enjoy an "Assumption" by Guido, but she enjoyed still more Titian's "Diana and her Nymphs." Titian's "classical elegance" left Stowe's "eye or mind" fully satisfied. He was "a Greek painter, the painter of an etherealized sensuousness, which leaves the spiritual nature wholly unmoved."[35]

If the angelic Raphael is insufficient to satisfy Stowe's high demands, and the voluptuous Titian's Greekness is appropriate to her taste, why are aristocratic youths to shun the Greeks in their education and be immersed in revelations? May Stowe's character of soul and concern for the poor be so secure as to require no special bulwarks? The defense of the aristocracy suggested that precisely their high ideals would be the source of elevation for the many. But it is not likely that the aristocracy will give itself to a morality from which the teacher is exempt. We can only conclude that the provisional nature of that defense is a consequence of the aristocracy's relationship to the project of humane progress. The English aristocracy, in itself, was not defended. Only aristocracy by nature was defended. But aristocracy by nature is not hemmed in by social conventions and prescribed modes of interaction with the many. Only English or constitutional aristocracy is restrained by such conventions. Natural aristocracy may require a specific education to attain appropriate goals of civilization, but that education would be akin to Stowe's own education. It would emphasize openness, profound psychology, and refined secular taste. English aristocracy, on the other hand, requires to be directed by a specific morality whose purpose is to incline the aristocracy in the channels prescribed by the goals of civilization appropriate to natural aristocracy.

In the end, the defense of English aristocracy is a criticism, a criticism equally aimed at noble Christians in America. The fact that they occupy a specific social position both deflects their judgment and makes it all the more difficult for them to undertake right action privately. What is really private, to Stowe, is what remains socially invisible, even when it has public consequences. No English aristocrat could ever achieve that degree of effectiveness save by abandoning his patrimony. Yet, abandoning his patrimony impairs his ability to do good and thus defeats its purpose. That Shaftesbury, Sutherland, and others are to be commended for what they do is proved by the very great difficulty they face in doing anything at all.

Having achieved this much by way of argument, Stowe must demonstrate two things. First, she must show that her own teaching is a suitable means of addressing and encouraging others, whatever their social circumstances. This she accomplished in her defense of the melodrama. Secondly, she must demonstrate that her own deeds—her private deeds—can in fact remain invisible yet contribute to the end consistently with her teaching. This she accomplished with her apology for consistency. These culminating defenses are given amidst occasional reflections on the continuing public meetings. But unlike the Stafford House meeting, they are not connected to the explanation of those meetings. Indeed, beginning in Letter XXI and continuing in the odd numbered letters through XXVII, Stowe manages to minimize those public meetings—where consistency was the theme—and deliver an apology for her own consistency at the same time. Meanwhile, the even numbered letters, beginning with the complete defense of melodrama in Letter XXII, through Letter XXVIII, offer specific examples of "doing good." Before we analyze these defenses, therefore, we must analyze her account of the final public meetings.

I. FALSE IMPRESSIONS

Letter XIX is a vehicle for correction of several previous impressions. It serves, therefore, as an introduction to the concluding letters. The chief correction we have already noted:

> Not everything found in the works of the "old masters" may have been seen by the masters themselves, Shakespeare in particular. Thus, the discovery of a political aesthetics may be said to have originated when Stowe opened the letter by renouncing any interest in "death and the past." She was, she held, "busy in seeing life and the present."[36] This radical break with her former pietistic posture also ended in the abandonment of Gothic individualism. She thought that Macaulay's account of Europe's cathedrals—they all arose at once under the direction of a few minds—ought to be believed even if not true. And, "I'm going to believe it." Thus easily does she abandon her architectural authority, Billings, whose antiquarianism was doubtless too confining for the creative impulses of liberal history. Having patiently elaborated those "perfect models" of the past, she flightily abandoned them, thereby declaring her independence. That this *follows* her defense of aristocracy prepares us for that version of her theory specifically suited to her own time. Hence, she turned to the education of aristocratic youth. But it also prepares us for an account of her campaign, which account was thus liberated from the concerns of British politics. Her own account, in other words, matures in a manner that exactly parallels the account Professor Stowe gave and emphasizes the same American independence of things British. Nonetheless, what she has to say differs.

Forrest Wilson thought Calvin Stowe had proved an embarrassment to his wife, and that the final letters especially belied the unanimity of sentiment Calvin had claimed in his "Introduction."[37] And on the surface this may seem to be the case. Stowe opens Letter XXI with only the briefest notice of the meeting at the Congregational Union on May 13th and with no notice at all of the remarks of Angell and Calvin Stowe. This is all the more dramatic as Calvin reports one of his lengthiest and most complex speeches on this occasion. It was the first in his dialectical triad. Stowe, however, reports little more than the strong impression of "how much of one blood the two countries are . . . the Christians of America and England are one."[38] Of course, Calvin went great lengths to establish such an identity, whereas their hosts had said very little. Thus, Stowe's remarks really indicate that she is following Calvin, without acknowledging it. His remarks had been unprovoked and challenged the British to be consistent. By ignoring this she created a context which generated surprise at the heat of the Exeter Hall attack. In the context of the letter, she partially atones for her oversight by commencing her own apology for consistency.

In this same letter, Stowe recorded the "great antislavery meeting in Exeter Hall." She does full justice to the character of Exeter Hall society.

> A crowded meeting [at Exeter Hall] gives one perhaps a better idea of the force of English democracy—of that kind of material that goes to make up the mass of the nation—than anything else.[39]

But she could probably have anticipated this well in advance. Calvin certainly must have. He had attended such a meeting seventeen years before, while abroad purchasing a library for Lane Theological Seminary and compiling his report on European education. He wrote to his wife at that time.

> I sent Henry a copy of the London Times containing an account of the meeting of the Protestant Association in Exeter Hall, which I attended. It was perhaps the must turbulent meeting I ever witnessed and I hope I may never see another.[40]

Yet he was to see another, and that on the very subject he had previously reproved. In the same letter he condemned the ultra-abolitionists who manifested the "same nasty radicalism, the same dogmatic narrowness" he had seen in America. That he came back to Exeter Hall prepared seems a justified conclusion. In 1853 they sought to advance abolitionism without advancing nasty dogmatism. It was this same unruly element of "democracy" that Stowe reports as if she sensed it in the air of the place.

Stowe approached the "densely crowded" hall with some hesitation, feeling slightly ill. She delayed entering until services had begun, thus explaining why she missed Shaftesbury's "most able speech." The press, as we noted, reported this as a *"grande entrée"* but we may take her at her word. Her entrance brought from the crowd a cheer the vehemence of which made her tremble. This far exceeded similar things she had heard in Scotland.

> I do not believe that there is in all America more vehemence of democracy, more volcanic force of power than comes out of one of these great gatherings in our old fatherland. I saw plainly enough where Concord, Lexington, and Bunker Hill came from; and it seems to me there is enough of this element of indignation . . . to found half a dozen more republics.[41]

The crowd was such that one "could easily see" how a sudden panic or great excitement would create a terrible scene. To this point, not one word had been written about the subject of the meeting. In effect, therefore, Stowe demonstrates that Calvin's approach was intentional. Since he could not fail to see the effect of their presence, he could only seek to direct the excitement into safe channels. Her report of the speeches parallels the turning away from America and toward Britain. But she is able to suggest this only because she neglects the other speeches in Calvin's triad, which plainly show his attack was not simply related to Exeter Hall and was in some measure gratuitous.

Thus, after noting the "denunciatory" and painful character of the English speeches (which pained "the national feelings of an American"), she minimized what Calvin said and reported no reaction at all. She admitted that the meeting was very long, but it was long because of reaction to Calvin's speech, which she described in a single, lengthy sentence.

> Mr. S. spoke on this point, that the cotton trade of Great Britain is the principal support to slavery and [he] read extracts from Charleston papers in which they boldly declared that they do not care for any amount of moral indignation wasted upon them by nations who, after all, must and will buy the cotton they raise.

Now this statement is admirably suited to achieve the effect Stowe has anticipated. A vehement and dogmatic crowd must react with anger to such a challenge. But the statement is not identical to Professor Stowe's version. In particular he used the newspapers only to show the "economic effect" of the cotton trade and cited no such bold declarations from slaveholders. *She implied that they took it all in stride.* She therefore paused to present her defense of melodrama. And in Letter XXIII but one line suggests the dimensions of the Exeter Hall affair. Commenting on an interview with the Hungarian exile, Kossuth,[42] she noted that "he seemed quite amused at the sensation which had been excited by Mr. S.'s cotton speech in Exeter Hall."[43]

Her appreciation of the event was slowly building. Four days later returning to London after a visit to Clarkson's residence at Playford, she noted "some disturbance" on the subject, "different papers declaring themselves for or against it with a good deal of vivacity." Thus, finally she related Professor Stowe's speech at the *soirée* of May 25 as the conclusion of the whole affair. This meeting was "filled with throngs of people." The host's address "was one of the most beautiful, sensible, judicious, and christian" that was possible and it afforded her "unmingled pleasure." This address, in the "Introduction," represented the capitulation to the Stowes' argument. Her pleasure, therefore, was justifiable. Calvin's response is said to be, in effect, a continuation of the Exeter Hall address. Where he had offered a triad, the work of their own effort, she offers a dyad, extorted by circumstances. Indeed, she scrupulously emphasizes "his" opinions in the text and only faintly suggests her involvement in a footnoted "we."

> Mr. S. took occasion still further to explain his views with respect to the free-grown cotton movement in England, and its bearings on the future progress of the course of freedom.* [ ] **We* are happy to say that a large body of religious persons in Great Britain have become favorable to these views. A vigorous society has been

> established, combining India reform and free cotton with the anti-slavery cause. The Earle of Albemarle made, while we were in London, a vigorous India reform speech in the House of Lords, and Messrs. Bright and Cobden are fully in for the same object in the Commons. There is much hope in the movement.[44] (Emphasis supplied)

The assignment of responsibility to Calvin in the text accords with the description of his struggling with public demands. The claim of joint responsibility in the subsequently written note ("while we were in London" identifies the note as post-London) accords with the development of their private demands.

This weak claim in the footnote is bolstered by the evidence of an earlier passage attributed to May 23. There, Stowe and Professor Stowe met Cobden for breakfast and raised the question of free cotton without reference to Exeter Hall. This "comparison of views" left them happy with future prospects. The cause of their happiness is borne out in the suggestion in the footnote that Cobden pursued the matter in Commons. The story of Exeter Hall as she presents it is, therefore, the story of the relationship between private and public endeavors. The minimizing of the artfulness involved in the close of the campaign is intended to agree with the demand for invisibility in do-gooders. Private action as distinguished from public action may be given a greater scope to the very extent its privacy is guarded. Public action must follow channels. But private action may originate the public impulses that follow channels. To close the story of Exeter Hall with an intermingling of India reform, free cotton, and anti-slavery is to describe the recommended approach for the reformer. It also pegs the hope for reform on the encouragement of general public tendencies as opposed to single, spectacular action.

Stowe was not embarrassed by her husband. Their two accounts differ, but are not contradictory. Their differences result entirely from the essentially public character of the one and the primarily private character of the other. But for the artfulness of the triad, the creation of a public context, the Stowes' private efforts could have no hope of success. The reformer presupposes a suitable public context for their private endeavors. And the work of creating a suitable public context falls to those sufficiently artful to point public sentiment in the right direction. Here the campaign ends, for in itself it can achieve no more. But the task of reconciling public and private demands and the nature of the teaching suited to creation of a public context remain to be mastered.

The nature of consistency must reflect the pressures of an existing public context as well as the demands of moral sentiments. Stowe sought to establish the means by which this may be achieved. The apology for consistency began with and centered on the question of Quaker consistency in abstinence from slave-grown produce. It opened upon a visit to the Quaker residence called "Paradise." It seemed, at first, an apology for inconsistency. Throughout the trip the Stowes had been drawn to the question of Quaker abstinence. The consistency with which Quakers pursued their aim seemed sometimes to compromise their own interests. Nonetheless, Stowe could readily envision the consequences if everyone were so guided. She thought, though, that "great practical difficulties" would prevent it, "especially in America." Hence she suggested the mean of partial abstention and the development of free-labor produce. This mean would compromise the antislavery principle unless it is not "an actual sin to eat, drink, or wear anything that has been the result of slave labor." If it were a complete asceticism would be requied, and that would still be insufficient. For the ascetic principle leads to avoidance of all products that result from unjust and inequitable arrangements, while the choices men face are rather between competing systems, with the standards of justice always inclining the decision toward the more just.

They attended another "Friends' meeting" in which they separated into men's and women's groups. She was called upon to express her opinion of "free labor." But she demurred, preferring to learn from them especially about their "consistency and self-denial."[45] This re-directs their question, since they asked about free labor, not free cotton, doubtless concerned with the conditions of labor in England as that was discussed in *Uncle Tom's Cabin*. But she framed the question to suit her own purposes and then refrained from criticizing by withholding the general sentiments she had reported in Letter XXI. She gave no report of the Friends' response to her willingness to learn. We may presume that she remained untaught.

Nonetheless, Stowe offered a practical example of what consistency is about, confronting the snares of this world. And thus she indirectly answered the original question. Turning immediately to an apparently new subject—without taking leave of the Quaker meeting—she abruptly stated, "I have been quite amused with something which happened lately." The tale opens with a description of the habit of the English press in discussing private details of the life of aristocracy, a custom not practiced in America. "Dear old England" made her "so much one of the family" that she received the same treatment. An announcement was made in the *Times* that she was having a dress made; but it went on to describe the circumstances: one of "the most shockingly distressed dens of London, of poor, miserable white slaves, worse treated than the plantation slaves of America."[46]

There followed a letter from a dressmaker's apprentice, deploring the fact. Stowe protested her ignorance, explaining that she dealt only with "a very respectable woman," who came to her apartment and took measurements and material. Since the article appeared she had received numerous pleas to take up the cause of white slavery and "employ my talents equally against oppression under every form." Only thus could she have proved what was presumed, that she must have intended only the best and blundered innocently. She worried about what to do. The advice of the *Times*, "in order to be consistent," was that she adopt the cause "immediately." She disagreed.

> What an unreasonable creature! Does he suppose me so lost to all due sense of humility as to take out of his hands a cause he is pleading so well? If the plantation slaves had such a friend as the *Times*, and if every overworked female cotton picker could write as clever letters as this dressmaker's apprentice, and get them published in as influential papers, and excite as general a sensation by them as this seems to have done, I think I should feel there was no need of my interfering in a work so much better done. Unfortunately, our female cotton pickers do not know how to read and write, and it is against the law to teach them; and this instance shows that the law is a sagacious one, since, doubtless, if they could read and write most embarrassing communication might be made. Nothing shows more plainly, to my mind, than this letter, the difference between the working class in England and the slave. The free workman or workwoman of England or America, however poor, is self-respecting; is, to some extent, clever and intelligent; is determined to resist wrong, and, as this incident shows, has abundant means for doing so.[47]

This whimsical reply defends Stowe's privacy. But the true defense is the use to which that privacy is put. The whimsical reply would not be nearly so comic if she had not indirectly shown earlier that she had made an inquiry to ascertain the truth of the charge. "The person who had been so unfortunate as to receive the weight of my public patronage . . . protested her innocence . . . with as much fervor as if I had been appointed on a committee of parliamentary inquiry."[48] This is her *only* concession that she investigated the charge before responding.

In the following letter Stowe presented a detailed description of the millinery profession in London and the great improvements that had been made. The information doubtless came in response to her plight and general investigation. Hence, her response to the *Times* was made from a posture of self-assurance and confidence that she was engaged in no inconsistency—even if the dress she wears is mingled with injustice. On the strength of this private consistency, she rejected the demand for public consistency and established the principle that the true standard of consistency is fidelity to the weightier cause. That is, the reformer is not bound to a public attack on every injustice however great or small. He need only attack those injustices the toleration of which would imperil the polity itself. *And even if he succeeds in demanding absolute fidelity to principle from himself—privately—he must not make absolute commitment the basis of the public context for reform.* The question of free labor versus slave labor was not to be raised to a principle in itself but was rather to be understood in relation to a fundamental objective. The apology for consistency is a demonstration that it is necessary for the reformer, if he is genuinely consistent, to sometimes appear publicly inconsistent.

In defending the form of her teaching in *Uncle Tom's Cabin* Stowe seems to be involved in a fascinating dialectic. While denying that her novel presents a simplistic morality, she must also defend the necessity of this simplistic appearance—a series of "monochromatic" characters as the *Edinburgh Review* put it. That surely accounts for the nature of her apology for consistency, reflecting the pressures of an existing public context as well as the demands of moral principle. The rejection of Quaker absolutism actually rests on moral grounds: that absolutism offers a simplistic view of the demands of justice. Then, when it is occasion not to act but to create the public context for action, she, too, apparently speaks in simplistic terms. Hence, *Uncle Tom's Cabin*.

Stowe was under the necessity, therefore, to defend her use of an approach she had denied to the Quakers. Further, we noted at the beginning of this section that, while *Uncle Tom's Cabin* sought to convince the slaveholder (America) of the evil of slavery, "Sunny Memories" sought to convey, privately, the ground of that opposition. The former task was undertaken through an explicitly public teaching, one that worked to perfection the simplistic black-white contrast. We have also seen Stowe advert to that method throughout "Sunny Memories," if less obviously. The surest example is the contrast between Scott and Shakespeare and the living and the dead. By affording us this close-up look at her method, she brings us to an understanding of how it points to something beyond itself. But in the process of doing so she has taught us to prefer the private sphere of perfected activity to the public realm. Still, she confessed that the essential objective of the black-white contrast is to convey a simplistic public teaching. She had therefore placed herself under the necessity of defending her recourse to a practical method the theoretical appropriateness of which is doubtful. She was called upon to demonstrate the distinction between her own absolutism and that of the unfeigning Quakers or, the distinction between her own simplistic teaching and that of a Bunyan, unseasoned by Defoe or Shakespeare.[49]

NOTES

1. April, 1855, p. 160ff. In addition, that essay interpreted "Sunny Memories" much more in the way Stowe intended—a rare occurrence.

2. Hedrick suggests that by landing at Liverpool rather than Glasgow, Stowe may have established some distance between herself and the Glasgow Female New

Association for the abolition of slavery, which was "viewed with suspicion by Garrison." Hedrick, *Harriet Beecher Stowe*, p. 236.

3. In the book, Stowe never explained how occasion for this campaign arose. These reflections, therefore, stand as an initial correspondence though, in fact, Stowe had corresponded with most if not all of these persons about her trip before she embarked.

4. The next soiree she reported—that of April 19th, as Calvin reports—is mentioned under date of April 26th in a letter that is undated. She spoke of it as if it had occurred on the 26th, thus justifying its place in the letter, following the account of correspondence. Later in that letter, under date of April 21, she related the trip to Aberdeen and thereby honored the strict chronology, if not explicitly.

5. *SM*, I, p. 316.

6. C. E. Stowe to H. B. Stowe, 5-18-42, op. cit.

7. *SM*, I, p. 319.

8. Note that in his essay, "The Religious Element in Education," Calvin Stowe urges the inclusion of the Bible in materials to be studied as part of the public education system then just developing in the United States.

9. The point again echoes Calvin's essay, ibid.

10. Compare Calvin's 1833 essay on the subject, discussed in book I, part II. Of course, he discussed America primarily.

11. *SM*, II, p. 101.

12. Ibid., p. 123.

13. Ibid., p. 124. "The current of novel writing is reversed. Instead of milliners and chambermaids being bewitched with the adventures of countesses and dukes, we now have fine lords and ladies hanging enchanted over the history of John the carrier, with his little Dot, dropping sympathetic tears into little Charlie's washtub, and pursuing the fortunes of a poor dressmaker's apprentice, in company with poor Smike, and honest John Brodie and his little Yorkshire wife."

14. Reform Bill: 1832; British Emancipation: 1833.

15. *SM*, II, p. 133.

16. Forrest Wilson, *Crusader in Crinoline* , p. 364 and, quoting Buchanan, p. 386. The best testimony of the Stowe party's impression of Ambassador Ingersoll's antagonism is found in Beecher's *Diary*, under date of May 28: "Sherman and I drove to Ingersoll's, to get my passports. He knew me, & directed all his conversation to Mr. Sherman. In the course of conversation he took occasion with a bad taste that no Englishman or Frenchman could ever have been guilty of, to allude to an article in the Morning Chronicle of yesterday unfavorable to Mr. Stowe, & was on the point of reading an extract, when I took the wind out of his sails by quoting Argyle's remark which he had made that morning at the table that the Animus of that piece was ______________. They could not endure that a dissenting chn (churchman) should produce so high a type of piety. Shaftsbury said if Uncle Tom had been an Episcopalian & St. Clare a Bishop they would have liked it very well.—This took Ingersoll aback—he read his extract but it was collapsed. It closed with the sentence, 'If we must choose between Mrs. Stowe and St. Paul, we really believe we should prefer the latter.'—Sherman coolly remarked—'No doubt—Mrs. Stowe would be probably of the same opinion.' Ingersoll is a fawning sycophant."

17. The account is given in Letter XVI, the central letter of the entire campaign. The Stafford House affair was the occasion for formal presentation of the "Affectionate Address," the subject of damning and praising in the American press for the previous six months. This particular occasion was the most noteworthy and controversial of the entire tour. Stowe silently indicated this fact by de-emphasizing the Exeter Hall rally and making the account of the Stafford House gathering the only extensive account of a public affair during the last half of the campaign. But she publicly reduced its dimensions by what she had to say of it and by intentionally omitting singular details.

18. That was surely the reason Stowe sent him a copy from the first printing of the novel. Cf. Carlisle, *Travels in America*.

19. According to Charles Beecher's most helpful *Diary*, Stowe actually did have this experience of first disliking and then liking works by Rubens. She shared her particular judgments with a critic and gained immense confidence when he "explained" the difference in her reactions. He informed her that, while Rubens *painted* the second picture, another artist *designed* it. Needless to say, this detail did not enter into the published version. Cf., p. 148.

20. Hedrick recognizes that Stowe's attention to works of art in "Sunny Memories" is significant, but misses the political message which is part of the significance. Hedrick, *Harriet Beecher Stowe*.

21. Stowe's philosophizing on harmony of expression may have been influenced by Archibald Alison's essay "On Taste." Camfield points out her mention of this essay in an autobiographical sketch published in 1863 and quotes the following from Alison: "'The principle which governs this ideal composition is that of unity of expression; that he admits into his sketch no feature or colour which does not correspond with the character which interests him; and that he is at last only satisfied when he has formed the conception of one uniform and harmonious whole'" [Archibald Alison, *Essays on the Nature and Principles of Taste*, 2 vols., 6th edition (Edinburgh: Archibald Constable, 1825)]. Camfield, "Moral Aesthetics," p. 337.

22. *SM*, I, p. 292.

23. Ibid., p. 293. Stowe's emphasis. This is the *unique* use of "regime" in the book, in the center of the central chapter of the discussion of the campaign. The focus is clearly on the nature of the American Constitution. Compare the end of this present book II, part I. Cf. concerning the "restlessness of the Americans," see Tocqueville, *Democracy in America*, Ch. 6, section on "Activity Prevailing in All Parts of the Political Body in the United States . . . " and, in particular, Ch. 9, section on "Accidental or Providential Causes Helping to Maintain a Democratic Republic in the United States," where, among other things, it is observed: "In Europe we habitually regard a restless spirit, immoderate desire for wealth, and an extreme love of independence as great social dangers. But precisely those things assure a long and peaceful future for the American republics. . . . What a happy land the New World is, where man's vices are almost as useful to society as his virtues!" (284, Tocqueville [Mayer] 1988 [1969]).

24. Ibid., I, pp. 289–90. According to the press, Shaftsbury did not read the address itself. He only acknowledged its existence and Mrs. Stowe's presence. Stowe's anticipation of the event is instructive: "I sought a little private conversation with the duchess in her boudoir, in which I frankly confessed a little anxiety, respecting

the arrangements of the day: having lived all my life in such a shady and sequestered way, and being entirely ignorant of life, as it exists in the sphere in which she moves, such apprehensions were rather natural. She begged that I would make myself entirely easy, and consider myself as among friends; that she had invited a few friends to lunch, and that afterwards others would call; that there would be a short address from the ladies of England read by Lord Shaftsbury, which would require no answer. I could not but be grateful for the consideration thus evinced."

25. Ibid., p. 295.

26. Cf. Stowe's tribute to Lady Shaftsbury: "But in the English nation it is a noticeable fact, that the long struggle by which liberal ideas and the rights of the common people have been steadily advanced has found some of its most efficient supporters among the nobility." Harriet Beecher Stowe, "Tribute of a Loving Friend to the Memory of a Noble Woman," *The Atlantic Monthly* 23 (1869): 242–43.

27. See especially the "complete" catalogue by William Young Ottley. William Young Ottley, *Engravings of the Marquis of Staffords's Collection of Pictures in London, Arranged According to Schools and in Chronological Order: With Remarks on Each Picture* (London: P. w. Tompkins, 1818).

28. Recent Stowe scholarship, especially by feminist scholars, has delved into both the influence of this nineteenth-century convention upon Stowe and her role in shaping the convention. Cf. Amy Schrager Lang, "Slavery and Sentimentalism: The Strange Career of Augustine St. Clare," *Women's Studies* 12 (1986); Sachs, "Describing a Sphere"; Hedrick, *Harriet Beecher Stowe*; and Weinstein, "Educating Sympathy," among others.

29. Interestingly, none of the critics who debate Stowe's position on colonization seem to have investigated "Sunny Memories" on this point.

30. Cf. *SM*, I, p. 303 and II, p. 87.

31. As noted earlier, Newman provides perhaps the most intriguing discussion of Stowe's defense of the Highland clearances. Newman, "Stowe's Sunny Memories."

32. Marotta provides an intriguing discussion of Stowe's views on and use of pre- and post-Raphaelite art in chapter 4 of his dissertation. Marotta, "The Literary Relationships of George Eliot and HBS."

33. Of course, "the first that I had ever seen" is not the exact equivalent of "that I had seen for the first time." One may see the first painting he had ever seen twenty years later and still report that it was the first he had ever seen.

34. *SM*, I, p. 322. Those critics who see Stowe as a utopian would do well to take these words into their account.

35. Ibid., pp. 323–24.

36. Ibid., II, p. 6.

37. *Crusader in Crinoline*, pp. 378–80. Cf. The Letter to the Ladies New Anti-Slavery Society of Glasgow. Several Stowe scholars differ from Wilson's perspective on this point; for example, Reynolds writes, "Apparently [Calvin Stowe] accorded his wife the same respect she showed him." Moira Davison Reynolds, *Uncle Tom's Cabin and Mid-Nineteenth-Century United States: Pen and Conscience* (Jefferson, NC: McFarland, 1985), p. 141. Also, Springer quotes from a letter by Stowe to George Eliot (dated April 20, 1873) in which she said that her husband "is on all subjects my teacher, my medium of conversation with the great world of thought—I cannot image how I could live without him to tell me what I want to know." Marlene Springer,

"Stowe and Eliot: An Epistolary Friendship," *Biography* 9, no. 1 (1986): 75. Stowe's most recent biographer, Hedrick, also differs from Wilson on this point, as noted earlier in this text. Hedrick, *Harriet Beecher Stowe.*

38. *SM*, II, p. 24.

39. Ibid., p. 32.

40. C. E. Stowe to H. B. Stowe, July 20, 1836, London (Stowe-Day).

41. *SM*, II, p. 33.

42. Louis (Lajos) Kossuth led the insurrection of 1848–1849 in Hungary and subsequently—an exile—campaigned extensively in the United States and in other nations in Western Europe.

43. *SM*, II, p. 55.

44. Ibid., p. 109. The statement, "while we were in London," suggests that this note was written after the tour. But the letter is datelined "London." The note must have been written for publication.

45. Ibid., p. 83.

46. Ibid., p. 84.

47. Ibid., pp. 85–86.

48. Ibid., p. 84.

49. Christian's abandonment of his family is the consequence of a naive faith which was rewarded in the end by the salvation of that very family and their happy reunion in heaven. Uncle Tom, on the other hand, abandons his family without real assurance of their eventual earthly salvation.

24

The Defense of Melodrama

Stowe responded to the challenge by creating an archetypal melodrama.[1] The melodrama is confined to Letter XXII and the discussion of a tour of Windsor Castle. This aesthetic pleasure was preferred to an invitation to join a group of dignitaries going to see off an emigrant ship.

The defense of melodrama is a defense in the highest sense, a demonstration of its virtue. Although, like the *Apology* of Socrates, it must reveal some concern with responding to charges made by critics regarding its propriety or conformity with established canons, its true defense resides in its founding of superior standards. The superiority of melodrama resides in its capacity to cultivate just sentiment without respect to place. That is, it completely abstracts from the regnant morality[2] and attendant social conditions but thereby arouses the sentiment of justice. Its absolutism is only apparent, for it can never be applied in any given circumstance. Thus, it affords no excuse for or incentive to authoritarianism or despotism.[3] Melodrama creates or purveys the kind of education suited to pure or well-intentioned souls in an imperfect world.[4] As a consequence, it is a vehicle of perfection or at least improvement in an imperfect world to the precise extent that it is teachable. Since it is teachable to the many, the many are therefore improvable. Men are not, for example, capable of complete abstinence from slave-grown produce where slavery exists. Yet, most men are capable of abhorring slavery. And to the extent the abhorrence is cultivated will they find themselves less inclined to encourage slavery by usage of such products. Thus, the initial abstraction from place and circumstance, affording the liberty to cultivate fervent sentiment, is the means which affords an eventual improvement of circumstances.[5] To many this will seem the presentation of an at best dubious claim—the social usefulness of hypocrisy. But a distinction is to be made between hypocrisy and the salutary nature of melodramatic sentiment after the defense is completed. For the present, it is well to carry further the idea of the relationship between place and sentiment. Stowe gives examples.

Discussing Shakespeare's "Merry Wives," Stowe reported the approach to Windsor, the anticipation of it, as coloring everything they encountered.[6] Where Shakespeare showed the incongruity between the human souls and the environment, she shows only agreement. She shows, at least, the overriding importance of agreement in the soul. It is a kind of environmental determinism in reverse.

> About nine o'clock we found ourselves in the cars, riding through a perpetual garden of blooming trees and blossoming hedges, birds in a perfect delight. Our spirits were all elated. Good, honest, cackling Mrs. Quickly herself was not more disposed to make the best of everything and everybody than we were. (Mrs. Quickly, of course, wished to do the best by everyone by winning to several suitors the hand of a single maiden!) *Mr. S., in particular,* (This was but two days after the Exeter Hall affair. Calvin was evidently well pleased with himself.) was so joyous that I was afraid he would break out into song, after the fashion of Sir Hugh Evans [the parson],—
>
> "melodious birds sung madrigals
> whenas I sat in Pabylon," etc.
> (III, i, 8–30, emphasis supplied.)

Again, the slight defects of Stowe's excellent memory cause a change in the quotation which brings it nearer to the meaning of her explicit reflections. Shakespeare's parson spoke in the present tense of the bird's song, intermitted a phrasal pause after "madrigals," and separated "when" from "as" in his Welsh praise of "Pabylon." Stowe's construction provides a continuous conception. By changing the independent relative pronoun plus adverb (in effect, a "genitive of place where"), she removes all sense of the incongruity in the parson's situation (His saintly person amidst the pleasures of Babylon!) as he prepares to fight a duel. Her reading shows the birds merely having sung *while* or "when as" he "sat in Babylon": whereas Shakespeare's version emphasizes the birds present singing while he sat *there,* in Babylon. The differences may be more meaningful if we alter the figure.

> We were locked arm in arm in battle,
> (circumstanced) under a canopy of nightingales
>
> as opposed to,
>
> We were locked arm in arm in battle
> (in the place) where the nightingales canopied.

In the last version it is a matter of complete indifference whether the nightingales actually witnessed the mortal struggle. One but identifies the place where the struggle occurred with such incidental detail as is appropriate. Stowe uses Evan's song, therefore, to reveal that the soul's sentiments are independent of the circumstances in which those sentiments are formed or held.[7] The Puritan in Babylon is yet a Puritan!

Calvin's joyousness is, in fact, the opposite of Evan's disposition. Evans sang, perhaps, to avoid crying; or his song was a cry, the cry of the saintly heart in Babylon. He spoke of himself as "full of chollors" and "trempling of mind," giving full force to the incongruity between his profession and his circumstances. "How melancholies I am," said he. And, starting up his song after promising to "knock Dr. Caius' urinals about his knave's costard" as soon as he has "good opportunity" to do so, he pauses to note, "Mercy on me! I have a great disposition to cry" (we may note, incidentally that the duel is brought on by Mrs. Quickly's attempt to do the best for everyone!) Now, this passage hardly seems apt to describe Calvin's joyousness! Indeed, it was Stowe, musing over Gray's "Elegy" in a country churchyard, who had "such 'dispositions to melancholies' as Sir Hugh Evans," that she allowed Calvin to return to London for a "peace meeting" (how differently Evans and Calvin approached their duels—and how different the outcome! This "peace meeting," by the bye, is not reported elsewhere, nor elaborated upon here) and remained herself to indulge her sentiments. After this indulgence, it was disappointing, *though not wholly destructive*, to learn that she was not in *the* "country churchyard." (According to Beecher's *Diary*, she was! But her version is more instructive. It is another proof of the detachment of noble sentiment from actual circumstances. Cf. the entry of May 17.)

> However . . . we could both console ourselves with the reflection that the emotion was admirable, and wanted only the right place to make it the most appropriate in the world.[8]

Evans could well have learned from this moral to consider his circumstances with less foreboding. For he saw only the drama and not the melodrama of his situation. There is always some compromising drama beneath the melodrama—some nasty "real life" considerations. One of the first reflections at the palace was occasioned by a reunion with the same picture of Charles I on horseback we had seen at Warwick. But its charm and special status were gone, as it no longer faced opposite Cromwell. Though the kindly sentiments expressed earlier may have been the most appropriate in the world, they were so only because of the place where they were formed. There were even many other views of Charles, and of his family, but the charm did not return. Now what was true of the life of Charles at Windsor was still true of the tyrant Charles at Warwick. The drama was unchanging.

Only the sentiment changed. Where, therefore, Stowe seems to confess a connection between place and sentiment, she in fact only confesses sentiment's independence of place. In doing so she demonstrates the drama beneath the melodrama.

The defense of melodrama is conveyed through a discussion of art and the critic's reaction to it. It is a question of "how much in a picture belongs to the idiosyncrasies of the viewer." Similarly, "much in painting and poetry depends upon the frame of mind in which we see or hear." The critic's task is especially difficult, for if he is proof against bias, he is an incompetent. But if he is capable of "moods and tenses," if he is sensitive, "how can we know that he does not impose his peculiar mood as a general rule?" This is still more true in melodrama—the black-white contrast—which obscures the drama of an event and hence expresses *only* sentiments, or moods and tenses. Since the premise of the syllogism is that the emotions of "fine art" are restive under the sway of restraint and rule, there seems no hope at all for the critic. To look at Zuccarelli, or read the *Lotus Eaters* or *Castle of Indolence*, when the soul and body are fatigued, for example, produces quite a differing image than is received with the "strong nerves of our more healthful and hilarious seasons." Stowe makes herself an example of these effects for the purpose of elaborating her defense.

After viewing much more, and being "most fatigued," the party came to the marble monument to Princess Charlotte. The work presents death, from an earthly and heavenly aspect, in two groups, the one above the other. It was a strict black-white contrast. The whole party was captivated by and enjoyed the scene.

After the presentation of this result, Stowe became rhetorical and appealed to the reader to discover poetic principle in the sanctuary. Appealing to "any one who can judge of poetry" whether the conception were not "poetical," and to any one with a "heart" whether it is not "pathos," she defended a "high poetic merit *in the mere conception*" (emphasis supplied). At some length she adduces and praises the poetic value of the work and then confesses she has reason to be thus rhetorical.

> Well, you will ask, why are you going on in this argumentative style? Who doubts you? Let me tell you, then, a little fragment of my experience. We saw this group . . . the *last thing*, before dinner, *after a most fatiguing* forenoon of sightseeing, when we were both tired and hungry,—a most unpropitious time, certainly,—and yet it enchanted our whole company; what is more, it made us all cry—a fact of which I am not ashamed, yet.[9] (Emphasis supplied)

But they learned "only the next day," from an artist, an authority, that the work was of "miserable taste" and utterly shocking. The work was "melodramatic—terribly so!"

At this first assault Stowe withdrew from the field. Confessing ignorance—or, at least, a "not very clear idea" of the meaning of the term, she thought it better to "reconsider my tears." But instead she offers a reconsideration of the authority's objection, concludes that "I see no sense in it," and launches her defense. If a work be "strongly suggestive, poetic, and pathetic," it holds some space in the "world of art." The "artists," therefore, must not be allowed to severely narrow the "rules of the game." Artists concentrate, after all, on works of imagination only because of their importance *vis-à-vis* nature, and, hence, a true conception of life's drama.

> But they let the works of nature alone, because they know there is no hope for them, and content themselves with enacting rules in literature and art, which make all the perfection and grace of the past so many impassable barriers to progress in the future. Because the ancients kept to unity of idea in their groups, and attained to most beautiful results by doing so, shall no modern make an antithesis in marble?

Stowe decided to remain wedded to her own opinion, "like an obstinate republican." The relating of this struggle is entirely melodramatic, the very good and innocent fending off the chains of the very bad. The end of this melodrama, too, is republican happiness ever after—save, its artfulness (the obscuring of the drama beneath the melodrama) is intentionally revealed by the artist in the last sentence as a means of cautioning the reader to take it as an instructive device and not as a lesson in itself.

We might say, she reminds the reader that the authority's critique, "It is melodramatic—terribly so!" could have been misspoken. It may reveal an imperfection in the attempt and not an imperfection in the form, since her staged defense is melodramatic, perfectly so. The last sentence reads:

> So, you see, like an obstinate republican, as I am, I defend my right to have an opinion about this monument, *albeit the guide book, with its usual diplomatic caution,* says, *"It is in very questionable taste."* (Emphasis supplied)

It was not in innocence if in goodness she appreciated the work. It required not the authority of the next day to stage the confrontation. Thus, the defense of melodrama is not the stated defense. It is the act of appreciation itself, against the strictures of the guidebook, that constitutes a defense of melodrama—not unarmed ignorance but armed wisdom. Stowe knew in advance, in other words, not only that the work was in questionable taste, but exceptionally so, since the extreme statement in the guidebook belies its "usual diplomatic caution" (what must we think if the whole story were a fiction? If there were no such sculpture, properly speaking, but rather the coenotaph of the Princess Caroline, housed in the castle's chapel?

Cf. Beecher's *Diary* entry for May 17). Her prior knowledge reveals that melodrama is but a vehicle for assaulting established authorities and, more importantly, that the true judgment of art (of a regnant morality) cannot be entrusted to artists who are, by definition, ignorant of nature.

An effective defense of melodrama, however, cannot consist in that mere assertion, so much as it can in the artful presentation of innocence, besieged by sophistication, emerging triumphant in the end. The trick is to give to the *in fact* sophisticated—those who are in fact superior to constituted authority—the very appearance of innocence, thus concealing both their wisdom and strength. From the point of view of philosophic insight, there is no better place for a Puritan to be than in Babylon! Precisely because the melodrama obscures the "drama of life," our capacity to understand what is by nature heightens our understanding of the "drama of life," which reveals an unsuspected kinship with the melodrama. For, to philosophic insight, the drama of life is melodramatic—terribly so.[10]

I. CORRECTED IMPRESSIONS

Before undertaking a discussion of the summary letters of "Sunny Memories" we must derive the standards of art or melodrama and respond to the criticism that this is a teaching of hypocrisy—a worship of the high and a practice of the low. At least four standards are suggested in the text. First, a work of art must be "strongly suggestive, poetic, and pathetic."[11] These three concerns are offered as fulfilling a single condition. Taking our lead from the terms themselves, we may say the condition is the artful presentation of what *is* in a manner that satisfies or invokes human sensibilities.[12] Secondly, it must be a work of imagination that is cognizant of the limits of artistic expression. It must, therefore, point beyond itself to nature or what may not be within the power of the artist as such to grasp but is nonetheless the true standard of human judgment.[13] Thirdly, a work of art must offer "perfection and grace" as an end to be attained but not yet possessed. And, fourthly, a work of art must strive for beauty of result.

Now, each of these standards serves as a limiting condition upon the other three. Thus, for example, anything that impugns human sensibility, if depicted with great grace and beauty, cannot qualify as a work of art. Similarly, nothing that is strongly suggestive of the human condition, deprived of perfection and beauty, is a work of art. Evidently, Stowe's obstinate republicanism is not a defense of radical individualism, which, by its nature, denies the existence of art as such.

A consequence of these standards would be an art which constantly memorializes men as better than they are while faithfully describing their weaknesses.[14] As such it would give rise to criticism of the incongruity between the preachings and practices of men. The artist, first, would be accused of hypocrisy. And men, second, to the extent they patronized or generated such art through their sentiments, would be accused of hypocrisy. And the cry would doubtless be raised that much injustice in the world could be eliminated if men were only to reconcile their unlimited ambitions to their limited and sullied capacities.

It is precisely to the refutation of this claim that this defense—and the liberal history of "Sunny Memories"—was dedicated. We saw Calvin's version in the "Introduction," that to abandon human conscience to the temptations of commerce was to abandon humankind. We saw, also, Stowe's provisional version in Letter X, that to give a laborer a clean collar was to elevate his vision. We may now see what both intend: that the relationship between opinion and deed is such that any effort to reconcile opinion to the level or standard of deeds as they exist at any given moment is to lapse into a mere primitivistic positivism; that is, a mere doing of whatever men do simply because it has been done. And in America in 1854 that means acceptance of slavery. It is the abandonment of standards of right. The absolutism of melodrama avoids hypocrisy precisely because, while saving a standard of right, it denies the title of absolute right to any existing deed or circumstance. A memorializing of what men can be is identical to lamenting what they are. And though that memorializing, since it is only art, does not present the complete picture of life, it does serve to undermine pretense of right (genuine hypocrisy) and to stave off despotism.[15]

NOTES

1. She had, of course, already created an archetypal melodrama in *Uncle Tom's Cabin.* Shipp opens his dissertation with a brief recounting of several critical definitions of melodrama as a genre. He finds that "All of these definitions appear, to some degree, to be applicable to Mrs. Stowe's story, but the incompleteness of the correspondence suggests one of two possibilities: either Mrs. Stowe wrote an imperfect melodrama or these definitions are themselves imperfect." Shipp goes on, then, to develop a new definition of melodrama, which grows out of an analysis of *Uncle Tom's Cabin,* and of its dramatizations. His assessment contrasts sharply with that of many Stowe scholars who fault the melodrama of *Uncle Tom's Cabin* for weakening its impact. Rather, he concludes it was the perfect and deliberate choice of genre for her message. Shipp, "*UTC* and the Ethos of Melodrama," p. 53.

2. Brooks disagrees: cf. note 4 below. Brooks, *The Melodramatic Imagination.*

3. See chapter 23, note 34.

4. Cf. Shipp: "Melodrama is a fundamentally egalitarian genre that burdens and empowers the individual by asserting both his responsibility and his ability to choose the actions that define him," and Brooks: "While its social implications may

be variously revolutionary or conservative, [melodrama] is in all cases radically democratic, striving to make its representations clear and legible to everyone. We may legitimately claim that melodrama becomes the principal mode for uncovering, demonstrating, and making operative the essential moral universe in a post-sacred era." Shipp, "*UTC* and the Ethos of Melodrama," p. 195. Brooks, *The Melodramatic Imagination*, p. 15. Cox applies Brooks's description of melodrama to Stowe's novel and concludes: "If ever a book had melodramatic structure, it is *Uncle Tom's Cabin*, and certainly in its manifest intention it is radically democratic in its universally clear and legible effort to express an essential moral universe in post-sacred era. . . . The radical democracy of *Uncle Tom's Cabin* is at once liberal and conservative—liberal in its determination to extend humanity into the excluded slave population, and conservative in its direct insistence upon reasserting the sacred as the essence of social justice." James M. Cox, "Harriet Beecher Stowe: From Sectionalism to Regionalism," *Nineteenth Century Fiction* 38, no. 4 (1984): 455.

5. Cf. McNeil: " . . . Stowe confidently used melodrama as an instrument for moral awakening. . . . Emotions are a direct route to morality, and melodrama can set the reader on that road." Helen McNeil, "Romance, Research, Melodrama," *Encounter* 53, no. 1 (1979): 75. Williams also makes use of Brooks's analysis and lists numerous luminaries of American literature, stage, and film, who along with Uncle Tom, " . . . all share the common function of revealing moral good in a world where virtue has become hard to read." Linda Williams, *Playing the Race Card: Melodrama of Black and White from Uncle Tom to O. J. Simpson* (Princeton: Princeton University Press, 2001), p. 19.

6. Lines 62–79, Yale edition, which is based on the Oxford Shakespeare. The Folio edition follows this reading. Windsor was said to be the representative palace in the same way Warwick was the representative feudal state. But, also, Windsor had been memorialized by Shakespeare's *Merry Wives of Windsor*. That makes it an apt vehicle for the demonstration of what Shakespeare had to contribute to the melodramatic art—a "disposition to make the best of everything and everybody." Throughout "Sunny Memories" this play, written for the "taste" of the "vestal virgin," is invoked three times more frequently, as I believe, than any other. In Letter XXII Stowe actually quotes the poet's portrait of the palace. It is Act V, Scene V, at that point at which Anne Page dispatches the pretended fairies to find and torment Sir John Falstaff with accusation of lust and concupiscence. The passage reads as follows:

> Search Windsor Castle, elves, within and out:
> Strew good luck, ouphs, in every sacred room,
> That it may stand till the perpetual doom,
> In state as wholesome as in state 'tis fit,
> Worthy the owner, and the owner it.
> The several chairs of order look you scour
> With juice of balm and every precious flower;
> Each fair instalment, coat, and several crest,
> With loyal blazon, ever more be blest!
> And nightly, meadow-fairies, look you sing,
> Like to the Garter's compass, in a ring:
> More fertile fresh than all the field to see;

And, *Honi Soit qui mal y pense* write
In emerald tufts flowers purple blue and white;
Like sapphire, pearl, and rich embroidery,
(Buckled below fair knighthood's bending knee:)
Fairies use flowers for their charactery.

The bracketed line in the quotation is omitted by Stowe. The only other change in the text occurs in the first line, where "within and out" became "within, without." The change in the first line saves the meter and the meaning. The change at line 78 alters the meter of the passage as a whole and of the immediate circumstance (unless "charactery" is read as three rather than four syllables). And it substitutes continuation of rhymed couplets for the break in the pattern Shakespeare had employed. The difference could be attributed to Stowe's citing the passage from memory without checking it, as Stowe scholars usually suggest. But we have already seen in the use of "Beaver Brook" that her "memory" is informed by the principle of poetic composition.

We need not, however, rely on this direct evidence to reveal the intentionality and purpose of the changes. A more slightly noticed, a more subtle change produces so strong an inference of change in the obvious case as to override all reservation. Lines 75–76 in Stowe's version read "And *Honi soit qui mal y pense,* write/In emerald tufts, flowers, purple, blue, and white." The simple elimination of the comma after "And," the addition of a comma after "pense," and the insertion of a comma between "flowers" and "purple" completely alter the meaning of the passage. In the original the fairies are commanded to write the words "*Honi soit qui mal y pense,*" using multi-colored flowers and emerald tufts. Stowe, on the other hand, declares "shame on whomever thinks evil" of such writing. And she commands the writing to be done in flowered characters without regard to that opinion. With that in mind, the omitted line seems clearly inappropriate in Stowe's version. For Shakespeare, the fairies' work prepares the way for the deeds of knights. Adapting nature's finery to the stated purpose is likened to buckling "sapphire, pearl, and rich embroidery" beneath the "fair knighthood's bending knee." The finery of the good and the defenders of the good, to Shakespeare, is strictly subordinated to the ends of goodness. Stowe replaces the phrasal pause at the end of line 76 with a mere comma and continues as though completing the elaboration of the finery with which fairies write. Thus, the flowered characters are left standing—on their own as it were—and "*honi soit qui mal y pense.*"

7. Cf. Shipp: " . . . the characters in melodrama are defined by the actions they take . . . rather than by their 'inner lives' . . . although the characters are not necessarily directly responsible for their environment, they are responsible for the actions they take in it." Shipp, "*UTC* and the Ethos of Melodrama," pp. 181–82.

8. *SM*, II, pp. 49–50.

9. Ibid., p. 46.

10. Hedrick correctly perceived the tendency of Stowe's anecdote: "Stowe includes in *Sunny Memories* a telling anecdote in which she was chastised by an 'artist' for her raptures over a 'melodramatic' Victorian sculpture. . . . This story illustrates the process through which *Uncle Tom's Cabin* would be relegated to that same category beneath contempt, 'melodrama,' and the book's power to evoke a powerful response from the reader would become a reason to despise it as unartistic. When the

authority to judge what passed from the people to artists and critics, a cultural divide opened between popular entertainment and high art.

"In *Sunny Memories* Stowe both observes the increasing codification of high culture and takes steps to undercut it. . . . Stowe simultaneously undercuts her pretensions to high culture and maintains her foothold in it. . . . By speaking in a colloquial, 'folksy' voice about what was increasingly becoming high, inaccessible art, Stowe's intent was not to debunk the art but rather to encourage a 'spontaneous' reaction to it—although in this increasingly self-conscious cultural encounter, it is hard to know what spontaneity might look like." Hedrick, *Harriet Beecher Stowe*, p. 268–69.

Williams also mentions this incident; while she recognizes that Stowe's relating of it is a subterfuge ("What interests me in this anecdote is . . . Stowe's desire to present herself as not quite comprehending what it means"); however, she does not entirely recognize Stowe's defense of melodrama ("Without specifically taking up the defense of the term, Stowe nevertheless defends the right of an artist to break the 'classical' rules of unity and decorum, even if it means 'being melodramatic'"). Williams, *Playing the Race Card*, p. 11.

11. Cf. Brooks: "In psychic, in ethical, in formal terms, [melodrama] may best be characterized as an expressive genre . . . [it] is the expressionism of the moral imagination." Brooks, *The Melodramatic Imagination*, p. 55. Also Williams: "[Melodrama's] sensations are the means to something more important: the achievement of a felt good, the merger—perhaps even the compromise—of morality and feeling into empathetically imagined communities forged in the pain and suffering of innocent victims, and the actions of those who seek to rescue them." Williams, *Playing the Race Card*, pp. 20–21.

12. Cf. Brooks: "[Melodrama] always makes an implicit claim that the world of reference—'real life'—will, if properly considered, live up to the expectations of the moral imagination: that the ordinary and humble and quotidian will reveal itself full of excitement, suspense, and peripety, conferred by the play of cosmic relations and forces." Brooks, *The Melodramatic Imagination*, p. 54.

13. Cf. Mason: " . . . melodrama is a means of revealing the nature of virtue." Mason, *Melodrama and the Myth of America*, p. 17. Also Brooks: "[Melodrama] is about virtue made visible and acknowledged." Brooks, *The Melodramatic Imagination*, p. 27.

14. Cf. Shipp: " . . . the melodramatist . . . empowers the most ordinary character by portraying him as potentially capable of achieving a result in any circumstance, however extreme; when the character fulfills his potential and achieves a result, the melodramatist magnifies the achievement because he has placed it in an extraordinary circumstance; at the same time, the melodramatist reminds his audience of the magnitude of personal responsibility by presenting his characters as being required to act positively even in the most difficult circumstances. A character in melodrama can and must choose the actions, hence results, that define him, and he is required to do so regardless of the pressure he feels from circumstances." Shipp, "*UTC* and the Ethos of Melodrama," pp. 190–91.

15. See book II, part I, chapter 22, on the teachability of melodrama. To judge how radical is this defense, one may contrast it with Hadass' account of Greek tragedy:

> For discussion and reflection there is always room, for Greek tragedy never presents a white hero opposed to a black villain. Where it may seem to do so, as in Sophocles' *Antigone*, we may be sure we are misreading the play, for the Greeks wrote tragedy, not melodrama. The spectacle of virtue always triumphant could only corroborate smugness; the spectacle of flawless virtue crushed to earth would only be shocking, as Aristotle points out. If in the elemental struggle against destiny man seems doomed to defeat, that is the way life looked to tragedians. Their gloom is no fatalistic pessimism but an adult confrontation of reality, and their emphasis is not on the grimness of life but on the capacity of great figures to adequate themselves to it. The tragedy is accentuated by the large stature of its persons. The little man's woe's may be pathetic, but not tragic. Merely by naming Agamemnon the poet has his grand figure, and needs waste no space to build him up. Usually (but not always) he has another asset, which a modern playwright would hardly regard as such, the audience's probable familiarity with the outlines of the story. They came to see, not how the story would turn out, for the heroic legends were conned in childhood, but how the heroes cam to do what it was known they did, and what the meaning of it might be. Everyone knew that Orestes murdered his mother; but under what pressure could a son be brought to do such a thing, and what is its meaning? Greek tragedies are not mysteries (unless in the medieval sense). The "recognition" or "change of fortune" is not, as it is likely to be with us, at the end, but nearer the middle of the play. Generally the play ends on a note of calm, all passion purged.

Moses Hadas, *A History of Greek Literature* (New York: Columbia University, 1950), p. 75. Cf. book I, part I, especially the final chapter and Uncle Tom's death and book II, part II.

25

Pre-Utopian Reflections

The account of the London campaign closed with the same kind of chronological confusion that characterized the Scottish campaign. At the center of the confusion lay the strong possibility that the visit to Windsor Castle occurred during one of those eternal moments necessary to profound reflection. The confusion begins in Letter XXVII with the apparent assignment of Monday, May 29 for the date of Calvin's last appearance and public speech. The assignment of this date is made difficult by the assignment of dates to other events in Letters XXVIII and XXX. In particular, Letter XXX is addressed to Calvin, since embarked for America, and is *the* summary letter of the campaign.

> According to your request I will endeavor to keep you informed of all our goings on after you left, *up to the time of our departure for Paris.* We have borne in mind your advice to hasten away to the continent. (135, emphasis supplied)

This letter officially closes the campaign. Calvin departed on May 26. Stowe left for Paris on June 4. She had ten days on which to report, and she scrupulously logs each entry with reference to date and time. It is partly the extant letter Calvin wrote while shipboard, dated June 4, which allows us to penetrate the veil of this confusion of dates, which has him speaking at Willis's rooms *after* his departure.

> Monday night I was sick and vomited three or four times. . . . Expect to arrive Monday [June 6].[1]

Calvin's extra-textual testimony, however, only adds to the inconsistencies of the text itself.

"Sunny Memories" introduces another character, Charles Beecher, writing in a "Journal" at the close of the London campaign and thereafter. Beecher reports the departure for Paris as Saturday, June 4, in contrast with Stowe's anticipated Friday, June 5. The imaginary two days give time for visits to the churchyard of "Grays Elegy" and to Windsor Castle, both *in Calvin's company.* Forrest Wilson attempted to bypass these difficulties (which are really opportunities) by going back to Letter XXVII and correcting May 29 to May 25. Then, taking June 4 from Beecher's "Journal" he says she had nine days free to roam. But he was misled by her citation of *Friday* for the day of departure. Wilson brings the visit to Windsor Castle up to follow the *soirée,* though it was reported in Letter XXII, dated May 18, and though it is placed fifty pages and five letters earlier. In fact there *was* a visit to Windsor, and it did occur on May 17. The evidence for this is revealed in Beecher's actual *Diary,* on which the "Journal" was based. Once again, then, we see that the difficulties present in the text were intentionally introduced by Stowe as an indication of her purpose in writing "Sunny Memories."

This signpost allows us to minimize the hyperbole in Stowe's post-London confession:

> I scarcely consider myself to have seen anything of art in England. The calls of the living world were so various and *exigeant,* I had little leisure for reflection, that although I saw many paintings, I could not study them; and many times I saw them in a state of the nervous system too jaded and depressed to receive the full force of the impression. (XXXI)

All or nearly all that was done in and written of the London campaign was in the service of the exigencies of the "living world," of practical politics. The defense of melodrama was founded on the same principle that sustained Stowe's defense of her consistency in the dress-making scandal. In each case, the particular issue or dramatic circumstance was not to be elevated to a principle itself, but was rather to serve as an instrument for the expression of principle still more fundamental. Stowe's appeal to and defense of the workingmen and workingwomen is subordinated to the purposes of her campaign. The concluding letters of "Sunny Memories" substantiate this claim and reveal still more clearly those lights by which Stowe was guided as they are distinguished from the light she held before others.

Behind the elevation of Great Britain—and her classes—lay the elevation of the United States. The "vast power, physical and moral, and intellectual" exerted by the comparatively small Great Britain is a harbinger of American force.[2] But the expectation of American fulfillment of this promise must clearly abstract from the critique of American lapsarianism. The practical difficulties that confronted the campaign, the diplomatic niceties which restrained it, and the political objective which inspired it are but so many opportunities to praise the United States. The three chief diplomatic questions of the day are all touched upon in the closing letters. The Cuban question—which involved threats both of an American attempt to purchase or otherwise acquire the island from Spain and of the illegal slave trade—was shown to be affected by the campaign.[3] The related question of the effect of slavery and cotton sales on British-American relations was dismissed with the reflection that the source of any possible ill will could not persist in America.

> Were it possible that America were always to tolerate and defend slavery, this might be. But this would be self-destruction. It cannot, must not, will not be. We shall struggle, and shall overcome; and when the victory has been gained we shall love England all the more for her noble stand in the conflict. (136, vol. II)

The third diplomatic question involved Stowe's conspicuous absence from the Queen's "drawing room," and the absence of any audience with the Queen during the tour. The American minister later vaunted this as an achievement of diplomatic art, but Stowe—in nearly her last word of the campaign—shows complete disinterest in the royal tradition. Her republican simplicity disdained mere "parade and ceremony," of which she had to endure "very little" in England.[4] The three "questions of the day" had been preceded by the tale of a note that Stowe was to have edited and presented to the Duchess of Sutherland on behalf of the "Black Swan," an ex-slave woman of remarkable vocal capacities. Two women had assisted the singer. The Duchess preferred the note "just as she wrote it," a fact which Stowe explains: "People always like simplicity and truth better than finish."[5]

Simplicity *and* finish do conclude the London campaign—though with characteristic obliqueness. And the casual and reflective letters that follow the campaign—more nearly a travelogue—take advantage of this clear-cut conclusion to make clear Stowe's own lights. The campaign's conclusion builds around a final characterization of British aristocracy, its relationship to workingmen, and its expression in the form of government that characterizes that powerful but tiny isle. Letter XXV signals this development. Stowe reiterated those qualities the British, as such, can bring to the relief of slavery. Opposing the munificent offer to establish a college in and to support emigration to Antigua, Stowe demanded what we might call by analogy *indigenation*.

> My impression was, that Canada would be a much better place to develop the energies of the race. *First*, on account of its cold and bracing climate; *second*, because, having never been a slave state, the white population there are more thrifty and industrious, and of course the influence of such a community was better adapted to form thrift and industry in the negro. (87, vol. II)

Rejecting an appropriateness of climate for races while maintaining an appropriateness of climates for human character types, and building upon particular cultural virtues while seeking a universal manifestation of those virtues—those are the contributions Stowe would derive from the British.

We have shown before—in the account of Calvin's triad of speeches—that the foundation of British liberality was now American principle, even if that principle might be said to have originated in Britain. Because the British claim to liberal principle seemed somehow suspect, Stowe suggested a ground upon which to establish British compatibility with or adaptability to American principle. Letter XXIX cites the proof of stability in the midst of European chaos in 1848—a revolutionary era. Shaftesbury was reported to have likened the quiet and happiness of British monarchy to the repose of the republican "President of the United States in his drawing room."[6] The singular happiness of averting proletarian rebellion was the decisive proof that the regime was not oppressive. But this was not a complete proof. There was wanted such evidence of a change in course as to support the premise that this momentary result—the happiness of workingmen—might be a permanent characteristic. The latter evidence came in the form of the adaptation of universal moral arguments to particular political events. Stowe identified the early anti-slave trade and abolition crusades as commencing this process. And we have already discussed the numerous "humanitarian" reforms following in this train. The virtue of these movements stems less from their particular achievements than their general effect. Because they described society's "religious obligations . . . to *every* human soul," they necessarily "educated parliament" and the community. In the end Stowe derived the British contribution to the anti-slavery crusade from what she regarded as the present conjunctures of forces and principles in British politics.

Although the campaign had understated the role of the British form of government in this plan, her expectations were informed by what she conceived to be the inclinations and capacities of the British government. The British workingmen are cared for by British aristocrats—not neglected. And the precise habits or principles that permit aristocrats to transcend class interests enable men to discover their mutual obligations beyond natural boundaries. Not until the closing letter, when Stowe had returned to England on her way home from the continent, did she directly draw this conclusion: British aristocracy has been trained by its association with democracy.

> It has occurred to me, that the superior stability of the English aristocracy, as compared with that of other countries, might be traced, in part, to their relations with the representative branch of the government. . . . Thus the same ties bind them to the people which bind our own representatives—a peculiarity

> which, I believe, never existed permanently with the nobles in any other country. By this means the nobility, when they enter the House of Lords, are better adapted to legislate wisely for the interests, not of a class, but of the whole people.

This appraisal must seem naive to those who know, however little predictable it was in 1853, that the power of the Lords was broken once and for all hardly more than fifty years after this passage was written. But they misperceive. The true panegyric in this passage is for the Commons—where not many a workingman sat—and the notion of representation in particular. The British aristocrat was trained, little by little, to find the justification for his position and privilege in the principle of representation and not in heredity.

Stowe closed with a visit to the Parliament houses—which she preferred to the Queen's "drawing room." Nothing brings out her praise of England so strongly as this visit. And in this visit nothing is praised so strongly as that eminent conservative, Edmund Burke. Cromwell, who perhaps originated the representation we know, may not be included in the great hall that will memorialize the great men of England. Will Burke be included? Macaulay thought him the greatest man living in the late eighteenth century and "superior to every orator, ancient or modern" in fullness of understanding and "richness of imagination."[7] But Macaulay would never have praised Burke for the deed for which Stowe remembers him.

> I seemed to see all that brilliant scene when Burke spoke there amid the nobility, wealth, and fashion of all of England, in the Warren Hastings trial. That speech always made me shudder. I think that there was never anything more powerful than its conclusion. (138, vol. II)

The great commoner, standing at the bar of the Lords to impeach the Governor-General of India! And what was his conclusion?

> There is one thing, and one thing only, which defies all mutation; that which existed before the world, and will survive the fabric of the world itself; I mean justice; that justice, which emanating from the Divinity, has a place in the breast of every one of us, given us for our guide with regard to ourselves and with regard to others, and which will stand after this globe is burned to ashes . . . [8]

To insist on one rule of right for Indiaman and Englishman alike and one rule of law for Englishman and Indiaman seems scarcely distinguishable from enfranchising the *sans culottes*. Burke was impressed with the danger, if not the identity of the case.

> My lords, . . . if it should so happen that we shall be subjected to some of those frightful changes which we have seen—if it should happen that your lordships,

> stripped of all the decorous distinctions of human society, should, by hands at once base and cruel, be led to those scaffolds and machines of murder . . .
>
> . . . a great consolation it is, which often happens to oppressed virtue and fallen dignity; . . . that the very oppressors and persecutors themselves are forced to bear testimony in its favour.[9]

The great cause, for which sake Burke invited the lords to this martyrdom, is the refutation of Hastings's argument that the rule of right must differ as between a people in its nonage and civilized peoples. A final quotation from Burke shall reveal the magnitude of the charge.

> My lords, if the prisoner can succeed in persuading us that these people have no laws, no rights, not even the common sentiments of men, he hopes your interest in them will be considerably lessened. He would persuade you that their sufferings must be assuaged by their being nothing new; and that having no right to property, to liberty, to honour, or to life, they must be pleased with the little that is left to them . . .[10]

Hastings attempted to deny the natural rights of peoples of dissimilar or deficient civilization. Burke called on the lords to affirm their rights. The lords acquitted Hastings. Burke asked the lords to loose the jaws and stare into the mouths of the lions of France and modern universalism, for the sake of eternal justice. He asked them to stare down the lord-killers. The lords declined the sacrifice.

The great moment of English parliamentary endeavor is Burke's defeat in the trial of Warren Hastings. The Burke who—as far as any gentleman also in the government decently could—supported the American Revolution; the Burke who reviled the French revolution; Burke is the decisive model of the representative principle. Stowe seems to adopt his demand: the nonmutability of natural right is the firm principle of social intercourse. Here was the most clear-cut testing of the changeability of natural right the world has yet seen—surpassing even the Melian dialogue.[11] On one side we have the eminent "conservative" Burke pleading the eternity and universality of natural right, and on the other, Warren Hastings pleading the exigencies of British empire. And all of this erupts in the midst of the world-changing turmoil of the American and French revolutions. To Stowe, Burke's victory would have been a victory of that view of natural rights which admits of no exceptions. It was as such, like the anti-Mexico campaign, a blast in the modern attack on imperialism—while regarding that attack to originate in the American Revolution.

The connection between the praise of Burke and the praise of representation should be apparent: Burke defended the notion that the governor *should* take an "interest" in the governed. We understand representation to be based on respect for the many. Natural rights demand that all legitimate government be conceived as representative. And just so far as government recedes from the representative form is it understood to recede from justice.

When Stowe escaped the exiguous requirements of her campaign, she became a tourist. She visited France first, where she writes of being wearied by the naive imitation of classical style in French art. Along with naive imitation goes a focus on superficialities, "that passion for the outward and the visible," which permeates not just French art, but all French life.[12] This criticism of France is balanced by high praise in the final letter. But the praise is understood to be rooted in this initial criticism. We will return to this shortly.

In the Swiss countryside and mountains Stowe deliberated on the significance of the god-man-nature conception. For example, god-the-creator-of-man (the theological conception which dominated the campaign) now has ceded to the conception of man-the-discoverer-of-god-in-nature. It is again legitimate to speak of the poetry and artistry of God. Indeed, it is even difficult to conceive of god-the-creator-of-man as a rival to this conception, if one view only the human beings whose immediate contact with nature has worn their souls to dullness.[13] We would not be amiss to see the tendency of Stowe's remarks in the continental letters, the final letters, to be distancing her from ordinary mortals. Indeed, in Letter XXXV she seemed to attribute to everyone *but* herself an argument distinctly her own.

> If this power of producing the beautiful has been always so fascinating that the human race for its sake have bowed down at the feet even of men deficient in moral worth, if we cannot forbear loving the painter, poet, and sculptor, how much more shall we love God, who, with all goodness, has also all beauty! (250, vol. II)

She receded into her own soul but only at the price of losing the authority to speak for others. Her carriage driver delighted to explain "the localities" to her, though she was not without some confidence herself.

> Of course mademoiselle could do no less than be exceedingly grateful, since a peasant on his own ground is generally better informed than a philosopher from elsewhere. (208, vol. II)

That which the peasant is generally able to explain on his own ground, however, is not of interest to the philosopher. Stowe sought a foundation for her theology beyond the mutations of men, and a revelation can provide this foundation.

> I saw that cold, distant, unfeeling fate, or that crushing regularity of power and wisdom, which was all the ancient Greek or modern Deist can behold of God;

> but I beheld, as it were, crowned and glorified, one who had loved with our loves, and suffered with our sufferings. (215, vol. II)

It is unclear why Stowe's theology is opposed *only* to the two dominant strains of the *rationalist* tradition (this is true in Calvin's work also, but in that case the reason is clear). But there is certainly a suggestion that this theology in some way *completes* the two strains of rationalism, skepticism and determinism.

Stowe reached this point by some degree of detachment from public or political concerns. This procedure suggests that such moral and political arrangements as had been made—summarized in representation—were sufficient to safeguard the human element as such. We might take the concluding praise of Burke to be founded on principles not unlike those ascribed to Chamonix mules however unflattering. They were, says she, "safe and stupid as any conservative in any country."[14] Their determined adherence to precedence makes them quite predictable. This, not their safety nor their stupidity, is their great virtue. For one is required but to set them straight on the path in the beginning, a "delicate point."[15] What the first mule does all following will do. The lead mule must accordingly be blessed with more than the usual "native originality." Stowe's delightfully seri-comic presentation of Rousse, the lead mule in their caravan, and the dangers attending the ascending of mountains in such fashion never quite crossed the line into the realm of analogy. But the general conclusion drawn is nonetheless instructive.

> Yet I suppose we are no more really dependent upon God's providence in such circumstances, than in many cases where we think ourselves most secure. Still the thrill of this sensation is not without its pleasure, especially with such an image of almighty power and glory constantly before one's eyes as Mont Blanc. (223, vol. II)

We imagine, we might say, the social caravan in the train of Burke to be ascending toward a principle of universal justice—once, that is, Burke has been set straight on the path.

This is, for the first time in this work, an admittedly unrestrained application of interpretation. The opportunity for such a hell-bent-for-leather approach emerges from the apparent divergence between the goal of Stowe's private reflection and what we have understood to be the goal of society. At every step, as in the above citation, Stowe reaffirmed a subjection to or faith in God. Faith in God, however, remains an indefinite conception to mankind, which, in its indefiniteness, contrasts strongly with the definiteness of universal justice. No intelligent human being can fail to see that the latter is problematic. But the problematic is not as such indefinite. And it follows that it can retain its power to move human society even after it loses its power to move the intelligent mind. I will quote at length the crucial passages following upon the last quoted.

> There is another curious fact, and that is, that every prospect loses by being made definite. As long as we can only see a thing by glimpses, and imagine that there is a deal more that we do *not* see, the mind is kept in a constant excitement and play; but come to a point where you can fairly and squarely take in the whole, and there your mind falls listless. It is the greatest proof to me of the infinite nature of our minds, that we almost instantly undervalue what we have thoroughly attained.

> I remember, once after finishing a very circumstantial treatise on the nature of heaven,[+] being oppressed with a similar sensation of satiety,—that which hath not entered the heart of man to conceive must not be mapped out,—hence the wisdom of the dim, indefinite imagery of the scriptures . . . (Ch. 33, p. 225, vol. II, original emphasis)

The journey to Mont Blanc provided the occasion for these reflections. The failure of the possession to match the grandeur of the anticipation created the problem.

I submit that we see plainly phrased the second critique of utopian politics, this time in philosophical rather than political terms. The critique is founded on nothing less than Uncle Tom's ratification of the principle that the whole world is "as empty as an egg shell."[16] We saw, however, that that statement was problematic in itself. What, therefore, these passages suggest is the dual necessity for humankind to strive for the whole and to refuse to the attainment of any particular state or thing the characterization as whole, final, or complete. If our minds are indeed infinite, it must follow that history can no more come to an end than thought or consciousness itself. Universal justice would not be the *final* consciousness. The defect of fatedness was the denial of thought. The defect of enlightenment—"power and wisdom" systematized—was the attempt to complete thought. Stowe's theology attempts a re-opening of minds. But the re-opening depends on a refusal to characterize the nature of heaven—a refusal to map out the inconceivable! If the *satiety* experienced by Stowe upon the completion of her "treatise on the nature of heaven" depended upon her achieving the object of her quest, she instructs men in general to refuse to attempt what she has achieved herself.

When Stowe descends the mountain she provides for a solution to the paradox she has created. For no intelligent human being, surely, will desist from pursuing what is known to be accessible merely because the possession may not be so sweet as the anticipation. Sweet anticipation already condemns one to the sentence of disappointment, for it demands the quest. But Stowe is not without device. She "mentally

---

[+] This treatise is not know to be extant. The place it would occupy in *Uncle Tom's Cabin* remains vacant—properly so in terms of this analysis.

compared Mont Blanc and Niagara" as she descended. The two she takes to be identical:

> that class of things which mark eras in a mind's history, and open a new door which no man can shut. (228, vol. II)

But Niagara (*properly American* though also English), *even when possessed, continues to offer a "vague and dreamy indefiniteness"* impossible to profound (emphasis supplied). Skillfully, she turns her honest friend from the desire to possess Niagara to the desire to imitate it. God-the-creator-of-poetic-man is not at the center of this discussion, because still higher tasks are reserved to man.[17] The beauty of God's poetry prepares the formation of man's soul.

> In this infancy of his existence, man creates pictures, statues, cathedrals; but when he is made "ruler over many things," will his Father intrust to him the building and adorning of worlds? the ruling of the glorious, dazzling forces of nature? (229, vol. II)

If Rousse, set straight on the path, can lead men toward universal justice by way of building universes, there will be no end to the human quest apart from the end of humankind itself. An ideal, necessarily indefinite and impossible of achievement—rather than impossible by agreement or convention—will inform human life. And knowledge of the impossibility of profounding this ideal will yet dull the taste of its anticipation. The human things will have been returned to the realm of shadows—a goddess wrongly omitted from the Greek pantheon, "the sister of Thought and Peace."[18]

Here should perhaps conclude the analysis of "Sunny Memories." But when Stowe described the "infancy" of man she omitted, among his works, those works of mind suggested by poetry. Need we add to "pictures, statues, [and] cathedrals" songs? Or, may man be at once infant and adult—infant in his imitations yet mature in his conceptions? Stowe closed this letter with reflections on the world's "progressive men." She meant Luther and Calvin, the fathers of the Reformation. The first she called a "poet" who "fused the mass." The last was a "philosopher" who "crystallized" the enthusiasm into an enduring view of the world. Stowe, while recognizing the defects of Calvinism as a "system," urges as she does in *Oldtown Folks*[19] that Calvinism "will never cease from the earth, because the great fundament facts of nature are Calvinistic . . ." These facts of nature, however, are not knowable only by Christians. They have been proved by Greek tragedians, Mahomet, Napoleon, and Cromwell. Calvinism is based rather on an understanding of nature than of God. Our poet must be responsible for what we know of God. What is central to this conception is man—both poet and philosopher. Stowe's account makes explicit the apparent relationship by describing the effects.

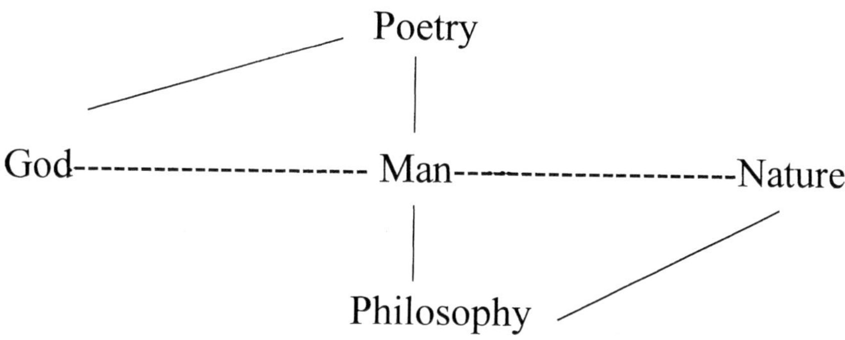

Figure 25.1

Is there evil in the world? His goodness will amend it. Is there some good that is desired? Nature will be the test of it.[20] We have in *Uncle Tom's Cabin* the complete account of the whole.[21]

Just as Stowe had criticized France earlier, in Letter XLVIII she criticized New England and for the opposite reason though on the same grounds. New England, she said, starves, withers the appetite for beauty in her human souls. "I know, because I have felt it." It is a stain on the New England Character, therefore, that this "immortal" element in man cannot be nourished there. The "Yankee mother" is but an apostrophization of womankind.[22] Similarly, the ancient Greeks, almost complete as human beings, had the defect of gods who were but apostrophizations of deity. As beautiful as they were, one can take little comfort in the example of these "islands where flesh and blood became semi-spiritual, and where the sense of beauty was an existence . . ."[23] We recall that the original criticism of France stemmed from its tireless imitation of the Greeks. It appears that the French were imitators of defects—however glorious. The appearance of the criticism of Greece should announce the reappraisal of France.

> The great men of France have always seemed to be in confusion as to whether they made God or he made them. There is a great resemblance in some points between the French and the ancient Athenians; there was the same excitability; the same keen outward life; the same passion for ideas; the same spending of life in hearing or telling some new thing; the same acuteness of philosophical research. The old Athenians first worshipped, and then banished their great men,—buried them and pulled them up, and did generally a variety of things which we Anglo-Saxons should call fantastic. There is a difference, that the Athenians had the advantage of coming first. (XLVIII, p. 399, vol. II)

If there is a difference between this criticism and the first it is that the French are not so sternly rebuked for their "keen outward life," their love of adorning the superficial. Related to that is the fact that they now possess "acuteness of philosophical research." There followed a lengthy discussion of French art and manners, culminating in the praise of "republicanism" in France from whom "Americans might learn many lessons."[24]

What is *the* French virtue? Consistent attachment to liberty and the capacity to pursue an ideal. Not very surprisingly, the work closed by directly connecting this factor with the struggle against slavery. Again, not surprisingly, the series of criticisms that began with New England closed with a criticism of Americans, especially "northern free states," and a contrast between the French and the Anglo-Saxons on this score. These terms seem to boil down to one: the American Constitution. By implicitly contrasting the defects of the Constitution with "devotion to abstract principle," Stowe suggested the work she had labored to present as an American alternative or completion.

> What do we see in our own history? Our northern free states denouncing slavery as a crime, confessedly inconsistent with their civil and religious principles, yet, for commercial and pecuniary considerations, deliberately entering into a compact with slaveholders tolerating a twenty years' perpetuation of the African slave trade . . .
> [Article I, section 9, the Constitution]
> the rendering of fugitives . . .
> [Article IV, section 2, clause 3]
> the suppression of servile insurrections, . . .
> [Article IV, section 4[25]]
> and allowing to the slaveholders a virtual property basis of representation.
> [Article I, section 2, clause 3]
> (XLVIII, p. 417, vol. II)

It cannot for a moment be doubted that Stowe wished, as did Calvin in his triad, to characterize the American Constitution specifically. For "our history" offers far many more and much more diverse examples of Yankee perfidy in dealing with the problem of slavery than those derived directly from the Constitution. Indeed, the most recent example at that time, the Compromise of 1850, was the immediate target of *Uncle Tom's Cabin*. Stowe made her point succinctly.

> As a race the French are less commercial, more ideal, more capable of devotion to abstract principles, and of following them consistently, irrespective of expediency.

We cannot now resolve at what cost expedients are ignored. We know that this letter is followed by the disclosure of the true virtue of British aristocrats. In that light we might say the French have one great virtue; they freed themselves from the stain of slavery without much agonizing. Similarly, the Americans had one great defect: they had not been able to free themselves from the stain of slavery under the guiding influence of even the most salutary principles. Stowe closed this work by pulling down the shade over her own lights and leaving the reader to guide himself by the light of a needed, if provisional, reform. We ought to note that a tale of this nature could not end more simply.

NOTES

1. ALS, June 4, 1853, from S. S. *Canada*. Stowe-Day.
2. *SM*, Letter XXV, II, pp. 86–87.
3. Ibid., Letter XXX, II, p. 138.
4. Ibid., p. 142. There is at least oblique evidence that Stowe is sincere in her protestation. She seemed indeed to be very engaged during her campaign, with little time for show. In October, 1853, *The Anti-Slavery Advocate* noted that "she warmly approved of the efforts of the Dublin Ladies Anti-Slavery Society to circulate anti-slavery information amongst Irish emigrants previous to their embarkation for America, saying that this class were likely to exercise a very powerful influence for good or evil, in the United States." This is cited by the editors of the Tappan correspondence in the context of contrasting Stowe's effectiveness with Daniel O'Connell's rabble-rousing. The discussion envelops the period of the campaign. Abel and Klingberg, eds., *A Side-Light on Anglo-American Relations*, p. 30, editor's note 27.
5. *SM*, Letter XXX, II, p. 136.
6. Ibid., p. 132.
7. Thomas Babington Macaulay, *Essays and Lays of Ancient Rome* (London: Longmans, Green and Company, 1895), pp. 650, 659.
8. Burke's *Works*, "Trial," Monday, June 16, 1794, Ninth Day of Reply, vol. 12, p. 396. Edmund Burke, *The Works of the Right Honorable Edmund Burke* (Boston: Little, Brown and Company, 1865).
9. Ibid.
10. Ibid., vol. 11, "Trial," First Day of Reply, Wed. May 28, 1794, p. 204.
11. Cf. Macaulay, *Essays*, pp. 610–611: ". . . tried by the lower standard of Indian Morality, he might be considered as a man of integrity and honor."
12. *SM*, Letter XXXI, pp. 165–167.
13. Ibid., XXXII, II, p. 209.
14. Ibid., XXVIII II, p. 218.
15. Ibid., p. 221.
16. See book I, Part I, chapter 13.
17. And so "Sunny Memories" come full circle. The stormy ship life aboard the *Niagara* presents the very challenge which our contemplation of Niagara provides occasion to resolve.
18. *SM*, II, p. 230.
19. Chapters 32–34.
20. Letter XLVIII provides the best example of the kind of attitude required of men toward divine and natural things, especially where they are united, as in the person of Christ.

21. See ch. 23.

22. *SM*, Letter XLVIII, II, p. 392; this would explain *her* absence from Cloudland, the utopia of *Oldtown Folks*.

23. Ibid., p. 394.

24. Ibid., p. 414.

25. This would not generally be conceded to stem from the intent alleged by Stowe.

II

SALVATION

26

Anutopia

> Let mortals never take a vow in jest
> Be faithful and not behind in doing that
> As Jephtah was in his first offering.
>
> —"Paradiso," Canto VI, 65

A separate place must be assigned to the interpretation of Stowe's version of utopian dreaming on account of the radical difference between *Oldtown Folks* (where it is presented) and her other works, above all the three pivotal anti-slavery books.[1] Here, as indeed in all of her major works after "The Two Altars," slavery's ill was not neglected. But the purpose of *Oldtown Folks* is not to account for some feature or defect of America here or there but rather to explain the entire generation of those passions and opinions which eventuated first in the founding and latterly in abolition, but about which some uncertainty remained even after the Civil War.[2] The confused virtues and vices of modernity were summarized in the novel in the personage of the village do-nothing, Sam Lawson. The novel closes with Sam, grown older, passionately yearning to fly to "Otawhity" (Tahiti), where *labor* is not necessary. Sam was irresolute, however, from the lingering suspicion that he ought to be able *to do* something for the folks there in order to earn so high a reward. The confused passions of Law-sons are sorted out in the novel, in the form of three prototype regimes: Oldtown, Needmore, and Cloudland. Stated only in the "Preface" but hoveringly present throughout is a fourth, actual regime: America at the moment of the founding.

Stowe promised in her preface to give a true reflection, a non-romantic picture of things American. While to do so necessitated "some serious thinking," she would remain passive, intervening in the narrative only to develop characters and otherwise remaining as "passive as a looking glass."[3] As if to make good on this promise, she wrote from start to finish under a pseudonym, "Horace Holyoke." (She entered the novel only at one point, when a conversation from which our narrator had removed himself was related in the first person plural. Either this was our real author speaking, or this work carved out a space for miracle. Cf. pp. 201–3.) Nevertheless, the work was published under her admitted authorship, "the author of *Uncle Tom's Cabin.*" What she achieved by her affectation was an emphasis upon the reader's need to seek his own reflection in her reverse-images. To sort out three types of regime is to sort out the virtues and vices of the human soul. By refusing to intervene actively in the narrative the author left to each reader to judge his own capacity for this work. Yet, Horace did not keep his word, for he intervened in dramatic fashion in the central chapter of the book:

> Reader, this is to be a serious chapter, and I advise all those people who want to go through the world without giving five minutes' consecutive thought to any subject to skip it. They will not find it entertaining, and it may perhaps *lead them to think* on puzzling subjects, even for so long as half an hour; and who knows what may happen to their brains, from so unusual an exercise? (367, emphasis supplied)

This unveiled warning (or is it a dare?) centers the task of sorting out the three regimes on the task of comprehending the foundations of Oldtown, the *ancien regime.*

We do not have the space to provide a thorough exegesis of *Oldtown Folks.* We will, accordingly, follow our narrator's lead and concentrate on the central chapter, "My Grandmother's Blue Book." Before doing so, however, we will offer a brief summary of the novel's symbolism and consider Flaubert's skepticism about the possibility of achieving through literature what the author seems bent on achieving and which Stowe had already achieved in her earlier works.

Flaubert, like Nietzsche, faulted Stowe's work for its commerce with things low.[4] Unlike Nietzsche, he grounded his critique on an understanding of the conditions of genuine literary merit as well as on a notion of the high as the truest reflection of human things. As we have seen above, Stowe's response to both begins with a demonstration that much confusion attends the recognition of the high. Flaubert had assumed that a focus on kings, gods, and demi-gods was a sufficient guarantee against confusion. His real challenge to Stowe, like Nietzsche's, is that she must demonstrate the insufficiency of ordinary, conventional human judgments about the high things. Like Nietzsche, Flaubert never made his challenge public. While Nietzsche's critique was contained in a note he chose not to publish, Flaubert's was contained in a series of letters to his lover.[5]

Flaubert produced his silent criticism as he worked on his novel, *Madame Bovary*, whose heroine, Emma, is in many ways every bit as misplaced, conventionally, as was Uncle Tom. Stowe's Emily Rossiter, in *Oldtown Folks*, every bit as tortured by French rationalism as Flaubert's Emma, recreates Emma's moral dilemmas and disasters as if Stowe had read her silent critic's mind. Stowe's Emily is, however, almost a side-show in her full discussion of the possibilities of the human soul. Flaubert's Emma is the whole story. This dramatic difference underlies Stowe's response to Flaubert and Nietzsche, as it responds to modern utopianism. She holds, in effect, that they are grossly mistaken to take the narrow limits of modernity as in fact narrowing the possibilities of the human soul.

We will state Flaubert's criticism explicitly, the better to comprehend the thoroughness of Stowe's response. Flaubert acknowledged at the outset an unfavorable prejudice to *Uncle Tom's Cabin*. True literature, he maintained, could never affect the masses so broadly as that book had done. The whole cannot be spoken, for art is limited even where ideas are not. Above all, metaphysical ideas do not conform well to the pen, because *la force plastique* always fails to reproduce what is not clear in the mind. Nevertheless, he promised his lover that he would read *l'Oncle Tom, en anglais*.

Flaubert's skepticism was not complete. He thought that ideas could be made amusing, provided that they flowed from one another *comme cascade en cascade* and led the reader among "trembling phrases and boiling metaphors." Such metaphysical art must be defended against narrow ideas and narrow literature. The attempt to stifle it is a species of treason against the soul. Socrates' death weighs heavily on mankind. The crucifixion of *l'homme-parole* was no less than an attempt to kill God. Republican ideas are especially obnoxious on that score, their virtuous declamations stifling. Republicans imagine that society is stoppered by "two or three rotten pegs," and that all drains away if they are pulled out. Judging by old ideas, they regard society as an artificial creation of man, something produced by design.

To Flaubert individual will no more affects the existence or destruction of civilization than the composition of the atmosphere. Man, he held, would cultivate here and there only to have *la force humaine* continue to act in his absence as if he had not been, rolling over his memory with all the dead leaves. Grass would cover every particular *coin de culture*. Every particular people would disappear under new conquests, every religion under new philosophies. The problem with *l'Oncle Tom*, as he reported in the following letter, was precisely that it was narrow in this way. Written from a "moral and religious point of view," it ought to have been written from a "human point of view."

Flaubert did not require to see a slave tortured in order to sympathize with him. Still less need that slave be a good man, good father and husband, singing hymns and reading the Evangel, and pardoning his captors. Such things derive from what is sublime, from an exception, hence *une chose special, fausse*. While there are *grandes qualités de sentiment* in the book, they were better employed for a goal less narrow. After the slaves are gone, the book will be false, a mere chronicle of the hatreds of a bygone era. What brings the book's success? Just this: it is contemporary. The truth in itself, the eternal, *le beau,* could never stir the masses to such a point. *Mais il fallait faire rire le parterre, comme dit Rousseau.* The lovely things in the book are sacrificed to its narrow moralizing.

> Puisque Tom est un mystique, je lui aurais voulu plus lyrisme (il eut été peut-être moins vrai comme nature). . . . Les réflexions de l'auteur m'ont irrité tout le temps, est-ce qu'on a besoin de faire réflexions sur l'esclavage? Montrez-le, voilà tout. . . . L'auteur dans son oeuvre doit être comme Dieu dans l'univers, présent partout, et visible nulle part . . . l'art grec était dans ce principe-là, et pour y arriver plus vite il choisissait ses personnages dans des conditions sociales exceptionnelles, rois, dieux, demi-dieux; on ne vous intéressait pas avec vous-mêmes, le divin était le but.

The great fault of *l'Oncle Tom,* therefore, lay in its sacrificing beautiful characterizations and ideas to the natural, the human, all too human praise of mere morality.

Arch defenders of Stowe's literary merit can point to Flaubert's concession that the sublime Tom was perhaps natural as grudging evidence of Stowe's success. Or, they can capture the anomaly of his utopian expectation that American slavery, as distinct from America, was going to disappear anyway as the complete evidence of his innocent understanding of human things. Or, they may attempt to insist on the revelatory status of his notion that to make the vulgar laugh is the same as to make them cry for a slave. On the other hand, they who yet harbor serious suspicions of Stowe's literary merit may find in Flaubert's analysis the articulate expression of their own reservations. He would have shown them a way to distinguish, to dissociate art (talent as we are blindly wont to say today) from literary merit. Both would be wrong.

Flaubert's criticism stands or falls entirely on the truth of his claim that the praise of mere morality is undignified, incapable of revealing the deepest recesses of the human soul.[6] It is at this point that Stowe meets his argument, the ultimate challenge to her political philosophy. The vision of anutopia is meant to prove that the praise of mere morality is indeed dignified. Stowe does so in a novel in which her presence is like *Dieu dans l'univers.*

Oldtown Folks praises mere morality. It also explains its doing so. The condition for understanding the praise of mere morality as the central task of the book is to master its symbolism. It is rich and extensive. We cannot present the whole of it here, but its leading themes should serve the purpose of this analysis. The end envisioned in Stowe's political philosophy is most clearly revealed in *Oldtown Folks.* Starting with the title that work is an account of three historical or moral stages: Oldtown, Needmore, and Cloudland. These are the names of the three villages which frame the drama. The story is an account of the impossible tensions that emerge from unreflective abandonment of the *ancien régime*. The Cloudland utopia[7] is revealed as incapable of generation and hence no true city.[8] We are thereby prepared for anutopia, the ultimate life of decency and order, which is proof against the false dreams of rationalized life. The neologism, anutopa, is an appropriate characterization of Stowe's vision. It is a double negative. Since *u-topos* originally meant no-where, the refutation of utopia comes to stand for a definite somewhere. Stowe's political philosophy is not a conservative defense of the status quo (as the attack on slavery alone ought to reveal).[9] It was rather a defense, a demonstration of the permanent necessity of a moral and prudential judgment in human affairs and of those political conditions that could best guarantee these conditions of decency.

Decency, above all else, belongs to the *ancien régime*, and the modern challenge is to recover or preserve it, while maintaining the new, cosmopolitan foundation of political life. The very question suggests that the original rebellion against the *ancien régime* erroneously jettisoned its certain virtues along with its certain vices.[10] The drama of *Oldtown Folks* discloses one view of how this came about, its unwanted consequences, and the necessary corrective. The drama fittingly turns on the central problem of the education of the young, their preparation for life in a given regime. It naturally gives rise to comparison of the competing alternatives. The heroes are three children who mature to adulthood under the new order, but who experience either directly or indirectly each of the alternatives.

The children's roots are in Oldtown, the narrator's by birth and the others by fortuitous adoption. The real Oldtown of the novel is only the decayed shell of the earlier Oldtown. The influence of the original, however, is still very much visible. Contemporary Oldtown is in a state of transition, at the point of choosing whether to take the left fork, through the forms of Needmore and Cloudland, or the right fork into a form still unclear. We require even more to discern why this choice must be made than how. Because we cannot behold a city in motion, undergoing its revolutions, the author provides that view of the changing city that is writ upon the changing souls of the children.

Oldtown comes into view first. It is the home of young Horace Holyoke at the time of the ratification of the Constitution. Next in order comes Needmore, where the young orphans, Harry and Tina Percival, are thrown upon the charity of strangers. Because of the insufficiency of Needmore the orphans escape to Oldtown. In Needmore the brother and sister, alone in the world, had been separated into the households of Crab Smith and Asphyxia Smith, themselves brother and sister. If Crab and Asphyxia were well studied they "would be found to be the result and out-come of certain moral and social forces, justly to discriminate which might puzzle a philosopher" (261). What are the elements of the puzzle? The family is untenable in Needmore. Individuals there have cut loose from the old-time religion and live grasping lives of self-interested acquisitiveness. Among them children can receive no further education than hard work to procure life's necessaries. Wives and mothers are but chattel to husbands and fathers. Indeed, there seem no fathers, properly speaking, because of the fathers' jealousy of every motherly attention to sons as so much attention stolen from themselves.[11] Women are free only to the extent they are manly and independent. Asphyxia Smith followed this course. The path to independence for sons is to run away. Crab Smith's son followed this course. Needmore's intransigent preference for self-interest, the subordination of benevolence to self-interest,[12] erodes every communal tie. What Needmore needs, beyond material sufficiency, is just such a communal tie.

The orphans escaped to Horace's home, his grandmother's home, in Oldtown. There they discovered what Needmore lacked. Needmore had once been an Oldtown too. The flight of the children (from "nowhere to oblivion") therefore represents a return to the kind of world Needmore once was, a world in which children may be educated. Needmore lost this capacity when, striking out for individual liberty, it heedlessly cast aside every justification for morality as mere convention. Needmore had placed self-interest in the place of virtue or morality, on the thought that it was aiming more directly at the end of which virtue or morality was but a means. The return to Oldtown represents the discovery that virtue or morality is not a mere pretext for satisfying the strongest passions of the strongest individuals, not merely a means.

Yet, Oldtown is in its own way insufficient, since mere morality is not true or necessary in the way that it thinks. The end sought by Needmore, to found the human on the necessary, remains valid. Howard White, writing of Shakespeare's *Pericles*, maintained that "Pericles knows, like the old democratic statesman of Athens whom he is not, that the divine does not relate to rank or birth." The education of Oldtown is in error to the precise extent it aims merely at replicating its still efficacious ranks and hierarchies. The education the children require may be the education of Oldtown, but only as it aims at what is human in them. Mere morality is an end, but not a comprehensive end. When Flaubert said, *le divin est le but,* he meant that the significance of the moral lies in what it posits beyond itself. Needmore's mistaken identification of the end produced its turn toward the low, the abandonment of education.[13]

The human foundations are re-laid at Oldtown. The necessity of morality is reaffirmed. To be moral or virtuous is not a matter of choice or will for human beings. It is rather a necessary means to enact the human. Grounding the defense of liberty on this tenet, Stowe had to demonstrate why the antique expression of morality was insufficient. While defending the old inasmuch as it was human, she did not entirely accept the refrain in *Pericles'* chorus:

> The purchase is to make men glorious;
> et bonum quo antiquio eo melius.[14]

Her demonstration of a high moral standard for modernity, however, required her to reveal not only the insufficiency of the beastly alternative in Needmore but the impossibility of the divine alternative in Cloudland, on the mountaintops. The account of Oldtown, accordingly, is at once a defense and a criticism. While the defense chains us to mere morality, the criticism sustains the identical search for something better which motivated change in Needmore, only this time along a higher road.

Oldtown, even more than Needmore and Cloudland, is revealed through our narrator's eyes. His view is singular. He was convinced that "so much of the human" (1) informs every individual life, whatever its obscurity, that a full understanding of it "would command the interest of all others" (1).[15] Since each individual is also "part and parcel" of the greater picture of his regime, the account of individuals at Oldtown is an account of the New England regime. In general, the regime was "a sort of half Hebrew theocracy, half ultra-democratic republic of little villages" (1). Originally, the souls of New Englanders were fused by "conceptions of an endless life" (4) and the notion "that the ruling forces which impelled them were the sublimities of the world to come" (4). Their Christian, should we say Judaeo-Christian, republic formed their entire moral horizon, and, wholly apart from other civilizations,

> [t]hey formed a commonwealth where vice was wellnigh impossible; where such landmarks and boundaries and buttresses and breastworks hedged in and defended the morality of a community, that to go very far out of the way would require some considerable ingenuity and enterprise. (4)

Original Oldtowners lived in a comprehensive community, where men's ideas of human and divine things were expressed with a singular clarity and forcefulness. It is almost incomprehensible, therefore, that this community's moral foundation was eroded. With a certainty that reminds of the vagueness of the decline of the best regime in Plato's *Republic*, however, the narrator assures the reader that the "traditional faith" of Oldtown was modified. Apparently, the modification stemmed from what Flaubert called the constant activity of *la force humaine*. Individual temperaments, for example, gradually and irresistibly brought about changes. So certain is the operation of this force, and the chance but necessary incidence of conflict between individual "nature" and professed belief, that "practically the whole faith of the man changes without his ever being aware of the fact himself." Humanity itself, therefore, resists the permanent establishment of a comprehensive moral order.

At first appearance not doubt but merely the conditions of human life seem to undermine the prospects of virtue. Still, there is something strange in the fact that susceptible temperaments seemed especially numerous in the "third generation of Massachusetts clergy" (5). In that generation the Arminian heresy arose. And as appearance would suggest, these were all men who had been precisely educated well and who conducted themselves well. Their skepticism was "secret." But they changed the faith, replacing the "soul stirring spiritual mysteries" of the confession with a complete focus on "moralities, virtues, and decorums" (5). This sounds rather like Montesquieu's distinction between morals and manners. In this context, however, the morals express "soul stirring mysteries" which have the power to raise doubt in the souls of those with "philosophic temperaments." Not merely the conditions of human life undermine the prospects of virtue. Rather, the inherently philosophic character of morality in the deep sense of religion sows doubt, if not as well as, at least after it sows certainty.[16]

The education, the teaching, required to lead men to virtue seems also to open them, if not to vice, then at least to skepticism about the necessity of virtue. In this sense one may say that morality in the deep sense is nihilistic. Stowe's conclusion leads in another direction, however. Horace's dying father had indeed been one of "those silent, peculiar natures whose thoughts and reasonings too often wander up and down the track of commonly received opinion, as Noah's dove of old, without finding rest for the sole of their foot" (14). His grandmother, who was now to raise and educate him, however, was of a different stamp. She could not often enough comply with the dictates of the opinions she had received. An "earnest Puritan Calvinist," she had "positive opinions on every subject" (19) and expressed them forcibly and vigorously. While nourished, educated in the principles of the original Oldtowners, her piety could nonetheless digest the principles of the young Turks, gaining only further liberty from breaking up "the crust of formalism and mechanical piety" (25). Grandmother Badger's piety is at the heart of the new foundation of morality. It is the subject of *Oldtown Folks'* central chapter, to which we will turn shortly. It remains, however, to describe old education at Oldtown and the newer education at Cloudland.

The old education had a more profoundly human foundation than reformers suspected. Those elements of the old theology which acted as "a subtle poison" on some natures belong to the realm of nature. They are "the great unanswerable questions" which "perplex every thinking soul." Puritan religion stated them with "the severest and most appalling distinctness." In fact, they underlie every religion. These "awful questions" belong as much to "deism as to the strictest orthodoxy." New England made them explicit and awakened the natural "perception and consciousness" of men there. For nature's teaching is more inexorably Calvinist than the confession (26).

The Calvinist doctrine of election is a moral counterpart to the natural hierarchy, the rule of the strongest or best. The distinction between morals and manners points to the need to efface the sharpness of the natural distinction. For manners, the outward evidence of the soul's submission to truth, aim at making all equally respectful of the forcefulness of truth, the forcefulness of human conditions. The old education accomplished this by centering social life on the meeting-house,[17] wherein all doffed their peculiarities and united in a "neighborhood charity" which affirmed the root of their differences in their common humanity. It was a "powerful and efficient means of civilization" (59).

The mere morality arrived at by means of vigorous manners is distinguished from the profound questions which underlie it. Since nature, no less than the Calvinist God, does not make its elections in accord with conventionally assigned positions, and since it defies human logic to ascertain the responses to these unanswerable questions, none can identify the elect by any rule of human prudence. The civilizing influence of mere morality depends, therefore, on its ability to preserve openness in the face of questions. But that means the manners must at one and the same time demonstrate the acceptance of the hierarchical relationships and deny the evidence of certainty for any given hierarchy. The old education failed to achieve this, for the equality of the meeting-house was vitiated by the assumption that God's spokesman stood apart from his fellow worshippers. In time, and even among Congregationalists, the minister came to stand as the sign of all authority in every New England village. Indeed, his very cocked hat and gold-headed cane came to represent unanswerable authority. Oldtown in the era of the American Revolution, however, stood at the gates of change. Among them the minister was already losing the prestige of former eras, though without loss of deference.[18] He would be "nothing but a citizen" even in Oldtown's next generation. His words would then "be sifted and examined just like the words of any other citizen." It was the task of the Oldtown education to anticipate the advent of this complete meeting-house equality.

Just as Oldtown education of the latter day preserved the meeting-house and its awful questions, so too it preserved the original settlers' focus on the family. Hence, the emphasis on the formation of children. Here the emphasis lay on gentleness of manners. The earlier indulgence of childhood innocence was strongly contrasted with latter day insistence on childish responsibility for original sin. Oldtown, as a latter day exception, seeks to preserve the original manners in the face of the emergence of combative religion and philosophy. It did so even though it too harbored in the breast of the family that "quiet brooding on the very deepest problems of mental and moral philosophy."

Talk about the family always seems to lead to mothers. *Oldtown Folks,* however, is the one important novel wherein mothers as such play an insignificant role (save for Grandmother Badger, who appears more as grandmother than mother). There is but one saintly mother (the mother of Harry and Tina Percival), whose early death leaves her represented only in the form of her orphaned off-spring. As for the rest, the one significant natural mother (the narrator's mother) is insignificant in the drama of the novel. The mothers who remain are all unnatural—step-mothers—more precisely, foster mothers who run the gamut of human possibilities from Asphyxia of Needmore to the Greek and Latin scholar-teacher-maid-mother of Cloudland. The natural mothers, whether living or dying, surrender their children to foster mothers and seem strangely incapable of raising their own children. This is a new theme for Mrs. Stowe, and it introduces a free field for consideration of a grandmother, whose tasks seem less defined by nature, in the limited sense, than by nature in the broad, species-caring sense. Besides, everyone knows that mothers are more demanding than grandmothers. For a grandmother it is sufficient that a child do what is right, no matter what he wants. The focus on grandmothers helps to draw out the "grandmotherly gentleness" of Cotton Mather's religious teaching.[19]

Oldtown education was a latter day exception to the rigors of New England theology, because it was molded on the lines of grandmotherly gentleness. Oldtown was able to resist the "disintegrating process" begun by Jonathan Edwards's application of "rationalistic methods to the accepted doctrines of religion."[20] His demand that each man name for himself the ground upon which he stands relative to God and nature ultimately cut through that bulwark which, for a time, preserved intact the civilized meeting-house manners. Edwards attempted to demonstrate the acceptability of a certain hierarchy, but succeeded only in denying the certain evidence of any hierarchy. Grandmother Badger is only a temporary exception. Oldtown, too, will eventually succumb, as her skeptical sons reveal. They cannot reconcile a view of the defense of civilization as "pleasant humbug" with the willing acceptance of that defense. "In this life, where nobody knows anything about anything, a capacity for humbugs would be a splendid thing to have." This prayer, oft repeated since, is vain for the awakened. But grandmother held Oldtown together just long enough to send the youngsters off to Cloudland, in search of a reason to preserve civilizing manners without preserving the inherent contradiction between morals and manners.

Horace later recalled the grandmotherly teaching without its contradiction. He recited from memory Cotton Mather's account of the planting of New England. He could not remember the first two points, the questions of theological doctrine. Points three to six recite the case for virtue and prosperity. Such lessons were "often repeated," above all to the young, whose manners could be correct even when their originating morals were not recalled. Mather taught the "idea of self-sacrifice," "a reverence for self-denial," and "the conception of a life which should look, not mainly to selfish interest, but to the good of the whole human race." In this the primitive early times did not become "mere stolid, material toil."

> It was toil and manual labor ennobled by a new motive . . . every man, woman, and child, . . . was part and parcel of a great new movement in human progress. (329)

Progress consisted of raising human beings to the life of "doing something." This was not merely the Protestant work ethic. The life of "doing something" became the "greatest public amusement," or at least "an Engrossing interest." Because rapaciousness was excluded, what had to be done was a general as well as a particular good. The "fathers" aimed at such an "equality of conditions" and "the means of securing the good of life so free to all" that none should fail of "opportunity for a prosperous seeking of his fortunes." Needmore's wealth lacked this capacity to be turned to the general good. Grandmotherly gentleness, what we called mitigating moral graces in the parallel discussion above, aimed at this end but actually had no true foundation for doing so. The omission of Mather's doctrinal basis shows this. Nor does reliance upon "Mr. Locke's" fine ideas on education seem to serve the purpose. If Cloudland cannot provide a vigorous pursuit of self-interest combined with a true foundation for turning it toward the general good, it would be necessary to reconsider the necessity of outward evidence of the soul's submission to truth.

Cloudland education may be summarized in an impoverished but brief manner. It sought the foundation of civilized life in the prevalence of rational manners. Correcting Needmore's erroneous focus on mere means as the substance of rationality, it replaced doctrinal purity with rational precision. Further, it sustained a social life whose manners were compatible with rational precision. Deference to the reasoned argument became inseparable from deference to men, the rational beings. Openness to truth became indistinguishable from openness to every hardy assertion of truth. The desire for knowledge led to desire to associate with knowers and seekers of knowledge. Doubt of oneself became solicitousness for others, while the unwillingness to be seduced by error produced manly independence of judgment.

Among themselves Cloudlanders were equal and charitable. They regarded their charities with the pride befitting their confidence about their own judgments of what was due to each. Cloudland was a stable, orderly society in which virtue was uncontradicted by the appeal of vice. Its virtue was not a reproach to vice, but rather a preference of what is high. In these circumstances the child heroes of *Oldtown Folks* grew to maturity and completed their education. One would think they could remain forever in this utopia, in which the manners necessary to civilization are compatible with the unanswered questions to which they point.

The children received their education in terrible questions under the best circumstances. They entered the "unknown tragedy" of human life with a teaching which made clear that every human faces "the necessity of crossing the shoreless ocean alone on his own raft." Like many ten- and twelve-year-old New Englanders, they "trembled at the possibilities of final election or reprobation" (436). But they did so under the care of a teacher conversant with the natural expression of such possibilities. The "theologic systems" taken alone had the defect of having always "been the work of man alone." The men who produced them were innocent of "moral and intellectual companionship with woman" (438). In Cloudland, while the teacher was a man, the best student was a woman,[21] the import of which was not lost on the republic's newest citizens.

> Plato says somewhere that the only perfect human thinker who will ever arise will be the MAN-WOMAN, or a human being who unites perfectly the nature of the two sexes.[22] (439, original capitalization)

Their education in self-sufficiency aimed at something beyond mere morality or necessity.

Cloudland's education also lay in the hands of a minister who had substituted "rational statement" for Calvinistic fears. The "Socratic" but republican minister had solved the problem of evil. Moral evil was a necessary result of the desire, or "motive," which lay at the heart of a human being. This clear answer laid the foundation for hope about the human condition; moral evil could be rectified as far as desire could be tutored. Parson Avery's work consisted of tutoring men's desires. His motto, Cloudland's epitaph, came from Goethe: "'Blessed is the man who believes he has an idea by which he may help his fellow-creatures'" (443). Avery's anticipation of the "millennium" expressed his belief in the efficacy of his own work. To the extent this utopia could extend beyond Cloudland, he joined the legions of millennialists who awaited "Beaver Brook's" "overplus of joy and peace" (444) as the consummation of the tendencies of human society. The "saintly race of perfected human beings" (444) was for all the earth, not just Cloudland. Uniformity of soul would once for all exorcise ambiguity.

Cloudland's teacher (Rossiter) nettled Cloudland's minister (Avery) because of his skepticism about the possibility of extending their felicity beyond their mountaintop retreat. The minister was partly correct. The complete liberty of thought that characterized their discussions did represent the thrust of "those pure republican principles in which the *individual* is *everything*" (446, original emphasis). His voice reflected the revolutionary "period in American history" (446). Still, what he shared with teacher Rossiter in Cloudland was but utopian dreaming elsewhere. Cloudland succeeds in making the high accessible to the low. So, too, would men in Spain be "infinitely better off for this life at least," if Spain had "schoolmasters and ministers working together" as these two did (448).

Despite Cloudland's success, it was dogged by an unseen threat, something calling into question its complete applicability to things human. The manners appropriate to rational individualism do indeed produce high-toned civilization, for so long as the desires of individuals are such as may be readily tutored by "rational statements." But erotic desires are more intransigent.[23] One reason the young heroine of *Oldtown Folks* was sent to Cloudland along with the young males was that, at Oldtown, her masters had seemed unable to work with her "without making fools of themselves." The Cloudland master promised to turn her out of his academy "a Spartan," saved from the error of the age. Non-Spartans commenced their life of liberty with a "repeal of the ten commandments, especially the seventh." The master at Cloudland did succeed in resisting Tina's intense charms. His accomplished virtue proved a bulwark, for he too was indeed moved. At Cloudland everyone sought the perfection of the man-woman nature, a self-sufficiency beyond the necessities of eros.

They had no protection against the visitor from outside, however. The accomplished erotic man carried away Cloudland's sole apparent chance for an indigenous mother. His passionate tyranny exposed Cloudland's defect: it could not reproduce itself. As determinedly individualist as any Cloudlander, Jonathan Edwards's own grandson, our story's Aaron Burr (here named Ellery Davenport), proved that liberty to discuss unanswerable questions is no match for sheer will, especially erotic will, where answers are above all necessary. The devotee of will always conquers where there are no answers.

> He saw into politics with unerring precision, and knew what was in men, and whither things were tending. His unbelief was purely and simply what has been called in New England the natural opposition of the heart to God.[24] He loved his own will, and he hated control, and he determined *per fas aut nefas* to carry his own plans in this world, and attend to the other when he got into it. (497)

The appearance of the villain in Cloudland prepares the return to the realm of mere morality, the discovery that maybe "natural laws were meant as servants of man's moral life." The human that is present in the moral does not point to a rational substitute for the moral or religious foundation of manners. It points to the necessity of the moral or religious. The completion of a Cloudland education is a return from utopia to anutopia, which parallels the return from Needmore to Oldtown. The children's education had been in "such a wholesome and innocent state of society" that they had no foundation, in "experience or habits of thought, for the conception of anything like villainy." Their education was completed by the discovery of what they lacked: a defense for virtue as a reproach to vice.

Even Cloudland's master, Jonathan Rossiter, descended the mountain to enunciate his discovery of the error of abstracting from eros. He discovered an openness to new, "infernal" ideas that "always turn out to the disadvantage" of woman. He called for inflexible and eternal moral laws as corrective, in spite of the knowledge that such laws "are in our own hands." We may at least say that the moral laws should not be intentionally transient. That leaves us to search for moral laws that can have the force of natural laws, in spite of our enlightenment. To find them we must reconsider mere morality and have no place to turn but back to "Grandmother's Blue Book."

The return to "Grandmother's Blue Book" is an attempt to recover for America the human from Oldtown. It begins the ascent from Oldtown by the right fork, correcting its defect while avoiding those of Needmore or Cloudland. The defect of grandmother's "Blue Book" was that it taught the inefficacy of mere morality, at the same time that it sustained manners wholly appropriate to mere morality. Stowe's task was to save the manners of the "Blue Book" by giving them a new moral justification.[25] Otherwise, the abandonment of "Blue Book" religion would entail the abandonment of mere morality. To highlight this prospect, the central chapter of *Oldtown Folks* demonstrates the best and worst case of "Blue Book" religion, leaving the reader to reflect on how to preserve the best. Accordingly, we present here a bare summary of this "serious and puzzling" discussion.

In the first half of the chapter the plight of Grandmother Badger's piety is clear. Her contradictory acceptance of the harshest views of human life and the necessity of pietistic charity toward her fellows was founded on an underlying consistency running deep in New England theology. Pitying charity reflected the accepted truth that practical instruction in virtue is of no consequence. This discovery belongs to New Englanders. They abandoned the "Old World" to build a community which focused on the "Whence, the Why, and the Whither" (367) of human things. This may seem like the building of a philosophic community or nation of philosophers. In fact they moved away from philosophy itself and sought to create a particular community, our philosophic arch-villain of Cloudland to the contrary notwithstanding. This getting away from philosophy can be a most philosophic act. New Englanders confronted the harshness of nature and of their theology without relying on the "opiate" features of religion, "poetic drapery," for support, thus to assure their contact with "absolute truth" (368). That truth ought to be found agreeable was to them an impractical desire. Motivated by necessity rather than the likelihood of a happy outcome, they valued duty above enjoyment. They built their life upon the notion that human life was a "ghastly risk," an "inconceivable misfortune for the greater part" (368). The most fortunate humans, in grandmother's eyes, were infants whose premature deaths granted escape from "the awful ordeal." All others could contend with it only through inquiry. She read religiously from the works of Rollin, Hume, and Edwards. The rigorous observance of her reading contrasted sharply with the non-systematic approach of her earthly duties.

Grandson Horace's passion for reading soon bore him to her shelf. There he met her most carefully studied volume, Bellamy's *True Religion Delineated and Distinguished from all Counterfeits*, the "Blue Book." It was a vigorous popular expression of the deepest reflections of New England theology. One example of its "deep mysteries" was the query, Is human being worse than not to be after the Fall? Yes, for mankind's present state is like that of the damned. How might a just God have done this, and ought men to be grateful for it? The unsatisfactory solution failed to allay the doubts raised by this query for thousands of "reflecting minds." God's initial grace to man was worthy and man owes Him thanks for such high consideration. That gratitude is not effaced by the apostasy; God is blameless of the evil man suffers as a result of his own deeds. Should not man's degraded status, then, remove all motive "to propagate their kind"? No answer need be given, for the inquiry itself reveals the depths men probed "in those days." Bellamy's hypothetical objector then doubted that children were a blessing. Children may be a blessing to their parents in this life, and even if most do perish thereafter they do not suffer harm at God's hands.

Concluding passages reveal how "the origin of evil" was conceived. God designed the human constitution as he deemed it "best on the whole." What might be better than the happiness of His highest creatures? A more important end was God's opportunity, at the judgment, to display his entire perfection. Mortal weakness serves to emphasize divine perfection. The "Blue Book" also developed "all the mazes of mental philosophy" and "problems of mystical religion." It brought readers to wonder whether love of God may be founded in self-love. Whether human impotency is moral only? What are differences between Calvinists and Arminians? Does love of the neighbor differ from natural compassion and any love based on self-love? This was the fare of a "plain farmer's wife" and others, who made it a daily study. The reader may judge their characters.

The "Blue Book" was published twenty-six years prior to the Declaration of Independence. It thoroughly penetrated the generation which made the Revolution.

> They were a set of men and women brought up to *think,*—to think not merely on agreeable subjects, but to wrestle and tug at the very severest problems. Utter self-renunciation, a sort of grand contempt for personal happiness when weighed with things greater and more valuable, was the fundamental principle of life in those days. (374, original emphasis)

Trained to Divine indifference to human happiness, these men did not lack the courage to part with an earthly regime. The tendency of their religious thought can be measured by the tendency of their earthly principles. The "Blue Book," like Edwards's works, reflected the influence of "monarchical and aristocratic institutions." The systematic theology was built under the pervasive influence of custom, literature, poetry, and art in the age of kings who could "do no wrong" (374). Divine sacrifice in man's behalf (the love of Christ) was not yet an emphasis of theology, which, unlike the Bible, "is the outgrowth of the human mind" and arises "from the movement of society" (375).

Cromwell's revolution introduced forces of change in political relations, which had their ultimate consequence and did not lead to disintegration precisely because "Puritans transferred to God" the characteristics that had belonged to their king (375). Their theology was born of the overthrow of their king. Hence, blind, impartial nature did not become a standard permitting men to arrogate all rights to their own persons. The human mind clings to the familiar, acceding to change only by slow degrees. Where the Puritans preserved a king, the French revolution preserved nothing; stability followed the Puritan revolt, anarchy followed the French. The idea of a divine sovereignty held together a community whose foundation had shifted by steadying within them "a faculty robbed of its appropriate object" (376). The appropriate object of the human faculty for reverence is what is high.

Puritans clung to their God in spite of the monstrous portrait of his character because of the "indestructible nature" of that within man which submits to what is divine. Descendants of the Puritans, as Stowe herself, proclaimed, "God is dead; long live God," because they retained civilizing manners. The "Old World" theologies were slowly ameliorated as the influence of the American Revolution acted upon "the principles of true Christian democracy," which they practiced, to alter the base of New England theology.

> Never again shall we see that union of perfect repose in regard to outward surroundings and outward life with that intense activity of the inward and intellectual world, that made New England, at this time, the vigorous, germinating

> seed-bed for all that has since been developed of politics, laws, letters, and theology, through New England to America and through America to the world. (421)

An accurate portrait of New England in the revolutionary era exceeds the capacity of art. For even the common people often spoke with as complete frankness on moral-religious questions as all did on ordinary political questions. The unresolved ambiguity of the human character held center stage. The resulting dialectic altered the theology of grandmother's "Blue Book." Grandmother's theological syllogisms were answered by her grandson's syllogisms based on the natural condition of humanity, as they debated the finitude of sins, punishments, and beings. The debate was curious. Mother would not yield, while grandson would not insist, for "moral earnestness" prevails over "mere intellectual cleverness" (377).

Unavoidably, however, the "consent of the governed" and the "happiness" of all or most had to undermine the "divine right and prerogative of the King Eternal" (377). Jonathan Edwards's account of "true virtue" offered the contradiction between human virtue consisting in "devotion to the general good" and divine virtue consisting in "supreme" self-regard (377–78). Edwards's account crumbled before the necessity of divine sacrifice for the general good. The mere human foundation of theology exposes it to conflict with the precepts of Christ. New England fostered deep human sadness. That was true tragedy. Yet, the free and courageous thinking it engendered produced characters able to make a better world.

The first half of Grandmother's "Blue Book" closes with this promise. The second half demonstrates the alternative, thus to prove the necessity of founding decent human life on a combination of grandmother's moral earnestness and the determination that the need to protect human nature had moral significance. This is Stowe's understanding of the American revolution.[26] It founded the reproach to vice on anticipation of the best in man, as a permanent human practice. Calvin Stowe's argument was nearly identical. He substituted the political or moral art for the possibility of divine miracle. That is the substance of Stowe's anutopian vision. It is the meaning of the praise of mere morality. Additionally, there is no other alternative to the tragedy of "making light of serious things."

The Oldtown family participated fully in the tragedy of deep human sadness, a sadness brought on by the illusory hope of an escape from the ambiguities of mere morality. The minister of nearby Adams reproduced all the virtues and contradictions of the era in his own person. Dr. Moses Stern was the ultimate expression of serious, even prophetic theological thought in New England.[27] The period was rife with the skepticism of the revolutionary era, the skepticism of Paine's *Age of Reason*, and ministers rose to the defense. Dr. Stern met skepticism on the ground of the identity between Calvinism's harsh view and what every schoolboy could see of the work of "Nature's Author." This was a point on which our narrator, the master of Cloudland, and the arch villain all could agree. But Horace believed neither his "grandmother nor Dr. Stern." His young mind found no answer for the seething questions. He desired intensely not to resolve his own fate but "to know the real truth from some unanswerable authority." He desired "a visible, tangible communion with God." Stern's teaching touched different chords. The farmer, thwarted by nature, can see the operation of laws neither wholly within his control nor adapted to his purpose, and he may believe their author to consult something other than human happiness.

The stern Moses struck free from the Fall of Adam and taught the farmers of Adams that all matter and mind are moved by the efficient agency of God, albeit without particular regard for human designs and, accordingly, without interfering with free agency. Moses's consummation of the Puritan revolution democratized Eden, thus showing how Calvinism finally frees man from God. His law holds that all men are Adamites, confronting the original alternative, submission or willing. While he liberated men from conscience, he submitted them to the torture of consciousness of simultaneous helplessness and responsibility. Man is good only so far as nature is good, but man must exercise the choice. While he will likely do wrong, he must nonetheless guard against choosing wrong. Stern's entire being was freighted with the mission of this teaching.

Stern's renown spread, inciting awe and opposition. He wove his interpretation of the Bible into its literal appearance and conquered opinion with the impossible choice between his harsh views and the Bible's authority. He preached for effect and not for the sake of mere morality. He was incorruptible and therefore irresistible, since he who is unmoved by ordinary desires "is generally king of the neighborhood" (382). While Stern never sought to advance himself, he ultimately had to submit to students attracted by his preaching. They met his refusal to teach them with greater insistence. And they carried his courageous teaching everywhere.

Even after the old-time religion had wilted, and manners had changed, he moved about as an anachronistic example of the hard times. Stern preserved clerical pre-eminence at Adams long after republican ways had prevailed everywhere else. His theology provided a sharp contrast with the refined, safe theology of a republican era, which had lost the sense of the need to defend principle. Freely defending unpopular truths, Moses showed no respect for the tyranny of democratic opinion. He applied his inflexible teaching of human vulnerability to himself, resolving every impulse in the "utter, absolute, unconditional" (384) submission of will. Moses died in doubt of his own salvation, regarding it a matter of the prerogative of "the King Eternal." Abstracting from the frightful in this, our narrator finds "something also which is grand, and in which we can take pride, as the fruit of our human nature" (384). Unfortunately, it is liable to undermine the foundations needed to cherish that nature.

The tragedy in "our Oldtown family" was the personal tragedy of Emily Rossiter, who was raised by an aunt and uncle in Adams (Zedekiah Farnsworth and his wife). The uncle had the character of intense self-reliance necessary to the battle with nature. The aunt was a mirror image of her husband, uncompromising in her judgments of herself and others. The orphaned Rossiter was a sensitive child, accustomed to warmth of feelings and some indulgences. She could not develop naturally and healthily with her guardians. Additionally,

> [t]he problem of education is seriously complicated by the peculiarities of womanhood. If we suppose two souls, exactly alike, sent into bodies, the one of a man, the other of a woman, that mere fact alone alters the whole mental and moral history of the two (hence, the significance of Stowe's writing under a pseudonym) (385).

We learn here not only that the goal of the man-woman nature is unrealistic. Stern's young scholars were the souls identical to Emily's in male bodies. They were "marked men," but Stern's teaching did not corrupt them. Why his effect on a bright young woman should be corrupting is a question of serious import.

Aunt Farnsworth's attempt to counteract the danger of Emily's extraordinary beauty made Emily doubt her aunt's sincerity. Thus, she sought warmth and society outside the family. Aunt Farnsworth possessed no manners to reflect her own sensitivity to Emily's charms. Her love was held in check by the teaching of self-restraint. Emily's plight produces a general reflection: the "overaction and misapplication" of the mind's "noblest faculties" produces sad effects (386).

The problem lay much in the fact that both Farnsworths were ruled completely by Stern's preaching. They required Emily to study it meticulously. Most youth escaped the freezing fears of such teachings through thoughtlessness. Emily's above the ordinary mental vigor and "Greek passion for ideas" rendered her incapable of becoming inured to the stern challenge (386). Moses's hardy, independent manner of thought inspired as many disciples as the content of his weekly sermons. The inspired auditor would turn the monologue into a dialectic within his own soul. Thus did Emily. Between eleven and thirteen years of age she suffered the agonizing conflict between a "strong sense of justice" and the acceptance of cruel and frightful injustices on the authority of the Bible (387). Her guardians saw her struggles as the approach of submission and the hope of salvation.

Emily's cup attained the full measure in the premature, unregenerate death of her brother, whose utter loss was a *fait accompli*. Stern's teaching did violence to the sentiments of human nature. He insisted on the literal rendering of *Revelation* 19:3: "'And again they said Alleluia. And her smoke rose up for ever and ever'" (387). Men were required to emulate the "heavenly hosts" in happily anticipating the eternal punishment of the impenitent. Stern would have regarded Uncle Tom's insistence that "forever is a dre'ful word" as sinful. Moses's teaching could have justified the slaves' natural desire for retribution, considering it as ghastly error to memorialize men as better than they are. There was no room for Uncle Tom's recognition of differences of "nature" among men. This is what Stowe purges from the old education. Emily parted with old education from this sermon. Her falling away produced a despondency that was to be cured by a trip to Boston. During the trip worldly influences exercised their power over Emily's soul.

Emily encountered the stirring ideas which led to the "French and American revolution." She learned French. While Voltaire was "cold and cynical," Rousseau's warmth spoke to her nature. *La Nouvelle Hélöise* discussed the very problem "raised by her theological education." She cured her despondency by adopting "the faith of the Savoyard Vicar," "the philosophy of *Émile*," and Stern's "utter self-reliance" (389). Nietzsche is wrong. Stowe does not praise this combination.[28] The fact that Emily chooses Émile's philosophy, and not Sophie's, suggests that Rousseau's praise of mere morality was inadequate. *Au fond*, he, too, failed to admit the significance of differences of soul among men. If that were not convincing enough, the sequel will tell all.

When Emily returned to Adams she concealed her unbelief in French passages in her sermons note-book. In one such passage she placed honor to God above honor to the scripture (a pale shadow of the "*scepticisme involontaire*" of the Savoyard's "*religion naturelle*") adding, "*j'aimerais mieux croire la Bible falsifiée ou inintelligible que Dieux injuste ou malfaisant.*" Where the maker requires of the created being services for which the being is not suited, it is natural to demand, "*pourquoi m'as tu fait ainsi?*" (389). Emily's convictions pointed away from the goal at which Puritanism aimed, when aided by the Declaration. That was to assimilate disinterestedness and benevolence (requiring services perhaps better than man was suited for), thus saving the noblest dimension of the human soul for the life of action. But the new piety had to contend against two staunch enemies: intolerant protestantism and skepticism. At least, it had to emerge in the midst of their contentions.

Emily-Émile closed the silent era of her Adams's life by running away, without leaving a trace. All that was known was that friends she had known in Boston returned to France at the same time. In fact, Emily had become the first Oldtown victim of the villain of Cloudland. Inspired by the conviction that human life could be lived free of conventional morality and its untenable justification, she entered a "true marriage" and way of life based on rational manners. Her life became a protest against the oppressive "laws of human society on this subject." Marriage, the convention designed to tutor eros, however, refuses above all conventions to be reduced to natural law.

The denouement was predictable. To the arch villain "the affair was a simple gratification of passion" (581). The principles to which he appealed were but efficient instruments for the achievement of his will. The foundation of his will to power was the conviction "that there was no subject which had not its right and wrong side, each of them capable of being unanswerably sustained." His extraordinary mental powers could "dazzle and confound his own moral sense with his own reasonings." "He had entirely obliterated conscience." Therefore he eventually grew weary at seeing arguments "he maintained only for convenience . . . regarded by Emily so seriously, and with an earnest eye to logical consequences." To him the only logical consequence was that Nietzsche attributed to Rousseau: "the libertinism of passion." The arch villain abandoned Emily when he "tired of playing the moral hero" (582). How ironic: he could sustain her illusion of free, natural existence only by "playing the *moral* hero." Emily Rossiter's degradation was the failure of French rationalism. It was signaled in her partner's subsequent appearance as the villain of Cloudland.

Stern's harsh version of the "Blue Book" opened the way to Emily's seduction by romanticism, just as surely as Cloudland's utopian dream would do. The only alternative is to carve out indulgent space for the faculties of soul involved under the protective cover of the "Blue Book," a grandmotherly "Blue Book." Grandmother Badger had instinctively perceived the inseparability of the low and the high among human things. The central chapter of *Oldtown Folks* closed with Mehitable Rossiter pouring this tale of deep sadness into the ear of the villain of Cloudland, not knowing it was he who had seduced her sister, Emily, and would next seduce her foster daughter (Tina Percival), the maiden of Cloudland.

The end of the central chapter, chapter 29, returns to the end of chapter 28, where Miss Rossiter had begun the confession. The chapters fit end to end, disclosing the true place of "Grandmother's Blue Book." Chapter 28, "Raid on Oldtown," portrayed indignation over an attempt by kidnappers to steal the free family of Aunt Nancy Prime and sell the children into slavery. These petty villains were caught by a band of citizens and the children rescued. The chapter focused on the importance of children in the church, using Cotton Mather and the English church to show the gentle nature they received. In chapter 29, then, the emphasis is reversed to show that the new church (of Edwards and Stern) rather estranges than nurtures them. Chapter 30 returns to the theme of nurture. The question as to who or what gets the blame for the estrangements is subordinated to the question of nurture, the preservation of civilizing manners here and now.

The saving grace of "Blue Book" morality was its accomplishment of a union of "the utmost extremes of the material (Needmore) and the spiritual (Cloudland)." While the original founding was steeped in "religious enthusiasm," it was distinguished from similar foundings, as in Canada, which connected religious enthusiasm with asceticism. The latter failed because of its teaching that "contempt of the body and of material good" was virtuous and the related injunction against marriage for its teachers. But the "Old Testament" founding of "Blue Book" morality always spoke of "material prosperity . . . as the lawful reward of piety." Marriage was an honor and "a numerous posterity a thing to be desired." Then these intellectual and emotional "Jews" added "intense spiritualism" to "this broad physical basis."

In the latter day the combined virtues of the original founding divided into the streams of the skeptical and material (Franklin), on the one hand, and the uniquely spiritual (Edwards), on the other hand. The combination of these two represents the New England character, "in which every *ism* of social or religious life had had its origins,—that land whose hills and villages are one blaze and buzz of material and manufacturing production." In short, the upper crust of this life was the focus on the material. But the tradition of religious revivals inaugurated by Edwards always tapped a "deep spiritual *undercurrent* of thought and emotion," which formed a permanent substream for "intense material industries." The religious revival was a provisional means of making the spiritual "visible and tangible."

> Plato says that we all once had wings, and that they still tend to grow out in us, and that our burnings and aspirations for higher things are like the teething pangs of children. We are trying to cut our wings. Let us not despise these teething seasons. Though the wings do not become apparent, they may be starting under many a rough coat, and on many a clumsy pair of shoulders. (468)

The confused intermingling of differing souls or natures is the only appropriate description of human political life here and now. Perhaps Tina's clinging to an unhappy marriage to the arch villain illustrates this point. The objective of mere morality, memorializing men as better than they are, is not for the mere sake of preserving civilizing manners. Aspirations for higher things feed upon the pretensions that there are higher things.[29] To the extent Stowe's teaching is serious at this point, the criticisms of Nietzsche, as of Flaubert, strongly resemble the complaint of aviation's old enemy: "If God had meant for man to fly, He would have given him wings."

Whether Plato's *Phaedrus*, and Stowe's adaptation of its teaching, in fact envisions the era of transcontinental journeys, and for whom, is another question. The vision of anutopia, however, is not incompatible with Socrates' retraction of his beautiful, dithyrambic praise of disinterestedness as a surer, non-mantic foundation for the human concern for goodness. The retraction gave way to a purer and yet more poetic praise of love, self-interest, as the foundation of the good. That self-interest, however, is the self-interest of the best soul. The truer, more poetic speech had to reveal that there is no foundation for goodness for most humans in order to reveal the true human good. Or, to be more precise, insofar as there is a true human good, humans are of such a nature, and that good is of such a nature, that only the false speech is indeed true where the question at stake is the preservation of those conditions that permit open expression of love of the good. The protection of human nature is the means to defend the highest human activities. Stowe pointed to this when, in "Sunny Memories," she wrote that "the waters of scepticism were waning in America." It was her belief that some piety was necessary to the formation of a transcendent logic.

Socrates, in the *Phaedrus*, also spoke of the problem of writing about the human things, perhaps with his death in mind, as Flaubert may have thought, but surely still more with the question in mind, how is it possible to combine the true and the false speech, thus to tell the truth, given the inability to choose one's words to fit each and every reader? Words are addressed to the "soul." Because of differences in souls nothing written ever speaks "clearly and simply." Written words serve rather to remind the reader of what he knows. A written teaching cannot be a new teaching, in that sense. The questions to which its words give rise receive only dumb silence in response. The written treatise cannot produce the dialectic needed for learning. It can however produce the dialectic needed for remembering. She who knows the just, the noble, and the beautiful writes only for amusement, to store up treasures for her own memory, the memories of souls like her own. The written word speaks, then, to souls like the soul of the speech—complex speeches for complex souls and simple speeches for simple souls. Whatever fame a good writer deserves stems not from what he has written but from his serious speech about those things. To judge Stowe's many amusing stories by their own forms, or their popularity, or anything other than the questions they are able to raise for inquiring souls is to judge them by a standard lower than that to which she and her husband held themselves.

Still, Stowe's works were explicitly (but not merely) didactic, written "for a purpose" which was a public purpose. The ultimate expression of that purpose is the vision of anutopia, the attempt to demonstrate a form of political existence which would permit the highest expression of the possibilities of human perfection. The attainment of that vision depended upon the rejection of every nihilistic attempt to discover or implement a uniform status for every human soul.[30] This, in turn, affirmed the existence of differences in soul as itself the source of every true conception of human perfection. The public purpose aimed at leads to recognition of differences in soul, which itself serves the highest private purpose. Stowe's didactic work served to remind of what she knew about the possibilities of the human soul (as her writing under an open pseudonym has suggested).

Thus do we see Harriet patiently and plainly demonstrating to her own and every subsequent generation the utter impossibility of an utopia. Her proof is in measure absolute precisely because it is founded on the simplest and most natural of considerations. Utopia is a "nowhere" which never is, nor can be anywhere, merely because it cannot reproduce itself. That is, a concern for the preservation of the species in its essential nature was regarded by her as utterly incompatible with utopian ambition. The concern with the preservation of the species, in the view of the utopian himself, is but mere dross encumbering the wholly abstracted embodiment of individual want. We should readily comprehend this argument, reformulated as it is now in the midst of our own lively and dominant concerns. But if our own concerns express a lingering passion for utopia, we are checked short by the notion of anutopia, which insists that the grounds of human existence are unchanged and unchanging. Life in anutopia is the life in which not Christian but Platonic souls can yearn to fly, even if they received no wings from God.

NOTES

1. All references are to the 1869 edition of *Oldtown Folks* published by Fields, Osgood, & Co., and are noted parenthetically.

2. *Oldtown Folks* has received minimal commentary by Stowe scholars and those few who have analyzed it tend to see it mainly as an example of New England regionalism. Foster is typical in seeing the novel as "one of the unquestionable, but still generally unacknowledged, masterpieces of New England, indeed of American literature"; overlooking its rich allegory, he views Stowe's main contribution here as giving us "a balanced and immediate sense of the vital and complex Puritan period." Charles Foster, *The Rungless Ladder: Harriet Beecher Stowe and New England Puritanism* (Durham, NC: Duke University Press, 1954), pp. 176, 242–43. In his introduction to the 1966 edition of the novel, May provides an overview of its critical reception to that point and adds his own assessment: "*Oldtown Folks* is not a good novel. It is, however, an important and highly interesting book . . . [it] is far more than expert local color; it is more even than intellectual history. It is a record of the intense and painful experience of a gifted woman to find her way through the difficult issues of her day." May, "Introduction," p. 6. Sawaya likewise misses the allegory but does acknowledge *Oldtown Folks* as "the serious historical and moral document," which he reports that Stowe intended it to be, but which she feared would not be recognized as such by her readers. Sawaya, "The Home Front," p. 16. Hartshorne is something of an exception; she does acknowledge that the novel is highly allegorical, reading it largely as a complex mixture of fairy tales; however, she has not captured its deep political and philosophical import in her analysis.

Hartshorne, "'Without Divine Intervention.'" Guilbert explicates the novel, along with *The Minister's Wooing* and *The Pearl of Orr Island*, primarily as Stowe's attempt to rewrite the history of the United States to allow for a more inclusive place for women ("In *The Minister's Wooing* and *Oldtown Folks*, Stowe imagines the colonial past to be the benign matriarchal ancestor of modern women's culture, rather than a patriarchal obstacle that must be overthrown, revised, or co-opted by women.") Juliette Guilbert, "Rewriting the Republic: American Women's Historical Fiction, 1824–1869" (Ph.D. diss., Yale University, 1999), p. 168. Marotta states that the novel is "by general consent" thought to be Stowe's "masterpiece," but does not cite the source for his conclusion. Marotta, "The Literary Relationship of George Eliot and HBS," p. 191. Suckow christens the book "a lost classic" and "a 'seminal' novel of American life," categorizing it as "all these things—environmental, historical, religious, a novel of character." Ruth Suckow, "An Almost Lost American Classic," *College English* 14, no. 6 (1953): 316 (hereafter cited as "An Almost Lost American lassic"). Forrest Wilson offers a clue by quoting the following from one of Stowe's letters in which she wrote of *Oldtown Folks*: "Under all the drollery that is to be found in it, this book will be found to have in it the depths of the most solemn tragedy of life, and I shall make it my means of saying many things which I hope will be accepted pacifically on all sides." Wilson, *Crusader in Crinoline*, p. 531.

3. For, as Calvin Stowe wrote in 1882, "It is only when a man looks through a glass which is perfectly clear and pure, that he sees things as they are; if the glass be in the least degree distorted or discolored, every object seen through it will necessarily partake of the distortion and discoloration." Calvin E. Stowe, introduction to *Philosophy of the Plan of Salvation*, ed. James B. Walker (New York: M. W. Dodd and R. Carter, 1843; reprint, New York: Chautauqua Press, 1887), p. 15. Pagination refers to the Chautauqua Press edition.

4. Kadish criticizes Flaubert's analysis, contending that it was a "highly gendered" reading, and disparaging his placement of aesthetic concerns above moral or humanistic concerns. Doris Y. Kadish, "Gendered Readings of *Uncle Tom's Cabin*: The Example of Sand and Flaubert," *Nineteenth-Century French Studies*, no. 3 & 4 (1998).

5. G. Flaubert to Louise Colet, November 22 and December 9, 1852 (published in Gustave Flaubert, *Correspondence*, ed. Jean Bruneau [Gallimard, 1980]).

6. Given Brooks's analysis of the French origins of melodrama, it is ironic that Flaubert does not recognize the transcendent possibilities of the genre, of which Brooks writes: "The melodramatists refuse to allow that the world has been drained of transcendence; and they locate that transcendence in the struggle of the children of light with the children of darkness, in the play of ethical mind." Brooks, *The Melodramatic Imagination*, p. 22.

7. Hedrick, however, locates in Cloudland Stowe's birthplace, saying that here "Stowe found the millennial community in the Litchfield of her youth." Hedrick, *Harriet Beecher Stowe*, p. 344. While Stowe may certainly have sketched Cloudland to resemble aspects of Litchfield (as several other critics also suggest), by naming it Cloudland she clearly intends a cautionary tale, not a hoped-for utopia. In addition to the evidence present in *Oldtown Folks* itself, we can adduce this from Stowe's essay, "The Lady Who Does Her Own Work," who gently calls her husband back to reality from his "cloudland" where he loves "to sail away in dreamy quietude, forgetting the war, the price of coal and flour, the rates of exchange, and the rise and fall

of gold." Stowe, *Household Papers and Stories,* p. 85. Westbrook also errs in his assessment of Cloudland not only as a replication of Litchfield but also as "a New Jerusalem." Perry D. Westbrook, *The New England Town in Fact and Fiction* (London and Toronto: Associated University Presses, 1982), p. 104.

8. Cf. Fisher (writing about Catharine Beecher's *Treatise on Domestic Economy*): ". . . the center of any political representation must include continuity, and therefore reproduction." Fisher, *Hard Facts,* p. 88.

9. Nor is the "radical, millennial vision held in check by conservative political impulses," which Hedrick finds in this and "so many of her novels." Hedrick, *Harriet Beecher Stowe,* p. 342.

10. How Rousseauian, Nietzsche might sneer! And what is worse, it derives inspiration from Schiller:

> In life, avails the right of force.
> The bold the timid worries;
> Who rules not, is a slave of course,
> Without design each thing across
> Earth's stage forever hurries.
> Yet what would happen if the plan
> Which guides the world now first began,
> Within the moral system lies
> Disclos'd with clearness to our eyes.

"The Philosophers," *Poems of Schiller,* tr. by Edgar A. Bowring (Philadelphia: J. B. Lippincott, 1851), p. 273.

11. Cf. Sawaya: " . . . throughout the book, there are more models of failed fathers than of successful fathers." Sawaya, "The Home Front," p. 61.

12. Although Crab Smith praised the dying mother who landed on his doorstep for having enough money to pay for her coffin, he nonetheless removed and sold her wedding ring for that purpose (or so informed the children!).

13. "Of all the change that art can make in men for the better, what can be done by education is certainly the most important part. It is the one single thing that can be done to raise the human soul." Howard B. White, "The Blind Mole," in *Copp'd Hills toward Heaven: Shakespeare and the Classical Polity* (Hague: Martinus-Nijhoff, 1970), p. 11.

14. Shakespeare, "Pericles, Prince of Tyre," Act I, lines 9–10; *et bonum . . . : "and the more ancient a good thing is the better it is."*

15. Cf. Suckow: " . . . the characters of *Oldtown Folks,* while sharply set in time and place—as all human life is set, . . .—are treated as eternal souls. Here lies my most compelling reason for affirming that *Oldtown Folks* is needed in a contemporary consideration of literature . . . " Suckow, "An Almost Lost American Classic," p. 325.

16. Tang ventures near to, without quite reaching, this conclusion when he comments that to Stowe, "Puritanism contributed to its own demise, promoting irreligious feelings among potential adherents." Tang, "Revolutionary Legacies," p. 219. Camfield comes closer still in writing that Stowe "advocated an intuitive rather than a rational approach to religion and to morality because she found that the 'habit of doubting' required by rationality destroyed her own faith.

"Reason's inability to resolve doubt, Stowe implies, prevents moral action. . . . As an alternative to this kind of intellectual paralysis, Stowe adopted the radical intuitionism inherent but usually dormant in Common Sense philosophies, developing it into a pietistic alternative to America's increasing skepticism." Camfield, "Moral Aesthetics," p. 342.

17. See Sawaya on the meeting-house as enforcer of unity and enabler of democracy and equality, chapter 7, note 1.

18. Tang finds that "the diminishing status of the clergy" was central to Stowe's thought. Tang, "Revolutionary Legacies," p. 214.

19. Cf. Guilbert: "Horace Holyoke suggests that the advantage of the motherly Mather's doctrine is its assumption that regeneration is, like maternity, a visible affair: simply by virtue of being born to and nurtured by the Christian Church, one can claim a connection to it. Edwards denies this self-evident link between the Church and her children, and offers in its place the unverifiable relationship between a father and his offspring. It is the job of nineteenth-century grandmothers to re-establish the visible matrilineal tradition of New England faith." Guilbert, "Rewriting the Republic," p. 178.

20. Numerous Stowe scholars have attempted to analyze her attitude toward Edwards. To cite but one example here, Kimball shows that in many ways Stowe "blamed him for the decline of Puritanism" and made many of the villains in her works "Edwardsian or related to Edwards in some way," but asserts in addition that "Edwards profoundly influenced Stowe in his emphasis on the affections." Kimball, "HBS's Revision of New England Theology," pp. 67, 68.

21. Quite a few Stowe scholars have described what they perceive as Stowe's belief that the softening influence of women was needed, in order to ameliorate the harshness of Calvinism. Tang's commentary is representative: "Bridging the gulf between Calvinist harshness and secular, democratic chaos was the exemplary New England woman, busy at her hearth, delivering equal doses of compassion and old-time religion . . . [but Stowe] became ensnared between the dilemmas of supporting a religious patriarchy to guide a reckless democracy and advocating the need for women to reform the very theological and political systems that confined them." Edward Tang, "Making Declarations on Her Own: Harriet Beecher Stowe as New England Historian," *New England Quarterly* 71, no. 1 (1998): 95. Smith hones in on the "idyllic nature" of the coeducation depicted in *Oldtown Folks* and the benefits to the youthful male scholars of "young women and their insights in their reading" (p. 235). Smith's broader argument is that, throughout her *oeuvre*, Stowe explores the need for and insight to be gained if a man reads as a woman, or a free man as a slave, or a European American as an African American." Smith, "The Sentimental Novel."

22. Hence, the significance of Stowe's writing under a pseudonym, rather than Hedrick's assessment that "speaking in a male voice was the price of admission to the *Atlantic* club" or Foster's notion that Stowe used "male spokesmen through whom she could speak her opinions without assuming immediate responsibility for them." Hedrick, *Harriet Beecher Stowe*, p. 314. Foster, *The Rungless Ladder*, p. 174.

23. Cf. Calvin Stowe: "Self-interest is no security at all against the influence of passion . . . " Stowe, "The Religious Element in Education," p. 13.

24. For an enlightening discussion of this natural opposition, see Calvin Stowe's preface to *The Philosophy of the Plan for Salvation*.

25. In Tang's account, Stowe "speculated that Calvinism, to survive in the nineteenth century, required increased accessibility to the people at large. On the other hand, she argued that democracy itself lacked a moral force that the older values and beliefs could provide." Tang, "Revolutionary Legacies," p. 215.

26. It is this understanding, and certainly not that proposed by Marotta, who maintains that "Stowe did not write in praise of the Christian achievement [i.e., America as the New Jerusalem]; rather, . . . she criticized American reality by juxtaposing it to those Biblical types it claimed to fill, revealing it not as Jerusalem but as Babylon. This was the outlook and the strategy that produced her first novel, and that was at the basis of all her novels. . . . Stowe's works, so occupied with depicting the surfaces of this new country . . . succeed above all else in showing the failure of this novelty, at the same time proposing a fictional New Jerusalem, one to be entered only in reading novels" (p. 256–57). Through the "power of [her] imagination" Stowe "discovered an America commensurate with the New Jerusalem [she] hoped for, and in [her] fiction, gave others the chance to discover it too" (p. 262). Marotta, "The Literary Relationship of George Eliot and HBS."

27. May, Kimball, and Tang each assert that Stowe modeled Stern on the theologian Nathaniel Emmons. May, "Introduction." Kimball, "HBS's Revision of New England Theology." Tang, "Making Declarations."

28. Stowe does not, as Smith would have it, make *La Nouvelle Hélöise* into "an alternate—and more humane—spiritual text for women." It is evident that the *use* of *Émile*'s philosophy qualifies the citation of *La Nouvelle Héloïse*, while invoking the continuing theme of the man-woman. Smith, "The Sentimental Novel," p. 233. Lombard's brief speculation on "the role the French Romantics played in formulating the social idealism and religious outlook of Harriet Beecher Stowe" comes a bit, but only a bit, closer to an accurate assessment in his suggestion that "Emily's desire to seek a deeper meaning in French Romanticism and its glorification of the role of intuition in religion . . . represents a phase of Mrs. Stowe's own quest for inner peace of soul and a better society." Charles M. Lombard, "Harriet Beecher Stowe's Attitude towards French Romanticism," *CLA Journal* 11 (1967/68): 236.

29. Cf. Camfield, discussing the influence of Alison's philosophy of moral sentiment on Stowe: " . . . human abilities to feel . . . lead human beings to virtue. . . . This is the moral aesthetic that drives *Uncle Tom's Cabin*. By engaging her readers human affections in her purified representations of life, Stowe attempts to train her readers beyond the human, toward the divine." Camfield, "Moral Aesthetics," pp. 340–41.

30ˆ. Cf. Shipp: "Acknowledging the sacred quality of all human life need not blind the audience to distinctions between those lives which are better lived than others." Shipp, "*UTC* and the Ethos of Melodrama," p. 149.

27

Coda

Was Harriet Stowe a Racist?

The foregoing argument should plainly demonstrate that Harriet was not a racist. In order to secure the case, however, it will not be amiss to point readers to a still more obvious demonstration of the prosaic facts of the matter. We can ascertain from Stowe's direct and non-literary reflections upon race and culture the character of her own evolving sentiments. We have that evidence in the form of her first book, published when she was but twenty-two years old, and the subsequently much-revised re-issue of that book. That initial work was the *Primary Geography for Children, on an Improved Plan* published in 1833. Although this work was issued with her sister Catharine's name as senior author, we know in fact that it is Harriet's work, as is also the very extensively revised *New Geography for Children* published in 1855 in the aftermath of the many works generated by *Uncle Tom's Cabin*.

A project awaits an enterprising scholar to perform a full-fledged comparison of these two works, the interest of which extends far beyond the question of racial characterization. Let it suffice for us to note, however, that the two works describe but five races among men, "the European, the Asiatic, the African, the American, and the Malayan." Despite the many and varied descriptions of race employed by Stowe in her popular works, therefore, her technical account admits only these five, and they remain unchanged from their formulation in chapter 13 of 1833 in the chapter 22, 1855 version. Almost everything else about the two chapters does change after twenty-two years of reflection and growth.

The single, most important change occurs in the iconography of race between the two. The first edition used but four images to convey the European, the Asiatic, the African, and the American. No representation of the

Malayan was provided, but they were declared "handsome" as not being very dark. The four images convey quite clearly the loveliness and sophistication of the European contrasted with the primitive and the exotic of the remaining three. Moreover, the language in the 1833 edition literally announces the Europeans, but only, curiously, those "in the Barbary States, in Egypt, and in Abyssinia," as having "features more regular and beautiful than those of any other class." The use of "class" instead of "race" does not necessarily confine this appraisal to the subset thus named. For, the "white people in America belong to this class," and the Europeans in the broader sense display a variety of complexions from dark to light. There is a clear prejudice of color in the early work. Nevertheless, negative ascriptions are far more generalized. No further characterizations are offered in chapter 13, although in other chapters Africa (the "country") is said to be "the most degraded and uncivilized of any of the four quarters of the globe" (chapter 19), the Americans of the South are a "lazy and miserable set of people" after the depredations of the Spanish (chapter 28), while the many tribes in the Cape Colony "are very stupid and ignorant" (chapter 19). The Greeks, long under the thumbs of the Turks, are "very ignorant," and the poor Russians (Europeans) are "very dirty," "ignorant and wretched" (chapter 21). Finally, in Mexico the "tribes of Indians" are very degraded and ignorant," while the "white people are very lazy and very vicious too and very few of them have any learning" (chapter 22).

The first throw of Stowe's geography, in other words, sprinkled generously glib generalizations about peoples and their ways, and conveyed a distinct sense of the superior *appearance* of the European. At no time, however, does that attitude crystallize into a purely racial (and Eurocentric) set of preferences. Indeed, the strongest preferences operating are "republicanism" and "Christianity," the absence of which alone seems to keep all mankind from living together happily. Even the account of the regional differences in the United States are presented with a minimal degree of differentiation in point of moral worth, albeit the northern hive is "industrious," while the southern hive—albeit pleasant and friendly enough—has a great indisposition to labor on account of slavery.

What, then, required revision in 1855? Two things stand out most dramatically. First, the presentation of the United States is given pride of place, being presented earlier rather than later and with a far more detailed presentation of regional differences, now adducing moral worth as a criterion. Secondly, the "Races of Men" was completely revised after the initial paragraph and including the graphic representation. These changes operate together to create a distinct impression and incidentally also tie the new version fast to the project of *Uncle Tom's Cabin*.

In 1855 the discussion of the United States opened in chapter 5, as the first substantive chapter following the presentation of the technical criteria for geography. It was previously chapter 23, following the presentation of world geography. The latter now follows instead. Moreover, the earlier order of presentation was "New England States," "Southern States," "Middle States," and "Western States." The new arrangement is "New England States," "Middle States," "Western States," and "Southern or Slave States." The southern states are demoted, while their chief defect is elevated to a primary focus of concern. The New England states again appear as a seedbed of industriousness and education, imparted to the middle and western states through emigration. Intelligence and prosperity prevail. Without detailing the account, it should suffice to observe that the presentation effectively suggests a providential ordering moving in a straight line from the Puritan settlements right through the growing empire of liberty. The slave empire is an exception to all this. Of the slave states it may be said that "states that are cultivated in this way never prosper as those do which are cultivated by freemen." And she provides reasons, the chief of which is the moral degradation of the slave owners and their children, and the next of which is the evil or injustice of slavery. The lengthy presentation eventuates in an invocation of the prayers of all "good people" for the abolition of slavery.

Stowe subtly signals that her account should be taken as just such a prayer. Where in 1833 she described the Ohio River straightforwardly in terms of its relationship to the Mississippi and surrounding territory, in 1855 she added a single phrase, "the name *Ohio* means *beautiful*" (chapter 9). That follows, of course, the usage in *Uncle Tom's Cabin* that derived from Tocqueville. Thus, what Stowe learned in the intervening years strengthened her approach and was ratified in 1855.

We see this in its fullness when she attains command of the graphic representations in her book, a command she did not have in 1833. In the chapter on the "Races of Men" (22), we now find a single illustration providing five profiles representative of all the races, each of which is dramatically improved over the original illustration, conveying personal attraction and a bourgeois appearance of strength of character. But even of this improved representation, Stowe was moved to comment in the text: "The picture of the Indian and African is like some of the worst looking of their kind, for there are some of them that look as well as the European race excepting their dark skins." The prejudice of color survives, but its significance is attenuated. This is revealed when we consider the "student questions" that accompanied the representations in the original edition, one of which was, "Are any of these people handsome?" The 1855 edition indicates how Stowe *would* dispose the answer to that question, just as in 1833 the comment about the unrepresented "Malayan race" aimed to broaden the notion of handsome. This account becomes especially compelling when we revisit the Malayans in 1855, not in the discussion of the "Races of Men" but in the discussion of the "Austral Asia" islands (chapter 20), where a new illustration of "Polynesian" princes evokes the observation: "You see how stupid and brutal they look"! Stowe who had previously celebrated such people as "handsome" now confronts their "cannibalism" and primitivism with "stupid and brutal." It is clear that the terms are not mutually incompatible for Stowe, just as in the case of Mexico in 1833 she could speak disparagingly both of the white people and the Indians.

Stowe was free in her use of racial characterizations, but not merely stereotypical in doing so. Indeed, a careful analysis of the political instruction conveyed in her geography texts would lead us to see the method of liberalism in her approach. To that end, we must conclude that not only was Harriet not a racist, but her purpose was directly to confront racism per se.

28

Postscript

I wish to say a chance and final word about Stowe's art concerning a factor that is key to understanding Stowe's art. Her talent for characterization was in fact a function of strongly developing plots; that is, telling a good story. A single incident from *Uncle Tom's Cabin* provides an example of just how integral Stowe's characterization was both to her story and to her project. The character of John, the Drover was dramatically unnecessary. Nonetheless, that character allowed Stowe, without a personal intervention, Flaubert to the contrary notwithstanding, to pose the question of slavery's impropriety in a fashion far more radical than we would ever have accepted had we been conscious of it. This bit of manipulation makes the reader indignant to be reminded of slavery's evil because, of course, he always thought just so! In short, Stowe's apparent simplicity makes all of her readers philosophers. That is good for independent-minded republicans who hate, above all, being openly manipulated. This allows them to find the necessity to defend, all by themselves, the truth that, of course, everybody's always known.

Bibliography

Abel, Annie Heloise and Frank J. Klingberg, eds. *A Side-light on Anglo-American Relations, 1839–1858.* Lancaster, PA: The Association for the Study of Negro Life and History, 1927.

Alison, Archibald. *Essay on the Nature and Principles of Taste.* 2 vols. 6th edition. Edinburgh: Archibald Constable, 1825.

Allen, William B. "The Manners of Liberalism: A Question of Limits." *Improving College and University Teaching* 30, no. 4 (Fall 1982): 163–70.

Ammons, Elizabeth. "Stowe's Dream of the Mother-Savior: *Uncle Tom's Cabin* and American Women Writers before the 1920s." In *New Essays on Uncle Tom's Cabin*, edited by Eric J. Sundquist, 155–95. Cambridge: Cambridge University Press, 1986.

———. "*Uncle Tom's Cabin*, Empire and Africa." In *Approaches to Teaching Uncle Tom's Cabin*, edited by Elizabeth Ammons and Susan Belasco, 68-76. New York: Modern Language Association, 2000.

Ammons, Elizabeth and Susan Belasco, eds. *Approaches to Teaching Uncle Tom's Cabin.* New York: Modern Language Association, 2000.

Anderson, Beatrice A. "Uncle Tom: A Hero at Last." *ATQ* 5 (1991): 95–108.

Arner, Robert D. "Jeffersonian Idealism and the Southern Frontier: A Reading of *Uncle Tom's Cabin.*" In *New Historical Perspectives: Essays on the Black Experience in Antebellum America*, edited by Gene D. Lewis, 59-80. Cincinnati: Friends of Harriet Beecher Stowe House and Citizens' Committee on Youth, 1984.

Baldwin, James. "Everybody's Protest Novel." *Partisan Review* 16 (1949): 578–85.

Banfield, Edward C. *The Heavenly City.* 1968. Reprint, Boston: Little, Brown, 1970.

Banks, Marva. "*Uncle Tom's Cabin* and Antebellum Black Response." In *Readers in History: Nineteenth-Century American Fiction and the Contexts of Response*, edited by James L. Machor, 209–27. Baltimore: Johns Hopkins University Press, 1993.

Bardes, Barbara and Suzanne Gossett. *Declarations of Independence: Women and Political Power in Nineteenth Century American Fiction.* New Brunswick: Rutgers University Press, 1990.

Baring-Gould, William S. and Cecil Baring-Gould, eds. *The Annotated Mother Goose.* New York: Bramhall House, 1962.

Baym, Nina. *American Women Writers and the Work of History, 1790-1860.* New Brunswick: Rutgers University Press, 1995.

Beecher, Catharine Esther and Harriet Beecher Stowe. *The American Woman's Home, or, Principles of Domestic Science.* New York: J. B. Ford & Company, 1869. Reprint, Hartford, CT: Stowe-Day Foundation, 1975. Citations refer to reprint edition.

———. *Primary Geography for Children, on an Improved Plan.* Cincinnati: Corey & Fairbank, 1833.

Beecher, Charles. *Anti-Slavery Tract No. 17.* New York: American Anti-Slavery Society, n.d.

———. *Diary.* Hartford, CT: Stowe-Day Foundation.

Beecher, Edward. *Narrative of Riots at Alton, in Connection with the Death of Reverend Elijah P. Lovejoy.* Philadelphia: George Holton, 1838.

Beecher, Lyman. *A Plea for the West.* Cincinnati: Truman & Smith, 1835.

Bellin, Joshua D. "Up to Heaven's Gate, Down in Earth's Dust: The Politics of Judgment in *Uncle Tom's Cabin.*" *American Literature* 65, no. 2 (June 1993): 275–95.

Bense, James. "Myths and Rhetoric of the Slavery Debate and Stowe's Comic Vision of Slavery." In *The Stowe Debate: Rhetorical Strategies in Uncle Tom's Cabin,* edited by Mason I. Lowance, Ellen E. Westbrook, and R. C. De Prospo, 187–204. Amherst: University of Massachusetts Press, 1994.

Berghorn, Donna. "'The Mother's Struggle': Harriet Beecher Stowe and the American Anti-Slavery Debate." Ph.D. diss., University of Pennsylvania, 1988.

Betts, S. M. "Harriet Beecher Stowe." In *Eminent Women of the Age.* Hartford, CT: 1868.

Billings, Robert William. *The Baronial and Ecclesiastical Antiquities of Scotland.* Edinburg and London: Published for the author by W. Blackstone and Sons, 1848–1852.

Boller, Paul F., Jr. "Uncle Tom as a Black Hero." In *Not So! Popular Myths about America from Columbus to Clinton* by Paul F. Boller, 66–71. New York: Oxford University Press, 1995.

Boots, Cheryl Charline. "Earthly Strains: The Cultural Work of Protestant Sacred Music in Three Nineteenth-Century American Popular Novels (James Fenimore Cooper, Harriet Beecher Stowe, Deborah Dunham Kelley-Hawkins)." Ph.D. diss., Boston University, 2000.

Boreham, F. W. *The Gospel of Uncle Tom.* London: The Epworth Press, 1956.

Boyd, Richard. "Models of Power in Harriet Beecher Stowe's *Dred.*" *Studies in American Fiction* 19, no. 1 (Spring 1991): 15–36.

Brommell, Nicholas K. *By the Sweat of the Brow: Literature and Labor in Antebellum America.* Chicago: University of Chicago Press, 1993.

Brooks, Peter. *The Melodramatic Imagination: Balzac, Henry James, Melodrama, and the Mode of Excess.* New Haven: Yale University Press, 1976.

Brown, Gillian. *Domestic Individualism: Imagining Self in Nineteenth-Century America.* Berkeley: University of California Press, 1990.

Buell, Lawrence. "Rival Romantic Interpretations of New England Puritanism: Hawthorne Versus Stowe." *Texas Studies in Literature and Languages* 25, no. 1 (Spring 1983): 77–99.

Burke, Edmund. *The Works of the Right Honorable Edmund Burke*. Boston: Little, Brown and Company, 1865.

Bush, Harold K. "The Declaration of Independence and *Uncle Tom's Cabin*: A Rhetorical Approach." In *Approaches to Teaching Uncle Tom's Cabin*, edited by Elizabeth Ammons and Susan Belasco, 172–83. New York: Modern Language Association of America, 2000.

Camfield, Gregg. "The Moral Aesthetics of Sentimentality: A Missing Key to *Uncle Tom's Cabin*." *Nineteenth-Century Literature* 43, no. 3 (December 1988): 319–45.

Carleton, George Washington. *Suppressed Book about Slavery*. New York: Carleton, 1864. Reprint, New York: Arno Press, 1968. Citations refer to reprint edition.

Carlisle, George William Frederick Howard, Earl of. *Travel in America, Poetry of Pope. Two Lectures Delivered to the Leeds Mechanics' Institute and Literary Society, December 5th and 6th, 1850*. New York: G. P. Putnam, 1851.

Carlyle, Thomas. "Occasional Discourse on the Nigger Question." In *English and Other Critical Essays*, by Thomas Carlyle. 1915. Reprint, London: J. M. Dent & Sons, 1925. Citations refer to the reprint edition.

Caskey, Marie. *Chariots of Fire: Religion and the Beecher Family*. New Haven: Yale University Press, 1978.

Choate, Rufus. "The Importance of Illustrating New England History by a Series of Romances Like the Waverly Novels." In *The Works of Rufus Choate*, edited by Samuel Gilman Brown, vol. 1, 319–46. Boston: Little, Brown and Company, 1862.

Cotugno, Clare Degree. "Form and Reform: Transatlantic Dialogues, 1824–1876." Ph.D. diss., Temple University, 2001.

Cox, James M. "Harriet Beecher Stowe: From Sectionalism to Regionalism." *Nineteenth Century Fiction* 38, no. 4 (March 1984): 444–66.

Crane, Gregg David. *Race, Citizenship, and Law in American Literature*. New York: Cambridge University Press, 2002.

Davis, Richard Beale. "Mrs. Stowe's Characters-in-Situation and a Southern Literary Tradition." In *Essays in Honor of Jay B. Hubbell*, edited by Clarence Gohdes, 108–25. Durham: Duke University Press, 1967.

Donovan, Josephine. *Uncle Tom's Cabin: Evil, Affliction, and Redemptive Love*. Boston: Twayne Publisher, 1991.

Duvall, Severn. "*Uncle Tom's Cabin*: The Sinister Side of the Patriarchy." *New England Quarterly* (March 1963): 2–33. Reprinted in *Images of the Negro in American Literature*, edited by Seymour L. Gross and John Edward Hardy. Chicago: University of Chicago Press, 1966. Citations refer to reprint edition.

Ellis, Lisa A. "The Popularity of *Uncle Tom's Cabin*: Escapism and Ethnocentrism in Mid-Nineteenth Century France." Master's thesis, Hunter College of the City University of New York, 1999.

Ferry, Luc. *Man Made God: The Meaning of Life*. Translated from the original, *L'Homme-Dieu, ou Le sens de la vie*. Paris: Grasset, 1996. Translation edition, Chicago: University of Chicago Press, 2002.

Fiedler, Leslie. "Home as Heaven, Home as Hell: *Uncle Tom's Cabin*." In *Rewriting the Dream: Reflections on the Changing American Literary Canon*, edited by W. M. Verhovoeven, 22–42. Amsterdam: Rodopi, 1992.

———. *The Inadvertent Epic: From Uncle Tom's Cabin to Roots*. New York: Simon and Schuster, 1982.

———. *Love and Death in the American Novel*. New York: Criterion Books, 1960. Revised edition, New York: Stein and Day, 1966. Citations refer to Stein and Day edition.

Fields, Annie. *Life and Letters of Harriet Beecher Stowe*. Boston: Houghton, Mifflin and Company, 1987.

Fisher, Philip. *Hard Facts: Setting and Form in the American Novel*. New York: Oxford University Press, 1985.

Flaubert, Gustave. *Correspondance*. Edited by Jean Bruneau. 4 vols. Paris: Gallimard, 1973–1980.

Fluck, Winfried. "The Power and Failure of Representation in Harriet Beecher Stowe's *Uncle Tom's Cabin*." *New Literary History* 23 (1992): 319–38.

Foner, Philip, ed. *The Life and Writings of Frederick Douglass*. 5 vols. New York: International Publishers, 1950.

Foster, Charles H. *The Rungless Ladder: Harriet Beecher Stowe and New England Puritanism*. Durham: Duke University Press, 1954.

Furnas, J. C. *Goodbye to Uncle Tom*. New York: W. Sloane Associates, 1956.

Gilbertson, Catherine. *Harriet Beecher Stowe*. 1937. Reprint, Port Washington, NY: Kennikat Press, Inc., 1968.

Gossett, Thomas F. *Uncle Tom's Cabin and American Culture*. Dallas: Southern Methodist University Press, 1985.

Graham, Thomas. "Harriet Beecher Stowe and the Question of Race." *New England Quarterly* 46 (1973): 614–22.

Grant, David. "*Uncle Tom's Cabin* and the Triumph of Republican Rhetoric." *New England Quarterly* 71, no. 3 (September 1998): 429–48.

Gruner, Mark Randall. "Stowe's *Dred*: Literary Domesticity and the Law of Slavery." *Prospects* 20 (1995): 1–37.

Guilbert, Juliette. "Rewriting the Republic: American Women's Historical Fiction, 1824–1869." Ph.D. diss., Yale University, 1999.

Hada, Kenneth. "The Kentucky Model: Economics, Individualism, and Domesticity in *Uncle Tom's Cabin*." *Papers on Language and Literature* 35, no. 2 (Spring 1999): 167–86.

Hadas, Moses. *A History of Greek Literature*. New York: Columbia University Press, 1950.

———. "Paginism at Bay." In *A History of Latin Literature*. New York: Columbia University Press, 1950.

Hamilton, Cynthia. "*Dred*: Intemperate Slavery." *Journal of American Studies* 34, no. 2 (2000): 257–77.

Harker, John Stanley. "The Life and Contributions of Calvin Ellis Stowe." Ph.D. diss., 1951.

Hartshorne, Sarah Dickson. "'Without Divine Intervention': Three Novels by Harriet Beecher Stowe Herself." Ph.D. diss., Brown University, 1990.

———. "'Woe Unto You that Desire the Day of the Lord:' Harriet Beecher Stowe and the Corruption of Christianity in *Dred, A Tale of the Great Dismal Swamp*." *Anglican and Episcopal History* 64 (1995): 280–99.

Hedrick, Joan. *Harriet Beecher Stowe: A Life*. New York: Oxford University Press, 2001.

Hegel, G. W. F. *The Phenomenology of Mind*. Translated by J. B. Baillie. 2nd edition. New York: The MacMillan Company, 1931.

Hovet, Theodore R. "Modernization and the American Fall into Slavery in *Uncle Tom's Cabin*." *New England Quarterly* 54, no. 4 (1981): 499–518.

Hudson, Benjamin F. "Another View of 'Uncle Tom.'" *Phylon* 24, no. 1 (First Quarter 1963): 79–87.

Ipema, Tim M. "The Voice of Protest in *Uncle Tom's Cabin* and *Native Son*." Master's thesis, Eastern Illinois University, 1990.

Jaffa, Harry V. *Bicentennial Cerebration*. Durham: Carolina Academic Press, 1978.

———. *Crisis of the House Divided*. Seattle: University of Washington Press, 1973.

Johnson, Charles. Introduction to *Uncle Tom's Cabin*, by Harriet Beecher Stowe, v–xv. 1853. Reprint, Oxford: Oxford University Press, 2002.

Jones, Horace Perry. "The Southern Press Follows Harriet Beecher Stowe Abroad." *The McNeese Review* 27 (1980): 36–44.

Joswick, Thomas P. "'The Crown without the Conflict': Religious Values and Moral Reasoning in *Uncle Tom's Cabin*." *Nineteenth Century Fiction* 39, no. 3 (December 1984): 253–74.

Kadish, Doris Y. "Gendered Readings of *Uncle Tom's Cabin*: The Example of Sand and Flaubert." *Nineteenth-Century French Studies* 26, nos. 3 & 4 (Spring-Summer 1998): 308–20.

Karafilis, Maria. "Spaces of Democracy in Harriet Beecher Stowe's *Dred*." *Arizona Quarterly* 55, no. 3 (Autumn 1999): 23–49.

Kay, Jacqueline. "Literary Images of Slavery and Resistance: The Case of *Uncle Tom's Cabin* and *Cecilia Valdes*." *Slavery & Abolition* [Great Britain] 5, no. 2 (1984): 105–17.

Kazin, Alfred. *God and the American Writer*. New York: Alfred A. Knopf, 1997.

Keck, Stephen. "Slaves or Labourers: Revisiting the 1852 Debate between Sir Arthur Helps and 'A Carolinian' (Edward J. Pringle)." *Proceedings of the South Carolina Historical Association* (1997): 12–23.

Kerr, Howard. "'The Blessed Dead': The Transformation of Occult Experience in Harriet Beecher Stowe's *Oldtown Folks*." In *Literature and the Occult: Essays in Comparative Literature*, edited by Luanne Frank, 174–187. Arlington: University of Texas at Arlington, 1977.

Kimball, Gayle. "Harriet Beecher Stowe's Revision of New England Theology." *Journal of Presbyterian History* 58, no. 1 (1980): 64–81.

———. *The Religious Ideas of Harriet Beecher Stowe: Her Gospel of Womanhood*. New York: Mellen Press, 1982.

Kirkham, E. Bruce. *The Building of Uncle Tom's Cabin*. Knoxville: University of Tennessee, 1977.

———. "Harriet Beecher Stowe and the Genesis, Composition, and Revision of *Uncle Tom's Cabin*." Ph.D. diss., University of North Carolina, 1968.

———. "Harriet Beecher Stowe: Autobiography and Legend." In *Portraits of a Nineteenth Century Family*, edited by Earl Royce and Diana Royce. Hartford, CT: Stowe-Day Foundation, 1976.

Kosnik, Kristin Costello. "The Alien in Our Nation: Complicating Issues of 'Passing' and Miscegenation in the American Narrative." Ph.D. diss., Columbia University, 2001.

Kristol, Irving. "A Few Kind Words for Uncle Tom." *Harper's Magazine* 230 (February 1965): 95–99.

Lang, Amy Schrager. "Slavery and Sentimentalism: The Strange Career of Augustine St. Clare." *Women's Studies* 12 (1986): 31–54.

Lant, Kathleen Margaret. "The Unsung Hero of *Uncle Tom's Cabin*." *American Studies* 28 (1987): 47–71.

Lee, Maurice Sherwood. "Quarreling with Politics: Antebellum Literature and the Limits of the Slavery Debate (Herman Melville, Harriet Beecher Stowe, Frederick Douglass, Ralph Waldo Emerson)." Ph.D. diss., University of California, Los Angeles, 2000.

Levin, David. "American Fiction as Historical Evidence: Reflections on *Uncle Tom's Cabin*." *Negro American Literature Forum* 5, no. 4 (Winter 1971): 132–36.

Levine, Robert. *Martin Delany, Frederick Douglass, and the Politics of Representative Identity*. Chapel Hill: University of North Carolina Press, 1997.

Lewis, Gladys Sherman. "Message, Messenger, and Response: Puritan Forms and Cultural Reformation in Harriet Beecher Stowe's *Uncle Tom's Cabin*." Ph.D. diss., Oklahoma State University, 1992.

Lieber, Francis to George Ticknor. ALS. March 14, 1853. Huntington Library, LI 4381.

Loebel, Thomas Leon. "Legal Fictions: Representing Justice in Nineteenth-Century American Literature." Ph.D. diss., State University of New York at Buffalo, 1996.

Lombard, Charles. "Harriet Beecher Stowe's Attitude toward French Romanticism." *CLA Journal* 11 (1967/68): 236–40.

Lowance, Mason, Ellen E. Westbook, and R. C. De Prospo, eds. *The Stowe Debate: Rhetorical Strategies in Uncle Tom's Cabin*. Amherst: University of Amherst Press, 1994.

Macaulay, Thomas Babington. *Essays, and Lays of Ancient Rome*. London: Longmans, Green and Company, 1895.

Macfarlane, Lisa Watt. "If Every I Get to Where I Can: The Competing Rhetorics of Social Reform in *Uncle Tom's Cabin*." *ATQ* n.s. 4 (June 1990): 135–47.

Madison, Ellen Louise. "A Parallel Text Edition of *Uncle Tom's Cabin*: Materials for a Critical Text." Ph.D. diss., University of Rhode Island, 1986.

Malraux, André. *Les Chens qu'on abat*. Paris: Gallimard, 1971.

Marks, Pamela Ann. "A Voice in Ramah: Rhetorical Structure and Cultural Context in *Uncle Tom's Cabin*." Ph.D. diss., University of Rhode Island, 1991.

Marotta, Kenny Ralph. "The Literary Relationship of George Eliot and Harriet Beecher Stowe." Ph.D. diss., Johns Hopkins University, 1974.

Martineau, Harriet. "Achievements of the Genius of Scott." In *Miscellanies* by Harriet Martineau, 27–56. Boston: Hilliard, Gray, & Co., 1836.

Mason, Jeffrey D. *Melodrama and the Myth of America*. Bloomington: Indiana University Press, 1993.

May, Henry F. Introduction to *Oldtown Folks*, by Harriet Beecher Stowe, 3–43. Cambridge, MA: The Belknap Press of Harvard University Press, 1966.

McNeil, Helen. "Romance, Research, Melodrama." *Encounter* 53, no. 1 (1979): 76–80.

Meyer, Michael. "Toward a Rhetoric of Equality: Reflective and Refractive Images in Stowe's Language." In *The Stowe Debate: Rhetorical Strategies in Uncle Tom's Cabin*, edited by Mason I. Lowance, Ellen E. Westbrook, and R. C. De Prospo, 236–254. Amherst: University of Massachusetts Press, 1994.

Moers, Ellen. *Harriet Beecher Stowe and American Literature*. Hartford, CT: The Stowe-Day Foundation, 1978.

Mullen, Harryette. "Runaway Tongue: Resistant Orality in *Uncle Tom's Cabin, Our Nig, Incidents in the Life of a Slave Girl,* and *Beloved.*" In *The Culture of Sentiment: Race, Gender and Sentimentality in Nineteenth-Century America*, edited by Shirley Samuels, 244–264. New York: Oxford University Press, 1992.

Nell, William C. *The Colored Patriots of the American Revolution*. With an introduction by Harriet Beecher Stowe. Boston: R. F. Wallcut, 1855.

Nelson, John Herbert. *The Negro Character in American Literature*. Lawrence: University of Kansas, Department of Journalism Press, 1926.

Newman, Judie. Introduction to *Dred: A Tale of the Great Dismal Swamp*, by Harriet Beecher Stowe, 9–25. Halifax, England: Ryburn Publishers, 1992.

———. "Stowe's Sunny Memories of Highland Slavery." In *Special Relationships: Anglo-American Antagonisms and Affinities, 1854–1936*, edited by Janet Beer, 28–41. Manchester: Manchester University Press, 2002.

Nietzsche, Friedrich. *The Use and Abuse of History*. Indianapolis: Bobbs Merrill, 1957.

———. *The Will to Power*. New York: Random House, 1967.

"Novels: Their Meaning and Mission." *Putnam's Monthly Magazine* 4 (October 1854): 389–96.

Oliver, Egbert S. "The Little Cabin of Uncle Tom." *College English* 26, no. 5 (February 1965): 355–61.

Ottley, William Young. *Engravings of the Marquis of Stafford's Collection of Pictures in London, Arranged According to Schools and in Chronological Order: With Remarks on Each Picture*. London: P. W. Tompkins, 1818.

Petersen, William J. "Naturally Different: Calvin and Harriet Beecher Stowe." In *Twenty-Five Surprising Marriages: Faith-Building Stories from the Lives of Famous Christians*, by William J. Petersen, 166–81. Grand Rapids, MI: Baker Books, 1997.

Phelps, Amos A. *Letters to Professor Stowe and Dr. Bacon on God's Real Method with Great Social Wrongs in Which the Bible Is Vindicated from Grossly Erroneous Interpretations*. New York: William Harned, for American Anti-Slavery Society, 1858.

Pierson, Michael D. "Antislavery Politics in Harriet Beecher Stowe's *The Minister's Wooing* and *The Pearl of Orr Island*." *American Nineteenth Century History* 3, no. 2 (Summer 2002): 1–24.

Powell, Timothy Burgess. "The Beautiful Absurdity of American Identity: Confliction Constructions of the Nation in 19th Century American Literature." Ph.D. diss., Brandeis University, 1995.

Rexroth, Kenneth. *The Elastic Retort: Essays in Literature and Ideas*. New York: The Seabury Press, 1973.

———. "*Uncle Tom's Cabin*." *Saturday Review of Literature* (January 11, 1969): 71.

Reynolds, Moira Davison. *Uncle Tom's Cabin and Mid-Nineteenth-Century United States: Pen and Conscience*. Jefferson, NC: McFarland, 1985.

Rhodes, James Ford. *History of the United States from the Compromise of 1850 to the McKinley-Bryan Campaign of 1896*. 8 vols. 1892–1919. Reissue, Port Washington, NY: Kennikat Press, Inc., 1967. Citations refer to Kennikat Press edition.

Riss, Arthur. "Racial Essentialism and Family Values in *Uncle Tom's Cabin*." *American Quarterly* 46, no. 4 (December 1994): 513–44.

Roberts, Diane. *The Myth of Aunt Jemima: Representations of Race and Region*. New York: Routledge, 1994.

Rodgers-Webb, Angelix Tina. "Looking Forward and Backward: The Utopian Impulse in American Women's Fiction from Stowe to Gilman (Harriet Beecher Stowe, Charlotte Perkins Gilman, Sarah Orne Jewett, Mary Wilkins Freeman, Louisa May Alcott)." Ph.D. diss., The University of Southern Mississippi, 2001.

Romero, Lora. "Bio-Political Resistance and Domestic Ideology and *Uncle Tom's Cabin*." *American Literary History* 1 (1989): 715–34.

Rourke, Constance. *Trumpets of Jubilee*. New York: Harcourt, Brace and World, Inc., 1963.

Ryan, Susan M. "Charity Begins at Home: Stowe's Antislavery Novels and the Forms of Benevolent Citizenship." *American Literature* 72, no. 4 (December 2000): 752–82.

Sachs, Elizabeth Evans. "Describing a Sphere: A Definition of Space in American Women's Domestic Fiction in the Nineteenth Century." Ph.D. diss., University of Wisconsin, 1992.

Sarson, Steven. "Harriet Beecher Stowe and American Slavery." *New Comparison* 7 (Summer 1989): 33–45.

Saunders, Catherine Elizabeth. "Houses Divided: Sentimentality in the Function of Biracial Characters in American Abolitionist Fiction." Ph.D. diss., Princeton University, 2002.

Savery, Paige. "Life of Calvin Ellis Stowe: A Chronology." Unpublished chronology. Stowe-Day Foundation, Hartford, CT.

Sawaya, Frances Josephine. "The Home Front: Domestic Nationalism and Regional Women's Writing, 1869–1913." Ph.D. diss., Cornell University, 1992.

Schiller, Friedrich. *The Poems of Schiller*. Translated by Edgar Alfred Bowring. Philadelphia: J. B. Lippincott, 1851.

Shipp, Robert Hosford. "*Uncle Tom's Cabin* and the Ethos of Melodrama." Ph.D. diss., Columbia University, 1986.

Short, Bryan C. "Stowe, Dickinson, and the Rhetoric of Modernism." *Arizona Quarterly* 47, no. 3 (Autumn 1991): 1–16.

Siebald, Manfred. "Harriet Beecher Stowe: *Uncle Tom's Cabin* (1852)—Walking through Fire and Singing of Heaven: Harriet Beecher Stowe's Vision of Heaven." In *Journey to the Celestial City: Glimpses of Heaven from Great Literary Classics*, edited by Wayne Martindale, 103–18. Chicago: Moody, 1995.

Smiley, Jane. "Say It Ain't So, Huck." *Harper's Magazine* 292 (January 1996): 61–67.

Smith, Gail K. "The Sentimental Novel: The Example of Harriet Beecher Stowe." In *The Cambridge Companion to Nineteenth-Century American Women's Writing*, edited by Dale M. Bauer and Philip Gould, 221–43. Cambridge: Cambridge University Press, 2001.

Smylie, James H. "*Uncle Tom's Cabin* Revisited: The Bible, the Romantic Imagination, and the Sympathies of Christ." *Interpretation* 27 (1973): 67–85.

Springer, Marlene. "Stowe and Eliot: An Epistolary Friendship." *Biography* 9, no. 1 (1986): 59–81.

Steele, Thomas J. "Tom and Eva: Mrs. Stowe's Two Dying Christs." *Negro American Literature Forum* 6, no. 3 (Autumn 1972): 85–90.

Steptoe, Robert B. "Sharing the Thunder: The Literary Exchanges of Harriet Beecher Stowe, Henry Bibb, and Frederick Douglass." In *New Essays on Uncle Tom's Cabin*, edited by Eric J. Sundquist, 135–154. Cambridge: Cambridge University Press, 1986.

Stowe, Calvin E. "The Advantages and Defects of the Social Condition in the United States of America." *American Biblical Repository* 2nd ser., vol. 1 (January 1839): 130–61.

———. "Dissertation on the Use of Wit in Matters of Religion." Manuscript. Stowe-Day Library, Hartford, CT, June 7, 1823.

———. "The Four Gospels as We Now Have Them in the New Testament and the Hegelian Assaults on Them." *Bibliotheca sacra* 8 (1851): 503–29.

———. "Importance of Studying the Bible in Connexion with the Classics." *American Biblical Repository* (October 1832): 724–43.

———. Introduction to *Philosophy of the Plan of Salvation* by James B. Walker. New York: M. W. Dodd and R. Carter, 1843. Reprint, New York: Chautauqua Press, 1887. Citations refer to reprint edition.

———. *Origin and History of the Books of the Bible*. Hartford, CT: Hartford Publishing Company, 1867.

———. *The Religious Element in Education. An Address Delivered before the American Institute of Instruction at Portland, ME, August 30, 1844*. Boston: William D. Ticknor & Company, 1844.

———. "Remarks Made While Pursuing a Course of Theological Studies." Manuscript. Hartford Theological Seminary, Hartford, CT, 1829.

———. *Report on Elementary Public Instruction in Europe, Made to the Thirty-Sixth General Assembly of the State of Ohio*. December 19, 1837. Reprint, Harrisburg: Packer, Barrett and Parke, 1838. Citations refer to reprint edition.

———. to H. B. Stowe. ALS. July 20, 1836. London. Stowe-Day Library, Hartford, CT.

———. to H. B. Stowe. ALS. June 4, 1853. From S. S. Canada. Stowe-Day Library, Hartford, CT.

———. to H. B. Stowe. ALS. June 4, 1853. S. S. Niagara.

———. to H. B. Stowe. ALS. July 11, 1853. Andover. Stowe-Day Library, Hartford, CT.

———. to H. B. Stowe. ALS. February 8, 1857. Andover. Stowe-Day Library, Hartford, CT.

Stowe, Charles Edward. *The Life of Harriet Beecher Stowe*. Boston: Houghton, Mifflin, 1889.

Stowe, Harriet Beecher. "Anti-Slavery Literature." *The Independent* (New York) (February 21, 1856): 1.

———. *Dred: A Tale of the Great Dismal Swamp*. Boston: Sampson and Company, 1856.

———. *First Geography for Children*. Boston: Phillips, Sampson, and Company, 1855.

———. *Household Papers and Other Stories*. Boston: Houghton, Mifflin and Company, 1896. Reprint, New York: AMS Press, Inc., 1967. Citations refer to reprint edition.

———. *The Key to Uncle Tom's Cabin*. Boston: John P. Jewett and Company, 1853. Reprint, Port Washington, NY: Kennikat Press, 1968. Citations refer to reprint edition.

———. "Let Every Man Mind His Own Business." In *The Christian Keepsake and Missionary Annual*, 239–64. Philadelphia: W. Marshall and Company, 1839.

——. *Letter to the Ladies New Anti-Slavery Society of Glasgow, the Contents of Which Are Designed Equally for the Anti-Slavery Societies of England and Scotland.* Glasgow: John Maclay, 1853.
——. "Literary Epidemics." Part 2. *New York Evangelist* (July 13, 1843): 1.
——. *My Wife and I: or, Harry Henderson's History*. Boston: Houghton, Mifflin and Company, 1871.
——. *New Geography for Children*. London: Sampson, Low, Son & Company, 1855.
——. *Oldtown Folks.* Boston: Fields, Osgood, 1869.
——. *Poganuc People: Their Loves and Lives.* New York: Fords, Howard and Hulbert, 1878. Reprint, with introduction by Joseph S. Van Why, Hartford, CT: Stowe-Day Foundation, 1987. Citations refer to reprint edition.
——. Preface and introduction to *A Library of Famous Fiction, Embracing the Nine Standard Masterpieces of Imaginative Literature.* New York: J. B. Ford & Company, 1873.
——. *Sunny Memories of Foreign Lands.* 2 vols. Boston: Phillips, Sampson, and Company, 1854.
——. "To the Editor of the *Cincinnati Journal and Luminary*." *Cincinnati Journal and Luminary* (July 21, 1836).
——. "Tribute to a Loving Friend to the Memory of a Noble Woman." *The Atlantic Monthly* 23 (February 1869): 242–250.
——. "Two Altars; or, Two Pictures in One." *New York Evangelist* (June 12 and June 19, 1851).
——. *Uncle Tom's Cabin; or, Life among the Lowly*. Boston: J. P. Jewett, 1852. Reprint, with introduction by John A. Woods, London: Oxford University Press, 1965. Citations refer to Oxford edition.
——. *The Works of Charlotte Elizabeth*. 2nd edition. New York: M. W. Dodd, 1845.
——. to C. E. Stowe. ALS. 1851. Andover. Stowe-Day Foundation Library, Hartford, CT.
——. to "My Lord ____." January 20, 1853. Huntington Library.
——. to H. W. Beecher. ALS. January 13, 1854. Stowe-Day Library, Hartford, CT.
——. to Duchess of Sutherland. ALS. September 15, 1856. University of Virginia Library, Charlottesville, VA. Copy at Stowe-Day Library.
——. to "Editor of the Brooklyn Magazine." ALS. April 2, 1885. University of Virginia Library, Charlottesville, VA.
Stowe, Lyman Beecher. *Saints, Sinners and Beechers*. New York: Blue Ribbon Books, Inc., 1934.
Strauss, Leo. *Natural Right and History.* Chicago: University of Chicago, 1953.
Strout, Cushing. "*Uncle Tom's Cabin* and the Portent of the Millennium." *The Yale Review* n.s. 57 (1968): 375–85.
Suckow, Ruth. "An Almost Lost Classic." *College English* 14, no. 6 (1953): 315–25.
Sundquist, Eric J., ed. *New Essays on Uncle Tom's Cabin.* Cambridge: Cambridge University Press, 1986.
Szczesiul, Anthony E. "The Canonization of Tom and Eva: Catholic Hagiography and *Uncle Tom's Cabin*." *ATQ* n.s. 10 (March 1996): 59–72.
Tang, Edward. "Making Declarations on Her Own: Harriet Beecher Stowe as New England Historian." *New England Quarterly* 71, no. 1 (March 1998): 77–96.
——. "Revolutionary Legacies: History, Literature and Memory in Nineteenth-Century America, 1820–1880." Ph.D. diss., New York University, 1996.

Tennyson, G. B. *Carlyle and the Modern World.* Lecture Delivered to the Carlyle Society, March 6, 1971. Edinburgh: Carlyle Society, 1971.

Thomas, Brook. *Cross-Examinations of Law and Literature: Cooper, Hawthorne, Stowe, and Melville.* New York: Cambridge University Press, 1987.

Tocqueville, Alexis de. *Democracy in America.* Translated by Henry Reeve. New York: Schocken Books, 1961.

Tocqueville, Alexis de. *Democracy in America.* Edited by J. P. Mayer, translated by George Lawrence. New York: Harper & Row, c1988, c1969.

Tompkins, Jane. *Sensational Designs: The Cultural Work of American Fiction, 1790–1860.* New York: Oxford University Press, 1985.

"Uncle Tomitudes." *Putnam's Monthly Magazine* 1 (January 1853): 97–102.

Venet, Wendy Hamand. *Neither Ballots Nor Bullets: Women Abolitionist and the Civil War.* Charlottesville: University Press of Virginia, 1991.

Wagenknecht, Edward. *Harriet Beecher Stowe: The Known and the Unknown.* New York: Oxford University Press, 1965.

Weeks, Stephen B. "Anti-Slavery in the South." *Southern History Association* 2, no. 2 (April 1898).

Weinstein, Daniel James. "Educating Sympathy: Imagination and Convention in Works by Harriet Beecher Stowe, Sarah Orne Jewett and Mary E. Wilkins Freeman." Ph.D. diss., State University of New York at Buffalo, 2000.

West, John. "Going Back to *Uncle Tom's Cabin.*" *Books & Culture* 26 (July/August 2003): 26.

Westbrook, Perry. *The New England Town in Fact and Fiction.* London and Toronto: Associated University Presses, 1982.

White, Herbert B. "The Blind Mole." In *Copp'd Hills toward Heaven: Shakespeare and the Classical Polity,* by Herbert B. White. The Hague: Martinus-Nijhoff, 1970.

——. *Peace among the Willows.* The Hague: Martinus-Nijhoff, 1968.

White, Isabella. "The Uses of Death in *Uncle Tom's Cabin.*" *American Studies* 26 (1984): 5–17.

Williams, Linda. *Playing the Race Card: Melodrama of Black and White from Uncle Tom to O. J. Simpson.* Princeton: Princeton University Press, 2001.

Wilson, Edmund. *Patriotic Gore: Studies in the Literature of the American Civil War.* New York: Oxford University Press, 1962.

Wilson, Gayle Edward. "'As John Bunyon Says': Bunyan's Influence on *Uncle Tom's Cabin.*" *ATQ* n.s. 1 (1987): 157–62.

Wilson, Robert Forrest. *Crusader in Crinoline, the Life of Harriet Beecher Stowe.* Philadelphia: J. B. Lippincott Company, 1941.

Yarborough, Richard and Sylvan Allen. "Radical or Reactionary? Religion and Rhetorical Conflict in *Uncle Tom's Cabin.*" In *Approaches to Teaching Uncle Tom's Cabin,* edited by Elizabeth Ammons and Susan Belasco, 57–67. New York: Modern Language Association of America, 2000.

Young, Elizabeth. *Disarming the Nation: Women's Writing and the American Civil War.* Chicago: University of Chicago Press, 1999.

Index

About the Author

William B. Allen is professor of political philosophy at Michigan State University and visiting senior scholar in the Matthew J. Ryan Center for the Study of Free Institutions and the Public Good at Villanova University. He also served previously on the National Council for the Humanities and as chairman and member of the United States Commission on Civil Rights.

He has published extensively, most notably, *George Washington: A Collection* and in 2008, *George Washington: America's First Progressive* and *The Personal and the Political: Three Fables by Montesquieu*. He previously published *Habits of Mind: Fostering Access and Excellence in Higher Education* (with Carol M. Allen).